BASIC ETHICS IN ACTION

Environmental Ethics

MICHAEL BOYLAN

Prentice
Hall

Upper Saddle River, New Jersey 07458

Library of Congress Cataloging-in-Publication Data

Boylan, Michael
  Environmental ethics / Michael Boylan.
    p. cm.—(Basic ethics in action)
  ISBN 0-13-776386-7
    1. Environmental ethics. I. Title. II. Series.

GE42.B69 2001
179'.1—dc21   00-062425

Editor-in-Chief: Charlyce Jones Owen
Acquisitions Editor: Ross Miller
Assistant Editor: Katie Janssen
AVP, Director of Manufacturing
  and Production: Barbara Kittle
Senior Managing Editor: Jan Stephan
Production Liaison: Fran Russello
Project Manager: Linda B. Pawelchak
Manufacturing Manager: Nick Sklitsis
Prepress and Manufacturing Buyer: Sherry Lewis
Cover Director: Jayne Conte
Cover Design: Bruce Kenselaar
Marketing Manager: Ilse Wolf
Copy Editing: JaNoel Lowe
Proofreading: Ann-Marie WongSam

Acknowledgments begin on page 425, which
constitutes a continuation of this copyright page.

This book was set in 10/12 Palatino by Pub-Set
and was printed and bound by Courier Companies, Inc.
The cover was printed by Phoenix Color Corp.

© 2001 by Michael Boylan
Published by Prentice-Hall, Inc.
A Division of Pearson Education
Upper Saddle River, New Jersey 07458

Printed in the United States of America
10 9 8 7 6 5 4 3 2 1

ISBN 0-13-776386-7

Prentice-Hall International (UK) Limited, *London*
Prentice-Hall of Australia Pty. Limited, *Sydney*
Prentice-Hall Canada Inc., *Toronto*
Prentice-Hall Hispanoamericana, S.A., *Mexico*
Prentice-Hall of India Private Limited, *New Delhi*
Prentice-Hall of Japan, Inc., *Tokyo*
Pearson Education Asia Pte. Ltd., *Singapore*
Editora Prentice-Hall do Brasil, Ltda., *Rio de Janeiro*

For Seán

Contents

chapter six

APPLIED ENVIRONMENTAL ETHICS   301

Preface

This book aspires to introduce the student to important ethical issues in the realm of environmental ethics. As such, it fits into the Applied Ethics branch of ethics. *Environmental Ethics* is the fourth book in the series *Basic Ethics in Action*. The composition of this series is ongoing. The central poles concern Medical Ethics, Business Ethics, and Environmental Ethics. There will be single-author books in this series from various philosophers and practitioners in the fields. The books will be in a normal and a condensed format.

The series is anchored by *Basic Ethics,* an essay on Normative Ethics and Metaethics. Instructors and students of ethics can use (a) *Basic Ethics* alone or with other primary texts in an ethics course, (b) *Basic Ethics* with one of the applied texts in the series in an ethics course that emphasizes an integration of theory and practice, or (c) one or more of the applied texts in courses concentrating on practice.

Distinctive Features of This Book

Environmental Ethics includes (a) an original interview with a prominent person who faces the practical challenges of ethical issues in the environment daily, (b) a methodology for linking theory to action, (c) an awareness throughout of gender issues as they relate to environmental ethics, and (d) a method for students to follow to write an essay using the information presented.

The book begins by introducing the student to my theory of worldview, or *Weltanschauung*. This concept is one of the unifying themes of *Basic Ethics*. I believe that acknowledging one's worldview and its relation to the common worldview (the worldview created by a particular community) is a crucial element in explaining and justifying what we value. This critical model, in turn, leads to what I call a linking principle to action. In the case of Environmental Ethics, I have constructed criteria that describe a value-duty relationship that I believe will allow students to move from theory to practice. A full exposition of this principle is found in Chapter Four.

Chapter One presents an interview with Tamar Datan, director of programs at the Nature Conservancy. She is a hands-on director who is constantly in the field engaged with the issues discussed in this book. I hope that students reading this interview will gain some perspectives on the central themes presented here from the point of view of a prominent practitioner in the field.

Chapter Two presents four traditional theories of ethics: Ethical Intuitionism, Virtue Ethics, Utilitarianism, and Deontology. At the end of this chapter begins the series of exercises to help students bridge the gap between Normative and Applied Ethics through a series of essays and cases. Some instructors may wish to go through these immediately as a type of propadeutic for reacting to moral problems. Others may wish to follow my plan by adding a little bit at a time.

Chapter Three suggests a linking principle from which readers might move from theory to practice. Prominent in this essay are my suggestions that there is a value-duty relationship. This connection occurs in an individual's personal worldview (especially through aesthetic value) and in the Shared Community Worldview Imperative that creates a basis for political action.

Chapter Four examines various worldview approaches to the environment from deep ecology, social ecology, and ecofeminism to explorations of worldview via religion and aesthetics.

Chapter Five addresses the issue of the ethical basis for environmentalism, a subtle issue. At its heart is the anthropocentric-biocentric debate. Exploring each position will allow the reader to side with one or the other position or to adopt a middle position such as James Sterba has suggested.

Finally, in Chapter Six, I highlight some pivotal problems in Environmental Ethics, including animal rights, biodiversity, and sustainable development. I believe that the disposition to these problems resonates to many other environmental issues. I hope that various instructors will ask students to investigate current environmental issues from the daily newspaper and supplement this presentation of ethical problems. This is an especially useful exercise since it engages students in integrating real-world experience with classroom theory. If we can do nothing else as instructors, we can create thoughtful, questioning students who will think for themselves, form reasoned beliefs, and have the inner courage to work for the adoption of those beliefs.

Each of the core chapters of the book has a section of case studies depicting situations related to topics discussed in the chapter's readings. These case studies are separated into two groups, macro cases and micro cases. The macro case takes the point of view of someone in a managerial or supervisory role and considers Environmental Ethics from a variety of perspectives of those in power. The point of view in the micro cases is of people who often are consonant with the principles of environmentalism but are not aware and/or committed to integrating their personal beliefs into personal action. Through these case studies, students have an opportunity to react to the readings and test their own attitudes by writing an essay.

Basic Ethics in Action has an argument-based style and tone and intends to challenge the reader to think about some of the various ethical implications involved in specific situations. I have found that discussion of the more controversial premises focuses debate in the classroom in a way that is satisfactory for both instructor and student.

Many may wish to read *Environmental Ethics* with an ethical theory text (such as *Basic Ethics*). Others may want to read *Environmental Ethics* with a companion volume or one of the focus volumes in the series. Still others may prefer to delve more deeply into issues of practice by finding topics that interest them and then doing their own inteviews of people in the field. I believe that getting a sense of what real life is like is important. It puts these cases and principles into a context that can be more easily integrated into the students' worldview. This is, after all, the purpose of a course on Environmental Ethics. It helps students refine their practical decision-making skills so that they might be better able to live following a worldview that is, above all else, good.

ACKNOWLEDGMENTS

A project like this creates many people to thank. I would first like to acknowledge all the contributors to this volume, especially Alan Gewirth, who composed an original essay for this text, and Murray Bookchin, who revised an earlier piece especially for this volume. Second, I would like to thank James P. Sterba, with whom I consulted on several points and whose discussion on the anthropocentric versus biocentric debate enhanced Chapter Five.

Third, I must mention the wonderful and growing group of people who are assembling to write volumes in this series. Each one of them has helped me understand and extend the concept of worldview through the Personal

Worldview Imperative and the Shared Community Worldview Imperative in new ways.

Fourth, I would like to thank Ross Miller, my editor at Prentice Hall, and his assistant Carla Worner. Ross has provided important direction to the series *Basic Ethics in Action*. Without Ross and Humanities Editorial Director Charlyce Jones Owen, this series would never have gotten off the ground. I extend my deepest appreciation to both of them.

I would also note the continued excellence of Linda B. Pawelchak, who has been the production editor since *Basic Ethics*. Her thoroughness has corrected many errors and this book has profited from her diligence and intelligence.

Finally, I would like to mention my family: Arianne, Seán, Éamon, and Rebecca. Their lives and the values they teach me are a constant source of strength and sustenance.

Michael Boylan

Contributors

Arne Naess was for many years the head of the philosophy department at the University of Oslo.

Bill Devall is professor of sociology at Humboldt State University.

George Sessions is professor of philosophy at Sierra College.

Murray Bookchin is co-founder and director emeritus of the Institute for Social Ecology.

Ecofeminism

Carolyn Merchant teaches in the Department of Conservation and Resources Studies at the University of California, Berkeley.

Karen J. Warren is associate professor of philosophy at Macalaster College.

Val Plumwood is an environmental philosopher from Australia.

Religion and Aesthetics

Eilon Schwartz teaches Jewish and environmental education at the Melton Center, School of Education, Hebrew University, Jerusalem. He is also the director of the Abraham Joshua Hershel Center for Nature Studies.

Annie L. Booth is in the environmental studies program at the University of Northern British Columbia.

Harvey M. Jacobs is associated with the Institute for Environmental Studies at the University of Wisconsin.

J. Baird Callicott is professor of philosphy and religious studies at the University of North Texas.

Janna Thompson teaches in the School of Philosophy, La Trobe University, Bundoora Campus, Bundoora, Victoria, Australia.

CHAPTER FOUR: A LINKING PRINCIPLE TO APPLIED ENVIRONMENTAL ETHICS

Michael Boylan is professor of philosophy at Marymount University.

CHAPTER FIVE: THE MORAL BASIS FOR ENVIRONMENTALISM

Anthropocentric Justification

Alan Gewirth is the Edward Carson Waller Distinguished Service Professor of Philosophy at the University of Chicago.

Onora O'Neill is professor of philosophy at Newnhaus College, Cambridge.

Holmes Rolston III is professor of philosophy at Colorado State University.

Paul Taylor is professor of philosophy at Brooklyn College, City University of New York.

Searching the Middle

James P. Sterba is professor of philosophy at the University of Notre Dame.
Brian K. Steverson is professor of philosophy at Gonzaga University.

CHAPTER SIX: APPLIED ENVIRONMENTAL ETHICS

Animal Rights

Peter Singer is the Ira W. Decamp Professor of Bioethics at the University Center for Human Values at Princeton University.
Tom Regan is professor of philosophy at North Carolina State University.
Mary Anne Warren is professor of philosophy at San Francisco State University.

Biodiversity

Paul M. Wood is on the faculty of forestry at the University of British Columbia.
Elliott Sober is professor of philosophy at the University of Wisconsin, Madison.

Sustainable Development

Wilfred Beckerman is an emeritus Fellow of Balliol College, Oxford.
Herman E. Daly teaches in the School of Public Affairs, University of Maryland/College Park.
Henryk Skolimowski is chair of Ecological Philosophy at Wydzial Organizacji I Zaradzania/Politechnika Lodzka//Piotrkowska.
Salah El Serafy was formerly a senior advisor at the World Bank.

chapter one

Introduction: Worldview and Applied Ethics

General Overview. This chapter offers the student a background in key concepts that will help her or him to understand the realm of Applied Ethics. At the end of the chapter is an interview with Tamar Datan, a prominent practitioner in the field of Environmental Ethics. Subsequent chapters provide a sketch of four traditional ethical theories as well as an essay on linking theory to practice in the field of Environmental Ethics.

I. THE STRATEGY OF APPLIED ETHICS.

Applied Ethics assumes a theory of Normative Ethics and a linking principle or principles by which the ethical principles or maxims can be applied in real-life situations. It is a difficult branch of ethics because it assumes a certain facility with the subject matter of ethics and with the general practical imperatives involved. The series of books *Basic Ethics in Action* addresses practical imperatives of Normative and Applied Ethics (with an emphasis on the professions in *Medical Ethics* and in *Business Ethics*). This book examines issues facing our responsibilities for the environment. Other books in the series address different ethical problems.

I believe that the logical order of presentation begins with an ethical theory that we have chosen, moves to "linking principles," and finishes with a practical directive to action. However, as neat and logical as this order of presentation is, we live in the genetic order of existence that is constantly changing and developing. We also find ourselves changing to keep up with these alterations and developments. This means that we must regularly take time to engage in an assessment of our personal understanding of ethical theory and practice. Both work together in Environmental Ethics to create an interdisciplinary attitude. Like all interdisciplinary perspectives, one side is often developed to the exclusion of the other.

For your study of this book, a certain amount of ethical material is prerequisite. This material concerns normative ethical theory. Although some of those issues are briefly addressed in this book (Chapter Two), the discussion is not meant to be comprehensive. My book, *Basic Ethics*, the anchor volume of this series, addresses in more detail the material that will help you better consider the problems inherent in Applied Ethics. Other books on ethical theory also address these issues. It would be very useful for the student to avail herself of one of these books to prepare herself for studying Applied Ethics. (The section "Evaluating a Case Study," a series of essays that follow the core chapters in this volume, gives help to the student in this regard.)

After studying the various ethical theories, you must choose which one to adopt. I believe this choice is very important and depends on some self-conscious understanding of your personal worldview. The next section of this chapter briefly discusses some important features of the personal worldview along with the Personal Worldview Imperative, which gives direction to the nature of the worldview a person should adopt.

Finally, after presenting the worldview and the Personal Worldview Imperative, I discuss how these might be integrated with action. At the end of this chapter, I present an interview with Tamar Datan to provide a perspective of the way an environmentalist works within the constraints of the real world. Chapters Two and Three will give more specific aspects of professional practice through a brief introduction to four influential ethical theories (Chapter Two) and through my essay (Chapter Three), "Worldview and the Value-Duty Link to Environmental Ethics," which discusses a linking principle between normative and applied ethics in environmental philosophy.

II. Personal Worldview Imperative.

A.

The World was all before them, where to choose
Thir place of rest, and Providence thir guide:
They hand in hand with wand'ring steps and slow,
Through Eden took thir solitary way.
—Milton, *Paradise Lost*

This is the way the world ends
This is the way the world ends
This is the way the world ends
Not with a bang but with a whimper.
    —T. S. Eliot, "The Hollow Men"

B.

Little Lamb, who made thee?
Dost thou know who made thee?
    —William Blake, "The Lamb"

That bit of filth in dirty walls,
And all around barbed wire,
And 30,000 souls who sleep
Who once will wake
And once will see
Their own blood spilled.
    —Hanus Hachenburg, "Terezin" (1944, just before his death
    in a Nazi concentration camp at the age of 14)

In these two groups of paired poems, each has a definite *point of view.* Group A begins with an optimistic view of a tragedy (the human fall in the Garden of Eden at the beginning of the world) followed by an angst-ridden view of the end of the world.

Group B presents an innocent view of gentle questioning about the causes of life from the mind of a carefree rural child followed by the queries of a soon-to-be Holocaust victim about the nature of life in death and death in life.

Each passage reflects a different set of assumptions held by the poet. In literature, we call this *voice.* As a writer of poetry and fiction (and occasional reviewer of literary novels), I can attest to the fact that the ultimate judgment that we make when reading a piece of fictive literature revolves around the author's voice.

Charles Dickens did not achieve fame for his stylistic writing. In fact, his sentences are often clumsy, and he uses many words improperly. His characters are often wooden and his plots predictable. What sets Dickens apart from others in his century (who were his superior in these departments) is his voice. Dickens's voice is that of a champion for the rights of children and for the rights of the oppressed and against those who through their machinations seek to overreach themselves and grasp goods meant for others. A reader of a Dickens novel is impressed with the clarity of moral vision that suffuses the pages. This sense of literary voice is what I will call the worldview, or *Weltanschauung.*

Voice demarcates the world we enter when we open the covers of a fiction book. The world it presents is an escape, and we assent to it or not according to a myriad of factors. The act of reading is a knowing *suspension of disbelief.* We willingly enter into the author's worldview and test what it is like to be there. This is more than merely becoming a murderer (in a mystery story), a member of the opposite sex, or a person of a different race, religion, or culture; it is accepting a network of beliefs that together express values concerning the critical concerns of life: ethics, politics, religion, aesthetics, and so forth. When the world we enter is welcoming (meaning that it *accords* with some deeply held tenets within our own worldview), we feel comfortable and react to that world positively. When that world is foreign and hostile (meaning that it does not accord with our deeply held tenets within our own worldview), we are uncomfortable and react negatively.

The composition of this worldview web of beliefs is not the same in everyone. Some (probably very few) may have a tree-structured logical pyramid of axiomatic primitives at the top and derivative theorems that follow from them. Others (many more) have an edifice that is *aporitic* in nature (meaning that a number of separate constructs owe their existence to specific problems that have arisen in each person's life). These aporitic constructs often exist in isolation from one another. I am reminded of Wemmick in *Great Expectations,* who had a life in Jaggers's office and another life with the aged-one in the "castle." Wemmick often advised Pip to bring up certain topics with him at one arena or the other, depending upon the answer Pip wanted to receive because in each place, Wemmick took on a different worldview. There was (almost) no integration between the two.

I am also reminded of the metaphorical descriptions used by John Ruskin in *The Seven Lamps of Architecture* in which he declares that the composition of a building should reflect all of the architect's value. Under this view, if the architect's worldview is not well integrated, during the process of design the architect must create a single vision that is true to his or her materials, function, and execution (or else the project will ultimately be a failure). The construction of a building is a metaphor for how we are to construct ourselves. It speaks to personal values and their relationships within our lives. In this way, we can be viewed as the architects of ourselves. Some might believe that this is rather ephemeral for hard-nosed philosophy, but I believe that the ideas of the worldview rest at the edge of traditional philosophical discourse.

It is important for the position I am defending that it be possible for an individual to evaluate her worldview and life plan in a holistic fashion with reason as one of several key components. This holistic approach means that one cannot separate worldview from philosophy. Some analytic philosophers have suggested that somehow it is possible for philosophy to work independently of any worldviews.[1]

These various views of analytic philosophy depict it as an objective tool that anyone can employ without assuming any of the characteristics, values,

---

[1]Kai Nielsen discussed this briefly in his article, "Philosophy and *Weltanschauung,*" *The Journal of Value Inquiry* 27 (1993): 179–86.

or worldview of the practitioner. This position seems wrong to me. I believe that the philosopher always brings his worldview along with him. This is not a position of epistemological relativism but merely an admission that the subjective and objective do not neatly segregate.[2]

Although they are subjective in nature, these worldviews are themselves subject to evaluative criteria. They are formal and logical principles that are virtually devoid of empirical content. These criteria can be put together to form the Personal Worldview Imperative: *All people must develop a single, comprehensive and internally coherent worldview that is good and that we strive to act out in our daily lives.*[3] In my opinion, every agent acting or potentially acting in the world falls under the normative force of the Personal Worldview Imperative. This principle could probably be analyzed to cover a wide range of axiological issues and may be the topic of some future work, but here I simply highlight three separate criteria that I believe are imbedded within the Personal Worldview Imperative and that bear closer examination.

The first criterion is: *We have a duty to develop and to act out our worldview.* This means that we are expected to *choose* and *fashion* a point of view that will do much to condition our day-to-day consciousness. It is not enough merely to accept another's general beliefs and attitudes about ethics, politics, aesthetics and religion. Doing so would be tantamount to becoming the slave of another. If some modicum of freedom and autonomy is a part of our human nature and if ultimately we are content only if we act out our human nature (assuming that all wish to be ultimately content), then we should all seek to exercise our freedom in the most practically fundamental way by choosing and fashioning a worldview.

Our power of choice in adopting a worldview may not be absolute, but that does not prevent us from exercising our freedom within a limited domain. Let us use another metaphor. Having a limited choice in adopting a worldview would be akin to moving into someone else's house. Suppose that the house had many features that we decided we did not like. We have some money, so we might remodel the house a room at a time, taking care that the remodeling concept is in accord with some larger plan or aesthetic point of view. The word *fashion* used earlier is meant to embody some of this sense of re-creation or remodeling.

---

[2]This is similar to Quine's insistence that analytic and synthetic truths do not easily segregate. See Willard Quine, "Two Dogmas of Empiricism," *From a Logical Point of View* (Cambridge, MA: Harvard University Press, 1953).

[3]Some might contend that my depiction of this imperative places an overreliance on form over content. It is a procedure and thus cannot have normative content. Against this attack, I reply that although the prescription, by itself, is procedural, it will result in some content. And, if taken in the Socratic spirit of living an examined life, the force of the normativity is toward participation in a process that must be sincere because it represents each of our very best versions of the "good, true, and beautiful."

Depending on our circumstances, this process of fashioning a world-view, like remodeling the house, could take a considerable length of time, especially given difficult exterior or interior factors. No two individuals' tasks are identical.

The second criterion is this: *We have a duty to develop a single worldview that is both comprehensive and internally consistent.* This second duty involves rather prudential concerns of what would count as a serviceable worldview. A worldview that is not unitary and comprehensive might not give us direction at some future time when such direction is sorely needed. We cannot depend on a worldview that is not comprehensive to help us grow and develop in life.

Likewise, a worldview that is not internally consistent might offer us contradictory directions of action in the future because each area of inconsistency (call them A and non-A) might develop a line of reasoning that maintains its original character (logical heritability). The resulting "offspring" of A and non-A would also be opposed. If these offspring are imperatives of action, then we are in a dilemma.[4] Such a worldview is inadequate because it may not be able to offer clear direction for action at some time in the future.

The third criterion is this: *We have a duty to create a worldview that is good.* This final criterion is the most difficult to justify in moral terms. Clearly, the word *good* in this instance may mean merely good for the agent's prudential interests. Certainly, we would not want to create a worldview that is self-destructive. Few would argue against the premise that our worldview ought to support a plan of life and development, which will be personally advantageous to us. But I assert that the type of worldview I am talking about should be ethically good as well. Such an ethical interpretation of the Personal Worldview Imperative is essential if this principle is to be of use in moral analysis.

III. WORLDVIEW INTEGRATION.

The basic approach to worldview integration was suggested in *Basic Ethics*. In that book, I argue that in constructing one's worldview, we might combine personal inclinations toward other essential values such as the principles of aesthetics, feminism, religion, and professional practices into a general system of ethics.

Many people actually reside in several self-contained worlds that dictate how they should act in this or that situation. These specifications can often be contradictory. For example, I have been a volunteer baseball coach for youth sports for a number of years. One day I had a baseball game scheduled on a field that was occupied by another team holding a practice. I approached the man running the practice and showed him my permit for the field. He

---

[4] A moral dilemma occurs when a person, through no fault of her own, finds herself in a situation in which the only available choices of action are both evil.

refused to leave and continued with his practice. When the umpires arrived for our game, they confirmed our reservation for the field. But the man holding the practice told us that we would have to call the police to have him evicted from the field.

I was not eager to call the police[5] and began to exhort the usurper in rational terms. First, I mentioned that he was not setting a good example of reasonableness and good will in front of the children of both teams. Both teams that rightfully had the field were being bullied by someone without a permit whose only claim to the field was that he was using it. I asked the man if he believed in societies without the rule of law—for that was what a *krateristic* (might makes right) position amounts to. Then I started naming various *krateristic* regimes in the twentieth century, starting with Joseph Stalin and Adolph Hitler. At the mention of those two names, the man yielded the field.

I found out later that the man was the coach of a church-sponsored team and was a prominent lay leader in that church. He was a respected corporate tax lawyer. I believe that when he was doggedly holding a field for which he had no permit, he was in the worldview of the aggressive corporate tax lawyer. However, when I began speaking about lawlessness and historical instances of how *kraterism* has resulted in tyranny, the worldview of the church leader took over and he yielded the field.

This man lived in at least two different worlds. Each world contained its own practices and endorsed different approaches to solving problems. It was also probable that each of these worlds had little interaction with the other. The Personal Worldview Imperative calls for us to create a single worldview. This means that people who hold multiple worldviews that refer, in turn, to multiple and contradictory practices must work to create unity and coherence among these. By integrating these various beliefs, general attitudes, and life values, these people confront the world more authentically than they did when their worldviews were fragmented. Such a process of integration obviously requires introspection and self-knowledge.

A similar example is someone who has a serviceable single worldview but makes certain exceptions now and again for activities that the worldview explicitly forbids. This is not an instance of weakness of the will (in which the person maintains her worldview but fails to follow its prescriptions because she is overwhelmed by contrary desires) but is a set of ad hoc amendments to the worldview that are patently inconsistent with its other tenets. Consider a person who has a general rule against belittling people because of their national origin or religion. But this person harasses an employee in a manner that directly contradicts his general rule. He forms a new amendment to his worldview that allows him to act in this way. Obviously, this

---

[5]I thought that calling the police to force the man from the field was merely to fight force with force and would represent a defeat for reason. Instead, I presented an argument in a controlled and level tone.

is an instance of incoherence and thus disallowed by the Personal Worldview Imperative.

In the process of integration, we relate the empirical world (in which we live and make sense of by continually wrestling and striving with these issues) to various more abstract principles in such a way that life becomes rationally comprehensible. I compare this process to an artist painting a picture or a poet writing a poem. In each case, we are (as Hamlet said) holding a mirror up to nature. However, the imitation itself—the artifact—may vary. Thus, Jan Van Eyck, Claude Monet, and Wassily Kandinsky might all paint one particular scene differently.

Consider John Donne, John Dryden, or Anthony Hecht. Each would create a poem describing a common event[6] but in his own way. The reason for this is that (a) each views the event in an objective way as to the measurement of sounds and colors but (b) each arranges these details somewhat differently according to an order based on a value-laden worldview. The result is an artifact about which the group could come to factual agreement queried in a court of law but which each would describe differently. The significance of the whole and of the way the parts are arranged to make up the whole varies.

Also consider the way different peoples have reacted to the human condition to create religion. If such a reaction were a transparent process of merely translating either a revelation (of God) or a reaction to some common human need, then we would expect that there would be one and only one religion, but this is obviously not the case. The reason is that (as with the painters and the poets) people react to the same revelation or human need differently.[7] Thus, we have various religions in the world (which are almost as numerous as the variety of artistic schools of expression).

These examples express some of the relationships among (a) worldview, (b) empirical events, and (c) other theoretical constructs. Together, I call these *interactions:* integration through the process of dialectical interaction.[8]

This integration has two important manifestations in the way we apply ethical theories. First is the way we integrate empirical events into theoretical categories (dialectical subsumption) given our worldview. Second is the way we match our ethical imperatives with our worldview. Let us discuss each of these briefly and then examine the process of applying an ethical theory.

The first manifestation is the way we integrate empirical events into theoretical categories (dialectical subsumption) given our worldview. *Dialectical*

---

[6]Obviously, this is a thought experiment. The point of putting people of different styles and historical eras together is to highlight how important the component of worldview is in the way we process empirical data.

[7]This analogy may be objectionable to advocates of a religion who believe that their particular version is the only one of any true value. They would object to the sort of aesthetic model I am creating here and prefer a more scientific one.

[8]See *Basic Ethics*, Chapter Eight, for an exposition of the various types of dialectical processes relevant here.

subsumption is the interactive process by which objects are schematized into our consciousness. The best way to describe dialectical subsumption is to contrast it to mechanical subsumption. In mechanical subsumption, a class, alpha, has certain membership requirements (e.g., possession of trait phi). When any x has phi, then it belongs to alpha. The entire process is termed *mechanical* because it is a simple mechanistic process of sorting things where they belong according to some preestablished set of rules. The decision procedure is certain so that the procedure could be performed on a sample space so that it would be exhaustive and complete. This model of mechanical subsumption may be possible in mathematics and computer modeling. It is often used to give fullness to certain theories in some of the social sciences (especially economics!).

Unfortunately, mechanical subsumption is largely a priori in character.[9] This means that instead of interacting with the data in a carefully refining, bootstraping operation, the practitioners intend a simple process of observing whether x possesses phi and, if it does, putting it into alpha.

Dialectical subsumption is more complicated than this. Let us consider two arguments along this line: (a) the ascription of properties to some object is a complicated process involving the worldview of the observer and (b) the manner by which the observer inserts the object into a category is also theory laden (meaning that it is connected to the observer's worldview).

A. First Form.

My first argument is that the ascription of properties is not a simple procedure. Although the painters Cranach and Turner may agree that the sunset is red, they may mean different things by this. Cranach may consider the sunset as a carefully circumscribed aspect of the third ground or background of the painting's composition while Turner may say that there is only one ground and that the sunset affects everything. The "what it is" is intricately connected to the "way it behaves." Thus, the ascription of properties includes more than a simple list of properties in some mechanical, objective manner. Instead, how the properties exist within the entire composition and the interaction of these into some environmental context must be considered. Both of these conditions are necessary to really understand the properties of some object.

An example of the linkage between the object and its activity is the identification of function along with morphology in evolutionary biology. Without function, the shapes, colors, and sizes are not completely described. The

---

[9]Although mechanical subsumption is widely used in diverse fields from legal positivism to econometrics to some theories of zoological systematics, it has been attacked by others as well. The reader is invited to examine some of these in context. Two diverse examples are cited in law by Ronald Dworkin, *Taking Rights Seriously* (Cambridge, MA: Harvard University Press, 1977), chaps. 2 and 3; and in evolutionary biology by Ernst Mayr, *Toward a New Philosophy of Biology* (Cambridge, MA: Harvard University Press, 1988), pt 5.

what it is is conditioned by the way it behaves. Both are necessary in order to understand homology in an evolutionary context. This means that the ascription of properties is not a simple, objective procedure without its connection to the observer's worldview. In the examples cited, a person's theoretical dispositions condition the way the person depicts the object itself.

These examples illustrate that the ascription of properties is not as straightforward as the mechanical subsumptionists would have us believe. Dialectical subsumption is a procedure that is informed by an individual's worldview. The way that the observer understands the object is colored by the way the observer understands the object to behave. The way that the object behaves is conditioned by the observer's theoretical assumptions about this object and objects like it. Finally, an individual's theoretical assumption about general laws governing existing entities is a major component of that person's worldview.

B. Second Form.

The manner by which we insert an object into a category is also theory laden (meaning that it is connected to the worldview of the observer). In many ways, this second mode of explaining dialectical subsumption is similar to the first. The second form involves fitting unknown objects into preestablished categories. This contrasts to the first form that seeks to identify objects and to ascribe to them certain traits and properties.

In biology, the second form is called *taxonomy* and the theory governing the process is called *systematics*. A person examining some individual object to determine what group it belongs to ascribes certain traits to it and uses that description to match (or approximate) its membership into some higher class (thus employing the first form). Sometimes this task is rather delicate; often the individual object is not clearly in a single subspecies but may possess traits of two or more subspecies. In these cases, the observer must make a judgment about the physical traits that are most significant, which is relative to the function of the part in question. Thus, the observer is ranking morphological traits based on theoretical assumptions about functional efficacy.

This is just like the first form in which the observer harbored certain more general theoretical assumptions to help form a judgment about what traits an object possessed and how the traits were to be described. In the second form, the observer uses a more general context (i.e., theoretical assumptions, part of the observer's worldview), which is the justification for putting the individual object into this or that taxonomological category.

Thus, both the ascription of properties to the object (the first form) and the act of placing the object into its appropriate category (the second form) are connected to the observer's worldview. This means that the mechanical subsumption model is false.

The alternative to the mechanical subsumption hypothesis is the *dialectical subsumption* thesis. According to it, the observer moves back and forth between the object and his understanding of the object (including all his theoretical assumptions) until the nature of the object can be determined. When a dissonance occurs between the object as preconceived and the object as dialectically understood, the latter trumps the former.

The second manifestation *is the way we match our ethical imperatives with our worldview.* The dialectical process of matching ethical imperatives with our worldview is outlined in Chapter Eight of *Basic Ethics.* What is the driving force behind this dialectic? What might cause an individual to accept certain courses of action and to reject others? For the answer to these questions, we must return to the Personal Worldview Imperative. This dissonance may occur when a theory suggests that the individual do x, but x is contrary to certain core values that this person holds. Let us examine two examples to see how dissonance occurs.

Example One.

Max is a guard at a Nazi concentration camp. His superiors have given him a directive to shoot a dozen Jewish prisoners because the camp needs fewer prisoners to meet their production requirements. Max marches the prisoners to a corner of the camp that is under repair and from which they could escape if he would turn away. He would never be detected if he shot his gun in the air and allowed them to escape because little attention is paid to the disposal of bodies (since this camp kills hundreds each day).

Max has been taught by his mother that human life is sacred. He knows that these Jews have committed no crimes except being at the wrong place at the wrong time. Therefore, Max believes that killing these people is wrong; he also believes that he has a prima facie duty to obey his superiors. It is a time of war and he has his orders. He is inclined to let the prisoners escape, but the law says he should not.

Example Two.

Sally is an American woman of European descent who grew up in poverty in Appalachia. She had always been close to her mother, who told her that African Americans and the affirmative action program were responsible for her father losing his job and committing suicide as a result. Sally is now a sergeant in the army and has some African Americans under her command. Military regulations require that all soldiers be treated equally regardless of race. However, she has the opportunity to make the lives of these African Americans in her command very difficult as a payback for what happened to her father. She is inclined to "give them hell," but the regulations say she should not.

These two examples are complementary. In the first case, Max's personal worldview may cause him to disobey the law to do the right thing. In the second case, Sally's personal worldview may cause her to disobey the law to do a bad thing. What are we to make of this?

The first question to be asked is whether the Personal Worldview Imperative has been engaged in either case. If Max or Sally had never examined their convictions, then they will probably act according to some idea of punishment should they break the law. In other words, if both are convinced that the law will not punish them, they will probably follow their worldview. But what of this worldview? How responsible are they for it? Was it not merely handed to them by another?

Socrates' dictum—the unexamined life is not worth living—lies at the heart of the Personal Worldview Imperative. I contend that if Max had examined his worldview as suggested by the Personal Worldview Imperative, he would have assumed ownership for his values. In that case, clearly he would not have performed the dissonant action of killing the prisoners. The conflict would be resolved in favor of the worldview.

Sally's case is more challenging; her worldview is incoherent. If she were to consider everything she believes in, that is, (a) that no biologically significant difference between the races exists, (b) that what happened to her father was an instance of an individual affected by a government policy (which was not established by African Americans), and (c) that no logical link exists between what happened to her father and these people now in her command, such an introspective inventory would surely cause Sally to change her worldview. According to the Personal Worldview Imperative, we must strive to make our worldview coherent. If Sally accepted this challenge, then she would alter her beliefs.

What if Sally does not alter them? In this case, she would be a pawn of her mother's value system. Her responsibility for her immoral treatment of her subordinates would still fall to her because she failed to examine her life (via the Personal Worldview Imperative). Her real flaw would be living an inauthentic existence as a slave to another (in this case, her mother). All the consequences of this initial choice also may be attributed to Sally. Sally is actually responsible even if the paradigm she used to guide her actions came from another.[10] This is the description of the material conditions of agency. How we treat Sally as to her culpability of action is another issue. We may determine that circumstances influenced her failure to examine her life.

---

[10]Of course, some would disagree that we really have as much choice as I have portrayed. A pointed rebuttal of my position in this regard has been made by Anita Allen, "Confronting Moral Theories: Gewirth in Context" in Michael Boylan, ed. *Gewirth: Critical Essays in Action, Rationality, and Community* (New York: Rowman and Littlefield, 1999).

I believe that all immoral worldviews that are examined according to the Personal Worldview Imperative will be revised. This is so because I believe that only moral worldviews will satisfy the conditions of rationality, such as those described in the Personal Worldview Imperative.

In this way, the Personal Worldview Imperative offers a necessary basis for any moral theory. Therefore, I can write this introduction without knowing the moral theory of a practitioner. If she has adopted the Personal Worldview Imperative completely, then it will condition the version of any ethical theory into one that will be serviceable to her or any other agent.

This does not mean that all theories are to be judged as equally correct (see my earlier discussion of painters and poets). No, an individual's worldview will dictate that Deontology, Utilitarianism, Intuitionism, or Virtue Ethics is *the* correct theory. The Personal Worldview Imperative allows this judgment to be made. However, the version of this theory (whichever is chosen) will also be conditioned by the Personal Worldview Imperative. An example of this is the emphasis upon both understanding as well as justification (see *Basic Ethics,* Chapter Eight).

In this way, the Personal Worldview Imperative is not a full-blown theory but an important element when considering questions of Metaethics, Normative Ethics, and Applied Ethics. It may offer a bridge between often inaccessible theories and the real lives of people who wish to consider ethical issues.

IV. DECISION MAKING.

Figure 1.1 is a version of the process that I believe should be performed when an individual decides to apply an ethical theory. The process begins when the individual must make a decision that has ethical implications. The process is a rather simplified version of how I believe we should apply any ethical theory.

What can be highlighted about this process is that it emphasizes the sincerity of the individual in following his conscience. *Conscience* means the gathering of a person's exact understandings. This congregation of knowledge is really one form of worldview. Thus, to act according to conscience (in this sense) means to act so that the person's core beliefs are not violated by the proposed action.

It is important to relate the gravity of the proposed action to the primary nature of the core beliefs. For example, if an individual were considering parting his hair from behind or eating a peach, the intended action is clearly rather trivial. If such actions were ethically offensive to the person's core beliefs, then there would be no question that they would be prohibited. Likewise, if the action in question were serious (e.g., Sally's dilemma

Step One: The person identifies the problematic situation in all its particularity, including any possible ethical issues.

Step Two: The agent identifies relevant moral rules in which he believes.

Step Three: The individual engages in dialectical subsumption of the ethical issues in step one, relating them to the rule identified in step two (see the last section for a discussion of dialectical subsumption).*

Step Four: The operation of step three will produce a provisional action directive (i.e., an ethical imperative for action).

Step Five: The individual matches his provisional action directive from step four with his worldview (as discussed in the last section).

Step Six (a): If the provisional action directive fits with his worldview according to the criteria of the Personal Worldview Imperative, he has an ethical imperative for action.

Step Six (b): If the provisional action directive does not fit with the individual's worldview according to the criteria of the Personal Worldview Imperative, he must return to step three.

Step Seven (a): If the difficulty can be resolved by further dialectical subsumption (following his worldview examination in step five), he has an ethical imperative for action.

Step Seven (b): If the difficulty cannot be resolved by further dialectical subsumption, the individual must return to step five and repeat the process.

Step Eight (a): If the difficulty can be resolved, he has an ethical imperative for action.

Step Eight (b): If the difficulty cannot be resolved, steps six (b) and seven (b) should be repeated until the problem is resolved or an impasse is reached.

Step Nine: In the event of an impasse, the individual should return to the process of choosing an ethical theory and repeat that process.

*When step three occurs as mechanical subsumption, the model is more similar to logically abstract supreme principle theory models discussed in *Basic Ethics,* Chapter Nine.

FIGURE 1.1 **The Process of Applying an Ethical Theory**

discussed earlier) and the worldview impediment were relatively trivial, the decision would be easy.[11]

---

[11]A further discussion of this type of analysis can be found in each of the accompanying volumes to this series. See the Evaluating a Case Study series of essays.

Motive/Action	Motive/Action	
	1. Good/Good	2. Good/Bad
	3. Bad/Good	4. Bad/Bad

FIGURE 1.2 **A Matrix of Actions and Motives**

When the ethical issue is serious and the conflicting value is primary (e.g., abortion, the death penalty, euthanasia), the situation is most challenging. When this occurs, the individual must do her best to be true to her conscience/worldview. If the worldview has been carefully crafted according to the steps listed in Figure 1.1, then this touchstone should represent the person's own best approximation of those values that together are most important in life.

If there truly is a right and a wrong in human conduct, we can imagine the four situations shown in Figure 1.2. In the first alternative, the individual has a good motive (one that is fully consonant with his worldview and the relevant ethical principle(s); see steps three and five in Figure 1.1) and a good action.

The second alternative suggests a good motivation with a bad action (the person sincerely believed that what she was doing was correct, but it really was not).[12] The significance of this second alternative contrasts with the third alternative (bad motivation and an accidentally good action). The real issue is engaged at this point. I believe that acting in accordance with one's worldview is the most important criterion. If this means that a person commits a bad action, then at least that person was doing the best she or he could; it was sincerely executed. The possibility that the action might turn out to be the best does not lend any credit to the individual who has acted against her best inclinations.[13]

The basis of this judgment is the Personal Worldview Imperative. When an individual accepts the fact that he must examine his life and develop a single, comprehensive, and internally coherent worldview that he must strive to act out in his life, he has self-consciously agreed that this exercise of autonomy and freedom is what we should do. Such behavior defines us as

---

[12]Whether something is or is not a good action in this context is a thought experiment to make a point about the relationships between conscience/worldview and the act itself. Some would contend that the only way to determine whether an action is right or wrong is to apply the appropriate operational criteria to it. In this case, there is no right or wrong apart from the successful execution of said operation. This point of view could negate the force of my thought experiment unless one were willing to allow the posit that an action was actually right apart from some agent's deliberations on the subject.

[13]For an example of this, see the excerpt from H. G. Wells's *The History of Mr. Polly,* in Michael Boylan, ed., *Perspectives in Philosophy* (New York: Harcourt Brace, 1993), pp. 379–88. Mr. Polly intends to commit suicide and ends up a hero. Was it right to treat him as a hero?

humans in a more comprehensive way than even saying we are "rational animals" because the Personal Worldview Imperative specifies the *manner* of executing our rationality. It is more holistic and ties people to abstract, atemporal logic; to an intellectual tradition; and to various cultural and personal values that jointly describe who we are.

As Figure 1.2 illustrates, an individual goes through this process by engaging in both dialectical subsumption (which commits that individual to creating a bridge between the particular action at hand and various principles that enrich and give meaning to her understanding of that action)[14] and in the worldview check. This check is analogous to the procedure of balancing a checkbook. We all do some quick mental arithmetic to estimate what our total should be and then we go through the mechanics of adding and subtracting. If our mechanical total is quite different from our original guess, we suspect a mistake and repeat the procedure. This process is similar to the worldview check, which offers a check and balance against improper calculations. This is so because we live in our worldview, and we accept it as being what we want—even if we do not always fully execute its demands.

We could use the vernacular expression Is this really *me?* to describe this interaction in another way. If it isn't me, then I should not do it—or I should redefine who me is. Thus, the ultimate authority of action is always the subject (the "me") because the me will be responsible. It is the "me" who will have to live with the action taken.

Thus, the short answer to how to apply an ethical theory is that an individual should strive to be (a) true to the moral theory she or he has chosen, (b) as thorough as possible (according to some sort of scale of proportionality of ethical gravity) in her or his application process (especially steps one through five in Figure 1.1), and (c) as open as possible to altering or changing her or his ethical theory according to the interactions of the *entirety* of her or his worldview. It seems to me that this is what we can and should expect of everyone, no more, no less.

---

[14]This process is also similar to Paul Ricoeur's view of the role of the productive imagination in the A-version of Kant's schematicism.

Interview with Tamar Datan

I. Introduction.

Tamar Datan is director of the Center for Compatible Economic Development and vice president of the Nature Conservancy. She works to design and implement innovative compatible development programs at priority conservation sites and is responsible for management of the Center's staff, budget, and various program activities. Prior to joining the Nature Conservancy in 1997, Datan served as manager of The Pew Charitable Trusts' Venture Fund and was responsible for nearly $100 million in grant awards.

Structure of the Interview.

I include interviews in *Basic Ethics in Action* because I believe it is important to match academic theory with actual practice by those who spend their lives *doing* what we are speculating about. My goal in these interviews is to survey many of the central themes of the book as they affect the person in the field. I hope that the student will find in this interview answers to some issues of practical importance in the way Environmental Ethics is actually practiced in the United States.

Q: I'd like to begin our interview by having you tell our readers a little about the job you do at the Nature Conservancy.
A: I work with communities to create solutions to the challenge of making economic development in their city, county, or region more compatible with its natural resources. This includes working with a broad cross-section of citizen leaders in the public and private sectors to help them seriously consider the intersecting threats and opportunities inherent in moving toward a healthy community, economy, and environment. We work with local communities—mostly in and around the Nature Conservancy's last great places. I seek to help those who are planning development to meet their employment and social goals within a context of responsible use of natural resources.

Q: One of the starting points in discussions of Environmental Ethics is always the source of value. On the one hand are those who say that the only

value the environment has is through its relationship to human interests and needs. This is often termed the *anthropocentric view.*

The contrasting position depicts nature as having intrinsic value apart from humans. This is often termed the *biocentric view.*

Each position has its adherents. On which side of the fence are you?
A: Both sides. I do not agree with the characterization of these positions as contradictory opposites (meaning that you must be on either one or the other side). Rather, I think that they are polar opposites (meaning that you may integrate aspects of each pole together to a greater or to a lesser degree). If they are polar opposites, then (unless you are an extremist) you should consider both points of view when considering an environmental issue. I believe that in the real world one ought to consider both the intrinsic value of nature and its value in providing for human life on earth.

The reason I am reluctant to choose one side or another is that I believe that at this point in human evolution, we have already had such a profound impact on our natural systems that it is impossible to separate one from the other. I also believe that humans could not exist without the natural environment.

Q: So you would support some arguments from each side?
A: Yes. For example, at the Nature Conservancy, we have been very involved in buying land and acquiring usage rights to protect our world for future generations. This is an anthropocentric argument to which I adhere.

On the other hand, when one looks to certain forests, it is clear that they function quite independently of humans. Given the wealth of life that depends on, and contributes to, these forests, I believe they have an intrinsic value independent of humans and would adhere to the view that such value is sufficient to justify the protection of these autonomous biomes.

Q: Well, if they both count, then we must assume that they form a sort of community. What type of community do you think it is?
A: Unfortunately, a community in which the humans have a grossly unequal impact. Perhaps there was a time many years ago in which the balance of the community comprising nature and humans was more equal. But we are a tool-making and controlling species and have become very capable of ignoring nature in our self-absorbed quest for dominion and domination.

Q: Does this mean that you think we are in a point of crisis?
A: Certainly. Humankind has been so restless and destructive of nature that we have put our planet in peril. We must act quickly. There is such urgency to our task that it dwarfs many subtle considerations that philosophers might be inclined to make. Action is imperative and, as such, it defines our mission.

Q: But what of this mission? One might ask whose mission? Some wish to efface the role of "self" in all affairs to a cosmic identification of self to include the entire environmental community. In this way the self transforms from personal ego to a sense of Hindu *atman* (or true self) that obliterates idiosyncratic personality in favor of a self that is blended with everything.

A: Certainly, that is one way of viewing the self, but the facts are that action drives us. You must appreciate that we are in crisis. When you are in crisis, the desired action is what is imperative above all else.

Q: All right, let's move to the action. Some want to link environmental action to social causes. They contend that the dominant theme of oppression creates a synonymy between social causes from Marxism to Feminism that seeks a linkage between their subordinated status and that of nature. For example, the ecofeminists contend that there cannot be an authentic ethics of ecology without the linkage to the plight of women. What do you think about this sort of linkage?

A: I do not doubt that many causes seek redress for unfair domination by an existing power structure. Many of these causes I support from the same impulses that have led me to devote my career to conservation. There is a deep idealistic strain in many environmentalists that longs for justice. This applies not only to the environment but to just causes for oppressed peoples anywhere.

However, I would like to raise a caution. If we in the environmental movement make certain preconditions on our agenda that a person must also sign on to these other movements as well, then we will complicate our task. Let me explain further. Say I am advocating that a certain development project retain a wetland; then I am arguing for an end (call it x) that has a certain cost (call it y). I must convince the developers that x is worth y. This is not an easy task. Unless unavoidable by virtue of environmental regulations, very few developers will voluntarily take additional steps to be sure their development is environmentally benign. But imagine how much *more* difficult the task of convincing the developers that x is worth y would be if I also have to convince them to take on additional social causes, as well.

Q: Tactics dictate that we focus on progress in each and every developmental situation.

A: Exactly. I am *not* saying that we should not be concerned about oppressed peoples everywhere, but I do believe that if environmentalists create new requirements for implementation of their goals, an already challenging mission becomes that much more difficult.

Q: Some have said that sustainable development is a problematic concept. On the one hand, "strong" sustainable development that maintains retaining a pristine or at least "relatively unaffected" environment seems to put a stop to development. It sets the needs of nature above the needs of humans. On the other hand, those same critics will say that "weak" sustainable

development offers nothing above traditional economic welfare maxi-mization. Thus, if sustainable development must either be strong or weak, it is a useless social goal. How do you respond to these arguments?

A: I think that they are incorrectly set. First, very few on the front lines of protecting the environment believe that we can maintain an unchanged en-vironment. Change is a given. Nature will be impacted by the change. All of us in the environmental movement understand this. Thus, the first disjunct you mention is false.

The second disjunct is also problematic. So-called weak sustainability (that I would prefer to call "compatible development") is *not* traditional eco-nomic welfare maximization. If it were not for the active intercession of en-vironment concerns in the planning and execution stages of development, we would be in even worse shape than we are now. Furthermore, a great many communities that are moving toward compatible development are doing so to ensure their economic futures. Whether in forestry, farming, or fishing, many economies rely on their natural resources for their livelihoods.

Q: So what you are saying is that it is all well and good to be utopian about the best possible situation that might exist, but we are now in the midst of a global ecological crisis and we cannot afford to turn our heads from the tasks at hand.

A: Exactly. In the world of action, tactics and strategy must be within a real-istic appraisal of the way things are. We cannot afford too many distractions. There is too much to lose. Thus, your "strong" sustainability position is un-realistic; even if an environment is currently relatively "pristine" or unaf-fected, it is only a matter of time before it is faced with natural and human interventions that will affect it. Everything has to be seen in terms of a nego-tiation between those who seek to gain by development and those who seek to protect (as much as possible) the environment from further devastation.

Let me also make clear that as a realist, I can accept the fact that devel-opment will continue and that the impetus for this development is from le-gitimate social aims: jobs and prosperity for communities. Helping people reshape their lives in a responsible way through development is also a part of my job.

Perhaps an example will illustrate my point. Often in our metropolitan areas around the United States there is growth pressure: more people, more jobs, more infrastructure. This is a fact. Where we come in is to try to deal with this fact and make the actualization of it as gentle on the environment as possible. In this example, one might suggest a strategy of minimal environ-mental disturbance through cluster development. This might make some sense but should also be considered within the context of a plan that takes the entire county or region into account. I believe planning should proceed from a vision of how the county or region could look in five, ten, twenty, fifty, one hundred years. This might seem to be a very long horizon, but (as I said earlier) humans have such a powerful impact on the environment that we ought to plan and act accordingly.

What we must avoid is letting actions create a de facto plan of how things should be without foresight or hindsight.

Q: Many developers often take short cuts in meeting the letter but not the spirit of the law. An individual I know who now works for the federal government at the Environmental Protection Agency has told me that many developers sidestep the regulations concerning maintenance of wetlands by creating surrogates that do not meet the intent of the law.
A: This gets us back to our example earlier of convincing people that x is worth y. But you know I believe that there is more sympathy for this position among regular people than among developers.

Q: How so?
A: It is my opinion that consumers are willing to spend more for products that are environmentally benign. The problem is that we have too few credible, comprehensive systems for delivering such goods to consumers. Europe is ahead of us in this regard. But if U.S. consumers knew that certain purchasing decisions could have a measurable impact on the health of the planet, I believe many would purchase accordingly, including paying more if necessary.

Q: How much more?
A: I don't know. But many assume that if they are environmentally conscious, their product will be unaffordable, or that environmentally irresponsible competition will overtake them. I don't believe that. In fact, I believe that in certain markets, for certain products, an environmental "good housekeeping seal" is a market advantage.

Q: My last question to you is what would you desire if you could control the direction of events in the next ten to thirty years in fulfilling your own personal mission?
A: I want to create new ideas and solutions for compatible economic development. I want to create real examples of businesses and jobs that are compatible with our natural resources. In your terms of worldview, I would like to figure out how we, as *homo sapiens,* can survive and thrive without compromising future generations.

chapter two

Four Traditional Ethical Theories

I. OVERVIEW.

This chapter introduces the reader to some basic terminology, theories, and primary readings. Each theory section is followed by an exercise intended to facilitate the reader's understanding of how to integrate that theory into his day-to-day understanding of how life might be if he were to adopt that particular theory. I believe that this worldview approach is essential in authentically choosing an ethical theory.

II. SOME KEY TERMS USED IN ETHICS.

A. Metaethics.

Metaethics refers to the most general investigation about how to go about creating and applying a theory that prescribes how we should act. Many issues and discussions have developed in this area of ethical study—more than can be set out in such a brief treatment as this; however, in the depiction of the ethical theories themselves, the reader should refer to Chapters One through Four of *Basic Ethics*.

One central issue concerns the *origins* of the theories. This, in turn, engenders several related questions: How do we know these theories are correct? How are these theories justified? What do these theories tell us about the world?

These (and other) questions are important because they set the stage for our being able to construct a normative theory of ethics. In this way, metaethics serves Normative Ethics just as philosophy of science serves those who create theories of science. There is a sense of creating the boundaries of acceptable discourse.

One of the principal questions in metaethics in the twentieth century has been whether one could derive an "ought" statement from an "is" statement. If you cannot, then "oughts" occur from nonfactual (i.e., nonrational) sources. Why do people hold such a position? Let's examine this through an example.

> *Premise*—John says to Mary, "There is a poisonous cobra under your chair."
> *Conclusion*—John then says, "You ought to get out of your chair and run" or, more simply, "Get out of your chair and run!"

What is the relationship between the premise and the conclusion? On first glance, it might seem as if the factual premise 1 implies the normative action-guiding conclusion. In this case, we would have an "is" (or factual statement) implying an "ought" (or prescriptive statement).

However, others might demur. They would say that this paradigm has suppressed premises. These might include the following:

1'.   A poisonous cobra will kill you.
1".   You do not wish to be killed.
1"'. The only way to avoid being killed is to get out of your chair and run.

Premise 1' and 1"' are both factual statements, but 1" is a suppressed premise that is also normative. The whole argument would go differently if one were to assert that *she or he were indifferent to being killed*. This means that 1" is really equivalent to "You *ought* not wish to be killed." In this way, the detractor would contend that a hidden *ought* has been smuggled into the premises. If this is true, one has not derived an ought from an is but an ought from an ought.

Thus, the detractor of there being a derivation of an *ought* from an *is* would assert that in every supposed example of such a purported derivation, there is a suppressed premise which contains a "hidden *ought*."

There are other important questions in metaethics. For example, perhaps the basis of ethical value cannot be determined rationally. Those who would make such an assertion fall into two camps: (a) the cognitivists who emphasize the role of rationally informed emotion such as sympathy and care (as in ethical feminism) and (b) the noncognitivists.

The noncognitivists believe that the basis of ethical theory is not legitimately in knowledge. In a deep sense, it is a matter of "taste." For example, few of us would contend that there is an intellectual basis for liking Fortnum and Mason's Irish Breakfast Tea over Bewley's variety of the same. Some prefer the softer taste of the former, while others choose the sharper, tannic aspect of the latter.

The noncognitivists contend that no matter how hard one tries, matters of value cannot be traced back to matters of fact. For example, in the preceding example concerning tea, one could say that good tea has a sharper, tannic taste; therefore, Bewley's is better. However, the critic would contend, how do we know that sharper and tannic are better and how do we measure them? This can be a problem, the noncognitivists contend. There is *no* pure standard for good tea that all would agree; this is why we have so many types of tea!

I will not elaborate on various other noncognitivist strategies—such as linguistic analysis and emotivism—here. For a more detailed treatment, I refer the reader to *Basic Ethics* or other general books that treat issues of metaethics.

B. Normative Ethics.

Normative Ethics concerns itself with creating[1] norms or standards of human conduct. Each of the theories in Normative Ethics comes complete with its own internal justification and metaethical assumptions. There are many important normative theories, but this abbreviated presentation presents only four: Intuitionism, Virtue Ethics, Utilitarianism, and Deontology. In addition to these traditional theories, various modifications of these theories have been made that include Feminism, Religion and Ethics, and Professional Ethics.[2] Each case has a prescriptive set of directives that are designed to offer judgments about our actions.

C. Applied Ethics.

Applied Ethics covers ethics in action. Actual ethical decision making occurs on this level. Ethics in action is a study of the way we *ought* to make decisions in the world when problems arise that have ethical content (i.e., touch on the right and wrong in human action). Just what counts as "right" and "wrong" is determined by a normative theory. Thus, Applied Ethics is an interdisciplinary arena in which all the rules of prudent professional decision making are

---

[1]I use the word *creating* here because (like Kant) I believe that we legislate moral maxims over a universal sample space. Those who would advocate Virtue Ethics or Utilitarianism would demur because for them the process is not one of creating but one of scientific discovery. Emotivists would also concur.

[2]It should be acknowledged that many advocates of feminism, religious ethics, and professional ethics would criticize me here by saying that their theories are not "overlays" to some other theory but should stand by themselves. I would concur that this is one way to view these theories. However, I would add that in my treatment, their status would be as an overlay to enrich other theories.

confronted with yet one more parameter: ethical considerations. Thus, from the outset, Applied Ethics deals with all the realities of real-life decisions.

The context that enables this choice to occur effectively is normative theory. Thus, Applied Ethics bounces back and forth between the front line of decision making and the Normative Ethics that supports this process. This series of books, *Basic Ethics in Action*, embodies this dynamic. It consciously moves back and forth between Normative and Applied Ethics.

III. ETHICAL INTUITIONISM.

Ethical Intuitionism can generally be described as a theory of justification for the immediate grasping of self-evident ethical truths. Ethical Intuitionism can operate on the level of general principles or on the level of daily decision making. In this latter mode, many of us have experienced a form of Ethical Intuitionism through the teaching of timeless adages such as, "Look before you leap," and "Faint heart never won fair maiden." The truth of these sayings is justified through intuition. Many adages or maxims contradict each other (such as these two), so that the ability to apply these maxims properly is also understood through intuition.

A Quick Exercise to Understand Ethical Intuitionism.

In practice, Ethical Intuitionism works from an established list of moral maxims that have no other justification other than they are immediately perceived to be true. To understand better how this ethical theory works, try the following exercise:

Step One: Make a list of general moral maxims that you believe will cover most moral situations (e.g., don't lie). Choose at least three but no more than ten.

Step Two: Establish a hierarchy among the maxims that applies for the most part.

Step Three: Create a moral situation that involves at least two moral maxims from your list. Determine which moral maxim best applies in the situation and state the reasons for your choice. How would you respond to someone who disagrees with your choice?

IV. VIRTUE ETHICS.

Virtue Ethics is also sometimes called *agent-based ethics.* Its position is that in living, a person should try to cultivate excellence in all that he does and all that others do. These excellences or virtues are both moral and nonmoral. Through conscious training, as a nonmoral example, an athlete can achieve excellence in a sport (nonethical example). In the same way, a person can achieve ethical excellence as well. The way these habits are developed and the community that nurtures them are all under the umbrella of Virtue Ethics.

Virtue Ethics works from an established list of accepted character traits called *virtues*. These traits are acquired by habit and guide the practitioner in making moral decisions. Aristotle described these character traits as being a mean between extremes. According to him, the good man so habituates his behavior to these virtues that he will carry out the good actions over and over again throughout his life.

A Quick Exercise to Understand Virtue Ethics.

To better understand what virtue ethics means, complete the following exercise:

Step One: Make a list of traits that you believe to be virtues. Make sure you have at least three virtues but no more than ten.

Step Two: Establish the mean by outlining how the virtues in step one are really somewhere in the middle of two extremes.

Step Three: Describe how you might ingrain this trait into your character. What consequences would this virtue have?

Step Four: Create a moral situation and show how Virtue Ethics would help you to resolve it. How does Virtue Ethics make a difference in this situation?

V. UTILITARIANISM.

Utilitarianism is a theory that suggests that an action is morally right when that action produces more total utility for the group as a consequence than any other alternative does. Sometimes this has been shortened to the slogan "the greatest good for the greatest number." This emphasis on calculating quantitatively the general population's projected consequential utility among competing alternatives appeals to many of the same principles that underlie democracy and capitalism (which is the reason that this theory has always been very popular in the United States and other Western capitalistic democracies).

A Quick Exercise to Understand Utilitarianism.

Since Utilitarianism commends the moral choice that produces the greatest happiness for the greatest number of people, under this system we must have a mechanism for determining (a) the alternatives involved, (b) a list of possible outcomes of the alternatives, (c) a clear definition of the population sample to be affected by the alternatives, and (d) a way to measure the possible impact that each alternative would have on the population sample so that it will become clear which alternative will yield the most pleasure/utility. The test chosen must be one that can be carried out and have relatively uncontroversial units by which the happiness-impact can be measured and examined. To better understand what is involved in choosing Utilitarianism as an ethical theory, try the following exercise.

Step One: Create a moral situation that involves a difficult choice of alternative actions. (Cases that pit the majority interests against rights of the minority are often good for this exercise.)

Step Two: List the possible alternatives and their projected outcomes.

Step Three: Define the population affected by your case.

Step Four: Propose a way to measure the happiness of the parties involved. Be sure that your measuring system can be quantified. What criticisms of your test could people make? How would you respond to their criticisms?

Step Five: Test your sample population and give the actual numbers of the happiness coefficients that each group will possess according to each alternative.

Step Six: Justify your choice from step five against possible attacks.

VI. DEONTOLOGY.

Deontology is a moral theory that emphasizes one's duty to do a particular action because the action itself is inherently right and not due to any calculation about the consequences of the action. Because of this nonconsequentialist bent, Deontology is often contrasted with Utilitarianism, which defines the right action in terms of its ability to bring about the greatest aggregate utility. In contradistinction to Utilitarianism, Deontology recommends an action based on principle. Principle is justified through an understanding of the structure of action, the nature of reason, and the operation of the will. The result is a moral command to act that does not justify itself by calculating consequences.

The moral principle is derived from and justified by the nature of reason and the structure of human action. Both its justification and its scope are general. The principle defines duty concerning moral situations in general. One way to understand this level of generality is to compare it to a scientific law, which is universal and absolute, covering all societies in all historical epochs.

One difficulty people often face with such a general principle is that moral cases are presented to us as particulars. In logic, general or universal propositions are contrasted to particular or individual propositions. They are different logical types and cannot be directly compared. The moral problem must be "translated" into general language at the same level as the moral principle, which allows a definitive outcome to be determined. However, this translation is not so easy. For example, consider Sally, who is contemplating an abortion. All particulars of her individual situation must be translated into the form of a general ethical principle or general ethical law.

For this example, let us assume Kant's Categorical Imperative as our general principle. This principle states that we should act only on that maxim through which we can at the same time will that it become a universal law. This principle prohibits murder[3] because a universal law allowing murder in some society is logically contradictory. (If everyone murdered everyone else, there would be no society.) Logically contradictory universal laws are immoral; therefore, murder is immoral.

Autonomy, however, is also dictated by the Categorical Imperative and becomes its cornerstone of a formulation of the Categorical Imperative that addresses people as ends, not means only.

An example of the problem of moving from the particular to the general level (necessary for applying the moral laws/principles of Deontology) is in the translation of abortion. Is abortion an instance of *killing* or of *autonomy?* If it is the former, it is prohibited. If it is the latter, it is permitted.

The real debate rests in the translation. Once a moral situation has been translated, the application to the ethical law is easy. The ethical law determines our duty in the situation, and we must do our duty or else we repudiate our human nature; we are, after all, rational beings.

A Quick Exercise to Understand Deontology.

To better understand how Deontology works, try the following exercise:

Step One: Choose a universal moral principle (it can be Kant's or any other principle stated in general "lawlike" terminology).

Step Two: Create a particular moral situation that involves a difficult choice of alternative actions. (Cases that pit two moral duties against each other are often good for this exercise.)

Step Three: Determine the possible alternative ways to translate the particular case into more general language (i.e., as an instance of truth telling, murder, autonomy).

---

[3]The mode of this prohibition is that all moral maxims generated from the notion of a universal society of murderers are shown to be incoherent. This means that a moral maxim such as "It is permissible to murder" is found to contain a logical contradiction. Like Plato, Kant believes that logical contradictions indicate immorality because morality means the right and wrong in human action. *Right* and *wrong* are determined by reference to logic. Illogic, therefore, is wrong. This is the driving force behind the universality of the Categorical Imperative in its various forms.

Step Four: Justify your translation and point out the flaws in alternative translations.

Step Five: Show how your translation fits a general corollary of the universal ethical principle. Explain how you arrived at the corollary and the outcome of translation to the corollary. What criticism of your translation, corollary derivation, or outcomes application could people make? How would you defend yourself against these criticisms?

The criteria for deciding between ethical theories are elaborated by metaethics. Once you endorse a theory, you must determine how to apply it.

One commonly held principle of application states that similar cases are to be treated similarly. Let this principle be termed the *just implementation of rules.* This principle is a purely formal principle of distributive justice.[4] (Distributive justice is that subbranch of ethics that provides criteria by which goods and services may be parsed to recipients.) As a formal principle, this tells us that no matter what the content of the rule, all things being equal, it is just to treat similar cases the same way.

The just implementation of rules is a necessary but not a sufficient principle. For example, if the Nazis held that the right to live is to be distributed only to non-Jews, then the application of the just implementation of rules would suggest that all Jews be killed!

What is needed are specifications on the *content* of the rule. When the content of the rule is included (as per the Personal Worldview Imperative), it is obvious that the imperative is inconsistent since no morally relevant difference exists between Jews and non-Jews. Since the Nazis contended that such a difference existed, they can be accused of being logically inconsistent.

Some might contend that makes no difference. These bestial creatures could care less. The answer would be that they diminish themselves—whether they know it or not—by violating the Personal Worldview Imperative.

Specifications on the content of the rule also address issues of what is the best system of distributive justice. Traditional candidates of distributive justice have included *capitalism* (to each according to his production), *socialism* (to each according to her need), *egalitarianism* (to each equally), *aristocracy* (to each according to his inherited station), and *kraterism* (to each according to her ability to snatch it for herself).

There are other allocation formulae (theories of distributive justice), but my list provides a range of approaches, which are often used to answer the question of how goods and services are to be distributed.

---

[4]Distributive justice is only one form of justice. The other most prominent form is retributive justice, which outlines how we are to punish others and the conditions on which these decisions are made and justified.

Once one has argued for and accepted a theory, then according to the just implementation of rules, he must apply it in a similar manner to all similar cases.

In the preceding example, the theory of justice one adopts constitutes the material element in the theory while the just implementation of rules represents merely a formal implementation tool.

This example is meant to illustrate the types of issues with which Normative Ethics concerns itself. In this domain, we are interested in creating norms for conduct, including a justification and defense of all issues involved with the creation, understanding, or general application of such ethical norms.

In subsequent chapters of this book, we will extend our exploration of both Normative Ethics and its interaction with actual decision making which is Applied Ethics. At the end of the core chapters of the book are exercises to integrate this process with the ability to create a coherent written evaluation of these case studies (a simulated action situation).

EVALUATING A CASE STUDY: DEVELOPING A PRACTICAL ETHICAL VIEWPOINT

Your goal in this book is to respond critically to case studies on various aspects of Environmental Ethics. To do this, you must be able to assess the ethical impact of some critical factor(s) in situations that pose ethical problems. One factor in assessing the case is the ethical impact of the project/policy/action. This chapter and Chapters Three through Six end with an "Evaluating a Case Study" section that focuses on a particular exercise. These sections include case studies to which you can apply the insight you gained from the readings and discussion in the chapter. Because the information presented in these "Evaluating a Case Study" sections is cumulative, you should be able to write a complete critical response to a case study by the end of Chapter Six.

Macro and Micro Cases.

Beginning with this chapter, each chapter will end with cases for you to consider. The cases section is divided into two categories, macro and micro. Each type of case employs a different point of view.

Macro Case. The macro case takes the perspective of someone in an executive position of authority who supervises or directs an organizational unit. His or her decisions will affect many people and resonate in a larger sociological sphere.

Micro Case. The micro case examines the perspective of someone at the proximate level of professional practice. Obviously, this case applies to more people than does the macro case.

Case Development. This book suggests one way to develop critical evaluations of ethical cases. In the "Evaluating a Case Study" sections, you will be asked to apply a specific skill to the cases presented. At the end of Chapter Six, you will be able to write an essay concerning the application of an ethical perspective to a specific problem.

Please note that although the cases presented here have fictional venues, they are based on composites of actual practice.

These end-of-chapter evaluations seek to bridge the gap between Normative Ethics and Applied Ethics. Skill in using Applied Ethics is very important, for this is where the practical decision making occurs. My approach in these essays is to allow you to employ techniques that you have been taught elsewhere in addition to those found in this text. Depending on your background in science or the public policy field, you can write a critical response to a case study that demonstrates your professional acumen along with your sensitivity to the ethical dimensions found in the situation you are examining. Classes that have few students with environmentally oriented backgrounds (such as in biology, ecology, and environmental policy) will deemphasize the fundamental details of science and concentrate instead on a less technical response.

Environmentalists often concentrate on the practices they so detest that they lose their ability to discern the rational grounds for their beliefs, a difficulty experienced in all professions.[1] But this is wrong. The "Evaluating a Case Study" sections will help you analyze both ethical and practical situations. The approach will invoke a technique that rates a proposal as having three levels of complexity: surface, medium, and deep. The level of interaction allows you to see at a glance how the competing areas of interest and ethical value conflict.

The five "Evaluating a Case Study" sections are intended to sequentially lead you to develop the abilities to write a critical response to a case study: (a) Developing a Practical Ethical Viewpoint, (b) Finding the Conflicts, (c) Assessing Embedded Levels, (d) Applying Ethical Issues, and (e) Structuring the Essay.

At the end of Chapters Three through Six, you will be presented case studies to which you can apply your newfound skills. By the end of the term, you should be able to create an ethical impact statement of some sophistication.

Let us begin first by choosing an ethical theory and proceed to develop a practical viewpoint. Few people bother to choose an ethical theory; most

---

[1]For a fuller discussion of this, see *Basic Ethics*, Chapter Seven.

pick up a few moral maxims that they apply when the occasion seems appropriate. The manner of this acquisition is often environment dependent, that is, having to do with their upbringing, friends, and the community(ies) in which they live. As such, their maxims reflect those other viewpoints.

The Personal Worldview Imperative enjoins us to develop a single comprehensive and internally coherent worldview that is good and that we will strive to act out in our lives (see Chapter One). One component of this worldview is an ethical theory. Thus, each us must *develop* an ethical theory. This does not mean that we must all start from scratch. Those before us have done much good work. But we must personally choose an ethical theory and assume ownership for it as being the most correct theory in existence. It is not enough merely to accept someone else's theory without any active work on our part. We must go through the process of personal introspection and evaluation to determine what we think is best and to be open to ways we can improve the theory (in concept or in practice).

This process of making an ethical theory our own can take years. This course is only a few months. Does this pose a problem? Not really when you consider that part of the process of making an ethical theory our own involves provisional acceptance and testing of various moral maxims. Obviously, this testing has a limit. We should not test whether it is morally permissible to murder by going out and murdering various people. The testing I am advocating is a way to examine various moral commands and evaluate whether their application is consonant with other worldview values we hold. The process will perhaps go back and forth in a progressive dialectic until we have accepted or rejected the commands.

To begin this process of testing, we must identify the most prominent ethical theories and their tenets. Many books survey and evaluate the major ethical theories. In this series of textbooks, *Basic Ethics in Action,* I have written one such survey entitled, *Basic Ethics.* I would suggest that you refer either to that book or to another like it to obtain enough information to enable you to begin the process of choosing an ethical theory.

For the purposes of this book, I have highlighted four major theories: Utilitarianism, Deontology, Ethical Intuitionism, and Virtue Ethics. To begin the process, I recommend that you choose a single theory from these four (or from among others your instructor may offer) as your critical tool as you prepare for class. How do I know which viewpoint to choose? This is a difficult question. It concerns the justification of the various ethical theories.

Many criteria can be used to justify an ethical theory. One criterion is Naturalism. Each theory presupposes a naturalistic or nonnaturalistic epistemological standpoint. Naturalism is complicated; for our purposes, let us describe it as a view that holds that no entities or events are in principle beyond the domain of scientific explanation. Cognitive claims are valid only if they are based on accepted scientific modes.

Ethical Naturalism states that moral judgments are also merely a subclass of facts about the natural world that can be studied scientifically. From this study, we can determine moral correctness as a corollary of certain facts that can be scientifically investigated (e.g., how much pleasure various alternatives will produce for the group). Thus, utilitarians believe that moral judgments *are* judgments about which alternative will be most beneficial to some group's survival.

A utilitarian might point to the scientific study of nature and say that the instinct to seek pleasure is evidenced in all species. Furthermore, an evolutionary advantage seems to exist for those species that act for the benefit of the group against those that do not act in this way.

Many sociobiologists make this sort of claim. The main imperative of evolutionary theory is that a person's own genes be passed on to another generation. If passing on a person's own genes is impossible, the next best thing is to pass on the genes of the individual's relatives. Thus, seemingly altruistic behavior (such as a bird that stays behind in dangerous situations so that the group might survive) is really selfish because helping the group *is* helping the bird to pass on its genes (or those of its relatives).

Sociobiology, of course, is not universally accepted, nor is it necessary for a utilitarian to be a sociobiologist. However, this example does illustrate a type of justification that the utilitarian might make. He could move from the concept of group happiness in animals and extrapolate to humans. The supporting data are scientific; therefore, the theory is naturalistic.

Deontologists may or may not be naturalists. Since Deontology involves a duty-based ethics, the key question to be asked concerns how we know whether a binding duty exists to do such and such. Are all moral "oughts" derivable from factual, scientifically ascertainable "is" statements? If they are, then the deontologist is a naturalist. If they are not, then the deontologist is not a naturalist.

In his book *Reason and Morality*, Alan Gewirth claims to derive ought from is. There is no reference to knowledge claims that are not compatible with the scientific inquiry of natural objects. This would make Gewirth a naturalist. Kant and Donagan are somewhat different. Each refers to supernatural entities that are not scientifically supported. Kant spends considerable effort trying to define these boundaries in the "Transcendental Dialectic" section of his book *The Critique of Pure Reason*. This aside, neither Kant nor Donagan considered that a problem about integrating the factual and the normative existed.

If you are inclined to view reality as an extension of evolutionary biology or to believe that group advantage immediately entails a moral ought, then you are leaning toward Utilitarianism. If you think that people should act from pure duty alone without reference to anything except the rightness of the action, then Deontology is probably your preference.

The is-ought problem was sharpened by intuitionist G.E. Moore,[2] who rejected Ethical Naturalism because he believed it contained a fallacy (which he dubbed *the naturalistic fallacy*). This fallacy claims that it is false to define goodness in terms of any natural property. This is so because good is not definable and because good is not subject to scientific examination. This is true because the factual realm is separate from the normative ought realm. The chasm between the two cannot be crossed.

Good for Moore is a unique, unanalyzable, non-natural property (as opposed, for example, to yellow which is a natural property). Clearly, scientific methods are of no use. Science can tell us things about yellow but can tell us nothing about the meaning of good. Other intuitionists also hold that we understand important moral terms and/or moral maxims by cognitive means that are not scientific. Generally, these are immediate and cannot be justified in factual "is" language.

Intuitionism is therefore a non-naturalistic theory. Still, it has some remote connections to Naturalism. For example, one can point to the *plausibility* of accepting certain common moral maxims—such as a prohibition against murder—by reference to other societies. (In other words, since all societies prohibit murder, the prohibition against murder must be immediately apparent to all.) However, plausibility is not the same thing as exhaustive scientific demonstration. Justification in Intuitionism lies in its alleged unarguable truth that can be grasped in principle immediately by all.

If you are having trouble adopting any of the other theories and believe that acceptance or rejection of an ethical theory comes down to some sort of brute immediate acceptance, then you will probably want to accept Intuitionism as your ethical theory.

Finally, we turn to Virtue Ethics. This theory seems at first to be naturalistic. Aristotle lends credence to this when he talks about relying on the common opinions of people about what is considered to be a virtue. The common opinions could be gathered and reviewed much as a sociologist or anthropologist might do, and this "scientific" method would yield definitive results. Aristotle believed that some common agreement existed about a core set of virtues.

Justification, therefore, was not an issue for Aristotle. If we accept a worldview such as Aristotle presents, then we would all agree that everyone considers courage (for example) to be a virtue. The confirming data can be

---

[2]I cannot stress too much the impossibility of completely pigeonholing philosophers. In some important ways, Moore was an intuitionist because "good" had to be accepted as an unanalyzable, unnatural fact. Toward the end of *Principia Ethica,* however, he sounds much like an agathistic utilitarian, one who wishes to maximize the group's good. This mixture of labels among philosophers shows only that labels are limited in what they can do.

Ross and Rawls have deontological and intuitionistic aspects to their theories. Therefore, one label alone cannot adequately capture the spirit of their philosophy. In an introductory text, such as this one, labels are used to simplify—but hopefully not obfuscate—the dynamics present in these thinkers.

gathered and scientifically studied; ergo, it is naturalistic. The proof depends on the community that values these traits. This emphasis on community makes Virtue Ethics a favorite theory among those who call themselves *communitarians.* The communitarian begins with the group and its institutions and depends on individual members to submit to the authority of the group (or to change the group in ways it accepts).

How does Communitarianism affect today's pluralistic society? Some might argue that consensus about the virtues no longer exists nor does a single community to which we all belong. If there is no consensus as Aristotle envisioned, then what constitutes a virtue may collapse into a form of Intuitionism. For example, I think that X is a virtue. You think Y is a virtue. X and Y are mutually exclusive traits. You and I come from different communities/societies; therefore, we cannot come to an agreement. All each of us can say is I am right and you are wrong. Personal insight (Intuitionism) is all we have to justify our practices (to ourselves and to others).

If you believe that courage, wisdom, self-control, piety, and so forth are virtues in every society, then perhaps you will choose Virtue Ethics as your model.

To help you choose an ethical theory, try this exercise. Examine one or more of the following moral situations and (a) interpret what is right and wrong according to each of the four theories, (b) then give an argument that might be proposed according to each theory, and (c) state your own assessment of the strengths of each theory.

Situation One.

You are the constable of a small, remote, rural town in Northern Ireland. The town is divided into the Catholics (20 percent minority) and the Protestants (80 percent majority). All Catholics live in one section of town on a peninsula jutting into the river just east of the main part of town.

One morning a young Protestant girl is found raped and murdered next to the town green. According to general consensus, a Catholic must have committed the crime. The Protestants form a citizens committee that demands the following of the constable: "We believe you to be a Catholic sympathizer, and we don't think you will press fast enough to bring this killer to justice. We know a Catholic committed the crime. We've sealed off the Catholic section of town; no one can go in or out. If you don't hand over the criminal by sundown, we will torch the entire Catholic section of town, killing all 1,000 people. Don't try to call for help. We've already disabled the telephone."

You made every effort to find out who did it, but you made no progress. You could not find out. At one hour before sundown, you don't know what to do. Your deputy says, "Why don't we just pick a random Catholic and tell them he did it? At least we'd be saving 999 lives."

"But then I'd be responsible for killing an innocent man!" you reply.

"Better one innocent die and 999 be saved. After all, there's no way the two of us can stop the mob. You have to give them a scapegoat," the deputy responds.

Describe how each ethical theory might approach this situation. Which one is most consonant to your own worldview, and why?

Situation Two.

You are a railroad switcher sitting in a tower and controlling a switch that allows trains to travel over the regular track or switches them to a siding. One morning you face a terrible dilemma. The N.Y. Zephyr is traveling at high speed on the main track, and a school bus filled with children (at least fifty) has stalled on the main track as it crosses Elm Street. The bus driver is trying to restart the engine, but the ignition will not turn over. It is clear to you that the bus will not get off the track in time. On the siding track is a homeless man who has fallen down and caught his foot on a rail tie. It is also clear that he is stuck.

In fifteen seconds, you must decide whether to use the switch to send the train to the siding—thereby killing the homeless man—or to do nothing and allow the train to take its normal course and thereby hit the bus and probably kill most if not all of the fifty school children on board.

Describe how each ethical theory might approach this situation. Which one is most consonant to your own worldview, and why?

Situation Three.

You are on the executive committee of the XYZ organization of health care professionals. Each year the committee gives an award to one of its members who displays high moral character in his or her work. This year you are among the four judges for the award. There is some disagreement among the judges, however, about what constitutes a good person. The judges, besides yourself, are Ms. Smith, Mrs. Taylor, and Mr. Jones. The candidates for the award are Mr. Big and Mrs. Little.

Ms. Smith says that the award should go to Mr. Big because he saved a man from drowning. However, Mr. Jones demurred, saying that Mr. Big's motives are suspect because the man he saved was in the midst of a very big financial deal with Mr. Big. If the man had been allowed to drown, Mr. Big would have lost a lot of money. Ms. Smith said motives are not important but that the goodness of the act counts and the man who was saved runs a big business in town. Many people besides Mr. Big would have been hurt if he had not saved the man.

Mr. Jones said the award should go to Mrs. Little because she performed a kind act of charity in chairing the town's United Way Campaign this last year. Surely such an act could not be said to benefit Mrs. Little in any way (unlike Mr. Big).

Mrs. Taylor says that she is somewhat unsure about either Mr. Big or Mrs. Little because both of them have been recommended on the basis of a single good act. Mrs. Taylor believed that it would be better to choose a candidate who has shown over time to have performed many good actions and to be of good character. "After all," she said, "a single swallow does not make a spring." Mr. Jones and Ms. Smith scratched their heads at this remark and turned to you. Who is right?

Describe how each ethical theory might approach this situation. Which one is most consonant to your own worldview, and why?

Choosing an ethical theory is only the first step in developing a practical ethical viewpoint. A link between the normative theory and application of the theory is needed. In Chapter One, I outlined my basic position concerning a personal worldview and how it might be utilized when applying an ethical theory. In the last section of Chapter One, I outlined a principle of fair competition that I believe can be used to apply the general theory chosen to the moral decision at hand.

The point is that one important aspect of developing a practical ethical viewpoint is to challenge ourselves to think about and provisionally accept certain tenets necessary to effectively apply ethical principles to practice. These concepts should allow individuals to connect normative theories to the real-life problems that confront them.

Before addressing ethical cases, try first to provisionally accept one moral theory. Then try to determine what connecting principles or concepts are necessary to translate theory to practice. Concentrate your efforts on these connections. They will be very useful to you as you address what you see as the important issues residing in each case.

chapter three

Worldview Arguments for Environmentalism

General Overview. This chapter presents various approaches to Environmental Ethics via worldview. Readers of this and other volumes in this series know that I believe worldview to be an essential component in confronting philosophical problems of value. Through the Personal Worldview Imperative, I march with those who believe that problems of value require that one *live* his or her philosophy—not simply profess it. This is an ancient, fundamental meaning of philosophy that I believe should be revived today.

I introduce this chapter with a key figure and a precursor to much environmental thinking, Aldo Leopold (1887–1948). He wrote (among other things) the famous essay, "The Land Ethic." In it Leopold argues that our relationship with the land is an ethical one in which we understand ourselves as being a part of a biotic community that includes the land. "Right" and "wrong" are to be understood through the well-being of the community as a whole. Under this understanding, a person could justify farming, hunting, or other use of natural resources so long as the integrity, stability, and beauty of the particular natural community has been maintained. Such an outlook has been called *ethical holism* because ethical judgments about projects involving nature are made from this perspective. Leopold creates a backdrop for many of the selections in this chapter.

The next set of selections introduce *deep ecology*. One of the essential movements that these philosophers make is to reidentify the locus of value away from the individual human to some other unit. One is reminded (by analogy) of Hegel's assertion (in the *Phenomenology of Spirit*) that the family is the basic unit and of the communitarians who assert that some particular (robustly defined) community is the basic unit of human value. Utilitarians also tend to identify human communities as primitive units—though their "community" is rather changeable (since group calculations of happiness are subject to revision and alteration). In these cases, the individual's desires and plans can be overridden by those of the group.

The deep ecologists go one step further and identify the biosphere as the basic unit. Thus, not only an individual's desires but also the self-interested desires of all the human community can be overridden. This approach can vary from a modest set of nested priorities to the cooperative social order that Murray Bookchin advocates. There are some differences between the deep ecologists and the social ecologists, who criticize the deep ecologists because they do not give adequate attention to the roles of capitalism and the state in nature's destruction. The deep ecologists reply that such an emphasis on human institutions makes social ecology rather anthropocentric rather than biocentric (as the deep ecologists advocate).

This link between the principles of deep ecology to the sociopolitical organization of society is developed further by the ecofeminists. By linking the subjugation of women to the subjugation of the environment, the ecofeminists advocate a position that calls for an examination of male-dominated social institutions as a key to solving the problems of women and the environment.

Finally, the last section of this chapter presents ways that the other (nonethical) basic values—religion and aesthetics—can make an impact on the environmental worldview. I begin with a Jewish perspective since much of the Jewish worldview permeates the other two Western religions of the region, Christianity and Islam. Eilon Schwartz invokes religious worldview values of Judaism to support an anthropocentric environmental ethics.

Next, I turn to perspectives from Native American peoples. Authors Annie L. Booth and Harvey M. Jacobs combine visions from various Native American nations to draw some pivotal contrasts with the worldview of the occidental culture. Although Native Americans were great hunters and fishermen, they did not overkill and lived in a sustainable balance with their environment.

In J. Baird Callicott's article, religious values on two continents (Africa and Australia) are shown to be causally significant to key tenets of environmental philosophy: seeing oneself as a part of a biocommunity and appreciating the special significance of certain geographic sites (including all the flora and fauna).

Finally, Janna Thompson offers an argument based on the connection of beauty to the moral good to support an environmental ethics position.

I. THE LAND ETHIC, DEEP ECOLOGY, AND SOCIAL ECOLOGY.

Overview. As I mentioned in the general introduction, Aldo Leopold's land ethic depends on our acceptance of the concept of a biotic community. Pivotal to this understanding is the notion of a land pyramid in which one distinguishes the importance of the pyramid's lower layers: the soil and the primary producers. Leopold speaks of these in terms of an energy circuit. Those at the top of the pyramid depend on the lower levels. If the lower levels are not nurtured, then those at the top are in jeopardy. Thus, a duty arises to the land and those primary producers at the bottom of the pyramid that is rooted in prudential interests.

Deep ecology is a movement that calls for us to reshape our worldviews and to reorganize our lives accordingly. Deep ecology shifts the emphasis from individualism and reductionistic thinking toward holistic and contextual thinking. If the basic unit of identification is the community (here the biotic ecosystem), then personal—even human—interests must take a back seat to the good of the whole. One proponent of such a plan is Arne Naess. Through a plan of conscious simplicity of life ("simple in means and rich in ends"), Naess proposes a profound and fundamental shift in the way we situate ourselves vis-à-vis the natural environment. In his essay, Naess contrasts the viewpoint of mainstream anthropocentric environmentalists (shallow ecology) with the position he is advocating (deep ecology). To this end, he calls for seven principles: (a) rejection of the man-in-environment image in favor of the relational, total-field image, (b) biospherical egalitarianism—in principle, (c) principles of diversity and symbiosis, (d) anticlass posture, (e) fight against pollution and resource depletion, (f) complexity, not complication, and (g) local autonomy and decentralization.

In other writings, Naess's contrast of the shallow and the deep leads to a redefinition of self along the lines of the Hindu concept of *atman,* or true self.[1] The *atman* represents one's true self, yet that self is cosmic. It has dissolved the ego and is released from concerns about self-interest. In this way, when an individual creates an ecophilosophy that abnegates the self, he is acting in the interests of the "self" (now understood as *atman*). From this standpoint, Naess redefines individual rights and responsibilities.

---

[1]Arne Naess, "Identification as a Source of Deep Ecological Attitudes," in Michael Tobias, ed., *Deep Ecology* (San Diego: Avant Books, 1985): 256–270.

Bill Devall and George Sessions expand on Naess by suggesting two core concepts on which to formulate a worldview: (a) self-realization and (b) biocentric equality. The first of these corresponds to the sense of self just described. The second is based on biocentric equality. This tenet of biocentric equality sounds much like Paul Taylor in Chapter Five. However, although Taylor asserts a type of biotic equality, he still roots his theory in a sense of basic and less basic needs (compare also to James Sterba). With the assertion of the cosmic self, the hierarchical structure that Taylor implies may transform to a "flatter" egalitarian landscape. In the end, Devall and Sessions advocate a simple lifestyle that has a minimum impact on other species.

Murray Bookchin enters this discussion by creating a link between ecological attitudes and general stances about the other social and political institutions of society. Bookchin's worldview has elements of Marxism and deep ecology that are united to a more general purpose: using the worldview created by these values to reform society from top to bottom. This view has been characterized as "social/political anarchism" and "libertarian social ecology." Unlike most Marxists, Bookchin does not believe in economic determinism or in the dictatorship of the proletariat. The aspect of Marx that Bookchin most admires is the analysis of social domination. We can easily see how accepting the tenets of deep ecology (especially the redefinition of self) can lead to a more cooperative social organization. This is really at the heart of Bookchin's approach.

The Land Ethic

Aldo Leopold

When god-like Odysseus returned from the wars in Troy, he hanged all on one rope a dozen slave-girls of his household whom he suspected of misbehavior during his absence.

This hanging involved no question of propriety. The girls were property. The disposal of property was then, as now, a matter of expediency, not of right and wrong.

Concepts of right and wrong were not lacking from Odysseus' Greece: witness the fidelity of his wife through the long years before at last his blackprowed galleys clove the wine-dark seas for home. The ethical structure of that day covered wives, but had not yet been extended to human chattels. During the three thousand years which have since elapsed, ethical criteria have been extended to many fields of conduct, with corresponding shrinkages in those judged by expediency only.

THE ETHICAL SEQUENCE

This extension of ethics, so far studied only by philosophers, is actually a process in ecological evolution. Its sequences may be described in ecological as well as in philosophical terms. An ethic, ecologically, is a limitation on freedom of action in the struggle for existence. An ethic, philosophically, is a differentiation of social from anti-social conduct. These are two definitions of one thing. The thing has its origin in the tendency of interdependent individuals or groups to evolve modes of co-operation. The ecologist calls these symbioses. Politics and economics are advanced symbioses in which the original free-for-all competition has been replaced, in part, by co-operative mechanisms with an ethical content.

The complexity of co-operative mechanisms has increased with population density, and with the efficiency of tools. It was simpler, for example, to define the anti-social uses of sticks and stones in the days of the mastodons than of bullets and billboards in the age of motors.

The first ethics dealt with the relation between individuals; the Mosaic Decalogue is an example. Later accretions dealt with the relation between the individual and society. The Golden Rule tries to integrate the individual to society; democracy to integrate social organization to the individual.

There is as yet no ethic dealing with man's relation to land and to the animals and plants which grow upon it. Land, like Odysseus' slave-girls, is still property. The land-relation is still strictly economic, entailing privileges but not obligations.

The extension of ethics to this third element in human environment is, if I read the evidence correctly, an evolutionary possibility and an ecological necessity. It is the third step in a sequence. The first two have already been taken. Individual thinkers since the days of Ezekiel and Isaiah have asserted that the despoliation of land is not only inexpedient but wrong. Society, however, has not yet affirmed their belief. I regard the present conservation movement as the embryo of such an affirmation.

An ethic may be regarded as a mode of guidance for meeting ecological situations so new or intricate, or involving such deferred reactions, that the path of social expediency is not discernible to the average individual. Animal instincts are modes of guidance for the individual in meeting such situations. Ethics are possibly a kind of community instinct in-the-making.

THE COMMUNITY CONCEPT

All ethics so far evolved rest upon a single premise: that the individual is a member of a community of interdependent parts. His instincts prompt him to compete for his place in the community, but his ethics prompt him also to co-operate (perhaps in order that there may be a place to compete for).

The land ethic simply enlarges the boundaries of the community to include soils, waters, plants, and animals, or collectively: the land.

This sounds simple: do we not already sing our love for and obligation to the land of the free and the home of the brave? Yes, but just what and whom do we love? Certainly not the soil, which we are sending helter-skelter downriver. Certainly not the waters, which we assume have no function except to turn turbines, float barges, and carry off sewage. Certainly not the plants, of which we exterminate whole communities without batting an eye. Certainly not the animals, of which we have already extirpated many of the largest and most beautiful species. A land ethic of course cannot prevent the alteration, management, and use of these 'resources,' but it does affirm their right to continued existence, and, at least in spots, their continued existence in a natural state.

In short, a land ethic changes the role of *Homo sapiens* from conqueror of the land-community to plain member and citizen of it. It implies respect for his fellow-members, and also respect for the community as such.

THE LAND PYRAMID

An ethic to supplement and guide the economic relation to land presupposes the existence of some mental image of land as a biotic mechanism. We can be ethical only in relation to something we can see, feel, understand, love, or otherwise have faith in.

The image commonly employed in conservation education is "the balance of nature." For reasons too lengthy to detail here, this figure of speech fails to describe accurately what little we know about the land mechanism. A much truer image is the one employed in ecology: the biotic pyramid. I shall first sketch the pyramid as a symbol of land, and later develop some of its implications in terms of land-use.

Plants absorb energy from the sun. This energy flows through a circuit called the biota, which may be represented by a pyramid consisting of layers. The bottom layer is the soil. A plant layer rests on the soil, an insect layer on the plants, a bird and rodent layer on the insects, and so on up through various animal groups to the apex layer, which consists of the larger carnivores.

The species of a layer are alike not in where they came from, or in what they look like, but rather in what they eat. Each successive layer depends on those below it for food and often for other services, and each in turn furnishes food and services to those above. Proceeding upward, each successive layer decreases in numerical abundance. Thus, for every carnivore there are hundreds of his prey, thousands of their prey, millions of insects, uncountable plants. The pyramidal form of the system reflects this numerical progression from apex to base. Man shares an intermediate layer with the bears, raccoons, and squirrels which eat both meat and vegetables.

The lines of dependency for food and other services are called food chains. Thus soil-oak-deer-Indian is a chain that has now been largely converted to soil-corn-cow-farmer. Each species, including ourselves, is a link in many chains. The deer eats a hundred plants other than oak, and the cow a hundred plants other than corn. Both, then, are links in a hundred chains. The pyramid is a tangle of chains so complex as to seem disorderly, yet the stability of the system proves it to be a highly organized structure. Its functioning depends on the co-operation and competition of its diverse parts.

In the beginning, the pyramid of life was low and squat; the food chains short and simple. Evolution has added layer after layer, link after link. Man is one of thousands of accretions to the height and complexity of the pyramid. Science has given us many doubts, but it has given us at least one certainty: the trend of evolution is to elaborate and diversify the biota.

Land, then, is not merely soil; it is a fountain of energy flowing through a circuit of soils, plants, and animals. Food chains are the living channels which conduct energy upward; death and decay return it to the soil. The circuit is not closed; some energy is dissipated in decay, some is added by absorption from the air, some is stored in soils, peats, and long-lived forests; but it is a sustained circuit, like a slowly augmented revolving fund of life. There is always a net loss by downhill wash, but this is normally small and offset by the decay of rocks. It is deposited in the ocean and, in the course of geological time, raised to form new lands and new pyramids.

The velocity and character of the upward flow of energy depend on the complex structure of the plant and animal community, much as the upward flow of sap in a tree depends on its complex cellular organization. Without this complexity, normal circulation would presumably not occur. Structure means the characteristic numbers, as well as the characteristic kinds and functions, of the component species. This interdependence between the complex structure of the land and its smooth functioning as an energy unit is one of its basic attributes.

When a change occurs in one part of the circuit, many other parts must adjust themselves to it. Change does not necessarily obstruct or divert the flow of energy; evolution is a long series of self-induced changes, the net result of which has been to elaborate the flow mechanism and to lengthen the circuit. Evolutionary changes, however, are usually slow and local. Man's invention of tools has enabled him to make changes of unprecedented violence, rapidity, and scope.

One change is in the composition of floras and faunas. The larger predators are lopped off the apex of the pyramid; food chains, for the first time in history, become shorter rather than longer. Domesticated species from other lands are substituted for wild ones, and wild ones are moved to new habitats. In this world-wide pooling of faunas and floras, some species get out of bounds as pests and diseases, others are extinguished. Such effects are seldom intended or foreseen: they represent unpredicted and often untraceable readjustments in the structure. Agricultural science is largely a race between the emergence of new pests and the emergence of new techniques for their control.

Another change touches the flow of energy through plants and animals and its return to the soil. Fertility is the ability of soil to receive, store, and release energy. Agriculture, by overdrafts on the soil, or by too radical a substitution of domestic for native species in the superstructure, may derange the channels of flow or deplete storage. Soils depleted of their storage or of the organic matter which anchors it, wash away faster than they form. This is erosion.

Waters, like soil, are part of the energy circuit. Industry, by polluting waters or obstructing them with dams, may exclude the plants and animals necessary to keep energy in circulation.

Transportation brings about another basic change: the plants or animals grown in one region are now consumed and returned to the soil in another. Transportation taps the energy stored in rocks, and in the air, and uses it elsewhere; thus we fertilize the garden with nitrogen gleaned by the guano birds from the fishes of seas on the other side of the Equator. Thus the formerly localized and self-contained circuits are pooled on a world-wide scale.

The process of altering the pyramid for human occupation releases stored energy, and this often gives rise, during the pioneering period, to a deceptive exuberance of plant and animal life, both wild and tame. These releases of biotic capital tend to becloud or postpone the penalties of violence.

This thumbnail sketch of land as an energy circuit conveys three basic ideas:

1. That land is not merely soil.
2. That the native plants and animals kept the energy circuit open; others may or may not.
3. That man-made changes are of a different order than evolutionary changes, and have effects more comprehensive than is intended or foreseen.

These ideas, collectively, raise two basic issues: Can the land adjust itself to the new order? Can the desired alterations be accomplished with less violence?

Biotas seem to differ in their capacity to sustain violent conversion. Western Europe, for example, carries a far different pyramid than Caesar found there. Some large animals are lost; swampy forests have become meadows or plowland; many new plants and animals are introduced, some of which escape as pests; the remaining natives are greatly changed in distribution and abundance. Yet the soil is still there and, with the help of imported nutrients, still fertile; the waters flow normally; the new structure seems to function and to persist. There is no visible stoppage or derangement of the circuit.

Western Europe, then, has a resistant biota. Its inner processes are tough, elastic, resistant to strain. No matter how violent the alterations, the pyramid, so far, has developed some new *modus vivendi* which preserves its habitability for man, and for most of the other natives.

Japan seems to present another instance of radical conversion without disorganization.

Most other civilized regions, and some as yet barely touched by civilization, display various stages of disorganization, varying from initial symptoms to advanced wastage. In Asia Minor and North Africa diagnosis is confused by climatic changes, which may have been either the cause or the effect of advanced wastage. In the United States the degree of disorganization varies locally; it is worst in the South-west, the Ozarks, and parts of the South, and least in New England and the North-west. Better land-uses may still arrest it in the less advanced regions. In parts of Mexico, South America, South Africa, and Australia a violent and accelerating wastage is in progress, but I cannot assess the prospects.

This almost world-wide display of disorganization in the land seems to be similar to disease in an animal, except that it never culminates in complete disorganization or death. The land recovers, but at some reduced level of complexity, and with a reduced carrying capacity for people, plants, and animals. Many biotas currently regarded as "lands of opportunity" are in fact already subsisting on exploitative agriculture, i.e., they have already exceeded their sustained carrying capacity. Most of South America is over populated in this sense.

In arid regions we attempt to offset the process of wastage by reclamation, but it is only too evident that the prospective longevity of reclamation projects is often short. In our own West, the best of them may not last a century.

The combined evidence of history and ecology seems to support one general deduction: the less violent the man-made changes, the greater the probability of successful readjustment in the pyramid. Violence, in turn, varies with human population density; a dense population requires a more violent conversion. In this respect, North America has a better chance for permanence than Europe, if she can contrive to limit her density.

This deduction runs counter to our current philosophy, which assumes that because a small increase in density enriched human life, that an indefinite increase will enrich it indefinitely. Ecology knows of no density relationship that holds for indefinitely wide limits. All gains from density are subject to a law of diminishing returns.

Whatever may be the equation for men and land, it is improbable that we as yet know all its terms. Recent discoveries in mineral and vitamin nutrition reveal unsuspected dependencies in the up-circuit: incredibly minute quantities of certain substances determine the value of soils to plants, of plants to animals. What of the down-circuit? What of the vanishing species, the preservation of which we now regard as an esthetic luxury? They helped build the soil; in what unsuspected ways may they be essential to its maintenance? Professor Weaver proposes that we use prairie flowers to reflocculate the wasting soils of the dust bowl: who knows for what purpose cranes and condors, otters and grizzlies may some day be used?

THE OUTLOOK

It is inconceivable to me that an ethical relation to land can exist without love, respect, and admiration for land, and a high regard for its value. By value, I of course mean something far broader than mere economic value; I mean value in the philosophical sense.

Perhaps the most serious obstacle impeding the evolution of a land ethic is the fact that our educational and economic system is headed away from, rather than toward, an intense consciousness of land. Your true modern is separated from the land by many middlemen, and by innumerable physical gadgets. He has no vital relation to it; to him it is the space between cities on which crops grow. Turn him loose for a day on the land, and if the spot does not happen to be a golf links or a "scenic" area, he is bored stiff. If crops could be raised by hydroponics instead of farming, it would suit him very well. Synthetic substitutes for wood, leather, wool, and other natural land products suit him better than the originals. In short, land is something he has "outgrown."

Almost equally serious as an obstacle to a land ethic is the attitude of the farmer for whom the land is still an adversary, or a taskmaster that keeps him in slavery. Theoretically, the mechanization of farming ought to cut the farmer's chains, but whether it really does is debatable.

One of the requisites for an ecological comprehension of land is an understanding of ecology, and this is by no means co-extensive with "education"; in fact, much higher education seems deliberately to avoid ecological concepts. An understanding of ecology does not necessarily originate in courses bearing ecological labels; it is quite as likely to be labeled geography, botany, agronomy, history, or economics. This is as it should be, but whatever the label, ecological training is scarce.

The case for a land ethic would appear hopeless but for the minority which is in obvious revolt against these "modern" trends.

The "key-log" which must be moved to release the evolutionary process for an ethic is simply this: quit thinking about decent land-use as solely an economic problem. Examine each question in terms of what is ethically and esthetically right, as well as what is economically expedient. A thing is right when it tends to preserve the integrity, stability, and beauty of the biotic community. It is wrong when it tends otherwise.

It of course goes without saying that economic feasibility limits the tether of what can or cannot be done for land. It always has and it always will. The fallacy the economic determinists have tied around our collective neck, and which we now need to cast off, is the belief that economics determines *all* land-use. This is simply not true. An innumerable host of actions and attitudes, comprising perhaps the bulk of all land relations, is determined by the land-users' tastes and predilections, rather than by his purse. The bulk of all land relations hinges on investments of time, forethought, skill, and faith rather than on investments of cash. As a land-user thinketh, so is he.

I have purposely presented the land ethic as a product of social evolution because nothing so important as an ethic is ever "written." Only the most superficial student of history supposes that Moses "wrote" the Decalogue; it evolved in the minds of a thinking community, and Moses wrote a tentative summary of it for a "seminar." I say tentative because evolution never stops.

The evolution of a land ethic is an intellectual as well as emotional process. Conservation is paved with good intentions which prove to be futile, or even dangerous, because they are devoid of critical understanding either of the land, or of economic land-use. I think it is a truism that as the ethical frontier advances from the individual to the community, its intellectual content increases.

The mechanism of operation is the same for any ethic: social approbation for right actions: social disapproval for wrong actions.

By and large, our present problem is one of attitudes and implements. We are remodeling the Alhambra with a steam-shovel, and we are proud of our yardage. We shall hardly relinquish the shovel which after all has many good points, but we are in need of gentler and more objective criteria for its successful use.

The Shallow and the Deep, Long-Range Ecology Movement: A Summary

Arne Naess

Ecologically responsible policies are concerned only in part with pollution and resource depletion. There are deeper concerns which touch upon principles of diversity, complexity, autonomy, decentralization, symbiosis, egalitarianism, and classlessness.

The emergence of ecologists from their former relative obscurity marks a turning-point in our scientific communities. But their message is twisted and misused. A shallow, but presently rather powerful movement, and a deep, but less influential movement, compete for our attention. I shall make an effort to characterize the two.

1. THE SHALLOW ECOLOGY MOVEMENT

Fight against pollution and resource depletion. Central objective: the health and affluence of people in the developed countries.

2. THE DEEP ECOLOGY MOVEMENT

(1) *Rejection of the man-in-environment image in favour of the relational, total-field image.* Organisms as knots in the biospherical net or field of intrinsic relations. An intrinsic relation between two things A and B is such that the relation belongs to the definitions or basic constitutions of A and B, so that without the relation, A and B are no longer the same things. The total-field model dissolves not only the man-in-environment concept, but every compact thing-in-milieu concept—except when talking at a superficial or preliminary level of communication.

(2) *Biospherical egalitarianism—in principle.* The 'in principle' clause is inserted because any realistic praxis necessitates some killing, exploitation, and suppression. The ecological field-worker acquires a deep-seated respect,

or even veneration, for ways and forms of life. He reaches an understanding from within, a kind of understanding that others reserve for fellow men and for a narrow section of ways and forms of life. To the ecological field-worker, *the equal right to live and blossom* is an intuitively clear and obvious value axiom. Its restriction to humans is an anthropocentrism with detrimental effects upon the life quality of humans themselves. This quality depends in part upon the deep pleasure and satisfaction we receive from close partnership with other forms of life. The attempt to ignore our dependence and to establish a master–slave role has contributed to the alienation of man from himself.

Ecological egalitarianism implies the reinterpretation of the future-research variable, 'level of crowding', so that *general* mammalian crowding and loss of life-equality is taken seriously, not only human crowding. (Research on the high requirements of free space of certain mammals has, incidentally, suggested that theorists of human urbanism have largely underestimated human life-space requirements. Behavioural crowding symptoms [neuroses, aggressiveness, loss of traditions . . .] are largely the same among mammals.)

(3) Principles of diversity and of symbiosis. Diversity enhances the potentialities of survival, the chances of new modes of life, the richness of forms. And the so-called struggle of life, and survival of the fittest, should be interpreted in the sense of ability to coexist and cooperate in complex relationships, rather than ability to kill, exploit, and suppress. 'Live and let live' is a more powerful ecological principle than 'Either you or me'.

The latter tends to reduce the multiplicity of kinds of forms of life, and also to create destruction within the communities of the same species. Ecologically inspired attitudes therefore favour diversity of human ways of life, of cultures, of occupations, of economies. They support the fight against economic and cultural, as much as military, invasion and domination, and they are opposed to the annihilation of seals and whales as much as to that of human tribes or cultures.

(4) Anti-class posture. Diversity of human ways of life is in part due to (intended or unintended) exploitation and suppression on the part of certain groups. The exploiter lives differently from the exploited, but both are adversely affected in their potentialities of self-realization. The principle of diversity does not cover differences due merely to certain attitudes or behaviours forcibly blocked or restrained. The principles of ecological egalitarianism and of symbiosis support the same anti-class posture. The ecological attitude favours the extension of all three principles to any group conflicts, including those of today between developing and developed nations. The three principles also favour extreme caution towards any over-all plans for the future, except those consistent with wide and widening classless diversity.

(5) *Fight against pollution and resource depletion.* In this fight ecologists have found powerful supporters, but sometimes to the detriment of their total stand. This happens when attention is focused on pollution and resource depletion rather than on the other points, or when projects are implemented which reduce pollution but increase evils of the other kinds. Thus, if prices of life necessities increase because of the installation of anti-pollution devices, class differences increase too. An ethics of responsibility implies that ecologists do not serve the shallow, but the deep ecological movement. That is, not only point (5), but all seven points must be considered together.

Ecologists are irreplaceable informants in any society, whatever their political colour. If well organized, they have the power to reject jobs in which they submit themselves to institutions or to planners with limited ecological perspectives. As it is now, ecologists sometimes serve masters who deliberately ignore the wider perspectives.

(6) *Complexity, not complication.* The theory of ecosystems contains an important distinction between what is complicated without any Gestalt or unifying principles—we may think of finding our way through a chaotic city—and what is complex. A multiplicity of more or less lawful, interacting factors may operate together to form a unity, a system. We make a shoe or use a map or integrate a variety of activities into a workaday pattern. Organisms, ways of life, and interactions in the biosphere in general, exhibit complexity of such an astoundingly high level as to colour the general outlook of ecologists. Such complexity makes thinking in terms of vast systems inevitable. It also makes for a keen, steady perception of the profound *human ignorance* of biospherical relationships and therefore of the effect of disburbances.

Applied to humans, the complexity-not-complication principle favours division of labour, *not fragmentation of labour.* It favours integrated actions in which the whole person is active, not mere reactions. It favours complex economies, an integrated variety of means of living. (Combinations of industrial and agricultural activity, of intellectual and manual work, of specialized and non-specialized occupations, of urban and non-urban activity, of work in city and recreation in nature with recreation in city and work in nature . . .)

It favours soft technique and 'soft future-research', less prognosis, more clarification of possibilities. More sensitivity towards continuity and live traditions, and—most importantly—towards our state of ignorance.

The implementation of ecologically responsible policies requires in this century an exponential growth of technical skill and invention—but in new directions, directions which today are not consistently and liberally supported by the research policy organs of our nation-states.

(7) *Local autonomy and decentralization.* The vulnerability of a form of life is roughly proportional to the weight of influences from afar, from outside the local region in which that form has obtained an ecological equilibrium.

This lends support to our efforts to strengthen local self-government and material and mental self-sufficiency. But these efforts presuppose an impetus towards decentralization. Pollution problems, including those of thermal pollution and recirculation of materials, also lead us in this direction, because increased local autonomy, if we are able to keep other factors constant, reduces energy consumption. (Compare an approximately self-sufficient locality with one requiring the importation of foodstuff, materials for house construction, fuel and skilled labour from other continents. The former may use only five per cent of the energy used by the latter.) Local autonomy is strengthened by a reduction in the number of links in the hierarchical chains of decision (For example a chain consisting of local board, municipal council, highest sub-national decision-maker, a state-wide institution in a state federation, a federal national government institution, a coalition of nations, and of institutions, e.g. E.E.C. top levels, and a global institution, can be reduced to one made up of local board, nation-wide institution, and global institution.) Even if a decision follows majority rules at each step, many local interests may be dropped along the line, if it is too long.

Summing up, then, it should, first of all, be borne in mind that the norms and tendencies of the Deep Ecology movement are not derived from ecology by logic or induction. Ecological knowledge and the lifestyle of the ecological field-worker have *suggested, inspired, and fortified* the perspectives of the Deep Ecology movement. Many of the formulations in the above seven-point survey are rather vague generalizations, only tenable if made more precise in certain directions. But all over the world the inspiration from ecology has shown remarkable convergencies. The survey does not pretend to be more than one of the possible condensed codifications of these convergencies.

Secondly, it should be fully appreciated that the significant tenets of the Deep Ecology movement are clearly and forcefully *normative*. They express a value priority system only in part based on results (or lack of results, cf. point [6]) of scientific research. Today, ecologists try to influence policy-making bodies largely through threats, through predictions concerning pollutants and resource depletion, knowing that policy-makers accept at least certain minimum *norms* concerning health and just distribution. But it is clear that there is a vast number of people in all countries, and even a considerable number of people in power, who accept as valid the wider norms and values characteristic of the Deep Ecology movement. There are political potentials in this movement which should not be overlooked and which have little to do with pollution and resource depletion. In plotting possible futures, the norms should be freely used and elaborated.

Thirdly, in so far as ecology movements deserve our attention, they are *ecophilosophical* rather then ecological. Ecology is a *limited* science which makes *use* of scientific methods. Philosophy is the most general forum of debate on fundamentals, descriptive as well as prescriptive, and political philosophy is one of its subsections. By an *ecosophy* I mean a philosophy of ecological harmony or equilibrium. A philosophy as a kind of *sofia* wisdom, is openly normative, it contains *both* norms, rules, postulates, value priority announcements *and* hypotheses concerning the state of affairs in our universe. Wisdom is policy wisdom, prescription, not only scientific description and prediction.

The details of an ecosophy will show many variations due to significant differences concerning not only 'facts' of pollution, resources, population, etc., but also value priorities. Today, however, the seven points listed provide one unified framework for ecosophical systems.

In general system theory, systems are mostly conceived in terms of causally or functionally interacting or interrelated items. An ecosophy, however, is more like a system of the kind constructed by Aristotle or Spinoza. It is expressed verbally as a set of sentences with a variety of functions, descriptive and prescriptive. The basic relation is that between subsets of premisses and subsets of conclusions, that is, the relation of derivability. The relevant notions of derivability may be classed according to rigour, with logical and mathematical deductions topping the list, but also according to how much is implicitly taken for granted. An exposition of an ecosophy must necessarily be only moderately precise considering the vast scope of relevant ecological and normative (social, political, ethical) material. At the moment, ecosophy might profitably use models of systems, rough approximations of global systematizations. It is the global character, not preciseness in detail, which distinguishes an ecosophy. It articulates and integrates the efforts of an ideal ecological team, a team comprising not only scientists from an extreme variety of disciplines, but also students of politics and active policy-makers.

Under the name of *ecologism,* various deviations from the deep movement have been championed—primarily with a one-sided stress on pollution and resource depletion, but also with a neglect of the great differences between under- and over-developed countries in favour of a vague global approach. The global approach is essential, but regional differences must largely determine policies in the coming years.

Selected Literature

Commoner, B., *The Closing Circle: Nature, Man, and Technology,* Alfred A. Knopf, New York 1971.
Ehrlich, P. R. and A. H., *Population, Resources, Environment: Issues in Human Ecology,* 2nd ed., W. H. Freeman & Co., San Francisco 1972.
Ellul, J., *The Technological Society,* English ed., Alfred A. Knopf, New York 1964.
Glacken, C. J., *Traces on the Rhodian Shore. Nature and Culture in Western Thought,* University of California Press, Berkeley 1967.
Kato, H., 'The Effects of Crowding', Quality of Life Conference, Oberhausen, April 1972.
McHarg, Ian L., *Design with Nature,* 1969. Paperback 1971, Doubleday & Co., New York.
Meynaud, J., *Technocracy,* English ed., Free Press of Glencoe, Chicago 1969.
Mishan, E. J., *Technology and Growth: The Price We Pay,* Frederick A. Praeger, New York 1970.
Odum, E. P., *Fundamentals of Ecology,* 3rd ed., W. E. Saunders Co., Philadelphia 1971.
Shepard, Paul, *Man in the Landscape,* A. A. Knopf, New York.

Deep Ecology

Bill Devall and George Sessions

The term *deep ecology* was coined by Arne Naess in his 1973 article, "The Shallow and the Deep, Long-Range Ecology Movements."[1] Naess was attempting to describe the deeper, more spiritual approach to Nature exemplified in the writings of Aldo Leopold and Rachel Carson. He thought that this deeper approach resulted from a more sensitive openness to ourselves and nonhuman life around us. The essence of deep ecology is to keep asking more searching questions about human life, society, and Nature as in the Western philosophical tradition of Socrates. As examples of this deep questioning, Naess points out "that we ask why and how, where others do not. For instance, ecology as a science does not ask what kind of a society would be the best for maintaining a particular ecosystem—that is considered a question for value theory, for politics, for ethics." Thus deep ecology goes beyond the so-called factual scientific level to the level of self and Earth wisdom.

Deep ecology goes beyond a limited piecemeal shallow approach to environmental problems and attempts to articulate a comprehensive religious and philosophical worldview. The foundations of deep ecology are the basic intuitions and experiencing of ourselves and Nature which comprise ecological consciousness. Certain outlooks on politics and public policy flow naturally from this consciousness. And in the context of this book, we discuss the minority tradition as the type of community most conducive both to cultivating ecological consciousness and to asking the basic questions of values and ethics addressed in these pages.

Many of these questions are perennial philosophical and religious questions faced by humans in all cultures over the ages. What does it mean to be a unique human individual? How can the individual self maintain and increase its uniqueness while also being an inseparable aspect of the whole system wherein there are no sharp breaks between self and the *other?* An ecological perspective, in this deeper sense, results in what Theodore Roszak calls "an awakening of wholes greater than the sum of their parts. In spirit, the discipline is contemplative and therapeutic."[2]

Ecological consciousness and deep ecology are in sharp contrast with the dominant worldview of technocratic-industrial societies which regards humans as isolated and fundamentally separate from the rest of Nature, as superior to, and in charge of, the rest of creation. But the view of humans as separate and superior to the rest of Nature is only part of larger cultural patterns. For thousands of years, Western culture has become increasingly obsessed with the idea of *dominance:* with dominance of humans over nonhuman Nature, masculine over the feminine, wealthy and powerful over the poor, with the dominance of the West over non-Western cultures. Deep ecological consciousness allows us to see through these erroneous and dangerous illusions.

For deep ecology, the study of our place in the Earth household includes the study of ourselves as part of the organic whole. Going beyond a narrowly materialist scientific understanding of reality, the spiritual and the material aspects of reality fuse together. While the leading intellectuals of the dominant worldview have tended to view religion as "just superstition," and have looked upon ancient spiritual practice and enlightenment, such as found in Zen Buddhism, as essentially subjective, the search for deep ecological consciousness is the search for a more objective consciousness and state of being through an active deep questioning and meditative process and way of life.

Many people have asked these deeper questions and cultivated ecological consciousness within the context of different spiritual traditions—Christianity, Taoism, Buddhism, and Native American rituals, for example. While differing greatly in other regards, many in these traditions agree with the basic principles of deep ecology.

Warwick Fox, an Australian philosopher, has succinctly expressed the central intuition of deep ecology: "It is the idea that we can make no firm ontological divide in the field of existence: That there is no bifurcation in reality between the human and the non-human realms . . . to the extent that we perceive boundaries, we fall short of deep ecological consciousness."[3]

From this most basic insight or characteristic of deep ecological consciousness, Arne Naess has developed two *ultimate norms* or intuitions which are themselves not derivable from other principles or intuitions. They are arrived at by the deep questioning process and reveal the importance of moving to the philosophical and religious level of wisdom. They cannot be validated, of course, by the methodology of modern science based on its usual mechanistic assumptions and its very narrow definition of data. These ultimate norms are *self-realization* and *biocentric equality.*

I. Self-Realization

In keeping with the spiritual traditions of many of the world's religions, the deep ecology norm of self-realization goes beyond the modern Western *self* which is defined as an isolated ego striving primarily for hedonistic gratification or for a narrow sense of individual salvation in this life or the next. This socially programmed sense of the narrow self or social self dislocates us, and leaves us prey to whatever fad or fashion is prevalent in our society or social reference group. We are thus robbed of beginning the search for our unique spiritual/biological personhood. Spiritual growth, or unfolding, begins when we cease to understand or see ourselves as isolated and narrow competing egos and begin to identify with other humans from our family and friends to, eventually, our species. But the deep ecology sense of self requires a further maturity and growth, an identification which goes beyond humanity to include the nonhuman world. We must see beyond our narrow contemporary cultural assumptions and values, and the conventional wisdom of our time and place, and this is best achieved by the meditative deep questioning process. Only in this way can we hope to attain full mature personhood and uniqueness.

A nurturing nondominating society can help in the "real work" of becoming a whole person. The "real work" can be summarized symbolically as the realization of "self-in-Self" where "Self" stand for organic wholeness. This process of the full unfolding of the self can also be summarized by the phrase, "No one is saved until we are all saved," where the phrase "one" includes not only me, an individual human, but all humans, whales, grizzly bears, whole rain forest ecosystems, mountains and rivers, the tiniest microbes in the soil, and so on.

II. BIOCENTRIC EQUALITY

The intuition of biocentric equality is that all things in the biosphere have an equal right to live and blossom and to reach their own individual forms of unfolding and self-realization within the larger Self-realization. This basic intuition is that all organisms and entities in the ecosphere, as parts of the interrelated whole, are equal in intrinsic worth. Naess suggests that biocentric equality as an intuition is true in principle, although in the process of living, all species use each other as food, shelter, etc. Mutual predation is a biological fact of life, and many of the world's religions have struggled with the spiritual implications of this. Some animal liberationists who attempt to side-step this problem by advocating vegetarianism are forced to say that the entire plant kingdom including rain forests have no right to their own existence. This evasion flies in the face of the basic intuition of equality.[4] Aldo Leopold expressed this intuition when he said humans are "plain citizens" of the biotic community, not lord and master over all other species.

Biocentric equality is intimately related to the all-inclusive Self-realization in the sense that if we harm the rest of Nature then we are harming ourselves. There are no boundaries and everything is interrelated. But insofar as we perceive things as individual organisms or entities, the insight draws us to respect all human and nonhuman individuals in their own right as parts of the whole without feeling the need to set up hierarchies of species with humans at the top.

The practical implications of this intuition or norm suggest that we should live with minimum rather than maximum impact on other species and on the Earth in general. Thus we see another aspect of our guiding principle: "simple in means, rich in ends." Further practical implications of these norms are discussed at length in chapters seven and eight.

A fuller discussion of the biocentric norm as it unfolds itself in practice begins with the realization that we, as individual humans, and as communities of humans, have vital needs which go beyond such basics as food, water, and shelter to include love, play, creative expression, intimate relationships with a particular landscape (or Nature taken in its entirety) as well as intimate relationships with other humans, and the vital need for spiritual growth, for becoming a mature human being.

Our vital material needs are probably more simple than many realize. In technocratic-industrial societies there is overwhelming propaganda and advertising which encourages false needs and destructive desires designed to foster increased production and consumption of goods. Most of this actually diverts us from facing reality in an objective way and from beginning the "real work" of spiritual growth and maturity.

Many people who do not see themselves as supporters of deep ecology nevertheless recognize an overriding vital human need for a healthy and high-quality natural environment for humans, if not for all life, with minimum intrusion of toxic waste, nuclear radiation from human enterprises, minimum acid rain and smog, and enough free flowing wilderness so humans can get in touch with their sources, the natural rhythms and the flow of time and place.

Drawing from the minority tradition and from the wisdom of many who have offered the insight of interconnectedness, we recognize that deep ecologists can offer suggestions for gaining maturity and encouraging the processes of harmony with Nature, but that there is no grand solution which is guaranteed to save us from ourselves.

The ultimate norms of deep ecology suggest a view of the nature of reality and our place as an individual (many in the one) in the larger scheme of things. They cannot be fully grasped intellectually but are ultimately experiential. We encourage readers to consider our further discussion of the psychological, social and ecological implications of these norms in later chapters.

As a brief summary of our position thus far, Figure 1 summarizes the contrast between the dominant worldview and deep ecology.

III. BASIC PRINCIPLES OF DEEP ECOLOGY

In April 1984, during the advent of spring and John Muir's birthday, George Sessions and Arne Naess summarized fifteen years of thinking on the principles of deep ecology while camping in Death Valley, California. In this great

Dominant Worldview	Deep Ecology
Dominance over Nature	Harmony with Nature
Natural environment as resource for humans	All nature has intrinsic worth/ biospecies equality
Material/economic growth for growing human population	Elegantly simple material needs (material goals serving the larger goal of self-realization)
Belief in ample resource reserves	Earth "supplies" limited
High technological progress and solutions	Appropriate technology; nondominating science
Consumerism	Doing with enough/recycling
National/centralized community	Minority tradition/bioregion

Figure 1

and special place, they articulated these principles in a literal, somewhat neutral way, hoping that they would be understood and accepted by persons coming from different philosophical and religious positions.

Readers are encouraged to elaborate their own versions of deep ecology, clarify key concepts and think through the consequences of acting from these principles.

Basic Principles

1. The well-being and flourishing of human and nonhuman Life on Earth have value in themselves (synonyms: intrinsic value, inherent value). These values are independent of the usefulness of the nonhuman world for human purposes.

2. Richness and diversity of life forms contribute to the realization of these values and are also values in themselves.

3. Humans have no right to reduce this richness and diversity except to satisfy *vital* needs.

4. The flourishing of human life and cultures is compatible with a substantial decrease of the human population. The flourishing of nonhuman life requires such a decrease.

5. Present human interference with the nonhuman world is excessive, and the situation is rapidly worsening.

6. Policies must therefore be changed. These policies affect basic economic, technological, and ideological structures. The resulting state of affairs will be deeply different from the present.

7. The ideological change is mainly that of appreciating *life quality* (dwelling in situations of inherent value) rather than adhering to an increasingly higher standard of living. There will be a profound awareness of the difference between big and great.

8. Those who subscribe to the foregoing points have an obligation directly or indirectly to try to implement the necessary changes.

Naess and Sessions Provide Comments on the Basic Principles

RE (1). This formulation refers to the biosphere, or more accurately, to the ecosphere as a whole. This includes individuals, species, populations, habitat, as well as human and nonhuman cultures. From our current knowledge of all-pervasive intimate relationships, this implies a fundamental deep concern and respect. Ecological processes of the planet should, on the whole, remain intact. "The world environment should remain 'natural'" (Gary Snyder).

The term "life" is used here in a more comprehensive nontechnical way to refer also to what biologists classify as "nonliving"; rivers (watersheds), landscapes, ecosystems. For supporters of deep ecology, slogans such as "Let the river live" illustrate this broader usage so common in most cultures.

Inherent value as used in (1) is common in deep ecology literature ("The presence of inherent value in a natural object is independent of any awareness, interest, or appreciation of it by a conscious being.").[5]

RE (2). More technically, this is a formulation concerning diversity and complexity. From an ecological standpoint, complexity and symbiosis are conditions for maximizing diversity. So-called simple, lower, or primitive species of plants and animals contribute essentially to the richness and diversity of life. They have value in themselves and are not merely steps toward the so-called higher or rational life forms. The second principle presupposes that life itself, as a process over evolutionary time, implies an increase of diversity and richness. The refusal to acknowledge that some life forms have greater or lesser intrinsic value than others (see points 1 and 2) runs counter to the formulations of some ecological philosophers and New Age writers.

Complexity, as referred to here, is different from complication. Urban life may be more complicated than life in a natural setting without being more complex in the sense of multifaceted quality.

RE (3). The term "vital need" is left deliberately vague to allow for considerable latitude in judgment. Differences in climate and related factors, together with differences in the structures of societies as they now exist, need to be considered (for some Eskimos, snowmobiles are necessary today to satisfy vital needs).

People in the materially richest countries cannot he expected to reduce their excessive interference with the nonhuman world to a moderate level overnight. The stabilization and reduction of the human population will take time. Interim strategies need to be developed. But this in no way excuses the present complacency—the extreme seriousness of our current situation must first be realized. But the longer we wait the more drastic will be the measures needed. Until deep changes are made, substantial decreases in richness and diversity are liable to occur: the rate of extinction of species will be ten to one hundred times greater than any other period of earth history.

RE (4). The United Nations Fund for Population Activities in their State of World Population Report (1984) said that high human population growth rates (over 2.0 percent annum) in many developing countries "were diminishing the quality of life for many millions of people." During the decade 1974–1984, the world population grew by nearly 800 million—more than the size of India. "And we will be adding about one Bangladesh (population 93 million) per annum between now and the year 2000."

The report noted that "The growth rate of the human population has declined for the first time in human history. But at the same time, the number of people being added to the human population is bigger than at any time in history because the population base is larger."

Most of the nations in the developing world (including India and China) have as their official government policy the goal of reducing the rate of human population increase, but there are debates over the types of measures to take (contraception, abortion, etc.) consistent with human rights and feasibility.

The report concludes that if all governments set specific population targets as public policy to help alleviate poverty and advance the quality of life, the current situation could be improved.

As many ecologists have pointed out, it is also absolutely crucial to curb population growth in the so-called developed (i.e., overdeveloped) industrial societies. Given the tremendous rate of consumption and waste production of individuals in these societies, they represent a much greater threat and impact on the biosphere per capita than individuals in Second and Third World countries.

RE (5). This formulation is mild. For a realistic assessment of the situation, see the unabbreviated version of the I.U.C.N.'s *World Conservation Strategy.* There are other works to be highly recommended, such as Gerald Barney's *Global 2000 Report to the President of the United States.*

The slogan of "noninterference" does not imply that humans should not modify some ecosystems as do other species. Humans have modified the earth and will probably continue to do so. At issue is the nature and extent of such interference.

The fight to preserve and extend areas of wilderness or near-wilderness should continue and should focus on the general ecological functions of these areas (one such function: large wilderness areas are required in the biosphere to allow for continued evolutionary speciation of animals and plants). Most present designated wilderness areas and game preserves are not large enough to allow for such speciation.

RE (6). Economic growth as conceived and implemented today by the industrial states is incompatible with (1)–(5). There is only a faint resemblance between ideal sustainable forms of economic growth and present policies of the industrial societies. And "sustainable" still means "sustainable in relation to humans."

Present ideology tends to value things because they are scarce and because they have a commodity value. There is prestige in vast consumption and waste (to mention only several relevant factors).

Whereas "self-determination," "local community," and "think globally, act locally," will remain key terms in the ecology of human societies, nevertheless the implementation of deep changes requires increasingly global action—action across borders.

Governments in Third World countries (with the exception of Costa Rica and a few others) are uninterested in deep ecological issues. When the governments of industrial societies try to promote ecological measures through Third World governments, practically nothing is accomplished (e.g., with problems of desertification). Given this situation, support for global action through nongovernmental international organizations becomes increasingly important. Many of these organizations are able to act globally "from grassroots to grassroots," thus avoiding negative governmental interference.

Cultural diversity today requires advanced technology, that is, techniques that advance the basic goals of each culture. So-called soft, intermediate, and alternative technologies are steps in this direction.

RE (7). Some economists criticize the term "quality of life" because it is supposed to be vague. But on closer inspection, what they consider to be vague is actually the nonquantitative nature of the term. One cannot quantify adequately what is important for the quality of life as discussed here, and there is no need to do so.

RE (8). There is ample room for different opinions about priorities: what should be done first, what next? What is most urgent? What is clearly necessary as opposed to what is highly desirable but not absolutely pressing?

NOTES

1. Arne Naess, "The Shallow and The Deep, Long-Range Ecology Movements: A Summary," *Inquiry* 16 (Oslo, 1973), pp. 95–100.

2. Theodore Roszak, *Where the Wasteland Ends* (New York: Anchor, 1972).

3. Warwick Fox, "Deep Ecology: A New Philosophy of Our Time?" *The Ecologist*, v. 14, 5–6, 1984, 194–200. Arnie Naess replies, "Intuition, Intrinsic Value and Deep Ecology," *The Ecologist*, v. 14, 5–6, 1984, pp. 201–204.

4. Tom Regan, *The Case for Animal Rights* (New York: Random House, 1983). For excellent critiques of the animal rights movement, see John Rodman, "The Liberation of Nature?" *Inquiry* 20 (Oslo, 1977). J. Baird Callicott, "Animal Liberation," *Environmental Ethics* 2, 4 (1980); see also John Rodman, "Four Forms of Ecological Consciousness Reconsidered" in T. Attig and D. Scherer, ed., *Ethics and the Environment* (Englewood Cliffs, N.J.: Prentice-Hall, 1983).

5. Tom Regan, "The Nature and Possibility of an Environmental Ethic," *Environmental Ethics* 3 (1981), pp. 19–34.

What Is Social Ecology?*

Murray Bookchin

We are clearly beleaguered by an ecological crisis of monumental proportions—a crisis that visibly stems from the ruthless exploitation and pollution of the planet. We rightly attribute the social sources of this crisis to a competitive marketplace spirit that reduces the entire world of life, including humanity, to merchandisable objects, to mere commodities with price tags that are to be sold for profit and economic expansion. The ideology of this spirit is expressed in the notorious marketplace maxim: "Grow or die!"—a maxim that identifies limitless growth with "progress" and the "mastery of nature" with "civilization." The results of this tide of exploitation and pollution have been grim enough to yield serious forecasts of complete planetary breakdown, a degree of devastation of soil, forests, waterways, and atmosphere that has no precedent in the history of our species.

In this respect, our market-oriented society is unique in contrast with other societies in that it places no limits on growth and egotism. The antisocial principles that "rugged individualism" is the primary motive for social

*Murray Bookchin has revised his essay especially for this volume.

improvement and competition the engine for social progress stand sharply at odds with all past eras that valued selflessness as the authentic trait of human nobility and cooperation as the authentic evidence of social virtue, however much these prized attributes were honored in the breach. Our marketplace society has, in effect, made the worst features of earlier times into its more honored values and exhibited a degree of brutality in the global wars of this century that makes the cruelties of history seem mild by comparison.

In our discussions of modern ecological and social crises, we tend to ignore a more underlying mentality of domination that humans have used for centuries to justify the domination of each other and, by extension, of nature. I refer to an image of the natural world that sees nature itself as "blind," "mute," "cruel," "competitive," and "stingy," a seemingly demonic "realm of necessity" that opposes "man's" striving for freedom and self-realization. Here, "man" seems to confront a hostile "otherness" against which he must oppose his own powers of toil and guile. History is thus presented to us as a Promethean drama in which "man" heroically defies and willfully asserts himself against a brutally hostile and unyielding natural world. Progress is seen as the extrication of humanity from the muck of a mindless, unthinking, and brutish domain or what Jean Paul Sartre so contemptuously called the "slime of history," into the presumably clear light of reason and civilization.

This image of a demonic and hostile nature goes back to the Greek world and even earlier, to the Gilgamesh Epic of Sumerian society. But it reached its high point during the past two centuries, particularly in the Victorian Age, and persists in our thinking today. Ironically, the idea of a "blind," "mute," "cruel," "competitive," and "stingy" nature forms the basis for the very social sciences and humanities that profess to provide us with a civilized alternative to nature's "brutishness" and "law of claw and fang." Even as these disciplines stress the "unbridgeable gulf" between nature and society in the classical tradition of a dualism between the physical and the mental, economics literally defines itself as the study of "scarce resources" (read: "stingy nature") and "unlimited needs," essentially rearing itself on the interconnection between nature and humanity. By the same token, sociology sees itself as the analysis of "man's" ascent from "animality." Psychology, in turn, particularly in its Freudian form, is focused on the control of humanity's unruly "internal nature" through rationality and the imperatives imposed on it by "civilization"—with the hidden agenda of sublimating human powers in the project of controlling "external nature."

Many class theories of social development, particularly Marxian socialism, have been rooted in the belief that the "domination of man by man" emerges from the need to "dominate nature," presumably with the result that once nature is subjugated, humanity will be cleansed of the "slime of history" and enter into a new era of freedom. However ambiguous these self-definitions of our major social and humanistic disciplines may be, they are still embedded in nature and humanity's relationships with the natural world, even as they try to sharply divide the two and impart complete autonomy to cultural development and social evolution.

Taken as a whole, it is difficult to convey the enormous amount of mischief this simplistic image of nature has done to our ways of thinking, not to speak of the ideological rationale it has provided for human domination. More so than any single notion in the history of religion and philosophy, the image of a "blind," "mute," "cruel," "competitive," and "stingy" nature has opened a wide, often unbridgeable chasm between the social world and the natural world, and in its more exotic ramifications, between mind and body, subject and object, reason and physicality, technology and "raw materials," indeed, the whole gamut of dualisms that have fragmented not only the world of nature and society but the human psyche and its biological matrix.

From Plato's view of the body as a mere burden encasing an ethereal soul, to René Descartes' harsh split between the God-given rational and the purely mechanistic physical, we are the heirs of a historic dualism: between, firstly, a misconceived nature as the opponent of every human endeavor, whose "domination" must be lifted from the shoulders of humanity (even if human beings themselves are reduced to mere instruments of production to be ruthlessly exploited with a view toward their eventual liberation), and, secondly, a domineering humanity whose goal is to "subjugate" the natural world, including human nature itself. Nature, in effect, emerges as an affliction that must be removed from the human condition by the technology and methods of domination that paradoxically justify human domination of humans in the name of "human freedom."

This all-encompassing image of an intractable nature that must be tamed by a rational humanity has given us domineering notions of reason, science, and technology—a fragmentation of humanity into hierarchies, classes, state institutions, gender, and ethnic divisions. It has fostered nationalistic hatreds, imperialistic adventures, and a global philosophy of rule that identifies order with dominance and submission. In slowly corroding every familial, economic, aesthetic, ideological, and cultural tie that provided a sense of place and meaning for the individual in a vital human community, this antinaturalistic mentality has filled the awesome vacuum created by an utterly nihilistic and antisocial development with massive urban entities that are neither cities nor villages, with ubiquitous bureaucracies that impersonally manipulate the lives of faceless masses of atomized human beings, with giant corporate enterprises that spill beyond the boundaries of the world's richest nations to conglomerate on a global scale and determine the material life of the most remote hamlets on the planet, and finally, with highly centralized State institutions and military forces of unbridled power that threaten not only the freedom of the individual but the survival of the species.

The split that clerics and philosophers projected centuries ago in their visions of a soulless nature and a denatured soul has been realized in the form of a disastrous fragmentation of humanity and nature, indeed, in our time, of the human psyche itself. A direct line or logic of events flows almost unrelentingly from a warped image of the natural world to the warped contours of the social world, threatening to bury society in a "slime of history" that is not of nature's making but of man's—specifically, the early hierarchies from which economic classes emerged; the systems of domination, initially of woman by man, that have yielded highly rationalized systems of exploitation; and the vast armies of warriors, priests, monarchs, and bureaucrats who emerged from the simple status groups of tribal society to become the institutionalized tyrants of a market society.

That this authentic jungle of "claw and fang" we call the "free market" is an extension of human competition into nature—an ideological, self-serving fiction that parades under such labels as social Darwinism and sociobiology—hardly requires emphasis any longer. Lions are turned into "Kings of the Beasts" only by human kings, be they imperial monarchs or corporate ones; ants belong to the "lowly" in nature only by virtue of ideologies spawned in temples, palaces, manors, and, in our own time, by subservient apologists of the powers that be. The reality, as we shall see, is different, but a nature conceived as "hierarchical," not to speak of the other "brutish" and very bourgeois traits imputed to it, merely reflects a human condition in which dominance and submission are ends in themselves, which has brought the very existence of our biosphere into question.

Far from being the mere "object" of culture (technology, science, and reason), nature is always with us: whether as the parody of our self-image, as the cornerstone of the very disciplines which deny it a place in our social and self-formation, even in the protracted infancy of our young which renders the mind open to cultural development and creates those extended parental and sibling ties from which an organized society emerged.

And nature is always with us as the conscience of the transgressions we have visited on the planet—and the terrifying revenge that awaits us for our violation of the ecological integrity of the planet.

What distinguishes social ecology is that it negates the harsh image we have traditionally created of the natural world and its evolution. And it does so not by dissolving the social into the natural, like sociobiology, or by imparting mystical properties to nature that place it beyond the reach of human comprehension and rational insight. Indeed, as we shall see, social ecology places the human mind, like humanity itself, within a natural context and explores it in terms of its own natural history, as well as its cultural history, so that the sharp cleavages between thought and nature, subject and object, mind and body, and the social and natural are overcome, and the traditional dualisms of Western culture are *transcended* by an evolutionary interpretation of consciousness with its rich wealth of gradations over the course of natural history.

Social ecology "radicalizes" nature, or more precisely, our understanding of natural phenomena, by questioning the prevailing marketplace image of nature from an ecological standpoint: nature as a constellation of communities that are neither "blind" nor "mute," "cruel" nor "competitive," "stingy" nor "necessitarian" but, freed of all anthropocentric moral trappings, a *participatory* realm of interactive life forms whose most outstanding attributes are fecundity, creativity, and directiveness, marked by complementarity that renders the natural world the *grounding* for an ethics of freedom rather than domination.

Seen from an ecological standpoint, life-forms are related in an ecosystem not by the "rivalries" and "competitive" attributes imputed to them by Darwinian orthodoxy, but by the mutualistic attributes emphasized by a growing number of contemporary ecologists—an image pioneered by Peter Kropotkin. Indeed, social ecology challenges the very premises of "fitness" that enter into the Darwinian drama of evolutionary development with its fixation on "survival" rather than differentiation and fecundity. As William Trager has emphasized in his insightful work on symbiosis:

> The conflict in nature between different kinds of organisms has been popularly expressed in phrases like the "struggle for existence" and the "survival of the fittest." Yet few people realized that mutual cooperation between organisms— symbiosis—is just as important, and that the "fittest" may be the one that helps another to survive.[1]

It is tempting to go beyond this pithy and highly illuminating judgement to explore an ecological notion of natural evolution based on the development of *ecosystems*, not merely individual species. This is a concept of evolution as the dialectical development of ever-variegated, complex, and increasingly fecund *contexts* of plant-animal communities as distinguished from the traditional notion of biological evolution based on the atomistic development of single life-forms, a characteristically entrepreneurial concept of the isolated "individual," be it animal, plant, or bourgeois—a creature which fends for itself and either "survives" or "perishes" in a marketplace "jungle." As ecosystems become more complex and open a greater variety of evolutionary pathways, due to their own richness of diversity and increasingly flexible forms of organic life, it is not only the environment that "chooses" what "species" are "fit" to survive but species themselves, in mutualistic complexes as well as singly, that introduce a dim element of "choice"—by no means "intersubjective" or "willfull" in the *human* meaning of these terms.

Concomitantly, these ensembles of species alter the environment of which they are part and exercise an increasingly *active* role in their own evolution. Life, in this *ecological* conception of evolution, ceases to be the passive *tabula rasa* on which eternal forces which we loosely call "the environment" inscribe the destiny of "a species," an atomistic term that is meaningless outside the context of an ecosystem within which a life-form is truly definable with respect to other species.[2]

Life is active, interactive, procreative, relational, and contextual. It is not a passive lump of "stuff," a form of metabolic "matter" that awaits the action of "forces" external to it and is mechanically "shaped" by them. Ever striving and always producing new life-forms, there is a sense in which life is self-directive in its own evolutionary development, not passively reactive to an inorganic or organic world that impinges upon it from outside and "determines" its destiny in isolation from the ecosystems which it constitutes and of which it is a part.

And this much is clear in social ecology: our studies of "food webs" (a not quite satisfactory term for describing the interactivity that occurs in an ecosystem or, more properly, an ecological *community*) demonstrate that the complexity of biotic interrelationships, their diversity and intricacy, is a crucial factor in assessing an ecosystem's stability. In contrast to biotically complex temperate zones, relatively simple desert and arctic ecosystems are very fragile and break down easily with the loss or numerical decline of only a few species. The thrust of biotic evolution over great eras of organic evolution has been toward the increasing diversification of species and their interlocking into highly complex, basically mutualistic relationships, without which the widespread colonization of the planet by life would have been impossible.

Unity in diversity (a concept deeply rooted in the Western philosophical tradition) is not only the determinant of an ecosystem's stability; it is the source of an ecosystem's fecundity, of its innovativeness, of its evolutionary potential to create newer, still more complex life-forms and biotic interrelationships, even in the most inhospitable areas of the planet. Ecologists have not sufficiently stressed the fact that a multiplicity of life-forms and organic interrelationships in a biotic community opens new evolutionary pathways of development, a greater variety of evolutionary interactions, variations, and degrees of flexibility in the capacity to evolve, and is hence crucial not only in the community's stability but also in its innovativeness in the natural history of life.

The ecological principle of unity in diversity grades into a richly mediated social principle, hence my use of the term *social* ecology.[3] Society, in turn, attains its "truth," its self-actualization, in the form of richly articulated, mutualistic networks of people based on community, roundedness of personality, diversity of stimuli and activities, an increasing wealth of experience, and a variety of tasks. Is this grading of ecosystem diversity into social diversity, based on humanly scaled, decentralized communities, merely analogic reasoning?

My answer would be that it is not a superficial analogy but a deep-seated continuity between nature and society that social ecology recovers from traditional nature philosophy without its archaic dross of cosmic hierarchies, mystical absolutes, and cycles. In the case of social ecology, it is not in the *particulars* of differentiation that plant-animal communities are ecologically united with human communities; rather, it is the *logic* of differentiation that makes it possible to relate the mediations of nature and society into a living continuum.

What makes unity in diversity in nature more than a suggestive ecological metaphor for unity in diversity in society is the underlying fact of wholeness. By wholeness I do not mean any finality of closure in a development, any "totality" that leads to a terminal "reconciliation" of all "Being" in a complete identity of subject and object or a reality in which no further development is possible or meaningful. Rather, I mean varying degrees of the actualization of potentialities, the organic unfolding of the wealth of particularities that are latent in the as-yet-undeveloped potentiality. This potentiality can be a newly planted seed, a newly born infant, a newly formed community, a newly emerging society—yet, given their radically different specificity, they are all united by a processual reality, a shared "metabolism" of development, a unified catalysis of growth as distinguished from mere "change" that provides us with the most insightful way of *understanding* them we can possibly achieve. Wholeness is literally the unity that finally gives order to the particularity of each of these phenomena; it is what has emerged from the process, what integrates the particularities into a unified form, what renders the unity an operable reality and a "being" in the literal sense of the term—an order as the actualized *unity* of its diversity from the flowing and emergent process that yields its self-realization, the fixing of its directiveness into a clearly contoured form, and the creation in a dim sense of a "self" that is identifiable with respect to the "others" with which it interacts. Wholeness is the *relative* completion of a phenomenon's potentiality, the fulfillment of latent possibility as such, all its concrete manifestations aside, to become more than the realm of *mere* possibility and attain the "truth" or fulfilled reality of possibility. To think this way—in terms of potentiality, process, mediation, and wholeness—is to reach into the most underlying nature of things, just as to know the biography of a human being and the history of a society is to know them in their authentic reality and depth.

The natural world is no less encompassed by this processual dialectic and developmental ecology than the social, although in ways that do not involve will, degrees of choice, values, ethical goals, and the like. Life itself, as distinguished from the nonliving, however, emerges from the inorganic latent with all the potentialities and particularities it has immanently produced from the logic of its own nascent forms of self-organization. Obviously, so does society as distinguished from biology, humanity as distinguished from animality, and individuality as distinguished from humanity in the generic sense of the word. But these distinctions are not absolutes. They are the unique and closely interrelated phases of a shared continuum, of a process that is united precisely by its own differentiations just as the phases through which an embryo develops are both distinct from and incorporated into its complete gestation and its organic specificity.

This continuum is not simply a philosophical construct. It is an earthy anthropological fact which lives with us daily as surely as it explains the emergence of humanity out of mere animality. Individual socialization is the highly nuanced "biography" of that development in everyday life and in everyone as surely as the anthropological socialization of our species is part of its history. I refer to the biological basis of all human socialization: the protracted infancy of the human child that renders its cultural development possible, in contrast to the rapid growth of nonhuman animals, a rate of growth that quickly forecloses their ability to form a culture and develop sibling affinities of a lasting nature; the instinctual maternal drives that extend feelings of care, sharing, intimate consociation, and finally love and a sense of responsibility for one's own kin into the institutional forms we call "society"; and the sexual division of labor, age-ranking, and kin-relationships which, however culturally conditioned and even mythic in some cases, formed and still inform so much of social institutionalization today. These formative elements of society rest on biological facts and, placed in the contextual analysis I have argued for, require ecological analysis.

In emphasizing the nature-society continuum with all its gradations and "mediations," I do not wish to leave the impression that the known ways and forms in which society emerged from nature and still embodies the natural world in a shared process of cumulative growth follow a logic that is "inexorable" or "preordained" by a telos that mystically guides the unfolding by a supranatural and suprasocial process. Potentiality is not necessity; the logic of a process is not a form of inexorable "law"; the truth of a development is what is *implicit* in any unfolding and defined by the extent to which it achieves stability, variety, fecundity, and enlarges the "realm of freedom," however dimly freedom is conceived.

No specific "stage" of a process necessarily yields a still later one or is "presupposed" by it—but certain obvious conditions, however varied, blurred, or even idiosyncratic, form the determining ground for still other conditions that can be expected to emerge. Freedom and, ultimately, a degree of subjectivity that make choice and will possible along rational lines may be desiderata that the natural world renders possible and in a "self"-directive way plays an active role in achieving. But in no sense are these desiderata predetermined certainties that must unfold, nor is any such unfolding spared the very real possibility that it will become entirely regressive or remain unfulfilled and incomplete. That the *potentiality* for freedom and consciousness exists in nature and society; that nature and society are not merely "passive" in a development toward freedom and consciousness, a passivity that would make the very notion of potentiality mystical just as the notion of "necessity" would make it meaningless by definition; that natural and social history bear existential witness to the potentiality and processes that form subjectivity and bring consciousness more visibly on the horizon in the very natural history of mind—all constitute *no guarantee* that these latent desiderata are certainties or lend themselves to systematic elucidation and teleological explanations in any traditional philosophical sense.

Our survey of organic and social experience may stir us to interpret a development we know to have occurred as reason to presuppose that potentiality, wholeness, and *graded* evolution are realities after all, no less real than our own existence and personal histories, but presuppositions they remain. Indeed, no outlook in philosophy can ever exist that is free of presuppositions, any more than speculation can exist that is free of some stimulus by the objective world. The only truth about "first philosophy," from Greek times onward, is that what is "first" in any philosophical outlook are the presuppositions it adopts, the background of unformulated experience from which these presuppositions emerge, and the intuition of a coherence that must be validated by reality as well as speculative reason.

One of the most provocative of the graded continuities between nature and society is the nonhierarchical relationships that exist in an ecosystem, and the extent to which they provide a grounding for a nonhierarchical society.[4] It is meaningless to speak of hierarchy in an ecosystem and in the succession of ecosystems which, in contrast to a monadic species-oriented development, form the true story of natural evolution. There is no "king of the beasts" and no "lowly serf"—presumably, the lion and the ant—in *ecosystem* relationships. Such terms, including words like "cruel nature," "fallen nature," "domineering nature," and even "mutualistic nature" (I prefer to use the word "complementary" here) are projections of our own social relationships into the natural world. Ants are as important as lions and eagles in ecosystems; indeed, their recycling of organic materials gives them a considerable "eminence" in the maintenance of the stability and integrity of an area.

As to accounts of "dominance-submission" relationships between *individuals* such as "alpha" and "beta" males, utterly asymmetrical relationships tend to be grouped under words like "hierarchy" that are more analogic, often more metaphoric, than real. It becomes absurd, I think, to say that the "dominance" of a "queen bee," who in no way knows that she is a "queen" and whose sole function in a beehive is reproductive, is in any way equatable with an "alpha" male baboon, whose "status" tends to suffer grave diminution when the baboon troop moves from the plains to the forest. By the same token, it is absurd to equate "patriarchal harems" among red deer with "matriarchal" elephant herds, which simply expel bulls when they reach puberty and in no sense "dominate" them. One could go through a whole range of asymmetrical relationships to show that, even among our closest primate relatives, which include the utterly "pacific" orangutans as well as the seemingly "aggressive" chimpanzees, words like "dominance" and "submission" mean very different relationships depending upon the species one singles out and the circumstances under which they live.

I cannot emphasize too strongly that hierarchy in society is an *institutional* phenomenon, not a biological one. It is a product of organized, carefully crafted power relationships, not a product of the "morality of the gene," to use E. O. Wilson's particularly obtuse phrase in his *Sociobiology*. Only institutions, formed by long periods of human history and sustained by well-organized bureaucracies and military forces, could have placed absolute rule in the hands of mental defects like Nicholas II of Russia and Louis XVI of France. We can find nothing even remotely comparable to such institutionalized systems of command and obedience in other species, much less in ecosystems. It verges on the absurd to draw fast-and-loose comparisons between the "division of labor" (another anthropocentric phrase when placed in an ecological context) in a beehive, whose main function is reproducing bees, not making honey for breakfast tables, and human society, with its highly contrived State forms and organized bureaucracies.

What renders social ecology so important in comparing ecosystems to societies is that it decisively challenges the very function of hierarchy as a way of *ordering* reality, of dealing with differentiation and variation—with "otherness" as such. Social ecology ruptures the association of order with hierarchy. It poses the question of whether we can experience the "other," not hierarchically on a "scale of one to ten" with a continual emphasis on "inferior" and "superior," but ecologically, as variety that enhances the unity of phenomena, enriches wholeness, and more closely resembles a food-web than a pyramid. That hierarchy exists today as an even more fundamental problem than social classes, that domination exists today as an even more fundamental problem than economic exploitation, can be attested to by every conscious feminist, who can justly claim that long before man began to exploit man through the formation of social classes, he began to dominate woman in patriarchal and hierarchical relationships.

We would do well to remember that the abolition of classes, exploitation, and even the State is no guarantee whatever that people will cease to be ranked hierarchically and dominated according to age, gender, race, physical qualities, and often quite frivolous and irrational categories, unless liberation focuses as much on hierarchy and domination as it does on classes and exploitation. This is the point where socialism, in my view, must extend itself into a broader libertarian tradition that reaches back into the tribal or band-type communities ancestral to what we so smugly call "civilization," a tradition, indeed an abiding human impulse, that has surged to the surface of society in every revolutionary period, only to be brutally contained by those purely societal forms called "hierarchies."

Social ecology raises all of these issues in a fundamentally new light, and establishes entirely new ways of resolving them. I have tried to show that nature is always present in the human condition, and in the very ideological constructions that deny its presence in societal relationships. The *notion* of dominating nature literally *defines* all our social disciplines, including socialism and psychoanalysis. It is the apologia *par excellence* for the domination of human by human. Until that apologia is removed from our sensibilities in the rearing of the young, the first step in socialization as such, and replaced by an ecological sensibility that sees "otherness" in terms of complementarity rather than rivalry, we will never achieve human emancipation. Nature lives in us ontogenetically as different layers of experience which analytic logic often conceals from us: in the sensitivity of our cells, the remarkable autonomy of our organ systems, our so-called layered brain which experiences the world in different ways and attests to different worlds, which analytic logic, left to its own imperialistic claims, tends to close to us—indeed, in the *natural history* of the nervous system and mind, which bypasses the chasm between mind and body, or subjectivity and objectivity, with an organic continuum in which body grades into mind and objectivity into subjectivity. Herein lies the most compelling refutation of the traditional dualism in religion, philosophy, and sensibility that gave ideological credence to the myth of a "domineering" nature, borne by the suffering and brutalization of a socially dominated humanity.

Moreover, this natural history of the nervous system and mind is a cumulative one, not merely a successive one—a history whose past lies in our everyday present. It is not for nothing that one of America's greatest physiologists, Walter B Cannon, titled his great work on homeostasis *The Widsom of the Body*. Running through our entire experiential apparatus and organizing experience for us are not only the categories of Kant's first *Critique* and Hegel's *Logic*, but also the *natural history of sensibility* as it exists in us hormonally, from our undifferentiated nerve networks to the hemispheres of our brains. We metabolize with nature in production in such a way that the materials with which we work and the tools we use to work on them enter reciprocally into the technological imagination we form and the social matrix in which our technologies exist. Nor can we ever permit ourselves to forget, all our overriding ideologies of class, economic interest, and the like notwithstanding, that we socialize with each other not only as producers and property owners, but also as children and parents, young and old, female and male, with our bodies as well as our minds, and according to graded and varied impulses that are as archaic as they are fairly recent in the natural evolution of sensibility.

Hence, to become conscious of this vast ensemble of natural history as it enters into our very beings, to see its place in the graded development of our social history, to recognize that we must develop new sensibilities, technologies, institutions, and forms of experiencing that give expression to this wealth of our inner development and the complexity of our biosocial apparatus is to go along with a deeper grain of evolution and dialectic than is afforded to us by the "epistemological" and "linguistic" turns of recent philosophy.[5] On this score, just as I would argue that science *is* the history of science, not merely its latest "stage," and technology *is* the history of technology, not merely its latest designs, so reason *is* the history of reason, not merely its present analytic and communicative dimensions. Social history includes natural history as a graded dialectic that is united not only in a continuum by a shared logic of differentiation and complementarity; it includes natural history in the social-ization process itself, in the natural as well as the social history of experience, in the imperatives of a harmonized relationship between humanity and nature that presuppose new ecotechnologies and ecocommunities, and in the desider-ata opened by a decentralized society based on the values of complementar-ity and community.

The ideas I have advanced so far take their point of departure from a radically different image of nature than the prevailing one, in which philo-sophical dualism, economics, sociology, psychology, and socialism have their roots. As a social ecologist, I see nature as essentially creative, directive, mu-tualistic, fecund, and marked by complementarity, not "mute," "blind," "cruel," "stingy," or "oppressive." This shift in focus from a marketplace to an ecological image of nature obliges me to challenge the time-honored notion that the domination of human by human is necessary in order to "dominate nature." In emphasizing how meaningless this rationale for hierarchy and domination is, I conclude—with considerable historical justification, which our own era amply illuminates with its deployment of technology primarily for purposes of social control—that the idea of dominating nature stems from human domination, initially in hierarchical forms as feminists so clearly un-derstand, and later in class and statist forms.

Accordingly, my ecological image of nature leads me to drastically re-define my conception of economics, sociology, psychology, and socialism, which, ironically, advance a shared dualistic gospel of a radical separation of society from nature even as they rest on a militant imperative to "subdue" nature, be it as "scarce resources," the realm of "animality," "internal nature," or "external nature." Hence, I have tried to re-vision history not only as an ac-count of power over human beings that by far outweighs any attempt to gain power over things, but also as power ramified into centralized states and urban environments, a technology, science, and rationality of social control, and a message of "liberation" that conceals the most awesome features of domination, notably, the traditional capitalist orthodoxies of our day.

At the juncture where nature is conceived either as a ruthless, compet-itive marketplace or a creative, fecund biotic community, two radically di-vergent pathways of thought and sensibility emerge, following contrasting directions and conceptions of the human future. One ends in a totalitarian and antinaturalistic terminus for society: centralized, statist, technocratic, corporate, and sweepingly repressive. The other ends in a libertarian and ecological beginning for society: decentralized, stateless, artistic, collective, and sweepingly emancipatory. These are not tendentious words. It is by no means certain that western humanity, currently swept up in a counterrevo-lution of authoritarian values and adaptive impulses, would regard a liber-tarian vision as less pejorative than a totalitarian one. Whether or not my own words seem tendentious, the full logic of my view should be seen: the view we hold of the natural world profoundly shapes the image we develop of the social worlds, even as we assert the "supremacy" and "autonomy" of culture over nature.

In what sense does social ecology view nature as a grounding for an ethics of freedom? If the story of natural evolution is not understandable in Locke's atomistic account of a particular species' evolution, if that story is basically an account of ecosystem evolution toward ever more complex and flexible evolutionary pathways, then natural history itself cannot be seen simply as "necessitarian," "governed" by "inexorable laws" and imperatives. Every organism is in some sense "willful," insofar as it seeks to preserve itself, to maintain its identity, to resist a kind of biological entropy that threatens its integrity and complexity. However dimly, every organism transforms the essential attributes of self-maintenance that earn it the status of a distinct form of life into a capacity to *choose* alternatives that favor its survival and well-being—not merely to react to stimuli as a purely physico-chemical ensemble.

This dim, germinal freedom is heightened by the growing wealth of ecological complexity that confronts evolving life in synchronicity with evolving ecosystems. The elaboration of possibilities that comes with the elaboration of diversity and the growing multitude of alternatives confronting species development opens newer and *more fecund pathways* for organic development. Life is not passive in the face of these possibilities for its evolution. It drives toward them actively in a shared process of mutual stimulation between organisms and their environment (including the living and non-living environment they create) as surely as it also actively creates and colonizes the niches that cradle a vast diversity of life-forms in our richly elaborated biosphere. This image of active, indeed striving, life requires no Hegelian "Spirit" or Heraklitean *Logos* to explain it. Activity and striving are presupposed in our very definition of metabolism. In fact, metabolic activity is coextensive with the notion of activity as such and imparts an identity, indeed, a rudimentary "self," to every organism. Diversity and complexity, indeed, the notion of evolution as a diversifying history, superadd the dimension of variegated alternatives and pathways to the simple fact of choice—and, with choice, the rudimentary fact of *freedom*. For freedom, in its most germinal form, is also a function of diversity and complexity, of a "realm of necessity" that is diminished by a growing and expanding multitude of alternatives, of a widening horizon of evolutionary possibilities, which life in its ever-richer forms both creates and in its own way "pursues," until consciousness, the gift of nature as well as society to humanity, renders this pursuit willful, self-reflexive, and consciously creative.

Here, in this ecological concept of natural evolution, lies a hidden message of freedom based on the "inwardness of life," to use Hans Jonas's excellent expression, and the ever greater diversification produced by natural evolution. Ecology is united with society in new terms that reveal moral tension in natural history, just as Marx's simplistic image of the "savage" who "wrestles with nature" reveals a moral tension in social history.

We must beware of being prejudiced by our own fear of prejudice. Organismic philosophies can surely yield totalitarian, hierarchical, and eco-fascistic results. We have good reason to be concerned over so-called nature philosophies that give us the notion of *Blut und Boden* and "dialectical materialism," which provide the ideological justification for the horrors of Nazism and Stalinism. We have good reason to be concerned over a mysticism that yields social quietism at best and the aggressive activism of reborn Christianity and certain Asian gurus at worst. We have even better reason to be concerned over the eco-fascism of Garrett Hardin's "lifeboat ethic" with its emphasis on scarce resources and the so-called tragedy of the commons, an ethic which services genocidal theories of imperialism and a global disregard for human misery. So, too, sociobiology, which roots all the savage features of "civilization" in our genetic constitution. Social ecology offers the coordinates for an entirely different pathway in exploring our relationship to the natural world—one that accepts neither genetic and scientistic theories of "natural necessity" at one extreme, nor a romantic and mystical zealotry that reduces the rich variety of reality and evolution to a cosmic "oneness" and energetics at the other extreme. For in both cases, it is not only our vision of the world and the unity of nature and society that suffers, but the "natural history" of freedom and the basis for an objective ethics of liberation as well.

We cannot avoid the use of conventional reason, present-day modes of science, and modern technology. They, too, have their place in the future of humanity and humanity's metabolism with the natural world. But we can establish new *contexts* in which these modes of rationality, science, and technology have their proper place—an *ecological* context that does not deny other, more qualitative modes of knowing and producing which are participatory and emancipatory. We can also foster a new sensibility toward otherness that, *in a nonhierarchical society,* is based on complementarity rather than rivalry, and new communities that, scaled to human dimensions, are tailored to the ecosystem in which they are located and open a new, decentralized, self-managed public realm for new forms of selfhood as well as directly democratic forms of social management.

Notes

1. William Trager, *Symbiosis,* New York: Van Nostrand Reinhold Co., 1970, vii.
2. The traditional emphasis on an "active" environment that determines the "survival" of a passive species, altered in a cosmic game of chance by random mutations, is perhaps another reason why the term "environmentalism," as distinguished from social ecology, is a very unsatisfactory expression these days.
3. My use of the word "social" cannot be emphasized too strongly. Words like "human," "deep," and "cultural," while very valuable as general terms, do not explicitly pinpoint the extent to which our image of nature is formed by the kind of society in which we live and by the abiding natural basis of all social life. The evolution of society out of nature and the ongoing interaction between the two tend to be lost in words that do not tell us enough about the vital

association between nature and society and about the importance of defining such disciplines as economics, psychology, and sociology in natural as well as social terms. Recent uses of "social ecology" to advance a rather superficial account of social life in fairly conventional ecological terms are particularly deplorable. Books like *Habits of the Heart* which glibly pick up the term serve to coopt a powerful expression for rather banal ends and tend to compromise efforts to deepen our understanding of nature and society as interactive rather than opposed domains.

4. Claims of hierarchy as a ubiquitous natural fact cannot be ignored by still further widening the chasm between nature and society—or "natural necessity" and "cultural freedom" as it is more elegantly worded. Justifying social hierarchy in terms of natural hierarchy is one of the most persistent assaults on an egalitarian social future that religion and philosophy have made over the ages. It has surfaced recently in sociobiology and reinforced the antinaturalistic stance that permeates so many liberatory ideologies in the modern era. To say that culture is precisely the "emancipation of man from nature" is to revert to Sartre's "slime of history" notion of the natural world that not only separates society from nature but mind from body and subjectivity from objectivity.

5. Our disastrously one-sided and rationalized "civilization" has boxed this wealth of inner development and complexity away, relegating it to preindustrial lifeways that basically shaped our evolution up to a century or two ago. From a sensory viewpoint, we live atrophied, indeed, starved lives compared to hunters and food cultivators, whose capacity to experience reality, even in a largely cultural sense, by far overshadows our own. The twentieth century alone bears witness to an appalling dulling of our "sixth senses" as well as to our folk creativity and craft creativity. We have never experienced so little so loudly, so brashly, so trivially, so thinly, so neurotically. For a comparison of the "world of experience we have lost" (to reword Peter Laslett's title), read the excellent personal accounts of so-called Bushmen, or San people, the Ituri Forest pygmies, and the works of Paul Radin on food-gatherers and hunters—not simply as records of their lifeways but of their epistemologies.

II. ECOFEMINISM.

Overview. Ecofeminism is a term coined by Françoise d'Eaubonne. The concept is that a connection exists between the aspects of domination that humans exert on the biosphere and that the male-dominated social system exerts on women. The various aspects of this logic of domination are central to ecofeminism.

Carolyn Merchant's essay shows how mainstream feminist theory might profit from adopting the ecofeminist model. Behind this model are assumptions that are not too dissimilar to Bookchin's previous essay except that the focus is on the domination of women in the context of domination in general. Merchant is interested in putting these connections into a comparative context with: (a) liberal feminism, (b) Marxist feminism, (c) radical feminism, and (d) socialist feminism. The ultimate end of this analysis is to create a synergy of interests, tactics, and intended results.

Karen J. Warren seeks to portray ecofeminism as an essential element to any environmental ethical theory. She identifies eight points of feminism that center on the pluralism and contextualism that are missing in the current social climate. A key feature that should be noted is that Warren does not believe that any objective social/ethical theory can ever be proposed. The question then becomes which biased theory is better. After proposing the feminist position, she emends each of the eight points with ecofeminism objectives to show how similar these two worldviews are and that they should therefore be accepted as a package.

Val Plumwood argues in her essay that the issues of discontinuity and of instrumentalism are among the most important ones to be addressed. *Discontinuity* refers to the seemingly arbitrary categories that serve to separate male/female, human/animal/plant, and so forth. In this way, the lessons of the deep ecologists are accepted. However, deep ecology goes too far in identifying the self with the biosphere and should instead critique social institutions and patriarchy, for they are the human institutions that promote instrumentalism. Men use women as the tools by which their purposes might be fulfilled. In the same way, humans use nature as a tool; but like the social ecologists, the ecofeminists emphasize the development of actual people (as opposed to the Hindu self of the deep ecologists) in a community (both social and natural).

Ecofeminism and Feminist Theory

Carolyn Merchant

The term *ecofeminisme* was coined by the French writer Françoise d'Eaubonne in 1974 to represent women's potential for bringing about an ecological revolution to ensure human survival on the planet.[1] Such an ecological revolution would entail new gender relations between women and men and between humans and nature. Liberal, radical, and socialist feminism have all been concerned with improving the human/nature relationship, and each has contributed to an ecofeminist perspective in different ways.[2] Liberal feminism is consistent with the objectives of reform environmentalism to alter human relations with nature through the passage of new laws and regulations. Radical ecofeminism analyzes environmental problems from within its critique of patriarchy and offers alternatives that could liberate both women and nature. Socialist ecofeminism grounds its analysis in capitalist patriarchy and would totally restructure, through a socialist revolution, the domination of women and nature inherent in the market economy's use of both as resources. While radical feminism has delved more deeply into the woman/nature connection, I believe that socialist feminism has the potential for a more thorough critique of the domination issue.

Liberal feminism characterized the history of feminism from its beginnings in the seventeenth century until the 1960s. Its roots are liberalism, the political theory that incorporates the scientific analysis that nature is composed of atoms moved by external forces with a theory of human nature that views humans as individual rational agents who maximize their own self-interest and capitalism as the optimal economic structure for human progress. Historically, liberal feminists have argued that women do not differ from men as rational agents and that exclusion from educational and economic opportunities have prevented them from realizing their own potential for creativity in all spheres of human life.[3]

For liberal feminists (as for liberalism generally), environmental problems result from the overly rapid development of natural resources and the failure to regulate environmental pollutants. Better science, conservation, and laws are the proper approaches to resolving resource problems. Given equal educational opportunities to become scientists, natural resource managers, regulators, lawyers, and legislators, women like men can contribute to the improvement of the environment, the conservation of natural resources, and the higher quality of human life. Women, therefore, can transcend the social stigma of their biology and join men in the cultural project of environmental conservation.

Radical feminism developed in the late 1960s and 1970s with the second wave of feminism. The radical form of ecofeminism is a response to the perception that women and nature have been mutually associated and devalued in Western culture and that both can be elevated and liberated through direct political action. In prehistory an emerging patriarchal culture dethroned the mother Goddesses and replaced them with male gods to whom the female deities became subservient.[4] The scientific revolution of the seventeenth century further degraded nature by replacing Renaissance organicism and a nurturing earth with the metaphor of a machine to be controlled and repaired from the outside. The Earth is to be dominated by male-developed and -controlled technology, science, and industry.

Radical feminism instead celebrates the relationship between women and nature through the revival of ancient rituals centered on Goddess worship, the moon, animals, and the female reproductive system. A vision in which nature is held in esteem as mother and Goddess is a source of inspiration and empowerment for many ecofeminists. Spirituality is seen as a source of both personal and social change. Goddess worship and rituals centered around the lunar and female menstrual cycles, lectures, concerts, art exhibitions, street and theater productions, and direct political action (web weaving in antinuclear protests) are all examples of the re-visioning of nature and women as powerful forces. Radical ecofeminist philosophy embraces intuition, an ethic of caring, and weblike human/nature relationships.

For radical feminists, human nature is grounded in human biology. Humans are biologically sexed and socially gendered. Sex/gender relations give men and women different power bases. Hence the personal is political. Radical feminists object to the dominant society's perception that women are limited by being closer to nature because of their ability to bear children. The dominant view is that menstruation, pregnancy, nursing, and nurturing of infants and young children should tie women to the home, decreasing their mobility and inhibiting their ability to remain in the work force. Radical feminists argue that the perception that women are totally oriented toward biological reproduction degrades them by association with a nature that is itself devalued in Western culture. Women's biology and nature should instead be celebrated as sources of female power.

Turning the perceived connection between women and biological reproduction upside down becomes the source of women's empowerment and ecological activism. Women argue that male-designed and -produced technologies neglect the effects of nuclear radiation, pesticides, hazardous wastes, and household chemicals on women's reproductive organs and on the ecosystem. They argue that radioactivity from nuclear wastes, power plants, and bombs is a potential cause of birth defects, cancers, and the elimination of life on Earth.[5] They expose hazardous waste sites near schools and homes as permeating soil and drinking water and contributing to miscarriage, birth defects, and leukemia. They object to pesticides and herbicides being sprayed on crops and forests as potentially affecting children and the childbearing women living near them. Women frequently spearhead local actions against spraying and power plant siting and organize others to demand toxic cleanups. When coupled with an environmental ethic that values rather than degrades nature, such actions have the potential both for raising women's consciousness of their own oppression and for the liberation of nature from the polluting effects of industrialization. For example, many lower-middle-class women who became politicized through protests over toxic chemical wastes at Love Canal in New York simultaneously became feminists when their activism spilled over into their home lives.[6]

Yet in emphasizing the female, body, and nature components of the dualities male/female, mind/body, and culture/nature, radical ecofeminism runs the risk of perpetuating the very hierarchies it seeks to overthrow. Critics point to the problem of women's own reinforcement of their identification with a nature that Western culture degrades.[7] If "female is to male as nature is to culture," as anthropologist Sherry Ortner argues,[8] then women's hopes for liberation are set back by association with nature. Any analysis that makes women's essence and qualities special ties them to a biological destiny that thwarts the possibility of liberation. A politics grounded in women's culture, experience, and values can be seen as reactionary.

To date, socialist feminists have had little to say about the problem of the domination of nature. To them, the source of male domination of women is the complex of social patterns called capitalist patriarchy, in which men bear the responsibility for labor in the marketplace and women for labor in the home.

Feminism and the Environment

	NATURE	HUMAN NATURE	FEMINIST CRITIQUE OF ENVIRONMENTALISM	IMAGE OF A FEMINIST ENVIRONMENTALISM
Liberal Feminism	Atoms Mind/body dualism Domination of nature	Rational agents Individualism Maximization of self-interest	"Man and his environment" leaves out women	Women participate in natural resources and environmental sciences
Marxist Feminism	Transformation of nature by science and technology for human use Domination of nature as a means to human freedom Nature is material basis of life: food, clothing, shelter, energy	Creation of human nature through mode of production, praxis Historically specific—not fixed Species nature of humans	Critique of capitalist control of resources and accumulation of goods and profits	Socialist/communist society will use resources for good of all men and women Resources will be controlled by workers Environmental pollution will be minimal since no surpluses will be produced Environmental research by men and women

Radical Feminism	Nature is spiritual and personal Conventional science and technology problematic because of their emphasis on domination	Biology is basic Humans are sexually reproducing bodies Sexed by biology/Gendered by society	Unaware of interconnectedness of male domination of nature and women Male environmentalism retains hierarchies Insufficient attention to environmental threats to women's reproduction (chemicals, nuclear war)	Woman/nature both valued and celebrated Reproductive freedom Against pornographic depictions of both women and nature Radical ecofeminism
Socialist Feminism	Nature is material basis of life: food, clothing, shelter, energy Nature is socially and historically constructed Transformation of nature by production	Human nature created through biology and praxis (sex, race, class, age) Historically specific and socially constructed	Leaves out nature as active and responsive Leaves out women's role in reproduction and reproduction as a category Systems approach is mechanistic not dialectical	Both nature and human production are active Centrality of biological and social reproduction Multileveled structural analysis Dialectical (not mechanical) systems Socialist ecofeminism

Yet the potential exists for a socialist ecofeminism that would push for an ecological, economic, and social revolution that would simultaneously liberate women, working-class people, and nature.

For socialist ecofeminism, environmental problems are rooted in the rise of capitalist patriarchy and the ideology that the Earth and nature can be exploited for human progress through technology. Historically, the rise of capitalism eroded the subsistence-based farm and city workshop in which production was oriented toward use values and men and women were economic partners. The result was a capitalist economy dominated by men and a domestic sphere in which women's labor in the home was unpaid and subordinate to men's labor in the marketplace. Both women and nature are exploited by men as part of the progressive liberation of humans from the constraints imposed by nature. The consequence is the alienation of women and men from each other and both from nature.

Socialist feminism incorporates many of the insights of radical feminism, but views both nature and human nature as historically and socially constructed. Human nature is seen as the product of historically changing interactions between humans and nature, men and women, classes, and races. Any meaningful analysis must be grounded in an understanding of power not only in the personal but also in the political sphere. Like radical feminism, socialist feminism is critical of mechanistic science's treatment of nature as passive and of its male-dominated power structures. Similarly, it deplores the lack of a gender analysis in history and the omission of any treatment of women's reproductive and nurturing roles. But rather than grounding its analysis in biological reproduction alone, it also incorporates social reproduction. Biological reproduction includes the reproduction of the species and the reproduction of daily life through food, clothing, and shelter; social reproduction includes socialization and the legal/political reproduction of the social order.[9]

Like Marxist feminists, socialist feminists see nonhuman nature as the material basis of human life, supplying the necessities of food, clothing, shelter, and energy. Materialism, not spiritualism, is the driving force of social change. Nature is transformed by human science and technology for use by all humans for survival. Socialist feminism views change as dynamic, interactive, and dialectical, rather than as mechanistic, linear, and incremental. Nonhuman nature is dynamic and alive. As a historical actor, nature interacts with human beings through mutual ecological relations. Socialist feminist environmental theory gives both reproduction and production central places. A socialist feminist environmental ethic involves developing sustainable, nondominating relations with nature and supplying all peoples with a high quality of life.

In politics, socialist feminists participate in many of the same environmental actions as radical feminists. The goals, however, are to direct change toward some form of an egalitarian socialist state, in addition to resocializing men and women into nonsexist, nonracist, nonviolent, anti-imperialist forms of life. Socialist ecofeminism deals explicitly with environmental issues that affect working-class women, Third World women, and women of color. Examples include support for the women's *Chipco* (tree-hugging) movement in India that protects fuel resources from lumber interests, for the women's Green Belt movement in Kenya that has planted more than 2 million trees in 10 years, and for Native American women and children exposed to radioactivity from uranium mining.[10]

Although the ultimate goals of liberal, radical, and socialist feminists may differ as to whether capitalism, women's culture, or socialism should be the ultimate objective of political action, shorter-term objectives overlap. In this sense there is perhaps more unity than diversity in women's common goal of restoring the natural environment and quality of life for people and other living and nonliving inhabitants of the planet.

NOTES

1. Françoise d'Eaubonne, "Feminism or Death," in Elaine Marks and Isabelle de Courtivron (eds.), *New French Feminisms: An Anthology* (Amherst: University of Massachusetts Press, 1980).

2. See Karen Warren, "Feminism and Ecology: Making Connections," *Environmental Ethics* 9 (no. 1: 1981): 3–20

3. See Alison M. Jaggar, *Feminist Politics and Human Nature* (Totowa, NJ: Rowman and Allanheld, 1983).

4. Merlin Stone, *When God Was a Woman* (New York: Harcourt Brace Jovanovich, 1976.)

5. See Dorothy Nelkin, "Nuclear Power as a Feminist Issue," *Environment* 23 (no. 1: 1981): 14–20, 38–39.

6. Carolyn Merchant, "Earthcare: Women and the Environmental Movement," *Environment* 22 (June 1970): 7–13, 38–40.

7. Donna Haraway, "A Manifesto for Cyborgs," *Socialist Review* 15 (no. 80: 1985): 65–107.

8. Sherry Ortner, "Is Female to Male as Nature Is to Culture?" in Michelle Rosaldo and Louise Lamphere (eds.), *Woman, Culture, and Society* (Stanford, CA: Stanford University Press, 1974), pp. 67–87.

9. Carolyn Merchant, "The Theoretical Structure of Ecological Revolutions," *Environmental Review* 11 (no. 4: Winter 1987): 265–74.

10. See Jeanne Henn, "Female Farmers—The Doubly Ignored," *Development Forum* 14 (nos. 7 and 8: 1986); and Gillian Goslinga, "Kenya's Women of the Trees," *Development Forum* 14 (no. 8: 1986): 15.

The Power and the Promise of Ecological Feminism

Karen J. Warren

INTRODUCTION

Ecological feminism (ecofeminism) has begun to receive a fair amount of attention lately as an alternative feminism and environmental ethic.[1] Since Françoise d'Eaubonne introduced the term *ecofeminisme* in 1974 to bring attention to women's potential for bringing about an ecological revolution,[2] the term has been used in a variety of ways. As I use the term in this paper, ecological feminism is the position that there are important connections—historical, experiential, symbolic, theoretical—between the domination of women and the domination of nature, an understanding of which is crucial to both feminism and environmental ethics. Here I discuss the nature of a feminist ethic and the ways in which ecofeminism provides a feminist and environmental ethic. I conclude that any feminist theory *and* any environmental ethic which fails to take seriously the twin and interconnected dominations of women and nature is at best incomplete and at worst simply inadequate. . . .

ECOFEMINISM AS A FEMINIST AND ENVIRONMENTAL ETHIC

A feminist ethic involves a twofold commitment to critique male bias in ethics wherever it occurs, and to develop ethics which are not male-biased. Sometimes this involves articulation of values (e.g., values of care, appropriate trust, kinship, friendship) often lost or underplayed in mainstream ethics.[3] Sometimes it involves engaging in theory building by pioneering in new directions or by revamping old theories in gender sensitive ways. What makes the critiques of old theories or conceptualizations of new ones "feminist" is that they emerge out of sex-gender analyses and reflect whatever those analyses reveal about gendered experience and gendered social reality.

As I conceive feminist ethics in the pre-feminist present, it rejects attempts to conceive of ethical theory in terms of necessary and sufficient conditions, because it assumes that there is no essence (in the sense of some transhistorical, universal, absolute abstraction) of feminist ethics. While attempts to formulate joint necessary and sufficient conditions of a feminist ethic are unfruitful, nonetheless, there are some necessary conditions, what I prefer to call "boundary conditions" of a feminist ethic. These boundary conditions clarify some of the minimal conditions of a feminist ethic without suggesting that feminist ethics has some ahistorical essence. They are like the boundaries of a quilt or collage. They delimit the territory of the piece without dictating what the interior, the design, the actual pattern of the piece looks like. Because the actual design of the quilt emerges from the multiplicity of voices of women in a cross-cultural context, the design will change over time. It is not something static.

What are some of the boundary conditions of a feminist ethic? First, nothing can become part of a feminist ethic—can be part of the quilt—that promotes sexism, racism, classism, or any other "isms" of social domination. Of course, people may disagree about what counts as a sexist act, racist attitude, classist behavior. What counts as sexism, racism, or classism may vary cross-culturally. Still, because a feminist ethic aims at eliminating sexism and sexist bias, and sexism is intimately connected in conceptualization and in practice to racism, classism, and naturism, a feminist ethic must be anti-sexist, anti-racist, anti-classist, anti-naturist and opposed to any "ism" which presupposes or advances a logic of domination.

Second, a feminist ethic is a *contextualist* ethic. A contextualist ethic is one which sees ethical discourse and practice as emerging from the voices of people located in different historical circumstances. A contextualist ethic is properly viewed as a *collage* or *mosaic*, a *tapestry* of voices that emerges out of felt experiences. Like any collage or mosaic, the point is not to have *one picture* based on a unity of voices, but a *pattern* which emerges out of the very different voices of people located in different circumstances. When a contextualist ethic is *feminist*, it gives central place to the voices of women.

Third, since a feminist ethic gives central significance to the diversity of women's voices, a feminist ethic must be structurally pluralistic rather than unitary or reductionistic. It rejects the assumption that there is "one voice" in terms of which ethical values, beliefs, attitudes, and conduct can be assessed.

Fourth, a feminist ethic reconceives ethical theory as theory in process which will change over time. Like all theory, a feminist ethic is based on some generalizations.[4] Nevertheless, the generalizations associated with it are themselves a pattern of voices within which the different voices emerging out of concrete and alternative descriptions of ethical situations have meaning. The coherence of a feminist theory so conceived is given within a historical and conceptual context, i.e., within a set of historical, socioeconomic circumstances (including circumstances of race, class, age, and affectional orientation) and within a set of basic beliefs, values, attitudes, and assumptions about the world.

Fifth, because a feminist ethic is contextualist, structurally pluralistic, and "in-process," one way to evaluate the claims of a feminist ethic is in terms of their *inclusiveness:* those claims (voices, patterns of voices) are morally and epistemologically favored (preferred, better, less partial, less biased) which are more inclusive of the felt experiences and perspectives of oppressed persons. The condition of inclusiveness requires and ensures that the diverse voices of women (as oppressed persons) will be given legitimacy in ethical theory building. It thereby helps to minimize empirical bias, e.g., bias rising from faulty or false generalizations based on stereotyping, too small a sample size, or a skewed sample. It does so by ensuring that any generalizations which are made about ethics and ethical decision making include—indeed cohere with—the patterned voices of women.[5]

Sixth, a feminist ethic makes no attempt to provide an "objective" point of view, since it assumes that in contemporary culture there really is no such point of view. As such, it does not claim to be "unbiased" in the sense of "value-neutral" or "objective." However, it does assume that whatever bias it has as an ethic centralizing the voices of oppressed persons is a *better bias*—"better" because it is more inclusive and therefore less partial—than those which exclude those voices.[6]

Seventh, a feminist ethic provides a central place for values typically unnoticed, underplayed, or misrepresented in traditional ethics, e.g., values of care, love, friendship, and appropriate trust.[7] Again, it need not do this at the exclusion of considerations of rights, rules, or utility. There may be many contexts in which talk of rights or of utility is useful or appropriate. For instance, in contracts or property relationships, talk of rights may be useful and appropriate. In deciding what is cost-effective or advantageous to the most people, talk of utility may be useful and appropriate. In a feminist *quo* contextualist ethic, whether or not such talk is useful or appropriate depends on the context; *other values* (e.g., values of care, trust, friendship) are *not* viewed as reducible to or captured solely in terms of such talk.[8]

Eighth, a feminist ethic also involves a reconception of what it is to be human and what it is for humans to engage in ethical decision making, since it rejects as either meaningless or currently untenable any gender-free or gender-neutral description of humans, ethics, and ethical decision-making. It thereby rejects what Alison Jaggar calls "abstract individualism," i.e., the position that it is possible to identify a human essence or human nature that exists independently of any particular historical context.[9] Humans and human moral conduct are properly understood essentially (and not merely accidentally) in terms of networks or webs of historical and concrete relationships.

All the props are now in place for seeing how ecofeminism provides the framework for a distinctively feminist and environmental ethic. It is a feminism that critiques male bias wherever it occurs in ethics (including environmental ethics) and aims at providing an ethic (including an environmental ethic) which is not male biased—and it does so in a way that satisfies the preliminary boundary conditions of a feminist ethic.

First, ecofeminism is quintessentially anti-naturist. Its anti-naturism consists in the rejection of any way of thinking about or acting toward nonhuman nature that reflects a logic, values, or attitude of domination. Its anti-naturist, anti-sexist, anti-racist, anti-classist (and so forth, for all other "isms" of social domination) stance forms the outer boundary of the quilt: nothing gets on the quilt which is naturist, sexist, racist, classist, and so forth.

Second, ecofeminism is a contextualist ethic. It involves a shift *from* a conception of ethics as primarily a matter of rights, rules, or principles predetermined and applied in specific cases to entities viewed as competitors in the contest of moral standing, *to* a conception of ethics as growing out of what Jim Cheney calls "defining relationships," i.e., relationships conceived in some sense as defining who one is.[10] As a contextualist ethic, it is not that rights, or rules, or principles are *not* relevant or important. Clearly they are in certain contexts and for certain purposes.[11] It is just that what *makes* them relevant or important is that those to whom they apply are entities *in relationship with* others.

Ecofeminism also involves an ethical shift *from* granting moral consideration to nonhumans *exclusively* on the grounds of some similarity they share with humans (e.g., rationality, interests, moral agency, sentiency, right-holder status) *to* "a highly contextual account to see clearly what a human being is and what the nonhuman world might be, morally speaking, *for* human beings."[12] For an ecofeminist, *how* a moral agent is in relationship to another becomes of central significance, not simply *that* a moral agent is a moral agent or is bound by rights, duties, virtue, or utility to act in a certain way.

Third, ecofeminism is structurally pluralistic in that it presupposes and maintains difference—difference among humans as well as between humans and at least some elements of nonhuman nature. Thus, while ecofeminism denies the "nature/culture" split, it affirms that humans are both members of an ecological community (in some respects) and different from it (in other respects). Ecofeminism's attention to relationships and community is not, therefore, an erasure of difference but a respectful acknowledgment of it.

Fourth, ecofeminism reconceives theory as theory in process. It focuses on patterns of meaning which emerge, for instance, from the storytelling and first-person narratives of women (and others) who deplore the twin dominations of women and nature. The use of narrative is one way to ensure that the content of the ethic—the pattern of the quilt—may/will change over time, as the historical and material realities of women's lives change and as more is learned about women-nature connections and the destruction of the nonhuman world.[13]

Fifth, ecofeminism is inclusivist. It emerges from the voices of women who experience the harmful domination of nature and the way that domination is tied to their domination as women. It emerges from listening to the voices of indigenous peoples such as Native Americans who have been dislocated from their land and have witnessed the attendant undermining of such values as appropriate reciprocity, sharing, and kinship that characterize traditional Indian culture. It emerges from listening to voices of those who, like

Nathan Hare, critique traditional approaches to environmental ethics as white and bourgeois, and as failing to address issues of "black ecology" and the "ecology" of the inner city and urban spaces.[14] It also emerges out of the voices of Chipko women who see the destruction of "earth, soil, and water" as intimately connected with their own inability to survive economically.[15] With its emphasis on inclusivity and difference, ecofeminism provides a framework for recognizing that what counts as ecology and what counts as appropriate conduct toward both human and nonhuman environments is largely a matter of context.

Sixth, as a feminism, ecofeminism makes no attempt to provide an "objective" point of view. It is a social ecology. It recognizes the twin dominations of women and nature as social problems rooted both in very concrete, historical, socioeconomic circumstances and in oppressive patriarchal conceptual frameworks which maintain and sanction these circumstances.

Seventh, ecofeminism makes a central place for values of care, love, friendship, trust, and appropriate reciprocity—values that presuppose that our relationships to others are central to our understanding of who we are.[16] It thereby gives voice to the sensitivity that in climbing a mountain, one is doing something in relationship with an "other," an "other" whom one can come to care about and treat respectfully.

Lastly, an ecofeminist ethic involves a reconception of what it means to be human, and in what human ethical behavior consists. Ecofeminism denies abstract individualism. Humans are who we are in large part by virtue of the historical and social contexts and the relationships we are in, including our relationships with nonhuman nature. Relationships are not something extrinsic to who we are, not an "add on" feature of human nature; they play an essential role in shaping what it is to be human. Relationships of humans to the nonhuman environment are, in part, constitutive of what it is to be a human.

By making visible the interconnections among the dominations of women and nature, ecofeminism shows that both are feminist issues and that explicit acknowledgment of both is vital to any responsible environmental ethic. Feminism *must* embrace ecological feminism if it is to end the domination of women because the domination of women is tied conceptually and historically to the domination of nature.

A responsible environmental ethic also must embrace feminism. Otherwise, even the seemingly most revolutionary, liberational, and holistic ecological ethic will fail to take seriously the interconnected dominations of nature and women that are so much a part of the historical legacy and conceptual framework that sanctions the exploitation of nonhuman nature. Failure to make visible these interconnected, twin dominations results in an inaccurate account of how it is that nature has been and continues to be dominated and exploited and produces an environmental ethic that lacks the depth necessary to be truly *inclusive* of the realities of persons who at least in dominant Western culture have been intimately tied with that exploitation, viz., women.

Whatever else can be said in favor of such holistic ethics, a failure to make visible ecofeminist insights into the common denominators of the twin oppressions of women and nature is to perpetuate, rather than overcome, the source of that oppression.

This last point deserves further attention. It may be objected that as long as the end result is "the same"—the development of an environmental ethic which does not emerge out of or reinforce an oppressive conceptual framework—it does not matter whether that ethic (or the ethic endorsed in getting there) is feminist or not. Hence, it simply is *not* the case that any adequate environmental ethic must be feminist. My argument, in contrast, has been that it *does* matter, and for three important reasons. First, there is the scholarly issue of accurately representing historical reality, and that, ecofeminists claim, requires acknowledging the historical feminization of nature and naturalization of women as part of the exploitation of nature. Second, I have shown that the conceptual connections between the domination of women and the domination of nature are located in an oppressive and, at least in Western societies, patriarchal conceptual framework characterized by a logic of domination. Thus, I have shown that failure to notice the nature of this connection leaves at best an incomplete, inaccurate, and partial account of what is required of a conceptually adequate environmental ethic. An ethic which *does* not acknowledge this is simply *not* the same as one that does, whatever else the similarities between them. Third, the claim that, in contemporary culture, one can have an adequate environmental ethic which is *not* feminist assumes that, in contemporary culture, the label *feminist* does not add anything crucial to the nature or description of environmental ethics. I have shown that at least in contemporary culture this is false, for the word *feminist* currently helps to clarify just *how* the domination of nature is conceptually linked to patriarchy and, hence, how the liberation of nature is conceptually linked to the termination of patriarchy. Thus, because it has critical bite in contemporary culture, it serves as an important reminder that in contemporary sex-gendered, raced, classed, and naturist culture, an unlabeled position functions as a privileged and "unmarked" position. That is, without the addition of the word *feminist*, one presents environmental ethics as if it has no bias, including male-gender bias, which is just what ecofeminists deny: failure to notice the connections between the twin oppressions of women and nature *is* male-gender bias.

One of the goals of feminism is the eradication of all oppressive sex-gender (and related race, class, age, affectional preference) categories and the creation of a world in which *difference does not breed domination*—say, the world of 4001. If in 4001 an "adequate environmental ethic" is a "feminist environmental ethic," the word *feminist* may then be redundant and unnecessary. However, this is *not* 4001, and in terms of the current historical and conceptual reality the dominations of nature and of women are intimately connected. Failure to notice or make visible that connection in 1990 perpetuates the mistaken (and privileged) view that "environmental ethics" is *not* a feminist issue, and that *feminist* adds nothing to environmental ethics. . . .[17]

NOTES

1. Explicit ecological feminist literature includes works from a variety of scholarly perspectives and sources. Some of these works are Leonie Caldecott and Stephanie Leland, eds., *Reclaim the Earth: Women Speak Out for Life on Earth* (London: The Women's Press, 1983); Jim Cheney, "Eco-Feminism and Deep Ecology," *Environmental Ethics* 9 (1987): 115–45; André Collard with Joyce Contrucci, *Rape of the Wild: Man's Violence against Animals and the Earth* (Bloomington: Indiana University Press, 1988); Katherine Davies, "Historical Associations: Women and the Natural World," *Women & Environments* 9, no. 2 (Spring 1987): 4–6; Sharon Doubiago, "Deeper than Deep Ecology: Men Must Become Feminists," in *The New Catalyst Quarterly*, no. 10 (Winter 1987/88): 10–11; Brian Easlea, *Science and Sexual Oppression: Patriarchy's Confrontation with Women and Nature* (London: Weidenfeld & Nicholson, 1981); Elizabeth Dodson Gray, *Green Paradise Lost* (Wellesley, Mass.: Roundtable Press, 1979); Susan Griffin, *Women and Nature: The Roaring Inside Her* (San Francisco: Harper and Row, 1978); Joan L. Griscom, "On Healing the Nature/History Split in Feminist Thought," in *Heresies #13: Feminism and Ecology* 4, no. 1 (1981): 4–9; Ynestra King, "The Ecology of Feminism and the Feminism of Ecology," in *Healing Our Wounds: The Power of Ecological Feminism*, ed. Judith Plant (Boston: New Society Publishers, 1989), pp. 18–28; "The Ecofeminist Imperative," in *Reclaim the Earth*, ed. Caldecott and Leland (London: The Women's Press, 1983), pp. 12–16. "Feminism and the Revolt of Nature," in *Heresies #13: Feminism and Ecology* 4, no. 1 (1981): 12–16, and "What is Ecofeminism?" *The Nation*, 12 December 1987; Marti Kheel, "Animal Liberation Is A Feminist Issue," *The New Catalyst Quarterly*, no. 10 (Winter 1987–88): 8–9; Carolyn Merchant, *The Death of Nature: Women, Ecology and the Scientific Revolution* (San Francisco, Harper and Row, 1980); Patrick Murphy, ed., "Feminism, Ecology, and the Future of the Humanities," special issue of *Studies in the Humanities* 15, no. 2 (December 1988); Abby Peterson and Carolyn Merchant, "Peace with the Earth: Women and the Environmental Movement in Sweden," *Women's Studies International Forum* 9, no. 5–6 (1986): 465–79; Judith Plant, "Searching for Common Ground: Ecofeminism and Bioregionalism," in *The New Catalyst Quarterly*, no. 10 (Winter 1987/88): 6–7; Judith Plant, ed., *Healing Our Wounds: The Power of Ecological Feminism* (Boston: New Society Publishers, 1989); Val Plumwood, "Ecofeminism: An Overview and Discussion of Positions and Arguments," *Australasian Journal of Philosophy*, Supplement to vol. 64 (June 1986): 120–37; Rosemary Radford Ruether, *New Woman/New Earth: Sexist Ideologies & Human Liberation* (New York: Seabury Press, 1975); Kirkpatrick Sale, "Ecofeminism—A New Perspective," *The Nation*, 26 September 1987): 302–05; Ariel Kay Salleh, "Deeper than Deep Ecology: The Eco-Feminist Connection," *Environmental Ethics* 6 (1984): 339–45, and "Epistemology and the Metaphors of Production: An Eco-Feminist Reading of Critical Theory," in *Studies in the Humanities* 15 (1988): 130–39; Vandana Shiva, *Staying Alive: Women, Ecology and Development* (London: Zed Books, 1988); Charlene Spretnak, "Ecofeminism: Our Roots and Flowering," *The Elmswood Newsletter*, Winter Solstice 1988; Karen J. Warren, "Feminism and Ecology: Making Connections," *Environmental Ethics* 9 (1987): 3–21; "Toward an Ecofeminist Ethic," *Studies in the Humanities* 15 (1988): 140–56; Miriam Wyman, "Explorations of Ecofeminism," *Women & Environments* (Spring 1987): 6–7; Iris Young, " 'Feminism and Ecology' and 'Women and Life on Earth: Eco-Feminism in the 80's'," *Environmental Ethics* 5 (1983): 173–80; Michael Zimmerman, "Feminism, Deep Ecology, and Environmental Ethics," *Environmental Ethics* 9 (1987): 21–44.

2. Francoise d'Eaubonne, *Le Feminisme ou la Mort* (Paris: Pierre Horay, 1974), pp. 213–52.

3. This account of a feminist ethic draws on my paper "Toward an Ecofeminist Ethic."

4. Marilyn Frye makes this point in her illuminating paper, "The Possibility of Feminist Theory," read at the American Philosophical Association Central Division Meetings in Chicago, 29 April–1 May 1986. My discussion of feminist theory is inspired largely by that paper and by Kathryn Addelson's paper "Moral Revolution," in *Women and Values: Reading in Recent Feminist Philosophy*, ed. Marilyn Pearsall (Belmont, Calif.: Wadsworth Publishing Co., 1986) pp. 291–309.

5. Notice that the standard of inclusiveness does not exclude the voices of men. It is just that those voices must cohere with the voices of women.

6. For a more in-depth discussion of the notions of impartiality and bias, see my paper, "Critical Thinking and Feminism," *Informal Logic* 10, no. 1 (Winter 1988): 31–44.

7. The burgeoning literature on these values is noteworthy. See, e.g., Carol Gilligan, *In a Different Voice: Psychological Theories and Women's Development* (Cambridge: Harvard University Press, 1982); *Mapping the Moral Domain: A Contribution of Women's Thinking to Psychological Theory and Education,* ed. Carol Gilligan, Janie Victoria Ward, and Jill McLean Taylor, with Betty Bardige (Cambridge: Harvard University Press, 1988); Nel Noddings, *Caring: A Feminine Approach to Ethics and Moral Education* (Berkely: University of California Press, 1984); Maria Lugones and Elizabeth V. Spelman, "Have We Got a Theory for You! Feminist Theory, Cultural Imperialism, and the Women's Voice," *Women's Studies International Forum* 6 (1983): 573–81; Maria Lugones, "Playfulness"; Annette C. Baier, "What Do Women Want In A Moral Theory?" *Nous* 19 (1985); 53–63.

8. Jim Cheney would claim that our fundamental relationships to one another as moral agents are not as moral agents to rights holders, and that whatever rights a person properly may be said to have are relationally defined rights, not rights possessed by atomistic individuals conceived as Robinson Crusoes who do not exist essentially in relation to others. On this view, even rights talk itself is properly conceived as growing out of a relational ethic, not vice versa.

9. Alison Jaggar, *Feminist Politics and Human Nature* (Totowa, N.J.: Rowman and Allanheld, 1980), pp. 42–44.

10. Henry West has pointed out that the expression "defining relations" is ambiguous. According to West, "the 'defining' as Cheney uses it is an adjective, not a principle—it is not that ethics defines relationships: it is that ethics grows out of conceiving of the relationships that one is in as defining what the individual is."

11. For example, in relationships involving contracts or promises, those relationships might be correctly described as that of moral agent to rights holders. In relationships involving mere property, those relationships might be correctly described as that of moral agent to objects having only instrumental value, "relationships of instrumentality." In comments on an earlier draft of this paper, West suggested that possessive individualism, for instance, might be recast in such a way that an individual is defined by his or her property relationships.

12. Cheney, "Eco-Feminism and Deep Ecology," p. 144.

13. One might object that such permission for change opens the door for environmental exploitation. This is not the case. An ecofeminist ethic is anti-naturist. Hence, the unjust domination and exploitation of nature is a "boundary condition" of the ethic; no such actions are sanctioned or justified on ecofeminist grounds. What it *does* leave open is some leeway about what counts as domination and exploitation. This, I think, is a strength of the ethic, not a weakness, since it acknowledges that *that* issue cannot be resolved in any practical way in the abstract, independent of a historical and social context.

14. Nathan Hare, "Black Ecology," in *Environmental Ethics,* ed. K. S. Shrader-Frechette (Pacific Grove, Calif.: Boxwood Press, 1981), pp. 229–36.

15. For an ecofeminist discussion of the Chipko movement, see my "Toward an Ecofeminist Ethic," and Shiva's *Staying Alive.*

16. See Cheney, "Eco-Feminism and Deep Ecology," p. 122.

17. I offer the same sort of reply to critics of ecofeminism such as Warwick Fox who suggest that for the sort of ecofeminism I defend, the word *feminist* does not add anything significant to environmental ethics and, consequently, that an ecofeminist like myself might as well call herself a deep ecologist. He asks: "Why doesn't she just call it [i.e., Warren's vision of a transformative feminism] deep ecology? Why specifically attach the label *feminist* to it . . .?" (Warwick Fox, "The Deep Ecology-Ecofeminism Debate and Its Parallels," *Environmental Ethics* 11, no. 1 [1989]: 14, n. 22). Whatever the important similarities between deep ecology and ecofeminism (or, specifically, my version of ecofeminism)—and, indeed, there are many—it is precisely my point here that the word *feminist* does add something significant to the conception of environmental ethics, and that any environmental ethic including deep ecology) that fails to make explicit the different kinds of interconnections among the domination of nature and the domination of women will be, from a feminist (and ecofeminist) perspective such as mine, inadequate.

Nature, Self, and Gender: Feminism, Environmental Philosophy, and the Critique of Rationalism

Val Plumwood

Environmental philosophy has recently been criticized on a number of counts by feminist philosophers. I want to develop further some of this critique and to suggest that much of the issue turns on the failure of environmental philosophy to engage properly with the rationalist tradition, which has been inimical to both women and nature. Damaging assumptions from this tradition have been employed in attempting to formulate a new environmental philosophy that often makes use of or embeds itself within rationalist philosophical frameworks that are not only biased from a gender perspective, but have claimed a negative role for nature as well. . . .

RATIONALISM AND THE ETHICAL APPROACH

The ethical approach aims to center a new view of nature in ethics, especially universalizing ethics or in some extension of human ethics. This approach has been criticized from a feminist perspective by a number of recent authors. I partly agree with and partly disagree with these criticisms; that is, I think that the emphasis on ethics as the central part (or even the whole) of the problem is misplaced, and that although ethics (and especially the ethics of noninstrumental value) has a role, the particular ethical approaches that have been adopted are problematic and unsuitable. I shall illustrate this claim by a brief discussion of Paul Taylor's *Respect for Nature*.[1] . . .

Paul Taylor's book is a detailed working out of an ethical position that rejects the standard and widespread Western treatment of nature as instrumental to human interests and instead takes living things, as teleological centers of life, to be worthy of respect in their own right. Taylor aims to defend a biocentric (life-centered) ethical theory in which a person's true human self includes his or her biological nature, but he attempts to embed this within a Kantian ethical framework that makes strong use of the reason/emotion dichotomy;[2] thus we are assured that the attitude of respect is a moral one because it is universalizing and disinterested, "that is, each moral agent who sincerely has the attitude advocates its universal adoption by all other agents, regardless of whether they are so inclined and regardless of their fondness or lack of fondness for particular individuals."[3] The essential features of morality having been established as distance from emotion and "particular fondness," morality is then seen as the domain of reason and its touchstone, belief. Having carefully distinguished the "valuational, conative, practical and affective dimensions of the attitude of respect," Taylor goes on to pick out the essentially cognitive "valuational" aspect as central and basic to all the others: "It is *because* moral agents look at animals and plants in this way that they are disposed to pursue the aforementioned ends and purposes"[4] and, similarly, to have the relevant emotions and affective attitudes. The latter must be held at an appropriate distance and not allowed to get the upper hand at any point. Taylor claims that actions do not express moral respect unless they are done as a matter of moral principle conceived as ethically obligatory and pursued disinterestedly and not through inclination, solely or even primarily:

> If one seeks that end solely or primarily from inclination, the attitude being expressed is not moral respect but personal affection or love. . . . It is not that respect for nature *precludes* feelings of care and concern for living things. One may, as a matter of simple kindness, not want to harm them. But the fact that one is so motivated does not itself indicate the presence of a moral attitude of respect. Having the desire to preserve or protect the good of wild animals and plants for their sake is neither contrary to, nor evidence of, respect for nature. It is only if the person who has the desire understands that the actions fulfilling it would be obligatory even in the absence of the desire, that the person has genuine respect for nature.[5]

There is good reason to reject as self-indulgent the "kindness" approach that reduces respect and morality in the protection of animals to the satisfaction of the carer's own feelings. Respect for others involves treating them as worthy of consideration for their own sake and not just as an instrument for the carer's satisfaction, and there is a sense in which such "kindness" is not genuine care or respect for the other. But Taylor is doing much more than this—he is treating care, viewed as "inclination" or "desire," as irrelevant to morality. Respect for nature on this account becomes an essentially *cognitive* matter (that of a person believing something to have "inherent worth" and then acting from an understanding of ethical principles as universal).

The account draws on the familiar view of reason and emotion as sharply separated and opposed, and of "desire," caring, and love as merely "personal" and "particular" as opposed to the universality and impartiality of understanding and of "feminine" emotions as essentially unreliable, untrustworthy, and morally irrelevant, an inferior domain to be dominated by a superior, disinterested (and of course masculine) reason. This sort of rationalist account of the place of emotions has come in for a great deal of well-deserved criticism recently, both for its implicit gender bias and its philosophical inadequacy, especially its dualism and its construal of public reason as sharply differentiated from and controlling private emotion.[6]

A further major problem in its use in this context is the inconsistency of employing, in the service of constructing an allegedly biocentric ethical theory, a framework that has itself played such a major role in creating a dualistic account of the genuine human self as essentially rational and as sharply discontinuous from the merely emotional, the merely bodily, and the merely animal elements. For emotions and the private sphere with which they are associated have been treated as sharply differentiated and inferior as part of a pattern in which they are seen as linked to the sphere of nature, not the realm of reason.

And it is not only women but also the earth's wild living things that have been denied possession of a reason thus construed along masculine and oppositional lines and which contrasts not only with the "feminine" emotions but also with the physical and the animal. Much of the problem (both for women and nature) lies in rationalist or rationalist-derived conceptions of the self and of what is essential and valuable in the human makeup. It is in the name of such a reason that these other things—the feminine, the emotional, the merely bodily or the merely animal, and the natural world itself—have most often been denied their virtue and been accorded an inferior and merely instrumental position. Thomas Aquinas states this problematic position succinctly: "the intellectual nature is alone requisite for its own sake in the universe, and all others for its sake."[7] And it is precisely reason so construed that is usually taken to characterize the authentically human and to create the supposedly sharp separation, cleavage, or discontinuity between all humans and the nonhuman world, and the similar cleavage within the human self. The supremacy accorded an oppositionally construed reason is the key to the anthropocentrism of the Western tradition. The Kantian-rationalist framework, then, is hardly the area in which to search for a solution. Its use, in a way that perpetuates the supremacy of reason and its opposition to contrast areas, in the service of constructing a supposedly biocentric ethic is a matter for astonishment.

Ethical universalization and abstraction are both closely associated with accounts of the self in terms of rational egoism. Universalization is explicitly seen in both the Kantian and the Rawlsian framework as needed to hold in check natural self-interest; it is the moral complement to the account of the self as "disembodied and disembedded," as the autonomous self of liberal theory, the rational egoist of market theory, the falsely differentiated self of object-relations theory. In the same vein, the broadening of the scope of moral concern along with the according of rights to the natural world has been seen by influential environmental philosophers as the final step in a process of increasing moral abstraction and generalization, part of the move away from the merely particular—*my* self, *my* family, *my* tribe—the discarding of the merely personal and, by implication, the merely selfish. This is viewed as moral progress, increasingly civilized as it moves further away from primitive self-ishness. Nature is the last area to be included in this march away from the unbridled natural egoism of the particular and its close ally, the emotional. Moral progress is marked by increasing adherence to moral rules and a move-ment away from the supposedly natural (in human nature), and the comple-tion of its empire is, paradoxically, the extension of its domain of adherence to abstract moral rules to nature itself.

On such a view, the particular and the emotional are seen as the enemy of the rational, as corrupting, capricious, and self-interested. And if the "moral emotions" are set aside as irrelevant or suspect, as merely subjective or per-sonal, we can only base morality on the rules of abstract reason, on the justice and rights of the impersonal public sphere.

This view of morality as based on a concept of reason as oppositional to the personal, the particular, and the emotional has been assumed in the frame-work of much recent environmental ethics. But as a number of feminist crit-ics of the masculine model of moral life and of moral abstraction have pointed out, this increasing abstraction is not necessarily an improvement.[8] The op-position between the care and concern for particular others and generalized moral concern is associated with a sharp division between public (masculine) and private (feminine) realms. Thus it is part of the set of dualistic contrasts in which the problem of the Western treatment of nature is rooted. And the op-position between care for particular others and general moral concern is a false one. There *can* be opposition between particularity and generality of con-cern, as when concern for particular others is accompanied by *exclusion* of others from care or chauvinistic attitudes toward them, but this does not au-tomatically happen, and emphasis on oppositional cases obscures the frequent cases where they work together—and in which care for particular others is essential to a more generalized morality. Special relationships, which are treated by universalizing positions as at best morally irrelevant and at worst a positive hindrance to the moral life, are thus mistreated. For as Blum stresses, special relationships form the basis for much of our moral life and concern, and it could hardly be otherwise.[9] With nature, as with the human sphere, the ca-pacity to care, to experience sympathy, understanding, and sensitivity to the situation and fate of particular others, and to take responsibility for others is an index of our moral being. Special relationship with, care for, or empathy with particular aspects of nature as experiences rather than with nature as ab-straction are essential to provide a depth and type of concern that is not oth-erwise possible. Care and responsibility for particular animals, trees, and rivers that are known well, loved, and appropriately connected to the self are an important basis for acquiring a wider, more generalized concern. (As we shall see, this failure to deal adequately with particularity is a problem for deep ecology as well.)

Concern for nature, then, should not be viewed as the completion of a process of (masculine) universalization, moral abstraction, and disconnection, discarding the self, emotions, and special ties (all, of course, associated with the private sphere and femininity). Environmental ethics has for the most part placed itself uncritically in such a framework, although it is one that is extended with particular difficulty to the natural world. Perhaps the kindest thing that can be said about the framework of ethical universalization is that it is seriously incomplete and fails to capture the most important elements of respect, which are not reducible to or based on duty or obligation any more than the most important elements of friendship are, but which are rather an expression of a certain kind of selfhood and a certain kind of relation between self and other. . . .

THE DISCONTINUITY PROBLEM

The problem is not just one of restriction *in* ethics but also of restriction *to* ethics. Most mainstream environmental philosophers continue to view environmental philosophy as mainly concerned with ethics. For example, instrumentalism is generally viewed by mainstream environmental philosophers as a problem in ethics, and its solution is seen as setting up some sort of theory of intrinsic value. This neglects a key aspect of the overall problem that is concerned with the definition of the human self as separate from nature, the connection between this and the instrumental view of nature, and broader *political* aspects of the critique of instrumentalism.

One key aspect of the Western view of nature, which the ethical stance neglects completely, is the view of nature as sharply discontinuous or ontologically divided from the human sphere. This leads to a view of humans as apart from or "outside of" nature, usually as masters or external controllers of it. Attempts to reject this view often speak alternatively of humans as "part of nature" but rarely distinguish this position from the obvious claim that human fate is interconnected with that of the biosphere, that humans are subject to natural laws. But on the divided-self theory it is the essentially or authentically human part of the self, and in that sense the human realm proper, that is outside nature, not the human as a physical phenomenon. The view of humans as outside of and alien to nature seems to be especially strongly a Western one, although not confined to the West. There are many other cultures which do not hold it, which stress what connects us to nature as genuinely human virtues, which emphasize continuity and not dissimilarity.

As ecofeminism points out, Western thought has given us a strong human/nature dualism that is part of the set of interrelated dualisms of mind/body, reason/nature, reason/emotion, masculine/feminine and has important interconnected features with these other dualisms.[10] This dualism has been especially stressed in the rationalist tradition. In this dualism what is characteristically and authentically human is defined against or in opposition to what is taken to be natural, nature, or the physical or biological realm. This takes various forms. For example, the characterization of the genuinely, properly, characteristically, or authentically human, or of human virtue, in polarized terms to exclude what is taken to be characteristic of the natural is what John Rodman has called "the Differential Imperative" in which what is virtuous in the human is taken to be what maximizes distance from the merely natural.[11] The maintenance of sharp dichotomy and polarization is achieved by the rejection and denial of what links humans to the animal. What is taken to be authentically and characteristically human, defining of the human, as well as the ideal for which humans should strive is *not* to be found in what is shared with the natural and animal (e.g., the body, sexuality, reproduction, emotionality, the senses, agency) but in what is thought to separate and distinguish them—especially reason and its offshoots. Hence humanity is defined not as part of nature (perhaps a special part) but as separate from and in opposition to it. Thus the relation of humans to nature is treated as an oppositional and value dualism.

The process closely parallels the formation of other dualisms, such as masculine/feminine, reason/emotion, and spirit/body criticized in feminist thought, but this parallel logic is not the only connection between human/nature dualism and masculine/feminine dualism. Moreover, this exclusion of the natural from the concept of the properly human is not the only dualism involved, because what is involved in the construction of this dualistic conception of the human is the rejection of those parts of the human character identified as feminine—also identified as less than fully human—giving the masculine conception of what it is to be human. Masculinity can be linked to this exclusionary and polarized conception of the human, via the desire to exclude and distance from the feminine and the nonhuman. The features that are taken as characteristic of humankind and as where its special virtues lie, are those such as rationality, freedom, and transcendence of nature (all traditionally viewed as masculine), which are viewed as not shared with nature. Humanity is defined oppositionally to both nature and the feminine.

The upshot is a deeply entrenched view of the genuine or ideal human self as not including features shared with nature, and as defined *against* or in *opposition to* the nonhuman realm, so that the human sphere and that of nature cannot significantly overlap. Nature is sharply divided off from the human, is alien and usually hostile and inferior. Furthermore, this kind of human self can only have certain kinds of accidental or contingent connections to the realm of nature. I shall call this the discontinuity problem or thesis and I argue later that it plays a key role with respect to other elements of the problem.

RATIONALISM AND DEEP ECOLOGY

Although the discontinuity problem is generally neglected by the ethical stance, a significant exception to its neglect within environmental philosophy seems to be found in deep ecology, which is also critical of the location of the problem within ethics. Furthermore, deep ecology also seems initially to be more likely to be compatible with a feminist philosophical framework, emphasizing as it does connections with the self, connectedness, and merger. Nevertheless, there are severe tensions between deep ecology and a feminist perspective. Deep ecology has not satisfactorily identified the key elements in the traditional framework or observed their connections to rationalism. As a result, it fails to reject adequately rationalist assumptions and indeed often seems to provide its own versions of universalization, the discarding of particular connections, and rationalist accounts of self.

Deep ecology locates the key problem area in human-nature relations in the separation of humans and nature, and it provides a solution for this in terms of the "identification" of self with nature. "Identification" is usually left deliberately vague, and corresponding accounts of self are various and shifting and not always compatible. There seem to be at least three different accounts of self involved—indistinguishability, expansion of self, and transcendence of self—and practitioners appear to feel free to move among them at will. As I shall show, all are unsatisfactory from both a feminist perspective and from that of obtaining a satisfactory environmental philosophy, and the appeal of deep ecology rests largely on the failure to distinguish them.

The Indistinguishability Account

The indistinguishability account rejects boundaries between self and nature. Humans are said to be just one strand in the biotic web, not the source and ground of all value and the discontinuity thesis is, it seems, firmly rejected. Warwick Fox describes the central intuition of deep ecology as follows: "We can make no firm ontological divide in the field of existence . . . there is no bifurcation in reality between the human and nonhuman realms. . . . to the extent that we perceive boundaries, we fall short of deep ecological consciousness."[12] But much more is involved here than the rejection of discontinuity, for deep ecology goes on to replace the human-in-environment image by a holistic or gestalt view that "dissolves not only the human-in-environment concept, but every compact-thing-in-milieu concept"—except when talking at a superficial level of communication.

Deep ecology involves a cosmology of "unbroken wholeness which denies the classical idea of the analyzability of the world into separately and independently existing parts."[13] It is strongly attracted to a variety of mystical traditions and to the Perennial Philosophy, in which the self is merged with the other—"the other is none other than yourself." As John Seed puts it: "I am protecting the rain forest" develops into "I am part of the rain forest protecting myself. I am that part of the rain forest recently emerged into thinking."[14]

There are severe problems with these claims, arising not so much from the orientation to the concept of self (which seems to me important and correct) or from the mystical character of the insights themselves as from the indistinguishability metaphysics which is proposed as their basis. It is not merely that the identification process of which deep ecologists speak seems to stand in need of much more clarification, but that it does the wrong thing. The problem, in the sort of account I have given, is the discontinuity between humans and nature that emerges as part of the overall set of Western dualisms. Deep ecology proposes to heal this division by a "unifying process," a metaphysics that insists that everything is really part of and indistinguishable from everything else. This is not only to employ overly powerful tools but ones that do the wrong job, for the origins of the particular opposition involved in the human/nature dualism remain unaddressed and unanalyzed. The real basis of the discontinuity lies in the concept of an authentic human being, in what is taken to be valuable in human character, society, and culture, as what is distinct from what is taken to be natural. The sources of and remedies for this remain unaddressed in deep ecology. Deep ecology has confused dualism and atomism and then mistakenly taken indistinguishability to follow from the rejection of atomism. The confusion is clear in Fox, who proceeds immediately from the ambiguous claim that there is no "bifurcation in reality between the human and nonhuman realms" (which could be taken as a rejection of human discontinuity from nature) to the conclusion that what is needed is that we embrace an indistinguishability metaphysics of unbroken wholeness in the whole of reality. But the problem must be addressed in terms of this specific dualism and its connections. Instead deep ecology proposes the obliteration of all distinction.

Thus deep ecology's solution to removing this discontinuity by obliterating *all* division is far too powerful. In its overgenerality it fails to provide a genuine basis for an environmental ethics of the kind sought, for the view of humans as metaphysically unified with the cosmic whole will be equally true whatever relation humans stand in with nature—the situation of exploitation of nature exemplifies such unity equally as well as a conserver situation and the human self is just as indistinguishable from the bulldozer and Coca-Cola bottle as the rocks or the rain forest. What John Seed seems to have in mind here is that once one has realized that one is indistinguishable from the rain forest, its needs would become one's own. But there is nothing to guarantee this—one could equally well take one's own needs for its.

This points to a further problem with the distinguishability thesis, that we need to recognize not only our human continuity with the natural world but also its distinctness and independence from us and the distinctness of the needs of things in nature from ours. The indistinguishability account does not allow for this, although it is a very important part of respect for nature and of conservation strategy.

The dangers of accounts of the self that involve self-merger appear in feminist contexts as well, where they are sometimes appealed to as the alternative to masculine-defined autonomy as disconnection from others. As Jean

Grimshaw writes of the related thesis of the indistinctness of persons (the acceptance of the loss of self-boundaries as a feminine ideal):

> It is important not merely because certain forms of symbiosis or "connection" with others can lead to damaging failures of personal development, but because care for others, understanding of them, are only possible if one can adequately distinguish oneself *from* others. If I see myself as "indistinct" from you, or you as not having your own being that is not merged with mine, then I cannot preserve a real sense of your well-being as opposed to mine. Care and understanding require the sort of distance that is needed in order not to see the other as a projection of self, or self as a continuation of the other.[15]

These points seem to me to apply to caring for other species and for the natural world as much as they do to caring for our own species. But just as dualism is confused with atomism, so holistic self-merger is taken to be the only alternative to egoistic accounts of the self as without essential connection to others or to nature. Fortunately, this is a false choice; as I argue below, nonholistic but relational accounts of the self, as developed in some feminist and social philosophy, enable a rejection of dualism, including human/nature dualism, without denying the independence or distinguishability of the other. To the extent that deep ecology is identified with the indistinguishability thesis, it does not provide an adequate basis for a philosophy of nature.

The Expanded Self

In fairness to deep ecology it should be noted that it tends to vacillate between mystical indistinguishability and the other accounts of self, between the holistic self and the expanded self. Vacillation occurs often by way of slipperiness as to what is meant by identification of self with the other, a key notion in deep ecology. This slipperiness reflects the confusion of dualism and atomism previously noted but also seems to reflect a desire to retain the mystical appeal of indistinguishability while avoiding its many difficulties. Where "identification" means not "identity" but something more like "empathy," identification with other beings can lead to an expanded self. According to Arne Naess, "The self is as comprehensive as the totality of our identifications. . . . Our Self is that with which we identify."[16] This larger self (or Self, to deep ecologists) is something for which we should strive "insofar as it is in our power to do so," and according to Fox we should also strive to make it as large as possible. But this expanded self is not the result of a critique of egoism; rather, it is an enlargement and an extension of egoism.[17] It does not question the structures of possessive egoism and self-interest; rather, it tries to allow for a wider set of interests by an expansion of self. The motivation for the expansion of self is to allow for a wider set of concerns while continuing to allow the self to operate on the fuel of self-interest (or Self-interest). This is apparent from the claim that "in this light . . . ecological resistance is simply another name for self defense."[18] Fox quotes with approval John Livingstone's statement: "When I say that the fate of the sea turtle or the tiger or the gibbon is mine, I mean it. All that is in my universe is not merely mine; it is *me*. And I shall defend myself. I shall defend myself not only against overt aggression but also against gratuitous insult."[19]

Deep ecology does not question the structures of rational egoism and continues to subscribe to two of the main tenets of the egoist framework—that human nature is egoistic and that the alternative to egoism is self-sacrifice. Given these assumptions about egoism, the obvious way to obtain some sort of human interest in defending nature is through the expanded Self operating in the interests of nature but also along the familiar lines of self-interest. The expanded-self strategy might initially seem to be just another pretentious and obscure way of saying that humans empathize with nature. But the strategy of transferring the structures of egoism is highly problematic, for the widening of interest is obtained at the expense of failing to recognize unambiguously the distinctness and independence of the other. Others are recognized morally only to the extent that they are incorporated into the self, and their difference denied. And the failure to critique egoism and the disembedded, nonrelational self means a failure to draw connections with other contemporary critiques.

The Transcended or Transpersonal Self

To the extent that the expanded Self requires that we detach from the particular concerns of the self (a relinquishment that despite its natural difficulty we should struggle to attain), expansion of self to Self also tends to lead into the third position, the transcendence or overcoming of self. Thus Fox urges us to strive for *impartial* identification with *all* particulars, the cosmos, discarding our identifications with our own particular concerns, personal emotions, and attachments. Fox presents here the deep ecology version of universalization, with the familiar emphasis on the personal and the particular as corrupting and self-interested—"the cause of possessiveness, war and ecological destruction."[20]

This treatment of particularity, the devaluation of an identity tied to particular parts of the natural world as opposed to an abstractly conceived whole, the cosmos, reflects the rationalistic preoccupation with the universal and its account of ethical life as oppositional to the particular. The analogy in human terms of impersonal love of the cosmos is the view of morality as based on universal principles or the impersonal and abstract "love of man." Thus Fox reiterates (as if it were unproblematic) the view of particular attachments as ethically suspect and as oppositional to genuine, impartial "identification," which necessarily falls short with all particulars.

Because this "transpersonal" identification is so indiscriminate and intent on denying particular meanings, it cannot allow for the deep and highly particularistic attachment to place that has motivated both the passion of many modern conservationists and the love of many indigenous peoples for their land (which deep ecology inconsistently tries to treat as a model). This is based not on a vague, bloodless, and abstract cosmological concern but on the formation of identity, social and personal, in relation to particular areas of land, yielding ties often as special and powerful as those to kin, and which are equally expressed in very specific and local responsibilities of care. This emerges clearly in the statements of many indigenous peoples, such as in the moving words of Cecilia Blacktooth explaining why her people would not surrender their land:

> You ask us to think what place we like next best to this place where we always lived. You see the graveyard there? There are our fathers and our grandfathers. You see that Eagle-nest mountain and that Rabbit-hole mountain? When God made them, He gave us this place. We have always been here. We do not care for any other place. . . . We have always lived here. We would rather die here. Our fathers did. We cannot leave them. Our children were born here—how can we go away? If you give us the best place in the world, it is not so good as this. . . . This is our home. . . . We cannot live any where else. We were born here and our fathers are buried here. . . . We want this place and no other. . . .[21]

In inferiorizing such particular, emotional, and kinship-based attachments, deep ecology gives us another variant on the superiority of reason and the inferiority of its contrasts, failing to grasp yet again the role of reason and incompletely critiquing its influence. To obtain a more adequate account than that offered by mainstream ethics and deep ecology it seems that we must move toward the sort of ethics feminist theory has suggested, which can allow for both continuity and difference and for ties to nature which are expressive of the rich, caring relationships of kinship and friendship rather than increasing abstraction and detachment from relationship.

THE PROBLEM IN TERMS OF THE CRITIQUE OF RATIONALISM

I now show how the problem of the inferiorization of nature appears if it is viewed from the perspective of the critique of rationalism and seen as part of the general problem of revaluing and reintegrating what rationalist culture has split apart, denied, and devalued. Such an account shifts the focus away from the preoccupations of both mainstream ethical approaches and deep ecology, and although it does retain an emphasis on the account of the self as central, it gives a different account from that offered by deep ecology. I conclude by arguing that one of the effects of this shift in focus is to make connections with other critiques, especially feminism, central rather than peripheral or accidental, as they are currently viewed by deep ecologists in particular.

First, what is missing from the accounts of both the ethical philosophers and the deep ecologists is an understanding of the problem of discontinuity as created by a dualism linked to a network of related dualisms. Here I believe a good deal can be learned from the critique of dualism feminist philosophy has developed and from the understanding of the mechanisms of dualisms ecofeminists have produced. A dualistically construed dichotomy typically polarizes difference and minimizes shared characteristics, construes difference along lines of superiority/inferiority, and views the inferior side as a means to the higher ends of the superior side (the instrumental thesis). Because its nature is defined oppositionally, the task of the superior side, that in which it realizes itself and expresses its true nature, is to separate from, dominate, and control the lower side. This has happened both with the human/nature division and with other related dualisms such as masculine/feminine, reason/body, and reason/emotion. Challenging these dualisms involves not just a reevaluation of superiority/inferiority and a higher status for the underside of the dualisms (in this case nature) but also a reexamination and reconceptualizing of the dualistically construed categories themselves. So in the case of the human/nature dualism it is not just a question of improving the status of nature, moral or otherwise, while everything else remains the same, but of reexamining and reconceptualizing the concept of the human, and also the concept of the contrasting class of nature. For the concept of the human, of what it is to be fully and authentically human, and of what is genuinely human in the set of characteristics typical humans possess, has been defined oppositionally, by *exclusion* of what is associated with the inferior natural sphere in very much the way that Lloyd, for example, has shown in the case of the categories of masculine and feminine, and of reason and its contrasts.[22] Humans have both biological and mental characteristics, but the mental rather than the biological have been taken to be characteristic of the human and to give what is "fully and authentically" human. The term "human" is, of course, not merely descriptive here but very much an evaluative term setting out an ideal: it is what is essential or worthwhile in the human that excludes the natural. It is not necessarily denied that humans have some material or animal component—rather, it is seen in this framework as alien or inessential to them, not part of their fully or truly human nature. The human essence is often seen as lying in maximizing control over the natural sphere (both within and without) and in qualities such as rationality, freedom, and transcendence of the material sphere. These qualities are also identified as masculine, and hence the *oppositional* model of the human coincides or converges with a masculine model, in which the characteristics attributed are those of the masculine ideal.

Part of a strategy for challenging this human/nature dualism, then, would involve recognition of these excluded qualities—split off, denied, or construed as alien, or comprehended as the sphere of supposedly *inferior* humans such as women and blacks—as equally and fully human. This would provide a basis for the recognition of *continuities* with the natural world. Thus reproductivity, sensuality, emotionality would be taken to be as fully and authentically human qualities as the capacity for abstract planning and calculation. This proceeds from the assumption that one basis for discontinuity and alienation from nature is alienation from those qualities which provide continuity with nature in ourselves.

This connection between the rationalist account of nature within and nature without has powerful repercussions. So part of what is involved is a challenge to the centrality and dominance of the rational in the account of the human self. Such a challenge would have far-reaching implications for what is valuable in human society and culture, and it connects with the challenge to the cultural legacy of rationalism made by other critiques of rationalism such as feminism, and by critiques of technocracy, bureaucracy, and instrumentalism.

What is involved here is a reconceptualization of the human side of the human/nature dualism, to free it from the legacy of rationalism. Also in need of reconceptualization is the underside of this dualism, the concept of nature, which is construed in polarized terms as bereft of qualities appropriated to the human side, as passive and lacking in agency and teleology, as pure materiality, pure body, or pure mechanism. So what is called for here is the development of alternatives to mechanistic ways of viewing the world, which are also part of the legacy of rationalism.

INSTRUMENTALISM AND THE SELF

There are two parts to the restructuring of the human self in relation to nature—reconceptualizing the human and reconceptualizing the self, and especially its possibilities of relating to nature in other than instrumental ways. Here the critique of the egoistic self of liberal individualism by both feminist and social philosophers, as well as the critique of instrumental reason, offers a rich set of connections and insights on which to draw. In the case of both of these parts what is involved is the rejection of basically masculine models, that is, of humanity and of the self.

Instrumentalism has been identified as a major problem by the ethical approach in environmental philosophy but treated in a rather impoverished way, as simply the problem of establishing the inherent worth of nature. Connection has not been made to the broader account that draws on the critique of instrumental reason. This broader account reveals both its links with the discontinuity problem and its connection with the account of the self. A closer look at this further critique gives an indication of how we might develop an account that enables us to stress continuity without drowning in a sea of indistinguishability.

We might notice first the strong connections between discontinuity (the polarization condition of dualism) and instrumentalism—the view that the excluded sphere is appropriately treated as a means to the ends of the higher sphere or group, that its value lies in its usefulness to the privileged group that is, in contrast, worthwhile or significant in itself. Second, it is important to maintain a strong distinction and maximize distance between the sphere of means and that of ends to avoid breaking down the sharp boundaries required by hierarchy. Third, it helps if the sphere treated instrumentally is seen as lacking ends of its own (as in views of nature and women as passive), for then others can be imposed upon it without problem. There are also major connections that come through the account of the self which accompanies both views.

The self that complements the instrumental treatment of the other is one that stresses sharply defined ego boundaries, distinctness, autonomy, and separation from others—that is defined *against* others, and lacks essential connections to them. This corresponds to object-relations account of the masculine self associated with the work of Nancy Chodorow and also to the self-interested individual presupposed in market theory.[23] This self uses both other humans and the world generally as a means to its egoistic satisfaction, which is assumed to be the satisfaction of interests in which others play no essential role. If we try to specify these interests they would make no essential reference to the welfare of others, except to the extent that these are useful to serve predetermined ends. Others as means are interchangeable if they produce equivalent satisfactions—anything which conduces to that end is as valuable, other things being equal, as anything else which equally conduces to that end. The interests of such an individual, that of the individual of market theory and of the masculine self as theorized by Chodorow, are defined as essentially independent of or disconnected from those of other people, and his or her transactions with the world at large consist of various attempts to get satisfaction for these predetermined private interests. Others are a "resource," and the interests of others connect with the interests of such autonomous selves only accidentally or contingently. They are not valued for themselves but for their effects in producing gratification. This kind of instrumental picture, so obviously a misdescription in the case of relations to other humans, is precisely still the normal Western model of what our relations to nature should be.

Now this kind of instrumental, disembedded account of the relation of self to others has been extensively criticized in the area of political theory from a variety of quarters, including feminist theory, in the critique of liberalism, and in environmental philosophy. It has been objected that this account does not give an accurate picture of the human self—that humans are social and connected in a way such an account does not recognize. People do have interests that make *essential* and not merely accidental or contingent reference to those of others, for example, when a mother wishes for her child's recovery, the child's flourishing is an essential *part* of her flourishing, and similarly with close others and indeed for others more widely ("social others"). But, the objection continues, this gives a misleading picture of the world, one that omits or impoverishes a whole significant dimension of human experience, a dimension which provides important insight into gender difference, without which we cannot give an adequate picture of what it is to be human. Instead we must see human beings and their interests as *esentially* related and interdependent. As Karen Warren notes, "Relationships are not something extrinsic to who we are, not an 'add on' feature of human nature; they play an essential role in shaping what it is to be human."[24] That people's interests are relational does not imply a holistic view of them—that they are merged or indistinguishable. Although some of the mother's interests entail satisfaction of the child's interests, they are not identical or even necessarily similar. There is overlap, but the relation is one of intentional inclusion (her interest is *that* the child should thrive, that certain of the child's key interests are satisfied) rather than accidental overlap.

This view of self-in-relationship is, I think, a good candidate for the richer account of self deep ecologists have sought and for which they have mistaken holistic accounts. It is an account that avoids atomism but that enables a recognition of interdependence and relationship without falling into the problems of indistinguishability, that acknowledges both continuity and difference, and that breaks the culturally posed false dichotomy of egoism and altruism of interests; it bypasses both masculine "separation" and traditional-feminine "merger" accounts of the self. It can also provide an appropriate foundation for an ethic of connectedness and caring for others, as argued by Gilligan and Miller.[25]

Thus is it unnecessary to adopt any of the stratagems of deep ecology—the indistinguishable self, the expanded self, or the transpersonal self—in order to provide an alternative to anthropocentrism or human self-interest. This can be better done through the relational account of self, which clearly recognizes the distinctness of nature but also our relationship and continuity with it. On this relational account, respect for the other results neither from the containment of self nor from a transcendence of self, but is an *expression of* self in relationship, not egoistic self as merged with the other but self as embedded in a network of essential relationships with distinct others.

The relational account of self can usefully be applied to the case of human relations with nature and to place. The standard Western view of the relation of the self to the nonhuman is that it is always *accidentally* related, and hence the nonhuman can be used as a means to the self-contained ends of human beings. Pieces of land are real estate, readily interchangeable as equivalent means to the end of human satisfaction; no place is more than "a stage along life's way, a launching pad for higher flights and wider orbits than your own."[26] But, of course, we do not all think this way, and instances of contrary behavior would no doubt be more common if their possibility were not denied and distorted by both theoretical and social construction. But other cultures have recognized such essential connection of self to country clearly enough, and many indigenous voices from the past and present speak of the grief and pain in loss of their land, to which they are as essentially connected as to any human other. When Aboriginal people, for example, speak of the land as part of them, "like brother and mother," this is, I think, one of their meanings.[27] If instrumentalism is impoverishing and distorting as an account of our relations to other human beings, it is equally so as a guiding principle in our relations to nature and to place.

But to show that the self can be essentially related to nature is by no means to show that it normally would be, especially in modern Western culture. What is culturally viewed as alien and inferior, as not worthy of respect or respectful knowledge, is not something to which such essential connection can easily be made. Here the three parts of the problem—the conception of the human, the conception of the self, and the conception of nature—connect again. And normally such essential relation would involve particularity, through connection to and friendship for *particular* places, forests, animals, to which one is particularly strongly related or attached and toward which one has specific and meaningful, not merely abstract, responsibilities of care.

One of the effects of viewing the problem as arising especially in the context of rationalism is to provide a rich set of connections with other critiques; it makes the connection between the critique of anthropocentrism and various other critiques that also engage critically with rationalism, such as feminism and critical theory, much more important—indeed essential—to the understanding of each. The problem of the Western account of the human–nature relation is seen in the context of the other related sets of dualisms; they are linked through their definitions as the underside of the various contrasts of reason. Since much of the strength and persistence of these dualisms derives from their connections and their ability to mirror, confirm, and support one another, critiques of anthropocentrism that fail to take account of these connections have missed an essential and not merely additional feature.

Anthropocentrism and androcentrism in particular are linked by the rationalist conception of the human self as masculine and by the account of authentically human characteristics as centered around rationality and the exclusion of its contrasts (especially characteristics regarded as feminine, animal, or natural) as less human. This provides a different and richer account of the notion of anthropocentrism, now conceived by deep ecology in terms of the notion of equality, which is both excessively narrow and difficult to articulate in any precise or convincing way in a context where needs are so different. The perception of the connection as at best accidental is a feature of some recent critiques of ecofeminism, for example the discussion of Fox and Eckersley on the relation of feminism and environmental philosophy.[28] Fox misses entirely the main thrust of the ecofeminist account of environmental philosophy and the critique of deep ecology which results or which is advanced in the ecofeminist literature, which is that it has failed to observe the way in which anthropocentrism and androcentrism are linked. It is a consequence of my arguments here that this critique needs broadening—deep ecology has failed to observe (and often even goes out of its way to deny) connections with a number of other critiques, not just feminism, for example, but also socialism, especially in the forms that mount a critique of rationalism and of modernity. The failure to observe such connections is the result of an inadequate historical analysis and understanding of the way in which the inferiorization of both women and nature is grounded in rationalism, and the connections of both to the inferiorizing of the body, hierarchical concepts of labor, and disembedded and individualist accounts of the self.

Instead of addressing the real concerns of ecofeminism in terms of connection, Fox takes ecofeminism as aiming to replace concern with anthropocentrism by concern with androcentrism. This would have the effect of making ecofeminism a reductionist position which takes women's oppression as the basic form and attempts to reduce all other forms to it. This position is a straw woman; the effect of ecofeminism is not to absorb or sacrifice the critique of anthropocentrism, but to deepen and enrich it.[29]

NOTES

The author would like to thank Jim Cheney and Karen Warren for comments on an earlier draft.

1. P. Taylor, *Respect for Nature* (Princeton, N.J.: Princeton University Press, 1986).

2. Ibid., 44.

3. Ibid., 41.

4. Ibid., 82.

5. Ibid., 85–86.

6. See, for example, S. Benhabib, "The Generalised and the Concrete Other," in *Women and Moral Theory*, ed. E. Kittay and D. Meyers (Totowa, N.J.: Rowman & Allenheld, 1987), 154–77; L. A. Blum, *Friendship Altruism, and Morality* (Boston: Routledge & Kegan Paul, 1980); and C. Gilligan, *In a Different Voice* (Cambridge, Mass.: Harvard University Press, 1982).

7. T. Regan and P. Singer, eds., *Animal Rights and Human Obligations* (Englewood Cliffs, N.J.: Prentice-Hall, 1976), 56.

8. See, for example, L. Nicholson, "Women, Morality, and History," *Social Research* 50 (1983): 514–36.

9. Blum, *Friendship, Altruism, and Morality*, 78–83.

10. K. Warren, "Feminism and Ecology: Making Connections," *Environmental Ethics* 9 (1987): 3–20, and "The Power and Promise of Ecological Feminism," *Environmental Ethics* 12 (1990): 121–46.

11. J. Rodman, "Paradigm Change in Political Science," *American Behavioral Scientist* 24 (1980): 54–55.

12. W. Fox, "Deep Ecology: A New Philosophy for Our Time?" *Ecologist* 14 (1984): 196.

13. Ibid., 197.

14. J. Seed, J. Macy, et al., *Thinking Like a Mountain: Towards a Council of All Beings* (Philadelphia: New Society Publishers, 1988), 36.

15. J. Grimshaw, *Philosophy and Feminist Thinking* (Minneapolis: University of Minnesota Press, 1986), 182–83.

16. Quoted in W. Fox, "Approaching Deep Ecology: A Response to Richard Sylvan's Critique of Deep Ecology," in *Environmental Studies Paper* 20 (Hobart: University of Tasmania Centre for Environmental Studies, 1986), 54.

17. Ibid., 13–19.

18. Ibid., 60.

19. Ibid.

20. W. Fox, *Towards a Transpersonal Ecology: Developing New Foundations for Environmentalism* (Boston: Shambhala, 1990), 12.

21. T. C. McLuhan, ed., *Touch the Earth* (London: Abacus, 1973), 28.

22. G. Lloyd, *The Man of Reason* (London: Methuen, 1984).

23. N. Chodorow, *The Reproduction of Mothering* (Berkeley: University of California Press, 1979).

24. Warren, "Power and Promise of Ecological Feminism," 143.

25. Gilligan, *In a Different Voice*; J. B. Miller, *Toward a New Psychology of Women* (Boston: Beacon Press, 1976).

26. M. Berman, *All That Is Solid Melts into Air: The Experience of Modernity* (New York: Simon and Schuster, 1982), 327.

27. B. Neidgie, *Kakadu Man* (Canberra: Mybrood P/L, 1985), 41; B. Neidgie and K. Taylor, eds., *Story About Feeling* (Wyndham: Magabala Books, 1989), 4, 146.

28. Fox, *Towards a Transpersonal Ecology*; R. Eckersley, "Divining Evolution," *Environmental Ethics* 11 (1989): 99–116.

29. This reductionist position has a few representatives in the literature, but it cannot be taken as representative of the main body of ecofeminist work.

III. Religion and Aesthetics.

Overview. I have often cited these categories of value as the fundamental components of worldview. It is therefore necessary that any chapter that seeks to examine the worldview arguments for environmentalism would examine specific religious and aesthetic arguments to that end.

In the first essay, Eilon Schwartz cites personal worldview religious values to support an environmental ethic. The Talmundic law *bal tashchit* (do not destroy) is a key maxim in contemporary Jewish environmental thought. The author points to biblical passages that refer to a prohibition against cutting down fruit-bearing trees, especially in time of war (when the need for lumber is high). This doctrine forbids wanton destruction and conspicuous consumption.

Schwartz then outlines a minimalist and a maximalist understanding of this doctrine. In the minimalist position, the environment is protected so long as it has economic or aesthetic worth (to humans). In the maximalist position, environmental destruction is prohibited for any reason short of fundamental human need. These positions are then fit into a modern context.

In the second essay, Annie L. Booth and Harvey M. Jacobs examine some common themes from Native American nations that might be termed an *environmental consciousness* or (as I prefer) an *environmental worldview*. The two principal threads of this worldview are aesthetic and religious. On the aesthetic side, the authors contrast a European aesthetic attitude with that of Native Americans. The European aesthetic sees a thriving ecosystem—whether it be a forested region, grassy plains, or various arid regions—as empty space. From this point of view, a developer gazes on a pristine mountain lake and sees in his mind's eye a resort or a factory or something that serves human interests. In contrast to this, the Native American aesthetic standpoint views nature with great wonder at its beauty. This beauty occasions joy and celebration. This is a contrast between an extrinsic, instrumental aesthetic and an intrinsic, reverential one.

Indeed, it is probably *because* of this aesthetic sensibility that many Native American nations created a dialectical religious relationship with God through the land and its flora and fauna. In this way, keeping a balance is essential because it involves a person's deepest religious values.

These two tenets of worldview as depicted by these authors create an interactive relationship with a vibrant whole of which humans form a part. Being a part is certainly different from being the ruler or the owner. Thus, Native American attitudes toward aesthetics and religion dictate that they pay heed to other living things. This is exemplified in their art (which often depicts animals animated in magical ways) and in a sense of balance. When the Europeans came to North America, they declared that the continent was virgin wilderness, not realizing that 90 million native people inhabited the land. But a person who inhabits space thinking she is "a part," not the "creator," can fit in and find an appropriate balance. Such a balance requires letting the land and its fauna and flora talk back—and *listening* to what they say.

In the next essay, J. Baird Callicott examines contrasting worldviews. In sub-Saharan Africa, the Yorba have a religious value system that is not pantheistic but does utilize nature as a vehicle through which communication with and reverence for ancestors may be achieved. Because of this worldview value, an associated understanding of the self as embedded in these various contexts emerges. Thus, the self is merely one piece of a multilayered ontological reality that includes nature as a conduit.

Another African people, the San, put people and animals on the same metaphysical level. Because of this, they have not sought to create more developed weapons for hunting, nor have they overhunted their prey. They live on a par with other animals. Together they form a single community.

In each of these cases from Africa, a community between humans and nonhumans is the result of religious values. This worldview component explains their ecological standpoint.

The Australian aborigines are the next group of people that Callicott examines. "The Dreaming" or "Dreamtime" plays a central role in the worldview of these people, sustaining a rich mythology through dreams. It is another reality that exists side by side everyday waking time reality.

The beings that inhabit dreamtime are mythic individuals who mingled with ancestral beings at particular geographic sites. Often the manner or figure of various characters took the form of animals. These wandering characters infuse meaning into the animals and physical geography that they inhabit in their sojourns. This may create a religious basis for a form of bioregional-ism. Again, a worldview tenet (in this case, the dreamtime) sets the stage for a particular sort of practical attitude, in this case a devotion for particular places as special (including all their fauna and flora).

Finally, Janna Thompson begins her essay with the assertion that nature is beautiful. This is a simple but powerful statement. G.E. Moore[1] viewed beauty (whether it was found in art or in nature) to be an intrinsic good. The ethical imperative, according to Moore, is to increase the total amount of good in the world. If all people have a duty to be ethical, then (by the same rea-soning), all people have a duty to promote and protect beauty (whether it be art or nature). By diminishing nature, a person diminishes the total amount of good in the world and thus violates Moore's dictum.

Thompson's argument also depends on whether beauty (in art or in na-ture) is intrinsically or instrumentally good. Much of this essay addresses this issue and seeks to create a standard that makes the aesthetic standard plausible.

Bal Tashchit:
A Jewish Environmental Precept

Eilon Schwartz

The talmudic law *bal tashchit* ("do not destroy") is the predominant Jewish pre-cept cited in contemporary Jewish writings on the environment. I provide an extensive survey of the roots and differing interpretations of the precept from within the tradition. The precept of *bal tashchit* has its roots in the biblical com-mand not to destroy fruit-bearing trees while laying siege to a warring city. The rabbis expand this injunction into the general precept of *bal tashchit*, a ban on any wanton destruction. Such a precept was interpreted in differing ways, along a continuum whose poles I describe as the minimalist and maximalist positions. In the minimalist position, interpreters limit the application of *bal tashchit* to only those situations in which natural resources and property are no longer viewed as having any economic or aesthetic worth. In the maximalist position, inter-preters expand the application of *bal tashchit* to any situation in which nature

---

[1]For a discussion of G. E. Moore, see *Basic Ethics*, Chapter One.

and property are being destroyed for something other than basic human needs. Finally, I compare and contrast the substance and style of the discussion of *bal tashchit* from within the Jewish tradition with the contemporary discussion of environmental ethics.

INTRODUCTION

No single Jewish concept is quoted more often in demonstrating Judaism's environmental credentials than the rabbinic[1] concept of *bal tashchit* ("do not destroy"). It appears in virtually all of the literature that discusses Jewish attitudes toward the environmental crisis. Yet, rarely are any more than a few sentences given to actually explain its history and its meaning. Such a superficial approach has been widespread in contemporary environmental ethics with regard to traditional cultures. Advocates of a particular culture bring prooftexts to show that the culture is part of the solution; critics use it to show that the culture is part of the problem. Neither approach allows a serious investigation of a cultural perspective different from our own, one which is based on different philosophical assumptions debated in a different cultural language.[2]

In keeping with Clifford Geertz's call for thick anthropological descriptions of culture, I have chosen to analyze *bal tashchit* as it unfolds throughout Jewish legal, or *halachic*,[3] history. Only by entering the classical world of Jewish texts is it possible to transcend apologetics and get a glimpse of a traditional cultural perspective on its own terms. In the process, I provide a richer understanding of the *content* and the *context* of Jewish cultural views of the natural world.

BAL TASHCHIT

Historically, Jews have been considered "a people of the book," based on the role texts have played in Jewish life. From the Bible, followed by the *Mishnah* and the *Gemora*, known collectively as the *Talmud*, continuing through medieval commentaries on these texts, and including compilations of questions posed to rabbis with their answers on the practical application of these ancient texts to new situations, Judaism has developed an elaborate interpretive tradition, rooted in the Bible and extending into modern times. Traditional texts beginning with the Bible are the core texts for subsequent *halachic* decisions.

Bal tashchit is based on a relatively small collection of sources. The original basis for it is biblical, although it is expanded by the rabbis far beyond the original context of the Bible. *Bal tashchit* is considered to have its roots as a *halacha* of the Bible, but to largely consist of prohibitions developed by the rabbis. In order to understand the *halachic* precept, it is necessary to explore both its biblical roots and its rabbinic interpretation.

The principle of *bal tashchit* originated in the attempt to explicate one specific biblical passage from Deuteronomy, which describes what constitutes proper behavior during time of war. I include two translations of the original Hebrew in order to emphasize the difficulty in understanding the Hebrew verses and the interpretative possibilities that emerge from the ambiguity of the text itself.

THE BIBLICAL SOURCE

When in your war against a city you have to besiege it a long time in order to capture it, you must not destroy its trees, wielding the axe against them. You may eat of them, but you must not cut them down. *Are trees of the field human to withdraw before you under siege?* Only trees which you know do not yield food may be destroyed: you may cut them down for constructing siegeworks against the city that is waging war on you, until it has been reduced. (Deuteronomy 20:19–20. New Jewish Publication Society translation)

When thou shalt besiege a city a long time, in making war against it to take it, thou shalt not destroy the trees thereof by forcing an axe against them: for thou mayest eat of them, and thou shalt not cut them down *for the tree of the field is man's life to employ them in the siege.* Only the trees which thou knowest that they be not trees for food, thou shalt destroy and cut them down; and thou shalt build bulwarks against the city that maketh war with thee, until it be subdued. (Deuteronomy 20:19–20, King James translation)

The passage deals with the propel ethical behavior with regard to trees during wartime. Fruit-bearing trees should not be chopped down while a city is under siege. Only non-fruit-bearing trees may be chopped down. The reason behind this prohibition seems to be cryptically supplied by the verse itself. In the King James translation the reason is that "the tree of the field is man's life," implying some causal relationship between the human being and trees, such that cutting down the tree is, in effect, damaging the human being as well. Yet, the other translation offers a different interpretation of the verse, translating the verse as a question rather than statement: "are trees of the field human to withdraw before you under siege?" It is a rhetorical question which denies a relationship between human beings and trees: implying that trees are not human beings and therefore should not be victims of human disputes.

The discrepancy between the translations echoes medieval commentators' varying interpretations of the verse. The J.P.S. translation seems to agree with Rashi's[4] interpretation of the verse. Rashi accentuates the categorical distance between the human being and the tree to create a rationale for why the tree should not be cut:

> The word 'ki' is used here in the sense of 'perhaps; should . . .': Should the tree of the field be considered to be (like) a human being, able to run away from you into the besieged town, to suffer there the agonies of thirst and hunger, like the townspeople—if not, why then destroy it? (Rashi's commentary on Deuteronomy 20:19)

Rashi's interpretation of the verse is based on his understanding of the Hebrew word *ki* as being interrogative, turning the text into a rhetorical question. Is the tree of the field to be part of the same (moral) world as the human being? No. The tree of the field is not the target of the siege; the people of the town are. One has no moral right to destroy the trees because of a dispute among human beings. The trees must not be destroyed because of human disputes.

Rashi in effect has argued for an environmental ethic which views (fruit) trees as having existence independent of human wants and needs. In spite of its strong anthropocentric language, Rashi's position gives ethical consideration to the trees, although it is still not clear why that should be so. The case is accentuated by the setting of the verse itself. In wartime, when human life is so endangered that values are often eclipsed altogether, it is difficult to maintain an ethical outlook on any issue, how much the more so with regard to nature. Indeed, some commentators were aware of, and concerned by, the radically nonanthropocentric nature of such a juxtaposition in which strategic considerations during war, considerations which might save human life, seem to be overruled by consideration for the trees' welfare. Samuel ben Meir [RaSHbaM] (1085–1144), for example, understands the word *ki* as "unless" and therefore interprets the verse as a prohibition against chopping down the fruit tree *unless* the enemy is using the trees as camouflage ("unless the human being is as a tree of the field"), in which case the trees may be removed.[5] Nahmanides [Ramban] (1194–1270) argues that if chopping trees is necessitated by the conquest, then it is obviously permissible to remove any and all trees.[6] Rashi's interpretation resists such an anthropocentric reading.

Yet, Rashi seems to have taken the verse out of context, for, if we accept Rashi's interpretation "is the human being a tree of the field?" how are we to understand the very next verse in which permission is given by God to cut down non-fruit bearing trees? What is the distinction between fruit-bearing and non-fruit-bearing trees that protects one and not the other? Rashi's interpretation does not offer a means for making such a distinction. Indeed, the text questions whether a human being is the tree of the field, whereas Rashi asks whether a tree of the field is like a human being. Rashi's reversal of the syntax of the sentence helps to support his interpretation, but is not supported by the original phrasing of the verse.

Ibn Ezra's (1089–1164) interpretation, later echoed by the King James version, attacks Rashi's position on both grammatical and logical grounds and offers an alternative possibility:

> In my opinion . . . this is the correct meaning: that from (the trees) you get food,
> therefore don't cut them down, 'for man is the tree of the field', that is—our lives
> as human beings depend on trees. (Ibn Ezra's commentary on Deuteronomy 20:19)

Human responsibility for the tree is based on human dependence upon the
tree. Trees are a source of food, and thus cutting them down reduces the food
supply available after the siege. Ramban goes on to suggest that such an act
is a sign of loss of faith, for the trees are being cut down to help in the siege.
The soldiers, not believing that God will lead them to victory, destroy their
own future food supply, fearful that the day of victory bill never come.[7]

Ibn Ezra's explanation makes sense in the context of the verse. Fruit trees
are not to be chopped down, for their importance as food for human beings
is clear. Non-fruit-bearing trees, on the other hand, were seen to have no immediate importance for the human being; therefore, it is permissible to chop
them down. The prooftext, "because the human being is a tree of the field,"
shows us our link to the natural world and how our abuses of nature can result in abuse of ourselves.

THE RABBINIC UNDERSTANDING AND EXPANSION OF THE TEXT

The rabbinic discussion of the text, and the rabbis' extrapolation of it into the
halachic precept of *bal tashchit,* although terse, expands the text in several, and
often conflicting, directions. Let us begin with the primary prooftext in the
Talmud for *bal tashchit.* It is an expansion on the *mishnaic* text which states: "He
who cuts down his own plants, though not acting lawfully, is exempt, yet
were others to [do it], they would be liable" (*Baba Kamma* 8:6[8]). Here it is clearly
stated that cutting down plants is acting unlawfully, presumably because of
bal tashchit. One who cuts down another's plants is monetarily liable. One
who cuts one's own plants, while not liable, is also a transgressor. In other
words, it is not merely a question of destroying another person's property.
Even destroying what appears to be one's own property is forbidden, although
seeking monetary penalty or compensation is inapplicable.

The *Talmud* proceeds to define what is permitted to be cut down and
what is forbidden:

> Rav said: A palm tree producing even one *kab* of fruit may not be cut down. An
> objection was raised [from the following]: What quantity should be on an olive
> tree so that it should not be permitted to cut it down? A quarter of a *kab*—Olives
> are different as they are more important. R. Hanina said: Shibbath my son did
> not pass away except for having cut down a fig tree before its time. Rabina, how-
> ever, said: If its value [for other purposes] exceeds that for fruit, it is permitted
> [to cut it down]. It was also taught to the same effect: 'Only the trees which you
> know' (Deuteronomy 20:20) implies even fruit-bearing trees; 'That they are not

trees for food (Deuteronomy 20:20) means a wild tree. But since we ultimately include all things, why then was it stated, 'that they are not trees for food'? To give priority to a wild tree over one bearing edible fruits. As you might say that this is so even where the value [for other purposes] exceeds that for fruits, it says 'only.' (*Baba Kamma* 91b–92a)

The talmudic passage here defines the worth of the tree in terms of its produce. A palm tree may be allowed to be cut down when it is producing less than one *kab* [2.2 liters] of fruit; an olive tree, which is deemed more important, presumably for economic reasons, can be cut down only when it is producing less than a quarter *kab*. Although such amounts might be an evaluation of the point at which a tree is still fulfilling its purpose in the world, it is just as likely that it is an evaluation of the point at which the tree is still economically valuable, as the claim that olives are "more important" suggests. Rabina offers a general rule of thumb: one may cut down a fruit tree whenever the value of the tree cut down is worth more than its production of fruit. The *Talmud* thus interprets the original biblical passage in the spirit of its economic reading of the law. "Trees for food" are not simply fruit-producing trees. They are trees that are producing enough fruit to be economically worthwhile. Thus, not only may non-fruit producing trees be chopped down, but fruit-producing trees that are not economically productive ultimately fall into the same category.

As stated in the mishnah above, one who unlawfully chops down another's tree is to be fined. One who chops down one's own trees, "although not acting lawfully, is exempt." In the talmudic commentary cited above, Rabbi Hanina makes a curious aside when he states that his son died because of having cut down a fig tree before its time, even though it was allowed since its economic worth cut down was greater than its worth as a fruit-producing tree. Death as divine punishment for cutting down the tree, even though it is permitted by the *halachah,* certainly demands that we relate to *bal tashchit* as something far more substantial than simply respecting the economic value of fruit-producing trees for human society. It is a mysterious theme that reappears often in the *halachic* literature. For example, the same story is related in another talmudic passage:

Raba, son of Rabbi Hanan, had some date trees adjoining a vineyard of Rabbi Joseph, and birds used to roost on the date trees [of Raba] and fly down and damage the vines [of Rabbi Joseph]. So Rabbi Joseph told [Raba:], 'Go cut them!' [Raba said:] 'But I have kept them four cubits away.' [Rabbi Joseph said:] 'This applies only to other trees, but for vines we require more,' [Raba said:] 'But does not our Mishnah say "this applies to all other trees"? [Rabbi Joseph said:] 'This is so where there are other trees or vines on both sides, but where there are trees on one side and vines on the other a greater space is required. Said Raba, 'I will not cut them down because Rav has said that it is forbidden to cut down a date tree which bears a *kab* of dates, and Rabbi Hanina has said, "My son Shikhath only died because he cut down a date tree before its time." You, sir, can cut them down if you like.' (*Baba Batra* 26a[9])

Here the date trees of Raba are the nesting ground for birds that are damaging the vineyards of Rabbi Joseph. The trees must be uprooted, for they are not planted the proper distance from the vineyard of Rabbi Joseph. Nevertheless, Raba refuses to uproot the trees, *even though it is halachically required,* because they are still producing the minimum *kab* of fruit, and Rabbi Hanina's son died for uprooting a date tree before its time. It has been suggested that such fear of cutting down trees might indicate the presence of pagan beliefs in the popular culture of the time.[10] They certainly suggest a more complex equation than a simple cost/benefit analysis. Raba does allow, however, Rabbi Joseph to dare to remove the trees.

So far we have examined two talmudic passages regarding *bal tashchit.* Although one deals with the responsibility of one property owner to his neighbor, and the other deals with responsibility independent of others, they both understand the meaning of the *halachah* in similar ways. Both deal solely with fruit trees. As is recalled from the original biblical prooftext, it is allowed to chop down non-fruit-bearing trees. Only fruit-bearing trees are forbidden. In the two talmudic passages, the rabbis limit the prohibition and, in the process, offer an interpretation of the reasoning behind *bal tashchit.* No tree is to be destroyed as long as it is economically worthwhile. However, if the value of the tree is greater for having been cut down (Rabina's dictum), or if the tree is causing damage to the value of another's property (Rabbi Joseph's complaint), then it is permissible to chop it down. The tree's worth, and in general the worth of nature, is ultimately evaluated in terms of its economic worth to humans. Notice the destruction of the bird's nesting place is of no moral concern in the text. Yet, although the cutting down of the tree is permitted, it appears to be problematic. The death of Rabbi Hanina's son offers a disturbing addendum to an otherwise utilitarian interpretation.

Up until now I have considered a rather narrow understanding of *bal tashchit,* focusing solely on its implications for duties and obligations concerning fruit-producing trees. The rabbis, however, did not understand *bal tashchit* as a precept solely concerned with fruit trees, but rather as a far-reaching principle that defines our responsibilities and obligations to the created world.

The initial discussion as to whether one is prohibited from cutting down trees takes place in a larger talmudic discussion as to whether one may harm oneself. The mishnaic text, which the *Talmud* then elaborates, parallels the previously quoted mishnah. They are here quoted together in context:

> . . . Where one injures oneself, though forbidden, he is exempt, yet, were others to injure him, they would be liable. He who cuts down his own plants [koreit], though not acting lawfully, is exempt, yet were others to [do it), they would be liable. (*Baba Kamma* 8:6)

Once again, there is a distinction between damage inflicted by another party and damage inflicted by oneself. Here one who injures another person is clearly liable. One who injures oneself, although liable, is not punishable in civil courts. But what is the connection between damage to plants and injury to persons? The link is explicated in the talmudic discussion:

> R. Eleazar said: I heard that he who rends [his garments] too much for a dead person transgresses the command, *bal tashchit*, and it seems that this should be the more so in the case of injuring his own body. But garments might perhaps be different, as the loss is irretrievable, for R. Johanan used to call garments 'my honourers,' and R. Hisda whenever he had to walk between thorns and thistles used to lift up his garments saying that whereas for the body [if injured] nature will produce a healing, for garments [if torn] nature could bring up no cure. (*Baba Kamma* 91b)

The talmudic text seeks to understand how some rabbis came to the conclusion that it was forbidden to injure oneself. Rabbi Eliezer asserts that ripping clothing, a traditional sign of mourning, when done too much transgresses *bal tashchit*. And, if ripping clothing is a transgression of *bal tashchit*, how much the more so is "ripping," or injuring, one's body? Therefore, injury to one's own body must be forbidden according to *bal tashchit*. Still, the *Talmud* points out, there is a distinction between garments and the body: ripping a garment can be irretrievable, whereas the body may heal. Indeed, Rabbi Hisda, when walking through scrub brush, used to lift up his garments, preventing them from ripping, while allowing his body to be cut and bruised, knowing that it would heal. Thus, injury to one's body is not prevented by *bal tashchit*, although the ripping of clothing is.

Such a conclusion—that is, that *bal tashchit* does not apply to the human being—is contradicted in another talmudic passage:

> Reb Judah said in Samuel's name: We may make a fire for an ill woman on the Sabbath [in the winter]. Now it was understood from him, only for an ill woman, but not for an invalid; only in winter, but not in summer. But that is not so; there is no difference between an ill woman and any [other] invalid, and summer and winter are alike. [This follows] since it was stated, R. Hiyya b. Abin said in Samuel's name: If one lets blood and catches a chill, a fire is made for him even on the Tammuz [summer] solstice. *A teak chair was broken up for Samuel; a table of juniper-wood was broken up for Rav Judah. A footstool was broken up for Rabah, where-upon Abaye said to Rabbah, 'But you are infringing on bal tashchit.' 'Bal tashchit in re-spect of my own body is more important to me,' he retorted.* (*Shabbat* 129a)

Here *bal tashchit* is used in reference to the breaking of furniture for warming an ill person on the Sabbath, and of course, in reference to human health. Notice that it has already been decided that one may disregard rules of the Sabbath in order to take care of the ill. The question now is whether the needs of the individual human being override the rules of *bal tashchit*, in this case, a prohibition on destroying furniture. If we interpret *bal tashchit* in utilitarian terms—that is, the economic worth of something to human beings—then there should be no question. The health of the human being obviously takes precedence over the furniture's existence. Indeed, Rabbah argues just that. However, the very presence of the question suggests that the answer is not taken for granted. There is a tension between an interpretation that evaluates all worth in terms of its use to human beings and one that sees worth independent of human wants and even needs.

But what is the connection between the biblical prohibition on cutting down fruit trees and the expanding rabbinic definition which, as we have so far seen, includes clothing, furniture, and even human beings? Maimonides [Rambam] (1135–1204) argues that the rabbinic prohibition of *bal tashchit* includes the destruction of household goods, the demolishing of buildings, the stopping of a spring, and the destruction of articles of food, as well.[11] Maimonides expands *bal tashchit* to include the destruction before its time of anything, natural or artificial. The world of creation includes the creation of the natural world and the world which humans have created from God's creation. There should be no needless destruction of any of the creation.

The central point, then, is how one is to evaluate "needless" or "wanton" destruction. As I have shown, there is some tension as to whether it is to be evaluated according to the effective use of human beings or there is an inherent value that exists apart from human use which must be balanced alongside human wants and needs. Although the dominant interpretation seems to be a utilitarian one, there is evidence of a differing interpretation.

Conspicuous Consumption

> R Hisda also said: when one can eat barley bread but eats wheaten bread he violates *bal tashchit*. R. Papa said: when one can drink beer but drinks wine, he violates *bal tashchit*. But this is incorrect: *Bal tashchit*, as applied to one's own person, stands higher. (*Shabbat* 140b)

How is one to evaluate what is permissible, and what is excessive, consumption? In this short piece, the rabbinic debate is presented clearly. Rabbi Hisda states that when one can eat barley bread, a poor man's bread, and instead chooses to eat wheaten bread, a more expensive bread, it is a violation of *bal tashchit*. In the same manner, Rabbi Papa claims that if one can drink beer, a poor man's beverage, and instead drinks wine, a more expensive drink, it is a violation of *bal tashchit*. One must provide for human needs. However, one is not permitted to consume beyond what is necessary to live. To do so would be *bal tashchit*—wanton destruction.

Such a view clearly has ascetic overtones. The link between *bal tashchit* and living a simple life certainly suggests that link between demanding less and not cutting down trees. However, motivation for a simple life has often come from social considerations as well. Excessive consumption means that one is using one's wealth on oneself, often flaunting one's wealth, at the expense of helping out those who are less fortunate. A talmudic passage emphasizes the point:

> At first the carrying out of the dead was harder for [the dead's] relatives than his death, so that they left him and ran away, until Rabban Gamaliel came and adopted a simple style and they carried him out in garments of linen, and all the people followed his example and carried out [the dead] in garments of linen. Said Rabbi Papa: And now it is the general practice [to carry out the dead] even in rough cloth worth [only] a *zuz*. (*Ketubot* 8b)

Although the text makes no mention of *bal tashchit*, later commentators use it as a prooftext in applying *bal tashchit* to excessive consumption. Rambam, for example, links the two in his discussion of the laws of mourning.[12] Here the norm for burial had become so cost prohibitive that the poor would abandon their dead, unable to afford such an expense. Rabbi Gamaliel successfully changed the practice from an excessive one to a modest one, which evolved into virtually an ascetic one. It is clear here that the motivation for simplicity is social.

Yet, for all that can be said for simplicity, the text is blunt as to which perspective wins out in the talmudic argument: "but this is incorrect. *Bal tashchit*, as applied to one's own person stands higher." The statement is quite powerful. It is considered *bal tashchit not to* drink the wine or eat the wheaten bread. Human comfort and enjoyment are to take precedence. Not according them priority limits human pleasure in the world, which is a form of destruction—destruction of human pleasure. Although there is a tradition of abstinence in Judaism, it is generally frowned upon. Human beings are to enjoy the bounty of creation. Although two traditions are clearly present, the one which places humans as the evaluator of worth is plainly dominant.

Maimonides canonizes this dominant tradition, leaving out the minority view. In three short *halachot* in his *Mishnah Torah* he summarizes the talmudic extrapolation of the biblical text.[13] There is no tension in Maimonides' summary. Wanton destruction is clearly defined as the cutting down of fruit trees when there is no economic justification for its removal. Although the rabbinic expansion of the text is presented, in fact the summary limits the text. Only when something is clearly of benefit, and its destruction does not bring about demonstrably more benefit, is its destruction considered *bal tashchit*. Any time there is economic again from its use, its destruction is justifiable.

THE RESPONSA LITERATURE

Two positions emerge from the rabbinic discussion on *bal tashchit*. The first, which is clearly the dominant position, I describe as the minimalist position. It limits *bal tashchit* as much as possible to only those situations that are clearly proscribed by the biblical injunction in Deuteronomy. Although seemingly expanding *bal tashchit* to encompass human creation and not simply nature, it in fact creates a clear hierarchy in which human utilitarian needs always override any inherent value of the created object. In contrast, the maximalist position does expand *bal tashchit* as a counterweight to human desires. Human needs define usage, although the definition of what constitutes human need is far from clear. Consumption should be limited to what is necessary, and the inherent value of the creation stands as a countermeasure to human usage.

The many interpretations offered in the literature on the human responsibility to the natural world thus cited leaves much latitude for the application of the concept of *bal tashchit* in Jewish law. An anthropocentric reading of the traditions leads to a minimalist application of the principle, with human considerations always determining the conduct toward nature. However, a reading of the tradition that gives a degree of inherent worth to the natural world independent of human use demands a much more complex negotiation between human wants and needs and nature, leading to what I call a maximalist application of the principle. The *halachic* process enabled each *posek*—each *halachic* authority—to offer his own interpretation of the concept through his own reading of the meaning of *bal tashchit* as it is expressed in the texts of biblical and rabbinic literature, and interpreted by later generations. Not surprisingly, different *Poskim*[14] chose to understand the *halachah* in the different ways suggested by the interpretations already cited. What follows is a representative survey of the responsa literature, according to the minimalist and maximalist traditions.

THE MINIMALIST TRADITION

One of the main *halachic* questions, once having accepted the idea of *bal tashchit* as relating to wanton destruction, is in what situations is it to be overridden. The *Tosafot,* for example, commenting on a talmudic passage, argue that *bal tashchit* is overridden by the obligation to honor royalty.[15] In *Sefer HaChasidim,* it is argued that rewriting a page of Torah only so that it looks better also overrides the commandment (*mitzvah*) of *bal tashchit*.[16] Ovadiah Yosef (1920–) claims that the fulfillment of a *mitzvah,* such as the breaking of the glass as part of the wedding ceremony, overrides *bal tashchit*.[17] He, like *Sefer HaChasidim,* also argues that *bal tashchit* is overridden in order to show honor to a *mitzvah,* such as by buying a newer, fancier *mezuzah*.[18]

It is also permissible to destroy property and even plants for educational reasons. Relying on a talmudic passage that allows one to rip clothing or break pottery in order to demonstrate anger as an educational tool (although it is forbidden to do such acts out of anger),[19] Abraham Isaac Kook (1865–1935) argues that one is allowed to destroy when one is teaching that something is forbidden so that two trees which are forbidden to be planted together under the laws of *kilayim* may be planted together and then uprooted to teach that such a planting is forbidden. The trees are deliberately planted and then uprooted to teach the *halachah*.[20]

Maimonides is asked whether a tree may be cut down which is in danger of falling and damaging a mosque which lies underneath. Here it is a question of whether *bal tashchit* applies when social relations between Jews and Moslems might be jeopardized by not removing the tree. Maimonides, in keeping with his radically minimalist position, answers that it is permitted to cut the tree down not only when there is damage inflicted, but also when there is the potential for damage.[21] Elsewhere Maimonides allows for the removal of a tree that threatens to break off in a storm and injure those walking past in the adjacent public area.

Judah Rosannes (1657–1727) holds that the prohibition is only on the chopping down of the entire tree, and there is therefore no problem with *bal tashchit* when chopping down branches from the tree.[22] Baruch Wiesel gives permission in his *Makor Baruch* (1755) to destroy an older house and build a newer one.[23]

Indeed, the anthropocentric view of *bal tashchit*, which sees nature as having been created for the use of human beings, is a central theme in the literature. Naphtali Zvi Berlin (1817–1893) states emphatically that the very purpose of a tree and its fruit is for it to be cut down for the use of human beings.[24] In his commentary on the Deuteronomy verse, Yaakov Tzvi from Kalenburg (d. 1865) states:

> It is not virtuous to use anything in a manner different from that which it has been created . . . also a tree, which was aimed in its creation to produce fruit as food for human beings to sustain them, it is forbidden to do anything to them which would harm human beings.[25]

Jonah ben Abraham Gerondi (1200–1263) holds that the body of a human being is to be considered part of the world of creation, hence part of that to which *bal tashchit* is to be applied. One has no right to cause it harm.[26] Menahem Azariah Da Fano (1548–1620) states that, although in general one should choose to be stringent with oneself, when it comes to financial losses to oneself, one is forbidden to be severe in order not to transgress *bal tashchit*.[27] Here we see once again the theme of human needs as a concern of *bal tashchit*, which takes precedence over other needs. Ephraim

Weinberger argues that any deprivation to the body's health is a transgression of *bal tashchit:*

> Even if he doesn't allow himself to eat foods that are good for his health and strengthen his body, although they are expensive, he transgresses the prohibition. Any abuse of bodily health in general is a transgression of *bal tashchit.*[28]

In a *responsa* about animal experimentation, Jacob Reischer states that even when there is only the possibility of medical or economic benefit, *bal tashchit* applied to human beings always takes precedence.[29] In the *Shulhan Arukh of the Rav*, in the laws of *bal tashchit* revealingly printed under "laws pertaining to the protection of the body and the spirit and laws of *bal tashchit*," Shneur Zalman of Lyady (1745–1813) states: ". . . and also those that destroy anything that it is destined for human beings to enjoy transgress *bal tashchit.*"[30]

The application of *bal tashchit* to the human being expresses the minimalist position quite well: although *bal tashchit* demands that nothing be wasted, it applies first and foremost to the human being. Although some have understood *bal tashchit* as applying to the preclusion of human *needs*, the most minimalist understanding maintains that preventing human *pleasure* by preventing human use of the world is an act of *bal tashchit*. The seemingly expansionist position that extends the precept of *bal tashchit* to all things, only to be circumvented by any human desire as the ultimate form of *bal tashchit*, is presented quite forcefully in both respects in *Sefer HaChinuch:*

> The root reason for the precept is known (evident): for it is in order to train our spirits to love what is good and beneficial and to cling to it; and as a result, good fortune will cling to us, and we will move well away from every evil thing and from every matter of destructiveness. This is the way of the kindly men of piety and the conscientiously observant; they love peace and are happy at the good fortune of people, and bring them near the Torah. They will not destroy even a mustard seed in the world, and they are distressed at every ruination and spoilage that they see: and if they are able to do any rescuing, they will save anything from destruction, with all their power.
>
> . . . Among the laws of the precept, there is what the Sages of blessed memory said: that the Torah did not forbid chopping down fruit trees if any useful benefit will be found in the matter: for instance, if the monetary value of a certain tree is high, and this person wanted to sell it, or to remove a detriment by chopping them down—for instance, if this was harming other trees that were better than it, or because it was causing damage in the fields of others. In all these circumstances, or anything similar, it is permissible.[31]

According to Zevi Ashkenazi (1660–1718), continuing the position alluded to by *Sefer Hachinuch*, the purpose of *bal tashchit* is not to prevent destruction so much as to teach human beings sensitivity.[32] Nature has no inherent value apart from its use by human beings.

THE MAXIMALIST TRADITION

Jacob Reischer is asked whether one may uproot trees from his garden which obstruct the view from his neighbor's house windows. Reischer rules that the trees are to be removed, but not before searching for another solution such as the replanting of the trees in an alternative location.[33] Jair Hayyim Bacharach (1638–1702) is asked whether one can remove a fruit tree whose branches obscure the view from one's own window. Note that here permission is being asked to remove a tree which is a nuisance oneself, as opposed to one which is a nuisance to one's neighbor. Bacharach makes two important points. The first, that since the nuisance can be dealt with through the pruning of the branches of the tree, which is not forbidden by *bal tashchit*, it is not permitted to chop the tree down. The second is that chopping down a tree is to be allowed for essential needs, but not for luxuries. Earlier, we saw that Rashba permitted the expansion of a house. Bacharach relies on this *responsum* to argue that, while there the chopping down of the tree was for an essential need, here it is not and therefore, based on the precedent of Rashba, it is not to be permitted.[34] Jacob Ettlinger is asked whether one may chop down elderly trees in order to build a home on the only piece of property which the individual is allowed to buy in town. Without having a home, he may not get a license to marry. Ettlinger allows for the trees to be chopped down, although he also points out that everything must be done to find an alternative, and that such permission is granted because not to would prevent the man from marrying. Although permission is granted, the tenor is one of limiting the exceptions to *bal tashchit*, rather than extending them.[35] Similarly, Moses Sofer gives permission to uproot a vineyard which is losing money, and to use the land for field crops instead. Nevertheless, he states that although usually it is forbidden to uproot the vineyard, for this particular time, since the economic loss is so great, permission is given.[36] Ovadiah Yosef also gives permission to chop down a fruit-bearing tree, in this example to expand one's home, while limiting the exceptions. Yosef allows the expansion of the house in this case in order to allow room for a family which has been blessed with many children. However, he asserts that it is forbidden to chop down the trees if one is expanding one's home for luxury, or for landscaping or general beautification. Once again, a distinction is made between perceived needs and wants.[37]

Citing the danger involved in chopping down trees, Pinhas Hai Anu (1693–1765) refuses to give permission to cut down a fig tree in order to build a storage shed.[38] Yaakov ben Shmuel from Tzoyemer (end of the seventeenth century) simply states that it is forbidden to chop down trees in order to build a home.[39] Interestingly, the same Naphtali Zevi Judah Berlin who stated that the purpose of a tree is to be cut down for the use of human beings gives the most maximalist of the interpretations of *bal tashchit*. Asked whether a tree may be removed to build a home, his answer is no. Berlin claims that one may cut down a tree only in cases explicitly spelled out by the *Talmud:* either when it damages other trees, in which case one tree has no precedence over another, or when it damages another's field.[40]

Berlin points out that there is a distinction between the chopping down of a tree and other transgressions of *bal tashchit* in that only the chopping down of a tree is punishable by flogging. Berlin also mentions the talmudic notion of there being danger involved in the chopping down of trees from the story of R. Hanina's son as reason to be particularly cautious.

The vast majority of examples from the literature with regard to the cutting down of trees refers explicitly to fruit trees or do not mention the kind of tree being discussed. The original distinction between fruit-producing trees and non-fruit-producing trees seems to be maintained. The *Tosafot*, however, commenting on a passage from the *Talmud* that "one who cuts down good trees will never see blessing in their lives" state—"One who cuts down even a non-fruit-producing tree." In other words, although not strictly forbidden, such an action will prevent the doer from being blessed in their life's deeds.[41] Although Greenwald (twentieth century) in his *responsum* makes a distinction between non-fruit-producing trees that have a use as trees for human beings, for example in providing shade, beauty, or even a pleasant aroma, and trees that have use only as firewood and should therefore be used for that purpose, the application of *bal tashchit* to non-fruit-producing trees is a direct rejection of Maimonides holding that *bal tashchit* does not apply to them.[42]

In the discussion of conspicuous consumption, which as an issue is directly linked to the maximalist position, two *responsa* are of interest. In the first, Joseph Karo (1488–1575) warns against the wasting of public monies on extravagances.[43] In the second, the first chief ashkenazic Rabbi of Israel, Abraham Yizhak Hacohen Kook, is asked whether there is any prohibition in the Torah to the improvement of the military cemetery. Kook answers that, while it is certainly a *mitzvah* to fix up the cemetery so that it is in honorable condition, it would be considered a violation of *bal tashchit* to invest large amounts of money in order that it be lavish.[44]

Finally, two different *responsa* apply *bal tashchit* to "ownerless property," which includes wild animals and vegetation, and abandoned property.[45] Such a view is in keeping with the idea that there is no such thing as ownerless property, since in fact, all the world is ultimately the property of God: "Because the earth is Mine."[46] It is a theocentric utilitarianism. As such, in the Sabbatical year, although all land becomes ownerless temporarily, that is, returned to God, its original owner, nevertheless *bal tashchit* continues to apply.

Although it is clear that even in those sources that have been attributed to a maximalist position there is a strong sense of a hierarchy in which human needs override other considerations, nevertheless, in the maximalist position there are other considerations that need to be weighed against the human. In all cases, human *needs* outweigh other considerations. However, there is a debate that takes place as to what defines *needs*. In addition, there seems to be a distinction made between trees, particularly fruit-bearing trees and other properties.

The *halachic* principle of *bal tashchit* has been open to different, often contradictory interpretations. From its beginning, tension existed with regard to how to understand the prohibition: whether such a prohibition was to define the world in terms of human use or whether such a prohibition demanded an evaluation of use that took into account more than human wants.

RELEVANCE TO CONTEMPORARY ENVIRONMENTAL ETHICS

Any analysis of the significance of *bal tashchit* must take into account both the *content* of the discussion—what has been said—and the *context* of the discussion—the cultural language of the debate. With regard to the *content*, several points can be made:

1. It is quite obvious from the survey of the literature that there is no one Jewish approach to *bal tashchit* and its application, but rather multiple approaches that are debated from within the tradition. In general, any claim to *the* Jewish view on an ethical situation should be held as suspect.

2. The discussion in many ways is remarkably similar to our contemporary discussion. Here too we see two poles on the continuum. The minimalist position has human needs and wants taking precedence over the rest of the creation; the maximalist position has human wants counterbalanced with the legitimate claims of the natural world. The tradition documents a debate between the two positions that has continued since rabbinic times.

3. The minimalist position is without question far more dominant within the tradition. This emphasis too parallels the contemporary debate. Those voices that question a utilitarian approach to the natural world are in the minority.

4. There is no hint in the maximal position of a holistic environmental ethic. This situation should not be particularly surprising in that the holistic environmental position is based on the science of ecology and the concept of species and on the assumption that human culture is a small part of the larger ecosystem. Premodern Aristotelian science, which is the scientific tradition within which *bal tashchit* developed, saw nature as static and species as eternal. *Bal tashchit* was applied on the level of the individual. Its concern was domesticated nature, nature in contact with day-to-day living.

5. There is also no hint in the *halachic* tradition of *bal tashchit* of the romantic idea of reconnecting humans to their natural selves. At least within the *halachic* discussion of *bal tashchit*, respect for nature in no way is connected to a desire to reconnect human culture with its natural, and truer, antecedents.

I believe that the absence of such a tendency reveals a strong preference in Jewish ethical philosophy to see morality as transcendent of the natural world and not immanent within it. The pagan-Jewish debate in many significant ways is connected to a debate about whether morality is defined by "what is"—a naturalist perspective—or by "what should be"—an idealistic model of moral philosophy. Although natural metaphors and images are present in the Jewish textual tradition,[47] particularly in the Bible, nature is primarily not considered to be a pristine state of the world, but a temporal reality that needs to be redeemed.

With regard to the *context*, any comparison of the contemporary discussion on environmental ethics and the traditional Jewish perspective will be limited. We can only understand another cultural perspective through the prism of our own cultural categories, and therefore any attempt to enter another cultural perspective can only be partial.[48] Only those parts of the tradition that can be explicated in contemporary terms can be translated into a contemporary context. The other parts can only be rumored. What I have so far considered is the part of the traditional discussion that appears to translate relatively easily into the contemporary cultural language and thus can be easily compared. The *content*, therefore, seems to be similar only when understood as emerging from a similar cultural context. However, the Jewish discussion is in many ways a discussion that is different in kind from the contemporary discussion and that defies a simple comparison.

Because the cultural *contexts* involve very different assumptions, comparison of the two languages of discourse can help locate some of the different cultural assumptions and can teach us about the outlooks of both traditional Jewish and contemporary culture. It helps us to glimpse at that which is incapable of being translated into contemporary categories.

1. Although primarily presented here as a moral discussion, the discussion of the *halachot* often seems legalistic to the modern ear, without regard to any ethical question. Although the discussion at times seems focused on the moral relationship to nature, with the biblical and rabbinic texts used as proof texts for the ethical position, at other times the discussion seems to be internally focused, allowing the texts to develop apart from any moral discussion. In short, the discussion of *bal tashchit* hints at a different type of moral discourse, neither utilitarian nor rights-based, neither anthropocentric nor biocentric.

2. The legal assumptions of the *halachic* tradition also sound strange to the modern individual. Much of the contemporary environmental discourse concerns the concept of rights. It has been pointed out by some legal historians that such an idea seems foreign to the traditional Jewish *halachic* tradition. Rather than focusing on rights, the tradition focuses on duties. Calling the *halachic* system a system based on duties, rather than rights, is also a partial translation of traditional categories, but it suggests the underlying assumption from which the *halachic* system works. The *halachah* extends beyond that which is forbidden and legislates normative behavior.[49]

3. The strikingly particularistic nature of the *halachic* discussion is also suggestive in terms of the demands of an environmental ethic. The *halachic* discussion continually focuses on a particular incident about a particular animal or a particular tree in a particular place. The discussion in those cases no longer revolves around the theoretical question of the human relationship to the natural world, but rather the trade-offs between human and other interests in particular situations. Jewish ethical philosophy is embodied in the material world. Although certain general principles are clearly established from the particular discussion, it is the unique situation which forms the basis of the discussion.

4. The particular nature of Jewish *halachic* discussion is connected to the centrality of community as a defining category. Mary Midgley points out in the debate around contemporary environmental ethics that traditional societies lived in "mixed communities" which allowed human sympathies to transcend the species boundary.[50] Callicott extends the concept of "mixed community" to the biotic community as well.[51] The *halachic* discussions around *bal tashchit* are testimony to a functioning mixed community. The species barrier is clearly transcended, since discussion includes concern for the community's trees (and, even more centrally, animals[52]) in the deliberation. As Callicott suggests, such a model has various concentric circles of interest, from the most immediate connection of family, but extending out in lesser degrees of concern beyond the species to animals and eventually to the biotic community. It is a morality based on relationships that emerge from particular communities in particular places. Such a dynamic of morality—rooted in relationships between human beings, humans and God, humans and animals, humans and nature—will lead to a very different kind of moral discourse.

In this discussion I have deliberately echoed a larger argument in ethics between rights-based ethics and the communitarian critique of the limits of such an approach. It should be noted, however, that communitarian positions on the environment, nevertheless, remain within an anthropocentric view of community that does not transcend the species barrier.[53] A religious culture that can see creation as having value independent of its utilitarian worth to human beings will philosophically find it much easier to view creation as having inherent worth.[54] Whether that potential can be realized is one of the major challenges facing the Jewish environmental community today.

Contemporary environmental ethics has a rich and complex discourse to describe contemporary society's relationships with the natural world. Yet, we have compromised such rigorous research when treating other cultural perspectives. Doing so caricatures traditional cultures and provides no significant insights into other perspectives. If looking at other cultural perspectives is to be a meaningful steppingstone in the rethinking of our own perspectives, we must recognize the limitations of cultural translation while at the same time attempting to describe the culture from within its own cultural language. Only then will we be able to peek into a truly other cultural world and glimpse a different way of seeing. The investigation of *bal tashchit* is offered as both an insight into a Jewish perspective and a glance at what nature looks like through different cultural eyes.

Notes

1. Although the term *rabbinic* has a more generic usage, in the context of this paper it refers to the individuals who wrote and codified the *Mishnah and Talmud.* The *Mishnah* is the name of the earliest major rabbinic works, first appearing toward the turn of the third century C.E. It is the core document of the talmudic tradition, composed in very terse language and arranged topic by topic over a wide range of subjects. The *Talmud* primarily refers to the *Mishnah* combined with its later rabbinic commentaries, the *Gemara.* The earliest one is the Jerusalem, or Palestinian, *Talmud,* dating from the first half of the fifth century. Some two centuries later the Babylonian *Talmud* was compiled. All talmudic references in this paper are to the Babylonian *Talmud.*

2. For a literature survey of the contemporary debate on the relationship of Judaism to the environment, and a discussion of the theological/moral issues which are at the root of such a relationship, see Eilon Schwartz. "Judaism and Nature: Theological and Moral Issues to Consider While Renegotiating a Jewish Relationship to Nature." *Judaism* 44 (Fall 1995): 437–47.

3. The *halacha* is the set of rules often known as "Jewish law" that governs Jewish life. The *halacha,* however, contains far more than what is usually suggested by the term *law,* as is demonstrated in this paper.

4. R. Solomon b. Issac [RaShI] (1040–1150). Perhaps the most influential biblical and talmudic exegete. French.

5. Samuel ben Meir, commentary on Deuteronomy 20:19, in *Torat Chaim* (Jerusalem: Hotzaat Mosad HaRav Kook, 1993). He is Rashi's grandson, one of the *Tosafists, halachic* commentators on the *Talmud* in twelfth to fourteenth-century France and Germany.

6. Nahmanides, commentary on Deuteronomy 20:19, in *Torat Chaim.*

7. Ibid.

8. All quotes from the *Mishnah* and the *Talmud* are taken from the Soncino translation, unless otherwise cited.

9. I have here changed parts of the Soncino translation, translating in a way similar to Adin Steinsaltz in his Hebrew translation of the *Talmud.*

10. Meir Ayele, "The Fear of Cutting Down Fruit-bearing Trees in the Response Literature," in *Tura* [Hebrew] (Kibbutz Hameuchad, 1989), pp. 135–40.

11. Moses Maimonides, *Judges, Mishnah Torah* [Hebrew] (Jerusalem: Hotzaat Mossad HaRav Kook, 1962), Laws of Kings 6:10. Perhaps the most influential Jewish philosopher ever.

13. Moses Maimonides, *Judges, Mishnah Torah* [Hebrew] (Jerusalem: Hotzaat Mossad HaRav Kook, 1962), Laws of Mourning 14:24.

13. Maimonides, *Mishnah Torah,* "The Book of Judges," Kings 6:8–10.

14. Scholars whose efforts were concentrated on determining the *halacha* in practice.

15. *Tosefot Baba Metzia* 32b.

16. Judah he-Hasid, *Sefer Ha Chasidim* (Jerusalem: Aharon Block, 1992), no. 339.

17. Ovadiah Yosef, *Yabiah Omer* (Jerusalem, 1993), pt. 4, *Even HaEzer,* no. 9. Former Sephardi Chief Rabbi of Israel.

18. Ovadiah Yosef, *Yabiah Omer,* pt. 3, Yoreh Deah, no. 18. A *mezuzah* is a parchment scroll containing portions of the Torah, fixed to the doorpost.

19. Shabbat 105b.

20. Abraham Isaac HaCohen Kook, *Mishpat Cohen* (Jerusalem, HaAguda L'Hotzaat Sifrei HaRav Kook, 1937), no. 21. Zionist leader. First Ashkenazi Chief Rabbi of Palestine.

21. Moses Maimonides, *Responsa* (Hebrew), trans. Jehoshua Blau (Jerusalem: *Mekize Nirdamim,* 1958), no. 112.

22. Judah B. Samuel Rosannes, *Mishneh la-Melekh,* commentary on Maimonides, *Mishnah Torah,* Isurei Mizbeah, 7:3 as it appears in *Baal Tashchit, Encyclopedia Talmudit* (Jerusalem: Hotzaat Encylopedia Talmudit, 1973). Turkish rabbi.

23. Baruch Baandit Wiesel, *Makor Baruch,* as cited in Meir Ayele. *The Fear of Chopping Down Fruit Trees in the Responsa Literature,* in *Tura: Studies in Jewish Thought* (Tel Aviv: Kibbutz HaMeuchad, 1989), p. 138.

24. Naphtali Zevi Judah Berlin, *Meshiv Davar* (Jerusalem, 1993), chap. 2, no. 56.

25. Yaakov Tzvi from Kalenburg, *HaKatav v'HaKabalah* (Nuremberg, 1924), Deuteronomy 20:19.

26. Jonah ben Abraham Gerondi, *Sefer Sha'arei Teshuva* (Jerusalem, 1960), chap. 3, no. 82. Spanish rabbi and moralist.

27. Menahem Azariah Da Fano, *Responsa,* 129, as quoted in Meir Zichal, *Environmental Protection in Jewish Sources* [Hebrew] (Ramat Gan: The Responsa Project, 1989), p. 31. Italian rabbi and kabbalist.

28. Ephraim Weinberger, *Yad Ephraim* (Tel Aviv: HaVaad HaTziburi LiHotzaat Kitvei HaRav Weinberger, 1976), no. 14. Former member of Tel Aviv rabbinic council.

29. Jacob Reischer, *Shevut Yaakov* (Jerusalem, 1972), pt. 3, no. 71.

30. Shneur Zalman of Lyady, "Laws of Protecting the Body and the Spirit and *Bal Tashchit*", *Shulhan Arukh of the Rav* (New York: Kehot Publication Society, 1975), 31:b. Founder of Habad Hasdism.

31. *Sefer Hachinuch: The Book of Education* (New York: Feldheim Publishers, 1989), no. 529.

32. Zevi Ashkenazi, *Haham Zevi,* as quoted in Zichal, *Environmental Protection in Jewish Sources,* p. 9.

33. Jacob Reischer, *Shevut Yaakov* (Jerusalem, 1972), pt. 1, no. 159.

34. Jair Hayyim Bacharach, *Havvot Yair* (Jerusalem, 1968), no. 195. German talmudic scholar.

35. Jacob Ettlinger, *Binyan Zion* (Jerusalem: Davar Jerusalem, 1989), no. 61.

36. Moses Sofer, *Responsa of Hatam Sofer* [Hebrew], (Jerusalem: Hotzaat Hod, 1972), Yoreh *Deah,* no. 102.

37. Ovadia Yosef, *Yabia Omer* (Jerusalem, 1969), vol. 5, *Yoreh Deah,* no. 12.

38. Pinhas Hai Anu from Ferrara, *Givat Pinhas,* pt. 8, no. 2, as it appears in Meir Ayele, "*Givat Pinhas*": *The Responsa of R. Pinhas Hai ben Menahem Anau of Ferrara,* in *Tarbitz.* Northern Italian rabbi.

39. Yaakov b. Rabbi Shmuel from Tzoyemer, *Beit Yaakov* (Diehernport, 1696), no. 140.

40. Naphtali Zevi Judah Berlin, *Meshiv Davar* (Jerusalem, 1993), chap. 2, no. 56.

41. Tosefot on Pesachim 50b.

42. Greenwald, *Keren LeDavid* (Satmar, 1928), *Orech Chaim,* no. 30. Hungarian rabbi.

43. Joseph Caro, *Avatak Rochel* (Leipzig, 1859), no. 18. Author of the *Shulkhan Aruch,* the authoritative code of Jewish law.

44. Abraham Isaac Kook, *Daat Kohen* (Jerusalem: Mossad Harav Kook, 1969), *Yoreh Deah,* no. 122.

45. Tzvi Pesach Frank, *Har Tzyi* (Jerusalem: Machon Harav Frank, 1973), Orech *Chaim 2,* no. 102; *Noda Yehuda, Yoreh Deah,* no. 10.

46. Leviticus 25:23.

47. It is quite significant that trees are a central metaphor in Judaism. As one example, the Torah, those parts of the Bible traditionally revealed directly to Moses on Mt. Sinai, is called "a tree of life." Trees played a central role in the economic life in the ancient land of Israel, and were thus proper metaphors for bridging between the socioeconomic life and the theological-moral one.

48. Michael Rosenak, "*Roads to the Palace*": *Jewish Texts and Teaching* (Providence and Oxford: Berghahn Books, 1995), p. 5.

49. Moshe Silberg, "Laws and Morals in Jewish Jurisprudence" in *Harvard Law Review* 75 (1961–1962): 306–31.

50. Mary Midgley, "The Mixed Community," in Eugene C. Hargrove, ed., *The Animal Rights/Environmental Ethics Debate* (Albany: State University of New York Press, 1992), pp. 211–25.

51. J. Baird Callicott, "Animal Liberation and Environmental Ethics: Back Together Again," in J. Baird Callicott, *In Defense of the Land Ethic: Essays in Environmental Philosophy* (Albany: State University of New York Press, 1989), pp. 49–51.

52. Paralleling the discussion of *bal tashchit* is the rabbinic precept of *tzar baalei chaim,* describing duties toward the prevention of animal suffering.

53. See Avner de-Shalit, *Why Posterity Matters: Environmental Policies and Future Generations* (London: Routledge, 1995).

54. This is perhaps the major point of Max Oelschlaeger, *Caring for Creation: An Ecumenical Approach to the Environmental Crisis* (New Haven: Yale University Press, 1994).

Ties That Bind: Native American Beliefs as a Foundation for Environmental Consciousness

Annie L. Booth and Harvey M. Jacobs

. . . Both deep ecologists and ecofeminists call for the development of a new human consciousness, one of humility, which recognizes the importance of all life, including the life of the organism Earth.[1] As radical activists and philosophers begin to articulate and implement their ideas for a truly ecological world, they find themselves drawn, again and again, to the beliefs and traditions of North America's Native Americans.[2] Native Americans are often portrayed as model ecological citizens, holding values and beliefs that industrialized humans have long since sacrificed in the pursuit of progress and comfort. This interest in Native American relationships with the natural world has an old history. As Cornell points out, influential members of the early American conservation movement were deeply impressed by Native Americans and their knowledge of and relations with the natural world.[3] Such interest is shared even by less radical elements in the environmental movement.[4]

Native American statements about the integrity and inherent importance of the natural world . . . stir many Western people, but there seems to be surprisingly little understanding of Native Americans' actual relationships with their environment. Even so, this does not keep elements of the environmental movement, mainstream and radical, recent and historical, from using Native Americans for their own ends. In this chapter we attempt to redress this situation by offering a synthetic, detailed discussion of Native American beliefs and relationships with the natural world as presented by Native Americans and by anthropologists and historians. As such, we take a broad approach to the nature of Native American culture, addressing it as a singular phenomenon. Although we are aware of the significant differences among Native American cultures, there is enough similarity in environmental views to warrant this type of cross-cutting approach. More detailed descriptions of the works used here are available in a related annotated bibliography.[5] It is our hope that this chapter will help the environmental movement develop an empathic and analytic understanding of traditions that they now use so loosely.

BELOVED MOTHER TO CONQUERED ENEMY

Although they varied significantly between different cultures, Native American relationships with the natural world tended to preserve biological integrity within natural communities, and did so over a significant period of historical time. These cultures engaged in relationships of mutual respect, reciprocity, and caring with an Earth and fellow beings as alive and self-conscious as human beings. Such relationships were reflected and perpetuated by cultural elements including religious belief and ceremonial ritual.[6]

We do not claim that natural communities remained unchanged by human activities, for they did change, considerably so, and in some instances, negatively so. However, the great majority of natural communities remained ecologically functional while supporting both Native American cultures and a great diversity of different plant and animal species.

In contrast, invading Europeans brought with them cultures that practiced relationships of subjugation and domination, even hatred, of European lands. They made little attempt to live *with* their natural communities, but rather altered them wholesale. The impoverishment of the ecological communities of sixteenth and seventeenth-century Europe was so great that, in contrast, early settlers of the New World found what they described as either a marvelous paradise or a horrendous wilderness, but certainly something completely outside their experience.[7]

Native American cultures had adapted their needs to the capacities of natural communities; the new inhabitants, freshly out of Europe, adapted natural communities to meet their needs. The differences between these two approaches have had profound impacts on the diversity and functioning of natural communities in North America.

NO SUCH THING AS EMPTINESS

In the songs and legends of different Native American cultures it is apparent that the land and her creatures are perceived as truly beautiful things. There is a sense of great wonder and of something which sparks a deep sensation of joyful celebration. Above all else, Native Americans were, and are, life-affirming; they respected and took pleasure in the life to be found around them, in all its diversity, inconsistency, or inconvenience. Everything had a place and a being, life and self-consciousness, and everything was treated accordingly. Hughes points out that only the newly arrived Europeans considered the land to be a "wilderness," barren and desolate.[8] To Native Americans, it was a bountiful community of living beings, of whom the humans were only one part. It was a place of great sacredness, in which the workings of the Great Spirit, or Great Mystery, could always be felt.

Hultkrantz argues that it is only because nature reflected the presence of the Great Mystery that it was considered to be sacred.[9] His interpretation suggests that the Indians' appreciation of nature, whether for its beauty or for its productivity, was influenced by the presence of other values. Hultkrantz felt that the Native American's relationship with nature reflected a dynamic tension, which was inherent in a relationship which both loves and exploits the natural world. This tension was reflected, in part, in the Native American's view of nature, which often included some quite terrifying aspects such as cannibalistic and malevolent spirits. Nature is both nurturing and attractive as well as destructive and dangerous.

In distinct contrast to Hultkrantz's interpretations, however, Native American writers focus on the wonders of the land. Standing Bear, a Lakota Sioux, wrote that Native Americans felt a special joy and wonder for all the elements and changes of season which characterized the land.[10] They felt that they held the spirit of the land within themselves, and so they met and experienced the elements and seasons rather than retreating from them. For Standing Bear and the Lakota, the Earth was so full of life and beings that they never actually felt alone.

[A] very central belief which seems consistent across many Native American cultures [is] that the Earth is a living, conscious being that must be treated with respect and loving care. The Earth may be referred to as Mother, or Grandmother, and these are quite literal terms, for the Earth is the source, the mother of all living beings, including human beings. Black Elk, a Lakota, asked, "Is not the sky a father and the earth a mother and are not all living things with feet and wings or roots their children?"[11] The Earth, and those who reside upon her, take their sacredness from that part of the Great Spirit which resides in all living beings. They are not the source of sacredness, but are no less sacred for that circumstance.

WE ARE THE LAND

The belief in a conscious, living nature is not simply an intellectual concept for Native American cultures. For most, perception of the landscape is important in determining perception of self. Vine Deloria, Jr., argues that Native Americans hold a perception of reality which is bound up in spatial references, references which refer to a physical place.[12] In Deloria's view, a spatial reference is important in establishing positive relationships with the natural world. Because of its basis in a particular land or place, a spatial orientation requires an intimate and respectful relationship with that land.

Not only do Native Americans see themselves as part of the land, they consider the land to be part of them. This goes beyond the romanticized love of nature that modern-day environmentalists are said to indulge in, for the

Native American faced the best and worst of the land, and still found it to be sacred, a gift from the Great Mystery of great meaning and value: it offered them their very being. In a very organic sense, the roots of the Native American peoples were always, and still are, in the natural communities in which they have lived.[13]

This theme is echoed by Luther Standing Bear when he describes the elders of the Lakota Sioux as growing so fond of the Earth that they preferred to sit or lie directly upon it.[14] In this way, they felt that they approached more closely the great mysteries in life and saw more clearly their kinship with all life. Indeed, Standing Bear comments that the reason for the white culture's alienation from their adopted land is that they are not truly of it; they have no roots to anchor them for their stay has been too short.[15]

This interconnection between person and land is not merely a thing of historical significance. Present-day Native Americans continue to acknowledge their ties to their land. Utes in the Southwest faced with the question of mining on their lands are deeply troubled, for the land is more than mere resource;[16] . . .

RELATIVES IN FUR MASKS

Recognizing that they were part of the land meant that many Native American cultures did not intellectually or emotionally isolate themselves from the land and her other inhabitants, as did European-derived cultures.

> The idea which appears over and over is "kinship" with other living beings. In the Native American system, there is no idea that nature is somewhere over there while man is over here, nor that there is a great hierarchical ladder of being on which ground and trees occupy a very low rung, animals a slightly higher one, and man a very high one indeed—especially "civilized" man. All are seen to be brothers or relatives (and in tribal systems relationship is central), all are offspring of the Great Mystery, children of our mother, and necessary parts of an ordered, balanced and living whole.[17]

Brown comments that while humans serve as the intermediary between earth and sky, this does not lessen the importance of other beings, as they are the links between humans and the Great Mystery.[18] To realize the self, kinship with all beings must be realized. To gain knowledge, humans must humble themselves before all creation, down to and including the lowliest ant, and realize their own nothingness. Knowledge may come through vision quests, and this knowledge is transmitted and offered by animals. Nature is a mirror which reflects all things, including that which it is important to learn about, understand and value throughout life.

Standing Bear explains that all beings share in the life force which flows from Wakan Tanka, the Great Mystery, including "the flowers of the plains, the blowing winds, rocks, trees, birds, animals," as well as man. "Thus all things were kindred and brought together by the same Great Mystery."[19] The other animals had rights, the right to live and multiply, the right to freedom, and the right to man's indebtedness. The Lakota Sioux, says Standing Bear, respected those rights.

Most Native American legends speak of other species as beings who could shed their fur mask and look human, as beings who once shared a common language with humans, and who continued to understand humans after the humans had lost their ability to understand them. Callicott quotes the Sioux holy man Black Elk, who describes the world as sharing in spiritedness.[20] Because everything shares in this spiritedness, it is possible for humans to enter into social and kin relations with other beings.

Martin, discussing subarctic bands, also notes that Native Americans felt and acknowledged a spiritual kinship with the animals they dealt with.[21] A sympathy built up between the human person who hunted and the animal persons who were hunted, a sympathy which pervaded human life. Animals lived in a world that was spiritual, although they assumed a fleshy body in the physical world. Their connection with the spiritual world made them mediators in all things to do with the spiritual world, such as when humans attempted to enter that world.

According to Nelson, the Alaskan Koyukon sense that the world they live in is a world full of aware, sensate, personified, feeling beings, who can be offended and who at all times must be treated with the proper respect.[22] The animals with which the Koyukons interact are among these powerful, watchful beings. Legend states that they once were human, becoming animals when they died. Animals and humans are distinct beings, their souls being quite different, but the animals are powerful beings in their own right. They are not offended at being killed for use, but killing must be done humanely, and there should be no suggestion of waste. Nor can the body be mistreated: it must be shown respect according to any number of taboos. Consequently a complex collection of rules, respectful activities, and taboos surround everyday life and assist humans in remaining within the moral code that binds all life. . . .

The practical consequences of such relationships with animals are profound. There is considerable archaeological evidence to suggest that the great prairies and the northeastern forests discovered by the Europeans were a product of modification. Hughes argues that the difference between these historical modifications and those made by the present-day inhabitants is demonstrated by the fact that the first Europeans found a forested and abundant country easily supporting the inhabitants, a country so different from fifteenth-century Europe that it was taken to be an unspoiled paradise.[23] Although animals were taken, sometimes in large numbers, rarely were species endangered or exterminated, for trying to exterminate a species would have meant trying to eliminate not only an essential of life, but a kindred being.

Hughes believes that the "ecological consciousness" of the Native American was in part due to their sense of kinship with the rest of the world, and in part made up of an extensive working knowledge and understanding of the world with which they lived. Much of this knowledge was codified and passed on through the medium of myths and legends handed down between generations. Such intimate knowledge permitted careful and judicious hunting, based on the knowledge of what animals resided in the area, how many there were, and how many were required to ensure a healthy population. Hunting territories were shared by families or bands, but misuse, such as excessive killing, might be grounds for war.

RECIPROCITY AND BALANCE IN ALL THINGS

Interactions with these important beings, these furcovered kin, required careful consideration. Reciprocity and balance were required from both sides in the relationships between humankind and other living beings. Balance was vital: the world exists as an intricate balance of parts, and it was important that humans recognized this balance and strove to maintain and stay within this balance. All hunting and gathering had to be done in such a way as to preserve the balance. Human populations had to fit within the balance. For everything that was taken, something had to be offered in return, and the permanent loss of something, such as in the destruction of a species, irreparably tore at the balance of the world. Thus, offerings were not so much sacrifices, as whites were inclined to interpret them, but rather a fair exchange for what had been taken, to maintain the balance. In this way, the idea of reciprocity emerges. From the Native American perspective, as Hughes puts it, "mankind depends on the other beings for life, and they depend on mankind to maintain the proper balance."[24] According to the Koyukons, for example, humans interact with natural things on the basis of a moral code, which, if properly attended to, contributes to a proper spiritual balance between humans and nonhumans.[25]

Momaday, a Kiowa writer and teacher, describes the necessary relationship as an act of reciprocal approbation, "approbations in which man invests himself in the landscape, and at the same time incorporates the landscape into his own most fundamental experience."[26] The respect and approval is two-way: humans both give and receive value and self-worth from the natural world. According to Momaday, this act of approbation is an act of the imagination, and it is a moral act. All of us are what we imagine ourselves to be, and the Native Americans imagine themselves specifically in terms of relationships with the physical world, among other things. Native Americans have been determining themselves in their imagination for many generations, and in the process, the landscape has become part of a particular reality. In a sense, for the Native American, the process is more intuitive and evolutionary than is the white Western rational linear process. The Native American has a personal investment in vision and imagination as a reality, or as part of a reality, whereas many whites believe such things have very little to do with what we call reality.

Toelken examines the idea of reciprocity between the Navaho people and what he describes as "the sacred *process* going on in the world."[27] Religion embodies a reciprocal relationship between the people and this process, and everything becomes a part of this circular, sacred give and take. Part of the idea of reciprocity is the necessity and importance of interaction. Participation in reciprocity is vital; a failure to interact, or a breakdown in interaction, leads to disease and calamity. Thus, everything that is used in everyday life is used for its part in that interaction; it becomes a symbol of sacred interaction and relationship between the people, the plants, the animals, and the land. Rituals such as those used for healing are not designed to ward off illness or directly cure the ill person. Rather, they are designed to remind the ill person of a frame of mind which is in proper relationship with the rest of the world, a frame of mind which is essential to the maintenance of good health. . . .

DEVELOPING AN ENVIRONMENTAL CONSCIOUSNESS

. . . For more than a century concerned Western environmentalists have held up Native Americans as one contemporary model of a way humans can learn to live in harmony with the natural world. Our detailed investigation of this assertion, cutting across Native American cultures, suggests that the basic premise of those holding this position is correct. However, it is likely that for many who hold this position, their conception of the Native American world view is limited in its appreciation of the depth and breadth of Native American integration with the land of which they are a part. For example, the extent to which Native Americans understand the Earth and all life upon it as fully alive and needing and deserving of a reciprocal, respectful relationship, and the thoroughly religious character of North American relationships with the natural world, demonstrate how far a construction of a Western environmental consciousness has to go to truly learn from and draw upon that which Native Americans have to teach.

Yet this is exactly the type of understanding which is reflected in the contemporary scholarship of environmental philosophy, particularly with regard to deep ecology and ecological feminism. Concerns and articulations of reciprocal respect for all life forms, a recognition of the Earth itself as a living being, and the recognition of the critical place of some form of spirituality in environmental consciousness permeate both strands of ecophilosophy. But these two approaches to a Western environmental consciousness have come to be characterized as oppositional, rather than integrative.[28] One lesson to be drawn from Native American beliefs is the unity of integrating these two approaches to ecophilosophy so they can work together in the construction of a Western environmental consciousness in which the Earth and all its beings, including humans, have a niche, and humans in particular have an awareness of the importance of all other life forms.

As we turn to Native American cultures for their wisdom, however, it is important to keep in mind that their cultures and relationship with the natural world will not provide any instantaneous solutions to the problems Western culture is presently facing. Cultures, or selected bits of one or two, cannot and should not be arbitrarily grafted onto one another.

Native American traditions, as in all cultures, are embedded in a particular context. The impact and meaning of a tradition stems from lifelong conditioning, preparation, and participation. It is built into the language, into the way day-to-day life is lived and experienced over time, and within a specific physical/social context. Attempts to borrow culture, whether it be wholesale or piecemeal, are doomed to failure.

If we ignore this fact, we risk harm not only to ourselves, but to Native Americans as well. There is a delicate line between respectful learning and intellectual plundering. Richard White questions our casual and constant habit of using the Native American as a symbol without reference or regard to real Native Americans or their attitudes and feelings.[29] In doing so, White argues, we are just as guilty of using and exploiting these cultures as we are when we steal their lands or their lives and spirits.

But there are less imperialistic approaches to Native American cultures. They can be studied as a contrast to our own destructive relationships with the natural world, and as a reminder that positive relationships can and do exist. An open-hearted and respectful investigation of Native American cultures, particularly when members of these cultures voluntarily share with us their understandings and perceptions, can help us discover new directions in which to travel to realize our own potentials.

Luther Standing Bear believed that it took generations of dying and being reborn within a land for that land to become a part of an individual and of a culture.[30] Deloria suggests that it is possible for peoples and lands to adapt and to relate to one another very powerfully, leading to a spiritual union which benefits both; a particular land determines and encourages the nature of a religion that will spring up upon it, and within a religion lies an entire way of life.[31] This is, in fact, exactly the premise of bioregionalists, who add a third strand to the deep ecology-ecofeminism discourse by stressing the need to become intimately aware of particular places, not just place in general.[32] The next step, then, in learning from Native Americans may be to move beyond general study to an examination of individual tribes and cultural groups to understand how the more universal themes addressed in this chapter were and are articulated in particular places.

All told, we may well be on the path to a sustainable Western environmental consciousness. At least in the case of Native Americans we appear to have encountered and long recognized enduring environmental wisdom, even if we have been unable to integrate it into the mainstream of Western culture. At present, the active discourse among deep ecologists, ecofeminists, and bioregionalists suggests serious work on the shaping of an environmental consciousness in a form appropriate to Western culture. We can and should look for assistance in this effort from Native Americans; they appear willing, even anxious, to aid, as long as in so doing we recognize the boundary between learning and exploiting.

NOTES

1. James E. Lovelock, *Gaia: A New Look at Life on Earth* (New York: Oxford University Press, 1979).
2. For one set of prominent examples see Devall, "The Deep Ecology Movement," and Green Party, *Politics For Life,* p. 13.
3. George L. Cornell, "The Influence of Native Americans on Modern Conservationists," *Environmental Review* 9 (1985): 105–17.
4. See for instance Stewart L. Udall, "Indians: First Americans, First Ecologists," in *Readings in American History—73/74* (Connecticut: Dushkin Publishing Group, 1973).
5. Annie L. Booth and Harvey M. Jacobs, *Environmental Consciousness: Native American Worldviews and Sustainable Natural Resource Management: An Annotated Bibliography,* CPL Bibliography no. 214 (Chicago: Council of Planning Librarians, 1988).
6. J. Donald Hughes, *American Indian Ecology* (El Paso: Texas University Press, 1983).
7. See William Cronan, *Changes in the Land: Indians, Colonists and the Ecology of New England* (New York: Hill and Wang, 1983); and Hughes, *American Indian Ecology.*
8. Hughes, *American Indian Ecology.*
9. Ake Hultkrantz, *Belief and Worship in Native North America* (Syracuse: Syracuse University Press, 1981).
10. Luther Standing Bear, *Land of the Spotted Eagle* (Lincoln: University of Nebraska Press, 1933).
11. John G. Neihardt, *Black Elk Speaks: Being the Life Story of a Holy Man of the Oglala Sioux* (New York: Pocket Books, 1975), p. 6.
12. Vine Deloria, Jr., *God Is Red* (New York: Grosset & Dunlap, 1973).
13. Paula Gunn Allen, *The Sacred Hoop: Recovering the Feminine in American Indian Traditions* (Boston: Beacon Press, 1986).
14. Standing Bear, *Land of the Spotted Eagle,* p. 192.
15. Ibid., p. 248.
16. Stephanie Romeo, "Concepts of Nature and Power: Environmental Ethics of the Northern Ute," *Environmental Review* 9 (1985): 160–61.
17. Paula Gunn Allen, "The Sacred Hoop: A Contemporary Indian Perspective on American Literature," in Geary Hobson (ed.), *The Remembered Earth* (Albuquerque: Red Earth Press, 1979), p. 225.
18. Joseph Epes Brown, *The Spiritual Legacy of the American Indian* (New York: Crossroad Publishing Co., 1985).
19. Standing Bear, *Land of the Spotted Eagle,* p. 193.

20. J. Baird Callicott, "Traditional American Indian and Traditional Western European Attitudes towards Nature: An Overview," in Robert Elliot and Arran Gare, eds., *Environmental Philosophy: A Collection of Readings* (University Park: Pennsylvania State University Press, 1983), pp. 231–59.

21. Calvin Martin, "Subarctic Indians and Wildlife," in C. Vecsey and R. W. Venables, eds., *American Indian Environments: Ecological Issues in Native American History* (Syracuse: Syracuse University Press, 1980), pp. 38–45.

22. Richard K. Nelson, *Make Prayers to the Raven* (Chicago: University of Chicago Press, 1983); Richard K. Nelson, "A Conservation Ethic and Environment: The Koyukon of Alaska," in Nancy M. Williams and Eugene S. Hunn, eds., *Resource Managers: North American and Australian Hunter Gatherers*, AAAS Selected Symposium no. 67 (Boulder: Westview Press, 1982), pp. 211–28.

23. J. Donald Hughes, "Forest Indians: The Holy Occupation," *Environmental Review* 2 (1977): 2–13.

24. Hughes, *American Indian Ecology*, p. 17.

25. Nelson, "A Conservation Ethic and Environment: The Koyukon of Alaska."

26. N. Scott Momaday, "Native American Attitudes towards the Environment," in Walter H. Capps, ed., *Seeing with a Native Eye* (New York: Harper & Row, 1976), p. 80.

27. Barre Toelken, "Seeing with a Native Eye: How Many Sheep Will It Hold?" in Walter H. Capps, ed., *Seeing with a Native Eye* (New York: Harper & Row, 1976), p. 14.

28. See for example Janet Biehl, "Ecofeminism and Deep Ecology: Unresolvable Conflict?" *Our Generation 19* (1988): 19–31; and Warwick Fox, "The Deep Ecology-Ecofeminism Debate and Its Parallels," *Environmental Ethics* 11 (1989): 5–25.

29. Richard White, "Introduction" [to special issue on the American Indian and the environment], *Environmental Review* 9 (1985): 101–103.

30. Standing Bear, *Land of the Spotted Eagle*, p. 248.

31. Deloria, *God Is Red*, p. 294.

32. See for example, Peter Berg, ed., *Reinhabiting a Separate Country* (San Francisco: Planet Drum Foundation, 1978); Kirkpatrick Sale, *Dwellers in the Land: The Bioregional Vision* (San Francisco: Sierra Club Books, 1985); James J. Parsons, "On 'Bioregionalism' and 'Watershed Consciousness,'" *The Professional Geographer* 37 (1985): 1–6; Peter Berg, Beryl Magilavy, and Seth Zuckerman, *A Green City Program for San Francisco Bay Area Cities and Towns* (San Francisco: Planet Drum Books, 1989).

African Biocommunitarianism and Australian Dreamtime

J. Baird Callicott

THE AFRICAN SCENE

A Paradox

While less rich in sheer numbers of living species than tropical South America, tropical Africa is the richest place on earth for what conservation biologists call "charismatic megafauna."[1] Indeed, the mere mention of Africa conjures images in the mind's eye of wildebeests, springboks, hippopotami, rhinoceroses, zebras, giraffes, elephants, ostriches, flamingos, crocodiles, lions, leopards, cheetahs, monkeys, baboons, gorillas, chimpanzees, and many other kinds of animals. On the other hand, mention of African culture evokes no thoughts of indigenous African environmental ethics. Nor have contemporary scholars looked to African intellectual traditions, as they have to Zen Buddhism, Taoism, and American Indian thought, when casting about for conceptual resources from which to construct an exotic environmental philosophy.

This combination of circumstances is at once paradoxical and discomfiting. How could African peoples be blessed with such a wonderful complement of fellow voyagers in the odyssey of evolution and not have mirrored that singular environmental endowment in their several cultural worldviews? Perhaps they have, and both the popular new environmental movement and scholars in the even newer field of comparative environmental ethics have simply neglected African ecophilosophy.

Of course, all of us *Homo sapiens* are Africans. Our species is one among the indigenous charismatic megafauna incubated in Africa. We evolved shoulder to shoulder with our phylogenetic first cousins, the gorillas and chimpanzees. After our African genesis, we gradually dispersed throughout the world. Perhaps for those of us in the diaspora the reverence for the wildlife of Africa is like reverence for the things of home. It would be surprising to learn that our fellow Africans whose forebears remained at home during the past hundred thousand years did not share those feelings and incorporate them in their philosophies and religions.

Given these reflections, one may be stunned to discover that, generally speaking, indigenous African religions tend to be both monotheistic and anthropocentric. Most posit the existence of a high God, both literally and figuratively speaking, who created the world. And most hold that the world was created with all its creatures for the sake of humanity. Apparently reinforcing anthropocentrism is ancestor worship—the belief nearly ubiquitous in Africa that the spirits of dead relatives haunt the living and must be ritually honored, served, and propitiated.

According to the distinguished British student of African religions Geoffrey Parrinder, "most African peoples have clear beliefs in a supreme God."[2] The African philosopher J. S. Mbiti goes beyond generalization to universalization. He states categorically that "All African peoples believe in God."[3]

As to anthropocentrism, Noel Q. King makes the following claim:

> Having studied these systems [of African thought] in all of their diversity, a student is able to recognize their unity and can only then legitimately look for a paradigm, a pattern. . . . The point of departure is anthropocentric; the central and ultimate concern is with woman and man, their fullness of being and power, their health in the widest sense.[4]

. . . Even Africans who regularly hunt for a living take an anthropocentric stance toward the environment. The Lele are village dwellers and subsist primarily on the maize cultivated by the female members of the tribe, but the ritual and psychological life of the Lele centers on hunting. Yet, according to the British anthropologist Mary Douglas,

> they frequently dwell on the distinction between humans and animals, emphasizing the superiority of the former and their right to exploit the latter. . . . Of God, Njambi, they say that he has created men and animals, rivers and all things. The relation of God to men is like that of their owner to his slaves. He orders them, protects them, sets their affairs straight, and avenges injustice. Animals of the forest are also under God's power, though they have been given to the Lele for food.

This way of thinking, Douglas notes, has ominous consequences for wildlife conservation: "Game protection laws enforced by the Administration [of the Belgian Congo in the 1940s and 1950s] strike the Lele as an impious contravening of God's act, since he originally gave all the animals in the forest to their ancestors to hunt and kill."[5]

Apparently, therefore, Africa looms as a big blank spot on the world map of indigenous environmental ethics for a very good reason. African thought orbits, seemingly, around human interests. Hence one might expect to distill from it no more than a weak and indirect environmental ethic, similar to the type of ecologically enlightened utilitarianism, focused on long-range human welfare. Or perhaps one could develop a distinctly African stewardship environmental ethic grounded in African monotheism from the core belief—of Judaism, Christianity, and Islam—in God, the Creator of Heaven and Earth.

While Christianity and Islam, especially the latter, are well established in Africa, the monotheism described in the scholarly literature on indigenous African religions has a flavor all its own. And the anthropocentrism characteristic of Western utilitarianism drags in its train a lot of conceptual baggage that seems out of place in an African context. African peoples are traditionally tribal, and the typically African sense of self is bound up with family, clan, village, tribe, and, more recently, nation. To such folk, the individualistic moral ontology of utilitarianism and its associated concepts of enlightened rational self-interest, and the aggregate welfare of social atoms, each pursuing his or her own idiosyncratic "preference satisfaction," would seem foreign and incomprehensible. . . .

The Unity in Diversity of African Thought

For many centuries, the Africans north of the Sahara, from Morocco to Egypt, have been of predominantly Arab descent and predominantly Muslim in outlook. . . .

Like Christianity, Islam is an aggressive, intellectually colonizing worldview. On the continent of Africa, before the perfection of medieval transport (the camel caravan) and modern mechanized transport, the formidable Sahara Desert represented a natural barrier to human information exchange—both genetic and cultural—and the inroads of Islam were limited to Arabic centers of trade on equatorial Africa's east coast. As commerce across the Sahara was established in the eleventh and twelfth centuries, and North African Muslims increasingly frequented the Sahel, or sub-Saharan region of Africa (now including Senegal, Mali, Niger, Chad, and the Sudan), Islam predictably spread to the interior of tropical melanotic Africa.[6] Further south, as the savannah thickens to bush and the bush gives way to the forests of moist equatorial Africa, the influence and purity of Islam diminishes. Islam becomes more and more mixed with traditional African beliefs, rites, and customs. The belt of rain forest girdling central Africa constitutes a second natural barrier to human cultural diffusion, and has historically served to limit the spread of Islam to the southerly latitudes of the continent.

Christianity has enjoyed a longer but much weaker tenure in Africa. By the fourth century it had spread south into Ethiopia, but that's about as far as it got until the era of aggressive European colonialism. During the heyday of European empire in Africa, conversion to Christianity was a necessity for upward mobility in the native petite bourgeoisie created by the colonial regimes. Conversion to Christianity also meant conversion to the full spectrum—medical, educational, political—of Western beliefs, attitudes, and values. Living, so to speak, by European colonialism, the growth and vigor of Christianity stagnated with African independence. In post-colonial Africa, Christianity remains a minority family of religions, mixed with and enriched by native beliefs and rituals. Many of the new and often ephemeral cults and sects, the springing up of which has been a curious aspect of recent African religious experience, exhibit Christian foundations and motifs to one degree or another.[7]

When one turns from the relative simplicity and familiarity of North African and Sahelian Islam and Ethiopian Christianity to consider indigenous African worldviews, one is overwhelmed and bewildered by the diversity of African languages, cultures, and religions. The distinguished student of African religions E. Thomas Lawson points out that in the Niger–Congo language family alone there are over nine hundred distinct tongues, each having numerous dialects, and that traditional native African social structures range from small bands of gatherer-hunters to large kingdoms, and from small encampments and villages to ancient cities with thousands of inhabitants.[8]

On the other hand, many scholars, while keenly aware of Africa's cultural diversity, have insisted on a complementary unity. Putative unity in diversity has been approached in two ways. Geoffrey Parrinder and J. S. Mbiti both find lowest common denominators in African belief systems, as just illustrated (indeed, in the case of the latter, universal denominators). Another approach, more typical of the social sciences than the humanities, attempts to construct a cognitive taxonomy, or "typology," by means of which the myriad tribal mythologies of Africa can be categorized, abstracted, and organized by genera and species. This half of the chapter will note the authoritative claims that there are common themes in indigenous African belief systems and then pursue them in detail through reference to specific representatives.

Yoruba Anthropo-theology

The Yoruba are an agricultural people of equatorial West Africa, whose traditional tribal territory today lies mostly in Nigeria. They are well covered in the literature on African culture and belief and well represent their region of the continent intellectually. Warranting mention is the fact that elements of Yoruba belief may be found in Brazil, Jamaica, Haiti, Cuba, and the United States, having crossed the Atlantic with the slave trade.[9]

As noted, most African belief systems include a high God. The Yoruba name for the Supreme 'Being is *Olorun* or *Olodumaré*, the names meaning, in different dialects, "Owner-of-the-Sky."[10] The conceptual difference just hinted at between the typically African notion of God and the Judeo-Christian Jehovah and Muslim Allah can be understood by noting a manifest difference. So fundamental to Jewish, Christian, and Muslim religious practice is the locus of worship—the synagogue, temple, church, or mosque—that we scarcely pause to note its significance. In these related religions indigenous to the

Middle East, the high God is the only God and the direct source of human blessing, grace, misfortune, and so on. God, by whatever name, is the central actor in history, from the initial creation of the universe to the vagaries of daily weather. Hence, God is the direct object of worship and prayer. But Olorun/ Olodumaré has "no shrines . . . erected in his honor, no rituals . . . directed toward him, no sacrifices . . . made to placate him."[11] According to Parrinder, this is typical: "The general picture in Africa is that regular communal prayers to God are rare. Temples and priests are few, and found only among certain tribes."[12] Yoruba religious sites (shrines, temples, and the like) and religious practice (prayers, rituals, divination, and sacrifice) are far from rare, but center on a variety of subordinate spirits—called the *orisa*—instead of on the high God. According to Noel King, comparativists have thus been led to declare Olorun/Olodumaré "otiose, 'superfluous, out of circuit, supernumerary.'"[13]

Naturally, there has been scholarly speculation about this religious happenstance. According to one hypothesis, belief in a Supreme Being is not native to tropical Africa. It was gradually acquired from the literary religions of the Middle East over many centuries of incidental cultural contact and diffusion.[14] Eventually, belief in a Supreme Being was tacked onto—or, to shift metaphors, papered over—the many forms of polyspiritualism native to the region, or so this story goes. Therefore, lip service is paid to the (originally foreign) high God throughout Africa, while sincere, genuinely native ritual service to the indigenous gods proceeds as before, hardly affected by the intellectually alien accretion.

According to a hypothesis favored by J. S. Mbiti and also the African scholars Joseph B. Danqua and E. Bolaji Idowu, however, belief in a high God is as indigenous to Africa as it is widespread. Further, the cult spirits are not separate entities existing apart from the Supreme Being. They are, rather, Spinozistic modes and attributes of the one high God.[15] As Christians manage to believe in one God and three divine persons—Father, Son, and Holy Spirit— so the Yoruba believe in one divinity, Olorun/Olodumaré, who has multiple personalities and manifestations: the *orisa*. One or another of the *orisa* may have particular sites of worship, be addressed in prayer or sacrifice, and ritually served, depending on locale, season, and circumstance. Thus Olorun/ Olodumaré is, according to this hypothesis, hardly neglected in actual Yoruba religious practice. On the contrary, all prayers, services, sacrifices, and rites are ultimately addressed to him in his various guises. . . .

Fundamental to Yoruba cosmology is a division between sky (*orun*) and earth (*aiye*). Chief of the sky spirits is, of course, the remote and unapproachable Olorun, its "owner." The *orisa* and/or . . . departed ancestors are also residents of the sky. The number of *orisa* is large and indeterminate. Some are worshiped only by one clan in one village; others restrict their influence to but one region of Yoruba-land; still others are known to all Yoruba.

Myth, of course, is never entirely systematic or internally consistent, and one should not be exasperated if in addition to Olorun/Olodumaré the Yoruba should also speak of another spirit who had a hand in creation, *Orisa-nla*, also called *Obatala*. This being seems to be next in the hierarchy of sky dwellers, and in some quarters is particularly associated with the shaping of the human body.

Orunmila is the chief god of divination—though one may inquire of other spirits about things hidden from human ken, like the future, the cause of illness, lost objects, and so on.

Esu is a complex Yoruba spirit whom the Christian and Muslim missionaries identified with Satan. This unfortunate association seems to have arisen because Esu tries to trick people into misconduct, as does the Christian–Muslim devil. (Anthropologists draw a parallel of their own, to the "trickster" figures like Coyote and Nanabushu in American Indian narrative cycles.) Unlike the devil, however, Esu's intent is good, not evil; he provides people with the occasion to exercise self-restraint, or, if they succumb to temptation, to expiate their miscreancy through sacrifices to the gods. Esu also mediates between the people and the spirits on high. . . .

In *Shango,* one finally comes upon a being in the Yoruba pantheon who seems to be a bona fide nature spirit; he is the storm god, whose most powerful manifestation is thunder and lightning. Among his symbols are rams and the double-headed axe. The rivers are his wives.

Ogun is also plausibly interpreted as a nature spirit. He is associated with wild animals and the hunt and with iron. His personality is violent and impulsive.

The ecological alter ego of Ogun is *Orisa-oko*, the peaceful and benign god of firming and cultivation.

The Yoruba, it would seem significant for this study, also believe that the earth is a maternal goddess, *Ile.* For reasons that remain obscure, smallpox was (until eliminated) believed to be the "arm" or sanction imposed by Ile on those who did not respect her. . . .

In any case, even from the scant information recounted here, one can see that the representative Yoruba cannot be simply assimilated to Judeo–Christian–Islamic monotheism. Therefore—given the very un-Western hierarchical pantheon, headed by a remote high God—a corresponding stewardship environmental ethic would not seem fitting. On the other hand, the *orisa* are on the whole not exactly nature spirits either, such as those encountered among native North Americans; thus an animist environmental ethic similar to that found in traditional Sioux or Ojibwa culture would appear no less forced and implausible.

Indeed, Yoruba belief does not fit into any of the three classic nineteenth-century religious categories just mentioned—monotheism, polytheism, and animism (or fetishism). The *orisa* seem more like deified ancestors than like "gods" or personified forms and forces of nature, even when they are linked with aspects of nature. Perhaps "ancestor worship" lies at the core of typically African systems of belief. . . .

Typical of the African outlook, the Yoruba worldview is this-worldly, not other-worldly. Since the dead are not packed off to another world, they remain concerned with and involved in the affairs of the living. (In this regard it is perhaps worth remembering that spirits reside in the sky, not in a realm beyond it.) Relations with socially important and influential relatives are maintained after they are deceased. The ritual nature of these relations has given rise to the common though somewhat misleading characterization of them as "ancestor worship."

But ancestor worship is a natural response to something in addition to the problem of what to do about the spirits of the dead when there is no Other World for them to go to. It is a natural response to a peculiar sense of personal identity or sense of self. Personal identity in Yoruba thinking is far more corporate than in modern Western atomic individualism. Mbiti has succinctly expressed the African view: "Whatever happens to the individual happens to the whole group, and whatever happens to the whole group happens to the individual."[16] Expressing the same thought more formally, the sociologist of religion Benjamin C. Ray writes, "African philosophy tends to define persons in terms of the social groups to which they belong. A person is thought of first of all as a *constituent* of a particular community, for it is the community that defines who he is and who he may become."[17]

An African's identity, nevertheless, is not confined to his or her role in the community. . . . Each individual is a distinct person, with his or her unique blend of personality, needs, desires, talents, and destiny. But, far more vividly than in the modern Western worldview, individuality is not only counterbalanced by community identity but one's unique individuality is defined in part by one's social relationships and expressed through social interaction.

This idea is especially reinforced by one aspect of Yoruba ancestor worship. The *ori* is the inner substance of an individual's essence—his or her soul, as it were. But the *ori* is also understood to be "the partial rebirth or reincarnation of a patrilineal ancestor."[18] Hence, what individuates one— one's *ori*—is drawn from a communal pool of personalities. Throughout one's life, one lives both as and for oneself and reexpresses the essence and destiny of a forebear. As Ray puts it, "Freedom and individuality are always balanced by destiny and community, and these in turn are balanced by natural and supernatural powers. Every person is a *nexus* of interacting elements of the self and the world which shape and are shaped by his behavior."[19] [Emphasis added.]

In this notion of embedded individuality—of individuality as a nexus of communal relationships—we may have the germ of an African environmental ethic. Add to the intense sense of social embeddedness an equally vivid sense of embeddedness in the *biotic* community, and anthropocentric African communitarianism might then be transformed into a nonanthropocentric African environmentalism. Indeed, traditional Africans may be better prepared to respond to contemporary ecology's story of a natural economy and social order than those of us who remain in the grip of the modern Western worldview. The traditional African is accustomed to think of personal identity and destiny as intimately bound up with community, while "the Western notion of individualism—the idea that men are essentially independent of their social and historical circumstances," as Ray characterizes it, may prevent unregenerately modern Westerners from internalizing the moral implications of ecology.[20]

A San Etiquette of Freedom

"San" is the preferred name of the south-central African people often called "bushmen," of which the Kalahari Desert !Kung are the best known. . . . Of all indigenous African peoples, the San may be an exception to the general non-association of traditional African cultures with responsible environmental attitudes and values.

Nonetheless, one looks in vain through the anthropological and ethnographic literature on the San for evidence of a sense of gratitude toward fellow members of the biotic community. . . .

The San seem to be no less matter-of-fact in their relations with supernatural entities. They believe in a creator high God who is, according to Lee, characteristically remote and inaccessible.[21] They also believe in a lower God who is something of a trickster. According to the folklorist Megan Biesele, this god began life as a human being and "later ascended to the sky and became divine." The stories of Kauha-the-trickster's tricks "are heard with anything but awed reverence. Instead, amused indignation greets the outrageous or bumbling adventures."[22]

Both Lee and Biesele report that according to San myth in the beginning all creatures were human beings, "persons of the early race."[23] In their originally human condition, moreover, the creatures who were eventually transformed into animals exhibited the personality traits that presently typify their species. One may immediately infer from this mythic particular that the San personify animal behavior. They regard the unusually diverse wildlife in their environment as a community of subjects—a community composed of beings animated by essentially the same consciousness enjoyed by a human being. This inference is confirmed by empirical studies of San beliefs about wildlife.[24] The San worldview puts human and nonhuman beings on the same metaphysical and psychological plane, the institution of insulting the meat notwithstanding. In some practical sense, therefore, the San regard themselves as "plain members and citizens" of the biotic community. . . .

For the San, success in hunting seems to be premised simply and squarely on skill and luck. As to skill, the San are perhaps most renowned for their ability to track and to read spoor. They are also very knowledgeable about animal behavior.[25] As to luck, that depends on the whereabouts of the game, which in turn depends on the moods, whims, and wiles of the beasts themselves, who are apparently believed to be no less interested in self-preservation than properly human beings are. In comparison with their North American counterparts, San hunter-gatherers seem to be members of a less enchanted, more everyday biotic community—though . . . one no less inwardly alive and shot through with subjectivity.

The difference may lie in the prehistoric human ecology of Africa and North America. In Africa, predatory *Homo sapiens* coevolved with the other fauna of the continent. In pre-Columbian North America, *Homo sapiens* were recent immigrants (by evolutionary measures of time), who encountered innocent, inexperienced populations of game. The encounter apparently led to tragedy—to the extinction of more than thirty genera of North American fauna and to a consequent post-Pleistocene New World human population explosion and crash.[26] The cultural evolution of explicit North American environmental ethics, such as that of the Ojibwa, may have been a dialectical response to this debacle.

Despite enthusiastic hunting by indigenous *Homo sapiens,* Africa retained into the historical period its populations of elephants, zebras, and camels, while similar fauna were extirpated in North America. In Africa the animals may have taken care of themselves—may have evolved defensive measures adequate to ensure their species' survival. If so, there would have been no cause, as there was in North America, for the cultural evolution of explicit indigenous environmental ethics. In any case, according to Richard Lee, "Whatever the nature of their gods and ghosts, the !Kung do not spend their time in philosophical discourse (except when anthropologists prod them). They are more concerned with the concrete matters of life and death, health and illness in their daily lives."[27]

However little reflection the traditional San may give the matter, they behave as though they regarded themselves as plain members and citizens of the biotic community. A window into San biocommunitarianism is provided by Elizabeth Marshall Thomas in a 1990 essay in *The New Yorker.* She writes,

> What mattered to the integrity of the environment was that human hunter-gatherers had been there long enough to count as ecologically indigenous. . . . The ecosystem absorbed the impact of its people, who in vast areas of the Kalahari are the only primates, as it absorbed the impact of, say, its lions.[28]

A major—and beneficial—impact of its people on the Kalahari ecosystem was secondary but critical. The San set fires, and the fire regime in the Kalahari is a principal determinant of the structure of the floral community, favoring grasses and suppressing thornbushes.[29] Because the former are palatable and nutritious for the antelope and other grazers, the traditional human population was indeed the keystone species, in large measure responsible for a productive, diverse, and healthy biotic community. . . .

However little the San folkloric record may reflect their respect for fellow members of the biotic community, the ecological and ethological records testify to an accommodation both with the game and with other predators. The prey species remained abundant. They were not overhunted. The San venatic equipment was simple, fit only for securing enough meat to supplement a diet consisting mostly of vegetable foodstuffs.[30] Continued development even of Stone Age technology is certainly conceivable. Why was it not pursued? Nor did the San attempt to eradicate species such as lions, leopards, and hyenas, which competed with the San for game. Here again, a systematic campaign of removal is conceivable, even with Stone Age weapons. Again, why was it not pursued? One can only assume that the San, as suggested by their scanty cosmogony, regarded themselves as one with the other fauna and practiced a quiet policy of live and let live with their nonhuman neighbors. . . .

AUSTRALIAN ABORIGINAL CONSERVATORS

The aboriginal peoples of Australia are also sometimes referred to as bushmen. And indeed, they have more than a few things in common with the San. The Australian aborigines were (and some still are) traditional hunter-gatherers, with all that that implies economically and socially.[31] The majority still live in arid environments. Ancestors play a prominent role in their belief systems. And the beings in their native mythologies were at first human and later took on animal form.

From the perspective of this study, however, the bushmen of Africa and the bushmen of Australia differ profoundly in their verbally manifest environmental attitudes and values. While the San seem to have been well integrated into the interspecies community of the Kalahari Desert and to have remained in balance with their nonhuman neighbors, San mythology lacks elaborately articulated paradigms of interspecies relationships and—unlike San painting—does not celebrate or sanctify the landscape. In contrast, the Australian aborigines verbally as well as graphically express a very intimate and morally charged sense of relationship with other species and with the topography of their territories. Accordingly, Australian aboriginal thought is beginning to attract the same sort of attention from contemporary environmentalists that North American Indian thought has enjoyed. Most notably, perhaps, the nature-poet laureate of the United States, Gary Snyder, has touched on the ecophilosophical significance of Australian aboriginal attitudes toward nature in his book of beautiful essays, *The Practice of the Wild.*

At first glance, like Africa, Australia confronts the casual student with a bewildering diversity of native peoples—about five hundred tribes (defined as a group of people speaking a mutually intelligible language), according to the dean of Australian anthropology, A. P. Elkin.[32] But a closer look reveals an anthropological commonality greater than in Africa or, for that matter, in the Americas. All native Australians are of one racial stock. All were foragers, practicing no gardening or herding. Further, Australian languages and social structures have many similar features. . . .

One also finds an amazing unity in the cognitive culture of Australian aboriginals. . . . It would seem appropriate to sketch the Australian aboriginal worldview in profile, illustrating it by reference to this or that tribal detail, since in its general features it seems to have been virtually omnipresent on the continent. The environmental attitudes and values implicit in this composite native Australian belief system may then be spelled out.

Elements of an Australian Worldview

Australian aboriginal mythology is referred to as "The Dreaming" or "Dreamtime"—alternative translations of the Aranda word *alcheringa*.[33] The contemporary convention of capitalizing these terms indicates that they are better understood as proper names than as descriptive nouns. "The Dreaming," read literally, suggests that Australian aboriginal mythology originated in and was sustained by dreams. However, while dreams per se seem to play a vital part in the spiritual life of native Australia, their role is not as large as the name would suggest.[34] "Dreamtime" seems to be the less misleading term, since the reference is to a special sort of time—the familiar time of the mythic human mind, a time that is at once long past and existing alongside the present, perhaps as dreams exist parallel to waking experience. Elkin captures its dual sense of both long ago and right now, and its similarity to dreams: "the eternal dream-time—a time which is past and yet present, partaking of the nature of the dreamlife, unfettered by the limitations set by time and space."[35] Gary Snyder characterizes Dreamtime as "the mode of the eternal moment of creating, of being, as contrasted with the mode of cause and effect in time." And he has insightfully suggested further similarities between dreams proper and Dreamtime, "a time of fluidity, shape-shifting interspecies conversation and intersexuality." In this realm there occurred "radically creative moves, whole landscapes being altered."[36]

In the beginning, there was the sky and the land. But the land was featureless. "Culture heroes" or "ancestral beings" traveled the land along specific routes or "tracks." As they went, they transformed it, establishing hills here, ravines there, water holes yonder, and other topographical formations. The Australian religions scholar Nancy Munn reports that in Walbiri mythology "the ancestor first dreams his . . . travels—the country, the songs and everything he makes—inside his head before they are externalized."[37] The doings of these mythic beings at various sites along their travel routes also establish the rites and ceremonies for their human progeny to reenact on location, so to speak. How the ancestral beings did the things they did, like cooking animals in their skins and observing incest taboos, establishes "the Laws" (mores) of the tribes. Part of what it means to be an aboriginal person is to observe the Law.[38] . . .

The ancestral beings were human but also had the characteristics of various animals—such as the emu, kangaroo, bandicoot, or red flying fox—into which they would eventually transform themselves. When their walkabouts were complete, each ancestral being "went down" or "in" at a certain spot.[39]

Such spots are called "increase sites." There the spiritual power, essence, or life force of the ancestor permanently resides. From that site are born both the animals whose specific form the ancestral being assumed and the people who also happen to be its progeny. Since these culture heroes are the ancestors both of certain people and of certain animals, those people and those animals are of one kind, so to speak. Thus arises Australian aboriginal totemism. Some people are emus, some are kangaroos, others bandicoots, still others red flying foxes, and so on. . . .

It is necessary to stress the site and species particularity of the ancestral beings. Each mythic person in the Dreamtime is associated with its peculiar species and its particular increase site, though other sites may be associated with its wanderings and doings. David Bennett notes, "For example, if in Aranda country there is a water hole that is the [increase] site of Karora, the bandicoot, then that is the source for bandicoots and humans of the bandicoot totem. It is not a site, for example, of green parrots or red flying foxes."[40] In some instances, the particularity may extend to individual spirits. . . .

For the most part, the members of one group will all belong to the same local totem. And it falls to them to maintain the sacred sites marking the adventures along the tracks of the ancestral being who went down in their territory, even when these places happen to be in the vicinity of another ancestral being's increase site. They must also perform a cycle of rites and ceremonies, the patterns for which were set out by the actions of their ancestral being. Most important, at the increase site of their totemic ancestor, they must perform the annual "increase ceremony."

The purpose of an increase ceremony is to ensure the plentifulness of a species—the totem species of the group performing the ceremony. The object is not to bring about an occurrence contrary to the usual workings of nature but to assist and encourage the natural course of events.[41] The traditional Australian aboriginals believe that the neglect of increase ceremonies will result in abnormal declines in the respective species populations. Such declines, when they occur, are blamed on those totemites who must have been derelict in their duties. The efficacy of the increase ceremonies, the other ceremonies, and the Law manifest the same principle in Australian aboriginal thought— the rejuvenation by means of reenactment of the events of the past. Thus continuity of all life through time can be maintained, and both the order of human society and the order of nature, in which human society is embedded and on which it depends, can be preserved. . . .

In addition to maintaining the totemic species population, the persons whose totem the species is are forbidden at times to kill and eat members of that species, or may eat only ceremonial morsels on ritual occasions. "For most groups," according to Bennett, "the totem may not be eaten or harmed in certain seasons or at certain locations."[42] And other taboos may restrict a person's activities in respect to his or her totem species, or in respect to the totems of certain classifications of kin.

As this brief sketch suggests, Australian aboriginal mythology is extremely rich, subtle, and complex. Indeed, Australian aborigines seem to have been at the opposite end of the spectrum of inclination to abstract speculation from their African counterparts. Aboriginal Australia evidently has consisted of a checkerboard of tribes and subgroups sharing a mythic worldview that is deeply rooted in the topography of the continent. Each local community provides a single tile, or small collection of tiles, in a single mosaic of ideas laid out on the landscape. . . .

The Dreamtime is also a map of the countryside. As the mythology celebrates the wanderings of the ancestral beings, the several cycles of songs coordinate the deeds of the heroes with landmarks. In journeying from place to place through the literally roadless outback, an aboriginal follows the tracks of an ancestral being, navigating from sacred site—distinguished by peculiar geographical features—to sacred site by means of the relevant song. Gary Snyder was particularly impressed with this aspect of the Dreamtime when he visited Australia. Each of the "special places" to which he was taken by his aboriginal guides was "out of the ordinary, fantastic even, and sometimes rich with life." Snyder mentions a place with "several unique boulders, each face and facet a surprise." He was charmed by "a sudden opening out of a hidden steep defile where two cliffs meet with just a little sandbed between, and some green bushes, some parrots calling, . . . [and by] a water hole you wouldn't guess was there, where a thirty-foot blade of rock stands on end, balancing."[43]

An Australian Environmental Ethic

If an environmental philosopher were to make up a "traditional" worldview from which environmental ethical implications would follow, he or she would find it hard to come up with anything more apt than what the Australian aboriginal peoples have actually articulated. Theirs is a worldview that at once unites human beings with the land and with the other forms of life on the land. . . .

The Australian aboriginal mind seems to have been deeply conservative—not, of course, in the contemporary political sense of the term but in its literal sense. In the Dreamtime, the past is in some way also the future, since the continued order of human life and of nature is perpetuated through the ritual reenactment of the heroic age. As Elkin succinctly puts it, "Sanctity, sanction, and life arise from the heroic and life-giving past. Conservatism and the maintenance of continuity with the past play an important part in the life . . . of the Aborigines."[44] Confirming Elkin, Berndt holds that "the 'deities' were not only creators but the stimulators of continuity: their power, released through human rituals, ensures the maintenance of the status quo."[45] Since natural features of the landscape are the enduring monuments to the deeds of the ancestral beings, then maintaining continuity with the past entails conserving the distinctive topography of Australia, be it forest, savannah, or desert.

One might therefore expect that contemporary Australian aboriginal groups would be at the forefront of resistance to land-defacing development in Australia. And according to Annette Hamilton, they are: From the aboriginal point of view, the acceptability of a development scheme

> depends on the nature of the development, where it is, and what level of local transformations may be expected. Is the proposed development going to affect a large and significant sacred site or complex? Will it involve going under the ground in a limited way (oil wells) or in a large way (open-cut mining)? Will it involve roads that cut across traditional ritual pathways for carrying ceremonial objects from place to place? Will it involve towers that overlook vast areas including sacred sites and tracks? Will it cut across dreaming tracks in such a way as to "break" them?[46]

Hamilton raises the question of whether or not one can legitimately speak of "management" by traditional Australian aboriginal peoples as well as conservancy. Though they did not cultivate crops or herd animals, Australian aborigines judiciously employed fire to promote the kind of vegetation useful to themselves and to other animal species.[47] Moreover, there is considerable support for the view that the spectrum of behaviors and behavioral limitations surrounding totemism helped to prevent the overexploitation of native species. If by "management" one means the conscious adaptation of means to ends, then the Dreaming was not management. But like the social representation of nature among the Ojibwa and the seminal representation of energy flows among the Tukano, the Australian Dreamtime seems to have been a crucial element in the ecological adaptation of the people to the land.

More than anyone else, David Bennett has concerned himself with the specifically environmental attitudes and values implicit in Australian aboriginal thought. He thinks that indeed there existed a "conservation effect," especially in regard to native beliefs and associated practices, that prohibited the overuse of economically exploited species. As Bennett characterizes Australian aboriginal taboos concerning other species, they seem functionally equivalent to the game laws enacted by Europeans and their cultural progeny.

Bennett believes that the Aranda and other groups placed a severe restriction on eating one's own totem species not out of respect either for the species or its several specimens but out of respect for one's future spirit children, who may currently be inhabiting the bodies of one's totem, and for one's ancestors. (Only a token amount of totem meat, as in the Christian eucharist, he claims, may be consumed on ceremonial occasions—although during periods of protracted drought the taboo on nonritual consumption by totemites could be violated with impunity.) But he argues that the effect of this prohibition—whether or not it was consciously motivated—was conservation: "In a land with relatively few individuals of some species, prohibiting a segment of the human population from eating that species eases the pressure of human predation and promotes the continued existence of that species."[48]

Further, the increase site itself and its environs were "posted," so to speak, and no hunting or gathering of anything was allowed in the precinct of the sanctum sanctorum. It also had to be approached along the ritual track that the ancestral being had established, and sometimes, according to Bennett, "the proper approach extends to walking backwards." In any case, the conservation effect of this taboo was the creation of "game reserves."[49] On this point, Bennett has the support of the Australian anthropologist T. G. H. Strehlow, who comments that "many of the finest water holes . . . provided inviolable sanctuaries for kangaroo," and "while there is no evidence to show that the Aranda *pmara kutata* [increase sites] had intentionally been created as game reserves," that was in fact the result.[50]

In line with Strehlow's suggestion that there may have been a program of game management encoded in the geomancy of the Australian aborigines, the Australian zoologist A. E. Newsome found that "in Aranda mythology, the major totemic sites for the red kangaroo coincide with the most favorable habitat for the species."[51] Totemic sites in places where there is no habitat for the totem species are not likely to have been instituted in the mythology. One would hardly expect to find an increase site for, say, waterfowl miles from the nearest water. So a coincidence such as Newsome notes is not really noteworthy. Rather, what is notable is the prohibition of exploitation in the best habitat. . . .

Another basic technique of European and Euro-American "rational" or "scientific" game management is the establishment of "closed seasons," coinciding with the nesting of fowl, the suckling of mammals, and so on. David Bennett reports that among the aborigines of central Australia, "between the performance of an increase ceremony and the time when the ceremony is considered to have had its effect, eating the totemic species is normally restricted."[52] The time when the ceremony is considered to have had its effect presumably is the time when the young actually start to appear. . . .

The main reasons for formulating an interspecies ethic are to preserve species, which the world is losing at an abnormal rate, and more generally to abate practices destructive of other aspects of the environment. And these desiderata the Australian aboriginal worldview seems admirably adapted, if not actually designed, to achieve. Deborah Rose is more on target, in comparing an

Australian aboriginal environmental ethic to the holistic Leopold land ethic rather than to an ethic primarily concerned with minimizing animal suffering.[53] Undeniably and unequivocally, Australian aboriginal totemism and associated increase ceremonies evidence a keen sense of kinship with and mutual dependency on other creatures, and express a concern for the flourishing of species populations. No less certainly, Australian aboriginal thought manifests a deep and abiding investment in place. The importance of "storied residence" for a "contextualized" environmental ethic has been stressed in the recent literature of environmental ethics and Deep Ecology.

For example, the American environmental philosopher Holmes Rolston, III, maintains that "an environmental ethic does not want merely to abstract out universals, if such there are, from all this drama of life, formulating some set of duties applicable across the whole." Then—without reference to (and almost certainly without a thought for) Australian aboriginal belief—he continues in terms that nevertheless evoke the mythogeography of aboriginal Australia:

> An ethic is not just a theory but a track through the world. . . . If a holistic ethic is really to incorporate the whole story, it must systematically embed itself in historical eventfulness, or else it will not really be objective. It will not be appropriate, well-adapted to the way humans actually fit their niches. . . . An environmental ethic needs roots in locality and in specific appreciation of natural kinds—not always rooted in a single place, but moving through particular regions and tracks of nature so as to make a narrative career, a storied residence.[54]

And one might say without undue exaggeration that for Gary Snyder "a sense of place" lies at the foundation of any genuine and practical environmental ethic. Bennett writes, "Land gives Aborigines their identity. They are at home."[55] Snyder's warm and personal portrait of his aboriginal hosts and their historically eventful storied residence in their Australian homelands brings vividly to life Bennett's dry declaration. Snyder writes:

> Our place is part of what we are. Yet even a "place" has a kind of fluidity: it passes through space and time—"ceremonial time". . . . It is not enough just to "love nature" or to want to "be in harmony with Gaia." Our relation to our natural world takes place in a *place,* and it must be grounded in information and experience.[56]

Perhaps more clearly and vividly than any other peoples on the planet, the Australian aboriginals have articulated their sense of self in terms of place. According to the Australian environmental philosopher Val Plumwood.

> Aboriginal culture [is] a model of bioregionalism. Identity is not connected to nature as a general abstract category (as urged upon us by the proponents of Deep Ecology), but to particular areas of land, just as the connection one has to close

relatives is highly particularistic and involves special attachments and obligations not held to humankind in general. And in complete contrast to Western views of land and nature as only accidentally related to self and as interchangeable means to human satisfaction, the land is conceptualized as just as essentially related to self as kin are, and its loss may be as deeply grieved for and felt as the death of kin.[57]

As this chapter ends, I pause to think of my own "place," my own spirit land. I find myself falling into a mode of consciousness that is human and natural, yet a mode of consciousness so unmodern and un-Western that imaginative immersion in a worldview from the other side of the earth is required to awaken it in me. I wonder what it would be like to stand in reverential silence in the fastness of a particular and familiar crane marsh and think to myself—and feel in my bones—that out of this watery wild both came I and the big birds trumpeting over the tamaracks. This place is the Crane, and I am a crane. Or so I dream.

NOTES

1. Brian J. Huntly, "Conserving and Monitoring Biotic Diversity: Some African Examples," in E.O. Wilson, ed., *Biodiversity* (Washington, D.C.: National Academy Press, 1988), pp. 248–60.

2. Geoffrey Parrinder, *African Traditional Religion* (New York: Harper & Row, 1976), p. 32.

3. J. S. Mbiti, *Introduction to African Religion* (London: Heinemann, 1975), p. 40.

4. Noel Q. King, *African Cosmos: An Introduction to Religion in Africa* (Belmont, CA: Wadsworth, 1986), p. 4.

5. Mary Douglas, "The Lele of Kasai," in Daryll Forde, ed., *African Worlds: Studies in the Cosmological Ideas and Social Values of African Peoples* (London: Oxford University Press, 1954), p. 9.

6. Benjamin C. Ray, *African Religions: Symbol, Ritual, and Community* (Upper Saddle River, NJ: Prentice Hall, 1976).

7. Ibid.

8. E.Thomas Lawson, *Religions of Africa: Traditions in Transformation* (San Francisco: Harper & Row, 1984), pp. 5–6.

9. King, *African Cosmos*; Lawson, *Religions of Africa*.

10. Lawson, *Religions of Africa*, p. 57.

11. Ibid., p. 58.

12. Parrinder, *African Traditional Religion*, p. 39.

13. King, *African Cosmos*, p. 9.

14. See C. G. Seligman, *Races of Africa* (London: Oxford University Press, 1930).

15. J. B. Danqua, *Akan Doctrine of God* (London: Frank Cass, 1968); E. B. Idowu, *Olodumaré: God in Yoruba Belief* (London: SCM Press, 1973); J.S. Mbiti, *African Religions and Philosophy* (New York: Anchor Books, 1970).

16. Mbiti, *African Religions*, p. 141.

17. Ray, *African Religions*, p. 132.

18. Ibid., p. 134.

19. Ibid., p. 132.

20. Ibid.

21. Laurens Van der Post, *The Lost World of the Kalahari* (New York: William Morrow, 1958), pp. 106–7.

22. Megan Biesele, "Aspects of !Kung Folklore," in Richard B. Lee and Irven DeVore, eds., *Kalahari Hunter-Gatherers: Studies of the !Kung San and Their Neighbors* (Cambridge: Harvard University Press, 1976), pp. 310, 308.

23. The quoted phrase is from Van der Post, *Lost World of the Kalahari,* p. 26.

24. Nicholas Blurton Jones and Melvin J. Conner, "!Kung Knowledge of Animal Behavior (or: The Proper Study of Mankind Is Animals)," in Lee and De Vore, eds., *Kalahari Hunter-Gatherers,* pp. 325–48.

25. Van der Post, *Lost World of the Kalahari,* p. 15.

26. See Paul S. Martin, "The Discovery of America," *Science* 179: 969–74.

27. Richard B. Lee, *The Dobe !Kung* (New York: Holt, Rinehart & Winston, 1984).

28. Elizabeth Marshall Thomas, "Reflections: The Old Way," *The New Yorker* (October 15, 1990), p. 80.

29. Thomas, "Reflections."

30. Lee, *The Dobe !Kung.*

31. See Richard B. Lee and Irven DeVore, eds., *Man the Hunter* (Chicago:Aldine, 1966).

32. A. P. Elkin, *The Australian Aborigines* (New York: Doubleday, 1964), p. 12.

33. See W. E. H. Stanner, *The White Man Got No Dreaming: Essays 1938–1973* (Canberra: Australian National University Press, 1979), pp. 23–40.

34. Ibid.

35. Elkin, *Australian Aborigines,* p. 206.

36. Gary Snyder, *The Practice of the Wild* (San Francisco: North Point Press, 1990), p. 84.

37. Nancy D. Munn, "The Transformation of Subjects into Objects in Walbiri and Pitjantjara Myth,"in M. Charlesworth, H. Morphy, D. Bell, and K. Maddock, eds., *Religion in Aboriginal Australia: An Anthology* (St. Lucia: University of Queensland Press, 1984), p. 61.

38. Annette Hamilton, "Culture Conflict and Resource Management in Central Australia," in Paul A. Olson, ed., *The Struggle for the Land: Indigenous Insight and Industrial Empire in the Semiarid World* (Lincoln: University of Nebraska Press, 1990).

39. See Munn,"The Transformation of Subjects into Objects," pp. 57–82, for a very thorough account of this process and its social and psychological implications.

40. David H. Bennett, *Inter-species Ethics: Australian Perspectives, A Cross-cultural Study of Attitudes Towards Nonhuman Animal Species* (Canberra: Preprint Series in Environmental Philosophy no. 14, Department of Philosophy. Australian National University, 1986), p. 103.

41. Bennett, *Inter-species Ethics;* and Elkin, *Australian Aborigines.*

42. Bennett, *Inter-species Ethics,* p. 108.

43. Snyder, *Practice,* p. 84.

44. Elkin, *Australian Aborigines,* p. 208.

45. R. M. Berndt,"Traditional Morality as Expressed through the Medium of an Australian Aboriginal Religion," in Charlesworth et al., eds., *Religion in Aboriginal Australia,* pp. 176–77.

46. Hamilton, "Culture Conflict,"p. 221.

47. See Rhys Jones, "Fire-stick Farming," *Australian Natural History* 16 (1969): 224–28; and D. R. Horton, "The Burning Question: Aborigines, Fire, and Australian Ecosystems," *Mankind* 13 (1982): 237–51.

48. Bennett, "Inter-species Ethics," p. 137.

49. Ibid., p. 130.

50. T. G. H. Strehlow, "Culture, Social Structure, and Environment in Aboriginal Central Australia," in R. M. Berndt and C. H. Berndt, eds., *Aboriginal Man in Australia* (Sydney: Angus & Robertson, 1965), p. 144.

51. A. E. Newsome, "The Eco-mythology of the Red Kangaroo in Central Australia," *Mankind* 12 (1980): 327.

52. Bennett, "Inter-species Ethics," p. 133.

53. Rose, "Exploring an Aboriginal Land Ethic."

54. Holmes Rolston III, *Environmental Ethics: Duties to and Values in the Natural World* (Philadelphia: Temple University Press, 1988), pp. 349–52.

55. Bennett, "Inter-species Ethics," p. 157.

56. Snyder, *Practice,* pp. 27, 39.

57. Val Plumwood, "Plato and the Bush: Philosophy and Environment in Australia," *Meanjin* 49 (1990): 531.

Aesthetics and the Value of Nature

Janna Thompson

Like many environmental philosophers, I find the idea that the beauty of wildernesses makes them valuable in their own right and gives us a moral duty to preserve and protect them to be attractive. However, this appeal to aesthetic value encounters a number of serious problems. I argue that these problems can best be met and overcome by recognizing that the appreciation of natural environments and the appreciation of great works of arts are activities more similar than many people have supposed.

I

Nature is beautiful. Few people would doubt that this claim, and the aesthetic value of an environment is something that often figures as a consideration in environmental planning and development. In this context, the beauty of a forest or river is treated alongside "recreational use" as an instrumental value: beauty is understood to be whatever happens to delight people. Because individuals are pleased by different things and fashions in taste are subject to change, an appeal to beauty thus seems to make a weak case for preservation. However, philosophers and environmentalists have sometimes argued that beauty is not a mere instrumental value and not merely a matter of personal taste, and that when properly appreciated, the existence of natural beauty is a good reason for its preservation. G. E. Moore regarded beauty, whether in nature or art, as an intrinsic good, something worthy of respect for its own sake, and therefore something we have an ethical duty to promote.[1] Eugene Hargrove develops this view into an argument for the preservation of nature: "Since the loss of both natural and artistic beauty represents a loss in the total good in the world, it is our duty to try to preserve both kinds of beauty as best we can."[2]

Like Moore, Hargrove is saying that a thing of beauty has a value in its own right. Aesthetic value cannot be reduced to the capacity to give us pleasure or feelings of awe and wonder. Their way of understanding beauty or, more generally, aesthetic value seems to answer much better to the desire of preservationists and deep ecologists to find noninstrumental ways of valuing nature.[3] Moreover, aesthetic worth is something that people can come to identify with and appreciate, and thus it seems that the appeal to the beauty of nature can provide a more satisfactory and defensible ground for preservation than do appeals to an inherent value that is independent of the human point of view. I have argued elsewhere that a conception of value in nature that transcends human concerns leaves it unclear what in nature is to be regarded as valuable in its own right, and thus does not provide us with the basis for a practical ethic.[4] For those who have similar concerns, Hargrove's attempt to derive an ethical position from the aesthetic value of nature seems like a promising direction to take: justice can be done to the deep ecological intuition that nature is intrinsically valuable and at the same time we can obtain, it seems, a well-grounded understanding of what our duties are. The critical issues are whether and how this promise can be fulfilled.

II

Most people can be persuaded that art has a value that is not merely instrumental. We do think that great works of art are worthy of respect, that we ought to make an effort to appreciate them (and that those who do not are Philistines), and that anyone who tries to destroy or damage them deserves moral condemnation. Because nature too is beautiful, it seems reasonable to insist that the same attitudes and prohibitions should be extended to natural things.

However, the success of this argument clearly depends upon our being able to establish that aesthetic value, whether in art or in nature, is intrinsic, noninstrumental, value. It also depends crucially on the objectivity of our value claims. The link that Moore and Hargrove want to make between aesthetic judgment and ethical obligation fails unless there are objective grounds—grounds that rational, sensitive people can accept—for thinking that something has value. If beauty in nature or in art is merely in the eyes of the beholder, then no general moral obligation arises out of aesthetic judgments, except the weaker obligation to preserve, if possible, what some individuals happen to value. A judgment of value that is merely personal and subjective gives us no way of arguing that everyone ought to learn to appreciate something, or at least to regard it as worthy of preservation.[5]

To insist that value judgments must be objective in this sense does not require us to suppose that beauty and other aesthetic values are real properties of objects. Nor do we have to suppose that the value of works of art or nature is independent of human perceivers. Claims to aesthetic objectivity clearly raise ontological questions about the nature of value. However, it is not necessary to settle metaphysical questions about beauty in order to defend the idea that our aesthetic judgments are, or can be, objective. We can and do give reasons for our aesthetic judgments. Critics are expected to provide a justification for why they think a work of art ought to be valued, and through appreciating what critics say and by training our perceptions and our responses, we can also learn to value it. The fact that this is so makes it possible to believe that aesthetic judgments can be objective even though there is a considerable amount of disagreement about what should be valued and why. The assumption that judgments about works of art can be objective is closely tied to the claim that art is intrinsically valuable. Making proper aesthetic judgments requires that people learn how to appreciate and enjoy an object for its own sake. They learn that they must accommodate their perceptions and reactions to the object and not expect immediate gratification. It is undeniable that great works of art do often give us enjoyment, but their value cannot be reduced to the production of pleasure, for our ability to enjoy them properly is predicated on developing a respect for the object as something valuable for what it is.

I will assume that these considerations provide a good, if not indisputable, case for thinking that some works of art ought to be respected by everyone, and that from this respect follows a moral obligation to protect and preserve them. The question remains whether an analogous case can be made for the preservation of natural beauty. There are two closely related reasons for doubt. The first lies behind a commonly held opinion that ethical appraisal is reserved for objects designed and produced by human beings. "Only *artifacts* which have been fashioned with the *intention* of being, at least, in part, objects of aesthetic judgment can be objects of aesthetic judgment," declares Mannison.[6] Is this refusal to regard aesthetic responses to nature as real judgments a mere prejudice? Callicott clearly thinks so, and deplores the equation of aesthetics with art criticism as "one more symptom of the cramped anthropocentrism and narcissism of our culture."[7] However, what I think motivates Mannison's declaration (at least in part) is a doubt about the objectivity of our aesthetic responses to nature. The intentions of artists, whether they are fulfilled and how, is an obvious focus for the criticism and justification of value claims in art. There is no such reference point for making judgments about objects that do not have human creators. To defend an environmental aesthetics which has ethical implications it is necessary to find an alternative ground for making and justifying *judgments* about aesthetic value in nature.

The second worry about the objectivity of aesthetic responses to nature is closely related. There is a disturbing variety in our ideas about what is beautiful in nature. Some people prefer the beauty of park lands, gardens, and other landscapes that have been shaped, civilized, and cultivated by human beings. John Passmore believes that gardens convert nature into "something at once more agreeable and more intelligible than a wilderness." "From wilderness," he says, "[we] are always in some measure alienated."[8] Others prefer the grand scenic wonders of nature: the roaring cataracts, the precipitous peaks, and the awesome abysses that have for the last two centuries been the objects of what Raymond Williams calls "conspicuous aesthetic consumption." On the other hand, such environmentalist ethicists as Callicott insist that we can and should learn to appreciate environments which at first sight seem ugly and hostile: for example, a mosquito-infested swamp.

The mere fact that people have different opinions about what is especially beautiful in nature does not mean that aesthetic judgments about nature are not objective—anymore than a variety of contrary opinion undermines the idea that art criticism can be objective. It does mean that we have to consider what reasons people can give for their preferences. Are there any good aesthetic reasons for judging some features of nature to be more aesthetically worthy than others? Does the wilderness lover have tastes that are superior to the lover of formal gardens, or for that matter, of city skylines? What is at stake is not merely particular views about what is beautiful. Those who, like Mannison, deny that our responses to nature count as aesthetic judgments are also doubting that our preferences are anything more than our personal likes and dislikes. To satisfy the objectivity requirement an environmental aesthetics must not only provide a general strategy for justifying value claims; it should also be able to make and justify, however tentatively, comparative evaluations of natural beauty. Let us consider how Hargrove, Callicott, and other advocates of an environmental aesthetic have met this challenge.

III

Most advocates of environmental aesthetics agree that the appreciation of beauty in nature requires a different approach and a different basis for judgment from that required for the appreciation of art. Callicott objects to the inclination of people in our culture to judge nature according to the standards of landscape art. A land aesthetic, he says, requires the development of a sensibility that is able to enjoy being in a natural environment with its sounds, scents, and feel—and not just looking at it.[9] It also requires a sensibility able to appreciate natural objects and environments that are not conventionally pretty or culturally valued. This kind of appreciation can be developed, he thinks, through a knowledge of ecological relationships and the natural history of an environment and the creatures in it:

> Our appreciation of the crane grows with the slow unraveling of earthly history. His tribe, we now know, stems out of the remote Eocene. The other members of the fauna in which he originated are long since entombed within the hills. When we hear his call, we hear no mere bird. He is the symbol of our untamable past, of that incredible sweep of millennia which underlines the daily affairs of birds and men.[10]

Because everything in nature has a natural history stretching back through millennia, Callicott seems to be suggesting that virtually any environment or creature can, or should, be an object of aesthetic appreciation. Allen Carlson develops this idea into what he calls "positive aesthetics." We make judgments about the value of works of art or objects of nature, he says, by reference to categories or standards. In the case of art the categories are provided by art criticism and art history. But, like Callicott, he insists that these standards are not appropriate to nature. Natural objects, whether environmental systems or species of plants or animals, should be appreciated for what they are: something we can discover by learning about their natural history and life cycle. The important difference between art and nature is, thus, that the categories we apply to nature essentially depend upon what exists. They have to be created to fit. The aesthetics of nature, Carlson says, is a positive aesthetics. "All virgin nature is essentially aesthetically good. The appropriate or correct aesthetic appreciation of the natural world is basically positive, and negative aesthetic judgments have little or no place."[11]

For Hargrove, the creativity of nature is the foundation for a positive aesthetics. Both nature and art exhibit creativity, he says, but need to be evaluated in different ways. Artistic creations are judged according to the standards of a tradition or the goals of an artist. But what nature brings forth is not designed in accordance with standards or goals. "Nature's existence precedes its essence, and therefore nature is its own standard of goodness and beauty, making ugliness impossible as a product of nature's own creative activity."[12] This means, he says, that it is even more important to preserve wild nature than it is to preserve objects of art, for natural beauty does not preexist in anyone's imagination. "It must exist physically in order to exist in any sense at all."[13] We not only have a moral duty to protect nature, but this duty takes precedence over our duty to protect works of art.

Positive aesthetics deals with the problem of finding an objective basis for judgments about natural beauty by pointing out that our appreciation of nature grows and deepens with knowledgeable experience of it. Scientific knowledge, particularly knowledge about the natural history of a particular environment or creature, plays a role analogous to the role of art history and art criticism. It makes proper appreciation possible and at the same time provides a basis for judgments about aesthetic worth. Positive aesthetics is also able to provide an answer to the question: "What in nature is beautiful?" All of wild nature is beautiful and thus deserves our appreciation and protection. The more wild, the better. Hargrove argues that those who force nature to serve their purposes, whether this purpose is aesthetic or economic, are not improving on nature. By constraining nature's creative freedom, they are detracting from the aesthetic value of nature. "The beauty of nature arises out of self-creation, which requires freedom from nonnatural influence."[14] Passmore's cultivated gardens, according to these standards, are less rather than more beautiful than wilderness.

The idea that all of nature, above all, wild nature, should be judged to be beautiful is extremely appealing, and not one that I want to dispute. What concerns me is not the positivity of positive aesthetics, but the question of whether its advocates have supplied us with an adequate basis for objective aesthetic judgments and discriminations. There are reasons for doubting this point.

IV

Cultivated nature can also be beautiful. To dispute Passmore's preference for informal gardens over wilderness, we must examine critically the claim that nature untouched by human activities is more aesthetically valuable than nature affected or shaped by human beings. One obvious difficulty for Carlson and Hargrove's positive aesthetics is defining what counts as wild nature. Most areas of the world that are regarded as wilderness areas are either the home of traditional cultures, or they were at some time, and the activities of these people, over thousands of years, have had an effect on the ecology (as in Australia where Aborigines have for centuries encouraged certain species of plants and animals by regularly burning off large areas of bush). If wild nature means areas that have never been affected by human beings, there is practically no wild nature in the world outside of Antarctica. I suspect that advocates of positive aesthetics would be happy to regard as wild nature areas that are or were inhabited by traditional cultures—and so they should. It would be difficult to regard Australian wilderness as less beautiful because generations of Aborigines made parts of it into a kind of park land.

Why not say the same of the environments affected by more recent settlement? Agriculture has sometimes produced landscapes that most people do find beautiful. On the other hand, some human activities have devastated the environment. But, whether an environment has been altered a lot or a little by human hands, it is not clear why this fact should make a difference to our view of it, as far as positive aesthetics is concerned. The creative power of nature is as manifest in its response to human interventions as it is in its response to contingencies that are completely natural. The worst of human interference is no more drastic than changes created by natural forces: volcanoes, hurricanes, continental drift. To all these changes nature adjusts in its creative, and sometimes unexpected, way. Some of the results may be bad for us—but this circumstance is no concern of nature's, and represents no diminution of its creative powers.

What I am suggesting is that if the free creativity of nature is the reason for finding wilderness beautiful, then we have no less of a reason for valuing environments affected by human beings and finding them beautiful. For one thing, because human beings too are part of nature, in an obvious way whatever we do can be regarded as a manifestation of the creativity of nature. Even granted the human-nature distinction, it is not clear why we can't regard the way in which nature responds to our interferences as another manifestation of its creativity, and therefore a proper object of respect and positive evaluation. Indeed, it is not clear why we should value environments affected by human beings less than environments that are free of such interference.

The problem that this extension of positive aesthetics poses is that if, according to its criteria for judgment, every manifestation of nature's creativity turns out to be of value, and if there is no way of justifying a preference for one manifestation over another, then positive aesthetics lacks what is required for objective aesthetic judgment. It gives us no way of making a case for valuing wilderness more than cultivated nature—not even a case for preferring a pristine environment to a trash dump overgrown with weeds. However, if positive aesthetics is not discriminating in its assignment of values, then it will not be able give us a reason for thinking that we have an ethical duty to preserve wilderness, or indeed anything else in nature.

Although my criticism of positive aesthetics is directed most obviously against Hargrove's insistence that the creativity of nature is what gives it value, the same point can be made against other attempts to provide reasons for valuing wild nature. Carlson points out that many people admire wild nature because it is both complex and orderly: systems and organisms are diverse and related in complex ways, and at the same time create a unity.[15] Let us allow that this claim is a reason for finding natural systems and processes aesthetically pleasing. But these are not qualities that distinguish wilderness areas from those systems that are not so natural. A system with introduced animals and plants can be complex and orderly; so can an area used for agriculture or even a lot full of weeds or a flower bed or a compost heap. It is true that a wilderness may contain more diversity than land used for agriculture, but this agricultural land is likely to have other qualities that we can value aesthetically: e.g., a pleasing color or design.

Can an appeal to natural history or ecology give us a reason why we should appreciate some environments more than others? A wilderness does have a different history, a different ecology, from a domesticated environment. The problem is to justify the idea that one history or ecology makes something more aesthetically valuable than another. A rural neighborhood, a city, a trash dump, or a garden all have a history, a complex relationship between parts, that we can come to appreciate.[16] It is not clear why a history of human interference should require us to value an environment less. Understanding how a land has been shaped by the deeds of past and present people can increase our appreciation of it just as understanding the natural history of the crane can heighten our aesthetic experience of it.

The problem is that science cannot provide us with the foundation that positive aesthetics needs for making objective evaluations. As far as evolutionary history is concerned, there is no reason for preferring one development of our evolutionary heritage over another. Species come and go, and human interference is simply contributing in its own way to the pageant of life and death on Earth. A knowledge of evolutionary history with its millions of years of contingencies and catastrophes might even encourage the view that the results of devastation and destruction are no less natural or aesthetically pleasing than the harmonious, untampered-with environments that environmentalists generally prefer.

My aim, however, is not to question the aesthetic tastes of those who advocate a positive aesthetics. I am arguing that these tastes have not been adequately justified. This problem is a serious one for those who want to draw ethical conclusions from aesthetic judgments, for the idea that things of beauty ought to be respected and protected depends on being able to make objective judgments about what is beautiful, and being able to do so in turn requires that we can make a case for saying that some things are distinguishable from others because of their particular beauty or aesthetic worth. Hargrove himself makes this point and adds that the problem can be solved by "accepting the view that there are degrees of beauty, that some objects are more beautiful than others, and that more beautiful objects ought to be given priority for preservation over less beautiful ones."[17] What I have argued is that neither he nor other advocates of positive aesthetics have as yet given us adequate resources for making such discriminations.

My criticisms might be taken to give ammunition to those who want to drive a wedge between art and nature: to those who say that only human products can have real aesthetic value. There are, however, some good reasons for rejecting this position. The first is the remarkable similarity between the way in which people learn to appreciate art, especially art that is difficult to appreciate, and the way in which they learn to appreciate and value natural environments that at first seem to them ugly or uninteresting. The first European settlers in Australia described the landscape as hostile, perverse, and depressing. There was little in this new world that answered to their pre-existing aesthetic categories. It took them some time to learn how to discover beauty in their new environment and to develop appropriate ways of perceiving and representing it. Their success depended upon the idea that there is something of value about the Australian bush worth the effort of discovery.[18] The idea that an aesthetic response to nature is merely a matter of personal taste does not do justice to the motivations that made this development possible. We need some account of why their efforts to appreciate the beauty of the bush were justified and worthwhile.

The second reason for rejecting the idea that art, but not nature, can be objectively evaluated is that the evaluation of art can also be a problematic exercise. The advocates of positive aesthetics tend to assume that criteria for evaluating human creations lie ready to hand. Carlson believes that art, unlike nature, can be measured according to preexisting aesthetic categories, and Hargrove's idea that artistic objects preexist in the imagination suggests that art (unlike nature) can be evaluated in terms of how well the actual product measures up to what the artist imagined. Both too readily accept the idea that the intentional nature of artistic products makes their evaluation different from the evaluation of natural objects, and given the problems with finding a foundation for natural value, the insistence on this difference can easily lead to scepticism about judgments of beauty in nature.

However, art, particularly the art we judge to be superior, is continually overstepping or rejecting the categories of criticism and the assumptions of a culture, or applying techniques or ideas in ways that no one anticipated. Artists can find that they have produced something different from, and sometimes better than, what they had intended. Creativity in art doesn't seem to be different in kind from the creativity of nature, and therefore the question of why we should value artistic objects, and why we should value them discriminately, is sometimes as urgent for art as it is for nature. For this reason, it seems to me that the best way of developing an environmental aesthetic is to try to apply to natural objects and environments some of the same kinds of reasoning that people use to discriminate great works of art from those which are merely pleasing or interesting.[19] Not all of the ways that we judge art are relevant to nature. Judgments that make essential reference to artists' intentions are clearly irrelevant. But not all judgments about art do or can depend upon reference to artists' intentions, and therefore the fact that natural things are not human products is not a reason for thinking that many of the same judgments we make about art cannot also be applied to nature.

The environmental aesthetic that I am advocating can be regarded as a way of developing a positive aesthetics. It is, at least, not incompatible with the projects of Carlson, Callicott, and Hargrove. However, it can, as I show, lead to somewhat different conclusions about what is beautiful.

V

The only way of demonstrating that something can be done is, sometimes, to do it. The ability to make good judgments about art is demonstrated in the practice of making and justifying judgments about particular works of art. So too our ability to make aesthetic judgments about nature is demonstrated by the way we make and justify judgments about particular environments or objects. Otherwise, my attempt to show that aesthetic judgment can be applied to nature will be incomplete, and in its details contentious. My aim is not to persuade everyone to agree with my particular judgments, but merely to show that we can be discriminating in our aesthetic appreciation of nature and justified in our discriminations. I proceed by making some fairly obvious comparisons between works of art that are regarded as superior and some natural environments.

Some art is great because it provides an inexhaustible feast for the senses, the intellect, and the imagination. Chartres Cathedral is an obviously impressive and inspiring monument. ("Its spires, like beacons, draw the traveller on, promising him comfort and sanctuary."[20]) Walking through it or around it, the observer continually discovers new aspects and arresting perspectives: the buttresses fanning out from its sides, the great spaces of the nave, the more intimate spaces of the chapels. Every detail, however small, is a delight and a source of new connections and interpretations: the "drunkeness of colour" in the stained glass windows, the fluid curves and lines in the stone carvings, and all of these details are a greater source of enjoyment because of their contribution to the whole.[21]

Some natural environments are equally magnificent and rich. The Grand Canyon of North America and the Olgas in Central Australia are two obvious examples. What makes them worth a pilgrimage, and the effort required to look at them closely, to wander around and through them, to spend time in their midst, is much the same thing that motivates people to make a pilgrimage to Chartres Cathedral or the Sistine Chapel. They are undeniably magnificent sights and there is no end to what we can discover there. Every perspective, every change in the weather or the position of the sun, is a new and unexpected revelation of line and color. As in the case of Chartres, the smallest details are beautiful in themselves: the swirls and knobs in the rock formed by erosion, the plants sheltering beneath overhangs, water finding its way down through the crevices in the rock. Geological and biological information contributes to the appreciation of these details and so does learning something about the meaning of the environment for early inhabitants. However, it is, above all, the experience of being in the midst of something so magnificent, overwhelming, and endlessly fascinating that persuades us that these natural environments are of great aesthetic worth.

The Olgas and the Grand Canyon are of greater aesthetic value than, say, a bluff on the Mississippi River, just as Chartres Cathedral is of more value than any cathedral in Minneapolis or Melbourne. This judgment does not mean that the river bluff is not beautiful in its own way. From a scientific point of view, it might be more interesting than the Olgas or the Grand Canyon. The fact remains that as far as aesthetic richness and grandeur is concerned, the latter are of greater worth.

To be great, works of art don't necessarily have to be obviously beautiful or immediately impressive. Some works of art are great because they portray something in a strikingly original way or because they present us with a new way of perceiving. They make the ordinary extraordinary, the mundane into something charged with meaning; they put together elements in a different way or present us with experiences that we have never had before. Van Gogh paintings or the music of Stravinsky are examples of art that pose this kind of challenge. They disturb and challenge our old habits of perception and imagination, and those who take the trouble to meet this challenge can feel that their organs of sensation have been altered, enhanced, and made more responsive and discriminating. The world becomes more vibrant and life a greater joy.

To take an example that I am familiar with, the eucalypt forests of south-eastern Australia present people with the same kind of challenge and the same kind of reward. There is nothing else like the color, light, and scents of a forest of mountain ash (*eucalyptus regnans*) or the hazy blue of a eucalypt-covered mountainside. European settlers found these environments to be a new world for the senses, and for those who learn to respond to it, an ordinary experience such as walking through a forest, catching the whiff of eucalypt on a warm breeze, or hearing a bell bird, sharpens the senses and lifts the spirit.

From this point of view, a forest of mountain ash is more beautiful than a boulevard of oaks or plane trees in the same way that a landscape painting by the Australian artists Arthur Streeton or Tom Roberts is better than the same scenes painted by an amateur artist.[22] The planted oaks and plane trees may be fine trees and the landscape that they are part of is agreeable; the amateur artist may also produce something that is pleasing to the eye. But it is Streeton and Roberts, and not the amateur artists, whose works are capable of changing our way of seeing, and it is the eucalypt forest, not the row of planted trees, that challenges and enhances our ability to use our senses.

Sometimes works of art are regarded as great not simply because they are beautiful, but also because of their cultural significance or connection with the past. By learning to appreciate, say, the works of early Renaissance painters or fine examples of Romanesque architecture, we are also learning to appreciate a tradition, a way of perceiving, and the preoccupations and problems of those who belonged to that tradition. Our response to art is also a response to these things—a way of connecting ourselves and our culture to the past; sometimes a way of appreciating the expression of people in cultures that are very different from our own. Through this experience we get a better sense of who we are and our relationship to our history and to other histories.

Nature also connects us with the past. Near Melbourne in southern Australia is a small grassland along the banks of the Merri Creek which seems, at first glance, an unremarkable piece of scenery. You have to go there and spend some time, look at how the colors change from season to season, hear the wind rustling the blades of grass, before you can fully appreciate its subtle beauty. But it is its cultural significance, as well as its beauty, that makes it of great aesthetic worth. It is one of the last remaining patches of the native grassland that once stretched over the basalt plain from Melbourne to South Australia. The Koori people hunted and gathered food on these grasslands and the wood for their shields was carved out of its ancient red gums. When the first European settlers arrived they looked out over "open plains as far as the eye can see westward."[23] A small field of kangaroo grass is a reminder of how things were, of the fact that this part of Victoria had a habitat that was unique. By learning how to appreciate its beauty and its connection to the past, we connect ourselves to the place we live, its peculiarities, its history, and its unique beauty.

From an aesthetic point of view, the Merri Creek grassland is more worthy of our appreciation than a city park. The park with its lush domesticated grass and beds of roses is pleasing to the eye. The subtle beauty of the grassland is not only more challenging, but the connection of this particular place with the past gives our experience a resonance and depth that we cannot obtain from the park. I am not saying that the grassland is of special significance simply because it has a past. All nature has a past—a history that stretches back into geological time. The grassland is special because it has a past that is or can be significant to the people who experience it, a past that connects them to their history and their land as the Koori knew it and as the first White settlers found it.

Works of art are sometimes of great value because they tacitly criticize a tradition or a way of life, and because they pose a challenge to the way we live or think. They force us to put our lives and our values in perspective, to recognize the existence of alternatives or the possibility of a happiness or simplicity that we have never experienced. Gaughin's paintings sometimes have that power, as do some of the novels of Dostoevksy.

Wild nature, above all, puts things in perspective. We live in a human world surrounded by human-made products, and however beautiful or terrible, predictable or unpredictable, these products are, they belong to us and reflect us back to ourselves. Wild nature is an environment that is not of our making; it is indifferent to our interests and cuts us down to size. Thoreau said that "we need to witness our own limits transgressed, and some life pasturing freely where we never wander."[24] The Australian poet Judith Wright sees wilderness as a necessary refuge from the human environment:

> The thought of "the calm, the leaf and the voice of the forest" is itself a refuge from stress, a wilderness at the back of the strained mind. When we finally know that the last forest has gone, that there is nowhere to go but along the runways of our steel and concrete anthills, that the last link with our past has snapped, then perhaps we may snap too. We will have no refuge left at all.[25]

Nature has aesthetic value, from this point of view, to the extent that it exists as a refuge, or at least as a counterweight to the human-made world. Some parts of nature do this better or more completely than others. The informal garden praised by Passmore is restful to the eye and the spirit, a nice place to go to relieve city stress, but it is still a human-made distraction; it is calculated to please, and thus it is not so capable as wilderness of posing a challenge or providing an alternative to civilization or to our self-conception.

This discussion suggests that the preference of advocates of positive aesthetics for undomesticated nature can in many cases be justified. Wilderness areas are likely to be more of an inexhaustible feast for the senses than parks or other settings shaped by human beings. The experience of wild nature is more likely to enhance our ability to use our senses than experiences of more tame environments, especially in Australia and the Americas, where people of European or Asian origin are still trying to come to terms with a new land and learning to find a way of appreciating it for what it is. For the same reason, land untouched by modern cultures is more likely to have a history and genesis of significance for us. By responding to it and appreciating its history, we are connecting ourselves with the land that was used by the native inhabitants and invested by them with meaning; we are connecting ourselves with the past of our own culture, with the land as it was first seen by the new settlers. Above all, wilderness is a continuing reminder of a nature outside of human control, a refuge from the preoccupations and priorities of the human world.

However, it does not follow that people who prefer gardens to wilderness are always mistaken. Considered aesthetic judgment could reach the conclusion that a particular garden is of great aesthetic worth and is more valuable in this respect than some wilderness areas. The approach to environmental aesthetics that I am advocating does not allow us to assume that (relatively) wild nature is always preferable to more domesticated environments, that a wilderness will always be worth more than a garden. Nor can we assume that all wilderness areas are equal in their aesthetic value (and indeed advocates of positive aesthetics are also not committed to this idea). Some will turn out to have more worth than others and will for that reason demand from us a greater duty of care. This does not mean that only those wilderness areas that are judged to be of great aesthetic worth should be preserved. There are lots of reasons for preserving wilderness, and there may be other grounds besides aesthetic ones for thinking that some aspects of nature have intrinsic value.

However, the aesthetic approach to the evaluation of nature does provide us with a way of arguing for the protection and preservation of some natural objects and environments. The comparisons and evaluations I have made do not provide a systematic or complete account of the reasons that we might give for valuing works of art or parts of nature. The creativity of both means that an a priori list of criteria of judgment is impossible. However, they do demonstrate that we can make aesthetic judgments about nature in the same way that we do about art. We can make and justify objective claims about the relative merits of natural things; we can give reasons for saying that some things in nature are of very great aesthetic worth. Discrimination is clearly compatible with the idea that all of nature is beautiful in some way or another. However, the fact that we can discriminate and justify our discriminations before others means that we can effectively argue that some parts of nature have a worth that demands respect. This respect brings with it ethical obligations. Everyone (whether they make the effort to appreciate this worth or not) has a duty to protect and preserve natural beauty that is at least as demanding as the duty to preserve great works of art.

The argument that connects aesthetic worth to ethical obligation can thus be shown to be valid in the case of nature, as in the case of art. This is the conclusion that advocates of positive aesthetics aimed to reach. My somewhat different approach can be regarded as a way of overcoming the principle difficulties that lie in the path of this argument. It shows that we can have objective grounds for regarding natural beauty as intrinsically valuable. This intrinsic value is not a nonanthropocentric value. An aesthetics of nature must appeal to what human beings, situated as they are, can find significant, enhancing, a joy for the senses, or a spur to the imagination and intellect, and the ethical obligations that follow from this appreciation are thus tied to human ways of perceiving and judging. Nevertheless, an environmental aesthetics requires of human perceivers that they learn how to value natural things for what they are. Like Hargrove, I favor this way of defending the idea that there are intrinsic values in nature. My version of environmental aesthetics shows, I hope, how the aesthetic approach can also serve as a useful starting point for a practical environmental ethics: not only by providing the discriminations that ethical judgment requires, but also by promoting a love and respect for nature.

Notes

1. G. E. Moore, *Principia Ethica* (Cambridge: Cambridge University Press, 1965), pp. 83–85.

2. Eugene C. Hargrove, *Foundations of Environmental Ethics* (Englewood Cliffs, N.J.: Prentice Hall), p. 192.

3. Beauty and aesthetic value are not the same thing. It is not difficult to think of artworks that have aesthetic value but are not beautiful. Nevertheless, as Hargrove remarks, other aesthetic evaluations that used to be applied to nature, such as "the sublime," have become incorporated into modern notions of natural beauty. I therefore make no attempt in this essay to discuss the relation between beauty and aesthetic value.

4. Janna Thompson, "A Refutation of Environmental Ethics," *Environmental Ethics* 12 (1990): 147–60.

5. Robert Elliot, in "Intrinsic Value, Environmental Obligation and Naturalness," *The Monist* 75 (1992): 138–60, argues that a subjective account of what is an intrinsic value is adequate for the purposes of aesthetics and environmentalism. For the above reasons, I doubt whether this claim is so. However, Elliot's and my accounts of intrinsic value may not be as far apart as they first seem, for he believes that the attribution of intrinsic value depends upon the existence of relevant properties or relations, and allows that the nature and relevance of the properties can serve as reasons for accepting and rejecting value claims.

6. Don Mannison, "A Prolegomenon to a Human Chauvinist Aesthetics," in D. Mannison, M. McRobbie, and R. Routley, eds., *Environmental Philosophy,* Monograph Series 2 (Canberra: Australia: Research School of Social Science, 1980), p. 212.

7. J. Baird Callicott, "The Land Aesthetic," *Environmental Review* 7 (1983): 346.

8. John Passmore, *Man's Responsibility for Nature: Ecological Problems and Western Tradition* (London: Duckworth, 1974), p. 37.

9. Callicott, "The Land Aesthetic," p. 350.

10. Ibid., p. 348. He is quoting from Aldo Leopold, *Sand County Almanac: With Essays on Conservation from Round River* (New York: Ballantine, 1970), pp. 102–03.

11. Allen Carlson, "Nature and Positive Aesthetics," *Environmental Ethics* 6 (1984): 5.

12. Hargrove, *Foundations of Environmental Ethics,* p. 184.

13. Ibid., p. 193.

14. Ibid.

15. Carlson, "Nature and Positive Aesthetics," p. 24.

16. Paul Ziff makes the point that "anything that can be viewed is a fit object for aesthetic attention. Garbage strewn about is apt to be as delicately variegated in hue and value as the subtlest Monet. Discarded beer cans create striking cubistic patterns" ("Anything Viewed," *Anti-Aesthetics: An Appreciation of the Cow with the Subtile Nose* [Dordrecht, Boston, London: D. Reidel, 1984], pp. 137–38).

17. Hargrove, *Foundations of Environmental Ethics*, p. 179.

18. Brian Elliot, *The Landscape of Australian Poetry* (Melbourne, Cambridge, Sydney: F. W. Chesire, 1967), and contributors to P. R. Eaden and F. H. Mares, eds., *Mapped But Not Known* (South Australia: Wakefield Press, 1986), discuss this aesthetic history. Hargrove, *Foundation of Environmental Ethics,* chap. 3, relates a similar development of North American sensibilities.

19. Mary McCloskey made this suggestion to me.

20. Robert Branner, *Chartres Cathedral* (New York: W. W. Norton & Co., 1969), p. 69.

21. See Henry Adams, "Mont Saint Michel and Chartres," *Works* (New York: Library of America, 1983), pp. 467–68.

22. Arthur Streeton and Tom Roberts were artists of the Heidelberg School who managed to evoke the light and color of the Australian bush in a way that remains inspiring.

23. According to the words of John Batman, the founder of the first Victorian colony.

24. Henry David Thoreau, *Walden* (Princeton: Princeton University Press, 1971), p. 318.

25. Judith Wright, "A Refuge in the Mind," *Victorian National Parks Association Newsletter,* 1989, p. 29.

EVALUATING A CASE STUDY: FINDING THE CONFLICTS

After establishing an ethical point of view (including a segue to application), we are ready to approach cases. The first stage in handling cases effectively is to analyze the situation according to normal practice and potential ethical issues. Obviously, sometimes ethical issues are involved in what one will do, and at other times they are not. It is your job to determine when ethical issues are involved. Let us consider specific cases.

Case 1.

You work in the Human Resource Development department of a company that has an annual awards picnic in June. One of the traditional practices is the release of thousands of balloons sending the company's name and mission to the four corners of the earth. You have heard, however, that such balloon launchings are biologically hazardous to wildlife. Although it makes a striking motivational situation, you believe that the company should reconsider this tradition.

What ethical issues are involved in this case? List them and connect them to a major ethical theory.

Case 2.

You work for Genie Biomedical Research whose mission is to create new techniques for gene therapy. The method for this experimentation is to work with monkeys (since their biological constitution is close to that of humans). Many of the procedures result in a monkey's painful death. If the mission of the company is successful, many inherited human disorders can be successfully treated, sparing humans the pain and disorientation of loss due to congenital conditions. Still, you wonder about the monkeys. Do the intended consequences of the research justify the experimental practices on monkeys?

Does this case involve any ethical issues? If so, what are they? What theories support your opinion?

An an aid for working through these two exercises, consider the following checklist for detecting ethical issues.

Checklist for Detecting Issues Concerning Professional Practice

Directions. Read your case carefully. Determine what (if any) relevant points of professional practice are at stake, and then decide which individual's perspective you will develop in your comments. Determine whether there are any clear violations of professional practice. Identify these violations and the various risks a person assumes when engaging in such behavior. Then consider whether the professional practice itself is immoral. Finally, if the practice is wrong, explain why it is and what major ethical theory judges it to be wrong. What arguments would a proponent of such a theory make?

Next follow the checklist for detecting ethical issues.

Checklist for Detecting Ethical Issues

Directions. Read your case carefully. Determine your ethical viewpoint (see "Developing a Practical Ethical Viewpoint," p. 30). Decide which individual's perspective you will develop in your comments. Create one or more detection questions that will identify ethical issues. These detection questions will follow from your own ethical perspective. For example, from my practical ethical perspective, I have chosen the following two detection questions to bring moral issues to my attention. These questions follow from a deontological viewpoint.

1. *Is any party being exploited solely for the advantage of another?* (Exploitation can include instances of lying, injuring, deliberately falsifying, creating an unequal competitive environment, and so forth.)

2. *Is every effort being made to assist and affirm the human dignity of all parties involved?* (Affirming human dignity can include instances of encouraging the fulfillment of legal and human rights as well as taking personal responsibility for results that are consonant with these principles. Thus, you cannot hide behind nonfunctioning rules.)

By asking these questions within the context of the case, I am able better to understand the moral dimensions that exist with other professional concerns.

A few other comments may be useful concerning my detection questions. Question 1 concerns "prohibitions" (i.e., actions that you must refrain from doing). Question 2 concerns "obligations" (i.e., actions that you are required to do). Anything that is not an ethical obligation or a prohibition is a "permission" (i.e., an action that you may do if you choose). Thus, if the case you present does not invoke a prohibition or an obligation, then you may act solely according to the dictates of your professional practice (such as those dictated as a governmental official or as an environmental scientist). It is often useful to group your detection questions as prohibitions and obligations, which emphasizes different types of moral duty.

Try creating detection questions and apply them to the earlier two cases. What do they reveal about the moral issues involved in the cases? How do different detection questions emphasize different moral issues? How different are these perspectives? How similar are they?

Once you have completed this preliminary ethical assessment, you can return to the ethical theory you have adopted and determine *how* and *why* the prohibitions and obligations are applicable to this theory.

Read the following macro and micro cases and follow the steps outlined:

A. Identify the professional practice issues at stake.
B. Identify your practical ethical viewpoint including any linking principles.
C. Determine which character's perspective you will adopt.
D. Identify two or more detection questions that define obligation and prohibition within the ethical theory you have chosen.
E. Apply the detection questions to the cases to bring attention to the ethical issues.
F. Discuss the interrelationships between the dictates of the ethical issues and those of the professional practice. How might they work together? How might they be opposed?

Macro and Micro Cases.*

Macro Case 1. The Chicago Housing Authority is planning to tear down several high-rise public housing projects and build single-family townhouses and duplexes to rent and sell to the public. The purpose of this endeavor is to

---

*For more on macro and micro cases, see the overview on p. 30.

create mixed communities, meaning that people of various income levels would be living together. You are the head of a natural ecology organization dedicated to making such community development as environmentally friendly as possible. The proposal that makes the most ecological sense has the least density of new housing. It would provide for more green urban park space (meaning retrieving land for natural usages including planting trees and reviving habitants long since destroyed). Also in favor of this proposal is the appeal the housing will have for middle- and upper-middle-income families. It will seem to bring the suburbs into the city. Everything seems directed to this proposal except that it could negatively impact the poor people who currently live in the housing projects. First, the planned spaces are not sufficient to house all of the poor who currently live in the projects. (At present, vague plans have been suggested, but the reality is that people who cannot rent or purchase the new housing must move somewhere else. There will be no room for them here.) Does this constitute an ethical problem? Second, the new properties may be so attractive that pressure will be brought to build even more luxurious dwellings with the result that the new community will gradually be transformed from mixed housing to homogeneous rich housing. Does this constitute an ethical problem?

As head of an environmental organization, your duty is to support the most environmental friendly program. Analyze this problem from the points of view of a deep ecologist and a social ecologist. Use the format of a position paper that your organization will submit to Janet Smiley, the head of the Chicago Housing Authority.

Macro Case 2. Analyze Macro Case 1 from an ecofeminist point of view. Then make a recommendation using a worldview listed in the section "Religion and Aesthetics" to base your recommendation to Ms. Smiley.

Macro Case 3. As head of the AFL-CIO's auto contract negotiation team, you are working on the latest round of contracts with the major auto companies. Keeping to your historical pattern, you have chosen one company with which to create a model contract on which your negotiations with other companies will be based. You have entered negotiations with Company X in this regard and are presently addressing the issue of outsourcing parts. Traditionally, the union has been against outsourcing because of the potential loss of U.S. jobs to foreign markets. However, Company X has offered an interesting proposal that would peg U.S. jobs at a permanent level (*permanent* means for the life of the contract) in return for the right to outsource parts. This proposal would be a step forward from past negotiations because you have never been given a pegged level of employment before. From the point of view of your union members, this is a great deal. However, the plants in the countries that will supply these parts operate on standards you do not think are ethical. They pay very low wages to their workers for very long hours, and they have no environmental regulations by which they must abide. The question is whether to accept a deal that is great for your workers but bad for foreign workers and the environment in that country? You must respond to Company X's proposal in forty-eight hours. Write your response, making clear your ethical position and any linking principles.

Macro Case 4. You are head of the World Maritime Commission's Department of Ecology. You are considering the case against one of the premier luxury cruise ship companies in the world, ABC Cruise Lines. The complaint is that ABC is in gross violation of the commission's waste disposal regulations and has egregiously polluted Prince William Sound in Alaska for the past twenty years. The company has admitted lax management but denies any systematic plan for pollution. However, the facts show that ABC has polluted four times as much as the next worst offender, which also faces charges. A tentative fine of $100 million has been assessed against ABC, which ABC says it cannot possibly pay, because it will lead to bankruptcy. If the cruise line goes bankrupt, 12,500 people will lose their jobs. ABC proposes that it be allowed to continue and that 5 percent of its net profits be diverted to an environmental fund for the next ten years. Critics say that this is merely a "slap on the wrist" that will do nothing to address the real problems. Environmental pollution is not a small matter. However, there is the issue of those who will be put out of work.

Write a recommendation for the other committee members to consider. Make clear the ethical position on which you base your recommendations.

Micro Case 1. You are a college senior about to enter the real world, and you have had several job offers. You have narrowed the list down to two; a nonprofit organization concerned with gender and social issues and a job on Wall Street as a stockbroker. As a stockbroker you will work long hours helping customers make money and perhaps growing rich yourself in the process. The former offer is for $30,000 a year, and the latter is for $50,000 a year (with the promise for lots more). There is nothing wrong about accepting either job. Both companies seem to be concerned about meeting their goals in a responsible way. However, a question that one of your philosophy professors put forth makes you wonder: What does it mean to simplify your life along the lines of Deep Ecology? Is this an important consideration for forming a worldview plan? What of the tenets of Social Ecology or Ecofeminism? What difference does it make? Write a diary entry that considers this choice, adding relevant details as necessary.

Micro Case 2. You are at the mall shopping for several pairs of new pants. One company, We Are Green, has attractive clothes that cost considerably more than the clothes in other stores. For example, a pair of pants that sells for $25 at another store costs $40 in the Green line. However, Green has an independent auditing company verify that all its clothes meet a core list of requirements for environmentally sensitive criteria. You believe that both lines of clothes are equally stylish, but you have only $50 to spend, so you can buy two pairs of pants from the other company or one pair of pants from Green. You like to support Green causes when you can, but you really need two pairs of pants. You become somewhat angry that the Green pants cost so much more. Perhaps these pants represent a luxury that you cannot afford. You decide to go to the coffee shop next door to think about it. You take out a pen and list arguments on your napkin. What should you do? Discuss the practical and ethical considerations to justify your decision.

Micro Case 3. You commute to work each day from your apartment in the suburbs to your job in one of the major metropolitan areas of the country (not New York), which has public transportation. You have considered using public transportation instead of driving a single occupancy vehicle to work. However, there is something empowering about knowing that your car is in the garage and that you can leave any time—just in case you have to (although you never have done so in the past three years). Often in the summer, the local Council of Governments issues a "code red" day, declaring that the pollution levels are at an unhealthy state; these days are becoming more and more frequent. In your locality, public transportation is half-price on these days. Should you change to public transit even though the commute would be forty-five minutes longer? Should you accept the loss of individual freedom that parking your wheels at home entails? Analyze the ethical components of this problem as well as their depth of embeddedness. Then choose one ethical viewpoint and use it to solve the problem.

Micro Case 4. An ounce of normal perfume based on flower sources requires 3,000 petals. You have recently heard about Aphrodisiac #18, a very potent perfume that not only requires 20,000 petals per ounce but also includes glands from 100,000 insects that are supposed to emit pheromones that will attract the opposite sex. You have sampled the "scratch and smell" ads and are convinced that this perfume is for you, but you also believe that this is a very wasteful product. On the other hand, the company that makes the product grows all the flowers on company lands, replanting them at regular intervals. It also breeds the insects for their glands. This is a "farmed" product, not an intrusion of natural, wild species. How is this any different from eating corn that has been bred to taste? Is there an ethical issue here? What would you say to those who say there is and those who say there is not?

chapter four

A Linking Principle to Applied Environmental Ethics

General Overview. Applied Ethics demands a way to move from normative theory to practice. In this series of books, *Basic Ethics in Action,* I suggest several such linking principles. For example, in *Medical Ethics,* I highlighted Deryck Beyleveld and Shaun Pattinson's essay on precautionary reason. In *Business Ethics,* I featured the principle of fair competition. Here, in *Environmental Ethics,* the link is the value-duty relationship. If a person is compelled to protect and defend what he values and if we can show (through an examination of the personal and shared community worldview) that the environment is valued, then it must be protected. I believe that this value-duty relationship means that the only thing all environmental advocates must prove is that we value the environment. To the extent that this is the case, a proportionate duty arises. The environment must be protected to the extent that humans value it. This relationship also elucidates other duties (through the Personal Worldview Imperative and the Shared Community Imperative) but this particular duty appears to be primary and therefore offers a clear justification for environmental protection.

Worldview and the Value-Duty Link to Environmental Ethics

Michael Boylan

This essay seeks to enunciate a practical link to applied Environmental Ethics through the Personal Worldview Imperative, the Shared Community Worldview Imperative, the value-duty relationship, and several other associated principles. It is the position of this essay that when created through one's personal worldview, the value-duty relationship will engender environmental duties on the agent and that these duties require the agent to enter into the dictates of the Shared Community Worldview Imperative. This process necessarily includes (through a series of intermediary steps) the duty to become involved in a political process that will seek to defend the environment.

This essay begins by presenting some key terms and distinctions. It proceeds to apply both through the Personal Worldview and the Shared Community Worldview.

I. Key Terms and Distinctions

To begin, let us consider several principles that I hold to be crucial when discussing questions of value.

A. First is the *Personal Worldview Imperative:* All people must develop a single comprehensive and internally coherent worldview that is good and that we strive to act out in our daily lives.[1] There are at least two divisions of the Personal Worldview Imperative; the first is a theoretical one that commands the agent to undergo a thorough self-examination of her values. This entails exposing what she believes in and organizing this inventory into some comprehensive and coherent whole. An underlying assumption of this theoretical stage is that the agent sees her own values in the context of her vision of the world.

---

[1]The argument for the Personal Worldview Imperative is given in the Introduction to *Basic Ethics* (Upper Saddle River, NJ: Prentice Hall, 2000).

The second stage is a practical one that commands the agent to act according to her basic values. This means that if she believes that killing animals is immoral, then she should not eat animals killed for human consumption or wear their skins.[2] It does no good for an individual to hold a belief but not practice it.

Both stages—reasoned beliefs and actions that follow from them[3]—are necessary for the ethical life.

B. This is not the end of the story, however. In the next stage, each agent (after he has created his personal worldview) must also engage other agents with whom he lives in his community[4] in creating a shared community worldview. This is dictated by the *Shared Community Worldview Imperative:* Each agent must strive to create a common body of knowledge that supports the creation of a shared community worldview (that is complete, coherent, and good) through which social institutions and their resulting policies might flourish within the constraints of the essential core commonly held values (ethics, aesthetics, and religion). There are several key elements to this imperative. First is the exhortation to create a common body of knowledge (discussed later).[5] This is an essential element so that positive group discussion can proceed. Second is a dialectical process of discussion among members of a single community and between members of various single communities that are united in another, larger heterogeneous community. This discussion should seek to form an understanding about the community's mission within the context of the common body of knowledge and the core values commonly held by members of the community. These values will include ethical maxims, aesthetic values, and religious values. Of course, there will be disagreements, but a process is enjoined that will create a shared worldview that is complete, coherent, and good.[6]

Third is that the result of this dialectical creation of a shared community worldview is to employ it in the creation (or revision of) social institutions

---

[2] A possible exception to this might be those who might eat the flesh or wear the skins of animals that die from some other cause. In this case, the person does not kill the animal but only uses what is already dead. However, this seems a very far-fetched idea. In this context we are reminded of Theophrastus, student of Aristotle, who preferred eating only the fruit that had already fallen.

[3] This position does not intend to exclude emotions within the context of reason. This is so because a person's worldview is representative of her entire person. Thus, there is some affinity between my depiction of the Personal Worldview Imperative and some versions of feminist ethics. For a further discussion of this, see *Basic Ethics*, chap. 5.

[4] By community, I mean (in ascending order) the family, the neighbors in his geographical region—some natural unit of a mile or so, his city, township, county, state, country, and the world itself. All are in communities that we cannot ignore. I believe that we should begin in the order I have listed because that order allows the most interaction of individuals in the political process.

[5] I discuss the common body of knowledge in greater detail as it pertains to logical argument in *The Process of Argument* (Englewood Cliffs, NJ: Prentice Hall, 1988), chap. 1.

[6] I discuss an example of how this shared community worldview might arise in my essay, "Affirmative Action: Strategies for the Future," *Journal of Social Philosophy* (in press).

that are responsible for setting policy within the community or social unit. It should be clear that this tenet seems highly inclined toward democracy; it is. However, it is not restricted to this. Even in totalitarian states, the influence of the shared community worldview is significant. One can, for example, point to the differences among communist states in Eastern Europe, the Soviet Union, China, North Korea, and Cuba during the 1960s to the 1980s. All were communist, yet major differences can be found in the way the totalitarian regimes operated in each instance because, even without the vote, the shared community worldview casts a strong influence on the operation of society's institutions and their resultant policies.

Finally, note that the actions of those institutions must always be framed within the core values of the people who make up the society. When the society veers too far in its implementation of the social worldview from the personal worldviews of its members, a realignment must occur. In responsive democracies, this takes the form of defeating incumbents in the next election. In totalitarian regimes, change also occurs but generally through coup d'état or armed revolution.

C. The next principle to consider is the *common body of knowledge,* a set of factual and normative principles about which there is general agreement among a community or between communities of people. This includes (but is not limited to) agreement on what constitutes objective facts and how to measure them. It also includes (but is not limited to) what values will be recognized as valid in the realms of ethics, aesthetics, and religion.[7]

At first glance, many would hold that the creation of the common body of knowledge is a very simple thing. In our contentious world, however, these points are not to be taken for granted. By engaging the issue head on, there is a much greater chance for meaningful dialogue among those involved in serious disputation.

The import of these distinctions in private and public morality is clear. The Personal Worldview Imperative is a command that each of us examine our own lives and strive to create coherence, completeness, and goodness among the myriad of value maxims that we hold. In the social sphere, the Shared Community Worldview Imperative demands that we seek to do the same with others. In this way, a set of concentric spheres of influence is created that should also include the even broader context of the environment. Figure 4.1 illustrates the way most people view relationships among themselves, their communities, and their environment. The large arrow representing the personal worldview

---

[7]This is not to suggest that I am arguing for a sharp distinction between analytic and synthetic truths; I agree with Quine's insistence that analytic and synthetic truths do not easily segregate. See "Two Dogmas of Empiricism," *From a Logical Point of View* (Cambridge, MA: Harvard University Press, 1953); however, the structure of deontic truths and other propositions do form a natural classification.

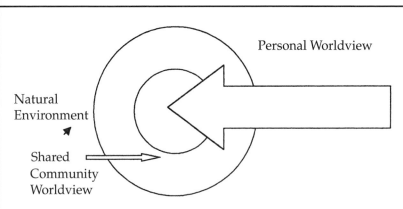

FIGURE 4.1 Relationships between Personal Worldview, Shared Community Worldview, and the Natural Environment

is meant to depict the high stake that each human places on her own view of reality (both facts and values).

The middle-size arrow represents the lesser stake that most people invest in the community. Finally, the smallest arrow seeks to illustrate the rather small role that most attribute to the environment.

Although Figure 4.1 may be factually true (though some will dispute this), this is not the way it *should* be. By investing so little worldview attention to the natural environment, many people are able to give it corresponding little value and respect.

From a biological point of view, however, even this minimalist position contains some strong duties.[8] None of us lives in some sort of hermetically sealed bubble with all we need inside. We are social animals; we live with other humans; we also live in community with all of nature. We cannot confine this concern to the immediate environments in which we live but must extend this to the entire world (and perhaps, by extension, the solar system, the galaxy, and beyond). Within our own world, warm waters off of Peru called El Niño affect the weather and the well-being of ecosystems from eastern Asia to North America to Europe. It may be a stretch to say that a butterfly suddenly falling from the sky in Brazil affects a farmer in Canada (as some of the purveyors of popular chaos theory have said), but it is a meteorological commonplace that regional weather and global weather are intricately connected.[9] The weather

---

[8]It is not the purpose of this essay to argue that *only* the minimalist position ought to be adopted but that this position is so basic that all rational agents must accept its authority. Adoption of such a strategy can lead to a wider range of assent (cf., common body of knowledge).

[9]One accessible overview of these relations can be found in Marcel Leroux, *Dynamic Analysis of Weather and Climate: Atmospheric Circulation, Perturbations, Climatic Evolution* (New York: John Wiley, 1998), especially part III.

is an important component of the well-being of the ecosphere (the combined ecosystems of the world). Therefore, at the very least, everyone must acknowledge that people do not act in isolation. Almost every action that we commit has personal, social, and ecological consequences.

D. A fourth principle that must be enunciated is the *Principle of Human Survival,* which says that humans may be obliged in their struggle for survival to kill animals and plants and to alter the natural landscape. In this way, humans are acting just as other animals do in their own quest for survival. It is also assumed that humans are justified in continuing in these practices past the point of basic primitive survival to some level of moderate, comfortable living.

The intent of the Principle of Human Survival is to highlight the fact that the natural world is not some pristine, static system but a robust, ever-changing arena of competition in which animals kill other animals, forests are destroyed by fires caused by lightning, and earthquakes violently alter the landscape. Humans are one component of this mix and are entitled to follow the same rules that other species follow. However, what makes humans unique is that they can reflect on what they do in such a way that they may refrain from certain actions for which they are naturally inclined because these actions conflict with other core values.

The reason for the abuse of this principle lies in these words: It is further assumed that humans are justified to continue in these practices past the point of basic, primitive survival to some level of moderate, comfortable living. These standards are somewhat plastic. What is comfortable to one person might be a studio apartment for two families but to another might be a house of 6,000 square feet on many acres of ground.

Clearly, the wide range of reference in the words "moderate" and "comfortable" is a problem. The worldviews of various people differ widely on what is an acceptable moderate use of resources. For example, I remember as a boy going to a friend's house for dinner and being shocked when my friend (who could not eat all of his dinner) simply took his plate to the garbage can and scraped it all away. In my Depression-era parents' house, we cut our food one bite at a time so that if we could not finish the food, we could save it for another meal or a leftover casserole. Throwing out food was *not* a part of our shared community worldview. If we had chicken or beef for dinner, the bones were collected for use in future soup dishes. In short, wasting food was absolutely forbidden. Both of my parents knew the experience of going to bed hungry. Thus, throwing away food, or wasting anything, was forbidden. I like to call this the *frugality ethic.* Behind this ethic is the basic economic problem: Humans have unlimited desires, but there are limited resources.

It is difficult to draw a precise line that demarcates moderate usage. Often economic necessity makes conservationists of us all. From anecdotal evidence from my friends who have lived in less-developed countries, it seems to me that in these countries many uses are made for everything. You eat the chicken or the contents of the can of beans. You use the carcass and the feathers of the dead animal for other practical uses. You also use the can for something, too. Nothing is wasted.

Thus, although the Principle of Human Survival is open to debate because of the rather amorphous term *moderate*, it does signify that extravagance and waste in our dealings with the natural world are wrong.

I suggest that readers think of the Principle of Human Survival in the way that we think of the doctrine of proportional retaliation in self-defense. When someone attacks you, you are permitted to respond in proportion to the attack. Thus, if a person is attacking your big toe (by stepping on it), your response would be different than if he were attacking your life. The exact line is plastic, but there is some general direction. In the same way, we can elucidate some community sense of what is an appropriate or moderate level of consumption—so long as the community in this case is sufficiently broad.

This is not a pure comparison because there are more objective touchstones in the self-defense case than in the moderate usage case, but some general directions can be seen.

E. The last principle that I would like to discuss in this section of the essay is the value-duty relationship. In some ways (for the purposes of my argument in this essay), this is the most important principle of all. I contend that when agent X values P (where P is an artifact, a natural object, an agent, or a human institution[10]), X assumes a corresponding duty to protect and defend P subject to the constraints of the Principle of Human Survival and the "ought implies can" doctrine.[11]

The import of the Value-Duty Doctrine is to assert that in the act of valuing, a person proceeds through various steps (refer to Figure 4.2).

Thus, according to this argument, when an individual perceives anything, she undergoes a process whereby she values it (positively or negatively) according to the standards of her personal worldview. If she values it to be good, then she has a duty to protect and defend it. The extent of this duty is proportional to the gradation of positive value that she assigns to it.

---

[10]This list is meant to be suggestive, not exhaustive of the entities that might fall under this principle.

[11]The "ought implies can doctrine" is generally attributed to Kant (though there is some dispute about this). It is a straightforward doctrine that says that no one can command you to do what is impossible for you to do. However, this becomes rather slippery when we analyze what "impossible" means. Often, this transforms to inconvenient, and thus guts the force of the doctrine.

1. X apprehends P (where X is an agent and P is an artifact, a natural object, an agent, or a human institution—among other things/processes/activities)—fact.

2. All apprehensions involve the internal value filter of the personal worldview—fact.

3. The act of valuation assesses a negative, neutral, or positive value according to a gradated scale that begins with disapproval, moves by steps to neutrality, and finally moves by steps of approbation to total approval—assertion.

4. When X apprehends P, X engages in a process of valuation according to the standards set by her personal worldview—1–3.

5. The act of positively valuing anything means that X is giving some gradated approval to P—assertion.

6. Giving approval to P means that X thinks P exists and that P is good—assertion.

7. When X encounters a P that is good, an interaction with P occurs—assertion.

8. The act of valuing P creates an ongoing interaction between X and that which X judges to be good (P)—5–7.

9. Ongoing interactions with what is judged to be good constitute striving to act out what is good in individual lives—assertion.

10. The Personal Worldview Imperative commands all people to develop a single comprehensive and internally coherent worldview that is good and that individuals strive to act out in their daily lives—fact.

11. The Personal Worldview Imperative commands that when X values P, X creates an ongoing interaction with P in X's daily life—8–10.

12. X cannot have an ongoing interaction with a P that is destroyed or no longer exists—fact.

13. When X is commanded to maintain an ongoing interaction with P, then X must maintain P's existence (as much as it is in X's power to do so.)—assertion.

14. Maintaining the existence of P (as much as it is in X's power) is to protect and defend P—fact.

15. The Personal Worldview Imperative commands individuals to protect and defend what they value—11–14.

16. When X is commanded to do Y, then X has a duty to do Y—fact.

17. When X apprehends P and judges it to be good (i.e., positively values P), then X incurs a duty to protect and defend P—4, 8, 11, 15, 16.

Figure 4.2 **Value-Duty Relationship**

II. APPLICATION THROUGH PERSONAL AND SHARED COMMUNITY WORLDVIEW

We now have the principles necessary to outline a theory of environmental duty via the worldview.

A. Application through Personal Worldview

In presenting the Personal Worldview Imperative, it has been my custom to highlight three areas of value: ethics, aesthetics, and religion. In keeping with this organization, I will examine each in order to determine which value areas (and their resultant duties) might arise.

The Realm of Ethical Values

Of course, a number of ways can be used to ground ethical value.[12] However, most traditional theories are grounded in aspects of *rationality*, which is often understood as the ability to demonstrate rudimentary skills in inductive and deductive logic. This, in turn, is operationally understood through an organism using language to communicate in ways that demonstrate these skills. Although there may be some debate at the fringes regarding some species of monkey, it is generally agreed that only humans are rational in just this way. If rationality alone is the ground for moral rights and duties, clearly there are only *moral* rights and duties to other humans.[13] If this position is correct, there are no moral duties to animals, plants, or the landscape, as such. One might construct a theory of duties to future generations or other such anthropocentric justifications that are really duties to people that include the environment as a part of that duty.

Another strategy along this line is a Virtue Ethics approach in which one of the virtues involves a certain disposition by humans to the environment. Bill Shaw makes one such argument in his essay, "A Virtue Ethics Approach to Aldo Leopold's Land Ethic."[14] Virtue Ethics is often used in conjunction with Communitariansim in traditional ethical theory. In this way, Shaw seeks to extend the usage to the natural community described by Leopold. Shaw seeks to examine the worldview change necessary to seriously consider adapting

---

[12]I provide a critical survey of many of the most prominent ethical theories in my book *Basic Ethics*.

[13]Of course, some would like to add emotion—rationally tethered emotion—and caring to this scheme. Others would add a faith-based religious element to the mixture. I have indicated a willingness elsewhere to accept these additions as overlays to traditional theories.

[14]William Shaw, "A Virtue Ethics Approach to Aldo Leopold's Land Ethic" *Environmental Ethics* 19.1 (1997), 53–68.

Virtue Ethics to Leopold's natural community. If such a view could be effected, then virtues such as respect or ecological sensitivity, prudence, and practical judgment might be adopted.

The problem, of course, is that Virtue Ethics requires some general agreement within the community about what constitutes a virtue. If a substantial shift in personal worldview among large numbers of people is a requirement, then it is certainly possible that the practical adoption of said virtue will never occur.

Even if one cannot go all the way to the worldview shift that Shaw is suggesting, it is still within the purview of most traditional lists of human virtue to adopt frugality as a desirable trait. By frugality, I mean an attitude of taking only what one needs, using it fully, not being wasteful. (Refer to the frugality ethic mentioned earlier.) For example, a frugal person does not take more food than he needs, does not build more housing space than he needs, does not buy more things than he needs. He, in turn, eats the food he has taken, uses the living space he has built, and utilizes the things he has until they are no longer functional. If large numbers of people exhibited such a virtue, then society would be less consumption driven and, by extension, exert less harmful pressure on the environment.

I believe that such a notion of frugality was a generally accepted virtue in the Depression era. As mentioned earlier, children of Depression era parents (like myself) were schooled in the virtue of the frugality ethic. Thus, a considerable number of people might already value measured and moderate use of our natural resources.

The only trouble with the virtue of frugality is that since 1980, conspicuous consumption appears to be more the norm than frugality. Instead of gas-efficient automobiles, the most popular models are sports utility vehicles that have low gas mileage and require a large amount of energy to produce. Suburbs are ringed with gigantic "trophy" houses of 6,000 to 7,000 feet that serve as domiciles for two or three people!

Thus, although I certainly argue in favor of considering frugality to be a virtue, I think that it may be becoming a minority position.

The alternative to these anthropocentric theories is a biocentric theory that sets the criteria for moral respect to be (among other things) (a) sentience, (b) active existence within a vital, powerful ecological system, or even (c) mere existence. The trouble with these accounts from my perspective is that they fail to provide a convincing reciprocal account that I believe is essential for any theory of ethics. For example, if I should refrain from killing the lion, should the lion refrain from killing me? Of course not because lions do not exhibit freedom (that comes from rationality alone). Lions act on a principle of survival. Humans also act on a principle of survival (as per the Principle of Human Survival). However, humans are free to use discretion (in situations of non-subsistence) about *what* they kill and *when*. This is different from other animals, plants, and the landscape.

Reciprocity requires that what is a duty to one agent is also a duty to another equal agent. One-sided (paternalistic) duties apply only to unequal entities (such as a parent to a child), but even these may not be strict moral duties.[15] And of course, the entire environmental ethics debate is about how humans should respect nature. If ethics presupposes free will and reciprocity of agency and if only humans exhibit this type of free will, then the best a biocentric theory can hope for is one-sided paternalistic quasi-moral duties. It seems to me that we get more justifiable environmental protection from anthropocentric moral theories than from biocentric ones.

The Realm of Aesthetic Values

In many ways, I believe the realm of aesthetic values to be the most promising strategy from the personal worldview perspective. Aesthetic values regarding nature may be understood in two ways: (a) artistic appreciation and (b) scientific appreciation.

In artistic appreciation, we point to the fact that nature is beautiful. Unlike ordinary artifacts in galleries and museums, this beauty is from an inscrutable maker. Still, the presence of a majestic landscape is powerful:

> Five years have passed: five summers with the length
> Of five long winters and again I hear
> These waters, rolling from their mountain-springs
> With a soft inland murmur. Once again
> Do I behold these steep and lofty cliffs,
> That on a wild secluded scene impress
> Thoughts of a more deep seclusion: and connect
> The landscape with the quiet of the sky.
> —William Wordsworth,
> *Lines Composed a Few Miles above Tintern Abbey*

Wordsworth and the other Lake Country poets exhibit an aesthetic appreciation that borders on worship. It is an odd individual, indeed, who would look at a parking lot or a mass of concrete and steel (such as midtown Manhattan) and exhort such lofty sensibilities—unless she were making an artistic judgment about architecture. But even then, considering the process of human city building and development, most would assert that the works of nature far outshine those of humankind.

According to the value-duty relationship, if a person values nature as beautiful, he is also saying that it is good and should be protected and defended.[16] The act of valuing incurs the duty of protecting/defending.

---

[15]For a discussion of unequal entities and their relationship to moral duties, see Deryck Beyleveld and Shaun Pattinson, "Precautionary Reason as a Link to Moral Action," *Medical Ethics*, ed. Michael Boylan (Upper Saddle River, NJ: Prentice Hall, 2000).

[16]One form of this argument is made by Janna Thompson, "Aesthetics and the Value of Nature" *Environmental Ethics* 17.3 (1995), pp. 291–306.

This works well for most who *do* view nature as beautiful and valuable. However, it ignores some who view it not as beautiful but as a market basket of raw resources just ripe for human development (exploitation). These individuals have no intrinsic aesthetic experience of nature but view only their own accomplishments as beautiful. They view a shopping center that sits on what once was a an aviary as a great feat of human engineering and know-how. For these individuals (I believe them to be a minority), no duty will arise from the aesthetic valuing of nature because they do not aesthetically value it.

In the mode of *scientific appreciation,* I believe there is also a large audience. The basic principle behind this mode is that when a person appreciates something intellectually, she automatically acquires a value for that thing as being beautiful. Many field biologists, for example, cite their love of the beauty of nature,[17] and by this they mean that the more they *understand* about the species/ecosystem they are observing, the more it enhances their appreciation/valuing of it.[18]

For this reason, I believe that most who understand or seek to understand something of the science of nature also value it aesthetically in this second mode. In this second mode, a person's rational appreciation of the intricate balance of natural systems creates within the subject an emotional response that I call *aesthetic.* The word *aesthetic* comes from the Greek meaning sensory perception. According to the *Oxford English Dictionary,* after 1830, a sentimental attachment also was associated with the word (although at first this was rather controversial). The point in this context is that a person's sensory experience could occasion an emotional response such as Wordsworth's rapture upon seeing the ruins of Tintern Abbey in southeastern Wales. We often attribute emotion to sense impressions that strike us forcefully.

In classical Greek, *aisthesis* and *noesis* were complementary concepts: When a person *sensed,* he was operating in a different mode than when he *thought.* But in the late eighteenth century when standards of artistic taste began being discussed using the word *aesthetics,* the gap between these two traditional antagonists narrowed. An individual could ratiocinate about what she sensed. A dialectical relationship between the two became a given in the

---

[17]There are many examples of this from Konrad Lorenz in *King Solomon's Ring* (New York: Plume, 1997) to E. O. Wilson in *The Diversity of Life* (New York: W.W. Norton, 1993). My point is that these scientists begin as observers but in the process begin to acquire an appreciation for the phenomenon that carries with it a valuing of this phenomenon. I call this valuing aesthetics in the mode of scientific appreciation.

[18]Some will say that "aesthetic" and "rational" appreciation are separate and rather unmixed. I counter to say that the two are intricately intertwined so that one reinforces the other. In this way, I support the position that Horace makes in the "Art of Poetry" in Q Horati Flacci, *Opera,* ed. E. C. Wickham, revised by H.W. Garrod (Oxford: Clarendon Press, 1975). Horace believes that poetry stimulates both rational and aesthetic responses but first must be beautiful to allow the other mode (reason) to function in conjunction with the former. Thus, art must both please and instruct, but it cannot instruct if it does not first please.

developing canons of nineteenth century criticism that led to Impressionism and Expressionism.

I am suggesting that we think seriously about this dialectical relationship—only this time, let us start it from *noesis*. Beginning with a scientific study of nature, the practitioner gains a heightened aesthetic appreciation of the phenomenon that is accompanied by sentiment. This valuing also incurs a duty to defend and protect based on the value-duty relationship.

I believe that we often begin with *noesis* and subsequently acquire *aisthesis*. Let's call this acquisition of aesthetic value mode two. (Mode one occurs when we begin with *aisthesis* and move to *noesis*.) I base my conjecture about how common mode two aesthetic acquisition is upon the large number of public television programs on nature to indicate the general interest in its operation. Viewers of these programs, too, will incur an aesthetic valuing that arises from their original rational quest. This aesthetic valuing creates a duty based on the value-duty relationship.

Taken together (mode 1 and mode 2), the aesthetic valuing of nature creates a duty to protect and defend it among a significant majority of people but not everyone (as mentioned).

The Realm of Religious Values

Religious duties are important; 80 percent of the world's population affirm belief in a monotheistic religion. The world's two largest religions, Christianity and Islam, accept the Jewish book of *Genesis* that asserts that God created the world from nothing. When God was finished, God declared it was good.[19] From this account alone, we have an assertion that all of nature is good (i.e., is to be valued). According to the value-duty relationship, this means that those who believe in *Genesis* should strive to protect and defend the environment out of a religious duty born of a religiously oriented valuing.

Most other religions ascribe to creation accounts that also would, on the same principle, incur duties to nature. In addition to this, other duties may also arise through the work of theologians who interpret the holy scriptures of the various religions. For example, in the *Mishnah* and the *Talmud*, a concept of *bal tashit* ("do not destroy') evolved.[20] This dictum argues against wanton destruction and conspicuous consumption (similar to the frugality ethic described earlier). In this way, a religious duty is formed to protect the environment from wanton destruction and to prevent people from being overly driven by consumption.

Between these two modes (the holy scriptures themselves in their creation accounts and the commentators on those scriptures), a large portion of

---

[19]*Genesis*, 1:31.

[20]For a discussion of this in more detail, see: Eilon Schwartz, "*Bal Tashit:* A Jewish Environmental Precept," in Chapter Three of this book.

the world's population (in principle)[21] incurs a duty to protect and defend the environment.

In the end, the duties incurred by the Personal Worldview Perspective greatly enhance the environment. Although duties can be formulated from all three principal domains of worldview value (ethics, aesthetics, and religion), I believe that the realm of aesthetics is the most promising to reach the greatest number.[22]

B. Application through Shared Community Worldview

Another source of duty to protect the environment comes from the shared community worldview. I will focus my comments in this section on examining the community's core values, questions of justice, and strategies and tactics for environmental protection.

Core Community Values

Core community values are the most prominent values that a group espouses as a part of its identity. They represent essential elements of that group's perceived mission or purpose. They include ethical, aesthetic, and religious values.

Core community values are developed in different ways. One way is from a discussion in the community about what is valuable in life. If we think of communities as social organizations that begin with the family and expand outward to include the city, county, state, nation, and the world,[23] then these discussions occur at these levels as well. Obviously, as we increase in levels of generality, the amount of personal interaction with the new level of community decreases. Thus, the sense that a dialectical interaction exists between individual and community best occurs at the family, neighborhood, and local town levels (including their various institutions such as schools and churches, synagogues, and mosques).

---

[21]I say "in principle" because there are many commands that organized religion(s) professes that are never realized. They seem to exist more in the realm of a utopian vision of things the way they *should* be but not the way they are. It has been my experience that many good people perform many noble actions because of their belief in organized religion. However, the numbers who respond in this way are nowhere near the 80 percent figure quoted earlier. This means that there are far more in organized religion who are willing to "talk the talk" but not willing to "walk the walk."

[22]This does not mean that I would dismiss ethics or religion. Indeed, they are valuable. The more people who can be garnered to defend and protect the environment, the better. It is just that the nature of the aesthetic impulse (given the value-duty relationship) is a compelling principle that is amenable to the creation of a common body of knowledge among many different peoples.

[23]I have obviously used the sociopolitical structure of the United States. This is easily adapted to countries that have a different political organization.

Another source of core community values might be through passively reading, listening, or viewing others discuss these issues. This might occur by attending a meeting and listening as a member of the audience or by reading, listening to, or viewing the popular media: newspapers, magazines, radio, and television.

Obviously, the potential also exists for propaganda and influence shaping (sometimes called *spinning*) from these sources as well. Thus, although they are a necessity of the modern age, they must be viewed with critical skepticism as well.

To better appreciate the dynamics of this process, let us turn to a concrete example. In Sleepy Hollow, a small town near Anywhere, USA, ABC Corporation has applied for a zoning variance to build one of its Floormart stores. Floormart has built its superstores around the country and undercut local merchants in cost, thus driving many of those merchants out of business. When people complain, Floormart replies, "We didn't drive the local merchants out of business; you [the people] did. You bought from us and stopped buying from them. It's the American way."

Your county planning board is holding a hearing to discuss the zoning proposal. At the meeting, advocates of both sides make their arguments. The proponents of Floormart proclaim that they can bring progress to Sleepy Hollow. "We can deliver you more goods and at a cheaper price than you've ever seen before. This will be the shot in the arm that this area has been waiting for!"

The opponents of Floormart say, "Floormart stores have driven local merchants out of business all around the country. At first, they will tell you that they can bring economic development to an area, but then they will offer such low wages that they will have to import workers who are willing to be exploited. And you know those six acres of woodlands at the edge of Johnson's farm? If they get this variance, it will all be asphalt and buildings. This project must be voted down, or we will lose everything that we cherish in Sleepy Hollow."

The proponents of the development appeal to the core prudential value of more money through more local development and cheaper costs for goods needed for day-to-day life. The opponents of development appeal to core values, as well (viz., looking after community jobs and not altering life as it is in Sleepy Hollow), both sociologically and ecoaesthetically.

Both sides appeal to issues that are meant to resonate within the community as represented at that meeting. Through an honest discussion that includes aspects of central worldview tenets, the debate will be engaged. This leads to the question of how worldview values are changed, which is a complicated process.[24] A shortened version is that there is an interaction between the proposal and a person's worldview. If the proposal creates a

---

[24]I outline this process in some detail in *Basic Ethics,* chap. 8.

significant dissonance, the person will reject it. However, if sufficient similarity is found via the common body of knowledge, then change is possible. More on this in the strategies and tactics section.

Questions of Justice

Justice is always in the province of shared community values. By *justice* (in this context), I am referring to distributive justice that is inherently an issue of allocation. There are, of course, many allocation principles. (I generally highlight the following list: to each equally (egalitarianism), to each according to his needs (socialism), to each according to his work or production (capitalism), to each according to his rank or station (aristocratism), and to each according to his ability to snatch it for himself (*kraterism*)). Connected to the principle of justice that is chosen is the question concerning the parties among whom the distribution is said to take place.

This is also a question about which communities to involve. Some candidates are (a) my family alone, (b) the local community at hand, (c) the county, (d) the state, (e) the country, (f) the world, (g) future generations in all of the preceding groups (i.e., my grandchildren, the grandchildren of each of the other categories in the same order).[25]

If a person were considering only her family, then the problem would concern it only. There are certainly microlevel problems about who gets to eat the tomatoes in the family garden. But the more pressing social issues occur when the community grows considerably larger. Many try to draw an artificial line that excludes considerations of all communities after items (e), (f), or (g). They do this based on some notion of national sovereignty. However, I believe this to be a mistake. The reason for this is that if natural resources are said to "belong" to humans at all, they belong only on the caveat that they are collectively owned. No person can say that he can properly own any natural thing himself (if ownership entails the ability to dispose of x as the owner pleases).[26] This is so because (a) natural resources are not discrete but interdependent and (b) the authority-granting ownership is a social institution that is thus ruled by principles of justice (a distribution principle that ought to consider all possible agents—now and in the future).

On the first point, natural resources are not discrete but interdependent. A person cannot utilize a natural resource as she pleases because what

---

[25]Some would say that this last category is rather peculiar since there are no *actual* members of the future generation. Since these people do not exist, how can anyone owe them a duty? This is true, but barring a cataclysm, there will be future generations. These individuals are connected to present peoples through the normal process of sexual reproduction. Such a relationship has long been held to carry normative force (cf. the Jewish doctrine of responsibility unto the third generation).

[26]Of course, if different definitions of ownership are given that are conditional on proper use, then I have no problem with private ownership. But many have traditionally taken the strong sense of ownership to justify all sorts of deleterious environmental action.

she does will affect the natural resources of the ecosystem, contiguous ecosystems, and even remote ecosystems. Thus, since the effects of resource utilization are communal, the obligations of stewardship/ownership are also communal.

Second, on the issue of justice, if we hold to the principle that I have enunciated elsewhere that, all things being equal, we must always begin with egalitarianism,[27] then considering all of these groups, we must modify absolute dominion over our property in favor of a limited use doctrine that considers all of the various stakeholders, both present and future.

Certainly, when we consider the fact that strong private property ownership is a given in most societies in the world, this is a radical proposition. I am arguing here (on the basis of egalitarian justice allocation of natural resources to all the peoples of the earth now and in the future) that individuals' ownership of anything in nature is conditional upon the conditions of this allocation.

If an individual is allocating natural resources, there is a difference between renewable and nonrenewable resources. The allocation of renewable resources is guided by the principle of sustainable development.[28] Humankind must "mother" its resources so that they continue to flourish under natural conditions. This means maintaining the integrity of wild species that have not been genetically engineered and are not endangered by such. The reasoning for this is that the mechanisms of nature are assumed to be more subtle and complex that we imagine and that creating an overly artificial breeding population will ultimately narrow the range of evolutionary fitness for that species. And since it is not just (under egalitarianism) to permit one person/company/country to "hog" nature's resources (i.e., claim an unequal share) and given the interdependence of resources argued for earlier, it is totally unacceptable for anyone or any community to deplete renewable resources. Thus, I am arguing that when allocating renewable resources, we must strictly adhere to sustainable development (including protection of wild species).

The argument for the permissibility of using nonrenewable resources is rather more difficult. If future generations stretch indefinitely in the future, then the utilization of nonrenewable resources automatically involves shortchanging someone else down the line. The obvious consequence of this is that utilization of nonrenewable resources is wrong because it violates the rights of future generations to utilize them. This right is supported by egalitarianism.

---

[27]"Affirmative Action," *Business Ethics,* ed. Michael Boylan (Upper Saddle River, NJ: Prentice Hall, 2001").

[28]One prominent critic of sustainable development as an independent concept apart from mere welfare maximization is Wilfred Beckerman, "'Sustainable Development': Is It a Useful Concept?" *Environmental Values* 3 (1994); pp. 191–209.

However, many of these nonrenewable resources are crucial for our survival. Practical arguments based upon human survival may refer to the "ought-implies-can" standard. I suggest that we should utilize only nonrenewable resources that can be recycled for continuous usage. This would cover metals but would say nothing about nonrecyclable minerals and petroleum. My response is that society must find alternatives to these so that we do not deplete the world of them.

Strategies and Tactics for Environmental Preservation

The final section of this essay briefly suggests directions for the future given the principles already enunciated.

First, I would say that the primary task is to formulate a dialogue within various communities about the shared worldview. This dialogue should proceed along the lines dictated by the Shared Community Worldview Imperative: Constructive dialogue must be engaged in communities at all levels about a common way to discuss environmental issues. The result of this dialogue must be a set of agreed-upon ethical maxims that address the relationship between humans and nature. These maxims need to recognize that nature is valuable. This value can be agreed to from ethical, aesthetic, and religious sources. Once nature's value is asserted, because of the value-duty relationship, the members of the community must admit to a duty to protect and defend nature that includes supporting sustainable development (along with protection for wild species) and a long-term commitment to use only nonrenewable resources that can be recycled.

Second, if the community in which we live is deaf to these appeals for dialogue, then we must resort to the time-proven practical devices of engaging in various high-profile antics that will shake up public consciousness so that we might begin anew with our discussion. (The limitation on these high-profile antics is that they do not create more harm than they are meant to alleviate—Greenpeace and People for the Ethical Treatment of Animals have been adept at making public statements that have shocked but not resulted in more harm than what they are protesting).

Because the value-duty relationship, the Personal Worldview Imperative, and the Shared Community Worldview Imperative dictate that each of us become practically, not just intellectually, involved in these issues, the result is that each of us must take some action. We cannot make an intellectual commitment only because intellectual acceptance of these imperatives dictates personal action.

Such is the task before us all. Real duties toward the environment have been enunciated via the Personal Worldview Imperative and the Shared Community Worldview Imperative; they enjoin action. We cannot fail to become involved or to heed our duty. The stakes are simply too high.

EVALUATING A CASE STUDY:
ASSESSING EMBEDDED LEVELS

The goal in this series of exercises is for you to be able to write an essay that critically evaluates an environmental problem involving ethical issues. Your essay should include an examination of professional practice as well as the ethical dimensions. In Chapter Three, we discussed how to bring the ethical dimensions to the fore through the use of detection questions. These were put side by side the principles of professional practice.

In this chapter, we compare these two types of issues. This comparison can be accomplished in multiple ways; the one offered here invokes a technique that rates professional practice as having three levels of complexity: surface, medium, and deep. The level of interaction allows you to see at a glance how professional practice issues, cost issues, and ethical issues conflict.

You need a model of some type to evaluate the professional practice issues, cost considerations, and ethical issues that may conflict. When ethical issues and practical issues conflict, you do not *automatically* choose either. Some ethical problems can be solved easily and do not require forgoing the dictates of the professional practice. At other times, an ethical problem must be solved in such a way that professional practices or cost considerations must be overridden.

You need a methodology for comparison. The *embedded concept model* is one such methodology. I illustrate how this works with several examples that employ a chart to clarify the ways the concepts conflict. You may also want to use this technology if you have access to one of the popular computer spreadsheet programs, but the use of a spreadsheet is not necessary. A more conventional approach is to discuss these differences. The spreadsheet is no substitute for solid narrative description, but at the very least it simplifies and makes visual the model I propose.

Case 1.

You are the environmental impact officer of a mining company that mines copper in Montana. The most efficient way to operate your mine is via strip mining, by which a portion of the earth (in this case an entire mountain) is removed to expose the ore-bearing earth underneath to cyanide and various other toxic chemicals that are captured within a clay-capped reservoir and treated according to Environmental Protection Agency guidelines. Your company is in legal compliance with all existing laws on the treatment of such waste, but your have learned that although it is in compliance, it is leaching toxic chemicals into the earth, which could infect the region's water table. To change this process is somewhat expensive but well within the company's ability. It involves creating a stronger more effective cap or seal to the leach pond. This probably will solve the problem, but it goes beyond what is required by law. Do you have a duty to do more than the law requires?

Let us examine this situation via professional practice issues, ethical issues, and cost issues. All three of these areas are important in forming an ethical decision.

Professional Practice Issues

1. A professional is required only to follow the law and the guidelines of its professional association. The mining company has obeyed all relevant regulations. However, the mining association has said repeatedly that it intends to be a friend to the environment. Critics say that this is hypocrisy, but you intend to take such statements seriously.
2. Going beyond the law and the association's guidelines could be perceived as raising the standard that other mining companies would be required to follow. Meeting this additional standard could require the use of funds that had not been budgeted.

Ethical Issues

1. When a company receives clearance to begin a mining operation, it must submit an environmental impact statement that promises to maintain the environment essentially as it was—as much as possible. Thus, the company is involved in keeping and maintaining a promise.
2. *Informed* consent is necessary for autonomous decision making.

Cost Issues

1. Creating a better leach pond seal for the waste products is possible but will cut into profits.
2. If profits fall, some people might lose their jobs.

In this simple case, the ethical guidelines override those of the cost or professional issues. That means the ethical guidelines are "easier" to solve. When a great disparity exists between the embeddedness of one alternative as opposed to the other, that direction should drive the decision. One should implement the other side as it is possible. This is not to suggest that either the professional or cost issues are unimportant. Rather, this analysis is useful to determine which are the most embedded.

Thus, in this case, the mining company's embedded status quo arguments are less embedded than implementing the use of the improved seal on its leach pond; therefore, the company should improve the leach pond seal because (a) the professional issues are not deeply embedded, (b) the ethical issues are deeply embedded, and (c) the cost issues are not deeply embedded (and one issue cuts both ways, that is, may actually be an advantage).

Analysis of the Illustration Practices at XYZ Mining

	SURFACE	MEDIUM	DEEP
Professional Practice Issues			
A professional is required to follow only the law and the professional association's guidelines		x	
The company may be accused of raising the standard	x		
Ethical Issues			
One's promise to leave the land as it was			x
Only a truly *informed* consent satisfies the conditions of autonomy (as well as the contract with the state)			x
Cost Issues			
New guidelines may affect future profits	x		
Additional costs may be incurred in implementing a new leach pond seal	x		

Case 2.

This case is not so simple. You are a regional director at the World Health Organization. One of your duties is to supervise the distribution of birth control devices to women in less-developed countries. The product of choice has been the intrauterine device (IUD) that has proved to be effective and inexpensive. The problem is that in the United States, several hundred users of the IUD have contracted pelvic inflammatory infections that have been linked to use of the IUD. These infections can cause sterility and death. As regional director, you must decide whether to continue to supply IUDs to women in less-developed countries.

There is also the ABC Corporation, a large multinational company that has a considerable inventory of IUDs that it cannot sell in the United States. The company would rather not write off its entire inventory and has consequently made a very attractive offer to sell the World Health Organization all of its existing inventory and to assist in distributing the product regionally.

As regional director, you must decide whether to accept ABC's offer to supply IUDs for the World Health Organization's program for women in less-developed countries.

Professional Practice Issues

1. As a professional in the public health field, your responsibility is to choose public policy that maximizes the health and minimizes the health risks in the general population.

2. Sexual activity without birth control in less-developed countries will lead to an increasing population that, in turn, will lead to severe poverty and mass starvation.
3. Mass starvation kills millions; pelvic inflammatory infections kill hundreds. Thus, it is better to save the many (in the spirit of the profession's mission).

Ethical Issues

1. Each person's life is precious.
2. The end of saving more lives does not justify the means of sacrificing others.

Cost Issues

1. ABC Corporation is willing to give the World Health Organization a substantial price break on its existing inventory of IUDs. This price break will allow the World Health Organization to serve more women of child-bearing age than its original strategic plan had projected. ABC's offer to assist in regional distribution will save the World Health Organization additional money.
2. White knights are not lining up at your door to help you fulfill the mission of this program.

This case differs from Case 1 because the professional, ethical, and cost guidelines are equally embedded. In this case, the dictates of the ethical imperative must be followed because it is more deeply imbedded in a person's worldview than is the imperative of professional practice or cost issues. The components of ethics enter the worldview generically as a feature of a person's humanity.[1] The imperatives of professionalism enter the worldview as one of many modes of personal fulfillment; the imperatives of cost enter the worldview as modes of day-to-day practical consumption.

Although many people may create pessimistic scenarios (such as state of nature) to the contrary, a decision such as this case will not cause your death or that of a family member. It may cause you to be discharged, drastically affecting your lifestyle. In the United States (at the writing of this book), making such a decision almost never causes an individual to face starvation.[2]

My experience has been that businesspeople are very prone to hyperbole when they describe the consequences of an ethical decision that entails the loss of money and worldly goods. This overstatement culture has the effect of blocking people from taking the right action because they fear exaggerated consequences.[3]

---

[1]For a further discussion of the mechanics, see Chapter One of *Basic Ethics.*

[2]Of course the dead hero problem comes in here. Would one prefer to be a live coward (here understood to mean a moral coward) or a dead hero (here understood to mean someone who has suffered for his or her beliefs) This is not an easy question and lies at the heart of all discussions of Environmental Ethics.

[3]It is not the worst thing in the world to have to step back and live on less. It has been my personal experience that the essential elements of personal happiness have no price tag. Truly supported caring relationships cannot be taken away from you no matter what hard times befall you (except through some unrelated event—such as disease or accident).

Analysis of Population Control in the Less-Developed Countries

	SURFACE	MEDIUM	DEEP
Professional Practice Issues			
Public health mission to preserve the health of as many as possible			x
Sexual activity without birth control leads to mass starvation			x
The end justifies the means			x
Ethical Issues			
Human life is precious			x
The end does not justify the means			x
Cost Issues			
ABC's inventory can be used to serve many women			x
The World Health Organization needs help from someone or it may be unable to continue this program			x

As with scientific theories, the dictates of a universally binding imperative founded on generic structures trump those of a particular person's individual interests. More details on this appear in the "Evaluating a Case Study" section in Chapter Five.

In this essay, the main concern is the ability to assess the levels of embeddedness. Some common mistakes that my students have made in performing this assessment follow:

1. *Not giving the imperatives of professional practice their due.* Remember that whether you assess imbeddedness via a spreadsheet or through discursive paragraphs, you are working from your original analysis of the problem. A failure to uncover all the important facets will be reflected in your depiction of embeddedness. You will notice gaps in the reasoning and will feel that something is missing. If this happens, go back over the issues lists. Rewrite the case in your own words; expand or recast the case in some way. By doing this, you become the author and are forced to recognize key elements in the case as presented.

2. *Seeing everything at the same level of imbeddedness.* You need to view embeddedness as a way to describe the degree to which an issue is essential to the case. A less essential issue should be given less consideration. To better understand the essential structure of a professional practice, prepare short justifications of your choice of that element as an issue in the case. As you prepare your justifications, think about each element in its relation to the whole. If that relation could not be different without seriously altering the whole, then

it is essential. If you can find substitutes that would work just as well, the relation is incidental.

3. *Listing too many professional, cost, and ethical issues.* This is the flip side
to step 1. You have given too much detail that is not essential to the case at
hand, or you are listing one issue in a number of different ways. In either
event, preparing an essential description of your elements (as in step 2) can
help you shorten your issue list to only those required for your evaluation.

Good solid work avoiding these mistakes will enable you to create a
more satisfactory result in the argumentative stage, in which you may finally
apply your ethical theory to your annotated imbeddedness charts.

Macro Cases.

Macro Case 1. As the secretary of the interior, you are about to draft
legislation to send to Congress outlining principles of land use in the nation's
national park system. The first issue you are considering is access to the parks
by vacationing citizens. The most popular parks in the system are well over
capacity. Cars move in gridlock along two-lane roads to famous landmarks
(such as Old Faithful). Your staff has prepared two solutions to this problem.
Jack Development suggested the first solution; he says that the nation's parks
are for its citizens to enjoy, but they aren't enjoying them by being stuck in long
traffic jams. The answer is to build six-lane roads through the park connected
by two-lane roads that will lead tourists to outlying areas. The cost of the project will be supported by increased user fees. "People will be willing to pay
more if you give them their money's worth," says Jack.

Cindy Conservation takes a contrary position; she says that Jack's plan
will ruin the natural beauty of the parks and harm wildlife tremendously.
What Cindy proposes is to limit entry to the parks through several embarka-
tion points. These points would lie just outside the park and consist of parking lots that have a set number of spaces. Cindy would like to set the figure
at 75 percent of current levels. From these points of entry, buses powered by
natural gas and electricity would ferry people to existing lodges and camp-
grounds. People could also bicycle into the park if they register first. Hiking
would also be permitted with proper registration. The point of this limitation
is to offer nature more protection by keeping private automobiles out of our
nation's parks. "The parks are being destroyed. We must reverse this trend,"
says Cindy.

You must craft either Cindy's or Jack's position. To do this, write a scene
in which Cindy and Jack argue their respective points of view before you. Be
sure that each uses practical, professional, and ethical arguments (with linking principles). Then write a summary of the position you will take and why.

Macro Case 2. You are the secretary of the interior, and the second half of the report you are sending to Congress concerns mining and oil rights for private companies on government land. Presently, these companies pay royalties, but they are nowhere near their market value. Thus, the government is (in effect) subsidizing them. Three groups are trying to lobby you concerning your policy recommendation. The first is an environmental group that exhorts you to stop all mining on federal lands. The second says that mining of reusable minerals (such as copper and gold) should be permitted, but that mining nonreusable minerals and petroleum should cease. This group also wants the royalties raised to market rates. A third group suggests that you leave things as they are because the economy is relatively good and the country cannot afford the human displacement that radical policies might cause.

Write arguments for all three positions, identifying the relevant issues concerning economic impact, professional issues, and ethical issues. After you have done this, write the position you will take to Congress. Be sure to adequately support your position.

Micro Cases.

Micro Case 1. You are visiting Lemar, your best friend, and Latasha, his wife. Lemar is reading the newspaper, and you are playing chess with Latasha. Suddenly, Lemar exclaims, "Hey, they're going to build a new power plant right here in Hudson County!"

"Oh yeah?" says Latasha. "Where?"

"Just off Route 123 near Backlick Road. On the old Miller Farm, I reckon."

"That's pretty close."

"Yeah. Close is right. Not more than a few miles away."

"What kind of plant are they going to build? Nuclear?"

"No—coal. Lots of cheap coal on the market right now. Going to change things around here, that's for sure." Each of them sighs as if to say, oh well, what can you do?

Then you say, "Is that all there is to it? Just shrug it off with a sigh?"

"What do you want?" asks Lemar. "People need their electricity."

You are taken aback. You want to mention something about values and principles, but you are not sure what to say. Are any ethical principles involved? Does it matter that the old Miller Farm is one of the most beautiful vistas in the valley? Does it matter that the plant will alter everyone's life with more noise, smoke, commotion, and outsiders coming in? What is important here?

Using the principles you have studied, discuss the ethical issues in this situation. Then identify any relevant ethical theory and associated cogent linking principles. With these data, create a response to Lemar and Latasha.

Micro Case 2. Your name is Carmelita. You live near San Francisco, and your town has a voluntary recycling law. The law says people should separate bottles and cans into a blue container and put newspapers into a yellow container. Yard waste is put into a can with a yard sticker (yearly cost is $25). All other garbage is put into a can with a general sticker (yearly cost $50). The problem is that your husband, Juan, likes to throw his refuse (no matter what it is) into the general garbage pile because he doesn't like to take the time to walk to the end of the kitchen and open the pantry door to find the recycling bins. You have confronted him about this several times, but he says that he can do what he wants because the law is voluntary and he pays the freight for general garbage when he could save money by using the free recycling bins—"It's my business if I want to pay, right?"

You think Juan is wrong and you want to appeal to his mother (the only person he will listen to). Make the argument in terms that will identify the ethical issues involved and connect a moral theory to the situation at hand via linking principles. Outline how you will approach Juan's mother with a few responses in case she disagrees.

chapter five

The Moral Basis for Environmentalism

General Overview. This chapter addresses one of the most important issues in environmental ethics: the foundation of moral value. The two traditional foundations are anthropocentric and biocentric. The anthropocentric argument bases moral value on nature's utility to humans. It sees nature as an entity or tool (albeit an important one) that humans utilize for their advantage and welfare. Under this scenario, a person's obligations are strictly prudential. A person does not want to spoil the thing he depends on for life. The future generation argument is simply an extension of this. A person does not want to spoil what his children or grandchildren depend on for life. (There is something wrong about bringing people into the world and then denying them what they depend on for their continued existence.)

The biocentric argument asserts a sort of egalitarianism between species: Each species is necessary for the ecosystem; therefore, each has an equal claim to continue to exist in a relatively unfettered manner. To support such a position, a person must attribute intrinsic value to the ecosystem as a whole. Obviously, various persons might view this in terms of a turf battle. (In all turf battles, however, the dictum "power rules" generally carries the day. Humans have the most power. Q.E.D.)

Can a middle ground be found? If common strategies for action are identical, then what is the importance of the reason? This is an important question.

I. Anthropocentric Justification

Overview. There are many forms of anthropocentric justification for environmental ethics. One of the most prominent is the duty to future generations. Alan Gewirth sets out this argument from the point of view of his theory of human rights and duties. In his theory, human rights require a sense of mutuality. One factor that complicates mutuality in the case of future generations is that it is hard to define a generation since the term is rather imprecise. There is no clear point of demarcation of a new generation. This problem of identifying what a generation is (much less a future generation) leads to the second point: Future generations do not exist so that to say that they have rights or duties is rather a stretch (keeping in mind the requirement for mutuality). Does this mean we do nothing? No. Gewirth suggests a transgenerational position that distinguishes two bases for positing duties to future generations. The first is humanistic because its first concern is the interests of human beings and their moral rights (both present and future). The second is naturalistic that posits nature as having an intrinsic claim. These two positions are examined and some suggestions are made about how each applies.

Onora O'Neill takes the position that all types of moral reasoning are anthropocentric because moral demands are made on agents. However, deep ecologists claim that if the source of obligation to the natural world rests ultimately in human agents, then there is little protection to the environment. Their claim is that the environment possesses a locus of real value. Various approaches to this end include realist, utilitarian, and rights-based arguments. The problem with these revolves around defending a metaphysical position that is questionable. Instead, O'Neill wishes to argue for an anthropocentrically based approach that reaches many of the same goals to which the biocentric realists aspire without the metaphysical baggage.

Human Rights
and Future Generations

Alan Gewirth

Human rights are rights that every human being has simply by virtue of being human. Does this apply to future generations of human beings as well as to present ones? Let us recognize, to begin with, that it is artificial and potentially misleading to talk of specific "generations" of humans. Humans do not come neatly packaged into discrete collections labeled "generations"; they exist as a continuum which is constantly being added to and subtracted from. When we talk of "generations," we often intend to distinguish temporally demarcated groups of humans by reference to some portentous set of events or circumstances that have some special importance in human history; thus we may talk of "the generation of the Great Depression," the "Vietnam Generation," and so forth. But when we talk of "future generations," such a demarcation is usually not intended. We usually mean groups of humans who will be living when all of "us" are presumably dead.

Nevertheless, insofar as the temporal demarcation involves relations of possible dependence, and especially of rights, among human beings, it carries moral significance, for then the well-being of a later group may be affected by the actions or inactions of earlier groups. So, to repeat the question, do future generations of humans, thus understood, have any human rights? The answer depends on the kinds of policies that ought to be followed in the present insofar as they may impinge on humans of the future.

One difficulty with an affirmative answer to this question bears on the requirement of mutuality. Human rights are universalistically mutual, in that they are rights of all humans against all humans: every human is both the subject or right-holder and the respondent or duty-bearer, so that there is a mutual sharing of the benefits of rights and the burdens of duties among all humans. On another construal, it is only governments that are the respondents or duty-bearers of human rights, since it is usually only they that have the power both to violate human rights and to implement them. Still, in principle, governments here act as the representatives of their citizens, so that it is still the latter that ultimately bear the burdens of being the respondents of human rights.

Future generations, however, cannot be properly construed as owing duties to the present generation, since they are in no position to implement the present generation's human rights. So the mutuality required for human rights seems lacking in their case.

We can solve this problem by taking a future-oriented, transgenerational view. Generation B, which exists later than Generation A, does not owe duties to Generation A because B cannot influence or implement A's rights. But B can implement the rights of the following generations C, D, and so forth, so that in this more complex way, mutuality is preserved: A owes duties to B, which in turn owes duties to C, and so forth. So, correlatively, B has rights against A, and C against B, and so forth. In addition, of course, there is required mutuality within each generation.

What is the nature of these rights? Broadly speaking, human rights can be divided into two kinds, negative and positive. Negative rights entail duties to refrain from interfering with the right-holder's having the objects of his rights: thus the right to life entails at least the duty to refrain from killing. Positive rights entail duties to help the right-holder to have the objects of her rights: thus the right to food entails, in certain circumstances, the duty to provide food, and so forth.

Future generations have both kinds of rights. Thus, for example, the present generation has the duty to refrain from so polluting the environment that the next generation will have dirty air, poisonous food, and so forth. This may well require sacrifices by the present generation; it has the duty to refrain from enriching itself in ways that will bring drastic harm to the future generations. This includes the duty to avoid saddling future generations with heavy debts incurred because the present generation will not tax itself to pay for its consumption of goods. Population growth incorporates another phase of these negative duties. While coercion should not be used in this sphere, other phases of these negative duties may well require political enactments that help to forestall nuclear disasters and prevent free marketeers, among others, from pursuing profits in ways that endanger future generations. In a still more directly political way, the present generation in a constitutional democracy has the duty to preserve its liberal institutions by refraining from corrupting or weakening those institutions. It also has the positive obligation to promote social justice in a way that benefits future generations as well as one's own, and to encourage economic development and political democracy in ways that will benefit future generations.

Serious problems of intergenerational justice arise when the positive rights of future generations are at stake. An emphatic example involves the kinds of steps taken by the government in one generation to provide benefits for a future generation. Stalin's drive to build a collectivist society by policies that led to the starvation of millions of "kulaks" was a drastic instance of violating the present generation's rights with the avowed aim of enabling a future generation to thrive. This point indicates the severe limits that must be set to the positive rights of future generations. They should indeed be helped to improve their well-being, but not at a price that violates the present generation's human rights. It is important to note that a similar conclusion applies when the envisaged benefits to the future generation are even admirable. The Egyptian pyramids and the Parthenon are wondrous creations; but their having been built with slave labor was a violation of human rights. This point may be criticized on the ground that the ancients had no idea of human rights and so cannot be condemned for what they did not know. But that some of the ancients did have this idea is suggested by the fact that their eminent philosophers saw the need to defend the institution of slavery. Moreover, the subsequent generations had no right that these monuments be built at such expense for their benefit.

It may be contended that criticism of the implementation of future generations' positive rights leads to a slippery slope: whenever one tries to improve the conditions of the next generation, this involves lowering the opportunities or benefits of the present generation. But this need not be so: it is not a zero-sum situation. In improving the chances or benefits of the next generation, one may also improve those of the present one. The right to education is an example; there are many others.

The whole idea that future generations have human rights may be criticized in the following way. In the argument for human rights, the agent or protagonist claims for himself rights to freedom and well-being as the necessary conditions of his agency, and he does so on the ground of his being a prospective purposive agent, so that he logically must accept that every prospective purposive agent has these rights. But the sense of "prospective" here is primarily individual: each agent regards himself as "prospecting" or looking ahead to fulfill his future purposes, beyond his actual present agency. This prospectiveness, however, does not apply to humans who are members of future generations; it is not to them as "prospective" future agents that the argument refers.

This objection overlooks the fact that future agents are still agents who will have the same agency needs as present agents, so that the argument also applies to them. A right is an individual's interest that ought to be protected for his own sake and controlled by him. Since future agents will have such interests, they have rights.

As was noted earlier, a main sphere of the application of human rights of future generations is environmental ethics. There is an important distinction, however, between two types of environmental ethics. One type is humanist: its basic concern is for the interests of human beings, and it regards the natural environment as providing means for the fulfillment of those interests. Since human rights are grounded in these human interests, the humanist type of environmental ethics is also focused on human rights. The natural environment is to be treated in a way that serves to fulfill human needs of well-being. On this view, then, the environment is the object of human rights, what they are rights to, while the subject of the rights, the right-holder, is humankind. The correlative duties incumbent on humans, including governments, are that the natural environment be treated in ways that fulfill human needs. The environment has no value independent of such humanist fulfillment. Future generations of humans have rights to be benefited by appropriate use of the natural environment.

This view sets both drastic limits and expansive opportunities for the human treatment of the natural environment. That environment must not be despoiled in ways that adversely affect the prospects of future generations as well as of the present one. But at the same time, within these limits, humans have the right to exploit natural resources in ways that contribute immeasurably to human well-being.

The alternative type of environmental ethics is naturalistic. It regards the natural environment as having value in itself, independent of any contributions it may make to fulfilling human needs. The environment is the subject of environmental rights, and humans are the respondents who have the correlative duty to preserve and enhance the environment.

The basis of the independent value attributed to the natural environment varies with different theories; it may be aesthetic, religious, organismic, or other. But central to many of these theories is the idea that the natural environment has a value, a grandeur, a nobility of structure and scope that makes it a fitting object of respect and indeed reverence. It is not to be used as a mere means to human ends; it is an end in itself that requires the utmost consideration and allegiance.

On the naturalist view, two aspects of the concept of rights can be fittingly applied to defend the idea of environmental rights as rights of the environment. One aspect is the point that rights are interests that ought to be protected. On the naturalist view, the environment has interests that are not primarily psychological but rather teleological: natural entities, especially biological ones, have patterns of inherent development that move normally to fruition (acorns become oak trees, and so forth). These entities can be approximately construed as having interests in such fruition, including their not being destroyed or mutilated. The other aspect is that of control. Although the environment usually cannot of itself control how humans will deal with it, both governmental and nongovernmental agencies can be appointed to represent its interests and thereby exercise appropriate control.

It is not always easy to distinguish between the humanist and the naturalist types of environmental ethics. Consider an analogy. The theoretical structure of physical science, amid its many complexities, is an enormously impressive system of ideas that has a profound intellectual beauty of so exalted a kind that knowledge of it is sometimes likened to a mystical experience. The system is constructed by human beings, but it has a significance and value that go beyond the uses made of it by human beings. At least since Aristotle such a system has been regarded as a good in itself, and devotion to its work as the highest human good.

It would be a misconception, then, to hold, with some pragmatists, that such a scientific system has value only insofar as it can be made to serve practical human needs. It does indeed involve obligations to future generations, but this is only to transmit and increase such knowledge, not to convert it into an engineering or other technological tool, let alone to subject it to obscurantist distortions. Nevertheless, it is sometimes held that the scientific system can be positively related to human needs: the basic need to know, to satisfy curiosity, to fulfill the profound desire to understand the world.

In a parallel way, it may be contended that the natural environment, entirely apart from its supplying food and other practical necessities for human beings, fulfills the human need to appreciate and to marvel at the majestic structure of the natural world. Human rights may also be invoked here because humans have a right to develop such appreciation. There is a correlative obligation to future generations to refrain from damaging the natural environment so that it can continue to be such an object of reverence.

The respect owed to the natural environment has certain implications for the rights of animals and other living beings. Entirely apart from the obligation to refrain from inflicting gratuitous pain on animals, there remains the question of the extent to which animals and even plants should be used to fulfill the imperative needs of human beings for food and clothing. Here the rights of present and future generations of human beings may come into conflict with the rights of animals. The basic argument for human rights shows why, in cases of such conflict, human rights must take precedence.

This consideration also bears on the question of whether the natural environment and its various parts have moral rights. For the naturalist, the intrinsic value of the environment provides sufficient justification for answering this question in the affirmative. It must be recognized, however, that even if we have duties toward animals, plants, and other parts of the environment, this does not prove that they have rights. The duties may derive not from the intrinsic worth of the environmental entities; it may not be for their own sake that we have duties toward them. The duties may derive instead from the complex ways in which, according to the humanist view, these entities subserve complex human needs. In this as in other cases, duties may not be correlative with rights.

Environmental Values, Anthropocentrism and Speciesism

Onora O'Neill

Most of us agree that we should value the environment, or at least some bits of the environment; fewer of us agree why we should do so. Leaving aside answers that appeal to sheer prudence or mere preference and looking at some of the array of answers offered under the heading of 'environmental ethics' leaves a great deal obscure.

One reason for valuing the environment might be that it is the locus of distinctive 'environmental values', which we can discover, recognise and then respect and preserve in appropriate ways—or, of course, and more worryingly, fail to respect and preserve. This conception of environmental values as real features of the natural world is often invoked on behalf of views that are broadly speaking vaguely realist and (at least) *biocentric*, or (more commonly) emphatically *ecocentric*, and supposedly reject *anthropocentric* positions. Advocates of realist forms of ecocentric ethics assert that intrinsic ecological values are objectively there in the natural world, whether or not there are any human beings who will recognise these values, and whether or not human beings who recognise the values act to preserve or respect them. Ecological realism can seem both thorough and objective. The values, whatever they may be, are part of the furniture of the universe and make their claims regardless of whether there is any audience, let alone an attentive audience, for the claims.

By contrast, living by an anthropocentric ethics is taken to put the environment, and above all the natural environment, at risk. If anthropocentric ethics derives its views of how we may act on the natural world from features of human life, it can supposedly accord the natural world little respect or protection. Such fears make it easy to understand the appeal of a realist and ecocentric ethic, which ostensibly puts real values, among them real environmental values, first, so is able both to underpin appeals for animal rights or liberation, and to support the wider ethical claims of various sorts of 'deep' or radical ecology.

The main drawback of appeals to real environmental values is that the ambitious claim that the environment, or nature, is the locus of distinctive, real values is so hard to establish. Yet unless we can show that there are indeed real environmental values, appealing to them will not provide *any* sort of reason for respecting or protecting the environment.[1] What makes it hard to establish these real values is the *realism* rather than the *ecocentrism,* a meta-physical difficulty that cannot be overcome by the merits of the cause which real environmental values are supposed to support. Appeals to a position which, if true, would have strong implications will establish nothing at all if the truth of the position cannot be shown. If no realist account of value, environmental or other, can be established, we have very strong reasons not to rely on one.

I cannot show that moral realism, and with it the view that there are real values located in the natural world, is false. What I shall try to show is that a plausible anthropocentric approach may provide a very great proportion of what many people hope to find in a realist and ecocentric approach, without making the same exacting metaphysical demands.

1. ANTHROPOCENTRISM, SPECIESISM AND RESULTS: UTILITARIANISM

If realist approaches to environmental ethics cannot be sustained, non-realist approaches may be more convincing. Yet the long-standing worry about non-realist approaches is that they are all anthropocentric,[2] in that they take human life (rather than some independent moral reality) as the starting point of ethical reasoning. Anthropocentric positions in ethics vary greatly. They include many forms of consequentialism (such as utilitarianism) as well as positions that take action rather than results as central (such as forms of contractualism, or action-based positions that take rights and obligations as the basic ethical categories).

A common criticism of anthropocentrist positions in ethics is that they all incorporate what has come to be called *speciesism.* The term *speciesism,* which was coined by analogue with terms such as *racism* or *chauvinism,* is usually used as a label for *unjustified* preference for the human species. The problem with any form of speciesism, critics complain, is that it accords humans moral standing, but unjustifiably accords animals of other species no, or only lesser, standing. On some views speciesism is also unjustifiable in its denial of moral standing to other aspects of the environment, ranging from plants and rivers to abstract entities such as species, habitats and ecosystems, bio-diversity and the ozone layer. Speciesism, as defined, is self-evidently to be condemned, since it builds on something that cannot be justified.

Unfortunately the term *speciesism* is also often used (derogatorily) for *any* preference for the human species, regardless of whether the preference is justified or not. This dual usage makes it easy to beg questions. In order to avoid begging questions I shall use the term *speciesism* strictly for *unjustified* views about the moral standing of certain species, and leave the question whether any preferences can be justified open for discussion. However, I shall use the terms *anti-speciesist* and *speciesist* descriptively to refer to those who do and do not accord non-human animals (full) moral standing. Speciesists in this merely descriptive sense would be guilty of speciesism only if the preference they accord humans cannot be justified.

The view that anthropocentric positions in ethics are invariably committed to speciesism, so unjustifiably blind to the claims of non-humans, is, I believe, unconvincing. Anthropocentrism views ethics as created by or dependent on human action; speciesism builds a preference for human beings into substantive ethical views. Many anthropocentric positions have benign implications for environmental issues, and specifically for the lives of non-human animals.

To show this it might seem reasonable to turn first to that supposedly *least* speciesist of anthropocentric positions, utilitarianism. Utilitarianism is anthropocentric in the straightforward and indispensable sense that it takes it that ethical argument is addressed to human agents, and that only humans can take up (or flout) utilitarian prescriptions.[3] However, Utilitarians claim to repudiate (human) speciesism because they offer reasons for according moral standing to all sentient animals. As Bentham put it, the way to determine moral standing is to ask not 'Can they *reason?* or can they *talk?* but can they *suffer?'*[4] By taking sentience rather than ability to reason as the criterion of moral standing, utilitarians can show the ethical importance of animal welfare; some of them even aim or claim to justify a conception of animal liberation.[5]

Still, it is worth remembering that utilitarianism needs only a little twist to reach conclusions which anti-speciesists do not welcome. John Stuart Mill agreed with Bentham that happiness was the measure of value, but thought that it came in various kinds, and that the higher kinds were restricted to humans. He concluded that it was better to be a human being dissatisfied than a pig satisfied.[6] Utilitarian reasoning about required trade-offs between different types of pleasure may demand that human happiness (of the higher sort) be pursued at the cost of large amounts of porcine misery. The readiness with which utilitarian thinking can return to prescriptions which favour humans is not unimportant: in a world in which xenotransplantation from pigs to humans may be possible, Millian and Benthamite forms of utilitarianism will perhaps reach quite different conclusions about permissible action.

Even if this difficulty were set aside, there are other reasons why Utilitarian thinking cannot provide a comprehensive environmental ethics. Utilitarianism relies on a subjective conception of value which allows it to take account of non-human pleasure and pain, but equally prevents it from valuing either particular non-sentient beings or dispersed and abstract features of the environment: anything that is not sentient cannot suffer or enjoy, so is denied moral standing. Oak trees, bacteria and Mount Everest, species and habitats, ecosystems and bio-diversity, the ozone layer and CO_2 levels are not sentient organisms, so utilitarians will conclude that they can have at most derivative value. They may value bacteria and habitats as constituting or providing the means of life for individual sentient animals; they may value bio-diversity as increasing the likelihood of future survival or pleasure for sentient animals: but they will not value these aspects of the environment except as means to pleasure or happiness in the lives of sentient beings.

A second, equally central feature of utilitarianism also suggests that, far from being the most environmentally benign of anthropocentric positions, it is inevitably highly selective in its concern for the environment. Utilitarian thinking, like other forms of consequentialism, insists that trading-off results is not merely permitted but required. Maximising happiness or welfare or pleasure can be achieved only by trading-off some outcomes to achieve others. There is no way in which to pursue the greatest happiness of the greatest number without pursuing happiness that will be enjoyed in some lives at the expense of suffering that is to be borne in other lives. Some of the outcomes that yield a lot of happiness (or welfare, or pleasure) in some lives—for example, economic growth and exclusive patterns of consumption—have high environmental costs which are not, or not fully, registered as suffering experienced in any sentient lives. Equally environmental damage that affects no sentient beings (e.g. destruction of arctic or desert wilderness with no or little destruction of sentient life) will not count as a cost or harm. More generally, maximising approaches that rely on a subjective measure of value will not merely *permit* but *require* pleasurable environmental damage whose costs escape their calculus.[7]

These worries might perhaps be assuaged to a limited degree by working out how environmental gain or damage could be more fully or better represented in utilitarian and cognate calculations.[8] But better representation of environmental gain or damage in utilitarian and kindred reasoning is still only representation of their effects on sentient lives: a subjective measure of value is still assumed. There is no guarantee that such measures of value will register all environmental gain or damage, and no guarantee that widely shared or trivial short-term pleasures that damage the environment will not outweigh the pains caused by that damage. The destruction of wilderness or environmentally sensitive areas will be a matter for concern only insofar as it is not outweighed by the pleasure of destroying them; the suffering caused by destruction of fragile habitats with few but rare sentient inhabitants might be outweighed, for example, by the pleasures of tourism or gold-mining.

Utilitarianism and environmentalism are therefore inevitably uneasy allies, not simply because some versions of utilitarianism reinstate conclusions anti-speciesists would not welcome, but mainly because of the larger implications of an ethical position which treats a system of trade-offs among expected pleasure and suffering for the sentient as ethical bed-rock.

2. ANTHROPOCENTRISM AND ACTION:
RIGHTS AND OBLIGATIONS

Some anthropocentric ethical positions may appear less hospitable to speciesism than utilitarianism is, in that they may be better structured to take account of a wider range of environmental concerns. For example, ethical reasoning that focuses on *action* rather than on *results* is quite evidently anthropocentric, since (as far as we know) only humans have full capacities for agency, and only they can heed (or flout) ethical prescriptions and recommendations. Yet such agent-centred reasoning may, I shall argue, offer a promising way of looking at environmental issues, and may even be less open than is utilitarian reasoning to the conclusions anti-speciesists dislike.

Most act-oriented ethical reasoning looks at required action, at rights and at obligations, rather than at preferred outcomes. It does not assume that there is any fundamental metric of value, objective or subjective; it does not identify required action by its contribution to results weighed in terms of that metric; it does not recommend or require that value be maximised by trading-off less valuable for more valuable results. Act-centred ethics, in its many forms, seeks to establish certain principles of obligation, or certain rights, which are to constrain not only individual action but institutions and practices. It accepts institutions or practices that permit or require systems of trading-off for certain domains of life, such as commercial life. However, there is no general reason why act-centred ethics should endorse institutions and practices that permit, let alone require, trading-off or maximising to regulate all domains of life, and no reason why the trade-offs which they permit should be conducted in terms of utilitarian conceptions of value (a monetary metric could often be appropriate). The best known forms of act-centred ethics, which treat rights or obligations as the fundamental ethical categories, limit the domains of life in which trading-off is even permitted, and since they provide no general measure of value, objective or subjective, don't provide a framework for introducing it into all domains of life.

Yet act-centred ethics is often seen as hostile to the environment, because its explicit anthropocentrist starting point is thought to entail an ineradicable preference for the human species. This criticism is often directed specifically at forms of act-oriented ethical reasoning which treat *rights* as central. Several criticisms are recurrent. First, although not all rights need be human rights, rights for other animals can be fitted in only with a bit of pushing and shoving.[9] Second, some supposedly central human rights (such as certain property rights)—and perhaps some animal rights (such as rights to habitat)—can have high environmental costs.[10] Third, rights-based thought appears every bit as blind as utilitarianism to concern for non-sentient particulars and abstract or dispersed features of the natural world.

However, these criticisms pale in the face of more general, structural problems in rights-based thought. The great advantage of rights-based ethics is that it is so beautifully adapted to making claims; its great disadvantage is that these claims can be made with flourish and bravado while leaving it wholly obscure who, if anyone, has a duty or obligation to meet them. Yet if nobody has obligations that correspond to a supposed right, then, however loudly it is claimed or proclaimed, the right amounts to nothing. Proclaiming rights is all too easy; taking them seriously is another matter, and they are not taken seriously unless the corollary obligations are identified and taken seriously. Although the rhetoric of rights has become the most widely used way of talking about justice in the last fifty years, it is the discourse of obligations that addresses the practical question *who ought to do what for whom?*[11] The anthropocentrism of rights discourse is, as it were, the wrong way up: it begins from the thought that humans are claimants rather than from the thought that they are agents. By doing so it can disable rather than foster practical thinking.

The profound structural difficulties of the discourse of rights can be obscured because many discussions of rights veer unselfconsciously between claims about *fundamental, natural* or *moral* rights and claims about *institutional* or *positive* rights. Identifying the obligations which are the counterparts to institutionalised or positive rights is unproblematic: here the move back to practical discourse is easily achieved. However, appeals to institutional and positive rights are not justifications of those rights: institutional and positive rights are the objects rather than the sources of ethical criticism and justification. In some societies some humans have had the positive rights of slave-masters, in others bears who kill or maim other animals have had positive rights to a trial. Neither fact establishes *anything* about the justice or the ethical acceptability of slavery or about the capacities of bears to act wrongly or unjustly, or their rights to due process. To establish what is right or wrong, just or unjust, rights-based reasoning would have to appeal to *fundamental, moral* or *natural* rights—yet these are the very rights whose counterpart obligations can so easily be overlooked, with the consequence that they are merely proclaimed and not taken seriously, and that a rhetorical rather than a practical approach to ethics is adopted.

These are ample reasons for act-oriented ethical reasoning to take obligations rather than rights as basic. A switch of perspective from recipience to action, from rights to obligations, carries no theoretical costs and may yield considerable gain: a focus on obligations will incorporate everything that can be covered by a focus on rights (since any genuine right must be matched by a converse obligation)[12] and can also incorporate any other less tightly specified obligations, which lack counterpart rights. (These obligations, traditionally termed *imperfect obligations,* may be the basis of certain virtues.[13]) By contrast, if rights are treated as basic, obligations without rights may simply be lost from sight.

Moreover, this switch of focus from rights to obligations is productive for environmental ethics, and for clarifying the differences between anthropocentrism and speciesism. The main advantage of taking obligations as basic is a simple gain in clarity about anthropocentrism. Even if some rights are not human rights, all obligations will be human obligations. Or, putting the matter more carefully, obligations can be held and discharged only where capacities for action and for reasoning reach a certain degree of complexity, and we have no knowledge of such capacities except among human beings and in the institutions created and staffed by human beings. Even among human beings these capacities are not universal. So in thinking about obligations, anthropocentrism about the locus of obligations is indispensable rather than inappropriate: without it obligations are not taken seriously. Since we cannot take rights seriously unless we take obligations seriously, anthropocentrism *about obligations* will be needed if we are to think seriously about any rights, including animal rights. This anthropocentrism about the locus of obligations accepts that all obligation-bearers are humans, more or less 'in the maturity of their faculties', but leaves open whether any right-holders are non-human, or lack 'mature' faculties.

In taking obligations seriously we have also to take an accurate view of the claims of entities which may end up on the receiving end of action, and it is here that issues about speciesism arise. Some of those on the receiving end will be individual human beings; others will be individual members of other species (sentient or non-sentient); yet others will be non-living features of the world (such as glaciers or volcanoes) or abstract and dispersed features of the world (such as species or bio-diversity, such as genetic traits or the ozone layer).

Noting the variety of beings who may be on the receiving end of action does not establish which of them have rights of which sorts. Some obligations to individuals, whether human or non-human, may have counterpart rights, which those individuals could claim or waive, or which could be claimed or waived on their behalves; other obligations may lack counterpart rights. Even where there are counterpart rights, they may not be vested in all the beings on the receiving end of required action. For example, there may be obligations to preserve bio-diversity or endangered species or genetic traits, and it is conceivable that we owe such action to certain others, but it barely makes sense to speak of these aspects or features of the natural world as having rights. Individual sentient animals, whether human or not, and other locatable features of the world, have a certain unity and certain capacities for independent activity and response, which enable us at least to make sense of ascribing rights to them. It is far less plausible to ascribe rights to particulars which lack all capacities to act, let alone to abstract or dispersed aspects of the natural world that lack unity as well as capacities for independent activity or response. Obligations may be directed to entities of any type, but the coherence of attributing rights to inanimate or to abstract or dispersed features of the natural world is questionable. So a second advantage of an obligation-based over a rights-based approach to environmental ethics is that it readily allows for obligations that are directed towards wide ranges of features of the natural world, to some of which a rights-based approach will be blind.

None of this is to deny that certain obligations may have counterpart rights. Yet even when they do there is advantage in treating obligations as the basic ethical notion. Once obligations have been established, a central task of those on whom they fall may be to work out where they must be directed and whether those who are on the receiving end of action, or others, have rights to their performance, in short to determine whether there are any right-holders. A second task may be to collaborate in the construction of institutions and the fostering of practices which make a reality of meeting obligations and of respecting any counterpart rights. These tasks may prove obscure and burdensome, but in beginning with obligations we at least see them as the tasks of identifiable agents, whether individual or collective. The discourse of obligations, *because rather than despite of its evident anthropocentrism,* has the practical merit that it addresses agents rather than claimants.

3. ENVIRONMENTAL OBLIGATIONS: REJECTING INJURY

These are the substantial advantages in taking obligations rather than rights as the basic category of act-oriented ethics. However, in acknowledging these advantages we do not yet know *which* obligations human agents and the agencies they construct hold, nor *which* (if any) of these obligations have counterpart rights, or *who* the holders of these rights may be. The advantages are, so to speak, *structural:* they allow one to approach ethical questions, including those of environmental ethics, in full recognition of the unavoidable core of anthropocentrism, namely that obligations must be held by humans (often working in and through institutions), and without assuming either that there are real values embedded in the environment or that there is some generally valid subjective metric of value. If these structural advantages are to be of practical use the next step must be to provide some account, if inevitably a sketchy and incomplete account, of at least some obligations which could be environmentally important.

A first move in trying to identify environmentally significant obligations might be to ask which sorts of fundamental, as opposed to positive and institutional, obligations *could* be taken seriously. Like rights, obligations may be divided into *fundamental (moral, natural)* obligations, and *positive* or *institutional* obligations which presuppose certain institutions and practices. Many of the obligations which we discuss on a daily basis are positive or institutional obligations. Their basis and their justification is tied to that of certain institutions, practices and roles; if the institutions, practices or roles lack justification, so may their derivative or component norms and obligations. If institutions, practices and roles, and with them their derivative norms and obligations, are to be justified, the justification will have to go deeper and appeal to *fundamental (moral, natural)*, or (we may wish to say) to *human* obligations, which are not so tied.

One feature of fundamental, human obligations which obligations of role or status lack, is that their principles must be *universal* obligations, in the sense that they could be accepted and adopted (not necessarily discharged) by all agents. Whereas institutional and positive obligations are always *special* obligations, held in virtue of *special* relationships or roles, or entered into by *specific* transactions (promises, contracts), a *fundamental human obligation* cannot presuppose the legitimacy of differentiations on which special obligations build, hence must be adoptable by all agents if by any.

These considerations provide a basis for identifying the underlying principles for many obligations. If fundamental, human obligations must be universal obligations, then their principles must be adoptable by all. Many principles of action can readily be adopted by each and by all: anybody and everybody can make it a principle not to commit perjury, to cultivate a good reputation or to refrain from lying (how far each individual succeeds in translating these principles into action is quite a different matter and will depend on many contingent circumstances). Other principles of action that can be adopted by some, even by many, cannot be thought of as universally adoptable. Consider, for example, a principle of injuring others: if we try to imagine a world of agents all of whom adopt this principle we are bound to fail because (since a hypothesis of universal failure is unreasonable) at least some people will succeed in injuring others, thereby rendering at least some others their victims, thereby preventing those others from acting, and in particular from acting on a principle of injuring. A principle of injuring cannot coherently be thought of as a principle all can adopt: to use an old technical term, it is not *universalisable.*

Many universalisable principles are entirely optional: their rejection is equally universalisable. For example, both the principle of fasting by day and the principle of eating by day are universalisable; either could be a principle for all, and the rejection of either could be a principle for all; neither day-time fasting nor day-time eating is a matter of obligation. By contrast, other universalisable principles are required because their rejection is not universalisable. For example, if principles of injuring, or of deceiving, or of doing violence are non-universalisable, their rejection must be a matter of obligation.

This line of thought establishes a good deal less than some people might hope. For example, by showing that there is an obligation to reject the principle of injury we do not establish any fundamental human obligation not to injure, but only a fundamental human obligation to reject injury, i.e. an obligation not to make injury a basic principle of lives and institutions. Those who adopt a principle of non-injury must prefer non-injury to injury in each and every context; they must be pacifists; they must not retaliate to injury against self and others, however catastrophic their restraint. By contrast, those who reject a principle of injury will indeed seek to limit injury, but may find that in certain cases this requires selective injury. Examples might be self-defence and the defence of innocent others, which in turn point to the construction of institutions which coerce, hence injure, in limited ways, where this will secure some overall limitation of injury. Rejecting injury is roughly a matter of refraining from *systematic* or *gratuitous* injury (either of these would count against any claim to have rejected the principle of injury), rather than a matter of blanket and undiscriminating commitment to non-injury.

Since injury takes many different forms, some direct and others indirect, a fundamental obligation to reject injury, hence not to injure gratuitously or systematically, will have numerous and powerful implications. *Rejecting direct injury* to others may require complex legal and political institutions that secure ranges of rights of the person and of political rights, as well as a social and economic order that secures at least a certain range of economic and social rights. *Rejecting indirect injury* is mainly a matter of limiting injury that arises from damage either to the social fabric or to natural and man-made environments. For present purposes, it is the rejection of injurious ways of damaging natural and man-made environments that is of central concern.

It is commonly supposed that speciesism follows from anthropocentric ethical reasoning that works along these lines. An argument that agents should not arrogantly assume that they may adopt principles which are unavailable for other agents seemingly will take no account of those who are not agents. Yet this form of anthropocentrism also has powerful anti-speciesist implications, and will establish considerable constraints on ways in which agents may use their environment.

Of course, an obligation-based ethic will not prescribe unlimited care for the environment. A commitment to reject injury does not require agents to refrain from all change to or intervention in the natural world. Since all living creatures interact with the natural world in ways that change it, it is incoherent to suppose that those of them who are agents should have obligations to refrain from all action that changes or damages any part of their environment. However, if the rejection of systematic or gratuitous injury to other agents is a fundamental obligation, then it will also be obligatory not to damage or degrade the underlying powers of renewal and regeneration of the natural world. The basic thought here is that it is wrong to destroy or damage the underlying reproductive and regenerative powers of the natural world because such damage may inflict systematic or gratuitous injury (which often cannot be foreseen with much accuracy or any detail) on some or on many agents. This argument is of course anthropocentric; but it is likely to have numerous anti-speciesist corollaries.

By this standard it might not be wrong to irrigate a desert or to bring land under plough—unless, for example, the cost of so doing is the permanent destruction of habitats, of species and of bio-diversity, which might lead to systematic or gratuitous injury to agents (and inevitably harms many other sentients). It might not be wrong to use an industrial process—unless, for example, that process would damage conditions of life, such as the ozone layer or the CO_2 level, in ways that will injure agents, (and inevitably harm many other sentients). In acting in disregard of such considerations we at the very least risk injuring agents gratuitously and at worst actually injure them systematically. Because these features form the shared environment of human and non-human life, arguments derived from the requirement of not making injury to humans basic to our lives are likely to have numerous anti-speciesist implications, even if they do not support a comprehensive anti-speciesism.

Moreover, these obligations point to a wide range of further and more specific obligations, and to ranges of institutional and positive obligations by means of which fundamental obligations may be discharged at a given time and place. These positive and institutional obligations might range from obligations to preserve or establish agricultural practices which do not irreversibly damage the bio-diversity of the natural world, to obligations to reject energy and transport policies which irreversibly damage the ozone layer or the CO_2 level, to obligations to work towards economic and social institutions and practices which are robust in the face of low-growth or no-growth economic policies. As is evident from these examples, a great merit of taking an obligation-based approach to environmental issues is that it is not blind to the importance of abstract and dispersed features of the environment.

Moreover, these ways of thinking about environmental obligations do not return us to patterns of cost-benefit analysis and maximising ways of thought. They simply spell out some constraints on what may be done in a given time and place, with its actual resources and population, if agents are not to act on the environment in ways that will or may injure systematically or gratuitously. The constraints that must be met by those who seek not to injure either systematically or gratuitously set complex tasks, which must be met in constructing and maintaining institutions and practices, as well as in individual decisions and action.

4. What about the Animals?

Still, this type of anthropocentrism will be only incompletely anti-speciesist; it will also have speciesist implications. As has often been noted, arguments that establish reasons to protect species, bio-diversity and habitats do not always provide reasons for protecting individual organisms, or for protecting individual sentient organisms. The advantage of a framework that takes account of action that affects abstract and dispersed features of the natural world has to be weighed against the seeming disadvantage of lacking comprehensive reasons for valuing individual non-human animals, or for thinking that they have fundamental rights.

The traditional move of anti-speciesists is to try to show that any failure to accord all sentient animals full moral standing, and so as having the same rights as humans, would amount to speciesism, so be unjustifiable. This is usually done by pointing to analogies between human and other animals that minimise the differences between them, so as to establish that non-human animals too have moral standing. If the appeal to analogy is to be plausible it has to be quite subtle, since it is not meant to leave us with the view (for example) that humans have no more obligations than non-human animals, and that a person torturing a cat is on a par with a cat torturing a bird. It is meant to be an appeal that leaves the indispensable anthropocentrism of ethical reasoning intact, while wholly derailing speciesist views by showing that any preferences for the human species that are implied are indeed unjustified. Humans are to be shown to resemble non-humans, who should therefore have the same rights—but not the same obligations.

Indeed, if the appeal to analogy is to be plausible, it will have to support even more differentiated conclusions. For anti-speciesists do not in fact seek to establish that non-human animals have *all* the rights of humans. They do not, for example, worry about animals lacking political or cultural rights. The rights that matter to anti-speciesists are mainly rights against certain sorts of ill treatment. It is not clear how very *general* arguments for the unimportance of the differences between human and non-human animals can be used to establish a very *selective* parity of rights and obligations.

Perhaps one could look for a more selective argument from analogy by emphasising that the boundary between (human) agents and (non-human) nonagents is pretty fuzzy. Although we do not hold non-human animals morally responsible in the ways in which we try to hold one another responsible, we do think of them as acting, and apply a wide range of evaluative vocabulary to them. We take a considerably different view of violent and destructive behaviour by non-human animals and of their peaceful behaviour; we take a considerably similar view of pain and distress in non-humans and humans. Perhaps then there is nothing implausible in the thought that quite specific obligations, for example not to do bodily injury, might hold between humans and great apes, or between humans and certain animals with whom they work and live. Where the boundary of such thoughts lie, and whether they could be used to put into question all the forms of cruelty to animals that anti-speciesists condemn is a harder question. As with all arguments from analogy, much will depend on the specificity and completeness of the comparisons.

Let us suppose that obligation-based thinking can be stretched only a certain distance towards the anti-speciesist goal, in that it offers no convincing arguments for a wholly general prohibition on, say, limiting animals' liberties or reducing their habitat, although it may offer quite good specific arguments against certain cruelties, or against cruelties to certain non-human animals. Would that be the end of the story?

There would be no reason for it to be the end of the story *either* if there are indirect arguments deriving from human obligations for extending animals wider protection, *or* if people choose to establish positive obligations to do so. For example, it might be that basic obligations to protect species and biodiversity will carry with them many derivative reasons to protect or benefit individual non-human animals. Or it might be that the ideals of certain cultures will provide reason to accord (some) non-human animals (some) further protections or concern. An anthropocentric starting point does not entail speciesism, and need not have relentlessly speciesist conclusions.

Still, many friends of non-human animals will think that this is simply not enough, because it will not establish fundamental rights for all individual non-human animals. (Utilitarians can hardly complain at this selectivity, since their own conclusions are highly selective for differing reasons). Yet, as soon as one considers the project of showing that all animals should have the same fundamental rights as humans it becomes evident that many of the rights that would be part and parcel of an obligation to reject injury to other humans are irrelevant for non-human animals. For example, rights to free speech or to a fair trial have no place in the lives of non-human animals. More generally, very many personal, political, economic, social, and cultural rights appear to have no useful place in the lives of non-human animals. Only a few personal rights such as a right not to be tormented, or a right not to be killed without reason, and possibly some analogues of (more controversial) economic or social rights, such as a right to an adequate habitat or to food, could even make sense for non-human animals; that they make sense does not, of course, show that any of them is a fundamental right.

Perhaps in the end we should ask whether all animal rights need be fundamental or moral rights, or whether all or many of them should be understood as the positive and institutional rights of a particular social order. For an obligation-based approach does not stand in the way of constructing institutional or positive rights for individual non-human animals, or for the individual non-human animals of certain species, even if it does not establish that all non-human animals have fundamental rights. (This thought might be congenial to some friends of non-human animals because it would allow us to think differently of animal killing by (say) subsistence farmers and pastoralists and by affluent societies, for whom vegetarian diets may be more feasible.) These are further reasons for thinking that an anthropocentric starting point clearly need lead to relentlessly speciesist conclusions.

No doubt this limited conclusion about animal rights will seem inadequate or disappointing to some. I take a more optimistic view. I set it against five considerable advantages of an obligation-based approach to ethical reasoning about the environment. The first advantage is that with this approach we do not attempt the Sysiphean metaphysical labours of showing that there are real environmental values embedded in the natural world. The second is that we do not have to approach environmental issues in terms of a subjective metric of value and the system of trade-offs which are implied in subordinating action to that conception of value, with all the risks for the environment and for individual non-human (and human!) animals that this can imply, even where 'environmentally sensitive' ways of costing results are used. The third is that we approach environmental issues in a sufficiently broad way to be able to take serious account of abstract and dispersed aspects of the environment. The fourth is that we do not lead with the confused anthropocentrism of a rhetoric of rights, so do not leave it perennially vague just who is obliged to do what for whom (even a comprehensive anti-speciesism will not be particularly attractive if its status is largely rhetorical). The fifth is that an obligation-based approach allows that individuals and groups may advocate and follow more comprehensively anti-speciesist ways of life than its basic arguments can establish.

To this I would like to add one consolation for those who are still sad at the thought that animal rights might be no more than positive and institutional rights, and that arguments for their importance could not demonstrate that sentient animals had complete moral standing. It is that this is where we would hope that all the best rights would end up, and that a derivative place in a process of justification need not entail a derivative place in our lives. It means only that good arguments for the construction of positive rights for non-human animals may not shadow arguments for constructing accounts of positive rights among (human) agents. There are plenty of other arguments that could be offered for constructing positive rights for certain non-human animals: some might derive from the positive obligations and rights of humans, others might be internal to ways of life, or invoke certain ideals or virtues. If we call to mind the systematic problems of realist, utilitarian and rights-based reasoning in addressing environmental issues, we may find merit in obligation-based reasoning, and welcome its various eco-friendly implications, even if they do not sustain the unrestricted conclusions anti-speciesists would most welcome.

NOTES

This paper arises from a presentation in the Allied Domecq public lecture series organised by Dr J. Smith for the Cambridge University Committee for Interdisciplinary Environmental Studies in the Lent term, 1996. I am grateful to him and to a lively audience, as well as to Dr T. Hayward, for searching comments.

1. Without the realism, appeals to environmental values are reifications which explain nothing. Just as we fail to explain why opium has its well known properties by citing its dormitive virtues, so we fail to show why we should value the environment if we merely invoke but do not establish environmental values.

2. The term anthropocentrism, rather than the more obvious humanism, has become conventional for ethical views that take human life as the starting point of ethical reasoning. The older term humanism is inappropriate for this purpose, since is taken to refer specifically to a set of claims about the human rather than divine basis of ethical relations.

3. I am grateful to Tim Hayward, who refereed this paper, for sending me a copy of his paper 'Anthropocentrism: A Misunderstood Problem', *Environmental Values* 6(1), in which he sharpens distinctions between anthropocentric and speciesist claims. I have found his thinking constructive and suggestive, and have drawn on it at several points.

4. Bentham, 1967, Ch. 17, p. 412 n. The position has its limits for environmental ethics: it puts the entire non-sentient world at the disposal of sentient beings.

5. The term liberation seems adrift in utilitarian waters: what is there in utilitarian right conduct to animals which would not be covered by the term animal welfare?

6. 'It is better to be a human being dissatisfied than a pig satisfied', Mill, 1962, p. 260.

7. Unless, of course, non-utilitarian considerations are introduced. Cf. Goodin, 1992, who introduces the non-subjective value of organic wholes into a broadly utilitarian account of environmental ethics in order to explain what is wrong about the destruction of wilderness that nobody is enjoying.

8. David Pearce et al., 1989, 1991, 1993, and 1995.

9. The pushing and shoving is usually accomplished by stressing the analogies between some non-human animals and some humans, while minimising the disanalogies between other non-human animals and other humans. Cf. Singer, 1976; Clark, 1977; Regan, 1983; Regan and Singer, 1989; more recently Singer and Cavalieri, 1993.

10. Cf. Aiken, 1992.

11. For more extensive argument on these points see O'Neill, 1996. Ch. 5.

12. The sole and for these purposes unimportant exceptions are so-called 'mere liberties' or 'unprotected rights', such as rights to pick up a coin from the pavement where there is no obligation on others to desist from picking it up if they can do so first.

13. See O'Neill, 1996, Ch. 7 for discussion of imperfect duties and virtues.

References

Aiken, William 1992. 'Human Rights in an Ecological Era', *Environmental Values* 1: 189–203.

Bentham, Jeremy 1967. *Introduction to the Principles of Morals and of Legislation*, in *A Fragment on Government and Introduction to the Principles of Morals and of Legislation*, ed. Wilfrid Harrison. Oxford: Blackwell.

Clark, Stephen 1977. *The Moral Status of Animals*. Oxford: Oxford University Press. *Environmental Values*, 1994, vol. 3, no. 4, special issue on Values and Preferences in Environmental Economics.

Goodin, Robert 1992, *Green Politics*. Oxford: Polity Press.

Hayward, Tim 1997. 'Anthropocentrism: A Misunderstood Problem', *Environmental Values* 6: 49–63.

O'Neill, Onora 1996. *Towards Justice and Virtue: A constructive account of practical reasoning*. Cambridge: Cambridge University Press.

Pearce, David, et al., 1989. *Blueprint for a Green Economy*. London: Earthscan.

Pearce, David, et al., 1991. *Blueprint 2: Greening the World Economy*. London: Earthscan.

Pearce, David, et al., 1993. *Blueprint 3: Measuring Sustainable Development*. London: Earthscan.

Pearce, David, et al., 1995. *Blueprint 4: Capturing Global Environmental Values*. London: Earthscan.

Regan, Thomas 1983. *The Case for Animal Rights*. Berkeley: University of California Press.

Regan, Thomas and Singer, Peter 1989. *Animal Rights and Human Obligations*. 2nd edn. Englewood Cliffs, NJ: Prentice Hall.

Singer, Peter 1976. *Animal Liberation*. London: Jonathan Cape.

Singer, Peter and Cavalieri, Paola 1993. *The Great Ape Project*. London: Fourth Estate.

II. Biocentric Justifications.

Overview. In the first essay, Holmes Rolston III argues for a biocentric justification for environmental ethics. He rejects the basis for much of traditional ethics that is based on human reason. Quoting Jeremy Bentham, Rolston asks, "The question is not, Can they reason? nor Can they talk? But, Can they suffer?"[1] Preventing and alleviating pain and ensuring a healthy, natural diet are two ways that humans can show their respect for all animal life. However, this respect does not stop with animals. Although plants and other living things cannot feel pain, they are part of an ecosystem that is really an intricate whole. Within this whole are various species of plants and animals that are alternately predators and prey; together they are all important, and their relationships should be preserved. This means that species and ecosystems must be valued intrinsically because they carry a strength (Latin: *valeo*, root for value).[2] One ought to value what works well and demonstrates a strength. Thus, we should respect the environment because of the intrinsic value that is demonstrated by its strength.

Paul W. Taylor's essay calls for a worldview that respects nature. He believes that the proper worldview will shape many of the smaller issues. One of the key elements of this worldview is a commitment to the biocentric outlook. In this outlook, we recognize what the entire biotic community has done for this world: It has allowed us (humans) to come into existence. Such a service to us ought to engender various duties or rules: (a) the Rule of Nonmaleficence, (b) the Rule of Noninterference, (c) the Rule of Fidelity, and (d) the Rule of Restitutive Justice. Taylor's essay consists of an amplification of these duties.

---

[1] J. Bentham, *Introduction to the Principles of Morals and Legislation* (New York: Hafner, 1789, p. 34).

[2] The sense in Latin is that to be strong and effective implies worth. It is a functional theory of value that fits in well when describing ecosystems.

Environmental Ethics: Values in and Duties to the Natural World

Holmes Rolston III

Environmental ethics stretches classical ethics to the breaking point. All ethics seeks an appropriate respect for life. But we do not need just a humanistic ethic applied to the environment as we have needed one for business, law, medicine, technology, international development, or nuclear disarmament. Respect for life does demand an ethic concerned about human welfare, an ethic like the others and now applied to the environment. But environmental ethics in a deeper sense stands on a frontier, as radically theoretical as it is applied. It alone asks whether there can be nonhuman objects of duty.

Neither theory nor practice elsewhere needs values outside of human subjects, but environmental ethics must be more biologically objective—nonanthropocentric. It challenges the separation of science and ethics, trying to reform a science that finds nature value-free and an ethics that assumes that only humans count morally. Environmental ethics seeks to escape relativism in ethics, to discover a way past culturally based ethics. However much our worldviews, ethics included, are embedded in our cultural heritages, and thereby theory-laden and value-laden, all of us know that a natural world exists apart from human cultures. Humans interact with nature. Environmental ethics is the only ethics that breaks out of culture. It has to evaluate nature, both wild nature and the nature that mixes with culture, and to judge duty thereby. After accepting environmental ethics, you will no longer be the humanist you once were.

Environmental ethics requires risk. It explores poorly charted terrain, where one can easily get lost. One must hazard the kind of insight that first looks like foolishness. Some people approach environmental ethics with a smile—expecting chicken liberation and rights for rocks, misplaced concern for chipmunks and daisies. Elsewhere, they think, ethicists deal with sober concerns: medical ethics, business ethics, justice in public affairs, questions of life and death and of peace and war. But the questions here are no less serious: The degradation of the environment poses as great a threat to life as nuclear war, and a more probable tragedy.

HIGHER ANIMALS

Logically and psychologically, the best and easiest breakthrough past the traditional boundaries of interhuman ethics is made when confronting higher animals. Animals defend their lives; they have a good of their own and suffer pains and pleasures like ourselves. Human moral concern should at least cross over into the domain of animal experience. This boundary crossing is also dangerous because if made only psychologically and not biologically, the would-be environmental ethicist may be too disoriented to travel further. The promised environmental ethics will degenerate into a mammalian ethics. We certainly need an ethic for animals, but that is only one level of concern in a comprehensive environmental ethics.

One might expect classical ethics to have sifted well an ethics for animals. Our ancestors did not think about endangered species, ecosystems, acid rain, or the ozone layer, but they lived in closer association with wild and domestic animals than we do. Hunters track wounded deer; ranchers who let their horses starve are prosecuted. Still, until recently, the scientific, humanistic centuries since the so-called Enlightenment have not been sensitive ones for animals, owing to the Cartesian legacy. Animals were mindless, living matter; biology has been mechanistic. Even psychology, rather than defending animal experience, has been behaviorist. Philosophy has protested little, concerned instead with locating values in human experiences at the same time that it disspirited and devalued nature. Across several centuries of hard science and humanistic ethics there has been little compassion for animals.

The progress of science itself smeared the human–nonhuman boundary line. Animal anatomy, biochemistry, cognition, perception, experience, behavior, and evolutionary history are kin to our own. Animals have no immortal souls, but then persons may not either, or beings with souls may not be the only kind that count morally. Ethical progress further smeared the boundary. Sensual pleasures are a good thing; ethics should be egalitarian, nonarbitrary, nondiscriminatory. There are ample scientific grounds that animals enjoy pleasures and suffer pains; and ethically there are no grounds to value these sensations in humans and not in animals. So there has been a vigorous reassessment of human duties to sentient life. The world cheered in the fall of 1988 when humans rescued two whales from winter ice.

"Respect their right to life": A sign in Rocky Mountain National Park enjoins humans not to harass bighorn sheep. "The question is not, Can they reason, nor Can they talk? but, Can they suffer?" wrote Jeremy Bentham, insisting that animal welfare counts too.[1] The Park Service sign and Bentham's question increase sensitivity by extending rights and hedonist goods to animals. The gain is a vital breakthrough past humans, and the first lesson in environmental ethics has been learned. But the risk is a moral extension that expands rights as far as mammals and not much further, a psychologically based ethic that counts only felt experience. We respect life in our nonhuman but near-human animal cousins, a semianthropic and still quite subjective ethics. Justice remains a concern for just-us subjects. There has, in fact, not been much of a theoretical breakthrough, no paradigm shift.

Lacking that, we are left with anomaly and conceptual strain. When we try to use culturally extended rights and psychologically based utilities to protect the flora or even the insentient fauna, to protect endangered species or ecosystems, we can only stammer. Indeed, we get lost trying to protect bighorns, because, in the wild, cougars are not respecting the rights or utilities of the sheep they slay, and, in culture, humans slay sheep and eat them regularly, while humans have every right not to be eaten by either humans or cougars. There are no rights in the wild, and nature is indifferent to the welfare of particular animals. A bison fell through the ice into a river in Yellowstone Park; the environmental ethic there, letting nature take its course, forbade would-be rescuers from either saving or killing the suffering animal to put it out of its misery. A drowning human would been saved at once. Perhaps it was a mistake to save those whales.

The ethics by extension now seems too nondiscriminating; we are unable to separate an ethics for humans from an ethics for wildlife. To treat wild animals with compassion learned in culture does not appreciate their wildness. Man, said Socrates, is the political animal; humans maximally are what they are in culture, where the natural selection pressures (impressively productive in ecosystems) are relaxed without detriment to the species *Homo sapiens,* and indeed with great benefit to its member persons. Wild animals cannot enter culture; they do not have that capacity. They cannot acquire language at sufficient levels to take part in culture; they cannot make their clothing or build fires, much less read books or receive an education. Animals can, by human adoption, receive some of the protections of culture, which happens when we domesticate them, but neither pets nor food animals enter the culture that shelters them.

Worse, such cultural protection can work to their detriment; their wildness is made over into a human artifact as food or pet animal. A cow does not have the integrity of a deer, or a poodle that of a wolf. Culture is a good thing for humans but often a bad thing for animals. Their biology and ecology—neither justice nor charity, nor rights nor welfare—provide the benchmark for an ethics.

Culture does make a relevant ethical difference, and environmental ethics has different criteria from interhuman ethics. Can they talk? and, Can they reason?—indicating cultural capacities—are relevant questions; not just, Can they suffer? *Equality* is a positive word in ethics, *discriminatory* a pejorative one. On the other hand, simplistic reduction is a failing in the philosophy of science and epistemology; to be "discriminating" is desirable in logic and value theory. Something about treating humans as equals with bighorns and cougars seems to "reduce" humans to merely animal levels of value, a "no more than" counterpart in ethics of the "nothing but" fallacy often met in science. Humans are "nothing but" naked apes. Something about treating sheep and cougars as the equals of humans seems to elevate them unnaturally and not to value them for what they are. There is something insufficiently discriminating in such judgments; they are species-blind in a bad sense, blind to the real differences between species, valuational differences that do count morally. To the contrary, a discriminating ethicist will insist on preserving the differing richness of valuational complexity, wherever found. Compassionate respect for life in its suffering is only part of the analysis.

Two tests of discrimination are pains and diet. It might be thought that pain is a bad thing, whether in nature or culture. Perhaps when dealing with humans in culture, additional levels of value and utility must be protected by conferring rights that do not exist in the wild, but meanwhile we should at least minimize animal suffering. That is indeed a worthy imperative in culture where animals are removed from nature and bred, but it may be misguided where animals remain in ecosystems. When the bighorn sheep of Yellowstone caught pinkeye, they were blinded, injured, and starving as a result, and three hundred of them, more than half the herd, perished. Wildlife veterinarians wanted to treat the disease, as they would have in any domestic herd, and as they did with Colorado bighorns infected with an introduced lungworm, but the Yellowstone ethicists left the animals to suffer, seemingly not respecting their life.

Had those ethicists no mercy? They knew rather that, although intrinsic pain is a bad thing whether in humans or in sheep, pain in ecosystems is instrumental pain, through which the sheep are naturally selected for a more satisfactory adaptive fit. Pain in a medically skilled culture is pointless, once the alarm to health is sounded, but pain operates functionally in bighorns in their niche, even after it becomes no longer in the interests of the pained individual. To have interfered in the interests of the blinded sheep would have weakened the species. Even the question, Can they suffer? is not as simple as Bentham thought. What we ought to do depends on what is. The *is* of nature differs significantly from the *is* of culture, even when similar suffering is present in both.

At this point some ethicists will insist that at least in culture we can minimize animal pain, and that will constrain our diet. There is predation in nature; humans evolved as omnivores. But humans, the only moral animals, should refuse to participate in the meat-eating phase of their ecology, just as they refuse to play the game merely by the rules of natural selection. Humans do not look to the behavior of wild animals as an ethical guide in other matters (marriage, truth telling, promise keeping, justice, charity). Why should they justify their dietary habits by watching what animals do?

But the difference is that these other matters are affairs of culture; these are person-to-person events, not events at all in spontaneous nature. By contrast, eating is omnipresent in wild nature; humans eat because they are in nature, not because they are in culture. Eating animals is not an event between persons but a human-to-animal event; and the rules for this act come from the ecosystems in which humans evolved and have no duty to remake. Humans, then, can model their dietary habits from their ecosystems, though they cannot and should not so model their interpersonal justice or charity. When eating, they ought to minimize animal suffering, but they have no duty to revise trophic pyramids whether in nature or culture. The boundary between animals and humans has not been rubbed out after all; only what was a boundary line has been smeared into a boundary zone. We have discovered that animals count morally, though we have not yet solved the challenge of how to count them.

Animals enjoy psychological lives, subjective experiences, the satisfaction of felt interests—intrinsic values that count morally when humans encounter them. But the pains, pleasures, interests, and welfare of individual animals are only one of the considerations in a more complex environmental ethics that cannot be reached by conferring rights on them or by a hedonist calculus, however far extended. We have to travel further into a more biologically based ethics.

ORGANISMS

If we are to respect all life, we have still another boundary to cross, from zoology to botany, from sentient to insentient life. In Yosemite National Park for almost a century humans entertained themselves by driving through a tunnel cut in a giant sequoia. Two decades ago the Wawona tree, weakened by the cut, blew down in a storm. People said, "Cut us another drive-through sequoia." The Yosemite environmental ethic, deepening over the years, answered, "No. You ought not to mutilate majestic sequoias for amusement. Respect their life." Indeed, some ethicists count the value of redwoods so highly that they will spike redwoods, lest they be cut. In the Rawah Wilderness in alpine Colorado, old signs read, "Please leave the flowers for others to enjoy." When the signs rotted out, new signs urged a less humanist ethic: "Let the flowers live!"

But trees and flowers cannot care, so why should we? We are not considering animals that are close kin, nor can they suffer or experience anything. Plants are not valuers with preferences that can be satisfied or frustrated. It seems odd to assert that plants need our sympathy, odd to ask that we should consider their point of view. They have no subjective life, only objective life.

Perhaps the questions are wrong, because they are coming out of the old paradigm. We are at a critical divide. That is why I earlier warned that environmental ethicists who seek only to extend a humanistic ethic to mammalian cousins will get lost. Seeing no moral landmarks, those ethicists may turn back to more familiar terrain. Afraid of the naturalistic fallacy, they will say that people should enjoy letting flowers live or that it is silly to cut drive-through sequoias, that it is aesthetically more excellent for humans to appreciate both for what they are. But these ethically conservative reasons really do not understand what biological conservation is in the deepest sense.

It takes ethical courage to go on, to move past a hedonistic, humanistic logic to a bio-logic. Pains, pleasures, and psychological experience will no further be useful categories, but—lest some think that from here on I as a philosopher become illogical and lose all ethical sense—let us orient ourselves by extending logical, propositional, cognitive, and normative categories into biology. Nothing matters to a tree, but much is vital to it.

An organism is a spontaneous, self-maintaining system, sustaining and reproducing itself, executing its program, making a way through the world, checking against performance by means of responsive capacities with which to measure success. It can reckon with vicissitudes, opportunities, and adversities that the world presents. Something more than physical causes, even when less than sentience, is operating within every organism. There is information superintending the causes; without it, the organism would collapse into a sand heap. This information is a modern equivalent of what Aristotle called formal and final causes; it gives the organism a telos, or end, a kind of (nonfelt) goal. Organisms have ends, although not always ends in view.

All this cargo is carried by the DNA, essentially a linguistic molecule. By a serial reading of the DNA, a polypeptide chain is synthesized, such that its sequential structure determines the bioform into which it will fold. Ever lengthening chains are organized into genes, as ever-longer sentences are organized into paragraphs and chapters. Diverse proteins, lipids, carbohydrates, enzymes—all the life structures—are written into the genetic library. The DNA is thus a logical set, not less than a biological set, and is informed as well as formed. Organisms use a sort of symbolic logic, using these molecular shapes as symbols of life. The novel resourcefulness lies in the epistemic content conserved, developed, and thrown forward to make biological resources out of the physicochemical sources. This executive steering core is cybernetic—partly a special kind of cause-and-effect system and partly something more. It is partly a historical information system discovering and evaluating ends so as to map and make a way through the world, and partly a system of significances attached to operations, pursuits, and resources. In this sense, the genome is a set of conservation molecules.

The genetic set is really a propositional set—to choose a provocative term—recalling that the Latin *propositum* is an assertion, a set task, a theme, a plan, a proposal, a project, as well as a cognitive statement. From this, it is also a motivational set, unlike human books, because these life motifs are set to drive the movement from genotypic potential to phenotypic expression. Given a chance, these molecules seek organic self-expression. They thus proclaim a lifeway; and with this an organism, unlike an inert rock, claims the environment as source and sink, from which to abstract energy and materials and into which to excrete them. It takes advantage of its environment. Life thus arises out of earthen sources (as do rocks), but life (unlike rocks) turns back on its sources to make resources out of them. An acorn becomes an oak; the oak stands on its own.

So far we have only description. We begin to pass to value when we recognize that the genetic set is a normative set; it distinguishes between what is and what ought to be. This does not mean that the organism is a moral system, for there are no moral agents in nature; but the organism is an axiological, evaluative system. So the oak grows, reproduces, repairs its wounds, and resists death. The physical state that the organism seeks, idealized in its programmatic form, is a valued state. Value is present in this achievement. *Vital* seems a better word here than *biological*. We are dealing not simply with another individual defending its solitary life but with an individual having situated fitness in an ecosystem. Still, we want to affirm that the living individual, taken as a point-experience in the web of interconnected life, is per se an intrinsic value.

A life is defended for what it is in itself, without necessary further contributory reference, although, given the structure of all ecosystems, such lives necessarily do have further contributory reference. The organism has something it is conserving, something for which it is standing: its life. Though organisms must fit into their niche, they have their own standards. They promote their own realization, at the same time that they track an environment. They have a technique, a know-how. Every organism has a good of its kind; it defends its own kind as a good kind. In that sense, as soon as one knows what a giant sequoia tree is, one knows the biological identity that is sought and conserved.

There seems no reason why such own-standing normative organisms are not morally significant. A moral agent deciding his or her behavior ought to take account of the consequences for other evaluative systems. Within the community of moral agents, one has not merely to ask whether x is a normative system but also, because the norms are at personal option, to judge the norm. But within the biotic community, organisms are amoral normative systems, and there are no cases in which an organism seeks a good of its own that is morally reprehensible. The distinction between having a good of its kind and being a good kind vanishes, so far as any faulting of the organism is concerned. To this extent, everything with a good of its kind is a good kind and thereby has intrinsic value.

One might say that an organism is a bad organism if, during the course of pressing its normative expression, it upsets the ecosystem or causes widespread disease. Remember, though, that an organism cannot be a good kind without situated environmental fitness. By natural selection the kind of goods to which it is genetically programmed must mesh with its ecosystemic role. In spite of the ecosystem as a perpetual contest of goods in dialectic and exchange, it is difficult to say that any organism is a bad kind in this instrumental sense either. The misfits are extinct, or soon will be. In spontaneous nature any species that preys upon, parasitizes, competes with, or crowds another will be a bad kind from the narrow perspective of its victim or competitor.

But if we enlarge that perspective, we typically have difficulty in saying that any species is a bad kind overall in the ecosystem. An "enemy" may even be good for the "victimized" species, though harmful to individual members of it, as when predation keeps the deer herd healthy. Beyond this, the "bad kinds" typically play useful roles in population control, in symbiotic relationships, or in providing opportunities for other species. The *Chlamydia* microbe is a bad kind from the perspective of the bighorns, but when one thing dies, something else lives. After the pinkeye outbreak among the bighorns, the golden eagle population in Yellowstone flourished, preying on the bighorn carcasses. For the eagles, *Chlamydia* is a good kind instrumentally.

Some biologist-philosophers will say that even though an organism evolves to have a situated environmental fitness, not all such situations are good arrangements; some can be clumsy or bad. True, the vicissitudes of historical evolution do sometimes result in ecological webs that are suboptimal solutions, within the biologically limited possibilities and powers of interacting organisms. Still, such systems have been selected over millennia for functional stability, and at least the burden of proof is on a human evaluator to say why any natural kind is a bad kind and ought not to call forth admiring respect. Something may be a good kind intrinsically but a bad kind instrumentally in the system; such cases will be anomalous however, with selection pressures against them. These assertions about good kinds do not say that things are perfect kinds or that there can be no better ones, only that natural kinds are good kinds until proven otherwise.

In fact, what is almost invariably meant by a bad kind is an organism that is instrumentally bad when judged from the viewpoint of human interests, often with the further complication that human interests have disrupted natural systems. *Bad* as so used is an anthropocentric word; there is nothing at all biological or ecological about it, and so it has no force in evaluating objective nature, however much humanistic force it may sometimes have.

A vital ethic respects all life, not just animal pains and pleasures, much less just human preferences. The old signs in the Rawah Wilderness—"Please leave the flowers for others to enjoy"—were application signs using an old, ethically conservative, humanistic ethic. The new ones invite a change of reference frame—a wilder ethic that is more logical because it is more biological, a radical ethic that goes down to the roots of life, that really is conservative because it understands biological conservation at depths. What the injunction "Let the flowers live!" means is this: "Daisies, marsh marigolds, geraniums, and larkspurs are evaluative systems that conserve goods of their kind and, in the absence of evidence to the contrary, are good kinds. There are trails here by which you may enjoy these flowers. Is there any reason why your human interests should not also conserve these good kinds?" A drive-through sequoia causes no suffering; it is not cruel. But it is callous and insensitive to the wonder of life.

SPECIES

Sensitivity to the wonder of life, however, can sometimes make an environmental ethicist seem callous. On San Clemente Island, the U.S. Fish and Wildlife Service and the Natural Resource Office of the U.S. Navy planned to shoot two thousand feral goats to save three endangered plant species (*Malacothamnus clementinus, Castilleja grisea,* and *Delphinium kinkiense*), of which the surviving individuals numbered only a few dozen. After a protest, some goats were trapped and relocated. But trapping all of them was impossible, and many thousands were killed. In this instance, the survival of plant species was counted more than the lives of individual mammals; a few plants counted more than many thousands of goats.

Those who wish to restore rare species of big cats to the wild have asked about killing genetically inbred, inferior cats presently held in zoos, in order to make space available for the cats needed to reconstruct and maintain a population that is genetically more likely to survive upon release. All the Siberian tigers in zoos in North America are descendants of seven animals; if these tigers were replaced by others nearer to the wild type and with more genetic variability, the species might be saved in the wild. When we move to the level of species, sometimes we decide to kill individuals for the good of their kind.

Or we might now refuse to let nature take its course. The Yellowstone ethicists let the bison drown, in spite of its suffering; they let the blinded bighorns die. But in the spring of 1984 a sow grizzly and her three cubs walked across the ice of Yellowstone Lake to Frank Island, two miles from shore. They stayed several days to feast on two elk carcasses, and the ice bridge melted. Soon afterward, they were starving on an island too small to support them. This time the Yellowstone ethicists promptly rescued the grizzlies and released them on the mainland, in order to protect an endangered species. They were not rescuing individual bears so much as saving the species.

Coloradans have declined to build the Two Forks Dam to supply urban Denver with water. Building the dam would require destroying a canyon and altering the Platte River flow, with many negative environmental consequences, including further endangering the whooping crane and endangering a butterfly, the Pawnee montane skipper. Elsewhere in the state, water development threatens several fish species, including the humpback chub, which requires the turbulent spring runoff stopped by dams. Environmental ethics doubts whether the good of humans who wish more water for development, both for industry and for bluegrass lawns, warrants endangering species of cranes, butterflies, and fish.

A species exists; a species ought to exist. An environmental ethics must make these assertions and move from biology to ethics with care. Species exist only instantiated in individuals, yet they are as real as individual plants or animals. The assertion that there are specific forms of life historically maintained in their environments over time seems as certain as anything else we believe about the empirical world. At times biologists revise the theories and taxa with which they map these forms, but species are not so much like lines of latitude and longitude as like mountains and rivers, phenomena objectively there to be mapped. The edges of these natural kinds will sometimes be fuzzy, to some extent discretionary. One species will slide into another over evolutionary time. But it does not follow from the fact that speciation is sometimes in progress that species are merely made up and not found as evolutionary lines with identity in time as well as space.

A consideration of species is revealing and challenging because it offers a biologically based counterexample to the focus on individuals—typically sentient and usually persons—so characteristic in classical ethics. In an evolutionary ecosystem, it is not mere individuality that counts; the species is also significant because it is a dynamic life-form maintained over time. The individual represents (re-presents) a species in each new generation. It is a token of a type, and the type is more important than the token.

A species lacks moral agency, reflective self-awareness, sentience, or organic individuality. The older, conservative ethic will be tempted to say that specific-level processes cannot count morally. Duties must attach to singular lives, most evidently those with a self, or some analogue to self. In an individual organism, the organs report to a center; the good of a whole is defended. The members of a species report to no center. A species has no self. It is not a bounded singular. There is no analogue to the nervous hookups or circulatory flows that characterize the organism.

But singularity, centeredness, selfhood, and individuality are not the only processes to which duty attaches. A more radically conservative ethic knows that having a biological identity reasserted genetically over time is as true of the species as of the individual. Identity need not attach solely to the centered organism; it can persist as a discrete pattern over time. From this way of thinking, it follows that the life the individual has is something passing through the individual as much as something it intrinsically possesses. The individual is subordinate to the species, not the other way around. The genetic set, in which is coded the telos, is as evidently the property of the species as of the individual through which it passes. A consideration of species strains any ethic fixed on individual organisms, much less on sentience or persons. But the result can be biologically sounder, though it revises what was formerly thought logically permissible or ethically binding. When ethics is informed by this kind of biology, it is appropriate to attach duty dynamically to the specific form of life.

The species line is the vital living system, the whole, of which individual organisms are the essential parts. The species too has its integrity, its individuality, its right to life (if we must use the rhetoric of rights); and it is more important to protect this vitality than to protect individual integrity. The right to life, biologically speaking, is an adaptive fit that is right for life, that survives over millennia. This idea generates at least a presumption that species in a niche are good right where they are, and therefore that it is right for humans to let them be, to let them evolve.

Processes of value that we earlier found in an organic individual reappear at the specific level: defending a particular form of life, pursuing a pathway through the world, resisting death (extinction), regenerating, maintaining a normative identity over time, expressing creative resilience by discovering survival skills. It is as logical to say that the individual is the species' way of propagating itself as to say that the embryo or egg is the individual's way of propagating itself. The dignity resides in the dynamic form; the individual inherits this form, exemplifies it, and passes it on. If, at the specific level, these processes are just as evident, or even more so, what prevents duties from arising at that level? The appropriate survival unit is the appropriate level of moral concern.

A shutdown of the life stream is the most destructive event possible. The wrong that humans are doing, or allowing to happen through carelessness, is stopping the historical vitality of life, the flow of natural kinds. Every extinction is an incremental decay in this stopping of life, no small thing. Every extinction is a kind of superkilling. It kills forms (species) beyond individuals. It kills essences beyond existences, the soul as well as the body. It kills collectively, not just distributively. It kills birth as well as death. Afterward nothing of that kind either lives or dies.

Ought species x to exist? is a distributive increment in the collective question, ought life on Earth to exist? Life on Earth cannot exist without its individuals, but a lost individual is always reproducible; a lost species is never reproducible. The answer to the species question is not always the same as the answer to the collective question, but because life on Earth is an aggregate of many species, the two are sufficiently related that the burden of proof lies with those who wish deliberately to extinguish a species and simultaneously to care for life on Earth.

One form of life has never endangered so many others. Never before has this level of question—superkilling by a superkiller—been deliberately faced. Humans have more understanding than ever of the natural world they inhabit and of the speciating processes, more predictive power to foresee the intended and unintended results of their actions, and more power to reverse the undesirable consequences. The duties that such power and vision generate no longer attach simply to individuals or persons but are emerging duties to specific forms of life. What is ethically callous is the maelstrom of killing and insensitivity to forms of life and the sources producing them. What is required is principled responsibility to the biospheric Earth.

Human activities seem misfit in the system. Although humans are maximizing their own species interests, and in this respect behaving as does each of the other species, they do not have any adaptive fitness. They are not really fitting into the evolutionary processes of ongoing biological conservation and elaboration. Their cultures are not really dynamically stable in their ecosystems. Such behavior is therefore not right. Yet humanistic ethical systems limp when they try to prescribe right conduct here. They seem misfits in the roles most recently demanded of them.

If, in this world of uncertain moral convictions, it makes any sense to assert that one ought not to kill individuals without justification, it makes more sense to assert that one ought not to superkill the species without superjustification. Several billion years' worth of creative toil, several million species of teeming life, have been handed over to the care of this late-coming species in which mind has flowered and morals have emerged. Ought not this sole moral species do something less self-interested than count all the produce of an evolutionary ecosystem as nothing but human resources? Such an attitude hardly seems biologically informed, much less ethically adequate. It is too provincial for intelligent humanity. Life on Earth is a many-splendored thing; extinction dims its luster. An ethics of respect for life is urgent at the level of species.

ECOSYSTEMS

A species is what it is where it is. No environmental ethics has found its way on Earth until it finds an ethic for the biotic communities in which all destinies are entwined. "A thing is right," urged Aldo Leopold, "when it tends to preserve the integrity, stability, and beauty of the biotic community. It is wrong when it tends otherwise."[2] Again, we have two parts to the ethic: first, that ecosystems exist, both in the wild and in support of culture; second, that ecosystems ought to exist, both for what they are in themselves and as modified by culture. Again, we must move with care from the biological assertions to the ethical assertions.

Giant forest fires raged over Yellowstone National Park in the summer of 1988, consuming nearly a million acres despite the efforts of a thousand fire fighters. By far the largest ever known in the park, the fires seemed a disaster. But the Yellowstone land ethic enjoined: "Let nature take its course; let it burn." So the fires were not fought at first, but in midsummer, national authorities overrode that policy and ordered the fires put out. Even then, weeks later, fires continued to burn, partly because they were too big to control but partly too because Yellowstone personnel did not really want the fires put out. Despite the evident destruction of trees, shrubs, and wildlife, they believe that fires are a good thing—even when the elk and bison leave the park in search of food and are shot by hunters. Fires reset succession, release nutrients, recycle materials, and renew the biotic community. (Nearby, in the Teton wilderness, a storm blew down fifteen thousand acres of trees, and some people proposed that the area be declassified from wilderness to allow commercial salvage of the timber. But a similar environmental ethic said, "No, let it rot.")

Aspen are important in the Yellowstone ecosystem. Although some aspen stands are climax and self-renewing, many are seral and give way to conifers. Aspen groves support many birds and much wildlife, especially beavers, whose activities maintain the riparian zones. Aspen are rejuvenated after fires, and the Yellowstone land ethic wants the aspen for their critical role in the biotic community. Elk browse the young aspen stems. To a degree this is a good thing, because it provides the elk with critical nitrogen, but in excess it is a bad thing. The elk have no predators, because the wolves are gone, and as a result the elk overpopulate. Excess elk also destroy the willows, and that destruction in turn destroys the beavers. So, in addition to letting fires burn, rejuvenating the aspen might require park managers to cull hundreds of elk—all for the sake of a healthy ecosystem.

The Yellowstone ethic wishes to restore wolves to the greater Yellowstone ecosystem. At the level of species, this change is desired because of what the wolf is in itself, but it is also desired because the greater Yellowstone ecosystem does not have its full integrity, stability, and beauty without this majestic animal at the top of the trophic pyramid. Restoring the wolf as a top predator would mean suffering and death for many elk, but that would be a good thing for the aspen and willows, the beavers, and the riparian habitat and would have mixed benefits for the bighorns and mule deer (the overpopulating elk consume their food, but the sheep and deer would also be consumed by the wolves). Restoration of wolves would be done over the protests of ranchers who worry about wolves eating their cattle; many of them also believe that the wolf is a bloodthirsty killer, a bad kind. Nevertheless, the Yellowstone ethic demands wolves, as it does fires, in appropriate respect for life in its ecosystem.

Letting nature take its ecosystemic course is why the Yellowstone ethic forbade rescuing the drowning bison but required rescuing the sow grizzly and her cubs, the latter case to insure that the big predators remain. After the bison drowned, coyotes, foxes, magpies, and ravens fed on the carcass. Later, even a grizzly bear fed on it. All this is a good thing because the system cycles on. On that account, rescuing the whales trapped in the winter ice seems less of a good thing, when we note that rescuers had to drive away polar bears that attempted to eat the dying whales.

Classical, humanistic ethics finds ecosystems to be unfamiliar territory. It is difficult to get the biology right and, superimposed on the biology, to get the ethics right. Fortunately, it is often evident that human welfare depends on ecosystemic support, and in this sense all our legislation about clean air, clean water, soil conservation, national and state forest policies, pollution controls, renewable resources, and so forth is concerned about ecosystem-level processes. Furthermore, humans find much of value in preserving wild ecosystems, and our wilderness and park system is impressive.

Still, a comprehensive environmental ethics needs the best, naturalistic reasons, as well as the good, humanistic ones, for respecting ecosystems. Ecosystems generate and support life, keep selection pressures high, enrich situated fitness, and allow congruent kinds to evolve in their places with sufficient containment. The ecologist finds that ecosystems are objectively satisfactory communities in the sense that organismic needs are sufficiently met for species to survive and flourish, and the critical ethicist finds (in a subjective judgment matching the objective process) that such ecosystems are satisfactory communities to which to attach duty. Our concern must be for the fundamental unit of survival.

An ecosystem, the conservative ethicist will say, is too low a level of organization to be respected intrinsically. Ecosystems can seem little more than random, statistical processes. A forest can seem a loose collection of externally related parts, the collection of fauna and flora a jumble, hardly a community. The plants and animals within an ecosystem have needs, but their interplay can seem simply a matter of distribution and abundance, birth rates and death rates, population densities, parasitism and predation, dispersion, checks and balances, and stochastic process. Much is not organic at all (rain, groundwater, rocks, soil particles, air), and some organic material is dead and decaying debris (fallen trees, scat, humus). These things have no organized needs. There is only catch-as-catch-can scrimmage for nutrients and energy, not really enough of an integrated process to call the whole a community.

Unlike higher animals, ecosystems have no experiences; they do not and cannot care. Unlike plants, an ecosystem has no organized center, no genome. It does not defend itself against injury or death. Unlike a species, there is no ongoing telos, no biological identity reinstantiated over time. The organismic parts are more complex than the community whole. More troublesome still, an ecosystem can seem a jungle where the fittest survive, a place of contest and conflict, beside which the organism is a model of cooperation. In animals the heart, liver, muscles, and brain are tightly integrated, as are the leaves, cambium, and roots in plants. But the so-called ecosystem community is pushing and shoving between rivals, each aggrandizing itself, or else seems to be all indifference and haphazard juxtaposition—nothing to call forth our admiration.

Environmental ethics must break through the boundary posted by disoriented ontological conservatives, who hold that only organisms are real, actually existing as entities, whereas ecosystems are nominal—just interacting individuals. Oak trees are real, but forests are nothing but collections of trees. But any level is real if it shapes behavior on the level below it. Thus the cell is real because that pattern shapes the behavior of amino acids; the organism, because that pattern coordinates the behavior of hearts and lungs. The biotic community is real because the niche shapes the morphology of the oak trees within it. Being real at the level of community requires only an organization that shapes the behavior of its members.

The challenge is to find a clear model of community and to discover an ethics for it: better biology for better ethics. Even before the rise of ecology, biologists began to conclude that the combative survival of the fittest distorts the truth. The more perceptive model is coaction in adapted fit. Predator and prey, parasite and host, grazer and grazed, are contending forces in dynamic process in which the well-being of each is bound up with the other—coordinated as much as heart and liver are coordinated organically. The ecosystem supplies the coordinates through which each organism moves, outside which the species cannot really be located.

The community connections are looser than the organism's internal interconnections but are not less significant. Admiring organic unity in organisms and stumbling over environmental looseness is like valuing mountains and despising valleys. The matrix that the organism requires to survive is the open, pluralistic ecological system. Internal complexity—heart, liver, muscles, brain—arises as a way of dealing with a complex, tricky environment. The skin-out processes are not just the support; they are the subtle source of the skin-in processes. In the complete picture, the outside is as vital as the inside. Had there been either simplicity or lockstep concentrated unity in the environment, no organismic unity could have evolved. Nor would it remain. There would be less elegance in life.

To look at one level for what is appropriate at another makes a mistake in categories. One should not look for a single center or program in ecosystems, much less for subjective experiences. Instead, one should look for a matrix, for interconnections between centers (individual plants and animals, dynamic lines of speciation), for creative stimulus and open-ended potential. Everything will be connected to many other things, sometimes by obligate associations but more often by partial and pliable dependencies, and, among other things, there will be no significant interactions. There will be functions in a communal sense: shunts and crisscrossing pathways, cybernetic subsystems and feedback loops. An order arises spontaneously and systematically when many self-concerned units jostle and seek to fulfill their own programs, each doing its own thing and forced into informed interaction.

An ecosystem is a productive, projective system. Organisms defend only their selves, with individuals defending their continuing survival and with species increasing the numbers of kinds. But the evolutionary ecosystem spins a bigger story, limiting each kind, locking it into the welfare of others, promoting new arrivals, increasing kinds and the integration of kinds. Species increase their kind, but ecosystems increase kinds, superposing the latter increase onto the former. Ecosystems are selective systems, as surely as organisms are selective systems. The natural selection comes out of the system and is imposed on the individual. The individual is programmed to make more of its kind, but more is going on systemically than that; the system is making more kinds.

Communal processes—the competition between organisms, statistically probable interactions, plant and animal successions, speciation over historical time—generate an ever-richer community. Hence the evolutionary toil, elaborating and diversifying the biota, that once began with no species and results today in five million species, increasing over time the quality of lives in the upper rungs of the trophic pyramids. One-celled organisms evolved into many-celled, highly integrated organisms. Photosynthesis evolved and came to support locomotion—swimming, walking, running, flight. Stimulus–response mechanisms became complex instinctive acts. Warm-blooded animals followed cold-blooded ones. Complex nervous systems, conditioned behavior, and learning emerged. Sentience appeared—sight, hearing, smell, taste, pleasure, pain. Brains coupled with hands. Consciousness and self-consciousness arose. Culture was superposed on nature.

These developments do not take place in all ecosystems or at every level. Microbes, plants, and lower animals remain, good of their kinds and, serving continuing roles, good for other kinds. The understories remain occupied. As a result, the quantity of life and its diverse qualities continue—from protozoans to primates to people. There is a push-up, lock-up ratchet effect that conserves the upstrokes and the outreaches. The later we go in time, the more accelerated are the forms at the top of the trophic pyramids, the more elaborated are the multiple trophic pyramids of Earth. There are upward arrows over evolutionary time.

The system is a game with loaded dice, but the loading is a pro-life tendency, not mere stochastic process. Though there is no Nature in the singular, the system has a nature, a loading that pluralizes, putting natures into diverse kinds: $nature_1$, $nature_2$, $nature_3$ . . . $nature_n$. It does so using random elements (in both organisms and communities), but this is a secret of its fertility, producing steadily intensified interdependencies and options. An ecosystem has no head, but it heads toward species diversification, support, and richness. Though not a superorganism, it is a kind of vital field.

Instrumental value uses something as a means to an end; intrinsic value is worthwhile in itself. No warbler eats insects to become food for a falcon; the warbler defends it own life as an end in itself and makes more warblers as it can. A life is defended intrinsically, without further contributory reference. But neither of these traditional terms is satisfactory at the level of the ecosystem. Though it has value *in* itself, the system does not have any value *for* itself. Though it is a value producer, it is not a value owner. We are no longer confronting instrumental value, as though the system were of value instrumentally as a fountain of life. Nor is the question one of intrinsic value, as though the system defended some unified form of life for itself. We have reached something for which we need a third term: systemic value. Duties arise in encounters with the system that projects and protects these member components in biotic community.

Ethical conservatives, in the humanistic sense, will say that ecosystems are of value only because they contribute to human experiences. But that mistakes the last chapter for the whole story, one fruit for the whole plant. Humans count enough to have the right to flourish in ecosystems, but not so much that they have the right to degrade or shut down ecosystems, not at least without a burden of proof that there is an overriding cultural gain. Those who have traveled partway into environmental ethics will say that ecosystems are of value because they contribute to animal experiences or to organismic life. But the really conservative, radical view sees that the stability, integrity, and beauty of biotic communities are what are most fundamentally to be conserved. In a comprehensive ethics of respect for life, we ought to set ethics at the level of ecosystems alongside classical, humanistic ethics.

VALUE THEORY

In practice the ultimate challenge of environmental ethics is the conservation of life on Earth. In principle the ultimate challenge is a value theory profound enough to support that ethics. In nature there is negentropic construction in dialectic with entropic teardown, a process for which we hardly yet have an adequate scientific theory, much less a valuational theory. Yet this is nature's most striking feature, one that ultimately must be valued and of value. In one sense, nature is indifferent to mountains, rivers, fauna, flora, forests, and grasslands. But in another sense, nature has bent toward making and remaking these projects, millions of kinds, for several billion years.

These performances are worth noticing, are remarkable and memorable—and not just because of their tendencies to produce something else; certainly not merely because of their tendency to produce this noticing in certain recent subjects, our human selves. These events are loci of value as products of systemic nature in its formative processes. The splendors of Earth do not simply lie in their roles as human resources, supports of culture, or stimulators of experience. The most plausible account will find some programmatic evolution toward value, and not because it ignores Darwin but because it heeds his principle of natural selection and deploys it into a selection exploring new niches and elaborating kinds, even a selection upslope toward higher values, at least along some trends within some ecosystems. How do we humans come to be charged up with values, if there was and is nothing in nature charging us up so? A systematic environmental ethics does not wish to believe in the special creation of values or in their dumbfounding epigenesis. Let them evolve. Let nature carry value.

The notion that nature is a value carrier is ambiguous. Much depends on a thing's being more or less structurally congenial for the carriage. We value a thing and discover that we are under the sway of its valence, inducing our behavior. It has among its strengths (Latin: *valeo*, "be strong") this capacity to carry value. This potential cannot always be of the empty sort that a glass has for carrying water. It is often pregnant fullness. Some of the values that nature carries are up to us, our assignment. But fundamentally there are powers in nature that move to us and through us.

No value exists without an evaluator. So runs a well-entrenched dogma. Humans clearly evaluate their world; sentient animals may also. But plants cannot evaluate their environment; they have no options and make no choices. A fortiori, species and ecosystems, Earth and Nature, cannot be bona fide evaluators. One can always hang on to the assertion that value, like a tickle or remorse, must be felt to be there. Its *esse* is *percipi*. To be, it must be perceived. Nonsensed value is nonsense. There are no thoughts without a thinker, no percepts without a perceiver, no deeds without a doer, no targets without an aimer.

Such resolute subjectivists cannot be defeated by argument, although they can be driven toward analyticity. That theirs is a retreat to definition is difficult to expose, because they seem to cling so closely to inner experience. They are reporting, on this hand, how values always excite us. They are giving, on that hand, a stipulative definition. That is how they choose to use the word *value*.

If value arrives only with consciousness, experiences in which humans find value have to be dealt with as appearances of various sorts. The value has to be relocated in the valuing subject's creativity as a person meets a valueless world, or even a valuable one—one able to be valued but one that before the human bringing of valuableness contains only possibility and not any actual value. Value can only be extrinsic to nature, never intrinsic to it.

But the valuing subject in an otherwise valueless world is an insufficient premise for the experienced conclusions of those who respect all life. Conversion to a biological view seems truer to world experience and more logically compelling. Something from a world beyond the human mind, beyond human experience, is received into our mind, our experience, and the value of that something does not always arise with our evaluation of it. Here the order of knowing reverses, and also enhances, the order of being. This too is a perspective but is ecologically better-informed. Science has been steadily showing how the consequents (life, mind) are built on their precedents (energy, matter), however much they overleap them. Life and mind appear where they did not before exist, and with them levels of value emerge that did not before exist. But that gives no reason to say that all value is an irreducible emergent at the human (or upper-animal) level. A comprehensive environmental ethics reallocates value across the whole continuum. Value increases in the emergent climax but is continuously present in the composing precedents. The system is value-able, able to produce value. Human evaluators are among its products.

Some value depends on subjectivity, yet all value is generated within the geosystemic and ecosystemic pyramid. Systemically, value fades from subjective to objective value but also fans out from the individual to its role and matrix. Things do not have their separate natures merely in and for themselves, but they face outward and co-fit into broader natures. Value-in-itself is smeared out to become value-in-togetherness. Value seeps out into the system, and we lose our capacity to identify the individual as the sole locus of value.

Intrinsic value, the value of an individual for what it is in itself, becomes problematic in a holistic web. True, the system produces such values more and more with its evolution of individuality and freedom. Yet to decouple this value from the biotic, communal system is to make value too internal and elementary; this decoupling forgets relatedness and externality. Every intrinsic value has leading and trailing *and*'s. Such value is coupled with value from which it comes and toward which it moves. Adapted fitness makes individualistic value too system-independent. Intrinsic value is a part in a whole and is not to be fragmented by valuing it in isolation.

Everything is good in a role, in a whole, although we can speak of objective intrinsic goodness wherever a point-event—a trillium, for example—defends a good (its life) in itself. We can speak of subjective intrinsic goodness when such an event registers as a point-experience, at which point humans pronounce both their experience and what it is to be good without need to enlarge their focus. Neither the trilliums nor the human judges of it require for their respective valuings any further contributory reference.

When eaten by foragers or in death resorbed into humus, the trillium has its value destroyed, transformed into instrumentality. The system is a value transformer where form and being, process and reality, fact and value, are inseparably joined. Intrinsic and instrumental values shuttle back and forth, parts-in-wholes and wholes-in-parts, local details of value embedded in global structures, gems in their settings, and their setting-situation a corporation where value cannot stand alone. Every good is in community.

In environmental ethics one's beliefs about nature, which are based upon but exceed science, have everything to do with beliefs about duty. The way the world is informs the way it ought to be. We always shape our values in significant measure in accord with our notion of the kind of universe that we live in, and this process drives our sense of duty. Our model of reality implies a model of conduct. Differing models sometimes imply similar conduct, but often they do not. A model in which nature has no value apart from human preferences will imply different conduct from one in which nature projects fundamental values, some objective and others that further require human subjectivity superimposed on objective nature.

This evaluation is not scientific description; hence it is not ecology per se but metaecology. No amount of research can verify that, environmentally, the right is the optimum biotic community. Yet ecological description generates this valuing of nature, endorsing the systemic rightness. The transition from *is* to *good* and thence to *ought* occurs here; we leave science to enter the domain of evaluation, from which an ethics follows.

What is ethically puzzling and exciting is that an *ought* is not so much derived from an *is* as discovered simultaneously with it. As we progress from descriptions of fauna and flora, of cycles and pyramids, of autotrophs coordinated with heterotrophs, of stability and dynamism, on to intricacy, planetary opulence and interdependence, unity and harmony with oppositions in counterpoint and synthesis, organisms evolved within and satisfactorily fitting their communities, and we arrive at length at beauty and goodness, we find that it is difficult to say where the natural facts leave off and where the natural values appear. For some people at least, the sharper *is–ought* dichotomy is gone; the values seem to be there as soon as the facts are fully in, and both values and facts seem to be alike properties of the system.

There is something overspecialized about an ethic, held by the dominant class of *Homo sapiens*, that regards the welfare of only one of several million species as an object and beneficiary of duty. If the remedy requires a paradigm change about the sorts of things to which duty can attach, so much the worse for those humanistic ethics no longer functioning in, or suited to, their changing environment. The anthropocentrism associated with them was fiction anyway. There is something Newtonian, not yet Einsteinian, besides something morally naive, about living in a reference frame in which one species takes itself as absolute and values everything else relative to its utility. If true to its specific epithet, which means wise, ought not *Homo sapiens* value this host of life as something that lays on us a claim to care for life in its own right?

Only the human species contains moral agents, but perhaps conscience on such an Earth ought not to be used to exempt every other form of life from consideration, with the resulting paradox that the sole moral species acts only in its collective self-interest toward all the rest. Is not the ultimate philosophical task the discovery of a whole great ethic that knows the human place under the sun?

NOTES

1. J. Bentham, *Introduction to the Principles of Morals and Legislation* (1789; New York: Hafner, 1948), 311.
2. A. Leopold, *A Sand County Almanac, and Sketches Here and There* (New York: Oxford University Press, 1949), 224–25.

"Respect for Nature: A Theory of Environmental Ethics"

Paul W. Taylor

HAVING AND EXPRESSING THE ATTITUDE OF RESPECT FOR NATURE

The central tenet of the theory of environmental ethics that I am defending is that actions are right and character traits are morally good in virtue of their expressing or embodying a certain ultimate moral attitude, which I call respect for nature. When moral agents adopt the attitude, they thereby subscribe to a set of standards of character and rules of conduct as their own ethical principles. Having the attitude entails being morally committed to fulfilling the standards and complying with the rules. When moral agents then act in accordance with the rules and when they develop character traits that meet the standards, their conduct and character express (give concrete embodiment to) the attitude. Thus ethical action and goodness of character naturally flow from the attitude, and the attitude is made manifest in how one acts and in what sort of person one is.

THE BIOCENTRIC OUTLOOK AND THE ATTITUDE OF RESPECT FOR NATURE

The attitude we think it appropriate to take toward living things depends on how we conceive of them and of our relationship to them. What moral significance the natural world has for us depends on the way we look at the whole system of nature and our role in it. With regard to the attitude of respect for nature, the belief-system that renders it intelligible and on which it depends for its justifiability is the biocentric outlook. This outlook underlies and supports the attitude of respect for nature in the following sense. Unless we grasp what it means to accept that belief-system and so view the natural order from its perspective, we cannot see the point of taking the attitude of respect. But once we do grasp it and shape our world outlook in accordance with it, we immediately understand how and why a person would adopt that attitude as the only appropriate one to have toward nature. Thus the biocentric outlook provides the explanatory and justificatory background that makes sense of and gives point to a person's taking the attitude.

The beliefs that form the core of the biocentric outlook are four in number:

1. The belief that humans are members of the Earth's Community of Life in the same sense and on the same terms in which other living things are members of that Community.
2. The belief that the human species, along with all other species, are integral elements in a system of interdependence such that the survival of each living thing, as well as its chances of faring well or poorly, is determined not only by the physical conditions of its environment but also by its relations to other living things.
3. The belief that all organisms are teleological centers of life in the sense that each is a unique individual pursuing its own good in its own way.
4. The belief that humans are not inherently superior to other living things.

To accept all four of these beliefs is to have a coherent outlook on the natural world and the place of humans in it. It is to take a certain perspective on human life and to conceive of the relation between human and other forms of life in a certain way. Given this world view, the attitude of respect is then seen to be the only suitable, fitting, or appropriate moral attitude to take toward the natural world and its living inhabitants.

THE BASIC RULES OF CONDUCT

. . . I shall now set out and examine four rules of duty in the domain of environmental ethics. This is not supposed to provide an exhaustive account of every valid duty of the ethics of respect for nature. It is doubtful whether a complete specification of duties is possible in this realm. But however that may be, the duties to be listed here are intended to cover only the more important ones that typically arise in everyday life. . . . [I]n all situations not explicitly or clearly covered by these rules we should rely on the attitude of respect for nature and the biocentric outlook that together underlie the system as a whole and give it point. Right actions are always actions that express the attitude of respect, whether they are covered by the four rules or not. They must also be actions which we can approve of in the light of the various components of the biocentric outlook.

The four rules will be named (1) the Rule of Nonmaleficence, (2) the Rule of Noninterference, (3) the Rule of Fidelity, and (4) the Rule of Restitutive Justice.

1. *The Rule of Nonmaleficence.* This is the duty not to do harm to any entity in the natural environment that has a good of its own. It includes the duty not to kill an organism and not to destroy a species-population or biotic

community, as well as the duty to refrain from any action that would be seriously detrimental to the good of an organism, species-population, or life community. Perhaps the most fundamental wrong in the ethics of respect for nature is to harm something that does not harm us.

The concept of nonmaleficence is here understood to cover only nonperformances or intentional abstentions. The rule defines a negative duty, requiring that moral agents refrain from certain kinds of actions. It does not require the doing of any actions, such as those that *prevent* harm from coming to an entity or those that help to *alleviate* its suffering. Actions of these sorts more properly fall under the heading of benefiting an entity by protecting or promoting its good. (They will be discussed in connection with the Rule of Restitutive Justice.)

The Rule of Nonmaleficence prohibits harmful and destructive acts done by moral agents. It does not apply to the behavior of a nonhuman animal or the activity of a plant that might bring harm to another living thing or cause its death. Suppose, for example, that a Rough-legged Hawk pounces on a field mouse, killing it. Nothing morally wrong has occurred. Although the hawk's behavior can be thought of as something it does intentionally, it is not the action of a moral agent. Thus it does not fall within the range of the Rule of Nonmaleficence. The hawk does not violate any duty because it *has* no duties. Consider, next, a vine which over the years gradually covers a tree and finally kills it. The activity of the vine, which involves goal-oriented movements but not, of course, intentional actions, is not a moral wrongdoing. The vine's killing the tree has no moral properties at all, since it is not the conduct of a moral agent.

Let us now, by way of contrast, consider the following case. A Peregrine Falcon has been taken from the wild by a falconer, who then trains it to hunt, seize, and kill wild birds under his direction. Here there occurs human conduct aimed at controlling and manipulating an organism for the enjoyment of a sport that involves harm to other wild organisms. A wrong is being done but not by the falcon, even though it is the falcon which does the actual killing and even though the birds it kills are its natural prey. The wrong that is done to those birds is a wrong done by the falconer. It is not the action of the Peregrine that breaks the rule of duty but the actions of the one who originally captured it, trained it, and who now uses it for his own amusement. These actions, it might be added, are also violations of the Rule of Noninterference, since the falcon was removed from its wild state. Let us now turn our attention to this second rule of duty.

2. *The Rule of Noninterference.* Under this rule fall two sorts of negative duties, one requiring us to refrain from placing restrictions on the freedom of individual organisms, the other requiring a general "hands off" policy with regard to whole ecosystems and biotic communities, as well as to individual organisms.

Concerning the first sort of duty, the idea of the freedom of individual organisms[,] . . . freedom is absence of constraint, [and] a constraint is any condition that prevents or hinders the normal activity and healthy development of an animal or plant. A being is free in this sense when any of four types of constraints that could weaken, impair, or destroy its ability to adapt successfully to its environment are absent from its existence and circumstances. To be free is to be free *from* these constraints and to be free *to* pursue the realization of one's good according to the laws of one's nature. The four types of constraints, with some examples of each, are:

1. Positive external constraints (cages; traps).
2. Negative external constraints (no water or food available).
3. Positive internal constraints (diseases; ingested poison or absorbed toxic chemicals).
4. Negative internal constraints (weaknesses and incapacities due to injured organs or tissues).

We humans can restrict the freedom of animals and plants by either directly imposing some of these constraints upon them or by producing changes in their environments which then act as constraints upon them. Either way, if we do these things knowingly we are guilty of violating the Rule of Noninterference.

The second kind of duty that comes under this rule is the duty to let wild creatures live out their lives in freedom. Here freedom means not the absence of constraints but simply being allowed to carry on one's existence in a wild state. With regard to individual organisms, this duty requires us to refrain from capturing them and removing them from their natural habitats, *no matter how well we might then treat them.* We have violated the duty of noninterference even if we "save" them by taking them out of a natural danger or by restoring their health after they have become ill in the wild. (The duty is not violated, however, if we do such things with the intention of returning the creature to the wild as soon as possible, and we fully carry out this intention.) When we take young trees or wildflowers from a natural ecosystem, for example, and transplant them in landscaped grounds, we break the Rule of Noninterference *whether or not we then take good care of them and so enable them to live longer, healthier lives than they would have enjoyed in the wild.* We have done a wrong by not letting them live out their lives in freedom. In all situations like these we intrude into the domain of the natural world and terminate an organism's existence as a wild creature. It does not matter that our treatment of them may improve their strength, promote their growth, and increase their chances for a long, healthy life. By destroying their status as wild animals or plants, our interference in their lives amounts to an absolute negation of their natural freedom. Thus, however "benign" our actions may seem, we are doing what the Rule of Noninterference forbids us to do.

Of still deeper significance, perhaps, is the duty of noninterference as it applies to the freedom of whole species-populations and communities of life. The prohibition against interfering with these entities means that we must not try to manipulate, control, modify, or "manage" natural ecosystems or otherwise intervene in their normal functioning. For any given species-population, freedom is the absence of human intervention of any kind in the natural lawlike processes by which the population preserves itself from generation to generation. Freedom for a whole biotic community is the absence of human intervention in the natural lawlike processes by which all its constituent species-populations undergo changing ecological relationships with one another over time. The duty not to interfere is the duty to respect the freedom of biologically and ecologically organized groups of wild organisms by refraining from those sorts of intervention. Again, this duty holds even if such intervention is motivated by a desire to "help" a species-population survive or a desire to "correct natural imbalances" in a biotic community. (Attempts to save endangered species which have almost been exterminated by past *human* intrusions into nature, and attempts to restore ecological stability and balance to an ecosystem that has been damaged by past *human* activity are cases that fall under the Rule of Restitutive Justice and may be ethically right. These cases will be considered in connection with that rule.)

The duty of noninterference, like that of nonmaleficence, is a purely negative duty. It does not require us to perform any actions regarding either individual organisms or groups of organisms. We are only required to respect their wild freedom by letting them alone. In this way we allow them, as it were, to fulfill their own destinies. Of course some of them will lose out in their struggle with natural competitors and others will suffer harm from natural causes. But as far as our proper role as moral agents is concerned, we must keep "hands off." By strictly adhering to the Rule of Noninterference, our conduct manifests a profound regard for the integrity of the system of nature. Even when a whole ecosystem has been seriously disturbed by a natural disaster (earthquake, lightning-caused fire, volcanic eruption, flood, prolonged drought, or the like) we are duty-bound not to intervene to try to repair the damage. After all, throughout the long history of life on our planet natural disasters ("disasters," that is, from the standpoint of some particular organism or group of organisms) have always taken their toll in the death of many creatures. Indeed, the very process of natural selection continually leads to the extinction of whole species. After such disasters a gradual readjustment always takes place so that a new set of relations among species-populations emerges. To abstain from intervening in this order of things is a way of expressing our attitude of respect for nature, for we thereby give due recognition to the process of evolutionary change that has been the "story" of life on Earth since its very beginnings.

This general policy of nonintervention is a matter of disinterested principle. We may want to help certain species-populations because we like them or because they are beneficial to us. But the Rule of Noninterference requires that we put aside our personal likes and our human interests with reference to how we treat them. Our respect for nature means that we acknowledge the sufficiency of the natural world to sustain its own proper order throughout the whole domain of life. This is diametrically opposed to the human-centered view of nature as a vast piece of property which we can use as we see fit.

In one sense to have the attitude of respect toward natural ecosystems, toward wild living things, and toward the whole process of evolution is to believe that nothing goes wrong in nature. Even the destruction of an entire biotic community or the extinction of a species is not evidence that something is amiss. If the causes for such events arose within the system of nature itself, nothing improper has happened. In particular, the fact that organisms suffer and die does not itself call for corrective action on the part of humans *when humans have had nothing to do with the cause of that suffering and death.* Suffering and death are integral aspects of the order of nature. So if it is ever the case in our contemporary world that the imminent extinction of a whole species is due to entirely natural causes, we should not try to stop the natural sequence of events from taking place in order to save the species. That sequence of events is governed by the operation of laws that have made the biotic Community of our planet what it is. To respect that Community is to respect the laws that gave rise to it.

In addition to this respect for the sufficiency and integrity of the natural order, a second ethical principle is implicit in the Rule of Noninterference. This is the principle of species-impartiality, which serves as a counterweight to the dispositions of people to favor certain species over others and to want to intervene in behalf of their favorites. These dispositions show themselves in a number of ways. First, consider the reactions of many people to predator–prey relations among wildlife. Watching the wild dogs of the African plains bring down the Wildebeest and begin devouring its underparts while it is still alive, they feel sympathy for the prey and antipathy for the predator. There is a tendency to make moral judgments, to think of the dogs as vicious and cruel, and to consider the Wildebeest an innocent victim. Or take the situation in which a snake is about to kill a baby bird in its nest. The snake is perceived as wicked and the nestling is seen as not deserving such a fate. Even plant life is looked at in this biased way. People get disturbed by a great tree being "strangled" by a vine. And when it comes to instances of bacteria-caused diseases, almost everyone has a tendency to be on the side of the organism which has the disease rather than viewing the situation from the standpoint of the living bacteria inside the organism. If we accept the biocentric outlook and have genuine respect for nature, however, we remain strictly neutral between predator and prey, parasite and host, the disease-causing and the diseased. To take sides in such struggles, to think of them in moral terms as cases of the maltreatment of innocent victims by evil animals and nasty plants, is to abandon the attitude of respect for all wild living things. It is to count the good of some as having greater value than that of others. This is inconsistent with the fundamental presupposition of the attitude of respect: that all living things in the natural world have the same inherent worth. . . .

3. *The Rule of Fidelity.* This rule applies only to human conduct in relation to individual animals that are in a wild state and are capable of being deceived or betrayed by moral agents. The duties imposed by the Rule of Fidelity, though of restricted range, are so frequently violated by so many people that this rule needs separate study as one of the basic principles of the ethics of respect for nature.

Under this rule fall the duties not to break a trust that a wild animal places in us (as shown by its behavior), not to deceive or mislead any animal capable of being deceived or misled, to uphold an animal's expectations, which it has formed on the basis of one's past actions with it, and to be true to one's intentions as made known to an animal when it has come to rely on one. Although we cannot make mutual agreements with wild animals, we can act in such a manner as to call forth their trust in us. The basic moral requirement imposed by the Rule of Fidelity is that we remain faithful to that trust.

The clearest and commonest examples of transgressions of the rule occur in hunting, trapping, and fishing. Indeed, the breaking of a trust is a key to good (that is, successful) hunting, trapping, and fishing. Deception with intent to harm is of the essence. Therefore, unless there is a weighty moral reason for engaging in these activities, they must be condemned by the ethics of respect for nature. The weighty moral reason in question must itself be grounded on disinterested principle, since the action remains wrong in itself in virtue of its constituting a violation of a valid moral rule. Like all such violations, it can be justified only by appeal to a higher, more stringent duty whose priority over the duty of fidelity is established by a morally valid priority principle.

When a man goes hunting for bear or deer he will walk through a woodland as quietly and unobtrusively as possible. If he is a duck hunter he will hide in a blind, set out decoys, use imitative calls. In either case the purpose, of course, is to get within shooting range of the mammal or bird. Much of the hunter's conduct is designed to deceive the wild creature. As an animal is approaching, the hunter remains quiet, then raises his rifle to take careful aim. Here is a clear situation in which, first, a wild animal acts as if there were no danger; second, the hunter by stealth is deliberately misleading the animal to expect no danger; and third, the hunter is doing this for the immediate purpose of killing the animal. The total performance is one of entrapment and betrayal. The animal is manipulated to be trusting and unsuspicious. It is deliberately kept unaware of something in its environment which is, from the standpoint of its good, of great importance to it. The entire pattern of the hunter's behavior is aimed at taking advantage of an animal's trust. Sometimes an animal is taken advantage of in situations where it may be aware of some danger but instinctively goes to the aid of an injured companion. The hunter uses his knowledge of this to betray the animal. Thus when the hunting of shorebirds used to be legally permitted, a hunter would injure a single bird and leave it out to attract hundreds of its fellows, which would fly in and gather around it. This way the hunter could easily "harvest" vast numbers of shorebirds. Even to this day a similar kind of trickery is used to deceive birds. Crow hunters play recordings of a crow's distress calls out in the field. The recording attracts crows, who are then easy targets to shoot. This aspect of hunting, it should be repeated, is not some peripheral aberration. Much of the excitement and enjoyment of hunting as a sport is the challenge to one's skills in getting animals to be trusting and unsuspecting. The cleverer the deception, the better the skill of the hunter. . . .

It is not a question here of whether the animal being hunted, trapped, or fished has a *right* to expect not to be deceived. The animal is being deceived in order to bring advantage to the deceiver and this itself is the sign that the deceiver considers the animal as either having no inherent worth or as having a lower degree of inherent worth than the deceiver himself. Either way of looking at it is incompatible with the attitude of respect for nature. . . .

Besides breaking the Rule of Fidelity, hunting, trapping, and fishing also, of course, involve gross violations of the Rules of Nonmaleficence and Noninterference. It may be the case that in circumstances where the only means for obtaining food or clothing essential to human survival is by hunting, trapping, or fishing, these actions are morally permissible. The ethical principles that justify them could stem from a system of human ethics based on respect for persons plus a priority principle that makes the duty to provide for human survival outweigh those duties of nonmaleficence, noninterference, and fidelity that are owed to nonhumans. But when hunting and fishing are done for sport or recreation, they cannot be justified on the same grounds.

There are cases of deceiving and breaking faith with an animal, however, which can be justified *within* the system of environmental ethics. These cases occur when deception and betrayal must (reluctantly) be done as a necessary step in a wider action of furthering an animal's good, this wider action being the fulfillment of a duty of restitutive justice. If breaking faith is a temporary measure absolutely needed to alleviate great suffering or to prevent serious harm coming to an animal, such an act may be required as an instance of restitutive justice. Putting aside for the moment a consideration of the idea of restitutive justice as it applies to environmental ethics, it may be helpful to look at some examples.

Suppose a grizzly bear has wandered into an area close to human habitation. In order to prevent harm coming not only to people but also to the bear (when people demand that it be killed), the bear may be deceived so that it can be shot with harmless tranquilizer darts and then, while it is unconscious, removed to a remote wilderness area. Another example would be the live-trapping of a sick or injured animal so that it can be brought to an animal hospital, treated, and then returned to the wild when it is fully recovered. Still another kind of case occurs when a few birds of an endangered species are captured in order to have them raise young in captivity. The young would then be released in natural habitat areas in an effort to prevent the species from becoming extinct.

These human encroachments upon the wild state of mammals and birds violate both the rule of Noninterference and the Rule of Fidelity. But the whole treatment of these creatures is consistent with the attitude of respect for them. They are not being taken advantage of but rather are being given the opportunity to maintain their existence as wild living things. . . .

. . . Hunters and fishermen often argue that they show true respect for nature because they advocate (and pay for) the preservation of natural areas which benefit wild species-populations and life communities. And it is quite true that the setting aside of many "wildlife refuges," both public and private, has resulted from their efforts. Wild animals and plants have benefited from this. What is being overlooked in this argument is the difference between doing something to benefit oneself which happens also to benefit others, and doing something with the purpose of benefiting others as one's ultimate end of action. Hunters and fishermen want only those areas of the natural environment protected that will provide for them a constant supply of fish, birds, and mammals as game. Indeed, sportsmen will often urge the killing of nongame animals that prey on "their" (the sportsmen's) animals. In Alaska, for example, hunters have persuaded state officials to "manage" wolves—the method used is to shoot them from helicopters—so as to ensure that a large population of moose is available for hunting. The argument that hunters and fishermen are true conservationists of wildlife will stand up only when we sharply distinguish conservation (saving in the present for future consumption) from preservation (protecting from both present and future consumption). And if the ultimate purpose of conservation programs is future exploitation of wildlife for the enjoyment of outdoor sports and recreation, such conservation activities are not consistent with respect for nature, whatever may be the benefits incidentally brought to some wild creatures. Actions that bring about good consequences for wildlife do not express the attitude of respect unless those actions are motivated in a certain way. It must be the case that the actions are done with the intention of promoting or protecting the good of wild creatures as an end in itself and for the sake of those creatures themselves. Such motivation is precisely what is absent from the conversation activities of sportsmen.

4. *The Rule of Restitutive Justice.* In its most general terms this rule imposes the duty to restore the balance of justice between a moral agent and a moral subject when the subject has been wronged by the agent. Common to all instances in which a duty of restitutive justice arises, an agent has broken a valid moral rule and by doing so has upset the balance of justice between himself or herself and a moral subject. To hold oneself accountable for having

done such an act is to acknowledge a special duty one has taken upon oneself by that wrongdoing. This special duty is the duty of restitutive justice. It requires that one make amends to the moral subject by some form of compensation or reparation. This is the way one restores the balance of justice that had held between oneself and the subject before a rule of duty was transgressed.

The set of rules that makes up a valid system of ethics defines the true moral relations that hold between agents and subjects. When every agent carries out the duties owed to each subject and each subject accordingly receives its proper treatment, no one is wronged or unjustly dealt with. As soon as a rule is willfully violated, the balance of justice is tilted against the agent and in favor of the subject; that is, the agent now has a special burden to bear and the victim is entitled to a special benefit, since the doing of the wrong act gave an undeserved benefit to the agent and placed an unfair burden on the subject. In order to bring the tilted scale of justice back into balance, the agent must make reparation or pay some form of compensation to the subject.

The three rules of duty so far discussed in this section can be understood as defining a moral relationship of justice between humans and wild living things in the Earth's natural ecosystems. This relationship is maintained as long as humans do not harm wild creatures, destroy their habitats, or degrade their environments; as long as humans do not interfere with an animal's or plant's freedom or with the overall workings of ecological interdependence; and as long as humans do not betray a wild animal's trust to take advantage of it. Since these are all ways in which humans can express in their conduct the attitude of respect for nature, they are at the same time ways in which each living thing is given due recognition as an entity possessing inherent worth. The principles of species-impartiality and of equal consideration are adhered to, so that every moral subject is treated as an end in itself, never as a means only.

Now, if moral agents violate any of the three rules, they do an injustice to something in the natural world. The act destroys the balance of justice between humanity and nature, and a special duty is incurred by the agents involved. This is the duty laid down by the fourth rule of environmental ethics, the Rule of Restitutive Justice.

What specific requirements make up the duty in particular cases? Although the detailed facts of each situation of an agent's wrongdoing would have to be known to make a final judgment about what sorts of restitutive acts are called for, we can nevertheless formulate some middle-range principles of justice that generally apply. These principles are to be understood as specifying requirements of restitution for transgressions of *any* of the three rules. In all cases the restitutive measures will take the form of promoting or protecting in one way or another the good of living things in natural ecosystems.

In working out these middle-range principles it will be convenient to distinguish cases according to what type of moral subject has been wronged. We have three possibilities. An action that broke the Rule of Nonmaleficence, of Noninterference, or of Fidelity might have wronged an individual organism, a species-population as a whole, or an entire community. Violations of the Rules in all cases are ultimately wrongs done to individuals, since we can do harm to a population or community only by harming the individual organisms in it (thereby lowering the median level of well-being for the population or community as a whole). The first possibility, however, focuses on the harmed individuals taken separately.

If the organisms have been harmed but have not been killed, then the principle of restitutive justice requires that the agent make reparation by returning those organisms to a condition in which they can pursue their good as well as they did before the injustice was done to them. If this cannot wholly be accomplished, then the agent must further the good of the organisms in some other way, perhaps by making their physical environment more favorable to their continued well-being. Suppose, on the other hand, that an organism has been killed. Then the principle of restitutive justice states that the agent owes some form of compensation to the species-population and/or the life community of which the organism was a member. This would be a natural extension of respect from the individual to its genetic relatives and ecological associates. The compensation would consist in promoting or protecting the good of the species-population or life community in question.

Consider as a second possibility that a whole species-population has been wrongly treated by a violation of either nonmaleficence or noninterference. A typical situation would be one where most of the animals of a "target" species have been killed by excessive hunting, fishing, or trapping in a limited area. As a way of making some effort to right the wrongs that have been committed, it would seem appropriate that the agents at fault be required to ensure that permanent protection be given to all the remaining numbers of the population. Perhaps the agents could contribute to a special fund for the acquisition of land and themselves take on the responsibility of patrolling the area to prevent further human intrusion.

Finally, let us consider those circumstances where an entire biotic community has been destroyed by humans. We have two sorts of cases here, both requiring some form of restitution. The first sort of case occurs when the destructive actions are not only wrong in themselves because they violate duties of nonmaleficence and noninterference but are wrong, all things considered. They are not justified by a rule of *either* environmental ethics *or* of human ethics. The second sort of case is one in which the actions are required by a valid rule of human ethics though they are contrary to valid rules of environmental ethics. Even when greater moral weight is given to the rule of human ethics, so that the actions are justified, all things considered, they still call for some form of restitution on grounds of justice to all beings having inherent worth. This idea holds also within the domain of human ethics.

A duty of restitutive justice (as a corollary of the Rule of Reciprocity) arises whenever one of the other valid rules of human ethics is broken. Even if the action was required by a more stringent duty, a human person has been unjustly treated and therefore some compensation is due her or him. That the action was morally justified, all things considered, does not license our over-looking the fact that someone has been wronged. Hence the propriety of de-manding restitution. So in our present concerns, even if the destruction of a biotic community is entailed by a duty of human ethics that overrides the rules of environmental ethics, an act of restitutive justice is called for in recog-nition of the inherent worth of what has been destroyed.

There are many instances in which human practices bring about the total obliteration of biotic communities in natural ecosystems. Whether or not these practices are justified by valid rules of human ethics, they all come under the Rule of Restitutive Justice. A northern conifer woodland is cut down to build a vacation resort on the shore of a lake. A housing development is constructed in what had been a pristine wilderness area of cactus desert. A marina and yacht club replace a tidal wetland which had served as a feeding and breed-ing ground for multitudes of mollusks, crustacea, insects, birds, fish, reptiles, and mammals. A meadow full of wildflowers, both common and rare, is bull-dozed over for a shopping mall. Strip mining takes away one side of a moun-tain. A prairie is replaced by a wheat farm. In every one of these situations and in countless others of the same kind, wholesale destruction of entire natural ecosystems takes place. Unrestrained violence is done to whole communities of plants and animals. Communities that may have been in existence for tens of thousands of years are completely wiped out in a few weeks or a few days, in some cases in a few hours. What form of restitution can then be made that will restore the balance of justice between humanity and nature? No reparation for damages can possibly be given to the community itself, which exists no more. As is true of a single organism that has been killed, the impos-sibility of repairing the damage does not get rid of the requirement to make some kind of compensation for having destroyed something of inherent worth.

If restitutive justice is to be done in instances of the foregoing kind, what actions are called for and to whom are they due? Two possibilities suggest themselves here. One is that compensation should be made to another biotic community which occupies *an ecosystem of the same type* as the one destroyed. If it is a northern conifer woodland, then the organizations or individuals who were responsible for its destruction owe it to the life community of another conifer woodland to help it in some way to further or maintain its well-being. Perhaps a partially damaged area of woodland could be restored to ecologi-cal health (removing trash that had been put there, cleaning up a polluted stream flowing through the area, stopping any further contamination by acid rain or other atmospheric pollution, and so on).

The other possible recipient of compensation would be any wild region of nature that is being threatened by human exploitation or consumption. Compensatory action would be taken in behalf of a biotic community some-where on Earth that might be damaged or destroyed unless special efforts are made to protect it. Acquiring the land and giving it legal status as a nature preserve would be suitable measures.

These suggested middle-range principles are all derived from the one broad Rule of Restitutive Justice: that any agent which has caused an evil to some natural entity that is a proper moral subject owes a duty to bring about a countervailing good, either to the moral subject in question or to some other moral subject. The perpetrating of a harm calls for the producing of a benefit. The greater the harm, the larger the benefit needed to fulfill the moral obligation.

It is worth adding here that all of us who live in modern industrialized societies owe a duty of restitutive justice to the natural world and its wild inhabitants. We have all benefited in countless ways from large-scale technology and advanced modes of economic production. As consumers we not only accept the benefits of industrialization willingly, but spend much of our lives trying to increase those benefits for ourselves and those we love. We are part of a civilization that can only exist by controlling nature and using its resources. Even those who go out to a natural area to enjoy "the wilderness experience" are recipients of the benefits of advanced technology. (What marvels of modern chemistry went into the creation of plastics and synthetic fabrics in their backpacks, tents, sleeping bags, and food containers!) None of us can evade the responsibility that comes with our high standard of living; we all take advantage of the amenities of civilized life in pursuing our individual values and interests. Since it is modern commerce, industry, and technology that make these amenities possible, each of us is a consumer and user of what the natural world can yield for us. Our well-being is constantly being furthered at the expense of the good of the Earth's nonhuman inhabitants. Thus we all should share in the cost of preserving and restoring some areas of wild nature for the sake of the plant and animal communities that live there. Only then can we claim to have genuine respect for nature.

III. SEARCHING THE MIDDLE

Overview. In many ways, it might seem that the chasm between the anthropocentrists and the biocentrists cannot be bridged. Each creates a starting point in a different place. This section seeks to highlight one attempt (by James P. Sterba) to reconcile what seems to be an irreconcilable conflict.

In his essay, Sterba creates a series of principles that rank goods of agency. This is similar to Gewirth's categories of goods (basic, nonsubtractive, and additive).[1] For example, Sterba sets out Principles of Human Defence and

---

[1]Gewirth's categories of goods are set out and discussed in *Basic Ethics* (Upper Saddle River, NJ: Prentice Hall, 2000) chaps. 4 and 8.

Preservation that allow killing or harming plants or animals for the sake of a basic good. However, on the other hand, if the good to be had is not essential (but additive and superfluous), then such a right is not justified (the Principle of Human Disproportionality). The intent of this approach is to create the foundation that supports principles on which both sides would agree. If Sterba is correct in this, and if we accept something similar to Leibnitz's principle of identity[2] and if both the anthropocentric and biocentric approaches (under a certain interpretation) imply a common conclusion, then a middle ground has been achieved.

Brian K. Steverson would demur. He finds Sterba to be an anthropocentrist who believes that human needs trump those of the animal/biotic kingdoms. If we are to consider only the environment (in an evenhanded way), then we will come to different conclusions. Specifically, Steverson criticizes Sterba's appeal to reciprocal altruism to justify the human preference permitted by the Principle of Human Preservation. He also claims that although it is reasonable from a nonanthropocentric position to select the Principle of Human Preservation, one could just as well select a principle of nonhuman preservation from that perspective.

In his reply, Sterba contends that Steverson is partially correct. Not all moral obligations can be given a reciprocal altruism foundation. But if only *some* can, then we have established a realistic possibility. This is not insignificant.

Second, Sterba defends a moral epistemological position (that implies a deontic standpoint) of the agent in question. How could an agent, for example, desire that his own basic goods not be fulfilled (even if it means killing another animal)? Certainly, lions and other animals are not saddled with such angst.

The answer to this debate requires the reader to choose a worldview perspective and then decide how everything else ought fit into it.

---

[2]In rough-and-ready fashion, this says that if x has properties F and if y has properties G and if F = G, then $x = y$. Such an exact formulation is really impossible in this case, but the intent is clear.

Reconciling Anthropocentric and Nonanthropocentric Environmental Ethics

James P. Sterba

A central debate, if not the most central debate, in contemporary environmental ethics is between those who defend an anthropocentric ethics and those who defend a nonanthropocentric ethics. This debate pits deep ecologists like George Sessions against reform or shallow ecologists like John Passmore.[1] It divides biocentric egalitarians like Paul Taylor from social ecologists like Murray Bookchin.[2] In this paper I propose to go some way toward resolving this debate by showing that when the most morally defensible versions of each of these perspectives are laid out, they do not lead to different practical requirements. In this way I hope to show how it is possible for defenders of anthropocentric and nonanthropocentric environmental ethics, despite their theoretical disagreement concerning whether humans are superior to members of other species, to agree on a common set of principles for achieving environmental justice.[3]

NONANTHROPOCENTRIC ENVIRONMENTAL ETHICS

Consider first the nonanthropocentric perspective. In support of this perspective it can be argued that we have no nonquestion-begging grounds for regarding the members of any living species as superior to the members of any other. It allows that the members of species differ in a myriad of ways, but argues that these differences do not provide grounds for thinking that the members of any one species are superior to the members of any other. In particular, it denies that the differences between species provides grounds for thinking that humans are superior to the members of other species. Of course, the nonanthropocentric perspective recognises that humans have distinctive traits which the members of other species lack, like rationality and moral agency. It just points out that the members of nonhuman species also have distinctive traits that humans lack, like the homing ability of pigeons, the speed of the cheetah, and the ruminative ability of sheep and cattle.

Nor will it do to claim that the distinctive traits that humans have are more valuable than the distinctive traits that members of other species possess because there is no nonquestion-begging standpoint from which to justify that claim. From a human standpoint, rationality and moral agency are more valuable than any of the distinctive traits found in nonhuman species, since, as humans, we would not be better off if we were to trade in those traits for the distinctive traits found in nonhuman species. Yet the same holds true of nonhuman species. Pigeons, cheetahs, sheep and cattle would not be better off if they were to trade in their distinctive traits for the distinctive traits of other species.[4]

Of course, the members of some species might be better off if they could retain the distinctive traits of their species while acquiring one or another of the distinctive traits possessed by some other species. For example, we humans might be better off if we could retain our distinctive traits while acquiring the ruminative ability of sheep and cattle.[5] But many of the distinctive traits of species cannot be even imaginatively added to the members of other species without substantially altering the original species. For example, in order for the cheetah to acquire the distinctive traits possessed by humans, presumably it would have to be so transformed that its paws became something like hands to accommodate its humanlike mental capabilities, thereby losing its distinctive speed, and ceasing to be a cheetah. So possessing distinctively human traits would not be good for the cheetah. And with the possible exception of our nearest evolutionary relatives, the same holds true for the members of other species: they would not be better off having distinctively human traits. Only in fairy tales and in the world of Disney can the members of nonhuman species enjoy a full array of distinctively human traits. So there would appear to be no nonquestion-begging perspective from which to judge that distinctively human traits are more valuable than the distinctive traits possessed by other species. Judged from a nonquestion-begging perspective, we would seemingly have to regard the members of all species as equals.[6]

Nevertheless, regarding the members of all species as equals still allows for human preference in the same way that regarding all humans as equals still allows for self preference. First of all, human preference can be justified on grounds of defence. Thus, we have

> *A Principle of Human Defence:* Actions that defend oneself and other human beings against harmful aggression are permissible even when they necessitate killing or harming animals or plants.[7]

This Principle of Human Defence allows us to defend ourselves and other human beings from harmful aggression first against our persons and the persons of other humans beings that we are committed to or happen to care about and second against our justifiably held property and the justifiably held property of other humans beings that we are committed to or happen to care about.

This principle is strictly analogous to the principle of self-defence that applies in human ethics[8] and permits actions in defence of oneself or other human beings against harmful human aggression.[9] In the case of human aggression, however, it will sometimes be possible to effectively defend oneself and other human beings by first suffering the aggression and then securing adequate compensation later. Since in the case of nonhuman aggression, this is unlikely to obtain, more harmful preventive actions such as killing a rabid dog or swatting a mosquito will be justified.

Second, human preference can also be justified on grounds of preservation. Accordingly, we have

> *A Principle of Human Preservation:* Actions that are necessary for meeting one's basic needs or the basic needs of other human beings are permissible even when they require aggressing against the basic needs of animals and plants.

Now needs, in general, if not satisfied, lead to lacks or deficiencies with respect to various standards. The basic needs of humans, if not satisfied, lead to lacks or deficiencies with respect to a standard of a decent life. The basic needs of animals and plants, if not satisfied, lead to lacks or deficiencies with respect to a standard of a healthy life. The means necessary for meeting the basic need of humans can vary widely from society to society. By contrast, the means necessary for meeting the basic need of particular species of animals and plants tend to be invariant.[10]

In human ethics, there is no principle that is strictly analogous to this Principle of Human Preservation. There is a principle of self-preservation in human ethics that permits actions that are necessary for meeting one's own basic needs or the basic needs of other people, even if this requires *failing to meet* (through an act of omission) the basic needs of still other people. For example, we can use our resources to feed ourselves and our family, even if this necessitates failing to meet the basic needs of people in Third World countries. But, in general, we don't have a principle that allows us to *aggress against* (through an act of commission) the basic needs of some people in order to meet our own basic needs or the basic needs of other people to whom we are committed or happen to care about. Actually, the closest we come to permitting aggressing against the basic needs of other people in order to meet our own basic needs or the basic needs of people to whom we are committed or happen to care about is our acceptance of the outcome of life and death struggles in lifeboat cases, where no one has an antecedent right to the available resources. For example, if you had to fight off others in order to secure the last place in a lifeboat for yourself or for a member of your family, we might say that you justifiably aggressed against the basic needs of those whom you fought to meet your own basic needs or the basic needs of the member of your family.[11]

Nevertheless, our survival requires a principle of preservation that permits aggressing against the basic needs of at least some other living things whenever this is necessary to meet our own basic needs or the basic needs of other human beings. Here there are two possibilities. The first is a principle of preservation that allows us to aggress against the basic needs of both humans and nonhumans whenever it would serve our own basic needs or the basic needs of other human beings. The second is the principle, given above, that allows us to aggress against the basic needs of only nonhumans whenever it would serve our own basic needs or the basic needs of other human beings. The first principle does not express any general preference for the members of the human species, and thus it permits even cannibalism provided that it serves to meet our own basic needs or the basic needs of other human beings. In contrast, the second principle does express a degree of preference for the members of the human species in cases where their basic needs are at stake. Happily, this degree of preference for our own species is still compatible with the equality of all species because favouring the members of one's own species to this extent is characteristic of the members of all species with which we interact and is thereby legitimated. The reason it is legitimated is that we would be required to sacrifice the basic needs of members of the human species only if the members of other species were making similar sacrifices for the sake of members of the human species.[12] In addition, if we were to prefer consistently the basic needs of the members of other species whenever those needs conflicted with our own (or even if we do so half the time), given the characteristic behaviour of the members of other species, we would soon be facing extinction, and, fortunately, we have no reason to think that we are morally required to bring about our own extinction. For these reasons, the degree of preference for our own species found in the above Principle of Human Preservation is justified, even if we were to adopt a nonanthropocentric perspective.[13]

Nevertheless, preference for humans can go beyond bounds, and the bounds that are compatible with a nonanthropocentric perspective are expressed by the following:

> *A Principle of Disproportionality:* Actions that meet nonbasic or luxury needs of humans are prohibited when they aggress against the basic needs of animals and plants.

This principle is strictly analogous to the principle in human ethics mentioned previously that prohibits meeting some people's nonbasic or luxury needs by aggressing against the basic needs of other people.[14]

Without a doubt, the adoption of such a principle with respect to nonhuman nature would significantly change the way we live our lives. Such a principle is required, however, if there is to be any substance to the claim that the members of all species are equal. We can no more consistently claim that the members of all species are equal and yet aggress against the basic needs of some animals or plants whenever this serves our own nonbasic or luxury needs than we can consistently claim that all humans are equal and aggress against the basic needs of some other human beings whenever this serves our nonbasic or luxury needs.[15] Consequently, if species equality is to mean anything, it must be the case that the basic needs of the members of nonhuman species are protected against aggressive actions which only serve to meet the nonbasic needs of humans, as required by the Principle of Disproportionality.[16]

So while a nonanthropocentric perspective allows for a degree of preference for the members of the human species, it also significantly limits that preference.[17]

It might be objected here that I have not yet taken into account the conflict within a nonanthropocentric ethics between holists and individualists. According to holists, the good of a species or the good of an ecosystem or the good of the whole biotic community can trump the good of individual living things.[18] According to individualists, the good of each individual living thing must be respected.[19]

Now one might think that holists would require that we abandon my Principle of Human Preservation. Yet consider. Assuming that people's basic needs are at stake, how could it be morally objectionable for them to try to meet those needs, even if this were to harm other species, whole ecosystems, or even, to some degree, the whole biotic community?[20] Of course, we can *ask* people in such conflict cases not to meet their basic needs in order to prevent harm to other species, ecosystems or the whole biotic community. But if people's basic needs are at stake, we can not reasonably demand that they make such a sacrifice. We could demand, of course, that people do all that they reasonably can to keep such conflicts from arising in the first place, for, just as in human ethics, many severe conflicts of interest can be avoided simply by doing what is morally required early on.[21] Nevertheless, when people's basic needs are at stake, the individualist perspective seems incontrovertible. We cannot reasonably require people to be saints.

At the same time, when people's basic needs are not at stake, we would be justified in acting on holistic grounds to prevent serious harm to a species, an ecosystem, or the whole biotic community. Obviously, it will be difficult to know when our interventions will have this effect, but when we can be reasonably sure that they will, such interventions (e.g. culling elk herds in wolf-free ranges or preserving the habitat of endangered species) would be morally permissible, and maybe even morally required.[22] This shows that it is possible to agree with individualists when the basic needs of human beings are at stake, and to agree with holists when they are not.

Yet this combination of individualism and holism appears to conflict with the equality of species by imposing greater sacrifices on the members of nonhuman species than it does on the members of the human species. Fortunately, appearances are deceiving here. Although the proposed resolution only justifies imposing holism when people's basic needs are not at stake, it does not justify imposing individualism at all. Rather it would simply permit individualism when people's basic needs *are* at stake. Of course, we could impose holism under all conditions. But given that this would, in effect, involve going to war against people who are simply striving to meet their own basic needs in the only way they can, as permitted by the Principle of Human Preservation, intervention is such cases would not be justified.

Nevertheless, this combination of individualism and holism may leave animal liberationists wondering about the further implications of this resolution for the treatment of animals. Obviously, a good deal of work has already been done on this topic. Initially, philosophers thought that humanism could be extended to include animal liberation and eventually environmental concern.[23] Then Baird Callicott argued that animal liberation and environmental concern were as opposed to each other as they were to humanism.[24] The resulting conflict Callicott called 'a triangular affair'. Agreeing with Callicott, Mark Sagoff contended that any attempt to link together animal liberation and environmental concern would lead to 'a bad marriage and a quick divorce'.[25] Yet more recently, philosophers such as Mary Ann Warren have tended to play down the opposition between animal liberation and environmental concern, and even Callicott now thinks he can bring the two back together again.[26] There are good reasons for thinking that such a reconciliation is possible.

Right off, it would be good for the environment if people generally, especially people in the First World, adopted a more vegetarian diet of the sort that animal liberationists are recommending. This is because a good portion of livestock production today consumes grains that could be more effectively used for direct human consumption. For example, 90% of the protein, 99% of the carbohydrate, and 100% of the fibre value of grain is wasted by cycling it through livestock, and currently 64% of the U.S. grain crop is fed to livestock.[27] So by adopting a more vegetarian diet, people generally, and especially people in the First World, could significantly reduce the amount of farmland that has to be keep in production to feed the human population. This, in turn, could have beneficial effects on the whole biotic community by eliminating the amount of soil erosion and environmental pollutants that result from raising livestock. For example, it has been estimated that 85% of U.S. topsoil lost from cropland, pasture, range land and forest land is directly associated with raising livestock.[28] So in addition to preventing animal suffering, there are these additional reasons to favour a more vegetarian diet.

But even though a more vegetarian diet seems in order, it is not clear that the interests of farm animals would be well served if all of us became complete vegetarians. Sagoff assumes that in a completely vegetarian human world people would continue to feed farm animals as before.[29] But it is not clear that we would have any obligation to do so. Moreover, in a completely vegetarian human world, we would probably need about half of the grain we now feed livestock to meet people's nutritional needs, particularly in Second and Third World countries. There simply would not be enough grain to go around. And then there would be the need to conserve cropland for future generations. So in a completely vegetarian human world, it seems likely that the population of farm animals would be decimated, relegating many of the farm animals that remain to zoos. On this account, it would seem to be more in the interest of farm animals generally that they be maintained under healthy conditions, and then killed relatively painlessly and eaten, rather than that they not be maintained at all.[30] So a completely vegetarian human world would not seem to serve the interest of farm animals.[31]

Nor, it seems, would it be in the interest of wild species who no longer have their natural predators not to be hunted by humans. Of course, where possible, it may be preferable to reintroduce natural predators. But this may not always be possible because of the proximity of farm animals and human populations, and then if action is not taken to control the populations of wild species, disaster could result for the species and their environments. For example, deer, rabbits, squirrels, quails and ducks reproduce rapidly, and in the absence of predators can quickly exceed the carrying capacity of their environments. So it is in the interest of certain wild species and their environments that humans intervene periodically to maintain a balance. Of course, there will be many natural environments where it is in the interest of the environment and the wild animals that inhabit it to be simply left alone. But here too animal liberation and environmental concern would not be in conflict. For these reasons, animal liberationists would have little reason to object to the proposed combination of individualism and holism within a nonanthropocentric environmental ethics.

ANTHROPOCENTRIC ENVIRONMENTAL ETHICS

But suppose we were to reject the central argument of the nonanthropocentric perspective and deny that the members of all species are equal. We might claim, for example, that humans are superior because they, through culture, 'realize a greater range of values' than members of nonhuman species or we might claim that humans are superior in virtue of their 'unprecedented capacity to create ethical systems that impart worth to other life-forms'.[32] Or we might offer some other grounds for human superiority.[33] Suppose, then, we adopt this anthropocentric perspective. What follows?

First of all, we will still need a principle of human defence. However, there is no need to adopt a different principle of human defence from the principle favoured by a nonanthropocentric perspective. Whether we judge humans to be equal or superior to the members of other species, we will still want a principle that allows us to defend ourselves and other human beings from harmful aggression, even when this necessitates killing or harming animals or plants.

Second, we will also need a principle of human preservation. But here too there is no need to adopt a different principle from the principle of human preservation favoured by a nonanthropocentric perspective. Whether we judge humans to be equal or superior to the members of other species, we will still want a principle that permits actions that are necessary for meeting our own basic needs or the basic needs of other human beings, even when this requires aggressing against the basic needs of animals and plants.

The crucial question is whether we will need a different principle of disproportionality. If we judged humans to be superior to the members of other species, will we still have grounds for protecting the basic needs of animals and plants against aggressive action to meet the nonbasic or luxury needs of humans?

Here it is important to distinguish between two degrees of preference that we noted earlier. First, we could prefer the basic needs of animals and plants over the nonbasic or luxury needs of humans when to do otherwise would involve *aggressing against* (by an act of commission) the basic needs of animals and plants. Second, we could prefer the basic needs of animals and plants over the nonbasic or luxury needs of humans when to do otherwise would involve simply *failing to meet* (by an act of omission) the basic needs of animals and plants.

Now in human ethics when the basic needs of some people are in conflict with the nonbasic or luxury needs of others, the distinction between failing to meet and aggressing against basic needs seems to have little moral force. In such conflict cases, both ways of not meeting basic needs are objectionable.[34]

But in environmental ethics, whether we adopt an anthropocentric or a nonanthropocentric perspective, we would seem to have grounds for morally distinguishing between the two cases, favouring the basic needs of animals and plants when to do otherwise would involve *aggressing against* those needs in order to meet our own nonbasic or luxury needs, but not when it would involve simply *failing to meet* those needs in order to meet our own nonbasic or luxury needs. This degree of preference for the members of the human species would be compatible with the equality of species insofar as members of nonhuman species similarly fail to meet the basic needs of members of the human species where there is a conflict of interest.[35]

Even so, this theoretical distinction would have little practical force since most of the ways that we have of preferring our own nonbasic needs over the basic needs of animals and plants actually involve aggressing against their basic needs to meet our own nonbasic or luxury needs rather than simply failing to meet their basic needs.[36]

Yet even if most of the ways that we have of preferring our own nonbasic or luxury needs does involve aggressing against the basic needs of animals and plants, wouldn't human superiority provide grounds for making such sacrifices? Or put another way, shouldn't human superiority have more theoretical and practical significance than I am allowing? Not, I claim, if we are looking for the most morally defensible position to take.

For consider: The claim that humans are superior to the members of other species, if it can be justified at all, is something like the claim that a person came in first in a race where others came in second, third, fourth, and so on. It would not imply that the members of other species are without intrinsic value. In fact, it would imply just the opposite—that the members of other species are also intrinsically valuable, although not as intrinsically valuable as humans, just as the claim that a person came in first in a race implies that the persons who came in second, third, fourth, and so on are also meritorious, although not as meritorious as the person who came in first.

This line of argument draws further support once we consider the fact that many animals and plants are superior to humans in one respect or another, e.g., the sense of smell of the wolf or the acuity of sight of the eagle or the photosynthetic power of plants. So any claim of human superiority must allow for the recognition of excellences in nonhuman species, even for some excellences that are superior to their corresponding human excellences. In fact, it demands that recognition.

Moreover, if the claim of human superiority is to have any moral force, it must rest on nonquestion-begging grounds. Accordingly, we must be able to give a nonquestion-begging response to the nonanthropocentric argument for the equality of species. Yet for any such argument to be successful, it would have to recognise the intrinsic value of the members of nonhuman species. Even if it could be established that human beings have greater intrinsic value, we would still have to recognise that nonhuman nature has intrinsic value as well. So the relevant question is: How are we going to recognise the presumably lesser intrinsic value of nonhuman nature?

Now if human needs, even nonbasic or luxury ones, are always preferred to even the basic needs of the members of nonhuman species, we would not be giving any recognition to the intrinsic value of nonhuman nature. But what if we allowed the nonbasic or luxury needs of humans to trump the basic needs of nonhuman nature half the time, and half the time we allowed the basic needs of nonhuman nature to trump the nonbasic or luxury needs of humans. Would that be enough? Certainly, it would be a significant advance over what we are presently doing. For what we are presently doing is meeting the basic needs of nonhuman nature, at best, only when it serves our own needs or the needs of those we are committed to or happen to care about, and that does not recognise the intrinsic value of nonhuman nature at all. A fifty-fifty arrangement would be an advance indeed. But it would not be enough.

The reason why it would not be enough is that the claim that humans are superior to nonhuman nature no more supports the practice of aggressing against the basic needs of nonhuman nature to satisfy our own nonbasic or luxury needs than the claim that a person came in first in a race would support the practice of aggressing against the basic needs of those who came in second, third, fourth, and so on to satisfy the nonbasic or luxury needs of the person who came in first. A higher degree of merit does not translate into a right of domination, and to claim a right to aggress against the basic needs of nonhuman nature in order to meet our own nonbasic or luxury needs is clearly to claim a right of domination. All that our superiority as humans would justify is not meeting the basic needs of nonhuman nature when this conflicts with our nonbasic or luxury needs. What it does not justify is aggressing against the basic needs of nonhuman nature when this conflicts with our nonbasic or luxury needs.

Now it might be objected that my argument so far presupposes an objective theory of value which regards things as valuable because of the qualities they actually have rather than a subjective theory of value which regards things as valuable simply because humans happen to value them. However, I contend that when both these theories are defensibly formulated, they will lead to the same practical requirements.

For consider. Suppose we begin with a subjective theory of value that regards things as valuable simply because humans value them. Of course, some things would be valued by humans instrumentally, others intrinsically, but, according to this theory, all things would have the value they have, if they have any value at all, simply because they are valued by humans either instrumentally or intrinsically.

One problem facing such a theory is why should we think that humans alone determine the value that things have? For example, why not say that things are valuable because the members of other species value them? Why not say that grass is valuable because zebras value it, and that zebras are valuable because lions value them, and so on? Or why not say, assuming God exists, that things are valuable because God values them?

Nor would it do simply to claim that we authoritatively determine what is valuable for ourselves, that nonhuman species authoritatively determine what is valuable for themselves, and that God authoritatively determines what is valuable for the Godhead. For what others value should at least be relevant data when authoritatively determining what is valuable for ourselves.

Another problem for a subjective theory of value is that we probably would not want to say that just anything we happen to value determines what is valuable for ourselves. For surely we would want to say that at least some of the things that people value, especially people who are evil or deficient in certain ways, are not really valuable, even for them. Merely thinking that something is valuable doesn't make it so.

Suppose then we modified this subjective theory of value to deal with these problems. Let the theory claim that what is truly valuable for people is what they would value if they had all the relevant information (including, where it is relevant, the knowledge of what others would value) and reasoned correctly.[37] Of course, there will be many occasions where we are unsure that ideal conditions have been realised, unsure, that is, that we have all the relevant information and have reasoned correctly. And even when we are sure that ideal conditions have been realised, we may not always be willing to act upon what we come to value due to weakness of will.

Nevertheless, when a subjective theory of value is formulated in this way, it will have the same practical requirements as an objective theory of value that is also defensibly formulated. For an objective theory of value holds that what is valuable is determined by the qualities things actually have. But in order for the qualities things actually have to determine our values, they must be accessible to us, at least under ideal conditions, that is, they must be the sort of qualities that we would value if we had all the relevant information and reasoned correctly.[38] But this is just what is valuable according to our modified subjective theory of value. So once a subjective theory of value and an objective theory of value are defensibly formulated in the manner I propose, they will lead us to value the same things.[39]

Now it is important to note here that with respect to some of the things we value intrinsically, such as animals and plants, our valuing them depends simply on our ability to discover the value that they actually have based on their qualities, whereas for other things that we value intrinsically, such as our aesthetic experiences and the objects that provided us with those experiences, the value that these things have depends significantly on the way we are constituted. So that if we were constituted differently, what we value aesthetically would be different as well. Of course, the same holds true for some of the things that we morally value. For example, we morally value not killing human beings because of the way we are constituted. Constituted as we are, killing is usually bad for any human that we would kill. But suppose that we were constituted differently such that killing human beings was immensely pleasurable for those humans that we killed, following which they immediately sprang back to life asking us to kill them again.[40] If human beings were constituted in this way, we would no longer morally value not killing. In fact, constituted in this new way, I think we would come to morally value *killing* and the relevant rule for us might be 'Kill human beings as often as you can.' But while such aesthetic and moral values are clearly dependent on the way we are constituted, they still are not anthropocentric in the sense that they imply human superiority. Such values can be recognised from both an anthropocentric and a nonanthropocentric perspective.

It might be objected, however, that while the intrinsic values of an environmental ethics need not be anthropocentric in the sense that they imply human superiority, these values must be anthropocentric in the sense that humans would reasonably come to hold them. This seems correct. However, appealing to this sense of anthropocentric, Eugene Hargrove has argued that not all living things would turn out to be intrinsically valuable as a nonanthropocentric environmental ethics maintains.[41] Hargrove cites as hypothetical examples of living things that would not turn out to be intrinsically valuable the creatures in the films *Alien* and *Aliens*. What is distinctive about these creatures in *Alien* and *Aliens* is that they require the deaths of many other living creatures, whomever they happen upon, to reproduce and survive as a species. Newly hatched, these creatures emerge from their eggs and immediately enter host organisms, which they keep alive and feed upon while they develop. When the creatures are fully developed, they explode out of the chest of their host organisms, killing their hosts with some fanfare. Hargrove suggests that if such creatures existed, we would not intrinsically value them because it would not be reasonable for us to do so.[42]

Following Paul Taylor, Hargrove assumes that to intrinsically value a creature is to recognise a negative duty not to destroy or harm that creature and a positive duty to protect it from being destroyed or harmed by others. Since Hargrove thinks that we would be loath to recognise any such duties with respect to such alien creatures, we would not consider them to be intrinsically valuable.

Surely it seems clear that we would seek to kill such alien creatures by whatever means are available to us, but why should that preclude our recognising them as having intrinsic value any more than our seeking to kill any person who is engaged in lethal aggression against us would preclude our recognising that person as having intrinsic value? To recognise something as having intrinsic value does not preclude destroying it to preserve other things that also have intrinsic value when there is good reason to do so. Furthermore, recognising a prima facie negative duty not to destroy or harm something and a prima facie positive duty to protect it from being destroyed or harmed by others is perfectly consistent with recognising an all-things-considered duty to destroy that thing when it is engaged in lethal aggression against us. Actually, all we are doing here is simply applying our Principle of Human Defence, and, as I have argued earlier, there is no reason to think that the application of this principle would preclude our recognising the intrinsic value of every living being.

In sum, I have argued that whether we endorse an anthropocentric or a nonanthropocentric environmental ethics, we should favour a Principle of Human Defence, a Principle of Human Preservation, and a Principle of Disproportionality as I have interpreted them. In the past, failure to recognise the importance of a Principle of Human Defence and a Principle of Human Preservation has led philosophers to overestimate the amount of sacrifice required of humans.[43] By contrast, failure to recognise the importance of a Principle of Disproportionality has led philosophers to underestimate the amount of sacrifice required of humans.[44] I claim that taken together these three principles strike the right balance between concerns of human welfare and the welfare of nonhuman nature.

Of course, the practical implications of these three principles would include proposals for conserving existing resources, particularly nonrenewable resources, proposals for converting to renewable resources, proposals for redistributing resources to meet basic needs of both humans and nonhumans, and proposals for population control, all implemented principally by educational changes and by changes in the tax and incentive structures of our society. In the longer work from which this paper is drawn, I go on to discuss these practical proposals in more detail. In this paper, what I have sought to do is provide the nonanthropocentric and anthropocentric grounding for such proposals in a common set of conflict resolution principles that are required for achieving environmental justice.

NOTES

Earlier versions of this paper were presented at the University of Notre Dame, Carleton University, Gonzaga University, Shawnee State University, the University of Washington, the Second World Congress on Violence and Human Co-existence held in Montreal and the Tenth International Social Philosophy Conference held in Helsinki. I would like to thank William Aiken, Robin Attfield, Kendall D'Andrade, Baird Callicott, Richard DeGeorge, Michael DePaul, Wendy Donner, Jay Drydyk, David Duquette, Haim Gordon, Eugene Hargrove, Harlan Miller, Maria Maimonova, Ronald Moore, Brian Norton, Phillip Quinn, Tom Regan, Kenneth Sayre, David Solomon, Brian Steverson, Paul Taylor, Aviezer Tucker, Alvin Plantinga, John Wagner and Laura Westra for their helpful comments.

1. See Passmore 1974 and Devall and Sessions 1985.

2. See Taylor 1986 and Bookchin 1991. It is also possible to view Passmore as pitted against Taylor and Bookchin as pitted against Sessions, but however one casts the debate, those who defend an anthropocentric ethics are still opposed to those who defend a nonanthropocentric ethics.

3. My reconciliation project contrasts with Bryan Norton's (Norton 1991). While Norton's reconciliation project seeks to achieve a reconciliation at the level of practical policies, mine seeks a reconciliation at the level of general principles as well. While Norton's reconciliation project tends to exclude deep ecologists, like George Sessions, and biocentric egalitarians, like Paul Taylor, from the class of environmentalists that he is seeking to reconcile, my reconciliation project explicitly includes them.

4. See Taylor 1986, pp. 129–135 and Routley and Routley 1979.

5. Assuming God exists, humans might also be better off if they could retain their distinctive traits while acquiring one or another of God's qualities, but consideration of this possibility would take us too far afield. Nonhuman animals might also be better off it they could retain their distinctive traits and acquire one or another of the distinctive traits possessed by other nonhuman animals.

6. I am assuming here that either we treat humans as superior overall to other living things or we treat them as equal overall to other living things. Accordingly, if there is no self-evident or nonquestion-begging grounds for claiming that humans are superior overall to other living things, then, I claim that we should treat humans as equal overall to all other living things.

7. For the purposes of this paper, I will follow the convention of excluding humans from the class denoted by 'animals'.

8. By human ethics I simply mean those forms of ethics that assume without argument that only human beings count morally.

9. Of course, one might contend that no principle of human defence applied in human ethics because either 'nonviolent pacifism' or 'nonlethal pacifism' is the most morally defensible view. However, I have argued elsewhere (Sterba 1992) that this is not the case, and that still other forms of pacifism more compatible with just war theory are also more morally defensible than either of these forms of pacifism.

10. For further discussion of basic needs, see Sterba 1988 pp. 45–50.

11. It is important to recognise here that we also have a strong obligation to prevent lifeboat cases from arising in the first place.

12. Notice that this is not an argument that since the members of other species aren't sacrificing for us, we don't have to sacrifice for them, but rather an argument that since the members of other species are not sacrificing for us, we don't have to sacrifice our basic needs for them. An analogous principle holds in human ethics.

13. The Principle of Human Preservation also imposes a limit on when we can defend nonhuman living beings from human aggression.

14. This principle is clearly acceptable to welfare liberals, socialists, and even libertarians. For arguments to that effect, see Sterba 1988. See also the special issue of the *Journal of Social Philosophy* (Vol. XXII No. 3) devoted to my book, including my 'Nine Commentators: A Brief Response'.

15. Of course, libertarians have claimed that we can recognise that people have equal basic rights while failing to meet, but not aggressing against, the basic needs of other human beings. However, I have argued at length that this claim is mistaken. See the references in the previous note.

16. It should be pointed out that although the Principle of Disproportionality prohibits aggressing against the basic needs of animals and plants to serve the nonbasic needs of humans, the Principle of Human Defence permits defending oneself and other human beings against harmful aggression of animals and plants even when this only serves the nonbasic needs of humans.

17. It might be objected here that this argument is still speciesist in that it permits humans to aggress against nonhuman nature whenever it is necessary for meeting our own basic needs or the basic needs of humans we happen to care about. But this objection surely loses some of its force once it is recognised that it is also permissible for us to aggress against the nonbasic needs of humans whenever it is necessary for meeting our own basic needs or the basic needs of humans we happen to care about.

18. Aldo Leopold's view is usually interpreted as holistic in this sense. Leopold wrote 'A thing is right when it tends to preserve the integrity, stability and beauty of the biotic community. It is wrong when it tends otherwise.' See Leopold 1949.

19. For a defender of this view, see Taylor 1986.

20. I am assuming that in these cases of conflict the good of *other* human beings is not at issue. Otherwise, as we have already noted, other considerations will apply.

21. For example, it is now quite clear that our war with Iraq could have been avoided if early on we had refused to support the military buildup of Saddam Hussein.

22. Where it most likely would be morally required is where our negligent actions have caused the environmental problem in the first place.

23. Peter Singer's *Animal Liberation* (1975) inspired this view.

24. Callicott 1980.

25. Sagoff 1984.

26. Warren 1983; Callicott 1989, Chapter 3.

27. *Realities for the 90's*, p.4

28. Ibid., p. 5

29. Sagoff 1984, pp. 301–5.

30. I think there is an analogous story to tell here about 'domesticated' plants.

31. Of course, if we permitted farmland and grazing land to return to its natural state, certain wild animals will surely benefit as a result, but why should we be required to favour the interests of these wild animals over the interests of farm animals, especially when favouring the latter serves our own interests as well? For further discussion, see Gruzalski 1983.

32. Rolston 1988, pp. 66–8; Bookchin 1991, p. xxxvi.

33. See the discussion of possible grounds of human superiority in Taylor, pp. 135–152 and in Norton 1987, 135–150.

34. This is clearly true for welfare liberals and socialists, and it can even be shown to be true for libertarians because most failings to meet the basic needs of others really turn out to be acts of aggressing against the basic needs of others. See note 14.

35. This is not an argument that any degree of preference for humans is acceptable, if the members of other species express the same degree of concern for their own members, but rather that this degree of preference for humans (failing to meet the basic needs of the members of other species in order to meet human needs) is acceptable if the members of other species express the same degree of concern for their own members.

36. The same holds true in human ethics where most of the ways that we have of preferring our own nonbasic needs over other humans actually involve aggressing against those needs to meet our own nonbasic or luxury needs rather than simply failing to meet them. See note 34

37. I am assuming here that part of what is required for reasoning correctly is that the reasoning be done in a nonquestion-begging way.

38. I'm assuming that objective value theorists would want to incorporate a condition of accessibility into their accounts. It is difficult for me to conceive what would be the point of a value theory for humans without such a condition.

39. Subjective and objective theories of value have tended to highlight different features of a defensible theory of value. A subjective theory of value stresses that what is valuable for us must be accessible to us. An objective theory stresses that what is valuable for us depends not just on us but on the qualities of things in the world.

40. One might object here that if humans immediately came back to life, they would not have been 'killed'. Possibly, but what if they came back to life five minutes later or ten minutes later or fifteen minutes later . . . In my judgment, a more telling objection is that creatures who came back to life in this way would no longer be humans. But irrespective of whether they are humans, given their constitution, they would favour the new moral rule about killing. And this is my point—that moral rules depend on one's constitution. Of course, nothing hangs on accepting this example. For my purposes, it suffices to recognise that our aesthetic judgments depend on the the way we are constituted.

41. Hargrove 1992, p. 147ff.

42. Ibid., p. 151

43. For example, Baird Callicott (1980) had defended Edward Abbey's assertion that he would sooner shoot a man than a snake.

44. For example, Eugene Hargrove argues that from a traditional wildlife perspective, the lives of individual specimens of quite plentiful nonhuman species count for almost nothing at all. See Chapter 4 of Hargrove 1989.

References

Bookchin, Murray 1991. *The Ecology of Freedom*. Montreal, Black Rose Books.

Callicott, J. Baird 1980. 'Animal Liberation: A Triangular Affair', *Environmental Ethics* **2:**311–328.

Callicott, J. Baird 1989. *In Defense of the Land Ethic*. Albany, SUNY Press.

Devall, Bill and Sessions, George (eds) 1985. *Deep Ecology: Living as if Nature Mattered*. Salt Lake City, Gibbs M. Smith.

Gruzalski, Bart 1983. 'The Case against Raising and Killing Animals for Food'. In H. Miller and W. Williams, *Ethics and Animals*, pp. 251–63. Clifton, Humana Press.

Hargrove, Eugene 1989. *Foundations of Environmental Ethics*. Englewood Cliffs, N.J., Prentice Hall.

Hargrove, Eugene 1992. 'Weak Anthropocentric Intrinsic Value'. In *After Earth Day*, edited by Max Oelschlaeger. Denton, Texas, University of North Texas Press.

Leopold, Aldo 1949. *A Sand County Almanac*, New York: Oxford University Press.

Norton, Bryan 1987. *Why Preserve Natural Variety?* Princeton, Princeton University Press.

Norton, Bryan 1991. *Toward Unity Among Environmentalists*. Oxford, Oxford University Press.

Passmore, John 1974. *Man's Responsibility for Nature*. London, Duckworth. *Realities for the 90's*. Santa Cruz, 1991.

Rolston, Holmes 1988. *Environmental Ethics*. Philadelphia, Temple University Press.

Routley, R. and Routley, V. 1979. 'Against the Inevitability of Human Chauvinism'. In *Ethics and Problems of the 21st Century* edited by K.E. Goodpaster and K.M. Sayre. Notre Dame, Notre Dame University Press.

Sagoff, Mark 1984. 'Animal Liberation and Environmental Ethics: Bad Marriage, Quick Divorce', *Osgood Hall Law Journal* 297–307.

Singer, Peter 1975. *Animal Liberation*. New York: New York Review.

Sterba, James 1988. *How To Make People Just*. Totowa, N.J., Rowman and Littlefield.

Sterba, James 1992. 'Reconciling Pacifists and Just War Theorists', *Social Theory and Practice* **18:**21–38.

Taylor, Paul 1987. *Respect for Nature*. Princeton, Princeton University Press.

Warren, Mary Ann 1983. 'The Rights of the Nonhuman World'. In *Environmental Philosophy*, edited by Robert Elliot and Arran Gare, pp. 109–134. London, Open University Press.

On the Reconciliation of Anthropocentric and Nonanthropocentric Environmental Ethics

Brian K. Steverson

James Sterba's recent essay in this journal, 'Reconciling Anthropocentric and Nonanthropocentric Environmental Ethics', represents the latest attempt to circumvent the decades old debate in environmental philosophy between the anthropocentrists and nonanthropocentrists, and to show that the axiological disagreement which has characterised the debate becomes moot as one proceeds to construct general normative principles and then to translate those principles into specific policy.[1] Sterba works to show that as regards principles of environmental justice, in their most morally defensible forms, both the anthropocentrist and nonanthropocentrist positions would ultimately concur on which such principles are acceptable. I have elsewhere argued that at least one such attempt to establish a convergence of anthropocentric and nonanthropocentric perspectives at the level of policy formation fails, and will here argue that Sterba's attempt at reconciling the two camps fails as well.[2] Though my critique of Sterba's argument is, of course, insufficient to show that no such reconciliation is possible, I think that it will provide grounds for recognising that such a unification project faces great difficulties, and that despite the growing weariness with the anthropocentric-nonanthropocentric debate, the foundational axiological division represented by the debate will remain a crucial point of contention for some time to come.

Sterba's approach is to interpret the nonanthropocentric-anthropocentric debate as a debate about the equality of species. Traditionally understood, the anthropocentrist is taken to believe that there exists a morally relevant inequality between humans and other species, while the nonanthropocentrist denies the existence of such an inequality. Sterba's project is to show that, despite their differences regarding species equality, both positions would allow for the exact same range of preferential satisfaction of human needs over those of members of nonhuman species. His general tack is this. He argues that even though the nonanthropocentrist is committed to species egalitarianism, that commitment does not preclude the possibility that preferential treatment of humans is morally justified in certain cases.[3]

From the other direction, he argues that despite the fact that the anthropocentrist holds to the belief in interspecific inegalitarianism, this general inequality does not license all forms of preferential treatment, since to do so would in effect translate the initial inequality into a right to domination, a move which Sterba argues is indefensible. The upshot is that when the most reasonable versions of both axiological positions are considered, agreement is reached as to which general principles of preferential treatment are acceptable. My argument is that Sterba overestimates the necessity of agreement between the two camps at this juncture. I will argue that the nonanthropocentrist has available good reasons for thinking that the kind of human preference embodied in the three principles Sterba defends is too broad, and that the anthropocentrist has good reasons for thinking that the restrictions on human preference found in those principles are too strict.

Sterba begins his reconciliation project with the nonanthropocentrist position. For Sterba, the important question to be addressed is whether such a commitment to species egalitarianism eliminates the possibility of justifiably preferring humans over nonhumans in situations of conflict. A first, and easy answer, is that in cases of self-defence, humans are justified in preferring their own lives or well-being over that of nonhumans when the latter pose a threat to humans. The principle runs this way:

> *A Principle of Human Defence:* Actions that defend oneself and other human beings against harmful aggression are permissible even when they necessitate killing or harming animals and plants.

As Sterba notes, this principle is perfectly analogous to the accepted principle of self-defence found in human ethics. Though nonanthropocentrists might demand that the domain of the set of actions counting as 'harmful aggression' be rather limited, they would obviously be committed to this principle.

A second type of justified preference occurs in cases where human preservation is at stake, though not due to the aggression of nonhumans. Sterba has in mind cases where the satisfaction of basic human needs requires the dissatisfaction of nonhuman basic needs, and sets out the following principle to cover such situations:

> *A Principle of Human Preservation:* Actions that are necessary for meeting one's basic needs or the basic needs of other human beings are permissible even when they require aggressing against the basic needs of animals and plants.

Unlike the Principle of Human Defence, no such strictly analogous principle exists in human ethics. Sterba states that there is a principle which allows for the committing of acts which are necessary to satisfy basic needs even when doing so results in a failure to meet the basic needs of others, but that, in general, no such principle pertaining to aggressing against the basic needs of others exists. Nevertheless, Sterba takes the Principle of Human Preservation to be a requirement if the human species is to survive.

'Happily', as Sterba describes it, the kind of human preference found in the Principle of Human Preservation is consistent with the nonanthropocentric commitment to species equality. Sterba's argument for why it is consistent rests on an appeal to the notion of 'reciprocity'. According to him, we would only be obligated to sacrifice our own basic needs for the sake of nonhumans' basic needs if they were doing the same, or were willing to do the same. In the absence of such reciprocal treatment on their part, we are not so obligated.

What is one to make of such an argument? Surely, there are types of obligations which exist only in the context of reciprocity (e.g. contractual obligations). However, ethical contractarians to the contrary, many would argue that not all obligations are grounded on the presence of reciprocity on the part of the party to which the obligations are owed (e.g. parents' obligations to their children). Why should we believe that a potential obligation to avoid aggressing against the basic needs of nonhumans should be such a reciprocity-based obligation? It seems as if Sterba has something like a naturalistic argument working here. The absence of interspecific sacrificial behaviour in nature eliminates the moral necessity of humans acting in that fashion, since such sacrificial behaviour has an 'unnatural' character.[4] It is unnatural because, if pursued consistently, it would result in extinction. Sterba writes,

> . . . if we were to prefer consistently the basic needs of members of other species whenever those needs conflicted with our own (or even if we do so half the time), given the characteristic behaviour of the members of other species, we would soon be facing extinction, and, fortunately, we have no reason to think that we are morally required to bring about our own extinction.

Assuming that Sterba is right to hold that there exists no reasonable justification for the view that humans have a moral obligation to bring about the extinction of the species (a safe assumption, no doubt), then it is permissible for humans to act so as to prevent their extinction, and the Principle of Human Preservation seems quite justified. Note, however, that all this line of reasoning, in itself, establishes is the *permissibility* of humans acting so as to prevent their own extinction. It does not establish the presence of an *obligation* on the part of humans to act so as to prevent their own extinction. Though an argument in support of such a view may be available (the beginnings of such an argument will be discussed later in connection with anthropocentrism and Sterba's Principle of Disproportionality), Sterba does not make such a claim. In the absence of such an obligation, acting so as to lead to our extinction remains, *prima facie*, permissible. An immediate implication of this possibility is that nonanthropocentrists, committed to species equality as they are, may consistently prefer the satisfaction of nonhuman basic needs over those of humans even if, following through with Sterba's logic, doing so entails the extinction of the human species.

Theoretically, Sterba's argument establishes very little regarding the nonanthropocentrists commitment to the Principle of Human Preservation since its complement, the Principle of Nonhuman Preservation, is an equally valid option. Any preference in the context of competing basic needs is permissible given the nonanthropocentrists' initial commitment to species equality. If some species must suffer, the equality of species plays no role in selecting which species will suffer; a coin toss would suffice. Consequently, though it is true that the nonanthropocentrist could justifiably accept the permissibility of sacrificing nonhuman basic needs for those of humans, they are not required to. Since sacrificing human basic needs for those of nonhuman species is equally permissible, the nonanthropocentrist could opt for that approach as a rule, or they could simply make alternating choices between the competing basic needs of humans and nonhumans. What is absent are reasons for believing that the nonanthropocentrist *ought* to prefer the Principle of Human Preservation on a consistent basis. To settle the dilemma consistently in favour of humans requires some independent argument to show that our obligation to prevent our own extinction is stronger than our obligation to prevent the extinction of other species. It is not apparent how a nonanthropocentrist, as defined by Sterba, could come up with such an argument, since no matter which argument is produced, it will involve some claim about the superior value of humans. So, though nonanthropocentrists *can* accept the Principle of Human Preservation, it is not clear that they *must*, or even should prefer it. The impact on Sterba's reconciliation project is this. The most that can be said for the nonanthropocentrist is that the Principle of Human Preservation is an acceptable principle, though not in any way more acceptable than the Principle of Nonhuman Preservation. As will be shown later in this essay, the anthropocentrist position, as Sterba presents it, embodies a strong presumption in favour of the Principle of Human Preservation, though it may fall short of making commitment to that principle absolutely obligatory. If such a difference in strength of commitment exists between the two perspectives, one can seriously question the extent to which reconciliation has been achieved.

The third principle of justice to which Sterba argues both nonanthropocentrists and anthropocentrists would be committed is this:

> *A Principle of Disproportionality:* Actions that meet nonbasic or luxury needs of humans are prohibited when they aggress against the basic needs of animals and plants.

Note that this principle makes a stronger claim than the first two in that it declares a particular kind of action to be *prohibited*, and not simply *permissible*. The importance of this will surface when the principle is considered from the anthropocentric perspective. That the nonanthropocentrist would be committed to such a principle is uncontroversial since, as Sterba notes, if the claim of species equality is to have any substance, one cannot accept the view that the satisfaction of any human need takes precedent over the satisfaction of nonhuman basic needs. Minimally, species equality requires a distinction between basic and nonbasic needs, and a weighting of the former over the latter; hence, the Principle of Disproportionality.

Both the Principle of Human Preservation and the Principle of Disproportionality trade upon the distinction between basic and nonbasic needs, at least as regards human needs. Making out such a distinction with precision is no easy task, and to demand that Sterba's argument include a precise explication of the distinction is misplaced, inasmuch as the generality of the principles of environmental justice he is concerned with require only a rough conceptual demarcation between basic and nonbasic needs. In fact, Sterba provides a working distinction when he addresses the moral importance of need satisfaction.

> Now needs, in general, if not satisfied, lead to lacks or deficiencies with respect to various standards. The basic needs of humans, if not satisfied, lead to lacks or deficiencies with respect to a standard of decent life. The basic needs of animals and plants, if not satisfied, lead to lacks or deficiencies with respect to a standard of healthy life. The means necessary for meeting the basic need of humans can vary widely from society to society. By contrast, the means necessary for meeting the basic need of particular species of animals and plants tend to be invariant.[5]

Since, for Sterba, the basic needs of humans are those connected with the maintenance of a 'decent life', it follows that nonbasic needs will be those not so connected. Likewise, nonhuman basic needs are those necessary for the maintenance of a 'healthy life', while nonhuman nonbasic needs (if there are any) will be those lacking such necessity.

Though this is not the place to critically assess Sterba's portrayal of the basic-nonbasic distinction, one comment pertinent to my critique is in order. In line with my earlier comment that in the context of agreeing to the Principle of Human Defence the nonanthropocentrist would undoubtedly opt for a narrow definition of 'harmful aggression', it is clear that as regards both the Principle of Human Preservation and the Principle of Disproportionality, the non-anthropocentrist would opt for an equally restrictive designation of which human needs count as basic, so as to guard against the potential for an overexpansion of the range of human aggression against nonhumans justified by the Principle of Human Preservation, as well as to guard against an undue shrinkage of the range of human aggression against nonhumans prohibited by the Principle of Disproportionality. Consequently, it is reasonable to presume that the nonanthropocentrist, at least, would require that both the Principle of Human Preservation and the Principle of Disproportionality be stated with greater precision than Sterba's current versions contain. It is interesting to note that Sterba employs different standards for qualifying basic needs. For humans, the standard is that of a *decent* life, whereas for nonhumans the standard is *healthy* life. Nonanthropocentrists might have reason to question such a 'double standard' in the light of their commitment to species equality, and wonder why the standard of *healthy* life is not sufficient for both human and nonhuman basic needs.

As regards nonanthropocentrism and Sterba's principles of justice, then, two general comments can be made. Though the nonanthropocentrist could accept the Principle of Human Preservation, they could just as easily accept the Principle of Nonhuman Preservation. The question is, which would the nonanthropocentrist most likely be committed to in practice? It is quite reasonable to presume that more often than not, the nonanthropocentrist would side with nonhuman species for various kinds of independent reasons, and that such a consistent preference for the basic needs of nonhumans over those of humans does not violate their commitment to species equality. As such, it is more reasonable to presume that the nonanthropocentrist would reject the Principle of Human Preservation, rather than accept it. As for the Principle of Disproportionality, Sterba is correct to believe that the nonanthropocentrist would be committed to it, but he fails to take into account that the version of that principle which the nonanthropocentrist would be committed to must be one which narrowly defines which human needs fall into the class of basic needs. Anticipating my treatment of the anthropocentric position, if the principle were expanded to include designations of basic and nonbasic needs, one would quickly discover that the nonanthropocentric version and the anthropocentric version have striking dissimilarities.

In addressing the anthropocentric side of his reconciliation project, Sterba's first step is to define what he takes to be its most defensible version. As a position on the equality of species, anthropocentrism is, of course, inegalitarian: humans possesses a superior value to that of nonhuman species. Nonetheless, Sterba's position is that this superiority in value cannot imply a total absence of intrinsic value on the part of members of nonhuman species. He gives two arguments for his view. The first is an analogy.

> The claim that humans are superior to the members of other species, if it can be justified at all, is something like the claim that a person came in first in a race where others came in second, third, fourth, and so on. It would not imply that the members of other species are without intrinsic value. In fact it would imply just the opposite—that the members of other species are also intrinsically valuable, although not as intrinsically valuable as humans, just as the claim that a person came in first in a race implies that the persons who came in second, third, fourth, and so on are also meritorious, although not as meritorious as the person who came in first.[6]

His second argument is based on the requirement that in order to have 'moral force' the anthropocentric claim of human superiority must be based on nonquestion-begging grounds. That is, whatever traits are selected as the basis for granting humans value superiority, one must be able to explain why those traits are sufficient to ground such superiority. For Sterba, no such nonquestion-begging explanation is forthcoming since nonhuman species possess their own distinctive traits which are as equally valuable to them as our distinctive traits are to us. His conclusion is that, '[j]udged from a nonquestion-begging perspective, we would seemingly have to regard the members of all species as equal'.[7]

Both arguments are, of course, open to possible criticism. One could question the adequacy of the race analogy as a model for the 'most morally defensible' version of anthropocentrism, and one could also propose reasons for thinking that simply possessing distinctive traits which are 'good for one-self' is an insufficient ground for attributions of intrinsic value. In this context, I will not pursue either line of discussion, but, instead, grant Sterba the claim that the most morally defensible version of anthropocentrism is one which, though it affords value superiority to humans, must grant some intrinsic value to members of nonhuman species. One quick comment, however, about this version of anthropocentrism. Recently, in the context of showing that environmental ethics rests on a mistaken requirement for an axiological theory capable of according differential intrinsic value to nature, Tom Regan has (per-suasively, I think) argued that, depending on which kind of object one has in mind when ascribing intrinsic value, the concept of intrinsic value is either a categorical one, or one for which there exists no nonarbitrary standard of com-parison by which to hierarchically rank intrinsically valuable things.[8] If Regan is correct, then, since it is characterised by a commitment to a theory of dif-ferential intrinsic value, Sterba's 'most morally defensible version of anthro-pocentrism' may itself embody an axiological mistake. But, I will leave that for another discussion.

The question, then, is whether the anthropocentrist, as described by Sterba, would be committed to the same principles of environmental justice as the nonanthropocentrist. As Sterba notes, the anthropocentrist would, of course, be committed to the Principle of Human Defence, and, not surpris-ingly given the superior value which their position attaches to being human, the anthropocentrist would find the Principle of Human Preservation quite acceptable. However, the latter claim misrepresents the nature of the anthro-pocentrist's commitment to the Principle of Human Preservation. Unlike the situation regarding non-anthropocentrism, the anthropocentrist does not have a choice between equally acceptable alternatives (the Principle of Human Preservation and the Principle of Nonhuman Preservation). If, as Sterba ar-gues, a consistent preference for either the basic needs of humans or those of nonhumans would result in the extinction of the other, the anthropo-centrist's commitment to the value superiority of humans clearly creates a strong presumption in favour of the Principle of Human Preservation The extent to which the anthropocentrist could opt for the Principle of

Nonhuman Preservation is dependent upon the weight attached to the value difference between humans and nonhumans. The greater the gap between the degree of intrinsic value afforded nonhuman and that assigned to humans, the less likely it is that the anthropocentrist would find the Principle of Nonhuman Preservation acceptable. As such, to say that both positions would find the Principle of Human Preservation *acceptable* is, as it turns out, not very significant since the nonanthropocentrist has an equally acceptable alternative, while the anthropocentrist is committed to the Principle of Human Preservation, at least regarding consistent preferences.

For Sterba, the critical question is whether the anthropocentrist would be committed to the previously stated Principle of Disproportionality, to some different version of it, or to no such principle whatsoever. As Sterba recognises, at first glance it might appear that, given the assumption that humans are of greater value than nonhumans, the Principle of Disproportionality would be antithetical to the anthropocentric position. A characteristic criticism of Western society by environmental philosophers has been that it embodies a form of anthropocentrism which has historically licensed uninhibited exploitation of nature. If only humans are of intrinsic value, than human exploitation of nonhumans is restricted only by the potential for direct or indirect harm to fellow humans. In the absence of that, nonhuman nature can be used for any purpose. But, as Sterba holds, there exists no nonquestion-begging argument in support of this radical form of anthropocentrism, so that the most defensible version of anthropocentrism is one which attributes intrinsic value to the members of nonhuman species, albeit, lesser intrinsic value than that of members of the human species. Given this, exploitation of nonhuman species in order to satisfy human needs requires justification. Such exploitation, when necessary to satisfy the basic needs of humans, is allowable due to the Principle of Human Preservation. The remaining question to be addressed, as Sterba notes, is whether the value superiority of humans justifies the exploitation of nonhumans in order to satisfy nonbasic human needs.

Sterba finds it important to distinguish between *aggressing against* the basic needs of members of nonhuman species and *failing to meet* those needs. In his opinion, this distinction does not carry any moral weight in the context of interhuman ethics where both aggressing against and failing to meet the basic needs of fellow humans in order to satisfy one's own nonbasic needs are deemed immoral. In the context of interspecific ethics, however, Sterba believes the distinction to be ethically important. His position is that, at least theoretically, there are legitimate grounds for favouring human nonbasic needs over the basic needs of nonhuman species when to do so involves only failing to meet their basic needs, but that no such grounds exist for justifying aggressing against the basic needs of members of nonhuman species in order to satisfy the nonbasic needs of humans. What legitimates the former? In Sterba's opinion, the fact that nonhuman species fail to meet the basic needs of humans when there is a conflict with their own needs (basic and nonbasic

I presume) entails that humans are under no such obligation themselves. This is simply the reciprocity argument again. Since nonhumans fail to sacrifice their own needs in order to avoid failing to meet the needs of humans, we do not act wrongly when we do the same. We have already seen the weakness of this argument in regards to the Principle of Human Preservation, and it fares no better here. The fact that members of nonhuman species, who are not moral agents, consistently prefer their own needs over those of humans or members of other species in general, does not entail that humans, who are moral agents, are free from any obligation to avoid failing to meet the basic needs of nonhumans in order to satisfy their own nonbasic needs.

Sterba recognises that most of the conflicts between human nonbasic needs and the basic needs of nonhuman species involves aggressing against the latter. Consequently, even if the theoretical distinction between 'aggressing against' and 'failing to meet' were to have ethical importance in the context of interspecific relations, it would have little if any practical significance. The question, then, to be addressed is whether there exist justifiable reasons for favouring human nonbasic needs over nonhuman basic needs when doing so requires aggressing against the latter. In other words, can the anthropocentrist reasonably reject the necessity of the Principle of Disproportionality? Sterba's position is that they cannot. They cannot because, given the version of anthropocentrism Sterba is working with, to allow that the needs of the members of nonhuman species can be aggressed against in order to satisfy any human needs, which would be the result of a denial of the Principle of Disproportionality combined with an acceptance of the Principle of Human Preservation, is, in effect, to deny that members of nonhuman species have any intrinsic value, a denial the anthropocentrist cannot make. Consequently, in order to respect the intrinsic value of members of nonhuman species, a line must be drawn. For Sterba, the Principle of Disproportionality represents that line.

Is it the case that the Principle of Disproportionality represents the absolute minimum which the anthropocentrist can consistently accept? Or, can the anthropocentrist consistently subscribe to a less restrictive principle which would allow for some human preference of their own nonbasic needs over the basic needs of members of nonhuman species? In Sterba's argument, there are two inequalities at work: humans are of greater intrinsic value than nonhumans, and the satisfaction of basic needs is of greater value than the satisfaction of nonbasic needs. All else being equal, one is justified in opting for the satisfaction of basic needs over that of nonbasic needs, and the satisfaction of human needs over nonhuman needs. The key to Sterba's argument is that the latter preference is insufficient to trump the former. But, is it? As Sterba recognises, the failure to satisfy any need results in a lack or deficiency. These lacks or deficiencies can be of various kinds (e.g. poor health, lack of psychological development, etc.), but they nonetheless represent a worsening of the being's condition in some shape or form. Even though, considered in themselves, the failure to satisfy basic needs may result in a greater, even much greater, harm than the failure to satisfy nonbasic needs, the failure to satisfy nonbasic needs can be construed as a harm. What the Principle of Disproportionality represents is a preference for avoiding the harms attendant upon the failure to satisfy the basic needs of lesser intrinsically valuable entities over the harm resulting from a failure to satisfy the nonbasic needs of beings of greater intrinsic value. The question is, what grounds are there for this preference?

Reading between the lines, Sterba's reasoning seems to be this. Differences in the intrinsic value of beings has no effect on the magnitude of the harm produced by the failure to satisfy basic needs as opposed to the magnitude of harm produced by the failure to satisfy nonbasic needs. The former is categorically larger and morally more important than the latter; hence, the categorical prohibition found in the Principle of Disproportionality. However plausible this reasoning might be, it simply is not the case that the anthropocentrist must be committed to it. The anthropocentrist could offer plausible arguments for holding the view that in certain kinds of cases it is worse to avoid aggressing against the basic needs of members of nonhuman species in order to satisfy nonbasic human needs than it is to satisfy the latter. Consider the utilitarian perspective. If humans are presumed to be of greater intrinsic value, then the enhancement of their condition, even if such enhancement is, in itself relatively small, might be of sufficient value as to outweigh the harm caused a being of much less intrinsic value, especially in cases where the benefits to the more intrinsically valuable entities are distributed over a larger number while the harm to the lesser intrinsically valuable entities is restricted to a small number of them. The general question is this: Should one always opt for a state of affairs in which one seeks to maximise the satisfaction of the basic needs of all intrinsically valuable entities, at the expense of the satisfaction of other needs of the more intrinsically valuable beings? Or, is it possible that an arrangement in which a portion of the basic needs of the lesser intrinsically valuable entities is not met in order to meet some nonbasic needs of more intrinsically valuable beings could produce a greater overall maximisation of intrinsic value? Put another way, are there any *a priori* reasons for believing that a world filled with a larger number of intrinsically valuable entities, the more intrinsically valuable of which are 'dissatisfied' in a number of ways, is of greater overall value than a world filled with a smaller number of intrinsically valuable entities, but one in which the more intrinsically valuable entities are more satisfied, have fewer lacks and deficiencies? There does not appear to be, and Mill's position on the relative value of a dissatisfied human life and the life of a satisfied pig could be offered up as a philosophical defence of the view that the alternate situation is morally preferable.

Sterba's version of anthropocentrism itself provides plausible grounds for denying the categorical prohibition present in the Principle of Disproportionality. If humans are deemed to be more intrinsically valuable, more 'meritorious', than nonhumans, that must be because they possess certain morally relevant traits, such as the capacity for rational, autonomous behaviour, self-consciousness, and a sense of psychophysical identity over time, which non-humans either do not possess or possess to a much lesser degree. If the possession of interests is a function of the presence of capacities like these, and one attaches moral significance to the possession of interests, then one could argue that taxonomic differences create differences in the kinds of interests at stake, and that sufficiently large differences in those interests has moral importance. So, one could reasonably argue that the interests of humans should be afforded greater moral weight than those of nonhuman species, how much greater weight depending on the phylogenetic differences present. Such a moral difference could easily be taken to outweigh any theoretical difference between basic and nonbasic needs, and in this way justify aggressing against the basic needs of members of some nonhuman species in order to satisfy the nonbasic needs of humans and perhaps other species. This recognition of morally relevant differences in the interests that can be ascribed to members of different species has, ironically, been recognised even by advocates of animal liberation/rights such as Peter Singer and Tom Regan.

What these considerations show is that the anthropocentrists have at their disposal the philosophical means by which to reject the categorical prohibition present in Sterba's Principle of Disproportionality in favour of a less restrictive principle which allows for, in certain well-defined cases, aggressing against the basic needs of members of nonhuman species in order to satisfy human nonbasic needs. As Sterba himself notes, 'To recognise something as having intrinsic value does not preclude destroying it to preserve other things that also have intrinsic value when there is good reason to do so.' If we substitute 'make better off' for 'preserve', and allow that the maximisation of the welfare of the most intrinsically valuable entities is a good reason, or that the inherent moral superiority of the interests of more intrinsically valuable beings demands our attention, then it does not appear that the anthropocentrist, upon pains of inconsistency, is committed to the Principle of Disproportionality. What we are left with is the reverse of the situation regarding the Principle of Human Preservation. There the anthropocentrist is strongly committed to the principle of justice under consideration, while the nonanthropocentrist is not. Here, the nonanthropocentrist is strongly committed to the principle, while the anthropocentrist is at best weakly committed to it. Again, if reconciliation is achieved, it is not very significant.

As mentioned at the outset, reconciliation projects such as those of Sterba and Norton are fuelled by the belief that when one moves beyond abstract, axiological debates about the value status of nonhuman nature relative to that of humans, one will discover that such debates have little or no effect on the formation of general principles by which to shape environmental policy. It would be quite nice, and quite philosophically convenient, if this were true. If it were true, then environmental ethicists could turn their attention to the admittedly more pressing issues of policy formation and environmental management, and, with great hope, reach some consensus as to how to proceed. However, the hope that foundational axiological differences might 'disappear' at the level of policy formation, or even at the level of general principles to guide policy formation, seems to me to be just that, a *hope*. The kind of theoretical 'reconciliation' or 'convergence' argued for by Sterba is too easily purchased. All it requires is an underestimation of the seriousness with which the nonanthropocentrist may hold to the belief in species equality, and a corresponding underestimation of the self-interested latitude which the notion of differential intrinsic value affords the anthropocentrist. Though for practical reasons, the differentially motivated environmental groups, organisations, and movements which now crowd the scene may have to make concessions to one another in order to achieve a politically effective level of cooperative activity, that is far from amounting to either a philosophical or operational 'reconciliation'.

NOTES

I would like to thank James Sterba, the journal referees, and the Editor for their helpful comments.

1. Sterba 1994. Norton 1991 is the most developed effort at showing that as regards substantive policy issues, the axiological debate between nonanthropocentrists and anthropocentrists becomes quite insignificant.

2. Steverson 1995.

3. On this point, Sterba is entering the debate regarding speciesism which dates back to the mid-1970s. Sterba's position, a view very similar to what James Rachels has labelled 'mild speciesism', has been criticised by Rachels and others. For example, see Rachels 1990. Rachels' point is to show that even mild speciesism is unacceptable from the standpoint of interspecific equality. If Rachels' assessment is correct, then Sterba is mistaken in the first place to believe that the nonanthropocentrist can accept a principle which shows preference for human interests. My approach will be to allow Sterba his view that preference for human interests is permissible, even for the nonanthropocentrist, but then to show that the claim of permissibility is too weak to support an effort of *reconciliation* of nonanthropocentrism and anthropocentrism.

4. As far back as 1979, Peter Singer, in the context of responding to objections to his argument for 'animal liberation', critically discussed the inadequacies of a naturalistic-contractarian approach such as this. See Singer 1979, pp. 68–71.

5. Sterba 1994, p. 231.

6. Ibid., p. 237.

7. Ibid., p. 230.

8. See Regan 1992.

References

Norton, Bryan 1991. *Toward Unity Among Environmentalists.* New York: Oxford University Press.

Rachels, James 1990. *Created From Animals: The Moral Implications of Darwinism.* New York: Oxford University Press.

Regan, Tom 1992. 'Does Environmental Ethics Rest on a Mistake?' *The Monist* **75:**161–83.

Singer, Peter 1979. *Practical Ethics.* Cambridge: Cambridge University Press.

Sterba, James P. 1994. 'Reconciling Anthropocentric and Nonanthropocentric Environmental Ethics'. *Environmental Values* 3:229–44.

Steverson, Brian K. 1995. 'Contextualism and Norton's Convergence Hypothesis', *Environmental Ethics* **17:**135–50.

Reconciliation Reaffirmed:
A Reply to Steverson

James P. Sterba

In 'On the Reconciliation of Anthropocentric and Nonanthropocentric Environmental Ethics,' Brian Steverson raises a number of important objections to my attempt to show that when a nonanthropocentric perspective and an anthropocentric perspective are each given its most morally defensible interpretation, they both support the following principles of environmental justice:

> *A Principle of Human Defence:* Actions that defend oneself and other human beings against harmful aggression are permissible even when they necessitate killing or harming animals or plants.
>
> *A Principle of Human Preservation:* Actions that are necessary for meeting one's basic needs or the basic needs of other human beings are permissible even when they require aggressing against the basic needs of animals and plants.
>
> *A Principle of Human Disproportionality:* Actions that meet nonbasic or luxury needs of humans are prohibited when they aggress against the basic needs of animals and plants. (Steverson, 1996)

Against my attempt to show that a nonanthropocentric perspective requires these principles, Steverson

i.   criticises my appeal to reciprocal altruism to justify the human preference permitted by the Principle of Human Preservation; and
ii. claims that while it is reasonable from a nonanthropocentric perspective to select the Principle of Human Preservation, one could just as well select a Principle of Nonhuman Preservation from that perspective.

Against my attempt to show that an anthropocentric perspective requires these principles, Steverson

i.   questions whether intrinsic value can comes in degrees as required to support the Principle of Disproportionality from an anthropocentric perspective.
ii. questions whether we are always prohibited from satisfying our nonbasic needs by aggressing against the basic needs of nonhuman nature as required by the Principle of Disproportionality, even assuming that nonhuman nature has intrinsic value. (Sterba, 1994, 1995)

These are very serious objections to my reconciliationist argument that go right to the heart of the matter. Unless there are adequate replies to these objections, there would be no point to pursuing my reconciliationist project further. So let me consider each of these objections in turn.

With respect to my appeal to reciprocal altruism to justify preferential treatment for humans, that is, my claim that the degree of human preference sanctioned by the Principle of Human Preservation is justified by the degree of reciprocal altruism that humans can reasonably expect from other humans, Steverson contends that it would be a mistake to ground all of our moral obligations in such reciprocity.[1]

Actually, I agree with Steverson here. I agree, that is, that not *all* of our moral obligations can be given a foundation in reciprocal altruism. What I have argued, however, is only that some of our obligations can be so grounded in the reciprocal altruism that we can reasonably expect of other humans, and Steverson offers no objection to this more limited appeal to reciprocal altruism.

With respect to my claim that it is reasonable to select the Principle of Human Preservation from a nonanthropocentric perspective, Steverson contends that it is equally reasonable from that perspective to select a Principle of Nonhuman Preservation, which maintains that actions that are necessary for meeting the basic needs of nonhumans are permissible even when they require aggressing against the basic needs of humans.

Here I doubt that Steverson is interpreting 'permissible' in the same sense or applying the notion in the same way in both of these principles. This is because as I interpret the Principle of Human Preservation, when it maintains that it is permissible to meet one's own basic needs or the basic needs of other humans even when this requires aggressing against the basic needs of animals and plants, it implies that other humans should not interfere with that aggression. Let us call this strong permissibility. Now, if we similarly interpret 'permissible' in the Principle of Nonhuman Preservation, it would imply that other humans should not interfere with any aggression that is directed against humans for the preservation of nonhumans, *even when that aggression happens to be directed against themselves*. Surely, this would be a very demanding requirement to impose on humans even from a nonanthropocentric perspective, and I doubt that Steverson wants to endorse it.

Alternatively, Steverson may want to interpret 'permissible' in the same way in both principles, but in such a way that it imposes almost no practical requirements on anyone. According to this interpretation, let us call it weak permissibility, its being permissible to meet one's own basic needs or the basic needs of other human beings by aggressing against the basic needs of nonhumans would be consistent with its being permissible for other humans to resist that aggression. And the same would hold true for the Principle of Nonhuman Preservation. Thus, its being permissible to meet the basic needs of nonhumans by aggressing against the basic needs of humans would be consistent with its being permissible for other humans to resist that aggression. On this interpretation of the two principles, since nothing is morally required or prohibited by them, what gets done obviously depends on the comparative power relations of the contending parties. Nevertheless, the problem with this interpretation is that it is certainly odd to think that morality imposes no prohibitions or requirements at all in such an area of severe conflicts of interest, given that it is in just such areas that we would expect morality to provide some sort of a resolution.

Another possibility is that Steverson may want to interpret 'permissible' as strong permissibility in both principles, but then limit the scope of application of the Principle of Nonhuman Preservation so that it would be permissible for humans to aggress against their own basic needs, (i.e., sacrifice them) in order to meet the basic needs of nonhumans, but not permissible for humans to aggress against the basic needs of other humans for that purpose. Yet while this limitation on the scope of the Principle of Nonhuman Preservation seems defensible from a nonanthropocentric perspective, it also seems defensible from an anthropocentric perspective, which, of course, is just what Steverson wanted to deny. Thus, it would seem that the only defensible interpretations of the Principle of Human Preservation and the Principle of Nonhuman Preservation turn out to support rather than oppose my reconciliationist argument.

In objecting to my claim that intrinsic value can come in degrees, Steverson cites Tom Regan as having shown that such a claim makes a category mistake, like claiming that two persons can be half-married to each other (Regan, 1992). Yet whether or not a category mistake is involved here depends on the particular notion of intrinsic value that one is using. In this context, there are at least two notions of intrinsic value that need to be distinguished. According to one notion of intrinsic value, which we can call agent-centred intrinsic value, to say that X *has intrinsic value* is to say that X *is good as an end for some agent Y* as opposed to saying that X *has instrumental value,* which is to say that X *is good as a means for some agent Y.* Now, according to this notion, intrinsic value does not come in degrees; one can't have more or less of it.[2] But there is another notion of intrinsic value, which we can call recipient-centred intrinsic value, according to which to say that X *has intrinsic value* is to say that *the good of X ought to constrain the way that others use X in pursuing their own interests.* Now it seems to me that recipient-centred intrinsic value, unlike recipient-centred intrinsic value, does allow for the possibility of different degrees of intrinsic value, provided that we can show that the good of some Xs should constrain others more than the good of other Xs. In fact, however, this is just what I have argued—that there *are* good reasons why the good of humans should constrain other humans more than the good of nonhumans. Specifically, they are the reasons of reciprocal altruism and what constitutes permissible defence and preservation as captured by the Principle of Human Defence and the Principle of Human Preservation. These reasons require a degree of preference for humans over nonhumans when the relevant needs of humans are at stake. Assuming, then, that it is possible to show in this way that humans are legitimately constrained more for the good of humans than by the good of nonhumans, it is possible to claim that humans have a greater degree of intrinsic value than nonhumans.[3]

Steverson further argues that those who accept an anthropocentric perspective would still have plausible grounds for rejecting the constraint of the Principle of Disproportionality, even assuming that nonhumans have intrinsic value, although less intrinsic value than humans. Specifically, Steverson denies that humans are always prohibited from satisfying their nonbasic needs by aggressing against the basic needs of nonhumans, despite the intrinsic value of nonhumans. But the only reason that Steverson offers for rejecting this prohibition is that the satisfaction of *many* nonbasic needs of humans may turn out in some utilitarian calculation to outweigh the frustration of a *few* basic needs of nonhumans.[4] Yet when this sort of reasoning is applied to humans, many utilitarians have been reluctant to embrace it (Hare, 1981). This is because it would seem to justify such practices as the sacrifice of the lives of Roman gladiators for the sake of the pleasures of the large crowds who witnessed those gladiator contests. Instead of defending the morality of such gladiator contests, utilitarians have been inclined to favour alternative social practices that preserve the lives of the few while still securing comparable pleasures for the many. It is also understandable why utilitarians have been reluctant to allow such trade-offs of the few for the many. The idea that a person's basic needs can be aggressed against to meet nonbasic needs of others seems opposed to the fundamental respect that we think is reasonably due to each and every person. So while utilitarians admit the theoretical possibility of such trade-offs, they tend to argue that, practically speaking, such trade-offs are unattainable, and so, even from a utilitarian perspective, the principles that we need to appeal to in order to carry on our affairs should not take such trade-offs into account (Hare, 1981).

Moreover, in considering such trade-offs with respect to our human/ nonhuman cases, it is difficult to see how the numbers could turn out to be the way that they must turn out in order to be justified—with the satisfaction of nonbasic needs of *many* humans weighed against aggression against the basic needs of only a *few* nonhumans. Usually the numbers seem to be the other way round, with aggression against the basic needs of many nonhumans weighed against the satisfaction of the nonbasic needs of only a few humans. Nevertheless, just as in the analogous case involving only humans, we may not be able to theoretically rule out the possibility of trade-offs involving aggression against the basic needs of a few nonhumans for the sake of the satisfaction of the nonbasic needs of many humans. Nevertheless, even from a utilitarian perspective, we can rule them out practically speaking, excluding them, as I have done, from the principles of environmental justice.

In formulating these answers to Brian Steverson's objections to my reconciliationist argument, I have been led to develop my argument further than I had previously done. Specifically, I have clarified the requirements for others that follow from the actions that are permitted by the Principle of Human Defence and the Principle of Human Preservation. I have also clarified the notion of intrinsic value that I am endorsing and the grounds on which my claim of greater intrinsic value for humans rests. So I obviously owe Steverson a debt of gratitude for eliciting these clarifications. My hope is that now that I have put the argument, with his help, in its present improved form, he and others will find the argument worthy of further development.

NOTES

1. For support here, Steverson cites Singer (1979: 68–71). Singer, however, is arguing against an attempt to base *all* of our moral obligations on reciprocity.

2. Under this interpretation, however, it is possible for something to have both intrinsic value and instrumental value, to be both an end and a means.

3. Given this notion of intrinsic value, I don't see how there is any category mistake in affirming degrees of intrinsic value. In 'Does Environmental Ethics Rest on a Mistake?' Tom Regan argues that the various notions of intrinsic value that do not allow for degrees of intrinsic value do not serve the goals of an environmental ethics very well. I think that he may be right about this, which may be a good reason in favour of my proposed notion of intrinsic value which does allow for degrees of intrinsic value.

4. Steverson also thinks that John Stuart Mill's claim in *Utilitarianism* that it is better to be Socrates dissatisfied than a pig satisfied also somehow supports a preference for nonbasic needs of humans over basic needs of nonhumans. But it isn't clear just how Mill's claim could provide this support. Mill makes his claim in the context of setting out his test of higher and lower pleasures:

> Of two pleasures, if there be one to which all or almost all who have experience of both give a decided preference . . . that is the more desirable pleasure.

Yet has any human ever really experienced what it is like being a pig? Mill considers cases in which humans actually do prefer lower to high pleasures and claims that the reason why they do so is because they have 'become incapable of the other.' But isn't that just what pigs are—animals that are incapable of our so-called higher pleasures. In order then to interpret Mill's claim so that his test of higher and lower pleasures applies to it, we must interpret it as claiming that it is better for people who are capable of both higher and lower pleasures to experience the higher pleasures (the Socrates-like pleasures) even if that leaves them somewhat discontent than it is for them to experience only lower pleasures (the pig-like pleasures) even if that leaves them perfectly content.

Unfortunately, the trade-offs that we are considering in the context of an environmental ethics are quite different. They are between at least two different entities, not one entity that is capable of being in one of two ways. In fact, aggressing against the basic needs of nonhumans to satisfy the nonbasic needs of humans will frequently involve killing off nonhumans to satisfy the nonbasic needs of humans. So we don't have a common entity that is capable of existing in one of two ways as we do in Mill's case. Accordingly, Mill's claim about the preferability of higher to lower pleasures cannot be used to support the satisfaction of nonbasic needs of humans by aggressing against basic needs of nonhumans.

References

Hare, R.M. 1981 *Moral Thinking*. Oxford: Oxford University Press.
Regan, Tom. 1992 'Does Environmental Ethics Rest on a Mistake?' *The Monist* **75**:161–83.

Singer, Peter. 1979 *Practical Ethics*. Cambridge: Cambridge University Press.
Steverson, Brian. 1996 'On the Reconciliation of Anthropocentric and Nonanthropocentric Environmental Ethics', *Environmental Values* **5**:349–61.
Sterba, James P. 1994 'Reconciling Anthropocentric and Nonanthropocentric Environmental Ethics', *Environmental Values* **3**:229–44.
Sterba, James P. 1995 'From Biocentric Individualism to Biocentric Pluralism', *Environmental Ethics* **17**:191–208.

EVALUATING A CASE STUDY: APPLYING ETHICAL ISSUES

You are finally at the last stage of the process of evaluating case studies. By this point, you have (a) chosen a practical ethical viewpoint (including the choice of an ethical theory and practical linking principles, whose point of view you will adopt), (b) listed professional, cost, and ethical issues, and (c) annotated the issues lists by examining how embedded each issue is to the essential nature of the case at hand. What remains is the ability to come to an action decision once these three steps have been completed. The final step is to discuss your conclusions.

To do this, you must enter an argumentative phase. In this phase, I suggest that you create brainstorming sheets headed by the possible courses of action open to you. Prepare an argument on each sheet to support that particular course of action utilizing the annotated charts you have already prepared. Then compare what you believe to be the pivotal issues that drive each argument. Use your chosen ethical theory to decide which issue is most compelling. Be prepared to defend your outcomes/action recommendation.

Let us return to the case of contraception in the less-developed countries. As you may recall, the case was as follows.[1] You are a regional director at the World Health Organization. One of your duties is to supervise the distribution of birth control devices to less-developed countries. The product of choice has been the intrauterine device (IUD), which has proved to be effective and inexpensive.

The problem is that in the United States, several hundred users of the IUD have contracted pelvic inflammatory infections that have been linked to use of the IUD.

As regional director, you must decide whether to continue to supply IUDs to women in less-developed countries.

ABC Corporation is a large multinational company that has a considerable inventory of IUDs that it cannot sell in the United States. The company would rather not write off its entire inventory and has consequently made a

---

[1]I have heard that many of the structural problems with the IUD that caused pelvic inflammatory infection have not been rectified. I am not competent to comment on this; nevertheless, for this case, let us assume that these problems still obtain.

very attractive offer to sell the World Health Organization all of its existing inventory and to assist in distributing the product regionally.

As regional director, you must decide whether to accept ABC's offer to supply IUDs to women in less-developed countries.

Remember that in this case, the professional practice cost considerations, and the ethical issues were both deeply embedded, which creates an intractable conflict; there is no simple way to justify one instead of the other.

What you must do is (a) consult your worldview and see what it dictates that you do and (b) consult the ethical theory of your deepest convictions and see what it would dictate that you do. Is there a synonymy between these? If not, then engage in a dialogue between your worldview and the professional practice. Let each inform on the other. In the end, you should be able to come to some resolution.[2]

One step in this direction is to examine the arguments that support each. What are the critical premises in these arguments?[3] In any argument, there is a conclusion. If you want to contrast two arguments, you must begin by contrasting two conclusions. Conclusions are supported by premises that (logically) cause the acceptance of the conclusion. Therefore, what you must do is to create at least two arguments that entail different conclusions. To do this, create brainstorming lists on the *key issue(s)* involved in the argument. The key issue is that concept that makes the difference. This case has a number of key issues. Let us try to construct arguments that are both for and against the position.

Sample "Pro" Brainstorming Sheet for the Position

Position to be supported. Accept ABC Corporation's offer and continue to provide IUDs in less-developed countries.

Key Thoughts on the Subject

1. As a public health professional, you are enjoined to benefit the greatest number of people possible in your health policy.

2. It is a fact that in less-developed countries, millions die of starvation each year. The simple cause of starvation is too many people for the available food. When you decrease the number of people (given a level food source), more people can eat.

3. There are "blips" to any project. In this case, it is a few hundred or so cases of pelvic inflammatory infection. These casualties pale when compared to the number who will benefit from continuing to provide IUDs.

---

[2]This dialectical interaction is described in Chapter Eight of *Basic Ethics*.
[3]See my book, *The Process of Argument* (Englewood Cliffs, NJ: Prentice Hall, 1988; rpt Lanham, MD: University Press of America, 1995) on the details of this process.

4. Utilitarian ethical theory dictates that the general good supersedes any individual's good.

5. In less-developed countries, the general good is advanced by continuing to distribute IUDs since more people (by far) benefit than are hurt.

6. ABC Corporation is willing to give a heavily discounted price on its present inventory and provide some regional assistance in the distribution of the product. This will allow the World Health Organization to reach more people than ever before and thus fulfill its mission.

Argument

1. In countries that have a limited amount of food that would feed only a certain population (n), increases in population ($n + x$), will result in x not having enough food to live—fact.

2. Many less-developed countries experience the condition mentioned in premise 1—assertion.

3. In many less-developed countries, x increase in population will result in x number of people starving to death—1, 2.

4. Many children who are born are not planned—assertion.

5. If one subtracts the number of unplanned births from the total birth rate, the number of births decreases significantly—assertion.

6. If all children were planned, the number (more than x) of births would decrease significantly—assertion.

7. If all children were planned, less-developed countries would not experience starvation (given constant crop production)—3–6.

8. The IUD is the most effective birth control device in the less-developed countries—assertion.

9. The imperative of professional conduct in public health is to help as many people as possible—fact.

10. Public health professional standards dictate that the IUD should be provided to women in less-developed countries—7, 8.

11. ABC Corporation has made an offer to substantially reduce the cost of its IUD inventory and to assist in regional distribution—fact.

12. ABC's offer will allow you to reach more women than you had before—fact.

13. Cost considerations bolster the professional practice standards—9–12.

14. The IUD poses potential health risks to some women (less than 5 percent)—fact.

15. The ethical imperative of Utilitarianism dictates that the right ethical decision is to advance the cause of the common good—fact.

16. Distributing IUDs helps more people in less-developed countries than it hurts—fact.

17. Utilitarianism dictates that the IUD should be provided to women in less-developed countries—11–13.

18. The regional director must continue the distribution of IUDs to less-developed countries—10, 13, 17.

Sample "Con" Brainstorming Sheet
Against the Position

Position to be supported. Reject ABC Corporation's offer and stop selling IUDs in less-developed countries.

Key Thoughts on the Subject

1. As a public health professional, you are enjoined to benefit the greatest number of people possible in your health policy.
2. It is a fact that in less-developed countries, millions die of starvation each year. The simple cause of starvation is too many people for the available food. When you decrease the number of people (given a level food source), more people can eat.
3. There are "blips" to any project. In this case, it is a few hundred or so cases of pelvic inflammatory infection. These casualties pale when compared to the number who will benefit from continuing to provide IUDs.
4. Human life is precious. No amount of practical gain can weigh against one human life.
5. Ends do not justify the means. One may have a very good end in mind, but unless the means to that end are just, the end cannot be willed.

Argument

1. In countries that have a limited amount of food that would feed only a certain population (n), increases in population ($n + x$) will result in x not having enough food to live—fact.
2. Many less-developed countries describe the conditions mentioned in premise 1—assertion.
3. In many less-developed countries, x increase in population will result in x number of people starving to deaths—1, 2.
4. Many children who are born are not planned—assertion.
5. If one subtracts the number of unplanned births from the total birth rate, the number of births decreases significantly—assertion.
6. If all children were planned, the number (more than x) of births would decrease significantly—assertion.
7. If all children were planned, less-developed countries would not experience starvation (given constant crop production)—3–6.
8. The IUD is the most effective birth control device in less-developed countries—assertion.
9. The imperative of professional conduct in public health is to help as many people as possible—fact.
10. Public health professional standards dictate that the IUD should be provided to women in less-developed countries—7, 8.
11. The IUD poses potential health risks to some women (less than 5 percent)—fact.

12. The ethical imperative of Deontology dictates that knowingly jeopardizing the essential health of any person is absolutely impermissible no matter what the practical advantage—assertion.

13. ABC Corporation's offer is attractive from a mere cost perspective—fact.

14. It is absolutely ethically impermissible (under Deontology) to provide IUDs to women in less-developed countries when the devices have been shown to be deleterious to the health of Americans—10, 11.

15. In cases of conflict, an absolute ethical imperative trumps an absolute professional standards imperative—assertion.

16. The director must reject ABC Corporation's offer and halt the distribution of IUDs to less-developed countries—10, 14, 15.

Obviously, the crucial difference in these two arguments is the choice of an ethical theory and the way each is interpreted. Thus, whether a person takes a pro or con position is a function of the underlying value system that person holds. The way a person chooses a value system and the broader practical viewpoint is through the person's worldview and its accompanying baggage.

You must determine how to apply your practical ethical viewpoint. This requires careful attention to the theory and the linking principles you have chosen and the way they affect your evaluation of actual cases. To be an authentic seeker of truth, you must engage in this dialectical process. To do less is to diminish yourself as a person.

You are now ready to evaluate a case study.

Macro and Micro Cases.*

Macro Cases.

Macro Case 1. You are the chairperson of an environmental impact study concerning a new dam on the Columbia River. Proponents of the dam say that they have developed a new "fish ladder" for spawning salmon that is easier than all previous designs. They describe it as beinging an "interstate highway" compared to other (older) designs. Proponents also cite the fact that the energy needs of the Pacific Northwest are ever increasing; present facilities will not meet demand. Either they must meet demand via hydroelectric plants or take the advice of the Hanford people and construct a nuclear power plant. Obviously, the latter is less attractive to people in the region. Everyone would be afraid of an accident.

On the other hand, the salmon ladders in the past have proved to be great barriers to spawning. Seventeen species of salmon are at dangerously low population levels, and this dam might tilt the balance.

---

*For more on macro and micro cases, see the overview on p. 30.

You must write an executive report to the committee for or against the dam. Should it be built? What factors are important for your decision? What moral principles are relevant? Will it make a difference if your stance toward environmental ethics is anthropocentric or biocentric?

Macro Case 2. You are the county commissioner and must recommend to the county council whether to go ahead on ABC Company's plan to open a new copper mine. All the data suggest that a rich lode is relatively near the surface of the earth. Your county has been economically depressed for twenty years since the sawmill closed. This new mine promises to bring three hundred jobs to a region that has been experiencing 21 percent unemployment (which would be higher except that many people have left). The mine could revitalize the region that has been teetering on extinction.

The problem is that the lode is not located near any existing road. In fact, half of the lode is under X-4 (a mountain in a chain that surrounds your Montana valley). The company proposes to level X-4 to build an access road and to make its strip mining enterprise more affordable. It would like to share the costs of this venture equally with the state. The state has already approved the money for it, but at a town meeting on this issue, people expressed very strong opposition to the prospect of leveling a two thousand-foot mountain. Certainly, all the other mountains in the chain will be left, but is it really right to demolish a mountain? You must report to the county commissioners, who have jurisdiction over issuing permits for this procedure. Is the prospect of more jobs more important than X-4? What ethical issues are at stake? Does it make a difference if you base recommendation on anthropocentric or biocentric principles? Why or why not?

Micro Cases.

Micro Case 1. Your name is Janet Belle. You live in a suburb of Chicago, Winetka, a wealthy suburb. You love your lawn and spend three hours a week caring for it—no lawn service for you! Your lawn is one of the few things in your life that brings you happiness. You mow, mulch, and fertilize your lawn. The problem is that the weed and feed mix you use—XYZ's Kill 'em and Grow 'em—has been cited as polluting Lake Michigan's water table. The lake has been so polluted lately that fish caught there have been deemed not fit for human consumption. Thousands of people in the northern suburbs have changed from XYZ's product on the advice of the Environmental Protection Agency. At first, you also tried other products, but none of them worked as well as XYZ. Almost everybody else has switched from XYZ, but why can't you just go on using it yourself? You can mix it in the garage so that your neighbors won't know that you're doing. After all, it works; you love your yard; and how much harm will only a few people continuing to use the forbidden brand cause? Analyze this from your point of view and from your grown child's point of view.

Micro Case 2.   You are ready to buy a car and are attracted to the new sports utility vehicle, Space Command Navigator. This is one of the largest and most powerful of its class. No one could look down at you in this baby—you are 10 feet off the ground! It gives you a feeling of power and command. Life has not been so good for you; you are a short person who is tired of looking up to others. You are also very average and are tired of people snubbing you. Here is your chance to look down on others. However, you note that the class of sports utility vehicles (really trucks) pollute the atmosphere much more than almost every other vehicle on the market and that the amount of energy necessary to construct one of these trucks is three to four times that necessary to build a comparable car. You know it is not the most "green" car, but what the heck? This is the vehicle of your dreams. Should you go purchase it? What are the ethical issues at stake? Does it make a difference if you base your environmental theory on anthropocentric or biocentric principles? Explain.

chapter six

Applied Environmental Ethics

General Overview. This chapter explores three particular issues involved in environmental ethics: animal rights, biodiversity, and sustainable development. There are, of course, many other important issues such as pollution (and resulting issues such as the ozone layer, hazardous waste disposal, and nuclear power) and the world population problem. However, I believe that these problems are contained within these more general environmental stances. For example, biodiversity and sustainable development are often appealed to when individuals protest an act of pollution by some industry or governmental entity.

The first issue to be examined is the human place in the biosphere. Are we the rulers at the top who may use everything else as means only? Are there any constraints on our use of nature (besides self-interested ones)? Do animals have moral rights? If so, how do we justify them? Do animals have any ethical rights (as humans have), or do they possess proportional rights (basing the proportion on their phylogenetic proximity to *homo sapiens*)? Do we want to say that various protists are to be given the same respect as a monkey? If so, why? If not, why? These are important questions, for they incline us to think about the foundations of morality. My own position, of course, is connected to the demonstrated ability to formulate a worldview (actually or potentially).

The second issue concerns biodiversity. This is a rather complicated issue on several accounts. First, the definition of *biodiversity* is not universally recognized. Do we mean diversity within the genetic population of one species or a proliferation of many different species? (I would vote for both.) Also, since biodiversity is a natural occurrence in nature, why do humans feel the necessity to preserve it in an artificial manner? Finally, what is the remedy? Is it appropriate to protect species or simply stop interfering with ecosystems? What difference would it make if one approach or the other were chosen?

Related to biodiversity is the issue of sustainable development. According to this concept, people harvest bioresources in such a way that those resources are replenished. For example, sustainable development would dictate that the pace of cutting down trees should equal the pace of replacing them with new adult trees. If we are concerned only with the development project at hand, perhaps we can term this weak sustainable development. But if we are concerned with the long term and the viability of an ecosystem/ biome, then a strong protectionist commitment must be taken. This lends allegiance to the maintenance of nature as we know it as long as possible. Such is the goal. Can we sustain it?

I. ANIMAL RIGHTS.

Overview. The status of animals (other than humans) has been a source of great controversy at least since the time that Theophrastus (Aristotle's student) declared himself to be a vegetarian on moral grounds. Certainly, humans have traditionally taken a view based on the so-called scale of nature (*scala naturae*). According to this scale, there is a linear progression of worth beginning with the soulless rocks and dirt and ascending to the plants (with their nutritive soul) to the animals (with their sensitive and/or motor soul) and ending with humans (with their rational soul). Augustine added to Aristotle's scale by setting angels and the company of heaven above humans and God on top, looking over everything. Because the scale of nature has sharp divisions and because the Judeo-Christian-Moslem traditions accept that God created humans in God's own image, it has been the assumption that this image refers to rationality and that this characteristic sets humans to be like God. Thus, because of this rationality, humans can claim to be different in kind from other living things. Proximately, they are just above the animals. Remotely, they are above the plants and the soulless things. This Aristotelian categorization has been with us for almost 2,400 years. Combined with the religious accounts of creation, it has set the prevailing public attitude about the uses of animals.

The reader must be careful, however, to sort out several different gradations of behavior toward animals. First is gratuitous cruelty, as when someone tortures an animal merely out of anger or sadism. Second is causing pain and/or death in experiments with animals to develop new medicines and other products for human use. Third is killing animals for their skins or other singular body part. Fourth is killing animals for food. Fifth is the subjugation of animals by humans who make the animals fit into our way of life (not to interrupt our neighborhoods or daily lives) or else pay the price. Each case involves us in different ethical issues. Where do we draw the line? Do we draw the line?

In the first article, Peter Singer argues that the foundation of respect is the ability to feel pain or to suffer (these are synonymous for Singer). He cites Bentham, who says, "The question is not, Can they *reason?* nor Can they *talk?* But, Can they *suffer?*"[1] Bentham puts the question in this way because he is keen on grounding conventional, societal rights on a principle of societal pleasure and pain. If pleasure and pain are the most primitive things we can say about humans and their *raison d'être*, then this is something that humans share with many animals. (Certainly, all vertebrates with central nervous systems can be said to feel systemic pain as a result of their biological "wiring.")

If Bentham is correct about the grounding of conventional, societal rights, and if many animals also feel pleasure and pain as humans do, then it would seem arbitrary to deny animals the rights we accord to humans. The only possible explanation would be some sort of unjustified discrimination analogous to racism or sexism. By denying these other animals rights, humans are involved in *speciesism*. We attribute all types of rights to ourselves but deny them to animals when the standard that grounds rights is the same for each. If Singer is correct about the foundation of rights, then clearly it is time for a change. Specifics on what changes they might be are discussed in Tom Regan's article.

Regan makes the case for (a) the total abolition of the use of animals in science, (b) the total dissolution of commercial animal agriculture, and (c) the total elimination of commercial and sport hunting and trapping. The reason for Regan's position is that animals should not be viewed as being the resources of humans. Those who view animals as resources often use Utilitarianism as the basis of their position (as per Singer's article). Regan rejects Utilitarianism for a rights-based theory designed to protect individual rights (be they human or some other animal). The ethical basis of this right comes from the notion that we are, each of us, the experiencing subject of a life— each of us a conscious creature having an individual welfare that has importance to us whatever our usefulness to others. Both animals and humans share

---

[1] J. Bentham, *Introduction to the Principles of Morals and Legislation* (New York: Hafner, 1789), p. 34.

in this moral basis for rights (according to Regan) so that both animals and humans are equally accorded moral rights.

Mary Anne Warren characterizes Regan's position as a "strong animal rights position." She disagrees with Regan that we should quickly reject the Aristotelian "reason standard" for determining moral worth. Thus, Regan's position for inherent worth as the basis for animal rights (described earlier) should be rejected. In its place, Warren argues for a "weak animal rights position" that any animal that is rational (i.e., pursues self-chosen satisfactions as a part of life) should be given the opportunity to explore those paths. Second, any creature capable of conscious pain and suffering should not be cruelly used. Third, no sentient animal should be killed without good reason.

All Animals Are Equal

Peter Singer

"Animal Liberation" may sound more like a parody of other liberation movements than a serious objective. The idea of "The Rights of Animals" actually was once used to parody the case for women's rights. When Mary Wollstonecraft, a forerunner of today's feminists, published her *Vindication of the Rights of Woman* in 1792, her views were widely regarded as absurd, and before long an anonymous publication appeared entitled *A Vindication of the Rights of Brutes*. The author of this satirical work (now known to have been Thomas Taylor, a distinguished Cambridge philosopher) tried to refute Mary Wollstonecraft's arguments by showing that they could be carried one stage further. If the argument for equality was sound when applied to women, why should it not be applied to dogs, cats, and horses? The reasoning seemed to hold for these "brutes" too; yet to hold that brutes had rights was manifestly absurd. Therefore the reasoning by which this conclusion had been reached must be unsound, and if unsound when applied to brutes, it must also be unsound when applied to women, since the very same arguments had been used in each case.

In order to explain the basis of the case for the equality of animals, it will be helpful to start with an examination of the case for the equality of women. Let us assume that we wish to defend the case for women's rights against the attack by Thomas Taylor. How should we reply?

One way in which we might reply is by saying that the case for equality between men and women cannot validly be extended to nonhuman animals. Women have a right to vote, for instance, because they are just as capable of making rational decisions about the future as men are; dogs, on the other hand, are incapable of understanding the significance of voting, so they cannot have the right to vote. There are many other obvious ways in which men and women resemble each other closely, while humans and animals differ greatly. So, it might be said, men and women are similar beings and should have similar rights, while humans and nonhumans are different and should not have equal rights.

The reasoning behind this reply to Taylor's analogy is correct up to a point, but it does not go far enough. There are obviously important differences between humans and other animals, and these differences must give rise to some differences in the rights that each have. Recognizing this evident fact, however, is no barrier to the case for extending the basic principle of equality to nonhuman animals. The differences that exist between men and women are equally undeniable, and the supporters of Women's Liberation are aware that these differences may give rise to different rights. Many feminists hold that women have the right to an abortion on request. It does not follow that since these same feminists are campaigning for equality between men and women they must support the right of men to have abortions too. Since a man cannot have an abortion, it is meaningless to talk of his right to have one. Since dogs can't vote, it is meaningless to talk of their right to vote. There is no reason why either Women's Liberation or Animal Liberation should get involved in such nonsense. The extension of the basic principle of equality from one group to another does not imply that we must treat both groups in exactly the same way, or grant exactly the same rights to both groups. Whether we should do so will depend on the nature of the members of the two groups. The basic principle of equality does not require equal or identical *treatment*; it requires equal consideration. Equal consideration for different beings may lead to different treatment and different rights.

So there is a different way of replying to Taylor's attempt to parody the case for women's rights, a way that does not deny the obvious differences between human beings and nonhumans but goes more deeply into the question of equality and concludes by finding nothing absurd in the idea that the basic-principle of equality applies to so-called brutes. At this point such a conclusion may appear odd; but if we examine more deeply the basis on which our opposition to discrimination on grounds of race or sex ultimately rests, we will see that we would be on shaky ground if we were to demand equality for blacks, women, and other groups of oppressed humans while denying equal consideration to nonhumans. To make this clear we need to see, first, exactly why racism and sexism are wrong. When we say that all human beings, whatever their race, creed, or sex, are equal, what is it that we are asserting? Those who wish to defend hierarchical, inegalitarian societies have often pointed out that by whatever test we choose it simply is not true that all humans are equal. Like it or not we must face the fact that humans come in different shapes and sizes; they come with different moral capacities, different intellectual abilities, different amounts of benevolent feeling and sensitivity to the needs of others, different abilities to communicate effectively, and different capacities to experience pleasure and pain. In short, if the demand for equality were based on the actual equality of all human beings, we would have to stop demanding equality.

Still, one might cling to the view that the demand for equality among human beings is based on the actual equality of the different races and sexes. Although, it may be said, humans differ as individuals, there are no differences between the races and sexes as such. From the mere fact that a person is black or a woman we cannot infer anything about that person's intellectual or moral capacities. This, it may be said, is why racism and sexism are wrong. The white racist claims that whites are superior to blacks, but this is false; although there are differences among individuals, some blacks are superior to some whites in all of the capacities and abilities that could conceivably be relevant. The opponent of sexism would say the same: a person's sex is no guide to his or her abilities, and this is why it is unjustifiable to discriminate on the basis of sex.

The existence of individual variations that cut across the lines of race or sex, however, provides us with no defense at all against a more sophisticated opponent of equality, one who proposes that, say, the interests of all those with IQ scores below 100 be given less consideration than the interests of those with ratings over 100. Perhaps those scoring below the mark would, in this society, be made the slaves of those scoring higher. Would a hierarchical society of this sort really be so much better than one based on race or sex? I think not. But if we tie the moral principle of equality to the factual equality of the different races or sexes, taken as a whole, our opposition to racism and sexism does not provide us with any basis for objecting to this kind of inegalitarianism.

There is a second important reason why we ought not to base our opposition to racism and sexism on any kind of factual equality, even the limited kind that asserts that variations in capacities and abilities are spread evenly among the different races and between the sexes: we can have no absolute guarantee that these capacities and abilities really are distributed evenly, without regard to race or sex, among human beings. So far as actual abilities are concerned there do seem to be certain measurable differences both among races and between sexes. These differences do not, of course, appear in every case, but only when averages are taken. More important still, we do not yet know how many of these differences are really due to the different genetic endowments of the different races and sexes, and how many are due to poor schools, poor housing, and other factors that are the result of past and continuing discrimination. Perhaps all of the important differences will eventually prove to be environmental rather than genetic. Anyone opposed to racism and sexism will certainly hope that this will be so, for it will make the task of ending discrimination a lot easier; nevertheless, it would be dangerous to rest the case against racism and sexism on the belief that all significant differences are environmental in origin. The opponent of, say, racism who takes this line will be unable to avoid conceding that if differences in ability did after all prove to have some genetic connection with race, racism would in some way be defensible.

Fortunately there is no need to pin the case for equality to one particular outcome of a scientific investigation. The appropriate response to those who claim to have found evidence of genetically based differences in ability among the races or between the sexes is not to stick to the belief that the genetic explanation must be wrong, whatever evidence to the contrary may turn up; instead we should make it quite clear that the claim to equality does not depend on intelligence, moral capacity, physical strength, or similar matters of fact. Equality is a moral idea, not an assertion of fact. There is no logically compelling reason for assuming that a factual difference in ability between two people justifies any difference in the amount of consideration we give to their needs and interests. *The principle of the equality of human beings is not a description of an alleged actual equality among humans: it is a prescription of how we should treat human beings.*

Jeremy Bentham, the founder of the reforming utilitarian school of moral philosophy, incorporated the essential basis of moral equality into his system of ethics by means of the formula: "Each to count for one and none for more than one." In other words, the interests of every being affected by an action are to be taken into account and given the same weight as the like interests of any other being. A later utilitarian, Henry Sidgwick, put the point in this way: "The good of any one individual is of no more importance, from the point of view (if I may say so) of the Universe, than the good of any other." More recently the leading figures in contemporary moral philosophy have shown a great deal of agreement in specifying as a fundamental presupposition of their moral theories some similar requirement that works to give everyone's interests equal consideration—although these writers generally cannot agree on how this requirement is best formulated.

It is an implication of this principle of equality that our concern for others and our readiness to consider their interest ought not to depend on what they are like or on what abilities they may possess. Precisely what our concern or consideration requires us to do may vary according to the characteristics of those affected by what we do: concern for the well-being of children growing up in America would require that we teach them to read; concern for the well-being of pigs may require no more than that we leave them with other pigs in a place where there is adequate food and room to run freely. But the basic element—the taking into account of the interests of the being, whatever those interests may be—must, according to the principle of equality, be extended to all beings, black or white, masculine or feminine, human or nonhuman.

Thomas Jefferson, who was responsible for writing the principle of the equality of men into the American Declaration of Independence, saw this point. It led him to oppose slavery even though he was unable to free himself fully from his slaveholding background. He wrote in a letter to the author of a book that emphasized the notable intellectual achievements of Negroes in order to refute the then common view that they had limited intellectual capacities:

> Be assured that no person living wishes more sincerely than I do, to see a complete refutation of the doubts I myself have entertained and expressed on the grade of understanding alloted to them by nature, and to find that they are on a par with ourselves . . . but whatever be their degree of talent it is no measure of their rights. Because Sir Isaac Newton was superior to others in understanding, he was not therefore lord of the property or persons of others.

Similarly, when in the 1850s the call for women's rights was raised in the United States, a remarkable black feminist named Sojourner Truth made the same point in more robust terms at a feminist convention:

> They talk about this thing in the head; what do they call it? ["Intellect," whispered someone nearby.] That's it. What's that got to do with women's rights or Negroes' rights? If my cup won't hold but a pint and yours holds a quart, wouldn't you be mean not to let me have my little half-measure full?

It is on this basis that the case against racism and the case against sexism must both ultimately rest; and it is in accordance with this principle that the attitude that we may call "speciesism," by analogy with racism, must also be condemned. Speciesism—the word is not an attractive one, but I can think of no better term—is a prejudice or attitude of bias in favor of the interests of members of one's own species and against those of members of other species. It should be obvious that the fundamental objections to racism and sexism made by Thomas Jefferson and Sojourner Truth apply equally to speciesism. If possessing a higher degree of intelligence does not entitle one human to use another for his or her own ends, how can it entitle humans to exploit nonhumans for the same purpose?

Many philosophers and other writers have proposed the principle of equal consideration of interests, in some form or other, as a basic moral principle; but not many of them have recognized that this principle applies to members of other species as well as to our own. Jeremy Bentham was one of the few who did realize this. In a forward-looking passage written at a time when black slaves had been freed by the French but in the British dominions were still being treated in the way we now treat animals, Bentham wrote:

The day *may* come when the rest of the animal creation may acquire those rights which never could have been withholden from them but by the hand of tyranny. The French have already discovered that the blackness of the skin is no reason why a human being should be abandoned without redress to the caprice of a tormentor. It may one day come to be recognized that the number of the legs, the villosity of the skin, or the termination of the *os sacrum* are reasons equally insufficient for abandoning a sensitive being to the same fate. What else is it that should trace the insuperable line? Is it the faculty of reason, or perhaps the faculty of discourse? But a full-grown horse or dog is beyond comparison a more rational, as well as a more conversable animal, than an infant of a day or a week or even a month, old. But suppose they were otherwise, what would it avail? The question is not, Can they *reason?* nor Can they *talk?* but, Can they *suffer?*

In this passage Bentham points to the capacity for suffering as the vital characteristic that gives a being the right to equal consideration. The capacity for suffering—or more strictly, for suffering and/or enjoyment or happiness—is not just another characteristic like the capacity for language or higher mathematics. Bentham is not saying that those who try to mark "the insuperable line" that determines whether the interests of a being should be considered happen to have chosen the wrong characteristic. By saying that we must consider the interests of all beings with the capacity for suffering or enjoyment Bentham does not arbitrarily exclude from consideration any interests at all—as those who draw the line with reference to the possession of reason or language do. The capacity for suffering and enjoyment is a *prerequisite for having interests at all*, a condition that must be satisfied before we can speak of interests in a meaningful way. It would be nonsense to say that it was not in the interests of a stone to be kicked along the road by a schoolboy. A stone does not have interests because it cannot suffer. Nothing that we can do to it could possibly make any difference to its welfare. The capacity for suffering and enjoyment is, however, not only necessary, but also sufficient for us to say that a being has interests—at an absolute minimum, an interest in not suffering. A mouse, for example, does have an interest in not being kicked along the road, because it will suffer if it is.

Although Bentham speaks of "rights" in the passage I have quoted, the argument is really about equality rather than about rights. Indeed, in a different passage, Bentham famously described "natural rights" as "nonsense" and "natural and imprescriptible rights" as "nonsense upon stilts." He talked of moral rights as a shorthand way of referring to protections that people and animals morally ought to have; but the real weight of the moral argument does not rest on the assertion of the existence of the right, for this in turn has to be justified on the basis of the possibilities for suffering and happiness. In this way we can argue for equality for animals without getting embroiled in philosophical controversies about the ultimate nature of rights.

In misguided attempts to refute the arguments of this book, some philosophers have gone to much trouble developing arguments to show that animals do not have rights. They have claimed that to have rights a being must be autonomous, or must be a member of a community, or must have the ability to respect the rights of others, or must possess a sense of justice. These claims are irrelevant to the case for Animal Liberation. The language of rights is a convenient political shorthand. It is even more valuable in the era of thirty-second TV news clips than it was in Bentham's day; but in the argument for a radical change in our attitude to animals, it is in no way necessary.

If a being suffers there can be no moral justification for refusing to take that suffering into consideration. No matter what the nature of the being, the principle of equality requires that its suffering be counted equally with the like suffering—insofar as rough comparisons can be made—of any other being. If a being is not capable of suffering, or of experiencing enjoyment or happiness, there is nothing to be taken into account. So the limit of sentience (using the term as a convenient if not strictly accurate shorthand for the capacity to suffer and/or experience enjoyment) is the only defensible boundary of concern for the interests of others. To mark this boundary by some other characteristic like intelligence or rationality would be to mark it in an arbitrary manner. Why not choose some other characteristic, like skin color?

Racists violate the principle of equality by giving greater weight to the interests of members of their own race when there is a clash between their interests and the interests of those of another race. Sexists violate the principle of equality by favoring the interests of their own sex. Similarly, speciesists allow the interests of their own species to override the greater interests of members of other species. The pattern is identical in each case.

Most human beings are speciesists. . . . [O]rdinary human beings—not a few exceptionally cruel or heartless humans, but the overwhelming majority of humans—take an active part in, acquiesce in, and allow their taxes to pay for practices that require the sacrifice of the most important interests of members of other species in order to promote the most trivial interests of our own species.

There is, however, one general defense of the practices . . . that needs to be disposed of before we discuss the practices themselves. It is a defense which, if true, would allow us to do anything at all to nonhumans for the slightest reason, or for no reason at all, without incurring any justifiable reproach. This defense claims that we are never guilty of neglecting the interests of other animals for one breathtakingly simple reason: they have no interests. Nonhuman animals have no interests, according to this view, because they are not capable of suffering. By this is not meant merely that they are not capable of suffering in all the ways that human beings are—for instance, that a calf is not capable of suffering from the knowledge that it will be killed in six months time. That modest claim is, no doubt, true; but it does not clear humans of the charge of speciesism, since it allows that animals may suffer in other ways—for instance, by being given electric shocks, or being kept in small, cramped cages. The defense I am about to discuss is the much more sweeping, although correspondingly less plausible, claim that animals are incapable of suffering in any way at all; that they are, in fact, unconscious automata, possessing neither thoughts nor feelings nor a mental life of any kind. . . .

Do animals other than humans feel pain? How do we know? Well, how do we know if anyone, human or nonhuman, feels pain? We know that we ourselves can feel pain. We know this from the direct experience of pain that we have when, for instance, somebody presses a lighted cigarette against the back of our hand. But how do we know that anyone else feels pain? We cannot directly experience anyone else's pain, whether that "anyone" is our best friend or a stray dog. Pain is a state of consciousness, a "mental event," and as such it can never be observed. Behavior like writhing, screaming, or drawing one's hand away from the lighted cigarette is not pain itself; nor are the recordings a neurologist might make of activity within the brain observations of pain itself. Pain is something that we feel, and we can only infer that others are feeling it from various external indications.

In theory, we *could* always be mistaken when we assume that other human beings feel pain. It is conceivable that one of our close friends is really a cleverly constructed robot, controlled by a brilliant scientist so as to give all the signs of feeling pain, but really no more sensitive than any other machine. We can never know, with absolute certainty, that this is not the case. But while this might present a puzzle for philosophers, none of us has the slightest real doubt that our close friends feel pain just as we do. This is an inference, but a perfectly reasonable one, based on observations of their behavior in situations in which we would feel pain, and on the fact that we have every reason to assume that our friends are beings like us, with nervous systems like ours that can be assumed to function as ours do and to produce similar feelings in similar circumstances.

If it is justifiable to assume that other human beings feel pain as we do, is there any reason why a similar inference should be unjustifiable in the case of other animals?

Nearly all the external signs that lead us to infer pain in other humans can be seen in other species, especially the species most closely related to us—the species of mammals and birds. The behavioral signs include writhing, facial contortions, moaning, yelping or other forms of calling, attempts to avoid the source of pain, appearance of fear at the prospect of its repetition, and so on. In addition, we know that these animals have nervous systems very like ours, which respond physiologically as ours do when the animal is in circumstances in which we would feel pain: an initial rise of blood pressure, dilated pupils, perspiration, an increased pulse rate, and, if the stimulus continues, a fall in blood pressure. Although human beings have a more developed cerebral cortex than other animals, this part of the brain is concerned with thinking functions rather than with basic impulses, emotions, and feelings. These impulses, emotions, and feelings are located in the diencephalon, which is well developed in many other species of animals, especially mammals and birds.

We also know that the nervous systems of other animals were not artificially constructed—as a robot might be artificially constructed—to mimic the pain behavior of humans. The nervous systems of animals evolved as our own did, and in fact the evolutionary history of human beings and other animals, especially mammals, did not diverge until the central features of our nervous systems were already in existence. A capacity to feel pain obviously enhances a species' prospects of survival, since it causes members of the species to avoid sources of injury. It is surely unreasonable to suppose that nervous systems that are virtually identical physiologically, have a common origin and a common evolutionary function, and result in similar forms of behavior in similar circumstances should actually operate in an entirely different manner on the level of subjective feelings.

It has long been accepted as sound policy in science to search for the simplest possible explanation of whatever it is we are trying to explain. Occasionally it has been claimed that it is for this reason "unscientific" to explain the behavior of animals by theories that refer to the animal's conscious feelings, desires, and so on—the idea being that if the behavior in question can be explained without invoking consciousness or feelings, that will be the simpler theory. Yet we can now see that such explanations, when assessed with respect to the actual behavior of both human and nonhuman animals, are actually far more complex than rival explanations. For we know from our own experience that explanations of our own behavior that did not refer to consciousness and the feeling of pain would be incomplete; and it is simpler to assume that the similar behavior of animals with similar nervous systems is to be explained in the same way than to try to invent some other explanation for the behavior of nonhuman animals as well as an explanation for the divergence between humans and nonhumans in this respect.

The overwhelming majority of scientists who have addressed themselves to this question agree. Lord Brain, one of the most eminent neurologists of our time, has said:

> I personally can see no reason for conceding mind to my fellow men and denying it to animals. . . . I at least cannot doubt that the interests and activities of animals are correlated with awareness and feeling in the same way as my own, and which may be, for aught I know, just as vivid.

The author of a book on pain writes:

> Every particle of factual evidence supports the contention that the higher mammalian vertebrates experience pain sensations at least as acute as our own. To say that they feel less because they are lower animals is an absurdity; it can easily be shown that many of their senses are far more acute than ours—visual acuity in

certain birds, hearing in most wild animals, and touch in others; these animals depend more than we do today on the sharpest possible awareness of a hostile environment. Apart from the complexity of the cerebral cortex (which does not directly perceive pain) their nervous systems are almost identical to ours and their reactions to pain remarkably similar, though lacking (so far as we know) the philosophical and moral overtones. The emotional element is all too evident, mainly in the form of fear and anger.

In Britain, three separate expert government committees on matters relating to animals have accepted the conclusion that animals feel pain. After noting the obvious behavioral evidence for this view, the members of the Committee on Cruelty to Wild Animals, set up in 1951, said:

> . . . we believe that the physiological, and more particularly the anatomical, evidence fully justifies and reinforces the commonsense belief that animals feel pain.

And after discussing the evolutionary value of pain the committee's report concluded that pain is "of clear-cut biological usefulness" and this is "a third type of evidence that animals feel pain." The committee members then went on to consider forms of suffering other than mere physical pain and added that they were "satisfied that animals do suffer from acute fear and terror." Subsequent reports by British government committees on experiments on animals and on the welfare of animals under intensive farming methods agreed with this view, concluding that animals are capable of suffering both from straightforward physical injuries and from fear, anxiety, stress, and so on. Finally, within the last decade, the publication of scientific studies with titles such as *Animal Thought, Animal Thinking,* and *Animal Suffering: The Science of Animal Welfare* have made it plain that conscious awareness in nonhuman animals is now generally accepted as a serious subject for investigation.

That might well be thought enough to settle the matter; but one more objection needs to be considered. Human beings in pain, after all, have one behavioral sign that nonhuman animals do not have: a developed language. Other animals may communicate with each other, but not, it seems, in the complicated way we do. Some philosophers, including Descartes, have thought it important that while humans can tell each other about their experience of pain in great detail, other animals cannot. (Interestingly, this once neat dividing line between humans and other species has now been threatened by the discovery that chimpanzees can be taught a language.) But as Bentham pointed out long ago, the ability to use language is not relevant to the question of how a being ought to be treated—unless that ability can be linked to the capacity to suffer, so that the absence of a language casts doubt on the existence of this capacity.

This link may be attempted in two ways. First, there is a hazy line of philosophical thought, deriving perhaps from some doctrines associated with the influential philosopher Ludwig Wittgenstein, which maintains that we cannot meaningfully attribute states of consciousness to beings without language. This position seems to me very implausible. Language may be necessary for abstract thought, at some level anyway; but states like pain are more primitive, and have nothing to do with language.

The second and more easily understood way of linking language and the existence of pain is to say that the best evidence we can have that other creatures are in pain is that they tell us that they are. This is a distinct line of argument, for it is denying not that non-language-users conceivably *could* suffer, but only that we could ever have sufficient reason to *believe* that they are suffering. Still, this line of argument fails too. As Jane Goodall has pointed out in her study of chimpanzees, *In the Shadow of Man*, when it comes to the expression of feelings and emotions language is less important than nonlinguistic modes of communication such as a cheering pat on the back, an exuberant embrace, a clasp of the hands, and so on. The basic signals we use to convey pain, fear, anger, love, joy, surprise, sexual arousal, and many other emotional states are not specific to our own species. The statement "I am in pain" may be one piece of evidence for the conclusion that the speaker is in pain, but it is not the only possible evidence, and since people sometimes tell lies, not even the best possible evidence.

Even if there were stronger grounds for refusing to attribute pain to those who do not have a language, the consequences of this refusal might lead us to reject the conclusion. Human infants and young children are unable to use language. Are we to deny that a year-old child can suffer? If not, language cannot be crucial. Of course, most parents understand the responses of their children better than they understand the responses of other animals; but this is just a fact about the relatively greater knowledge that we have of our own species and the greater contact we have with infants as compared to animals. Those who have studied the behavior of other animals and those who have animals as companions soon learn to understand their responses as well as we understand those of an infant, and sometimes better.

So to conclude: there are no good reasons, scientific or philosophical, for denying that animals feel pain. If we do not doubt that other humans feel pain we should not doubt that other animals do so too.

Animals can feel pain. As we saw earlier, there can be no moral justification for regarding the pain (or pleasure) that animals feel as less important than the same amount of pain (or pleasure) felt by humans. But what practical consequences follow from this conclusion? To prevent misunderstanding I shall spell out what I mean a little more fully.

If I give a horse a hard slap across its rump with my open hand, the horse may start, but it presumably feels little pain. Its skin is thick enough to protect it against a mere slap. If I slap a baby in the same way, however, the baby will cry and presumably feel pain, for its skin is more sensitive. So it is worse to slap a baby than a horse, if both slaps are administered with equal force. But there must be some kind of blow—I don't know exactly what it would be, but perhaps a blow with a heavy stick—that would cause the horse as much pain as we cause a baby by slapping it with our hand. That is what I mean by "the same amount of pain," and if we consider it wrong to inflict that much pain on a baby for no good reason then we must, unless we are speciesists, consider it equally wrong to inflict the same amount of pain on a horse for no good reason.

Other differences between humans and animals cause other complications. Normal adult human beings have mental capacities that will, in certain circumstances, lead them to suffer more than animals would in the same circumstances. If, for instance, we decided to perform extremely painful or lethal scientific experiments on normal adult humans, kidnapped at random from public parks for this purpose, adults who enjoy strolling in parks would become fearful that they would be kidnapped. The resultant terror would be a form of suffering additional to the pain of the experiment. The same experiments performed on nonhuman animals would cause less suffering since the animals would not have the anticipatory dread of being kidnapped and experimented upon. This does not mean, of course, that it would be *right* to perform the experiment on animals, but only that there is a reason, which is *not* speciesist, for preferring to use animals rather than normal adult human beings, if the experiment is to be done at all. It should be noted, however, that this same argument gives us a reason for preferring to use human infants—orphans perhaps—or severely retarded human beings for experiments, rather than adults, since infants and retarded humans would also have no idea of what was going to happen to them. So far as this argument is concerned nonhuman animals and infants and retarded humans are in the same category; and if we use this argument to justify experiments on nonhuman animals we have to ask ourselves whether we are also prepared to allow experiments on human infants and retarded adults; and if we make a distinction between animals and these humans, on what basis can we do it other than a bare-faced—and morally indefensible—preference for members of our own species?

There are many matters in which the superior mental powers of normal adult humans make a difference: anticipation, more detailed memory, greater knowledge of what is happening, and so on. Yet these differences do not all point to greater suffering on the part of the normal human being. Sometimes animals may suffer more because of their more limited understanding. If, for instance, we are taking prisoners in wartime we can explain to them that although they must submit to capture, search, and confinement, they will not otherwise be harmed and will be set free at the conclusion of hostilities. If we capture wild animals, however, we cannot explain that we are not threatening their lives. A wild animal cannot distinguish an attempt to overpower and confine from an attempt to kill; the one causes as much terror as the other.

It may be objected that comparisons of the sufferings of different species are impossible to make and that for this reason when the interests of animals and humans clash the principle of equality gives no guidance. It is probably true that comparisons of suffering between members of different species cannot be made precisely, but precision is not essential. Even if we were to prevent the infliction of suffering on animals only when it is quite certain that the interests of humans will not be affected to anything like the extent that animals are affected, we would be forced to make radical changes in our treatment of animals that would involve our diet, the farming methods we use, experimental procedures in many fields of science, our approach to wildlife and to hunting, trapping and the wearing of furs, and areas of entertainment like circuses, rodeos, and zoos. As a result, a vast amount of suffering would be avoided.

So far I have said a lot about inflicting suffering on animals, but nothing about killing them. This omission has been deliberate. The application of the principle of equality to the infliction of suffering is, in theory at least, fairly straightforward. Pain and suffering are in themselves bad and should be prevented or minimized, irrespective of the race, sex, or species of the being that suffers. How bad a pain is depends on how intense it is and how long it lasts, but pains of the same intensity and duration are equally bad, whether felt by humans or animals.

The wrongness of killing a being is more complicated. I have kept, and shall continue to keep, the question of killing in the background because in the present state of human tyranny over other species the more simple, straightforward principle of equal consideration of pain or pleasure is a sufficient basis for identifying and protesting against all the major abuses of animals that human beings practice. Nevertheless, it is necessary to say something about killing.

Just as most human beings are speciesists in their readiness to cause pain to animals when they would not cause a similar pain to humans for the same reason, so most human beings are speciesists in their readiness to kill other animals when they would not kill human beings. We need to proceed more cautiously here, however, because people hold widely differing views about when it is legitimate to kill humans, as the continuing debates over abortion and euthanasia attest. Nor have moral philosophers been able to agree on exactly what it is that makes it wrong to kill human beings, and under what circumstances killing a human being may be justifiable.

Let us consider first the view that it is always wrong to take an innocent human life. We may call this the "sanctity of life" view. People who take this view oppose abortion and euthanasia. They do not usually, however, oppose the killing of nonhuman animals—so perhaps it would be more accurate to describe this view as the "sanctity of *human* life" view. The belief that human life, and only human life, is sacrosanct is a form of speciesism. To see this, consider the following example.

Assume that, as sometimes happens, an infant has been born with massive and irreparable brain damage. The damage is so severe that the infant can never be any more than a "human vegetable," unable to talk, recognize other people, act independently of others, or develop a sense of self-awareness. The parents of the infant, realizing that they cannot hope for any improvement in their child's condition and being in any case unwilling to spend, or ask the state to spend, the thousands of dollars that would be needed annually for proper care of the infant, ask the doctor to kill the infant painlessly.

Should the doctor do what the parents ask? Legally, the doctor should not, and in this respect the law reflects the sanctity of life view. The life of every human being is sacred. Yet people who would say this about the infant do not object to the killing of nonhuman animals. How can they justify their different judgments? Adult chimpanzees, dogs, pigs, and members of many other species far surpass the brain-damaged infant in their ability to relate to others, act independently, be self-aware, and any other capacity that could reasonably be said to give value to life. With the most intensive care possible, some severely retarded infants can never achieve the intelligence level of a dog. Nor can we appeal to the concern of the infant's parents, since they themselves, in this imaginary example (and in some actual cases) do not want the infant kept alive. The only thing that distinguishes the infant from the animal, in the eyes of those who claim it has a "right to life," is that it is, biologically, a member of the species Homo sapiens, whereas chimpanzees, dogs, and pigs are not. But to use *this* difference as the basis for granting a right to life to the infant and not to the other animals is, of course, pure speciesism. It is exactly the kind of arbitrary difference that the most crude and overt kind of racist uses in attempting to justify racial discrimination.

This does not mean that to avoid speciesism we must hold that it is as wrong to kill a dog as it is to kill a human being in full possession of his or her faculties. The only position that is irredeemably speciesist is the one that tries to make the boundary of the right to life run exactly parallel to the boundary of our own species. Those who hold the sanctity of life view do this, because while distinguishing sharply between human beings and other animals they allow no distinctions to be made within our own species, objecting to the killing of the severely retarded and the hopelessly senile as strongly as they object to the killing of normal adults.

To avoid speciesism we must allow that beings who are similar in all relevant respects have a similar right to life—and mere membership in our own biological species cannot be a morally relevant criterion for this right. Within these limits we could still hold, for instance, that it is worse to kill a normal adult human, with a capacity for self-awareness and the ability to plan for the future and have meaningful relations with others, than it is to kill a mouse, which presumably does not share all of these characteristics; or we might appeal to the close family and other personal ties that humans have but mice do not have to the same degree; or we might think that it is the consequences for other humans, who will be put in fear for their own lives, that makes the crucial difference; or we might think it is some combination of these factors, or other factors altogether.

Whatever criteria we choose, however, we will have to admit that they do not follow precisely the boundary of our own species. We may legitimately hold that there are some features of certain beings that make their lives more valuable than those of other beings; but there will surely be some nonhuman animals whose lives, by any standards, are more valuable than the lives of some humans. A chimpanzee, dog, or pig, for instance, will have a higher degree of self-awareness and a greater capacity for meaningful relations with others than a severely retarded infant or someone in a state of advanced senility. So if we base the right to life on these characteristics we must grant these animals a right to life as good as, or better than, such retarded or senile humans.

This argument cuts both ways. It could be taken as showing that chimpanzees, dogs, and pigs, along with some other species, have a right to life and we commit a grave moral offense whenever we kill them, even when they are old and suffering and our intention is to put them out of their misery. Alternatively one could take the argument as showing that the severely retarded and hopelessly senile have no right to life and may be killed for quite trivial reasons, as we now kill animals.

Since the main concern of this book is with ethical questions having to do with animals and not with the morality of euthanasia I shall not attempt to settle this issue finally. I think it is reasonably clear, though, that while both of the positions just described avoid speciesism, neither is satisfactory. What we need is some middle position that would avoid speciesism but would not make the lives of the retarded and senile as cheap as the lives of pigs and dogs now are, or make the lives of pigs and dogs so sacrosanct that we think it wrong to put them out of hopeless misery. What we must do is bring nonhuman animals within our sphere of moral concern and cease to treat their lives as expendable for whatever trivial purposes we may have. At the same time, once we realize that the fact that a being is a member of our own species is not in itself enough to make it always wrong to kill that being, we may come to reconsider our policy of preserving human lives at all costs, even when there is no prospect of a meaningful life or of existence without terrible pain.

I conclude, then, that a rejection of speciesism does not imply that all lives are of equal worth. While self-awareness, the capacity to think ahead and have hopes and aspirations for the future, the capacity for meaningful relations with others and so on are not relevant to the question of inflicting pain—since pain is pain, whatever other capacities, beyond the capacity to feel pain, the being may have—these capacities are relevant to the question of taking life. It is not arbitrary to hold that the life of a self-aware being, capable of abstract thought, of planning for the future, of complex acts of communication, and so on, is more valuable than the life of a being without these capacities. To see the difference between the issues of inflicting pain and taking life, consider how we would choose within our own species. If we had to choose to save the life of a normal human being or an intellectually disabled human being, we would probably choose to save the life of a normal human being; but if we had to choose between preventing pain in the normal human being or the intellectually disabled one—imagine that both have received painful but superficial injuries, and we only have enough painkiller for one of them—it is not nearly so clear how we ought to choose. The same is true when we consider other species. The evil of pain is, in itself, unaffected by the other characteristics of the being who feels the pain; the value of life is affected by these other characteristics. To give just one reason for this difference, to take the life of a being who has been hoping, planning, and working for some future goal is to deprive that being of the fulfillment of all those efforts; to take the life of a being with a mental capacity below the level needed to grasp that one is a being with a future—much less make plans for the future—cannot involve this particular kind of loss.

Normally this will mean that if we have to choose between the life of a human being and the life of another animal we should choose to save the life of the human; but there may be special cases in which the reverse holds true, because the human being in question does not have the capacities of a normal human being. So this view is not speciesist, although it may appear to be at first glance. The preference, in normal cases, for saving a human life over the life of an animal when a choice *has* to be made is a preference based on the characteristics that normal humans have, and not on the mere fact that they are members of our own species. This is why when we consider members of our own species who lack the characteristics of normal humans we can no longer say that their lives are always to be preferred to those of other animals. . . . In general, though, the question of when it is wrong to kill (painlessly) an animal is one to which we need give no precise answer. As long as we remember that we should give the same respect to the lives of animals as we give to the lives of those humans at a similar mental level, we shall not go far wrong.

In any case, the conclusions that are argued for in this book flow from the principle of minimizing suffering alone. The idea that it is also wrong to kill animals painlessly gives some of these conclusions additional support that is welcome but strictly unnecessary. Interestingly enough, this is true even of the conclusion that we ought to become vegetarians, a conclusion that in the popular mind is generally based on some kind of absolute prohibition on killing. . . .

That is why I have chosen to discuss these particular forms of speciesism. They are at its heart. They cause more suffering to a greater number of animals than anything else that human beings do. To stop them we must change the policies of our government, and we must change our own lives, to the extent of changing our diet. If these officially promoted and almost universally accepted forms of speciesism can be abolished, abolition of the other speciesist practices cannot be far behind.

The Radical Egalitarian Case for Animal Rights

Tom Regan

I regard myself as an advocate of animal rights—as a part of the animal rights movement. That movement, as I conceive it, is committed to a number of goals, including:

1. the total abolition of the use of animals in science
2. the total dissolution of commercial animal agriculture
3. and the total elimination of commercial and sport hunting and trapping.

There are, I know, people who profess to believe in animal rights who do not avow these goals. Factory farming they say, is wrong—violates animals' rights—but traditional animal agriculture is all right. Toxicity tests of cosmetics on animals violate their rights; but not important medical research—cancer research, for example. The clubbing of baby seals is abhorrent; but not the harvesting of adult seals. I used to think I understood this reasoning. Not any more. You don't change unjust institutions by tidying them up.

What's wrong—what's fundamentally wrong—with the way animals are treated isn't the details that vary from case to case. It's the whole system. The forlornness of the veal calf is pathetic—heart wrenching; the pulsing pain of the chimp with electrodes planted deep in her brain is repulsive; the slow, torturous death of the raccoon caught in the leg hold trap, agonizing. But what is fundamentally wrong isn't the pain, isn't the suffering, isn't the deprivation. These compound what's wrong. Sometimes—often—they make it much worse. But they are not the fundamental wrong.

The fundamental wrong is the system that allows us to view animals as our resources, here for us—to be eaten, or surgically manipulated, or put in our cross hairs for sport or money. Once we accept this view of animals—as our resources—the rest is as predictable as it is regrettable. Why worry about their loneliness, their pain, their death? Since animals exist for us, here to benefit us in one way or another, what harms them really doesn't matter—or matters only if it starts to bother us, makes us feel a trifle uneasy when we eat our veal scampi, for example. So, yes, let us get veal calves out of solitary confinement, give them more space, a little straw, a few companions. But let us keep our veal scampi.

But a little straw, more space, and a few companions don't eliminate—don't even touch—the fundamental wrong, the wrong that attaches to our viewing and treating these animals as our resources. A veal calf killed to be eaten after living in close confinement is viewed and treated in this way: but so, too, is another who is raised (as they say) "more humanely." To right the fundamental wrong of our treatment of farm animals requires more than making rearing methods "more human"—requires something quite different—requires the *total dissolution of commercial animal agriculture.*

How we do this—whether we do this, or as in the case of animals in science, whether and how we abolish their use—these are to a large extent political questions. People must change their beliefs before they change their habits. Enough people, especially those elected to public office, must believe in change—must want it—before we will have laws that protect the rights of animals. This process of change is very complicated, very demanding, very exhausting, calling for the efforts of many hands—in education, publicity, political organization and activity, down to the licking of envelopes and stamps. As a trained and practicing philosopher the sort of contribution I can make is limited, but I like to think, important. The currency of philosophy is ideas—their meaning and rational foundation—not the nuts and bolts of the legislative process say, or the mechanics of community organization. That's what I have been exploring over the past ten years or so in my essays and talks and, more recently, in my book, *The Case for Animal Rights.*[1] I believe the major conclusions I reach in that book are true because they are supported by the weight of the *best arguments.* I believe the idea of animal rights has reason, not just emotion, on its side.

In the space I have at my disposal here I can only sketch, in the barest outlines, some of the main features of the book. Its main themes—and we should not be surprised by this—involve asking and answering deep foundational moral questions, questions about what morality is, how it should be understood, what is the best moral theory all considered. I hope I can convey something of the shape I think this theory is. The attempt to do this will be—to use a word a friendly critic once used to describe my work—cerebral. In fact I was told by this person that my work is "too cerebral." But this is misleading. My feelings about how animals sometimes are treated are just as deep and just as strong as those of my more volatile compatriots. Philosophers do—to use the jargon of the day—have a right side to their brains. If it's the left side we contribute or mainly should—that's because what talents we have reside there.

How to proceed? We begin by asking how the moral status of animals has been understood by thinkers who deny that animals have rights. Then we test the mettle of their ideas by seeing how well they stand up under the heat of fair criticism. If we start our thinking in this way we soon find that some people believe that we have no duties directly to animals—that we owe nothing to *them*—that we can do nothing that *wrongs them.* Rather, we can do wrong acts that involve animals, and so we have duties regarding them, though none to them. Such views may be called indirect duty views. By way of illustration:

Suppose your neighbor kicks your dog. Then your neighbor has done something wrong. But not to your dog. The wrong that has been done is a wrong to you. After all, it is wrong to upset people, and your neighbor's kicking your dog upsets you. So you are the one who is wronged, not your dog. Or again: by kicking your dog your neighbor damages your property. And since it is wrong to damage another person's property, your neighbor has done something wrong—to you, of course, not to your dog. Your neighbor no more wrongs your dog than your car would be wronged if the windshield were smashed. Your neighbor's duties involving your dog are indirect duties to you. More generally, all of our duties regarding animals are indirect duties to one another—to humanity.

How could someone try to justify such a view? One could say that your dog doesn't feel anything and so isn't hurt by your neighbor's kick, doesn't care about the pain since none is felt, is as unaware of anything as your windshield. Someone could say this but no rational person will since, among other considerations, such a view will commit one who holds it to the position that no human being feels pain either—that human beings also don't care about what happens to them. A second possibility is that though both humans and your dog are hurt when kicked, it is only human pain that matters. But, again, no rational person can believe this. Pain is pain wheresoever it occurs. If your neighbor's causing you pain is wrong because of the pain that is caused, we cannot rationally ignore or dismiss the moral relevance of the pain your dog feels.

Philosophers who hold indirect duty views—and many still do—have come to understand that they must avoid the two defects just noted—avoid, that is, both the view that animals don't feel anything as well as the idea that only human pain can be morally relevant. Among such thinkers the sort of view now favored is one or another form of what is called *contractarianism*.

Here, very crudely, is the root idea: morality consists of a set of rules that individuals voluntarily agree to abide by—as we do when we sign a contract (hence the name: contractarianism). Those who understand and accept the terms of the contract are covered directly—have rights created by, and recognized and protected in, the contract. And these contractors can also have protection spelled out for others who, though they lack the ability to understand morality and so cannot sign the contract themselves, are loved or cherished by those who can. Thus young children, for example, are unable to sign and lack rights. But they are protected by the contract nonetheless because of the sentimental interests of others, most notably their parents. So we have, then, duties involving these children, duties regarding them, but no duties to them. Our duties in their case are indirect duties to other human beings, usually their parents.

As for animals, since they cannot understand the contract, they obviously cannot sign; and since they cannot sign; they have no rights. Like children, however, some animals are the objects of the sentimental interest of others. You, for example, love your dog . . . or cat. So these animals—those enough people care about: companion animals, whales, baby seals, the American bald eagle—these animals, though they lack rights themselves, will be protected because of the sentimental interests of people. I have, then, according to contractarianism, no duty directly to your dog or any other animal, not even the duty not to cause them pain or suffering; my duty not to hurt them is a duty I have to those people who care about what happens to them. As for other animals, where no or little sentimental interest is present—farm animals, for example, or laboratory rats—what duties we have grow weaker and weaker, perhaps to the vanishing point. The pain and death they endure, though real, are not wrong if no one cares about them.

Contractarianism could be a hard view to refute when it comes to the moral status of animals if it was an adequate theoretical approach to the moral status of human beings. It is not adequate in this latter respect, however, which makes the question of its adequacy in the former—regarding animals—utterly moot. For consider: morality, according to the (crude) contractarian position before us, consists of rules people agree to abide by. What people? Well, enough to make a difference—enough, that is, so that collectively they have the power to enforce the rules that are drawn up in the contract. That is very well and good for the signatories—but not so good for anyone who is not asked to sign. And there is nothing in contractarianism of the sort we are discussing that guarantees or requires that everyone will have a chance to participate equitably in framing the rules of morality. The result is that this approach to ethics could sanction the most blatant forms of social, economic, moral, and political injustice, ranging from a repressive caste system to systematic racial or sexual discrimination. Might, on this theory, does make right. Let those who are the victims of injustice suffer as they will. It matters not so long as no one else—no contractor, or too few of them—cares about it. Such a theory takes one's moral breath away . . . as if, for example, there is nothing wrong with apartheid in South Africa if too few white South Africans are upset by it. A theory with so little to recommend it at the level of the ethics of our treatment of our fellow humans cannot have anything more to recommend it when it comes to the ethics of how we treat our fellow animals.

The version of contractarianism just examined is, as I have noted, a crude variety, and in fairness to those of a contractarian persuasion it must be noted that much more refined, subtle, and ingenious varieties are possible. For example, John Rawls, in his *A Theory of Justice,* sets forth a version of contractarianism that forces the contractors to ignore the accidental features of being a human being—for example, whether one is white or black, male or female, a genius or of modest intellect. Only by ignoring such features, Rawls believes, can we insure that the principles of justice contractors would agree upon are not based on bias or prejudice. Despite the improvement a view such as Rawls's shows over the cruder forms of contractarianism, it remains deficient: it systematically denies that we have direct duties to those human beings who do not have a sense of justice—young children, for instance, and many mentally retarded humans. And yet it seems reasonably certain that, were we to torture a young child or a retarded elder, we would be doing something that wrongs them, not something that is wrong if (and only if) other humans with a sense of justice are upset. And since this is true in the case of these humans, we cannot rationally deny the same in the case of animals.

Indirect duty views, then, including the best among them, fail to command our rational assent. Whatever ethical theory we rationally should accept, therefore, it must at least recognize that we have some duties directly to animals, just as we have some duties directly to each other. The next two theories I'll sketch attempt to meet this requirement.

The first I call the *cruelty-kindness* view. Simply stated, this view says that we have a direct duty to be kind to animals and a direct duty not to be cruel to them. Despite the familiar, reassuring ring of these ideas, I do not believe this view offers an adequate theory. To make this clearer, consider kindness. A kind person acts from a certain kind of motive—compassion or concern, for example. And that is a virtue. But there is no guarantee that a kind act is a right act. If I am a generous racist, for example, I will be inclined to act kindly toward members of my own own race, favoring their interests above others. My kindness would be real and, so far as it goes, good. But I trust it is too obvious to require comment that my kind acts may not be above moral reproach—may, in fact, be positively wrong because rooted in injustice. So kindness, not withstanding its status as a virtue to be encouraged, simply will not cancel the weight of a theory of right action.

Cruelty fares no better. People or their acts are cruel if they display either a lack of sympathy for or, worse, the presence of enjoyment in, seeing another suffer. Cruelty in all its guises *is* a bad thing—*is* a tragic human failing. But just as a person's being motivated by kindness does not guarantee that they do what is right, so the absence of cruelty does not assure that they avoid doing what is wrong. Many people who perform abortions, for example, are not cruel, sadistic people. But that fact about their character and motivation does not settle the terribly difficult question about the morality of abortion. The case is no different when we examine the ethics of our treatment of animals. So, yes, let us be for kindness and against cruelty. But let us not suppose that being for the one and against the other answers questions about moral right and wrong.

Some people think the theory we are looking for is *utilitarianism*. A utilitarian accepts two moral principles. The first is a principle of *equality: everyone's interests count, and similar interests must be counted as having similar weight or importance.* White or black, male or female, American or Iranian, human or animal: everyone's pain or frustration matter and matter equally with the like pain or frustration of anyone else. The second principle a utilitarian accepts is the principle of *utility: do that act that will bring about the best balance of satisfaction over frustration for everyone affected by the outcome.*

As a utilitarian, then, here is how I am to approach the task of deciding what I morally ought to do: I must ask who will be affected if I choose to do one thing rather than another, how much each individual will be affected, and where the best results are most likely to lie—which option, in other words, is most likely to bring about the best results, the best balance of satisfaction over frustration. That option, whatever it may be, is the one I ought to choose. That is where my moral duty lies.

The great appeal of utilitarianism rests with its uncompromising *egalitarianism:* everyone's interests count and count equally with the like interests of everyone else. The kind of odious discrimination some forms of contractarianism can justify—discrimination based on race or sex, for example— seems disallowed in principle by utilitarianism, as is speciesism—systematic discrimination based on species membership.

The sort of equality we find in utilitarianism, however, is not the sort an advocate of animal or human rights should have in mind. Utilitarianism has no room for the *equal moral rights of different individuals because it has no room for their equal inherent value or worth.* What has value for the utilitarian is the satisfaction of an individual's interests, not the individual whose interests they are. A universe in which you satisfy your desire for water, food, and warmth, is, other things being equal, better than a universe in which these desires are frustrated. And the same is true in the case of an animal with similar desires. But neither you nor the animal have any value in your own right. *Only your feelings do.*

Here is an analogy to help make the philosophical point clearer: a cup contains different liquids—sometimes sweet, sometimes bitter, sometimes a mix of the two. What has value are the liquids: the sweeter the better, the bitter the worse. The cup—the container—has no value. It's what goes into it, not what they go into, that has value. For the utilitarian, you and I are like the cup; we have no value as individuals and thus no equal value. What has value is what goes into us, what we serve as receptacles for; our feelings of satisfaction have positive value, our feelings of frustration have negative value.

Serious problems arise for utilitarianism when we remind ourselves that it enjoins us to bring about the best consequences. What does this mean? It doesn't mean the best consequences for me alone, or for my family or friends, or any other person taken individually. No, what we must do is, roughly, as follows: we must add up—somehow!—the separate satisfactions and frustrations of everyone likely to be affected by our choice, the satisfactions in one column, the frustrations in the other. We must total each column for each of the opinions before us. That is what it means to say the theory is aggregative. And then we must choose that option which is most likely to bring about the best balance of totaled satisfactions over totaled frustrations. Whatever act would lead to this outcome is the one we morally ought to perform—is where our moral duty lies. And that act quite clearly might not be the same one that would bring about the best results for me personally, or my family or friends, or a lab animal. The best aggregated consequences for everyone concerned are not necessarily the best for each individual.

That utilitarianism is an aggregative theory—that different individual's satisfactions or frustrations are added, or summed, or totaled—is the key objection to this theory. My Aunt Bea is old, inactive, a cranky, sour person, though not physically ill. She prefers to go on living. She is also rather rich. I could make a fortune if I could get my hands on her money, money she intends to give me in any event, after she dies, but which she refuses to give me now. In order to avoid a huge tax bite, I plan to donate a handsome sum of my profits to a local children's hospital. Many, many children will benefit from my generosity, and much joy will be brought to their parents, relatives, and friends. If I don't get the money rather soon, all these ambitions will come to naught. The once-in-a-lifetime-opportunity to make a real killing will be gone. Why, then, not really kill my Aunt Bea? Oh, of course I *might* get caught. But I'm no fool and, besides, her doctor can be counted on to cooperate (he has an eye for the same investment and I happen to know a good deal about his shady past). The deed can be done . . . professionally, shall we say. There is *very* little chance of getting caught. And as for my conscience being guilt ridden, I am a resourceful sort of fellow and will take more than sufficient comfort—as I lie on the beach at Acapulco—in contemplating the joy and health I have brought to so many others.

Suppose Aunt Bea is killed and the rest of the story comes out as told. Would I have done anything wrong? Anything immoral? One would have thought that I had. But not according to utilitarianism. Since what I did brought about the best balance of totaled satisfaction over frustration for all those affected by the outcome, what I did was not wrong. Indeed, in killing Aunt Bea the physician and I did what duty required.

This same kind of argument can be repeated in all sorts of cases, illustrating time after time, how the utilitarian's position leads to results that impartial people find morally callous. It is wrong to kill my Aunt Bea in the name of bringing about the best results for others. A good end does not justify an evil means. Any adequate moral theory will have to explain why this is so. Utilitarianism fails in this respect and so cannot be the theory we seek.

What to do? Where to begin anew? The place to begin, I think, is with the utilitarian's view of the value of the individual—or, rather, lack of value. In its place suppose we consider that you and I, for example, do have value as individuals—what we'll call *inherent value*. To say we have such value is to say that we are something more than, something different from, mere receptacles. Moreover, to insure that we do not pave the way for such injustices as slavery or sexual discrimination, we must believe that all who have inherent value have it equally, regardless of their sex, race, religion, birthplace, and so on. Similarly to be discarded as irrelevant are one's talents or skills, intelligence and wealth, personality or pathology, whether one is loved and admired—or despised and loathed. The genius and the retarded child, the prince and the pauper, the brain surgeon and the fruit vendor, Mother Theresa and the most unscrupulous used car salesman—all have inherent value, all possess it *equally,* and *all have an equal right to be treated with respect,* to be treated in ways that do not reduce them to the status of things, as if they exist as resources for others. My value as an individual is independent of my usefulness to you. Yours is not dependent on your usefulness to me. For either of us to treat the other in ways that fail to show respect for the other's independent value is to act immorally—is to violate the individual's rights.

Some of the rational virtues of this view—what I call the rights view—should be evident. Unlike (crude) contractarianism, for example, the rights view *in principle* denies the moral tolerability of any and all forms of racial, sexual, or social discrimination; and unlike utilitarianism, this view *in principle* denies that we can justify good results by using evil means that violate an individual's rights—denies, for example, that it could be moral to kill my Aunt Bea to harvest beneficial consequences for others. That would be to sanction the disrespectful treatment of the individual in the name of the social good, something the rights view will not—categorically will not—ever allow.

The rights view—or so I believe—is rationally the most satisfactory moral theory. It surpasses all other theories in the degree to which it illuminates and explains the foundation of our duties to one another—the domain of human morality. On this score, it has the best reasons, the best arguments, on its side. Of course, if it were possible to show that only human beings are included within its scope, then a person like myself, who believes in animal rights, would be obliged to look elsewhere than to the rights view.

But attempts to limit its scope to humans only can be shown to be rationally defective. Animals, it is true, lack many of the abilities humans possess. They can't read, do higher mathematics, build a bookcase, or make *baba ghanoush.* Neither can many human beings, however, and yet we don't say—and shouldn't say—that they (these humans) therefore have less inherent value, less of a right to be treated with respect, than do others. It is the *similarities* between those human beings who most clearly, most noncontroversially have such value—the people reading this, for example—it is our similarities, not our differences, that matter most. And the really crucial, the basic similarity is simply this; *we are each of us the experiencing subject of a life, each of us a conscious creature having an individual welfare that has importance to us whatever our usefulness to others.* We want and prefer things; believe and feel things; recall and expect things. And all these dimensions of our life, including our pleasure and pain, our enjoyment and suffering, our satisfaction and frustration, our continued existence or our untimely death—all make a difference to the quality of our life as lived, as experienced by us as individuals. As the same is true of those animals who concern us (those who are eaten and trapped, for example), they, too, must be viewed as the experiencing subjects of a life with inherent value of their own.

There are some who resist the idea that animals have inherent value. "Only humans have such value," they profess. How might this narrow view be defended? Shall we say that only humans have the requisite intelligence, or autonomy, or reason? But there are many, many humans who will fail to meet these standards and yet who are reasonably viewed as having value above and beyond their usefulness to others. Shall we claim that only humans belong to the right species—the species *Homo sapiens?* But this is blatant speciesism. Will it be said, then, that all—and only—humans have immortal souls? Then our opponents more than have their work cut out for them. I am myself not ill-disposed to there being immortal souls. Personally, I profoundly hope I have one. But I would not want to rest my position on a controversial, ethical issue on the even more controversial question about who or what has an immortal soul. That is to dig one's hole deeper, not climb out. Rationally, it is better to resolve moral issues without making more controversial assumptions than are needed. The question of who has inherent value is such a question, one that is more rationally resolved without the introduction of the idea of immortal souls than by its use.

Well, perhaps some will say that animals have some inherent value, only *less* than we do. Once again, however, attempts to defend this view can be shown to lack rational justification. What could be the basis of our having more inherent value than animals? Will it be their lack of reason, or autonomy, or intellect? Only if we are willing to make the same judgment in the case of humans who are similarly deficient. But it is not true that such humans—the retarded child, for example, or the mentally deranged—have less inherent value than you or I. Neither, then, can we rationally sustain the view that animals like them in being the experiencing subjects of a life have less inherent value. *All who have inherent value have it equally, whether they be human animals or not.*

Inherent value, then, belongs equally to those who are the experiencing subjects of a life. Whether it belongs to others—to rocks and rivers, trees and glaciers, for example—we do not know. And may never know. But neither do we need to know, if we are to make the case for animal rights. We do not need to know how many people, for example, are eligible to vote in the next presidential election before we can know whether I am. Similarly, we do not need to know *how many* individuals have inherent value before we can know that some do. When it comes to the case for animal rights, then what we need to know is whether the animals who, in our culture are routinely eaten, hunted, and used in our laboratories, for example, are like us in being subjects of a life. And we *do* know this. We do *know* that many—literally, billions and billions—of these animals are subjects of a life in the sense explained and so have inherent value if we do. And since, in order to have the best theory of our duties to one another, we must recognize our equal inherent value, as individuals, *reason*—not sentiment, not emotion—*reason compels us to recognize the equal inherent value of these animals.* And, with this, their equal right to be treated with respect.

That, *very* roughly, is the shape and feel of the case for animal rights. Most of the details of the supporting argument are missing. They are to be found in the book I alluded to earlier. Here, the details go begging and I must in closing, limit myself to four final points.

The first is how the theory that underlies the case for animal rights shows that the animal rights movement is a part of, not antagonistic to, the human rights movement. The theory that rationally grounds the rights of animals also grounds the rights of humans. Thus are those involved in the animal rights movement partners in the struggle to secure respect for human rights—the rights of women, for example, or minorities and workers. The animal rights movement is cut from the same moral cloth as these.

Second, having set out the broad outlines of the rights view, I can now say why its *implications for farming and science,* for example, are both clear and uncompromising. In the case of using animals in science, the rights view is categorically abolitionist. *Lab animals are not our tasters; we are not their kings.* Because these animals are treated—routinely, systematically—as if their value is reducible to their usefulness to others, they are routinely systematically treated with a lack of respect, and thus their rights routinely, systematically violated. This is just as true when they are used in trivial, duplicative, unnecessary or unwise research as it is when they are used in studies that hold out real promise of human benefits. We can't justify harming or killing a human being (my Aunt Bea, for example) just for these sorts of reasons. Neither can we do so even in the case of so lowly a creature as a laboratory rat. It is not just refinement or reduction that are called for, not just larger, cleaner cages, not just more generous use of anesthetic or the elimination of multiple surgery, not just tidying up the system. It is replacement—completely. The best we can do when it comes to using animals in science is—not to use them. That is where our duty lies, according to the rights view.

As for commercial animal agriculture, the rights view takes a similar abolitionist position. The fundamental moral wrong here is not that animals are kept in stressful close confinement, or in isolation, or that they have their pain and suffering, their needs and preferences ignored or discounted. *All* these *are* wrong, of course, but they are not the fundamental wrong. They are symptoms and effects of the deeper, systematic wrong that allows these animals to be viewed and treated as lacking independent value, as resources for us—as, indeed, a renewable resource. Giving farm animals more space, more natural environments, more companions does not right the fundamental wrong, any more than giving lab animals more anesthesia or bigger, cleaner cages would right the fundamental wrong in their case. Nothing less than the total dissolution of commercial animal agriculture will do this, just as, for similar reasons I won't develop at length here, morality requires nothing less than the total elimination of commercial and sport hunting and trapping. The rights view's implications, then, as I have said, are clear—and are uncompromising.

My last two points are about philosophy—my profession. It is most obviously, no substitute for political action. The words I have written here and in other places by themselves don't change a thing. It is what we do with the thoughts the words express—our acts, our deeds—that change things. All that philosophy can do, and all I have attempted, is to offer a vision of what our deeds could aim at. And the why. But not the how.

Finally, I am reminded of my thoughtful critic, the one I mentioned earlier, who chastised me for being "too cerebral." Well, cerebral I have been: indirect duty views, utilitarianism, contractarianism—hardly the stuff deep passions are made of. I am also reminded, however, of the image another friend once set before me—the image of the ballerina as expressive of disciplined passion. Long hours of sweat and toil, of loneliness and practice, of doubt and fatigue; that is the discipline of her craft. But the passion is there, too: the fierce drive to excel, to speak through her body, to do it right, to pierce our minds. That is the image of philosophy I would leave with you; not "too cerebral," but *disciplined passion*. Of the discipline, enough has been seen. As for the passion:

There are times, and these are not infrequent, when tears come to my eyes when I see, or read, or hear of the wretched plight of animals in the hands of humans. Their pain, their suffering, their loneliness, their innocence, their death. Anger. Rage. Pity. Sorrow. Disgust. The whole creation groans under the weight of the evil we humans visit upon these mute, powerless creatures. It *is* our heart, not just our head, that calls for an end, that demands of us that we overcome, for them, the habits and forces behind their systematic oppression. All great movements, it is written, go through three stages: ridicule, discussion, adoption. It is the realization of this third stage—adoption—that demands both our passion and our discipline, our heart and our head. *The fate of animals is in our hands. God grant we are equal to the task.*

NOTE

1. Tom Regan, *The Case for Animal Rights* (Berkeley: University of California Press, 1983).

A Critique of Regan's Animal Rights Theory

Mary Anne Warren

Tom Regan has produced what is perhaps the definitive defense of the view that the basic moral rights of at least some non-human animals are in no way inferior to our own. In *The Case for Animal Rights*, he argues that all normal mammals over a year of age have the same basic moral rights.[1] Non-human mammals have essentially the same right not to be harmed or killed as we do. I shall call this "the strong animal rights position," although it is weaker than the claims made by some animal liberationists in that it ascribes rights to only some sentient animals.[2]

I will argue that Regan's case for the strong animal rights position is unpersuasive and that this position entails consequences which a reasonable person cannot accept. I do not deny that some non-human animals have moral rights; indeed, I would extend the scope of the rights claim to include all sentient animals, that is, all those capable of having experiences, including experiences of pleasure or satisfaction and pain, suffering, or frustration.[3] However, I do not think that the moral rights of most non-human animals are identical in strength to those of persons.[4] The rights of most non-human animals may be overridden in circumstances which would not justify overriding the rights of persons. There are, for instance, compelling realities which sometimes require that we kill animals for reasons which could not justify the killing of persons. I will call this view "the weak animal rights" position, even though it ascribes rights to a wider range of animals than does the strong animal rights position.

I will begin by summarizing Regan's case for the strong animal rights position and noting two problems with it. Next, I will explore some consequences of the strong animal rights position which I think are unacceptable. Finally, I will outline the case for the weak animal rights position.

REGAN'S CASE

Regan's argument moves through three stages. First, he argues that normal, mature mammals are not only sentient but have other mental capacities as well. These include the capacities for emotion, memory, belief, desire, the use of general concepts, intentional action, a sense of the future, and some degree of self-awareness. Creatures with such capacities are said to be subjects-of-a-life. They are not only alive in the biological sense but have a psychological identity over time and an existence which can go better or worse for them. Thus, they can be harmed or benefited. These are plausible claims, and well defended. One of the strongest parts of the book is the rebuttal of philosophers, such as R. G. Frey, who object to the application of such mentalistic terms to creatures that do not use a human-style language.[5] The second and third stages of the argument are more problematic.

In the second stage, Regan argues that subjects-of-a-life have inherent value. His concept of inherent value grows out of his opposition to utilitarianism. Utilitarian moral theory, he says, treats individuals as "mere receptacles" for morally significant value, in that harm to one individual may be justified by the production of a greater net benefit to other individuals. In opposition to this, he holds that subjects-of-a-life have a value independent of both the value they may place upon their lives or experiences and the value others may place upon them.

Inherent value, Regan argues, does not come in degrees. To hold that some individuals have more inherent value than others is to adopt a "perfectionist" theory, i.e., one which assigns different moral worth to individuals according to how well they are thought to exemplify some virtue(s), such as intelligence or moral autonomy. Perfectionist theories have been used, at least since the time of Aristotle, to rationalize such injustices as slavery and male domination, as well as the unrestrained exploitation of animals. Regan argues that if we reject these injustices, then we must also reject perfectionism and conclude that all subjects-of-a-life have equal inherent value. Moral agents have no more inherent value than moral patients, i.e., subjects-of-a-life who are not morally responsible for their actions.

In the third phase of the argument, Regan uses the thesis of equal inherent value to derive strong moral rights for all subjects-of-a-life. This thesis underlies the Respect Principle, which forbids us to treat beings who have inherent value as mere receptacles, i.e., mere means to the production of the greatest overall good. This principle, in turn, underlies the Harm Principle, which says that we have a direct *prima facie* duty not to harm beings who have inherent value. Together, these principles give rise to moral rights. Rights are defined as valid claims, claims to certain goods and against certain beings, i.e., moral agents. Moral rights generate duties not only to refrain from inflicting harm upon beings with inherent value but also to come to their aid when they are threatened by other moral agents. Rights are not absolute but may be overridden in certain circumstances. Just what these circumstances are we will consider later. But first, let's look at some difficulties in the theory as thus far presented.

The Mystery of Inherent Value

Inherent value is a key concept in Regan's theory. It is the bridge between the plausible claim that all normal, mature mammals—human or otherwise—are subjects-of-a-life and the more debatable claim that they all have basic moral rights of the same strength. But it is a highly obscure concept, and its obscurity makes it ill-suited to play this crucial role.

Inherent value is defined almost entirely in negative terms. It is not dependent upon the value which either the inherently valuable individual or anyone else may place upon that individual's life or experiences. It is not (necessarily) a function of sentience or any other mental capacity, because, Regan says, some entities which are not sentient (e.g., trees, rivers, or rocks) may, nevertheless, have inherent value. It cannot attach to anything other than an individual; species, ecosystems, and the like cannot have inherent value.

These are some of the things which inherent value is not. But what is it? Unfortunately, we are not told. Inherent value appears as a mysterious non-natural property which we must take on faith. Regan says that it is a *postulate* that subjects-of-a-life have inherent value, a postulate justified by the fact that it avoids certain absurdities which he thinks follow from a purely utilitarian theory. But why is the postulate that *subjects-of-a-life* have inherent value? If the inherent value of a being is completely independent of the value that it or anyone else places upon its experiences, then why does the fact that it has certain sorts of experiences constitute evidence that it has inherent value? If the reason is that subjects-of-a-life have an existence which can go better or worse for them, then why isn't the appropriate conclusion that all sentient beings have inherent value, since they would all seem to meet that condition? Sentient but mentally unsophisticated beings may have a less extensive range of possible satisfactions and frustrations, but why should it follow that they have—or may have—no inherent value at all?

In the absence of a positive account of inherent value, it is also difficult to grasp the connection between being inherently valuable and having moral rights. Intuitively, it seems that value is one thing, and rights are another. It does not seem incoherent to say that some things (e.g., mountains, rivers, redwood trees) are inherently valuable and yet are not the sorts of things which can have moral rights. Nor does it seem incoherent to ascribe inherent value to some things which are not individuals, e.g., plant or animal species, though it may well be incoherent to ascribe moral rights to such things.

In short, the concept of inherent value seems to create at least as many problems as it solves. If inherent value is based on some natural property, then why not try to identify that property and explain its moral significance, without appealing to inherent value? And if it is not based on any natural property, then why should we believe in it? That it may enable us to avoid some of the problems faced by the utilitarian is not a sufficient reason, if it creates other problems which are just as serious.

Is There a Sharp Line?

Perhaps the most serious problems are those that arise when we try to apply the strong animal rights position to animals other than normal, mature mammals. Regan's theory requires us to divide all living things into two categories: those which have the same inherent value and the same basic moral rights that we do, and those which have no inherent value and presumably no moral rights. But wherever we try to draw the line, such a sharp division is implausible.

It would surely be arbitrary to draw such a sharp line between normal, mature mammals and all other living things. Some birds (e.g., crows, magpies, parrots, mynahs) appear to be just as mentally sophisticated as most mammals and thus are equally strong candidates for inclusion under the subject-of-a-life criterion. Regan is not in fact advocating that we draw the line here. His claim is only that normal mature mammals are clear cases, while other cases are less clear. Yet, on his theory, there must be such a sharp line *somewhere,* since there are no degrees of inherent value. But why should we believe that there is a sharp line between creatures that are subjects-of-a-life and creatures that are not? Isn't it more likely that "subjecthood" comes in degrees, that some creatures have only a little self-awareness, and only a little capacity to anticipate the future, while some have a little more, and some a good deal more?

Should we, for instance, regard fish, amphibians, and reptiles as subjects-of-a-life? A simple yes-or-no answer seems inadequate. On the one hand, some of their behavior is difficult to explain without the assumption that they have sensations, beliefs, desires, emotions, and memories; on the other hand, they do not seem to exhibit very much self-awareness or very much conscious anticipation of future events. Do they have enough mental sophistication to count as subjects-of-a-life? Exactly how much is enough?

It is still more unclear what we should say about insects, spiders, octopi, and other invertebrate animals which have brains and sensory organs but whose minds (if they have minds) are even more alien to us than those of fish or reptiles. Such creatures are probably sentient. Some people doubt that they can feel pain, since they lack certain neurological structures which are crucial to the processing of pain impulses in vertebrate animals. But this argument is inconclusive, since their nervous systems might process pain in ways different from ours. When injured, they sometimes act as if they are in pain. On evolutionary grounds, it seems unlikely that highly mobile creatures with complex sensory systems would not have developed a capacity for pain (and pleasure), since such a capacity has obvious survival value. It must, however, be admitted that we do not *know* whether spiders can feel pain (or something very like it), let alone whether they have emotions, memories, beliefs, desires, self-awareness, or a sense of the future.

Even more mysterious are the mental capacities (if any) of mobile micro-fauna. The brisk and efficient way that paramecia move about in their incessant search for food *might* indicate some kind of sentience, in spite of their lack of eyes, ears, brains, and other organs associated with sentience in more complex organisms. It is conceivable—though not very probable—that they, too, are subjects-of-a-life.

The existence of a few unclear cases need not pose a serious problem for a moral theory, but in this case, the unclear cases constitute most of those with which an adequate theory of animal rights would need to deal. The subject-of-a-life criterion can provide us with little or no moral guidance in our interactions with the vast majority of animals. That might be acceptable if it could be supplemented with additional principles which would provide such guidance. However, the radical dualism of the theory precludes supplementing it in this way. We are forced to say that either a spider has the same right to life as you and I do, or it has no right to life whatever—and that only the gods know which of these alternatives is true.

Regan's suggestion for dealing with such unclear cases is to apply the "benefit of the doubt" principle. That is, when dealing with beings that may or may not be subjects-of-a-life, we should act as if they are.[6] But if we try to apply this principle to the entire range of doubtful cases, we will find ourselves with moral obligations which we cannot possibly fulfill. In many climates, it is virtually impossible to live without swatting mosquitoes and exterminating cockroaches, and not all of us can afford to hire someone to sweep the path before we walk, in order to make sure that we do not step on ants. Thus, we are still faced with the daunting task of drawing a sharp line somewhere on the continuum of life forms—this time, a line demarcating the limits of the benefit of the doubt principle.

The weak animal rights theory provides a more plausible way of dealing with this range of cases, in that it allows the rights of animals of different kinds to vary in strength. . . .

WHY ARE ANIMAL RIGHTS WEAKER THAN HUMAN RIGHTS?

How can we justify regarding the rights of persons as generally stronger than those of sentient beings which are not persons? There are a plethora of bad justifications, based on religious premises or false or unprovable claims about the differences between human and non-human nature. But there is one difference which has a clear moral relevance: people are at least sometimes capable of being moved to action or inaction by the force of reasoned argument. Rationality rests upon other mental capacities, notably those which Regan cites as criteria for being a subject-of-a-life. We share these capacities with many other animals. But it is not just because we are subjects-of-a-life that we are both able and morally compelled to recognize one another as beings with equal basic moral rights. It is also because we are able to "listen to reason" in order to settle our conflicts and cooperate in shared projects. This capacity, unlike the others, may require something like a human language.

Why is rationality morally relevant? It does not make us "better" than other animals or more "perfect." It does not even automatically make us more intelligent. (Bad reasoning reduces our effective intelligence rather than increasing it.) But it is morally relevant insofar as it provides greater possibilities for cooperation and for the nonviolent resolution of problems. It also makes us more dangerous than non-rational beings can ever be. Because we are potentially more dangerous and less predictable than wolves, we need an articulated system of morality to regulate our conduct. Any human morality, to be workable in the long run, must recognize the equal moral status of all persons, whether through the postulate of equal basic moral rights or in some other way. The recognition of the moral equality of other persons is the price we must each pay for their recognition of our moral equality. Without this mutual recognition of moral equality, human society can exist only in a state of chronic and bitter conflict. The war between the sexes will persist so long as there is sexism and male domination; racial conflict will never be eliminated so long as there are racist laws and practices. But, to the extent that we achieve a mutual recognition of equality, we can hope to live together, perhaps as peacefully as wolves, achieving (in part) through explicit moral principles what they do not seem to need explicit moral principles to achieve.

Why not extend this recognition of moral equality to other creatures, even though they cannot do the same for us? The answer is that we cannot. Because we cannot reason with most non-human animals, we cannot always solve the problems which they may cause without harming them—although we are always obligated to try. We cannot negotiate a treaty with the feral cats and foxes, requiring them to stop preying on endangered native species in return for suitable concessions on our part.

> If rats invade our houses . . . we cannot reason with them, hoping to persuade them of the injustice they do us. We can only attempt to get rid of them.[7]

Aristotle was not wrong in claiming that the capacity to alter one's behavior on the basis of reasoned argument is relevant to the full moral status which he accorded to free men. Of course, he was wrong in his other premise, that women and slaves by nature cannot reason well enough to function as autonomous moral agents. Had that premise been true, so would his conclusion that women and slaves are not quite the moral equals of free men. In the case of most non-human animals, the corresponding premise is true. If, on the other hand, there are animals with whom we can learn to reason, then we are obligated to do this and to regard them as our moral equals.

Thus, to distinguish between the rights of persons and those of most other animals on the grounds that only people can alter their behavior on the basis of reasoned argument does not commit us to a perfectionist theory of the sort Aristotle endorsed. There is no excuse for refusing to recognize the moral equality of some people on the grounds that we don't regard them as quite as rational as we are, since it is perfectly clear that most people can reason well enough to determine how to act so as to respect the basic rights of others (if they choose to), and that is enough for moral equality.

But what about people who are clearly not rational? It is often argued that sophisticated mental capacities such as rationality cannot be essential for the possession of equal basic moral rights, since nearly everyone agrees that human infants and mentally incompetent persons have such rights, even though they may lack those sophisticated mental capacities. But this argument is inconclusive, because there are powerful practical and emotional reasons for protecting non-rational human beings, reasons which are absent in the case of most non-human animals. Infancy and mental incompetence are human conditions which all of us either have experienced or are likely to experience at some time. We also protect babies and mentally incompetent people because we care for them. We don't normally care for animals in the same way, and when we do—e.g., in the case of much-loved pets—we may regard them as having special rights by virtue of their relationship to us. We protect them not only for their sake but also for our own, lest we be hurt by harm done to them. Regan holds that such "side-effects" are irrelevant to moral rights, and perhaps they are. But in ordinary usage, there is no sharp line between moral rights and those moral protections which are not rights. The extension of strong moral protections to infants and the mentally impaired in no way proves that non-human animals have the same basic moral rights as people.

Why Speak of "Animal Rights" at All?

If, as I have argued, reality precludes our treating all animals as our moral equals, then why should we still ascribe rights to them? Everyone agrees that animals are entitled to some protection against human abuse, but why speak of animal *rights* if we are not prepared to accept most animals as our moral equals? The weak animal rights position may seem an unstable compromise between the bold claim that animals have the same basic moral rights that we do and the more common view that animals have no rights at all.

It is probably impossible to either prove or disprove the thesis that animals have moral rights by producing an analysis of the concept of a moral right and checking to see if some or all animals satisfy the conditions for having rights. The concept of a moral right is complex, and it is not clear which of its strands are essential. Paradigm rights holders, i.e., mature and mentally competent persons, are *both* rational and morally autonomous beings and sentient subjects-of-a-life. Opponents of animal rights claim that rationality and moral autonomy are essential for the possession of rights, while defenders of animal rights claim that they are not. The ordinary concept of a moral right is probably not precise enough to enable us to determine who is right on purely definitional grounds.

If logical analysis will not answer the question of whether animals have moral rights, practical considerations may, nevertheless incline us to say that they do. The most plausible alternative to the view that animals have moral rights is that, while they do not have *rights,* we are, nevertheless, obligated not to be cruel to them. Regan argues persuasively that the injunction to avoid being cruel to animals is inadequate to express our obligations towards animals, because it focuses on the mental states of those who cause animal suffering, rather than on the harm done to the animals themselves (p. 328). Cruelty is inflicting pain or suffering and either taking pleasure in that pain or suffering or being more or less indifferent to it. Thus, to express the demand for the decent treatment of animals in terms of the rejection of cruelty is to invite the too easy response that those who subject animals to suffering are not being cruel because they regret the suffering they cause but sincerely believe that what they do is justified. The injunction to avoid cruelty is also inadequate in that it does not preclude the killing of animals—for any reason, however trivial—so long as it is done relatively painlessly.

The inadequacy of the anti-cruelty view provides one practical reason for speaking of animal rights. Another practical reason is that this is an age in which nearly all significant moral claims tend to be expressed in terms of rights. Thus, the denial that animals have rights, however carefully qualified, is likely to be taken to mean that we may do whatever we like to them, provided that we do not violate any human rights. In such a context, speaking of the rights of animals may be the only way to persuade many people to take seriously protests against the abuse of animals.

Why not extend this line of argument and speak of the rights of trees, mountains, oceans, or anything else which we may wish to see protected from destruction? Some environmentalists have not hesitated to speak in this way, and, given the importance of protecting such elements of the natural world, they cannot be blamed for using this rhetorical device. But, I would argue that moral rights can meaningfully be ascribed only to entities which have some capacity for sentience. This is because moral rights are protections designed to protect rights holders from harms or to provide them with benefits which matter to *them.* Only beings capable of sentience can be harmed or benefited in ways which matter to them, for only such beings can like or dislike what happens to them or prefer some conditions to others.

Thus, sentient animals, unlike mountains, rivers, or species, are at least logically possible candidates for moral rights. This fact together with the need to end current abuses of animals—e.g., in scientific research . . .—provides a plausible case for speaking of animal rights.

CONCLUSION

I have argued that Regan's case for ascribing strong moral rights to all normal, mature mammals is unpersuasive because (1) it rests upon the obscure concept of inherent value, which is defined only in negative terms, and (2) it seems to preclude any plausible answer to questions about the moral status of the vast majority of sentient animals. . . .

The weak animal rights theory asserts that (1) any creature whose natural mode of life includes the pursuit of certain satisfactions has the right not to be forced to exist without the opportunity to pursue those satisfactions; (2) that any creature which is capable of pain, suffering, or frustration has the right that such experiences not be deliberately inflicted upon it without some compelling reason; and (3) that no sentient being should be killed without good reason. However, moral rights are not an all-or-nothing affair. The strength of the reasons required to override the rights of a non-human organism varies, depending upon—among other things—the probability that it is sentient and (if it is clearly sentient) its probable degree of mental sophistication. . . .

NOTES

1. Tom Regan, *The Case for Animal Rights* (Berkeley, University of California Press, 1983). All page references are to this edition.

2. For instance, Peter Singer, although he does nor like to speak of rights, includes all sentient beings under the protection of his basic utilitarian principle of equal respect for like interests. (*Animal Liberation* [New York: Avon Books, 1975], p. 3.)

3. The capacity for sentience like all of the mental capacities mentioned in what follows is a disposition. Dispositions do not disappear whenever they are not currently manifested. Thus, sleeping or temporarily unconscious persons or non-human animals are still sentient in the relevant sense (i.e., still capable of sentience), so long as they still have the neurological mechanisms necessary for the occurrence of experiences.

4. It is possible, perhaps probable that some non-human animals—such as cetaceans and anthropoid apes—should be regarded as persons. If so, then the weak animal rights position holds that these animals have the same basic moral rights as human persons.

5. See R. G. Frey, *Interests and Rights: The Case Against Animals* (Oxford: Oxford University Press, 1980).

6. See, for instance, p. 319, where Regan appeals to the benefit of the doubt principle when dealing with infanticide and late-term abortion.

7. Bonnie Steinbock, "Speciesism and the Idea of Equality," *Philosophy* 53 (1978):253.

II. BIODIVERSITY.

Overview. Biodiversity is a concept from evolutionary biology and environmentalism. In evolutionary biology, it is a dictum that there will always be diversity in species. This diversity interacts with environmental conditions to create pressure on certain reproductive groups within the species. This pressure defines fitness (the positive or negative ability of a certain biological reproductive grouping within a species to be more or less successful at reproducing within that pressure constraint). As the environment changes, the fitness of the subgroups also can change. This result is a rather plastic nature of species so that they might be more able to survive environmental changes (that are taken as a given). In nature, there is such intense competition for survival that extinction of species is a regular event. Thus, environmentalists approach the issue of biodiversity with some trepidation because (in one way) it is working against nature in which continued existence goes to those species that are sufficiently fit for some particular environment.

Nonetheless, the intervention of humans into the ecosystems of other animals has been so pervasive and the results of human intervention so disastrous as to make protection (even with its drawbacks of being artificial and unnatural) an important consideration. Just what type of protection is called for and how one justifies it in ethical terms is the subject matter of the essays in this section.

Paul M. Wood contends that the term *biodiversity* is used in different ways in the literature. One common confusion is between biological resources and biodiversity. The former are instrumentally valued, and this often blocks the worth of biodiversity, which operates as the source or ground of resources. Wood takes biodiversity to be the differences among biological species. Diversity, understood in this way, is essential for the long-term survival of biological resources. This means that protecting diversity is essential and should never be exchanged for increased harvesting of biological resources. Seen in this way, biodiversity is a firm constraint on public action, not merely a desirable goal to attempt to reach.

Elliott Sober begins his essay by differentiating two views toward protecting biodiversity: (a) we should protect biodiversity because of nature's instrumental value to humans and (b) we should protect biodiversity because of nature's intrinsic value. The former is not problematic concerning conservation and biodiversity, but the latter is. Sober cites a number of reasons to support his skepticism about intrinsic value in nature. Among these include the holistic emphasis in evolutionary biology that generally measures groups and their survival as a species as opposed to any particular individual. Another is that biodiversity seems paradoxically to value species more when the number of species decreases. For example, if there were 10 billion species, each might have a value n, but if the number of species were reduced to 100 million, then the value of each species would rise to $100n$. Thus, the value of any particular species increases as biodiversity decreases!

Finally, Sober points out that biologists and environmentalists do not value all species in the same way. Wild species are prized more than domesticated ones. But a bias cannot be supported on the principle of biodiversity alone. In the end Sober, supports the first justification for biodiversity.

Biodiversity as the Source of Biological Resources: A New Look at Biodiversity Values

Paul M. Wood

INTRODUCTION

There are many descriptions of biodiversity values in the literature. One more description, therefore, may appear redundant, requiring justification. My justification is simple: whereas previous authors have correctly claimed that biological *resources,* both actual and potential, are valuable, this claim tends to obscure the specific values of biological *diversity* itself. A sharper distinction needs to be drawn between the two sets of values. In this article I will claim that biological diversity is a concept on a higher logical plane than biological resources. In turn, this claim leads to a different conception of biodiversity's value: biodiversity is the *source* of biological resources and therein lies its value to humans.[1]

As such, biodiversity is a *necessary precondition* for the long term maintenance of biological resources. This conception of biodiversity and its instrumental value holds several implications for land-use decisions and land-management decisions. In particular, biological resources cannot be traded-off against increments of biodiversity as if the latter were substitutable items on the same logical plane as resources. Thus, cost-benefit analysis and similar evaluation techniques are useless for the purpose of determining whether or not to preserve another increment of biodiversity. In order to secure a supply of biological *resources* in the long term, the conservation of biological *diversity* can be seen as a constraint on the legitimate extent and degree of any one generation's use of relatively natural areas. The need for legal reform in constitutional democracies is strongly implied.[2]

Of course, in order to distinguish between the two sets of values, one first needs to clarify the distinction between biodiversity and biological resources. This is my first task. The second is to summarise the major values of biological resources for the purpose of setting them apart from the values of biodiversity. The third is to explicate exactly why biodiversity itself is so important. Finally, I highlight the significance of this conception of biodiversity values within a political decision-making context.

WHAT IS BIODIVERSITY?

Swanson et al. (1992: 407) assert that 'defining exactly what is meant by biodiversity [is] a notoriously intractable question'. Magurran (1988: 1) suggests that 'diversity has a knack of eluding definition'. Salwasser (1988: 87) states flatly that it 'defies definition'. Yet these authors and many others have provided general definitions. One of the best is this:

> Biological diversity encompasses all species of plants, animals, and microorganisms and the ecosystems and ecological processes of which they are parts. It is an umbrella term for the degree of nature's variety, including both the number and frequency of ecosystems, species or genes in a given assemblage. It is usually considered at three different levels: genetic diversity, species diversity, and ecosystem diversity. (McNeely et al. 1990: 17)

This is a carefully worded description. It does not claim that biodiversity consists of genes, species, and ecosystems, or ecological processes, but instead it encompasses them. McNeely et al. (1990: 18) later claim that these entities and processes are the 'physical manifestations' of biodiversity. What, then, is biodiversity itself, if these entities are only the manifestations of it? A clue is the word 'variety'. It is true that 'variety' is a rough synonym for 'diversity' (McMinn 1991: 1), but this does not take us very far. Similarly, 'number' and 'frequency' are important attributes of diversity, but they are not coextensive with the concept.

The main difficulty in defining biodiversity, I suggest, is its multidimensional character, along with the fact that the dimensions are not commensurable; they cannot be reduced to a single, and therefore commensurable, statistic. (If they were commensurable, the several dimensions could be collapsed into one.) The multidimensional character of diversity has long been recognised. Peet (1974: 285) described it as a 'number of concepts . . . lumped under the title of diversity' (see also: Hurlbert 1971; Patil and Taillie 1982a).[3]

Nevertheless, 'By tradition, diversity has been primarily viewed in ecology as a two-dimensional concept with components of richness and evenness' (Patil and Taillie 1982b: 566). Several reviews of the topic agree that the two basic concepts of biological variety are (a) richness, and (b) evenness, equitability, frequency, or some other measure of relative abundance (cf. Krebs 1985: 514; Magurran 1988: 7; Putnam and Wratton 1984: 320; Westman 1985: 444). Richness refers to the number of entities (of a kind) in a standard sample, and usually refers to richness of species in particular.[4] Evenness refers to the extent to which entities are found in equal relative abundances and, once again, usually refers to species. Some authors emphasise richness as the basic component of diversity while others emphasise evenness or some other notion of frequency.

Yet there are other dimensions of biodiversity, Franklin et al. (1981) and Franklin (1988), for example, suggest that biodiversity's three main characteristics are composition, structure, and function. Noss (1990) arranges these same three characteristics in a nested hierarchy. Many authors suggest that biodiversity also consists of ecological processes. Vane-Wright et al. (1991) and Williams et al. (1991) focus on cladistic hierarchies based on phylogenetic lineage. All these dimensions of biodiversity are important. They take on special significance in operational issues. But none is entirely coextensive with the concept of biodiversity.

I suggest there is a unifying conceptual theme that brings together the several dimensions of diversity. At the risk of stating the obvious, diversity has meaning only in association with some sort of entities. Entities are required before they can be described as being diverse. But it is somewhat less obvious that the entities under observation must also be different from one another before they can be described as diverse. Without the notion of a difference, the concept of diversity cannot gain a purchase, so to speak. At the core of the concept of diversity, therefore, the twin notions of entities and differences appear to be the essential components.[5]

Applying the twin notions of entities and differences to biological phenomena leads to a dichotomy concerning possible definitions of biodiversity. Does biodiversity refer to:

a. biological *entities* that are different from one another, or
b. *differences* among biological entities?

At first glance, this distinction may appear to be a moot point. But it makes an important difference to the conceptualisation of biodiversity. In (a) entities are emphasised, whereas in (b) emphasis is given to an environmental condition or state of affairs relative to biological entities. The two are corollaries of each other; they are the flip sides of the same coin. Nonetheless, I will argue that the latter conception is more consistent internally, and more consistent externally, with the various uses to which the term is applied. Consequently, for the specific purpose of evaluating biodiversity, I propose the following general definition of biodiversity:

> Biodiversity = differences among biological entities.[6]

Biodiversity, therefore, is not a property of any one biological entity. Rather, it is an emergent property of collections of entities. More precisely, it is the differences among them.

This definition may appear to be true in a trivial sense only. It certainly will not help in any field measurements of biodiversity. Yet this abstract definition permits a sharp cleavage between biodiversity *per se* and biological resources, and this sharp distinction is needed to separate the values of biodiversity from the values of biological resources.

THE VALUES OF BIODIVERSITY

McPherson (1985: 157) points out that 'there is little agreement on how to value biological diversity, who should value it, and what dimensions of it should be valued'. People have differing and often competing interests, he argues, and therefore 'no single group, whether ecologists, biologists, economists, or anthropologists, has proposed a set of reasons which are sufficiently compelling and appealing to generate the necessary support to ensure that all of the biological diversity they value will be maintained'. He concludes by noting that 'a general approach to valuing biological diversity has eluded scholars and policymakers alike'.

Nevertheless, numerous authors have attempted to describe the values of biodiversity.[7] Typically a list of several values is proposed, and each value is described. However, these lists of values are problematic for a number of reasons. The single largest problem is their lack of a clear distinction between the values of biological resources and the values of biological *diversity* itself.[8] Of course, this distinction can only be made if biodiversity is clearly distinguished from biological resources.

Most of the putative values of biodiversity, such as economic, recreational, aesthetic, and cultural values, can be attributed more meaningfully to biological resources. From this perspective, it comes as no surprise that people have differing and competing interests in these resources. As Ehrenfeld (1981: 177–207) points out, many arguments for the conservation of biodiversity (Ehrenfeld actually focuses on species) rely on attempts to assign some sort of resource value to apparently non-economic aspects of biodiversity. This strategy carries inherent weaknesses, as Ehrenfeld explains: these 'resource' values may not be able to compete with the values of development projects which deplete biodiversity; resource values might change and become more competitive, but would come too late due to the irreversibility of species losses (or other increments of biodiversity) or the irreversibility of many development projects; and the assignment of resource values permits ranking, thereby creating the possibility that one natural area might be pitted against another in decisions to conserve only the most valuable.

The following suggestions for clarifying the values of biodiversity therefore are predicated on the distinction between biodiversity *per se* and biological resources. I begin with a summary of the major values that have been attributed to biological entities as resources or potential resources, and then later I attempt to describe the values of biodiversity.

From a strictly anthropocentric (human-centered) perspective nature (apart from humans) is simply a source of valuable goods and services—i.e. resources. These goods and services span the entire range of human interests in nature from vital sources of food, shelter, and clothing to aesthetic and cultural values. Nature from this perspective is *instrumentally* valuable for human purposes. In summary, and for convenience, these values can be grouped into three broad categories:

(a) Some biological entities are valuable as resources. Wild biological resources are both directly and indirectly valuable for people. Directly, many wild plants, animals, and micro-organisms are used by people for food, shelter, fuelwood, clothing, medicines, and so on, and as the raw materials for manufactured products. They are consumed directly or exchanged in markets. Wild organisms and ecosystems are valued for recreational and aesthetic purposes, and for their cultural values. They can also serve as environmental indicators, either as 'early warning systems' for adverse environmental change (Newman and Schereiber 1984), or as indicators of ecosystem stress (Ehrenfeld 1976: 650).

Wild plants and animals also are indirectly valuable. They provide 'environmental services' such as water cleansing, watershed protection, regulation of hydrological cycles, the absorption of atmospheric carbon dioxide, the release of oxygen, the regulation of local climates (and perhaps even the world's climate—Lovelock 1979), the recycling of nutrients needed for plants, the production of soil, the prevention of soil erosion, the absorption and conversion of human-produced pollutants, and biological pest control.

(b) Some biological entities are valuable as potential resources. Wild plants, animals, and micro-organisms present opportunities for the discovery of new and valuable resources, including new materials such as organic chemicals (Altschul 1973), useful knowledge (Orians and Kunin 1985: 116–122), or genetic resources (Oldfield 1984). For example, the trend in industrialised agriculture is toward genetic uniformity in commercial crops with an accompanying increase in vulnerability to insect and disease pests and to adverse climatic

conditions (Oldfield 1984). Wild relatives of commercial crops are a source of fresh genetic material from which resistant and hardy varieties can be produced. In fact, 'nearly all modern crop varieties and some highly productive livestock strains contain genetic material recently incorporated from related wild or weedy species, or from more primitive genetic stocks still used and maintained by traditional agricultural peoples' (Oldfield 1984: 3). Wild genetic resources are now indispensable to modern agriculture (R. and C. Prescott-Allen 1986). Wild gene pools, therefore, are potential resources.

(c) Some biological entities have contributory value. Wild plants, animals, and micro-organisms also may have contributory value, in the sense that they contribute to the functioning of healthy ecosystems which in turn produce organisms and services that are more directly valued (Norton 1987: 60–63). The contributory value of 'non-resource' species cannot be overestimated. Of the world's 5 to 30 million species, relatively few are known to science and even fewer have been screened in modern times for useful resource materials. However, as contributors to the maintenance of resource goods and services, it is reasonable to presume that all species have contributory value.

Similarly, in order to maintain those *in situ* species and gene pools that are potential resources, their specific habitats, both biotic and abiotic, must be maintained. Consequently, those sympatric species (and their gene pools) that contribute to the maintenance of these habitats are valuable because they maintain potential biological resources; they are (once again) important for their contributory value.[9]

The above three categories are intended, in summary form, to describe the human-centered, instrumental values of biological entities. They do not describe the values of biodiversity *per se*. Yet the thread of an argument for the value of biodiversity can now be discerned: biodiversity can be seen as necessary for the maintenance of biological resources, thereby lending value to biodiversity by extension. Biological diversity, in other words, may be instrumentally valuable for obtaining something else—biological goods and services—that are more directly valued. Clearly, this is the beginning of a rationale for attributing value to some forms of biodiversity. But there are more detailed reasons for valuing biodiversity itself. I suggest these reasons can be placed into three groups, arranged in a hierarchy.

- At the primary level, biodiversity is valuable because it provides a range of resources, both actual and potential.
- At the secondary level, biodiversity is valuable for maintaining these actual and potential resources, and it does this by providing the preconditions for adaptive evolution. Thus biological entities are able to adapt to changing environmental conditions over time if the preconditions of biodiversity are provided.

- At the tertiary level, biodiversity is valuable as a precondition for the maintenance of biodiversity itself in a self-augmenting (i.e. positive) feedback mechanism. Conversely, a self-diminishing feedback mechanism may be activated if ecosystems are sufficiently disturbed.

Each of these three levels is discussed in more detail below.

1. Primary Level of Biodiversity: A Range of Actual and Potential Resources

As indicated above, biological resources are numerous and varied and therefore provide a *range* of resources. There are a number of reasons for attributing value to a range of resources, which I will discuss. But what needs to be emphasised here is, once again, the distinction between biological resources and biodiversity itself. I have pointed out the major ways in which biological entities are valuable as resources. But whereas biological entities and the differences among them exist in a necessarily reciprocal arrangement, biodiversity can be defined as 'differences among biological entities'. Consequently, a *range* of biological resources is a manifestation of the *differences* among biological entities, and this, of course, is biodiversity itself. To the extent that a range of biological resources is valuable, then that value is directly attributable to biodiversity.

Why is a range of resources valuable? I assume it is self-evident that, in general, a greater abundance and variety of resources is more valuable than fewer or less varied resources because the former allows more scope for serving purposes that people want. This is true for actual (i.e. currently used) resources.

A more interesting issue is the value of a range of *potential* resources. Many arguments supporting the conservation of biodiversity are based on the value of potential resources. There are two basic arguments here. The first is obvious: 'increments in diversity increase the likelihood of benefits to man' (Norton 1986: 117). The emphasis here is on the discovery of *new* resources. The possibility of discovering new medicines, new foodstuffs, new industrial raw materials, and many other types of commodities, is often cited as one of the strongest arguments in favour of preserving species and their genetic diversity (cf. Myers 1983). However, when species are viewed simply as potential commodities, then they must compete with other economic demands. There are costs associated with preserving potential resources, and the economic benefits of biodiversity-depleting development projects may outweigh these costs. Norton (1987: 124–127) refers to the potential commodity value of species as 'Aunt Tillie's Drawer argument', referring by analogy to the compulsive collector who saves pieces of junk 'in case I might need them someday'. Nevertheless, this value of biodiversity—the chance of discovering new resources—should not be underestimated.

The second value of a range of potential resources is less obvious: a range of potential biological resources is also required in order to maintain the current range of resources. Current biological resources, such as domesticated crops, are vulnerable to insect and disease pests and to adverse climatic conditions, as mentioned above. They are vulnerable primarily because they lack genetic diversity, and for the same reason, they rarely develop resistance or hardiness by natural selection (Oldfield 1984: 8). Consequently, an abundant supply of wild genetic resources is required in order to prevent the depletion of current resources. The greater the genetic diversity within these wild populations, the more likely it is that suitable genetic material will be found.

It should be noted that, for a number of technical reasons, biotechnology cannot reliably substitute for natural genetic variety (see generally: Baumann et al. 1996). In turn, the wild relatives of domestic crops are dependent on the communities and ecosystems of which they are a part. By extension, therefore, the diversity of species that are sympatric with the wild relatives of domestic crops are instrumentally valuable, as is the diversity of habitats required to support them.

2. Secondary Level of Biodiversity Value: Necessary Preconditions for Adaptive Evolution in Response to Change.

Frankel and Soulé (1981: 79) point out that there are two principal axioms in evolutionary theory: (a) genetic variation is required for a population to adapt to changes in its environment, and (b) natural selection of organisms is the means by which such adaptation occurs. While Sober (1984: 23) and others emphasise that evolution occurs by 'the natural selection of organisms', as compared to the selection of species or other collective entities, the overall effect is to allow these taxa to evolve in response to change.

As discussed, domestic biological resources tend to be vulnerable to new pests or adverse conditions due to their lack of genetic diversity and a concomitant inability to adapt by natural selection. Conversely, wild relatives of domestic crops are usually better able to survive changing conditions precisely because of the diversity of individuals within these wild populations, which is largely a manifestation of their underlying genetic diversity. The genetic diversity of these wild relatives of domestic crops is therefore an essential *precondition* that enables them to adapt.

Perhaps the one constant in nature is that it continues to change, over many spatial and temporal scales, and not necessarily in predictable patterns (see generally: Botkin 1990). Some of these changes are human-induced. Examples include the current threats of ozone depletion and global warming. To the extent that current biological resources are dependent on wild resources (actual and potential), and these wild resources in turn are dependent on their *in situ* communities and habitats, then humans are dependent on the ability of these entities to adapt to inevitable environmental change. *Humans are vitally reliant, therefore, on nature's ability to adapt.* But since diversity itself (particularly genetic diversity) is a necessary precondition for adaptive evolution, this places humans in a state of obligant dependency on biodiversity.

3. Tertiary Level of Biodiversity Value: Necessary Preconditions for the Self-Augmenting Maintenance of Biodiversity Itself.

It has been suggested that diversity begets diversity by way of positive feedback mechanisms. With a focus on species, for example, Whittaker (1970:103) argues that 'Species diversity is a self-augmenting evolutionary phenomenon; evolution of diversity makes possible further evolution of diversity'. The opposite might also be true: 'Diminutions in diversity affect the spiral in reverse. Losses in diversity beget further losses and the upward diversity spiral will be slowed and eventually reversed if natural and/or human-caused disturbances are severe and continued' (Norton 1986: 117).

Whittaker's hypothesis is controversial,[10] but three plausible explanations are worthy of note. The first suggests that disturbances, dispersal, and competition together serve as a diversity generator. Within ecological time frames, disturbances followed by successional stages create patchy landscapes, with measurable between-habitat diversity. But in turn, the colonisation and serial development of disturbed areas is dependent on a pool of nearby species that are able to disperse to, and compete within, the disturbed area throughout its successional stages.

> Thus the total diversity of an area provides the pool of competitors for niches in developing ecosystems. The larger the pool, the more likely it is that the system will evolve into a complex, highly interrelated system. A complex, highly interrelated system provides more niche opportunities for new species. (Norton 1986:115)[11]

Conversely, if an area is sufficiently disturbed, or if the landscape is fragmented (see generally: Harris 1984; MacArthur and Wilson 1967; Wilcove et al. 1986), then for any one ecosystem or habitat fragment, access to a larger species pool is at least partially cut off and a self-diminishing diversity spiral begins. Thus Wilcox (1984: 642) writes: 'The reduction in habitat size which accompanies insularization will result in . . . the tendency for a process (extinction of a species) normally occurring on a geological time scale to condense to an ecological time scale.'

A second explanation suggests that diversity is self-augmenting by way of lengthening and tighter packing of niche axes with subsequent specialisation and speciation—all operating in 'evolutionary time':

> Consider . . . the niche space for a group of organisms in a community. Along each axis of that space the number of species tends to increase in evolutionary time as additional species enter the community, fit themselves in between other species along the axis, and increase the packing of species along axes. Species can also be added as specialists on marginal resources, and they can be added by the evolution of new resource gradients and species adapted to utilizing them . . . Considered for a given group of organisms, diversity increases through evolutionary time by the 'lengthening' of niche axes, and by the addition of new axes—by the 'expansion' and complication of the niche space. (Whittaker 1970: 103)

A third explanation, drawing heavily on chaos theory and the science of complexity, is perhaps the most intriguing. Kauffman (1995), for example, maintains that Darwinian natural selection is insufficient to explain the diversity found in biological entities. Self-organisation, he argues, has played a far greater role in diversity generation than previously thought possible. At 'supracritical' levels of diversity, 'diversity feeds on itself, driving itself forward' (Kauffman 1995: 114).

Regardless of the explanations posited in the literature, the geological record provides strong evidence for the phenomenon of increasing diversity over time (Sepkoski 1984).

I have suggested that these three levels of biodiversity value can be arranged in a hierarchy. A hierarchical arrangement implies some sort of connection between the levels within the hierarchy. What sort of connection is implied here? Since the subject matter is about *values*, one perspective is to see the hierarchy as a series of instrumental values which culminates in the attainment of the highest level values, as is typical of value hierarchies. From this perspective,

a. the self-augmenting phenomenon of biodiversity, or the prevention of a self-diminishing spiral (i.e. the tertiary level of biodiversity value), is instrumentally valuable for maintaining the preconditions for adaptive evolution;

b. the preconditions of adaptive evolution (i.e. the secondary level of biodiversity value) are instrumentally valuable for maintaining the range of potential biological resources; and

c. the range of potential biological resources (i.e. the primary level of biodiversity value) is instrumentally valuable both for maintaining the current biological goods and services upon which humanity is dependent, and for increasing the current range of biological resources.

This can be expressed symbolically as:

$$3° \text{ value} \Rightarrow 2° \text{ value} \Rightarrow 1° \text{ value} \Rightarrow \text{current and new biological resources}$$

In short, biodiversity is a necessary precondition for biological resources; this is its value.[12]

This conception of the values of biodiversity carries a distinct advantage over the various lists of values that have been compiled in the literature. Most of these lists refer to economic, ecological, recreational, aesthetic, cultural and other categories of value. As I mentioned previously, the drawback with such lists is that they more accurately refer to biological resources, not biodiversity *per se*. I maintain that biodiversity can be distinguished from biological resources. Regardless of the differences among peoples' preferences, all people have at least some sort of interest in biological resources. After all, everyone's life is dependent on them. Consequently, when biodiversity is viewed as a necessary precondition for the continuing flow of biological resources, then it can be stated reasonably that it is generally in humanity's interests to maintain biodiversity."[13]

This conception of biodiversity transcends the problems that are inherent in the allocation of scarce resources among competing interests. To some extent, therefore, the conservation of biodiversity can be seen as a means for maintaining values that are universal and largely independent of the competition over scarce biological resources and land. Biodiversity is literally the *sine qua non* of renewable resource management.

IMPLICATIONS FOR LEGAL REFORM

If, as I have argued, biodiversity is a necessary precondition for the long term maintenance of biological resources, then two broad implications can be discerned. First, it behoves those of us in the present generation to preserve biodiversity. At the societal level, this is largely a prudential issue; we are likely to be better off in the long term by conserving biodiversity. Second, future generations are likely to be vitally dependent on the extent to which we in the present generation conserve biodiversity. This is an ethical issue. Identifying our obligations to future generations and clarifying cogent sustainability policies are closely parallel ideas. It is in this latter context that a new perspective on biodiversity values is needed.

Those land-use and land-management decisions that affect biodiversity are usually perceived in terms of trade-offs. The overall issue is seen as economic: scarce resources are to be distributed among persons in society, and human wants for resources are assumed to be unquenchable. From this perspective, conserving biodiversity usually means forgoing some opportunities for resource extraction. Or, to characterise the more frequent pattern, extracting resources often entails a loss of biodiversity. Either way, environmental decision-making is viewed as a problem of making appropriate trade-offs: a little less of this for a little more of that. Valuing biodiversity in terms of biological resources feeds this decision-making paradigm. By narrowly focusing on increments of biodiversity (i.e. a species here, an ecosystem there) and treating them *as if* they were biological resources alone, then it is possible to make trade-offs between biodiversity conservation and those resource extraction activities that deplete biodiversity.

Yet if biodiversity is more appropriately seen as a necessary precondition for the long term maintenance of biological resources, an entirely different decision-making paradigm emerges. Biodiversity can then be perceived as an essential environmental condition. Consider other essential environmental conditions: the rate of solar influx, the earth's orbit around the sun, and gravitational pull. We take them for granted and we need not concern ourselves with their conservation. Biodiversity is different precisely because humans now have the ability to change this environmental condition.

An essential environmental condition is not something to be traded-off against more attractive, short-term opportunities. If an environmental condition really is essential, then it needs to be maintained. Land-use and land-management decisions should be made with this constraint in mind. Put simply, this means that each generation needs to live within its ecological limits. Each generation should be free to make whatever environmental trade-offs are appropriate for promoting the public interest, provided that biodiversity is not depleted.[14] Or to express this as an ethical principle: *the conservation of biodiversity should take priority over any one generation's collective interests.*

Implementing this priority-of-biodiversity principle in law is more difficult.[15] The purpose of western governments is to promote the public interest, and the public interest is usually interpreted as the collective interests of extant individuals within the relevant government's jurisdiction. But the priority-of-biodiversity principle suggests a constraint on the public interest and therefore implies a limit on governmental authority.

In constitutional democracies, limits on state authority are recognised in one area only: constitutionally entrenched civil rights and freedoms. These rights and freedoms are the individual's safeguard against a 'tyranny of the majority'. Borovoy expresses the system this way:

> Majority rule is democracy's safeguard against minority dictatorship. And the fundamental rights such as freedom of speech, freedom of assembly, and due process of law are democracy's safeguard against majority rule itself from becoming a dictatorship. (Borovoy 1988: 200)

There is a connection between this self-limiting feature of constitutional democracies and the conservation of biodiversity. Valuing biodiversity as a necessary precondition for the long term maintenance of biological resources allows us to see biodiversity not as one more value to be traded-off against competing values, but rather as an essential environmental condition. Fulfilling our obligations to future generations therefore implies that no one government should permit itself to be persuaded by contemporary collective desires for resource extraction to the extent that biodiversity would be depleted. But since the *purpose* of any one government is precisely to promote these contemporary collective desires, the conservation of biodiversity needs to be placed beyond the immediate reach of governmental discretion. The legal mechanism in constitutional democracies is to limit state authority itself by constitutional decree. Constitutions prescribe the legitimate jurisdiction of state authority. Government actions in violation of constitutional limits are *ultra vires*—literally 'beyond jurisdiction'.

In effect, there is a strong parallel between the individual in contemporary societies and future generations: both need to be protected against a 'tyranny of the majority'.[16] Limits to state authority are required in both cases. In the specific case of biodiversity conservation, constitutional limits to state authority are needed in order to prevent the present generation from exerting the equivalent of a 'tyranny of the majority' over future generations by way of pre-emptive environmental decisions.

NOTES

The author would like to thank F. Bunnell, P. Dooling, L. Jacobs, W. Rees, T. Sullivan, and E. Winkler for helpful discussions on this topic, and G. Namkoong and D. VanDeVeer for commenting on earlier versions of this paper. B. Norton and an anonymous reviewer provided insightful and constructive comments.

1. This article focuses exclusively on anthropocentric (i.e. human-centered) values. Yet nothing in this article is intended to undermine either the validity or importance of possible intrinsic values in nature. The entire subdiscipline of environmental ethics is seeking both to articulate and justify these values, and the journal *Environmental Ethics* is a primary vehicle for expressing current thought in this arena. Nonetheless, as a *political* premise, the assertion of intrinsic values in nature is problematic. Scherer (1990: 4) expresses the problem this way: '[E]nvironmental ethicists have at most produced a *theory of value*. They have not produced a *theory of action* inferable from the former. . . . Important as it has been, their work has also shown its own shortcoming, for they have made painfully clear the difficulty of *inferring from the value of [nature]* to *how humans ought to act*.'

2. Obviously, biodiversity needs to be conserved worldwide, regardless of the type of governance in any one country. This article, however, discusses only those legal reforms that are required in western constitutional democracies.

3. Patil and Taillie (1982a) refer to diversity as a 'multidimensional' concept, by which I assume they mean a *polytypic* or *cluster* concept.

4. A distinction is sometimes drawn between species richness which refers to the number of species in a given number of individuals or unit of biomass, and species density, which refers to the number of species per unit of area (Hurlbert 1971: 581). For the purposes of this discussion, either interpretation is applicable.

5. While structure, function, and processes are important attributes of biodiversity, they are not essential for the definition of biodiversity. Given the specific composition of, say, an ecosystem, then structure, functions, and any attending processes cannot help but co-exist. In technical terms, structure, functions, and processes are *supervenient* on composition. Also, many biological entities are more abstract than simple physical entities. Examples are: species, other

taxa, and gradients of change within ecosystems. Most of these are also polytypic concepts (see note 3).

6. Williams et al. (1991) suggest a similar definition, but more narrowly confined to differences among species.

7. Cf. Ehrenfeld 1976, 1981, 1988; Ehrlich and Ehrlich 1981; Fitter 1986; Hanemann 1988; Hoffman 1991; Livingston 1981; Lovejoy 1986; McMinn 1991; McNeely 1988; McNeely et al. 1990; McPherson 1985; Myers 1979, 1983; Norse 1990; Norton 1985, 1986, 1987; Office of Technology Assessment 1988; Oldfield 1984; Orians and Kunin 1985; R. and C. Prescott-Allen 1982, 1986; Primack 1993; Randall 1985, 1988, 1991; Rolston 1985, 1988, 1989; Soulé 1985; and WRI/IUCN/UNEP 1991.

8. Another major problem, which cannot be discussed in detail here, is that a simple list of values presupposes that one value can be traded off against another in order to obtain the highest aggregate of value from nature in general or from any one area of land in particular. In short, a utilitarian decision-making philosophy is implied. Yet, if the conclusions of this article are correct, then biodiversity conservation must be preserved as an overarching principle for all land and resource use. A *lexicographic* ordering is implied for environmental decision-making.

9. These three categories are not mutually exclusive. It is possible for one species to be a resource, a potential resource, and have contributory value—all at the same time. Take the dominant tree species in a temperate coniferous forest for example. It could be a valuable timber resource (or aesthetic resource); it might also yield new products and therefore is a potential resource; and finally, its dominant presence contributes to the well-being of other species, some of which may, in turn, be resources or potential resources.

10. See Rosenzweig (1995) for review.

11. See generally Ricklefs and Schluter (1993) for more discussion.

12. A parallel argument can be made, and has been made, between the concept of *wildness* and resources. Birch (1990: 9) argues that 'although it [wildness] is at the heart of finding utility values in the first place, wildness itself cannot plausibly be assigned any utility value because it spawns much, very much, that is just plain disutility. It is for this reason that it is so puzzling, to the point of unintelligibility, to try to construe wildness (or wilderness) as a resource . . . To take the manifestation of wildness for the thing itself is to commit a category mistake.' Rolston (1983: 181–207) presents a similar argument, and states that 'wildness itself is of *intrinsic* value as the generating source [of resources]'. Oelschlaeger (1991: 1) discusses 'wild nature as the *source* of human existence'. See also Snyder (1990).

13. By emphasising biodiversity as a necessary precondition for the maintenance of biological resources, I am not suggesting that it is a sufficient condition. A number of social and political conditions, for example, may also be necessary (see especially Kaplan 1994). *Caring for the Earth: a strategy for sustainable living* (IUCN/UNEP/WWP 1991: 9) lists nine principles for sustainable resource use. Several of these could be restated as necessary conditions.

14. At a more practical level, not every gene, every individual organism, nor even every ecosystem can be preserved—nor would it be desirable to do so if possible. For management purposes, a unit of conservation must be identified. Here I am assuming that the biological species concept is an appropriate unit of conservation, meaning that every species should be conserved. This is a contentious point, but see Wilson (1992: 37–38) for comment on this issue. I should also hasten to add that I have a *wide* conception of species in mind: conserving a species entails the conservation of many other aspects of biodiversity, including, for example, a sufficient of genetic amplitude, a sufficient number of locally-adapted populations over each species' natural range, along with suitable biotic and abiotic habitat conditions. For obvious reasons, this cannot be fully articulated here.

15. See note number 2.

16. While the term 'tyranny of the majority' is usually interpreted literally in the sense of a majority outnumbering a minority, the term can also apply to a minority exercising unjust power over the interests of *disadvantaged* groups, even if the latter constitute a majority. South Africa's apartheid regime is an example in the recent past. The issue at stake here is the exercise of power, not numbers of people *per se*. For the topic at hand, it is likely that the number of people in the near future will outnumber extant individuals, despite the current rate of biodiversity loss. So in this case I am referring to the ability of the present generation to exercise power over future generations by way of unjustly usurping the ability of the environment to support them, and this is one form of tyranny of the majority.

References

Altschul, S. V. R. 1973. Exploring the herbarium. *Scientific American* **256**(6): 96–104.

Baumann, M., J. Bell, F. Koechlin, and M. Pimbert (eds) 1996. *The life industry: biodiversity, people and profits.* London: Immediate Technology Publications.

Birch, T.H. 1990. The incarceration of wildness: wilderness areas as prisons. *Environmental Ethics* **12:** 3–26.

Borovoy, A. 1988. *When freedoms collide: the case for our civil liberties.* Toronto: Lester and Orpen Dennys.

Botkin, D.B. 1990. *Discordant harmonies: A new ecology for the twenty-first century.* New York: Oxford University Press.

Ehrenfeld, D.W. 1976. The conservation of non-resources. *American Scientist* **64:** 648–656.

Ehrenfeld, D.W. 1981. *The arrogance of humanism,* New York: Oxford University Press. [Republication of 1978 original, with minor revisions]

Ehrenfeld, D.W. 1988. Why put a value on biodiversity? In: Wilson, E.O. and F.M. Peter (eds), *Biodiversity.* Washington, D.C.: National Academy Press, pp. 212–216.

Ehrlich, P. and Ehrlich, A. 1981. *Extinction: the causes and consequences of the disappearance of species.* London: Victor Gollancz.

Fitter, R. 1986. *Wildlife for man: how and why we should conserve our species.* London: Collins.

Frankel, O.H. and Soulé, M.E. 1981. *Conservation and evolution.* Cambridge: Cambridge University Press.

Franklin, J.F. 1988. Structural and functional aspects of temperate forests. In: Wilson. E.O. and F.M. Peter (eds), *Biodiversity.* Washington, D.C.: National Academy Press, pp. 166–175.

Franklin, J.F.; Cromack, K.; Denison, W.; McKee, A.; Maser, C.; Sedell, J.; Swanson, F. and Juday, G. 1981. *Ecological characteristics of old-growth Douglas-fir forests.* USDA Forest Service, General Technical Report PNW-118.

Hanemann, W.M. 1988. Economics and the preservation of biodiversity. In Wilson, E.O. and F.M. Peter (eds), *Biodiversity.* Washington, D.C.: National Academy Press, pp. 193–199.

Harris, L.D. 1984. *The fragmented forest: island biogeography theory and the preservation of biotic diversity.* Chicago: The University of Chicago Press.

Hoffmann, R.S. 1991. Global biodiversity: the value of abundance. *Western Wildlands.* Fall 1991, pp. 2–7.

Hurlbert, S.H. 1971. The non-concept of species diversity: a critique and alternative parameters. *Ecology* **52:** 577–586.

IUCN/UNEP/WWF (International Union for the Conservation of Nature and Natural Resources, United Nations Environment Programme, World Wildlife Fund) 1991. *Caring for the Earth: a strategy for sustainable living.* Gland, Switzerland: IUCN.

Kaplan, R.D. 1994. The coming anarchy: how scarcity, crime, overpopulation, tribalism, and disease are rapidly destroying the social fabric of our planet. *The Atlantic Monthly* **273**(2): 44–76.

Kauffman, S. 1995. *At home in the universe: the search for laws of self-organization and complexity.* New York: Oxford University Press.

Krebs, C.J. 1985. *Ecology: the experimental analysis of distribution and abundance* (3rd ed.). New York: Harper and Row.

Livingston, J. 1981. *The fallacy of wildlife conservation.* Toronto: McClelland and Stewart.

Lovejoy, T.E. 1986. Species leave the ark one by one. In Norton, B.G. (ed.). *The preservation of species: the value of biological diversity.* Princeton, N.J.: Princeton University Press, pp. 13–27.

Lovelock, J. 1979. *Gaia: a new look at life on Earth.* New York: Oxford University Press.

MacArthur, R.H. and Wilson, E.O. 1967. *The theory of island biogeography.* Princeton, N.J.: Princeton University Press.

Magurran, A.E. 1988. *Ecological diversity and its measurement.* Princeton, N.J.: Princeton University Press.

McMinn, J.W. 1991. *Biological diversity research: an analysis* U.S.D.A. Forest Service: General Technical Report SE-71.

McNeely, J.A. 1988. *Economics and biological diversity: developing and using economic incentives to conserve biological diversity.* Gland, Switzerland: IUCN.

McNeely, J.A.; Miller, K.R.; Reid, W.V.; Mittermeier, R.A. and Werner, T.B. 1990. *Conserving the world's biological diversity.* International Union for Conservation of Nature and Natural

Resources, World Resources Institute, Conservation International, World Wildlife Fund—US, and the World Bank.

McPherson, M.F. 1985. Critical assessment of the value of and concern for the maintenance of biological diversity. In: Office of Technology Assessment, 1986. *Technologies to maintain biological diversity.* Volume II, Contract Papers. Part E: Valuation of biological diversity. Washington, D.C.: U.S. Congress, pp. 154–245.

Myers, N. 1979. *The sinking ark.* Oxford: Pergamon Press.

Myers, N. 1983. *A wealth of wild species: storehouse for human welfare.* Boulder, Colorado: Westview Press.

Newman, J.R. and Schereiber, R.K. 1984. Animals as indicators of ecosystem responses to air emissions. *Environmental Management* 8(4): 309–324.

Norse, E.A. 1990. *Ancient forests of the pacific northwest.* Washington, D.C.: The Wilderness Society and Island Press.

Norton, B.G. 1985. Values and biological diversity. In: Office of Technology Assessment, 1986, *Technologies to maintain biological diversity.* Volume II, Contract Papers. Part E: Valuation of biological diversity. Washington, D.C.: U.S. Congress, pp. 49–91.

Norton, B.G. 1986. On the inherent danger of undervaluing species. In: Norton, B.G. (ed.), *The preservation of species: the value of biological diversity.* Princeton, N.J.: Princeton University Press, pp. 110–137.

Norton, B.G. 1987. *Why preserve natural variety?* Princeton, N.J.: Princeton University Press.

Noss, R.F. 1990. Indicators for monitoring biodiversity: a hierarchical approach. *Conservation Biology* 4(4): 355–364.

Oelschlaeger, M. 1991. *The idea of wilderness.* New Haven: Yale University Press.

Office of Technology Assessment (OTA) 1988. *Technologies to maintain biological diversity.* Philadelphia: Lippincott (originally published in 1987 by U.S. Government Printing Office, Washington, D.C.).

Oldfield, M.L. 1984. *The value of conserving genetic resources.* Washington, D.C.: U.S. Department of Interior, National Park Service.

Orians, G. and Kunin, W. 1985. An ecological perspective on the valuation of biological diversity. In: Office of Technology Assessment, 1986, *Technologies to maintain biological diversity.* Volume II, Contract Papers. Part E: Valuation of biological diversity. Washington, D.C.: U.S. Congress, pp. 93–148.

Patil, G.P. and Taillie, C. 1982a. Diversity as a concept and its measurement. *Journal of the American Statistical Association* 77(379): 548–561.

Patil, G.P. and Taillie, C. 1982b. Rejoinder [to immediately preceding critiques of their 1982a article]. *Journal of the American Statistical Association* 77(379): 565–567.

Peet, R.K. 1974. The measurement of species diversity. *Annual Review of Ecology and Systematics* **5**: 285–307.

Prescott-Allen, C. and Prescott-Allen, R. 1982. *What's wildlife worth? Economic contributions of wild plants and animals to developing countries.* London: Earthscan; International Institute for Environment and Development.

Prescott-Allen, C. and Prescott-Allen, R. 1986. *The first resource: wild species in the North American economy.* New Haven: Yale University Press.

Primack, R.B. 1993. *Essentials of conservation biology.* Sunderland, MA.: Sinauer Associates.

Putman, R.J. and Wratton, S.D. 1984. *Principles of ecology.* London: Croom Helm.

Randall, A. 1985. An economic perspective of the valuation of biological diversity. In: Office of Technology Assessment, 1986, *Technologies to maintain biological diversity.* Volume II, Contract Papers. Part E: Valuation of biological diversity. Washington, D.C.: U.S. Congress, pp. 3–47.

Randall, A. 1988. What mainstream economists have to say about the value of biodiversity. In: Wilson, E.O. and Peter, F.M. (eds), *Biodiversity.* Washington, D.C.: National Academy Press, pp. 217–223.

Randall, A. 1991. The value of biodiversity. *Ambio* 20: 64–68.

Ricklefs, R.E. and Schluter, D. (eds) 1993. *Species diversity in ecological communities: historical and geographical perspectives.* Chicago: The University of Chicago Press.

Rolston, H. III 1983. Values gone wild. *Inquiry,* 26: 181–207.

Rolston, H. III 1985. Valuing wildlands. *Environmental Ethics* 7: 23–48.

Rolston, H. III 1988. *Environmental ethics: duties to and values in the natural world.* Philadelphia: Temple University Press.

Rolston, H. III. 1989. Biology without conservation: an environmental misfit and contradiction in terms. In: Western, D. and Pearl, M. (eds) 1989. *Conservation for the twenty-first century.* New York: Oxford University Press, pp. 232–240.

Rosenzweig, M.L. 1995. *Species diversity in space and time.* Cambridge University Press.

Salwasser, H. 1988. Managing ecosystems for viable populations of vertebrates: a focus for biodiversity. In: Agee, J.K. and Johnson, D.R. (eds), *Ecosystem management for parks and wilderness.* Seattle: University of Washington Press, pp. 87–104.

Scherer, D. (ed.) 1990. *Upstream/Downstream: Issues in environmental ethics.* Philadelphia: Temple University Press.

Sepkoski, J.J. 1984. A kinetic model of Phanerozoic taxonomic diversity III. Post-Paleozoic families and mass extinctions. *Paleobiology* **10**: 246–67.

Snyder, G. 1990. *The practice of the wild.* San Francisco: North Point Press.

Sober, E. 1984. *The nature of selection: evolutionary theory in philosophical focus.* Cambridge, Massachusetts: The MIT Press.

Soulé, M. 1985. What is conservation biology? *BioScience* **35:** 727–734.

Swanson, T.; Aylward, B.; Grammage, S.; Freedman, S. and Hanrahan, D. 1992. Biodiversity and economics. In: Groombridge, B. (ed.) *Global biodiversity: status of the earth's living resources.* A report compiled by the World Conservation Monitoring Centre. London: Chapman and Hall, pp. 407–438.

Vane-Wright, R.I.; Humphries, C.J. and Williams, P.H. 1991. What to Protect?—Systematics and the Agony of Choice. *Biological Conservation* **55:** 235–254.

Westman, W.E. 1985. *Ecology, impact assessment, and environmental planning.* New York: John Wiley & Sons.

Whittaker, R.H. 1970. *Communities and ecosystems.* New York: MacMillan.

Wilcove, D.S.; McLellan, C.H. and Dobson, A.P. 1986. Habitat fragmentation in the temperate zone. In: Soulé, M. (ed.), *Conservation biology: the science of scarcity and diversity.* Sunderland, Massachusetts: Sinauer Associates, pp. 237–256.

Wilcox, B. 1984. In situ conservation of genetic resources: determinants of minimum area requirements. In: McNeely, J.A. and Miller, K.R. (eds). *National parks, conservation, and development: the role of protected areas in sustaining society.* Washington, D.C.: Smithsonian Institution Press, pp. 639–647.

Wilson, E.O. 1992. *The diversity of life.* Cambridge, MA: The Belknap Press of Harvard University Press.

WRI/IUCN/UNEP (World Resources Institute, International Union for the Conservation of Nature and Natural Resources, United Nations Environment Programme) 1991. *Global Biodiversity Strategy.* Washington, D.C.

Williams, P.H.; Humphries, C.J. and Vane-Wright, R.I. 1991. Measuring biodiversity: taxonomic relatedness for conservation priorities. *Australian Systematic Botany* **4**(4): 665–679.

"Philosophical Problems for Environmentalism"

Elliott Sober

INTRODUCTION

Preserving an endangered species or ecosystem poses no special conceptual problem when the instrumental value of that species or ecosystem is known. When we have reason to think that some natural object represents a resource to us, we obviously ought to take that fact into account in deciding what to do. A variety of potential uses may be under discussion, including food supply, medical applications, recreational use, and so on. As with any complex decision, it may be difficult even to agree on how to compare the competing values that may be involved. Willingness to pay in dollars is a familiar least common denominator, although it poses a number of problems. But here we have nothing that is specifically a problem for environmentalism.

The problem for environmentalism stems from the idea that species and ecosystems ought to be preserved for reasons additional to their known value as resources for human use. The feeling is that even when we cannot say what nutritional, medicinal, or recreational benefit the preservation provides, there still is a value in preservation. It is the search for a rationale for this feeling that constitutes the main conceptual problem for environmentalism.

The problem is especially difficult in view of the holistic (as opposed to individualistic) character of the things being assigned value. Put simply, what is special about environmentalism is that it values the preservation of species, communities, or ecosystems, rather than the individual organisms of which they are composed. "Animal liberationists" have urged that we should take the suffering of sentient animals into account in ethical deliberation. Such beasts are not mere things to be used as cruelly as we like no matter how trivial the benefit we derive. But in "widening the ethical circle," we are simply including in the community more individual organisms whose costs and benefits we compare. Animal liberationists are extending an old and familiar ethical doctrine—namely, utilitarianism—to take account of the welfare of other individuals. Although the practical consequences of this point of view may be revolutionary, the theoretical perspective is not at all novel. If suffering is bad, then it is bad for any individual who suffers. Animal liberationists merely remind us of the consequences of familiar principles.

But trees, mountains, and salt marshes do not suffer. They do not experience pleasure and pain, because, evidently, they do not have experiences at all. The same is true of species. Granted, individual organisms may have mental states; but the species—taken to be a population of organisms connected by certain sorts of interactions (preeminently, that of exchanging genetic material in reproduction)—does not. Or put more carefully, we might say that the only sense in which species have experiences is that their member organisms do: the attribution at the population level, if true, is true simply in virtue of its being true at the individual level. Here is a case where reductionism is correct.

So perhaps it is true in this reductive sense that some species experience pain. But the values that environmentalists attach to preserving species do not reduce to any value of preserving organisms. It is in this sense that environmentalists espouse a holistic value system. Environmentalists care about entities that by no stretch of the imagination have experiences (e.g., mountains). What is more, their position does not force them to care if individual organisms suffer pain, so long as the species is preserved. Steel traps may outrage an animal liberationist because of the suffering they inflict, but an environmentalist aiming just at the preservation of a balanced ecosystem might see here no cause for complaint. Similarly, environmentalists think that the distinction between wild and domesticated organisms is important, in that it is the preservation of "natural" (i.e., not created by the "artificial interference" of human beings) objects that matters, whereas animal liberationists see the main problem in terms of the suffering of any organism—domesticated or not. And finally, environmentalists and animal liberationists diverge on what might be called then $n + m$ *question.* If two species—say blue and sperm whales—have roughly comparable capacities for experiencing pain, an animal liberationist might tend to think of the preservation of a sperm whale as wholly on an ethical par with the preservation of a blue whale. The fact that one organism is part of an endangered species while the other is not does not make the rare individual more intrinsically important. But for an environmentalist, this holistic property—membership in an endangered species—makes all the difference in the world: a world with n sperm and m blue whales is far better than a world with $n + m$ sperm and 0 blue whales. Here we have a stark contrast between an ethic in which it is the life situation of individuals that matters, and an ethic in which the stability and diversity of populations of individuals are what matter.

Both animal liberationists and environmentalists wish to broaden our ethical horizons—to make us realize that it is not just human welfare that counts. But they do this in very different, often conflicting, ways. It is no accident that at the level of practical politics the two points of view increasingly find themselves at loggerheads. This practical conflict is the expression of a deep theoretical divide.[1]

THE IGNORANCE ARGUMENT

"Although we might not now know what use a particular endangered species might be to us, allowing it to go extinct forever closes off the possibility of discovering and exploiting a future use." According to this point of view, our ignorance of value is turned into a reason for action. The scenario envisaged in this environmentalist argument is not without precedent; who could have guessed that penicillin would be good for something other than turning out cheese? But there is a fatal defect in such arguments, which we might summarize with the phrase *out of nothing, nothing comes*: rational decisions require assumptions about what is true and what is valuable (in decision-theoretic jargon, the inputs must be probabilities and utilities). If you are completely ignorant of values, then you are incapable of making a rational decision, either for or against preserving some species. The fact that you do not know the value of a species, by itself, cannot count as a reason for wanting one thing rather than another to happen to it.

And there are so many species. How many geese that lay golden eggs are there apt to be in that number? It is hard to assign probabilities and utilities precisely here, but an analogy will perhaps reveal the problem confronting this environmentalist argument. Most of us willingly fly on airplanes, when safer (but less convenient) alternative forms of transportation are available. Is this rational? Suppose it were argued that there is a small probability that the next flight you take will crash. This would be very bad for you. Is it not crazy for you to risk this, given that the only gain to you is that you can reduce your travel time by a few hours (by not going by train, say)? Those of us who not only fly, but congratulate ourselves for being rational in doing so, reject this argument. We are prepared to accept a small chance of a great disaster in return for the high probability of a rather modest benefit. If this is rational, no wonder that we might consistently be willing to allow a species to go extinct in order to build a hydroelectric plant.

That the argument from ignorance is no argument at all can be seen from another angle. If we literally do not know what consequences the extinction of this or that species may bring, then we should take seriously the possibility that the extinction may be beneficial as well as the possibility that it may be deleterious. It may sound deep to insist that we preserve endangered species precisely because we do not know why they are valuable. But ignorance on a scale like this cannot provide the basis for any rational action.

Rather than invoke some unspecified future benefit, an environmentalist may argue that the species in question plays a crucial role in stabilizing the ecosystem of which it is a part. This will undoubtedly be true for carefully chosen species and ecosystems, but one should not generalize this argument into a global claim to the effect that *every* species is crucial to a balanced ecosystem. Although ecologists used to agree that the complexity of an ecosystem stabilizes it, this hypothesis has been subject to a number of criticisms and qualifications, both from a theoretical and an empirical perspective.[2] And for certain kinds of species (those which occupy a rather small area and whose normal population is small) we can argue that extinction would probably not disrupt the community. However fragile the biosphere may be, the extreme view that everything is crucial is almost certainly not true.

But, of course, environmentalists are often concerned by the fact that extinctions are occurring now at a rate much higher than in earlier times. It is mass extinction that threatens the biosphere, they say, and this claim avoids the spurious assertion that communities are so fragile that even one extinction will cause a crash. However, if the point is to avoid a mass extinction of species, how does this provide a rationale for preserving a species of the kind just described, of which we rationally believe that its passing will not destabilize the ecosystem? And, more generally, if mass extinction is known to be a danger to us, how does this translate into a value for preserving any particular species? Notice that we have now passed beyond the confines of the argument from ignorance; we are taking as a premise the idea that mass extinction would be a catastrophe (since it would destroy the ecosystem on which we depend). But how should that premise affect our valuing the California condor, the blue whale, or the snail darter?

THE SLIPPERY SLOPE ARGUMENT

Environmentalists sometimes find themselves asked to explain why each species matters so much to them, when there are, after all, so many. We may know of special reasons for valuing particular species, but how can we justify thinking that each and every species is important? "Each extinction impoverishes the biosphere" is often the answer given, but it really fails to resolve the issue. Granted, each extinction impoverishes, but it only impoverishes a little bit. So if it is the *wholesale* impoverishment of the biosphere that matters, one would apparently have to concede that each extinction matters a little, but only a little. But environmentalists may be loathe to concede this, for if they concede that each species matters only a little, they seem to be inviting the wholesale impoverishment that would be an unambiguous disaster. So they dig in their heels and insist that each species matters a lot. But to take this line, one must find some other rationale than the idea that mass extinction would be a great harm. Some of these alternative rationales we will examine later. For now, let us take a closer look at the train of thought involved here.

Slippery slopes are curious things: if you take even one step onto them, you inevitably slide all the way to the bottom. So if you want to avoid finding yourself at the bottom, you must avoid stepping onto them at all. To mix metaphors, stepping onto a slippery slope is to invite being nickeled and dimed to death.

Slippery slope arguments have played a powerful role in a number of recent ethical debates. One often hears people defend the legitimacy of abortions by arguing that since it is permissible to abort a single-celled fertilized egg, it must be permissible to abort a foetus of any age, since there is no place to draw the line from 0 to 9 months. Antiabortionists, on the other hand, sometimes argue in the other direction: since infanticide of newborns is not permissible, abortion at any earlier time is also not allowed, since there is no place to draw the line. Although these two arguments reach opposite conclusions about the permissibility of abortions, they agree on the following idea: since there is no principled place to draw the line on the continuum from newly fertilized egg to foetus gone to term, one must treat all these cases in the same way. Either abortion is always permitted or it never is, since there is no place to draw the line. Both sides run their favorite slippery slope arguments, but try to precipitate slides in opposite directions.

Starting with 10 million extant species, and valuing overall diversity, the environmentalist does not want to grant that each species matters only a little. For having granted this, commercial expansion and other causes will reduce the tally to 9,999,999. And then the argument is repeated, with each species valued only a little, and diversity declines another notch. And so we are well on our way to a considerably impoverished biosphere, a little at a time. Better to reject the starting premise—namely, that each species matters only a little—so that the slippery slope can be avoided.

Slippery slopes should hold no terror for environmentalists, because it is often a mistake to demand that a line be drawn. Let me illustrate by an example. What is the difference between being bald and not? Presumably, the difference concerns the number of hairs you have on your head. But what is the precise number of hairs marking the boundary between baldness and not being bald? There is no such number. Yet, it would be a fallacy to conclude that there is no difference between baldness and hairiness. The fact that you cannot draw a line does not force you to say that the two alleged categories collapse into one. In the abortion case, this means that even if there is no precise point in foetal development that involves some discontinuous, qualitative change, one is still not obliged to think of newly fertilized eggs and foetuses gone to term as morally on a par. Since the biological differences are ones of degree, not kind, one may want to adopt the position that the moral differences are likewise matters of degree. This may lead to the view that a woman should have a better reason for having an abortion, the more developed her foetus is.

Of course, this position does not logically follow from the idea that there is no place to draw the line; my point is just that differences in degree do not demolish the possibility of there being real moral differences.

In the environmental case, if one places a value on diversity, then each species becomes more valuable as the overall diversity declines. If we begin with 10 million species, each may matter little, but as extinctions continue, the remaining ones matter more and more. According to this outlook, a better and better reason would be demanded for allowing yet another species to go extinct. Perhaps certain sorts of economic development would justify the extinction of a species at one time. But granting this does not oblige one to conclude that the same sort of decision would have to be made further down the road. This means that one can value diversity without being obliged to take the somewhat exaggerated position that each species, no matter how many there are, is terribly precious in virtue of its contribution to that diversity.

Yet, one can understand that environmentalists might be reluctant to concede this point. They may fear that if one now allows that most species contribute only a little to overall diversity, one will set in motion a political process that cannot correct itself later. The worry is that even when the overall diversity has been drastically reduced, our ecological sensitivities will have been so coarsened that we will no longer be in a position to realize (or to implement policies fostering) the preciousness of what is left. This fear may be quite justified, but it is important to realize that it does not conflict with what was argued above. The political utility of making an argument should not be confused with the argument's soundness.

The fact that you are on a slippery slope, by itself, does not tell you whether you are near the beginning, in the middle, or at the end. If species diversity is a matter of degree, where do we currently find ourselves—on the verge of catastrophe, well on our way in that direction, or at some distance from a global crash? Environmentalists often urge that we are fast approaching a precipice; if we are, then the reduction in diversity that every succeeding extinction engenders should be all we need to justify species preservation.

Sometimes, however, environmentalists advance a kind of argument not predicated on the idea of fast approaching doom. The goal is to show that there is something wrong with allowing a species to go extinct (or with causing it to go extinct), even if overall diversity is not affected much. I now turn to one argument of this kind.

APPEALS TO WHAT IS NATURAL

I noted earlier that environmentalists and animal liberationists disagree over the significance of the distinction between wild and domesticated animals. Since both types of organisms can experience pain, animal liberationists will think of each as meriting ethical consideration. But environmentalists will typically not put wild and domesticated organisms on a par. Environmentalists typically are interested in preserving what is natural, be it a species living in the wild or a wilderness ecosystem. If a kind of domesticated chicken were threatened with extinction, I doubt that environmental groups would be up in arms. And if certain unique types of human environments—say urban slums in the United States—were "endangered," it is similarly unlikely that environmentalists would view this process as a deplorable impoverishment of the biosphere.

The environmentalist's lack of concern for humanly created organisms and environments may be practical rather than principled. It may be that at the level of values, no such bifurcation is legitimate, but that from the point of view of practical political action, it makes sense to put one's energies into saving items that exist in the wild. This subject has not been discussed much in the literature, so it is hard to tell. But I sense that the distinction between wild and domesticated has a certain theoretical importance to many environmentalists. They perhaps think that the difference is that we created domesticated organisms which would otherwise not exist, and so are entitled to use them solely for our own interests. But we did not create wild organisms and environments, so it is the height of presumption to expropriate them for our benefit. A more fitting posture would be one of "stewardship": we have come on the scene and found a treasure not of our making. Given this, we ought to preserve this treasure in its natural state.

I do not wish to contest the appropriateness of "stewardship." It is the dichotomy between artificial (domesticated) and natural (wild) that strikes me as wrong-headed. I want to suggest that to the degree that "natural" means anything biologically, it means very little ethically. And, conversely, to the degree that "natural" is understood as a normative concept, it has very little to do with biology.

Environmentalists often express regret that we human beings find it so hard to remember that we are part of nature—one species among many others—rather than something standing outside of nature. I will not consider here whether this attitude is cause for complaint; the important point is that seeing us as part of nature rules out the environmentalist's use of the distinction between artificial-domesticated and natural-wild described above. *If we are part of nature, then everything we do is part of nature, and is natural in that primary sense.* When we domesticate organisms and bring them into a state of dependence on us, this is simply an example of one species exerting a selection pressure on another. If one calls this "unnatural," one might just as well say the same of parasitism or symbiosis (compare human domestication of animals and plants and "slave-making" in the social insects).

The concept of naturalness is subject to the same abuses as the concept of normalcy. *Normal* can mean *usual* or it can mean *desirable*. Although only the total pessimist will think that the two concepts are mutually exclusive, it is generally recognized that the mere fact that something is common does not by itself count as a reason for thinking that it is desirable. This distinction is quite familiar now in popular discussions of mental health, for example. Yet, when it comes to environmental issues, the concept of naturalness continues to live a double life. The destruction of wilderness areas by increased industrialization is bad because it is unnatural. And it is unnatural because it involves transforming a natural into an artificial habitat. Or one might hear that although extinction is a natural process, the kind of mass extinction currently being precipitated by our species is unprecedented, and so is unnatural. Environmentalists should look elsewhere for a defense of their policies, lest conservation simply become a variant of uncritical conservatism in which the axiom "Whatever is, is right" is modified to read "Whatever is (before human beings come on the scene), is right."

This conflation of the biological with the normative sense of "natural" sometimes comes to the fore when environmentalists attack animal liberationists for naive do-goodism. Callicott writes:

> . . . the value commitments of the humane movement seem at bottom to betray a world-denying or rather a life-loathing philosophy. The natural world as actually constituted is one in which one being lives at the expense of others. Each organism, in Darwin's metaphor, struggles to maintain its own organic integrity. . . . To live *is* to be anxious about life, to feel pain and pleasure in a fitting mixture, and sooner or later to die. That is the way the system works. *If nature as a whole is good, then pain and death are also good.* Environmental ethics in general require people to play fair in the natural system. The neo-Benthamites have in a sense taken the uncourageous approach. People have attempted to exempt themselves from the life/death reciprocities of natural processes and from ecological limitations in the name of a prophylactic ethic of maximizing rewards (pleasure) and minimizing unwelcome information (pain). To be fair, the humane moralists seem to suggest that we should attempt to project the same values into the nonhuman animal world and to widen the charmed circle—no matter that it would be biologically unrealistic to do so or biologically ruinous if, per impossible, such an environmental ethic were implemented.
>
> There is another approach. Rather than imposing our alienation from nature and natural processes and cycles of life on other animals, we human beings could reaffirm our participation in nature by accepting life as it is given without a sugar coating. . . .[3]

On the same page, Callicott quotes with approval Shepard's remark that "the humanitarian's projection onto nature of illegal murder and the rights of civilized people to safety not only misses the point but is exactly contrary to fundamental ecological reality: the structure of nature is a sequence of killings."[4]

Thinking that what is found in nature is beyond ethical defect has not always been popular. Darwin wrote:

. . . That there is much suffering in the world no one disputes.

Some have attempted to explain this in reference to man by imagining that it serves for his moral improvement. But the number of men in the world is as nothing compared with that of all other sentient beings, and these often suffer greatly without any moral improvement. A being so powerful and so full of knowledge as a God who could create the universe, is to our finite minds omnipotent and omniscient, and it revolts our understanding to suppose that his benevolence is not unbounded, for what advantage can there be in the sufferings of millions of the lower animals throughout almost endless time? This very old argument from the existence of suffering against the existence of an intelligent first cause seems to me a strong one; whereas, as just remarked, the presence of much suffering agrees well with the view that all organic beings have been developed through variation and natural selection.[5]

Darwin apparently viewed the quantity of pain found in nature as a melancholy and sobering consequence of the struggle for existence. But once we adopt the Panglossian attitude that this is the best of all possible worlds ("there is just the right amount of pain," etc.), a failure to identify what is natural with what is good can only seem "world-denying," "life-loathing," "in a sense uncourageous," and "contrary to fundamental ecological reality."[6]

Earlier in his essay, Callicott expresses distress that animal liberationists fail to draw a sharp distinction "between the very different plights (and rights) of wild and domestic animals."[7] Domestic animals are creations of man, he says. "They are living artifacts, but artifacts nevertheless. . . . There is thus something profoundly incoherent (and insensitive as well) in the complaint of some animal liberationists that the 'natural behavior' of chickens and bobby calves is cruelly frustrated on factory farms. It would make almost as much sense to speak of the natural behavior of tables and chairs."[8] Here again we see teleology playing a decisive role: wild organisms do not have the natural function of serving human ends, but domesticated animals do. Cheetahs in zoos are crimes against what is natural; veal calves in boxes are not.

The idea of "natural tendency" played a decisive role in pre-Darwinian biological thinking. Aristotle's entire science—both his physics and his biology—is articulated in terms of specifying the natural tendencies of kinds of objects and the interfering forces that can prevent an object from achieving its intended state. Heavy objects in the sublunar sphere have location at the center of the earth as their natural state; each tends to go there, but is prevented from doing so. Organisms likewise are conceptualized in terms of this natural state model:

. . . [for] any living thing that has reached its normal development and which is unmutilated, and whose mode of generation is not spontaneous, the most natural act is the production of another like itself, an animal producing an animal, a plant a plant. . . .[9]

But many interfering forces are possible, and in fact the occurrence of "monsters" is anything but uncommon. According to Aristotle, mules (sterile hybrids) count as deviations from the natural state. In fact, females are monsters as well, since the natural tendency of sexual reproduction is for the offspring to perfectly resemble the father, who, according to Aristotle, provides the "genetic instructions" (to put the idea anachronistically) while the female provides only the matter.

What has happened to the natural state model in modern science? In physics, the idea of describing what a class of objects will do in the absence of "interference" lives on: Newton specified this "zero-force state" as rest or uniform motion, and in general relativity, this state is understood in terms of motion along geodesics. But one of the most profound achievements of Darwinian biology has been the jettisoning of this kind of model. It isn't just that Aristotle was wrong in his detailed claims about mules and women; the whole structure of the natural state model has been discarded. Population biology is not conceptualized in terms of positing some characteristic that all members of a species would have in common, were interfering forces absent. Variation is not thought of as a deflection from the natural state of uniformity. Rather, variation is taken to be a fundamental property in its own right. Nor, at the level of individual biology, does the natural state model find an application. Developmental theory is not articulated by specifying a natural tendency and a set of interfering forces. . . . The idea that a corn plant might have some "natural height," which can be augmented or diminished by "interfering forces" is entirely alien to post-Darwinian biology.

The fact that the concepts of natural state and interfering force have lapsed from biological thought does not prevent environmentalists from inventing them anew. Perhaps these concepts can be provided with some sort of normative content; after all, the normative idea of "human rights" may make sense even if it is not a theoretical underpinning of any empirical science. But environmentalists should not assume that they can rely on some previously articulated scientific conception of "natural."

APPEALS TO NEEDS AND INTERESTS

The version of utilitarianism considered earlier (according to which something merits ethical consideration if it can experience pleasure and/or pain) leaves the environmentalist in the lurch. But there is an alternative to Bentham's hedonistic utilitarianism that has been thought by some to be a foundation for environmentalism. Preference utilitarianism says that an object's having interests, needs, or preferences gives it ethical status. This doctrine is at the core of Stone's affirmative answer to the title question of his book *Should Trees Have Standing?*[10] "Natural objects *can* communicate their wants (needs) to us, and in ways that are not terribly ambiguous. . . . The lawn tells me that it wants water by a certain dryness of the blades and soil—immediately obvious to the touch—the appearance of bald spots, yellowing, and a lack of springiness after being walked on." And if plants can do this, presumably so can mountain ranges, and endangered species. Preference utilitarianism may thereby seem to grant intrinsic ethical importance to precisely the sorts of objects about which environmentalists have expressed concern.

The problems with this perspective have been detailed by Sagoff.[11] If one does not require of an object that it have a mind for it to have wants or needs, what *is* required for the possession of these ethically relevant properties? Suppose one says that an object needs something if it will cease to exist if it does not get it. Then species, plants, and mountain ranges have needs, but only in the sense that automobiles, garbage dumps, and buildings do too. If everything has needs, the advice to take needs into account in ethical deliberation is empty, unless it is supplemented by some technique for weighting and comparing the needs of different objects. A corporation will go bankrupt unless a highway is built. But the swamp will cease to exist if the highway is built. Perhaps one should take into account all relevant needs, but the question is how to do this in the event that needs conflict.

Although the concept of needs can be provided with a permissive, all-inclusive definition, it is less easy to see how to do this with the concept of want. Why think that a mountain range "wants" to retain its unspoiled appearance, rather than house a new amusement park? Needs are not at issue here, since in either case, the mountain continues to exist. One might be tempted to think that natural objects like mountains and species have "natural tendencies," and that the concept of want should be liberalized so as to mean that natural objects "want" to persist in their natural states. This Aristotelian view, as I argued in the previous section, simply makes no sense. Granted, a commercially undeveloped mountain will persist in this state, unless it is commercially developed. But it is equally true that a commercially untouched hill will become commercially developed, unless something causes this not to happen. I see no hope for extending the concept of wants to the full range of objects valued by environmentalists.

The same problems emerge when we try to apply the concepts of needs and wants to species. A species may need various resources, in the sense that these are necessary for its continued existence. But what do species want? Do they want to remain stable in numbers, neither growing nor shrinking? Or since most species have gone extinct, perhaps what species really want is to go extinct, and it is human meddlesomeness that frustrates this natural tendency? Preference utilitarianism is no more likely than hedonistic utilitarianism to secure autonomous ethical status for endangered species.

Ehrenfeld describes a related distortion that has been inflicted on the diversity/stability hypothesis in theoretical ecology. If it were true that increasing the diversity of an ecosystem causes it to be more stable, this might encourage the Aristotelian idea that ecosystems have a natural tendency to increase their diversity. The full realization of this tendency—the natural state that is the goal of ecosystems—is the "climax" or "mature" community. Extinction diminishes diversity, so it frustrates ecosystems from attaining their goal. Since the hypothesis that diversity causes stability is now considered controversial (to say the least), this line of thinking will not be very tempting. But even if the diversity/stability hypothesis were true, it would not permit the environmentalist to conclude that ecosystems have an interest in retaining their diversity.

Darwinism has not banished the idea that parts of the natural world are goal-directed systems, but has furnished this idea with a natural mechanism. We properly conceive of organisms (or genes, sometimes) as being in the business of maximizing their chances of survival and reproduction. We describe characteristics as adaptations—as devices that exist for the furtherance of these ends. Natural selection makes this perspective intelligible. But Darwinism is a profoundly individualistic doctrine.[12] Darwinism rejects the idea that species, communities, and ecosystems have adaptations that exist for their own benefit. These higher-level entities are not conceptualized as goal-directed systems; what properties of organization they possess are viewed as artifacts of processes operating at lower levels of organization. An environmentalism based on the idea that the ecosystem is directed toward stability and diversity must find its foundation elsewhere.

GRANTING WHOLES AUTONOMOUS VALUE

A number of environmentalists have asserted that environmental values cannot be grounded in values based on regard for individual welfare. Aldo Leopold wrote in *A Sand County Almanac* that "a thing is right when it tends to preserve the integrity, stability, and beauty of the biotic community. It is wrong when it tends otherwise."[13] Callicott develops this idea at some length, and ascribes to ethical environmentalism the view that "the preciousness of individual deer, *as of any other specimen*, is inversely proportional to the population of the species."[14] In his *Desert Solitaire*, Edward Abbey notes that he would sooner shoot a man than a snake.[15] And Garrett Hardin asserts that human beings injured in wilderness areas ought not to be rescued: making great and spectacular efforts to save the life of an individual "makes sense only when there is a shortage of people. I have not lately heard that there is a shortage of people."[16] The point of view suggested by these quotations is quite clear. It isn't that preserving the integrity of ecosystems has autonomous value, to be taken into account just as the quite distinct value of individual human welfare is. Rather, the idea is that the only value is the holistic one of maintaining ecological balance and diversity. Here we have a view that is just as monolithic as the most single-minded individualism; the difference is that the unit of value is thought to exist at a higher level of organization.

It is hard to know what to say to someone who would save a mosquito, just because it is rare, rather than a human being, if there were a choice. In ethics, as in any other subject, rationally persuading another person requires the existence of shared assumptions. If this monolithic environmentalist view is based on the notion that ecosystems have needs and interests, and that these take total precedence over the rights and interests of individual human beings, then the discussion of the previous sections is relevant. And even supposing that these higher-level entities have needs and wants, what reason is there to suppose that these matter and that the wants and needs of individuals matter not at all? But if this source of defense is jettisoned, and it is merely asserted that only ecosystems have value, with no substantive defense being offered, one must begin by requesting an argument: *why* is ecosystem stability and diversity the only value?

Some environmentalists have seen the individualist bias of utilitarianism as being harmful in ways additional to its impact on our perception of ecological values. Thus, Callicott writes:

> On the level of social organization, the interests of society may not always coincide with the sum of the interests of its parts. Discipline, sacrifice, and individual restraint are often necessary in the social sphere to maintain social integrity as within the bodily organism. A society, indeed, is particularly vulnerable to disintegration when its members become preoccupied totally with their own particular interest, and ignore those distinct and independent interests of the community as a whole. One example, unfortunately, our own society, is altogether too close at hand to be examined with strict academic detachment. The United States seems to pursue uncritically a social policy of reductive utilitarianism, aimed at promoting the happiness of all its members severally. Each special interest accordingly clamors more loudly to be satisfied while the community as a whole becomes noticeably more and more infirm economically, environmentally, and politically.[17]

Callicott apparently sees the emergence of individualism and alienation from nature as two aspects of the same process. He values "the symbiotic relationship of Stone Age man to the natural environment" and regrets that "civilization has insulated and alienated us from the rigors and challenges of the natural environment. The hidden agenda of the humane ethic," he says, "is the imposition of the anti-natural prophylactic ethos of comfort and soft pleasure on an even wider scale. The land ethic, on the other hand, requires a shrinkage, if at all possible, of the domestic sphere; it rejoices in a recrudescence of the wilderness and a renaissance of tribal cultural experience."[18]

Callicott is right that "strict academic detachment" is difficult here. The reader will have to decide whether the United States currently suffers from too much or too little regard "for the happiness of all its members severally" and whether we should feel nostalgia or pity in contemplating what the Stone Age experience of nature was like.

THE DEMARCATION PROBLEM

Perhaps the most fundamental theoretical problem confronting an environmentalist who wishes to claim that species and ecosystems have autonomous value is what I will call the *problem of demarcation*. Every ethical theory must provide principles that describe which objects matter for their own sakes and which do not. Besides marking the boundary between these two classes by enumerating a set of ethically relevant properties, an ethical theory must say why the properties named, rather than others, are the ones that count. Thus, for example, hedonistic utilitarianism cites the capacity to experience pleasure and/or pain as the decisive criterion; preference utilitarianism cites the having of preferences (or wants, or interests) as the decisive property. And a Kantian ethical theory will include an individual in the ethical community only if it is capable of rational reflection and autonomy. Not that justifying these various proposed solutions to the demarcation problem is easy; indeed, since this issue is so fundamental, it will be very difficult to justify one proposal as opposed to another. Still, a substantive ethical theory is obliged to try.

Environmentalists, wishing to avoid the allegedly distorting perspective of individualism, frequently want to claim autonomous value for wholes. This may take the form of a monolithic doctrine according to which the only thing that matters is the stability of the ecosystem. Or it may embody a pluralistic outlook according to which ecosystem stability and species preservation have an importance additional to the welfare of individual organisms. But an environmentalist theory shares with all ethical theories an interest in not saying that everything has autonomous value. The reason this position is proscribed is that it makes the adjudication of ethical conflict very difficult indeed. (In addition, it is radically implausible, but we can set that objection to one side.)

Environmentalists, as we have seen, may think of natural objects, like mountains, species, and ecosystems, as mattering for their own sake, but of artificial objects, like highway systems and domesticated animals, as having only instrumental value. If a mountain and a highway are both made of rock, it seems unlikely that the difference between them arises from the fact that mountains have wants, interests, and preferences, but highway systems do not. But perhaps the place to look for the relevant difference is not in their present physical composition, but in the historical fact of how each came into existence. Mountains were created by natural processes, whereas highways are humanly constructed. But once we realize that organisms construct their environments in nature, this contrast begins to cloud. Organisms do not passively reside in an environment whose properties are independently determined. Organisms transform their environments by physically interacting with them. An anthill is an artifact just as a highway is. Granted, a difference obtains at the level of whether conscious deliberation played a role, but can one take seriously the view that artifacts produced by conscious planning are thereby *less* valuable than ones that arise without the intervention of mentality? As we have noted before, although environmentalists often accuse their critics of failing to think in a biologically realistic way, their use of the distinction between "natural" and "artificial" is just the sort of idea that stands in need of a more realistic biological perspective.

My suspicion is that the distinction between natural and artificial is not the crucial one. On the contrary, certain features of environmental concerns imply that natural objects are exactly on a par with certain artificial ones. Here the intended comparison is not between mountains and highways, but between mountains and works of art. My goal in what follows is not to sketch a substantive conception of what determines the value of objects in these two domains, but to motivate an analogy.

For both natural objects and works of art, our values extend beyond the concerns we have for experiencing pleasure. Most of us value seeing an original painting more than we value seeing a copy, even when we could not tell the difference. When we experience works of art, often what we value is not just the kinds of experiences we have, but, in addition, the connections we usually have with certain real objects. Routley and Routley have made an analogous point about valuing the wilderness experience: a "wilderness experience machine" that caused certain sorts of hallucinations would be no substitute for actually going into the wild.[19] Nor is this fact about our valuation limited to such aesthetic and environmentalist contexts. We love various people in our lives. If a molecule-for-molecule replica of a beloved person were created, you would not love that individual, but would continue to love the individual to whom you actually were historically related. Here again, our attachments are to objects and people as they really are, and not just to the experiences that they facilitate.

Another parallel between environmentalist concerns and aesthetic values concerns the issue of context. Although environmentalists often stress the importance of preserving endangered species, they would not be completely satisfied if an endangered species were preserved by putting a number of specimens in a zoo or in a humanly constructed preserve. What is taken to be important is preserving the species in its natural habitat. This leads to the more holistic position that preserving ecosystems, and not simply preserving certain member species, is of primary importance. Aesthetic concerns often lead in the same direction. It was not merely saving a fresco or an altar piece that motivated art historians after the most recent flood in Florence. Rather, they wanted to save these works of art in their original ("natural") settings. Not just the painting, but the church that housed it; not just the church, but the city itself. The idea of objects residing in a "fitting" environment plays a powerful role in both domains.

Environmentalism and aesthetics both see value in rarity. Of two whales, why should one be more worthy of aid than another, just because one belongs to an endangered species? Here we have the $n + m$ question mentioned [earlier]. As an ethical concern, rarity is difficult to understand. Perhaps this is because our ethical ideas concerning justice and equity (note the word) are saturated with individualism. But in the context of aesthetics, the concept of rarity is far from alien. A work of art may have enhanced value simply because there are very few other works by the same artist, or from the same historical period, or in the same style. It isn't that the price of the item may go up with rarity; I am talking about aesthetic value, not monetary worth. Viewed as valuable aesthetic objects, rare organisms may be valuable because they are rare.

A disanalogy may suggest itself. It may be objected that works of art are of instrumental value only, but that species and ecosystems have intrinsic value. Perhaps it is true, as claimed before, that our attachment to works of art, to nature, and to our loved ones extends beyond the experiences they allow us to have. But it may be argued that what is valuable in the aesthetic case is always the relation of a valuer to a valued object. When we experience a work of art, the value is not simply in the experience, but in the composite fact that we and the work of art are related in certain ways. This immediately suggests that if there were no valuers in the world, nothing would have value, since such relational facts could no longer obtain. So, to adapt Routley and Routley's "last man argument," it would seem that if an ecological crisis precipitated a collapse of the world system, the last human being (whom we may assume for the purposes of this example to be the last valuer) could set about destroying all works of art, and there would be nothing wrong in this.[20] That is, if aesthetic objects are valuable only in so far as valuers can stand in certain relations to them, then when valuers disappear, so does the possibility of aesthetic value. This would deny, in one sense, that aesthetic objects are intrinsically valuable: it isn't they, in themselves, but rather the relational facts that they are part of, that are valuable.

In contrast, it has been claimed that the "last man" would be wrong to destroy natural objects such as mountains, salt marshes, and species. (So as to avoid confusing the issue by bringing in the welfare of individual organisms, Routley and Routley imagine that destruction and mass extinctions can be caused painlessly, so that there would be nothing wrong about this undertaking from the point of view of the nonhuman organisms involved.) If the last man ought to preserve these natural objects, then these objects appear to have a kind of autonomous value; their value would extend beyond their possible relations to valuers. If all this were true, we would have here a contrast between aesthetic and natural objects, one that implies that natural objects are more valuable than works of art.

Routley and Routley advance the last man argument as if it were decisive in showing that environmental objects such as mountains and salt marshes have autonomous value. I find the example more puzzling than decisive. But, in the present context, we do not have to decide whether Routley and Routley are right. We only have to decide whether this imagined situation brings out any relevant difference between aesthetic and environmental values. Were the last man to look up on a certain hillside, he would see a striking rock formation next to the ruins of a Greek temple. Long ago the temple was built from some of the very rocks that still stud the slope. Both promontory and temple have a history, and both have been transformed by the biotic and the abiotic environments. I myself find it impossible to advise the last man that the peak matters more than the temple. I do not see a relevant difference. Environmentalists, if they hold that the solution to the problem of demarcation is to be found in the distinction between natural and artificial, will have to find such a distinction. But if environmental values are aesthetic, no difference need be discovered.

Environmentalists may be reluctant to classify their concern as aesthetic. Perhaps they will feel that aesthetic concerns are frivolous. Perhaps they will feel that the aesthetic regard for artifacts that has been made possible by culture is antithetical to a proper regard for wilderness. But such contrasts are illusory. Concern for environmental values does not require a stripping away of the perspective afforded by civilization; to value the wild, one does not have to "become wild" oneself (whatever that may mean). Rather, it is the material comforts of civilization that make possible a serious concern for both aesthetic and environmental values. These are concerns that can become pressing in developed nations in part because the populations of those countries now enjoy a certain substantial level of prosperity. It would be the height of condescension to expect a nation experiencing hunger and chronic disease to be inordinately concerned with the autonomous value of ecosystems or with creating and preserving works of art. Such values are not frivolous, but they can become important to us only after certain fundamental human needs are satisfied. Instead of radically jettisoning individualist ethics, environmentalists may find a more hospitable home for their values in a category of value that has existed all along.

Notes

I am grateful to Donald Crawford, Jon Moline, Bryan Norton, Robert Stauffer, and Daniel Wikler for useful discussion. I also wish to thank the National Science Foundation and the Graduate School of the University of Wisconsin–Madison for financial support.

1. See, for example, J. B. Callicott, "Animal Liberation: A Triangular Affair," *Environmental Ethics* 2 (1980): 311–38.

2. D. Ehrenfeld, "The Conservation of Non-Resources," *American Scientist* 64 (1976): 648–56; R. M. May, *Stability and Complexity in Model Ecosystems* (Princeton, N.J.: Princeton University Press, 1973).

3. Callicott, "Animal Liberation," 333–34 (my emphasis).

4. P. Shepard, "Animal Rights and Human Rites," *North American Review* (1974): 35–41.

5. C. Darwin, *The Autobiography of Charles Darwin* (1876; London: Collins, 1958), 90.

6. The idea that the natural world is perfect, besides being suspect as an ethical principle, is also controversial as biology. In spite of Callicott's confidence that the amount of pain found in nature is biologically optimal, this adaptationist outlook is now much debated. See, for example, R. Lewontin and S. J. Gould, "The Spandrels of San Marco and the Panglossian Paradigm: A Critique of the Adaptionist Programme," *Proceedings of the Royal Society of London* 205 (1979): 581–98.

7. Callicott, "Animal Liberation," 330.

8. Ibid., 330.

9. Aristotle, *De Anima*, 415a26.

10. C. D. Stone, *Should Trees Have Standing? Toward Legal Rights for Natural Objects* (Los Altos, Calif.: William Kaufmann, 1974), 24.

11. M. Sagoff, "On Preserving the Natural Environment," *Yale Law Review* 84 (1974): 220–24.

12. See G. C. Williams, *Adaptation and Natural Selection* (Princeton, N.J.: Princeton University Press, 1966), and E. Sober, *The Nature of Selection* (Cambridge, Mass.: MIT Press, 1984).

13. A. Leopold, *A Sand County Almanac, and Sketches Here and There* (New York: Oxford University Press, 1949), 224–25.

14. Callicott, "Animal Liberation," 326.

15. E. Abbey, *Desert Solitaire* (New York, Ballantine, 1968), 20.

16. G. Hardin, "The Economics of Wilderness," *Natural History* 78 (1969): 176.

17. Callicott, "Animal Liberation," 323.

18. Ibid., 335.

19. R. Routley and V. Routley, "Human Chauvinism and Environmental Ethics," in *Environmental Philosophy*, Monograph Series 2, ed. D. S. Mannison, M. A. McRobbie, and R. Routley (Canberra: Philosophy Department, Australian National University, 1980), 154.

20. Ibid., 121–22.

III. SUSTAINABLE DEVELOPMENT.

Overview. Many of the same issues that lie at the heart of biodiversity also apply to sustainable development. The emphasis, however, is different. In biodiversity, the ultimate goal is to maintain the maximum possible diversity both within a species and within an ecosystem (maintaining the greatest diverse number of species). Sustainable development seeks to maintain things as they are—only the time horizon differs. Weak sustainable development seeks to maintain things as they are. When a development project x disturbs the environment to y degree, the environment must be restored to y degree in a clearly defined and reasonable time frame. Strong sustainable development seeks to extend the time frame indefinitely. Thus, strong development looks beyond any particular project and seeks to preserve the ecosystem forever.

Wilfred Beckerman begins this section by arguing against both strong and weak sustainable development as such. He argues that a strong sense of sustainable development that tries to protect the environment indefinitely for future generations is impractical and morally repugnant, for such a policy would divert important resources from other more pressing environmental concerns such as providing clean drinking water for less-developed countries.

Beckerman terms weak sustainable development in which compensation is made for resources consumed as being nothing more than human welfare maximization (in traditional economic models). If this is correct, then sustainable development, as such, is not a worthy goal. Rather, we should turn to human welfare maximization as the model of choice.

Herman E. Daly takes exception with Beckerman. Daly defends a position of strong sustainable development. He agrees that weak sustainability ought not be our goal but argues that strong sustainable development is no sloppier than any other economic concept such as the definition of money in the macroeconomic realm (viz., M-1, M-2, or M-1a). Thus, Daly engages Beckerman exactly on Beckerman's own terms (i.e., an economic analysis).

Henryk Skolimowski commends Beckerman for drawing to our attention some of the ambiguities inherent in present notions of sustainable development. Skolimowski believes that even if these concepts are ambiguous, they are useful. Although new economic theories mix many different ends (some prudential and some normative), they seek an integrated goal: the preservation of the species.

Finally, Salah El Serafy defends the concept of weak sustainability. One principal issue is the economists' definition of economic growth as referring merely to income levels. But we could just as easily insist that natural capital (i.e., nature's resources) be included in this mix. If we are committed not to diminish natural capital, we have already accepted the proper sense of weak sustainability (although El Serafy would prefer sustainable development). Although weak sustainability may be an economics-laden concept (which El Serafy defends), this should not deter us from also looking beyond the so-called facts of economics alone and consider normative concepts that lie at the base of strong sustainable development.

'Sustainable Development': Is It a Useful Concept?

Wilfred Beckerman[1]

1. 'SUSTAINABLE DEVELOPMENT': TECHNICAL CONDITION OR MORAL INJUNCTION?

During the last few years the fashionable concept in environmental discourse has been 'sustainable development'. It has spawned a vast literature and has strengthened the arm of empire builders in many research institutes, Universities, national and international bureaucracies and statistical offices. Environmental pressure groups present the concept of sustainable development as an important new contribution to the environmental debate. It is claimed that it brings new insights into the way that concern for the environment and the interests of future generations should be taken into account in policy analysis. But in fact it only muddles the issues. As two distinguished authorities in this area, Partha Dasgupta and Karl-Göran Mäler, point out '... most writings on sustainable development start from scratch and some proceed to get things hopelessly wrong. It would be difficult to find another field of research endeavour in the social sciences that has displayed such intellectual regress.'[2]

It seems high time, therefore, for somebody to spell out why, if the Emperor of Sustainable Development has any clothes at all, they are pretty threadbare. In this article I maintain that 'sustainable development' has been defined in such a way as to be either morally repugnant or logically redundant. It is true that, in the past, economic policy has tended to ignore environmental issues, particularly those having very long run consequences. It is right, therefore, that they should now be given proper place in the conduct of policy. But this can be done without elevating sustainability to the status of some overriding criterion of policy. After all I am sure that the reader can easily think of innumerable human activities that are highly desirable but, alas, not indefinitely sustainable!

In 1992, at Rio de Janeiro, the United Nations held a Conference on Environment and Development (UNCED), in which almost all the countries in the world participated. At this conference the countries adopted a major document of several hundred pages, known as 'Agenda 21', which set out, amongst other things, the agreed intentions of the countries to take account of environmental objectives in their domestic policies, to monitor their own developments from the point of view of their 'sustainability' taking full account of environmental changes, and to submit regular reports on these developments to a newly established 'Commission on Sustainable Development' (CSD).[3]

Agenda 21 is full of references to 'sustainable development'. For example, Chapter 8 states that 'Governments, in cooperation, where appropriate, with international organisations, should adopt a national strategy for sustainable development . . .'. It goes on to say that countries should draw up sustainable development strategies the goals of which '. . . should be to ensure socially responsible economic development while protecting the resources base and the environment for the benefit of future generations'. But what are socially responsible goals in this area, how far should we protect the resource base, whatever that means, and what are the legitimate interests of future generations that have to be protected?

All these, and many other, questions arise immediately one asks what exactly does 'sustainable development' mean, and what is so good about it? As many writers have pointed out, there is a danger that sustainable development is treated as a 'motherhood and apple pie' objective.[4] But, as Harvey Brooks puts it, 'For the concept of sustainability in the process of development to be operationally useful it must be more than just an expression of social values or political preferences disguised in scientific language. Ideally it should be defined so that one could specify a set of measurable criteria such that individuals and groups with widely differing values, political preferences, or assumptions about human nature could agree whether the criteria are being met in a concrete development program.'[5]

It may well be that this is asking too much of the concept of sustainable development and that it can be of some use without being fully operational. But, as it stands, the concept is basically flawed. This is because it mixes up together the technical characteristics of a particular development path with a moral injunction to pursue it. And a definition of whether any particular development path is technically sustainable does not, by itself, carry any special moral force. The definition of a straight line does not imply that there is any particular moral virtue in always walking in straight lines. But most definitions of sustainable development on the market tend to incorporate some ethical injunction without apparently any recognition of the need to demonstrate why that particular ethical injunction is better than many others that one could think up. One obvious rival injunction would be to seek the highest welfare for society over some specified time period.

The result of the fusion of technical characteristics with moral injunctions is that the distinction between positive propositions about the threat to the continuation of any development path and normative propositions concerning the optimality of any particular pattern of development is hopelessly blurred.[6] Instead, a sustainable development path should be defined simply as one that can be sustained over some specified time period, and whether or not it *ought* to be followed is another matter. It should be treated, in other words, as a purely technical concept—not that this necessarily makes it easy to define operationally.[7]

This is most clearly seen when evaluating the desirability of embarking on some specific project. Consider, for example, a simple mining project in a poor country. Implementing the project might be the best way for the people concerned to obtain some funds to keep alive and to build up productive facilities that would enable them to survive in the future. This might include investing in some other activity—such as promoting sustainable agriculture, or investing in their education and technical training. In this case although the project will not be technically sustainable, it ought to be carried out. In the economist's jargon it will be 'optimal'. And one can also imagine the opposite scenario of specific projects that might be sustainable—such as certain forestry projects where replanting can offset the cutting—but that are not 'optimal', perhaps because they are not worthwhile from an economic point of view and would involve the community in excessive costs of cutting and transport relative to the revenues it could earn from sale of the timber.

In other words, immediately one draws the distinction between sustainability, defined as a purely technical concept, and optimality, which is a normative concept, it is obvious that many economic activities that are unsustainable may be perfectly optimal, and many that are sustainable may not even be desirable, let alone optimal. As Little and Mirrlees put it in the context of project analysis 'Sustainability has come to be used in recent years in connection with projects. . . . It has no merit. Whether a project is sustainable (forever?—or just a long time?) has nothing to do with whether it is desirable. If unsustainability were really regarded as a reason for rejecting a project, there would be no mining, and no industry. The world would be a very primitive place.'[8]

2. CHANGING FASHIONS IN 'SUSTAINABLE DEVELOPMENT'

One of the most famous of the definitions of sustainable development is that contained in *Our Common Future*, the 1987 report of the World Commission on the Environment and Development.[9] This report, which is known as the 'Brundtland Report', after its chairperson, Mrs Brundtland, the Prime Minister of Norway, defined sustainable development as '. . . development that meets the needs of the present without compromising the ability of future generations to meet their own needs'. But such a criterion is totally useless since 'needs' are a subjective concept. People at different points in time, or in different income levels, or with different cultural or national backgrounds, will differ with respect to what 'needs' they regard as important. Hence, the injunction to enable future generations to meet their needs does not provide any clear guidance as to what has to be preserved in order that future generations may do so.

Over the past few years innumerable definitions of sustainable development have been proposed.[10] But one can identify a clear trend in them. At the beginning, sustainability was interpreted as a requirement to preserve intact the environment as we find it today in all its forms. The Brundtland report, for example, stated that 'The loss of plant and animal species can greatly limit the options of future generations; so sustainable development requires the conservation of plant and animal species'.

But, one might ask, how far does the Brundtland report's injunction to conserve plant and animal species really go? Is one supposed to preserve all of them? And at what price? Is one supposed to mount a large operation, at astronomic cost, to ensure the survival of every known and unknown species on the grounds that it might give pleasure to future generations, or that it might turn out, in 100 years time, to have medicinal properties? About 98 percent of all the species that have ever existed are believed to have become extinct, but most people do not suffer any great sense of loss as a result. How many people lose sleep because it is no longer possible to see a live Dinosaur?

Clearly, such an absolutist concept of 'sustainable development' is morally repugnant. Given the acute poverty and environmental degradation in which a large part of the world's population live, one could not justify using up vast resources in an attempt to preserve from extinction, say, every one of the several million species of beetles that exist. For the cost of such a task would be partly, if not wholly, resources that could otherwise have been devoted to more urgent environmental concerns, such as increasing access to clean drinking water or sanitation in the Third World.

As it soon became obvious that the 'strong' concept of sustainable development was morally repugnant, as well as totally impracticable, many environmentalists shifted their ground. A new version of the concept was adopted, known in the literature as 'weak' sustainability. This allows for some natural resources to be run down as long as adequate compensation is provided by increases in other resources, perhaps even in the form of man-made capital.[11] But what constitutes adequate compensation? How many more schools or hospitals or houses or factories or machines are required to compensate for using up of some mineral resources or forests or clean atmosphere? The answer, it turned out, was that the acceptability of the substitution had to be judged by its contribution to sustaining human welfare.

This is clear from one of the latest definitions provided by David Pearce, who is the author of numerous works on sustainability. His definition is that ''Sustainability' therefore implies something about maintaining the level of human well-being so that it might improve but at least never declines (or, not more than temporarily, anyway). Interpreted this way, sustainable development becomes equivalent to some requirement that well-being does not decline through time.'[12]

The first important feature of this definition is that it is couched in terms of maintaining 'well-being', not in terms of maintaining the level of consumption or GNP, or even in terms of maintaining intact the overall stock of natural capital, a condition that is found in many definitions of sustainable development including one to which David Pearce had earlier subscribed (though in collaboration with two other authors who clearly had a bad influence on him[13]). This implies, for example, that sustainable development could include the replacement of natural capital by man-made capital, provided the increase in the latter compensated future generations for any fall in their welfare that might have been caused by the depletion of natural capital. In other words, it allows for substitutability between different forms of natural capital and man-made capital, provided that, on balance, there is no decline in welfare.

But this amounts to selling a crucial pass in any struggle to preserve the independent usefulness of the concept of sustainability. For if the choice between preserving natural capital and adding to (or preserving) man-made capital depends on which makes the greatest contribution to welfare the concept of sustainable development becomes redundant. In the attempt to rid the original 'strong' concept of sustainable development of its most obvious weaknesses the baby has been thrown out with the bath water. For it appears now that what society should aim at is not 'sustainability', but the maximisation of welfare. In other words, it should pursue the old-fashioned economist's concept of 'optimality'.

3. Optimality and Sustainability for the Rational Individual

Suppose somebody wants to choose between two possible courses of action—e.g. which of two possible careers to pursue. Let us assume, for the sake of the argument, that the only difference between the two careers is the level of income she would earn in each and hence the level of consumption that she can enjoy, and that they are roughly the same as regards conditions of work, prestige, job satisfaction, life expectation, location and everything else. Let us also assume that her welfare at any point of time—her 'instantaneous welfare'—is correlated with her income at that point of time.[14] Suppose now that one of the careers will ensure her a steady but very modest level of income, and hence welfare, throughout her life, and the other will ensure her an income/welfare level that is higher than in the first alternative *in every single year of her life*, but that includes a decline in income/welfare in the middle of her life, say, when it may decline for a few years (possibly followed by a further rise, though this condition is not essential to the argument). Which path will she choose? Obviously she will choose the latter.[15] Her 'optimal' path is the one that maximises her welfare over her lifetime. In this simplified example, the 'present value' of her lifetime income must be higher in the latter case than in the former.

Why should she care about a temporary decline in her income/welfare if it is by choosing the path containing it that she will maximise the present value of her total welfare over the whole of her life? Insofar as the prospect of a temporary decline in income worried her she would simply invest more heavily in earlier years and use the subsequent extra income to boost her income in the years when income would otherwise decline. If this entailed too great a loss of welfare earlier —e.g. the subjective cost of the greater risk burden that such an investment policy would imply—the path containing the decline in income would be the one that maximised the present value of her welfare over her life.

Of course, in this example, the problem is simplified in two ways. First, it was assumed that the level of welfare expected in the non-sustainable path is greater in every year than it is in the sustainable path, in spite of the temporary decline in welfare in the former. Secondly, only one person is involved, so there is no need to take account of the way in which the two income paths differ with respect to their effect on the equality with which incomes are distributed among different members of the population, let alone between different generations. We shall examine the distributional considerations in the next section, when we consider welfare maximisation for society as a whole.

Meanwhile, as regards the first problem, suppose our rational individual is faced with a choice between two paths of income which intersect—i.e. one is higher than the other in some years but lower in others. In this case, to compare the 'present values' of the two income streams she would discount future incomes at whatever rate of interest she could get on her savings and investment. But, again, there seems to be no reason why the rational individual should attach special importance to a temporary decline in income during her lifetime. The time path of her income stream throughout her life will be taken care of in the discounting exercise. She will be free to borrow, or lend, in such a way as to allocate her consumption over time in such a way that it maximises the present value of her welfare.

4. OPTIMALITY FOR SOCIETY AND THE DISTRIBUTION PROBLEM

As regards the second simplification in our example, when one is concerned with optimality for society as a whole, rather than for an individual, account has to be taken of distributional considerations. This applies whether one is maximising welfare of society at any moment of time or maximising welfare over some time period. Making due allowance for distributional considerations means that when we are seeking to maximise total social welfare at any point of time we will be concerned with the manner in which the total consumption of society is distributed amongst the population at the point in time in question—e.g. how equally, or justly (which may not be the same thing) it is distributed. And if we are seeking to maximise welfare over time whilst making allowance for distributional considerations we would be concerned with the distribution of consumption over time—e.g. how equally, or justly, consumption is distributed between different generations.

Both procedures fit easily into welfare economics. Environmentalists may not be aware of the fact that it has long been conventional to include distributional considerations into the concept of economic welfare—which is a component of total welfare—that one seeks to maximise. In the opinion of the great economist A.C. Pigou, who might be regarded as the father of welfare economics, 'Any cause which increases the absolute share of real income in the hands of the poor, provided that it does not lead to a contraction in the size of the national dividend from any point of view, will, in general, increase economic welfare'.[16] Distributional considerations are even included in standard techniques of cost-benefit analysis pioneered by Ian Little and J.A. Mirrlees.[17] I myself have published estimates of growth rates of national income in different countries adjusted for changes in their internal income distributions, and others had already done so before me.[18]

Welfare can also be defined to include considerations of social justice and freedom, and so on. Of course, the more widely one draws the net of welfare to include such variables the greater the difficulty in making them all commensurate with each other. It is true that this makes it more difficult to define exactly what is meant by the 'maximisation' operation. But the same difficulty is encountered by any proposition to the effect that 'welfare' (or 'well-being') had declined in any specific time period.

How one should maximise the present value of society's welfare over time in a way that takes due account of the interests of future generations raises difficult, and relatively novel, problems of inter-generational justice that lie outside the scope of this article.[19] In the absence of any obvious consensus view to the contrary we shall assume here that a unit of *welfare* accruing to some future generation should be given the same weight in arriving at the present value of the stream of welfare over time as an equal unit of welfare accruing to the present generation. In other words, we should not discriminate against future generations. We should not, therefore, discount *welfare* for time per se. This means that we do not advocate 'pure' time preference, which is a preference for consumption now, rather than later, purely on account of its precedence in time. There may, of course, be good reasons for doing so, such as the possibility that the human race will become extinct in a relevant time period.[20] Or one may simply wish to impose on the discounting operation some particular ethical views concerning the relative importance—or lack of it—of *welfare* accruing to different generations.[21]

But although we shall abstain from any such discounting of welfare, this does not mean that we should not discount *consumption*. That is to say we have to allow for whatever increase in productivity we may expect to take place over time as a result of investment and technological progress. For an increase in productivity would mean that any particular item of consumption will be 'cheaper' in future than it is now (allowing for inflation, of course). Hence, we would not value a unit of consumption to be delivered in ten years' time, say, at the same price as we would value it for delivery today. For instead of paying now for it to be delivered in ten years' time one could invest the money so that in ten years' time one could buy it and still have something left over. In the long run, for society as a whole, how much is left over depends on the (real) rate of growth of the economy, since that determines, roughly speaking, the (real) rate of return we could get on our money today.

We might even want to go further than that in our discounting procedure. We might want to make an additional allowance for the fact that, as consumption levels rise, the welfare that one can obtain from additional ('marginal') units of consumption will fall. This application of the law of diminishing marginal utility would be one particular way of taking account of distributional concerns. That is to say, it would allow for the fact that higher consumption will not provide *proportionately* higher welfare to rich people as to poor people. Taking account of differences in the incomes accruing to different generations in this way would be the inter-temporal counterpart of some conventional cost-benefit methods of allowing for the way that, say, any specific project at any moment of time may confer benefits on different income groups in society by attaching weights to their income levels. In applying this procedure to inter-generational comparisons of income and welfare levels one would still not be discounting 'welfare' at all. One would be simply assuming that higher levels of consumption do not bring proportionately higher levels of welfare.

Finally, in the same way that we may assume that individuals derive less welfare from additional consumption the higher is their consumption, we may also decide that society as a whole derives less welfare from the sum of the welfare of its members if this is distributed unequally among them. In our estimate of the present value of welfare over time, therefore, one could then attach lower weight to a unit of welfare accruing to society when social welfare was expected to be high than in periods when it was expected to be low. But this would be nothing to do with discounting for time per se.[22]

Thus the use of a discount rate does not necessarily mean, as most environmentalists—and some philosophers—appear to believe, that we attach less value to the *welfare* of future generations simply because it comes later in time.[23] On the contrary, rationing investment according to the discount rate helps to ensure that we invest now in projects that will give future generations more welfare than if we invested, instead, in projects—some of which may be environmental projects—that yield lower returns. In this way it maximises the welfare of future generations. It is in no way 'unfair' to them since we would discount future returns in the same way even if we expected to live for another two centuries and hence be amongst the generation that has to bear the consequences of our present decisions.[24]

5. OPTIMALITY VERSUS SUSTAINABILITY

We have argued above that (a) distributional considerations can—and invariably are—included in the economist's concept of 'welfare'; (b) this applies also to the inter-generational distribution of income and welfare; and (c) one way of doing this (though not necessarily the only way) is by appropriate choice of the discount rate used to estimate the present value of welfare that society should seek to maximise. In view of this there does not appear to be any independent role left for 'sustainability' as a separate objective of policy, independent of maximisation of the present value of welfare. For if future generations have lower incomes as a result of any particular environmental policy this will show up—other things being equal—in a lower present value of income over whatever time period our views on inter-generational justice regard as relevant. We might also want to allow for the fact that marginal units of consumption probably add more to welfare at lower levels of consumption than at higher levels.

Nor does there seem to be any special role left to play for the particular possibility that future levels of welfare may include some decline. And this is related to the second important feature of the Pearce definition of sustainability quoted above, which is that wellbeing must never decline, 'or, not more than temporarily'.[25] Apart from the qualification about a temporary decline this is in line with most recent definitions of sustainable development. It is anyway implicit in any definition of sustainability that requires that any substitution of man-made capital for natural capital can only be justified if it makes an equal contribution to welfare. As John Pezzey rightly says in his survey of the various definitions used, most of them '. . . understand sustainability to mean sustaining an improvement (or at least maintenance) in the quality of life, rather than just sustaining the existence of life'. He goes on to adopt a 'standard definition of sustainable development' according to which welfare per head of population must never decline (as in the latest Pearce definition mentioned above, but without the 'temporary' qualification this had included).[26]

One is always free, of course, to define welfare however one wishes. But it would be very curious to insist on defining it to *include* all sorts of environmental, distributional, social, and other considerations, but to *exclude* changes in the level of welfare (as distinct from the level itself). Indeed, it seems self-contradictory to do so. If a decline in welfare did not affect welfare, why bother about it? And if it does affect welfare, why cannot it be included in the concept of welfare that one is trying to maximise? As indicated above, one might want to adopt a concept of welfare maximisation that left no room for incommensurate objectives, such as integrity, or freedom. In that case, it would be sensible to talk about maximising welfare subject to some constraint on these other incommensurate objectives. But there seems no reason to treat *changes* in welfare levels in this way.

Furthermore, not only does it seem illogical to exclude a decline in welfare from the concept of welfare that optimal policy should seek to maximise, it is not clear why some special moral significance should be attached to *declines* in the level of welfare. It is no doubt true that a very rich man may suffer some extra loss of welfare if he has had a bad year on the stock exchange and has had to sell his yacht. He would not miss the yacht so much if he had never had it before. But we cannot be expected to be very sorry for him. After all, how did he become rich if not as a result of a lot of *increases* in income in earlier years which, if we are to be consistent, should be given an additional value, on top of their effect in bringing him to a higher level. Anyway, it may well be that he will lose less welfare from having to give up the yacht—which may have been a nuisance and entailed all sorts of responsibilities—than the joy he experienced when he first got his new toy.

On the other hand, it may be argued that this does not apply to different generations. For if some particular generation experiences a decline in its welfare one cannot assume that it was the same generation that enjoyed the previous increases. Nevertheless, if future generations experience a dip in welfare in any period, we cannot be expected to be very sorry for them *irrespective of their welfare levels.* And even if we are there seems to be no justification for switching to a development path that yields a lower present value of welfare in order to avoid the temporary decline. For that would imply inflicting on some other generation a loss of welfare greater than the one that was incurred by some particular generation *solely because of the temporary decline.* And it is far from obvious that there is any moral justification for shielding future generations from any decline in income or welfare irrespective of whatever sacrifice of welfare this might inflict on other generations.

In other words, if we are to attach a separate value to *changes* in welfare, they need not be only negative. We should also include the increases in welfare—the rise that preceded the fall. Indeed, if the hypothecated temporary decline in welfare that is to be avoided at all costs is from a higher level of welfare than the one we enjoy now, the preceding generations must have experienced more increases in welfare than declines in welfare. On balance, therefore, the future generations that enjoyed the increases in welfare should be credited with even more welfare than the simple present value exercise would have permitted. As well as being credited with more welfare for reaching higher levels, they would be credited with even more welfare because they reached the higher levels in the only possible way, namely by experiencing more increases than declines!

Thus, the exclusion of *changes* in welfare—as distinct from the level of welfare—from the concept of welfare the present value of which society should seek to maximise is open to two objections. First, it appears to be simply logically self-contradictory. At the same time, if one is consistent one should take account of positive as well as negative changes in welfare, so that it is far from obvious how the incorporation of changes in welfare in the concept of welfare that society should maximise would affect its value. One might add a third objection, namely, why should negative changes in welfare be singled out for special treatment anyway?

Of course, if the decline in living standards of future generations continued to the point that human life on this planet was no longer possible, the simple optimisation rule comes up against another tricky question. This is whether it makes sense to talk about the loss of welfare caused by the extinction of the human race. As Thomas Nagel points out, 'none of us existed before we were born (or conceived), but few regard that as a misfortune'.[27] Would the non-existence of the human race constitute a negative item in the overall total of welfare? Perhaps the welfare of such wild-life that remained might be much higher?

6. Should 'Sustainability' Be a Constraint?

The preceding discussion should make it obvious—if it were not already so—that not only should we stick to welfare maximisation, rather than sustainability, as an over-riding objective of policy, but that sustainability cannot even be regarded as a logical constraint on welfare maximisation. Mimicry of the economist's use of the concept of a constraint is the latest twist in the evolution of the concept of sustainable development. It represents a further step in the retreat, under fire, by those environmentalists who have presented the 'sustainable development' concept as a great breakthrough in our thinking on the subject. First they retreat from strong sustainability to weak sustainability, and then from weak sustainability as an objective of policy to weak sustainability as just a constraint. The idea now is that welfare should be maximised but subject to the constraint that the path of development being followed be sustainable. However, this appears to represent a mis-interpretation of the concept of a 'constraint'.

Economic theory is dominated by the notion of how to make optimal choices when faced with constraints of one kind or another. For example, it is full of the analysis of how firms may seek to maximise profits *subject to constraints,* such as the prices they can charge for the goods they sell or the wages they need pay employees, and so on. Or households are treated as maximising utility *subject to constraints* in terms of their incomes and the prices of goods they buy, and so on. If, for example, the firm could relax the wage constraint and pay employees lower wages it could make higher profits. If a household could relax its income constraint by earning more, or by borrowing, it could increase welfare. In many other contexts, too, it might be analytically convenient to seek to maximise some objective, such as total economic welfare, subject to some constraint in terms of the other objectives, such as freedom, or justice.

But it is obvious that only if there is a conflict between the 'constraint' and what it is that one is trying to maximise does it make sense to use the term 'constraint'. For a constraint is something that, if relaxed, enables one to obtain more of whatever it is one is trying to maximise. Where there is no conflict, however, there is no scope for a 'constraint'.

Sustainable development could only constitute a constraint on welfare maximisation, therefore, if it conflicted with it. It is, of course, possible to define sustainable development in such a way that it does conflict with welfare maximisation over the time period in question. 'Strong sustainability', for example, would do so. For it is quite likely that the attempt to preserve all existing species and other environmental facilities would lead to a reduction in welfare as commonly defined. But, as we have seen, 'strong' sustainability has been more or less abandoned on account of its moral inacceptability. And the capital stock component of 'weak' sustainability obviously cannot conflict with welfare maximisation since the criterion of whether a substitution of man-made for natural capital is acceptable is whether it makes an adequate contribution to welfare.

For sustainability to constitute a constraint on welfare maximisation, therefore, some other source of conflict between sustainability and welfare maximisation has to be found. We have discussed at some length one that has been given much prominence, namely distributional considerations, particularly the inter-generational distribution of welfare. We have shown that whilst it is, of course, open to anybody to define welfare in such as way as to take no account of distributional considerations it would violate a long tradition in economics to the effect that income distribution was an integral part of welfare and that inter-temporal distribution can be handled through the appropriate choice of the discount rate. We have also argued the notion that declines in welfare—particularly temporary declines—should be given special consideration and constitute constraints on welfare maximisation is also open to serious objections.

The advocates of sustainable development as a constraint, therefore, face a dilemma. Either they stick to 'strong' sustainability, which is logical, but requires subscribing to a morally repugnant and totally impracticable objective, or they switch to some welfare-based concept of sustainability, in which case they are advocating a concept that appears to be redundant and unable to qualify as a logical constraint on welfare maximisation.

7. Sustainability and the Measurement of National Income

As pointed out above, most environmentalists mix up, in their own concept of sustainable development, the technical characteristics of a development path with its moral superiority. It is perhaps because of this confusion that they also mis-interpret perfectly legitimate technical definitions that some economists have proposed, such the definition of maintaining capital intact, or the conditions to be satisfied IF it is required to ensure constant levels of consumption per head, as carrying with them ethical force that their originators would not necessarily attach to them at all.

For example, a famous definition of income by the late Sir John Hicks, a Nobel Laureate in Economics, is that national income is the output of a nation's economy *after maintaining capital intact*—i.e. after allowing for the amount of capital used up in the course of producing the output in question. Obviously, if the capital that is gradually 'used up' in the course of time through wear and tear and so on is not replaced then, in the longer run, output will begin to decline and it will not be possible to maintain income levels. But this Hicksian definition of income, with its emphasis on the need to maintain capital intact in order to maintain income levels, is a purely technical definition of net income and has no moral connotation whatsoever.

More recently, other economists, notably Hartwick, Weitzman, and Solow, have shown precisely how to extend the concept of net national income and maintaining capital intact to encompass the depletion of natural capital through the extraction of minerals, and precisely how much investment is required in order to compensate for using up natural capital and to maintain constant levels of consumption per head.[28] But these technical definitions of income and of sustainable consumption paths are frequently quoted by environmentalists as if they imply some moral obligation never to consume more than income so defined and hence to always maintain capital intact and to follow a sustainable growth path as so defined. But the authors of these definitions usually had no intention of suggesting that they were also laying down the law as to what is morally imperative.

For example, in a much quoted article on 'Intergenerational Equity and Exhaustible Resources' Nobel Laureate Robert M. Solow states that he is merely exploring the consequences of a straightforward application of the famous second principle of justice associated with the political philosopher, John Rawls, to the problem of optimal capital accumulation spanning several generations.[29] He states that 'It will turn out to have both advantages and disadvantages as an ethical principle in this context' (page 30). He goes on to show that in the normal situations '. . . the max-min [*i.e.*the Rawlsian] criterion does not function very well as a principle of intergenerational equity. . . . It calls . . . for zero net saving with stationary technology, and for negative net saving with advancing technology.' This is hardly a ringing endorsement of the principle of never allowing consumption per head to be lower in any time period than in any other time period. But it does not prevent many environmentalists from writing that Solow has demonstrated the desirability of the principle of maintaining a constant level of consumption per head.[30] Most of them must be just quoting each other without bothering to read Solow in the original.

Thus the fact that eminent economists have helped provide a precise basis for estimating how much investment a society would need to make, under certain highly simplified conditions, in order to compensate for any reduction in the stock of natural capital and to maintain 'sustainable development' (defined as no fall in welfare levels), after taking due account of damage to the environment, does not imply that this represents some ethical injunction. This not only implies nothing at all about the optimality of sustainable growth paths, it does not even imply that making such estimates is worthwhile in practice.

Even the depreciation of man-made capital is not possible to estimate with much accuracy. For it does not correspond to any actual market transactions. The flow of goods and services entering into gross national product (GNP)—such as the food consumed, the machine tools built, the services provided to consumers, and so on—are almost all the subject of two-way market transactions involving a buyer and a seller. By contrast, the depletion of the capital stock is not, as a rule, the subject of any transactions between buyers and sellers. True, firms will show estimates of depreciation in their accounts, but, for many reasons that lie outside the scope of this paper, nobody in the trade would rely on these as being objective and accurate estimates of any conceptually valid true measure of capital consumption.[31] But at least the assets in question did go through the market at one time in their life, and in some cases it may be possible to use second-hand prices to estimate the value of capital goods that have been discarded.

By contrast most environmental assets never did pass through the market place at all. In almost all cases there are no market observations of the value to be attached to clean air or water or beautiful landscape. It is true that newly extracted supplies of minerals do pass through the market, but the known reserves are only the reserves that have been found worthwhile identifying given prices at any point of time. As I explained in detail about twenty years ago, insofar as demand may exceed supply for any length of time this will lead to a rise in price which, in turn, invariably sets in motion many feedback mechanisms to restore the balance between supply and demand. These include increases in exploration and discovery of new reserves, improvements in extraction and refinement techniques, but also economies and substitution in the use of the materials in question.[32] Also, there are obvious difficulties in using prices of minerals at any point of time as guide to the prices that they will fetch for the next few centuries, so that it is impossible to put any reasonable values on these resources.

8. CONCLUSIONS

What we have seen so far then is that:—

i. 'sustainability' should be interpreted purely as a technical characteristic of any project, programme or development path, not as implying any moral injunction of over-riding criterion of choice;

ii. the 'optimal' choice for society is to maximise the present value of welfare over whatever time period is regarded as relevant given one's views on inter-generational justice. This can make allowance for distributional considerations, including inter-temporal distribution, by attaching weights to the welfare accruing to different generations in any estimate of the present value of social welfare, as, for example, by appropriate choice of the discount rate;

iii. since, anyway, most environmentalists have now dropped 'strong' sustainability and now define the 'sustainability' condition in terms of how much contribution different components of the total capital stock contribute to welfare, insofar as society seeks to maximise welfare the sustainability condition becomes redundant and cannot even be treated as a 'constraint'.

None of the above conclusions means that we are not left with serious environmental problems when attempting to decide what is an *optimal* policy. As I have always maintained the world is faced with real environmental problems. Economists have been well aware of the fact that, left to itself, the environment will not be managed in a socially optimal manner. There are too many market imperfections. The most important is probably the absence of well-defined property rights. But in many cases—particularly with global environmental issues, such as the preservation of biodiversity or the prevention of excessive production of greenhouse gases—it is not easy to see what economic incentives can be devised and implemented internationally in order to secure socially optimal co-operative action. These are serious issues, many of them requiring extensive scientific research and economic research into, for example, the economic evaluation of environmental assets, or the costs of pollution reduction, or the relative efficacy of alternative schemes to achieve socially optimal levels of environmental protection.

Serious research into these and related environmental problems is being carried out in various institutions all over the world.[33] It is unfortunate that too much time and effort is also being devoted to developing the implications of the sustainable development concept, including innumerable commissions and committees set up to report on it and innumerable research programmes designed to measure it.[34] Outside a few devloping countries heavily dependent on limited supplies of some minerals or other primary product, the measurement of some wider concept of 'sustainable GNP' is a waste of time and effort and such estimates as have been made for developed countries are virtually worthless.

NOTES

1. Emeritus Fellow of Balliol College, Oxford. I wish to express my particular gratitude to John Pezzey who has helped me remedy some serious deficiencies in an earlier draft of this paper, as well as to an anonymous referee for several constructive comments. Needless to say I alone am responsible for all remaining defects.

2. Dasgupta and Mäler 1994.

3. The legal status of Agenda 21 is far from clear although it was later enshrined in a resolution of the Second Committee of the General Assembly of the UN (at its 51st meeting on the 16th December 1992). But this only urged governments and international bodies to take the action necessary to follow up the agreements reached in Rio, and there is no question of countries that do not take much notice of it being brought before the International Court of Justice! After all, most countries in the world are constantly in breach of various more binding commitments into which they have entered concerning human rights without ever being pursued in the courts or penalised in any way.

4. See, for example, Pearce Markandya and Barbier 1989, p. 1; Solow 1991; Pezzey 1992a, p.1.

5. Brooks 1992, p. 30.

6. See criticism along these lines by Dasgupta and Mäler (1990, p. 106), in which they take specific issue with a definition of SD by D. Pearce, Barbier and Markandya, which required no decline in the natural capital stock. This condition differs significantly from one proposed by the same authors but with their names in a different order, namely in Pearce, Markandya and Barbier 1989, p. 3. It is interesting that changing the order of the authors changes their views on the definition of SD.

7. Even at a technical level, whether some project or development programme is sustainable or not depends on numerous assumptions—e.g. concerning availability of inputs, of foreign loans, and so on.

8. Little and Mirrlees 1990, p. 365.

9. World Commission on Environment and Development, 1987.

10. An excellent recent survey is contained in Appendix 1 of Pezzey 1992a.

11. See Pezzey 1992a and Pezzey 1992b.

12. Pearce 1993, p. 48.

13. On page 48 of Pearce et al. 1989, this maintenance of the stock of natural capital seems to be the concept of sustainable development to which the authors subscribe, though wider concepts are also given their due.

14. We abstract here from the question of whether, at the margin, she derives as much welfare from a unit of consumption as from a unit of income devoted to investment.

15. This example does not depend at all on any assumptions about the individual's rate of time preference.

16. Pigou 1932, p. 89. The link between economic welfare and distribution is very forcibly expressed in, for example, de V. Graaff 1957, p. 92. Nowadays, of course, refinements to the theory enable one to combine changes in distribution with changes in real income in such a way as to weaken the force of Pigou's proviso concerning the importance of not reducing total real income.

17. See, in particular, Little and Mirrlees 1974.

18. See Beckerman 1978, chapter 4, 'The adjustment of growth rates for changes in income distribution'. In this study I adjusted the growth rates of nine OECD countries to take account of income distribution changes.

19. Some of the difficulties surrounding the problem of our obligations to future generations are discussed in Pasek 1992.

20. As proposed by Dasgupta and Heal 1979, p. 262.

21. One interesting attempt to relate alternative ethical views concerning inter-generational justice is in d'Arge, Schultze and Brookshire 1982.

22. See, for example, a formal exposition of this type of egalitarianism in Broome 1991, pp. 178–80.

23. See, for example, Partridge 1981. One distinguished philosopher who has made extensive criticisms along these lines is Derek Parfit, as in Parfit 1984, Appendix F.

24. We might, however, use a slightly lower discount rate to allow for the reduced risk of one's not surviving long enough to see the fruits of one's savings. I have attempted a fuller exposition of the discounting argument in Beckerman 1993.

25. And how temporary is the temporary decline in welfare that is permitted under the Pearce definition? If one cannot specify this precisely the condition is totally non-operational. By this I do not mean to suggest that one should give a precise number of years. What is required is a specification of the precise criteria by which one can determine whether any particular 'temporary' decline in welfare is optimal. Economists define the optimum output of any commodity as that output at which the marginal social cost of producing it equals the marginal social benefit. This definition does not tell us exactly how much of each commodity should be produced in terms of kilograms or gallons or any other units. But it gives a precise and operational definition. By contrast definitions of sustainable development that include vague qualifications about the acceptability of 'temporary' declines in social welfare, devoid of any criteria for deciding how temporary is temporary, are totally non-operational.

26. Pezzey 1992a, p. 11.

27. Nagel 1979, p. 3.

28. A relatively recent paper by R.M. Solow (1986) contains also the key references to contributions made by Hartwick, Weitzman, Dixit, and others.

29. Solow 1974, p. 30. More specifically, here, and elsewhere, Solow demonstrates that with growing population and technical progress, constant consumption per head may not be desirable. Elsewhere, he also explicitly states that 'there are social goals other than sustainability' (Solow 1992, p. 20).

30. See, for example, the generally excellent article by Mick Common and Charles Perrings (1992) where they write (p. 10) that 'Economists have always had to work hard to find a rationalization for the principle of constant consumption. In this instance, the rationalization was provided by Solow, who used the egalitarian arguments of Rawls (1971) to propose a "Rawlsian" maximin approach to the intertemporal distribution of consumption.'

31. Various other methods have been used to attempt to measure capital stocks and their depreciation, such as the use of fire insurance surveys. Or estimates have been made of the typical length of life of specific types of building or machinery or capital equipment and so on. But nobody would pretend that such estimates provide more than rough orders of magnitude at best.

32. I explained the theory and backed it up with the facts in my book *In Defence of Economic Growth*, chapter 8, 'Resources for Growth' (1974). For more recent data see, also, Beckerman 1992, Annex 2.

33. The Environment Directorate of the OECD, and the World Bank, frequently produce authoritative studies of economic valuation of environmental costs and benefits, including, for example, Munasinghe 1993; Pezzey 1992a; and Peskin and Lutz 1990. See also Barde and Pearce 1991, and the papers included in Part II of Costanza 1991.

34. These are among the tasks of the Convention on Biodiversity signed by over 150 countries at the 1992 UN Conference on Environment and Development at Rio de Janeiro.

References

Barde, Jean-Philippe and Pearce, David (eds) 1991. *Valuing the Environment*. London, Earthscan.

Beckerman, W. 1974. *In Defence of Economic Growth*. London, Jonathan Cape.

Beckerman, W. 1978. *Measures of Leisure, Equality and Welfare*. Paris, OECD.

Beckerman, W. 1992. *Economic Development and the Environment*, WPS 961, (August). Washington, D.C., The World Bank.

Beckerman, W. 1993. 'Environmental Policy and the Discount Rate', CSERGE Working Paper 93-12. University College London and the University of East Anglia, Norwich, Centre for Social and Economic Research on the Global Environment.

Brooks, Harvey 1992. 'Sustainability and Technology', in *Science and Sustainability*, p. 30. Vienna, International Institute for Applied Systems Analysis.

Broome, John 1991. *Weighing Goods*. Oxford, Blackwell.

Common, Mick and Perrings, Charles 1992. 'Towards an ecological economics of sustainability', *Ecological Economics* **6**.

Costanza, Robert (ed.) 1991. *Ecological Economics: The Science and Management of Sustainability*. New York, Columbia University Press.

d'Arge, R. C., Schultze, W. D., and Brookshire, D. S., 1982. 'Carbon Dioxide and Intergenerational Choice', *American Economic Review* **72** (May).

Dasgupta, Partha and Heal, G. M. 1979. *Economic Theory and Exhaustible Resources*. Cambridge, Cambridge University Press.

Dasgupta, Partha and Mäler, Karl-Göran 1990. 'The Environment and Emerging Development Issues', in *Proceedings of the World Bank Annual Conference on Development Economics 1990*. Washington D.C., The World Bank.

Dasgupta, Partha and Mäler, Karl-Göran 1994. 'Poverty, Institutions, and the Environmental-Resource Base', in Jere Behrman and T.N. Srinivasan. *Handbook of Development Economics*, Vol. 3. Amsterdam, North Holland (forthcoming).

de V. Graaff, Jan 1957. *Theoretical Welfare Economics*. Cambridge, Cambridge University Press.

Little, I. M. D. and Mirrlees, J. A. 1974. *Project Appraisal and Planning for Developing Countries*. London, Heinemann.

Little, I .M. D. and Mirrlees, J. A. 1990. 'Project Appraisal and Planning Twenty Years On', in *Proceedings of the World Bank Annual Conference on Development Economics, 1990*. Washington D.C., The World Bank.

Munasinghe, Mohan 1993. 'Towards Sustainable Development: The Role of Environmental Economics and Valuation', World Bank Environment Paper No. 3. Washington, D.C., The World Bank.

Nagel, Thomas 1979. *Mortal Questions*. Cambridge, Cambridge University Press.

Parfit, Derek 1984. *Reasons and Persons*. Oxford, Oxford University Press.

Partridge, E. (ed.) 1981. *Responsibilities to Future Generations*. New York, Prometheus Books.

Pasek, Joanna 1992. 'Obligations to Future Generations: A Philosophical Note', in *World Development*, **20**(4).

Pearce, David 1993. *Economic Values and the Natural World*. London, Earthscan.

Pearce, David, Markandya, A., and Barbier, E. 1989. *Blueprint for a Green Economy*. London, Earthscan.

Peskin, Henry and Lutz, Ernst 1990. 'A Survey of Resources and Environmental Accounting in Industrialized Countries'. Washington, D.C., The World Bank (August).

Pezzey, J. 1992a *Sustainable Development Concepts: An Economic Analysis*, World Bank Environment Paper No. 2. Washington D.C., The World Bank.

Pezzey, J. 1992b 'Sustainability: An Interdisciplinary Guide', *Environmental Values* **1**: 321–62.

Pigou, A. C. 1932. *The Economics of Welfare*, 4th edition. London, Macmillan.

Solow, R. M. 1974. 'Intergenerational equity and exhaustible resources', *Review of Economic Studies*, Symposium.

Solow, R. M. 1986. 'On the intergenerational allocation of natural resources', *The Scandinavian Journal of Economics* **88**.

Solow, R. M. 1991. 'Sustainability: An Economists's Perspective', lecture at the Woods Hole Oceanographic Institution Marine Policy Center, Maine.

Solow, R. M. 1992. 'An almost practical step toward sustainability', lecture on the occasion of the Fortieth Anniversary of Resources for the Future, Washington D.C. (October).

World Commission on Environment and Development 1987. *Our Common Future*. Oxford, Oxford University Press.

On Wilfred Beckerman's Critique of Sustainable Development

Herman E. Daly

Beckerman's discussion of sustainable development (*Environmental Values* **3**: 191–209) provides some useful clarifications, and a good occasion for making a few more. Since I advocate what he calls the 'sustainability as constraint' position, I will move straight to it, and begin with the dilemma in which he claims to have placed those like me:

> The advocates of sustainable development as a constraint, therefore, face a dilemma. Either they stick to 'strong' sustainability, which is logical, but requires subscribing to a morally repugnant and totally impractical objective, or they switch to some welfare-based concept of sustainability, in which case they are advocating a concept that appears to be redundant and unable to qualify as a logical constraint on welfare maximisation. (p.203)

I advocate strong sustainability, thereby receiving Beckerman's blessing in the realm of logic but provoking his righteous indignation in the realms of morality and practicality. Consequently I will focus on a reply to those charges. But first, I must congratulate him for his effective demolition of 'weak sustainability'. I hope he has more success than I have had in converting the many environmental economists who still cling to it.

Beckerman's concept of strong sustainability, however, is one made up by himself in order to serve as a straw man. In the literature, weak sustainability assumes that manmade and natural capital are basically substitutes. He got that right. Strong sustainability assumes that manmade and natural capital are basically complements. Beckerman completely missed that one. He thinks strong sustainability means that no species could ever go extinct, nor any nonrenewable resource should ever be taken from the ground, no matter how many people are starving. I have referred to that concept as 'absurdly strong sustainability' in order to dismiss it, so as to focus on the relevant issue: namely are manmade and natural capital substitutes or complements? That is really what is at issue between strong and weak sustainability. Since Beckerman got the definition right for weak sustainability his arguments against it are relevant, and as I said above, convincing. But since he got the definition of strong sustainability wrong, in spite of the obvious symmetry of the cases, his arguments against it are irrelevant. He indeed demonstrated that 'absurdly strong sustainability' is in fact absurd! Let me accept that, and move on to the real issue.

I did not even find the word 'complementarity' or its derivatives in the article, and that is the key to strong sustainability. If natural and manmade capital were substitutes (weak sustainability) then neither could be a limiting factor. If, however, they are complements (strong sustainability), then the one in short supply is limiting. Historically, in the 'empty world' economy, manmade capital was limiting and natural capital superabundant. We have now, due to demographic and economic growth, entered the era of the 'full world' economy, in which the roles are reversed. More and more it is remaining natural capital that now plays the role of limiting factor. The fish catch is not limited by fishing boats, but by remaining populations of fish in the sea. Economic logic says to economise on and invest in the limiting factor. For this reason we put the constraint on natural capital. Maximise current welfare subject to the constraint that natural capital be maintained intact over generations.

Let me agree with Beckerman not only in rejecting weak sustainability, but also in rejecting the attempt to define sustainable development in terms of welfare of future generations. To his reasons I would only add that the welfare of future generations is beyond our control and fundamentally none of our business. As any parent knows, you cannot bequeath welfare. You can only pass on physical requirements for welfare. Nowadays natural capital is the critical requirement. A bequest of a fishing fleet with no fish left is worthless. But even the bequest of a world full of both fish and fishing boats does not guarantee welfare. The future is always free to make itself miserable with whatever we leave to it. Our obligation therefore is not to guarantee their welfare but their capacity to produce, in the form of a minimum level of natural capital, the limiting factor. This can be operationalised in some simple rules of management. Projects should be designed (constrained) so that:

> *Output Rule:* waste outputs are within the natural absorptive capacities of the environment. (i.e., nondepletion of the sink services of natural capital).
>
> *Input Rules:* (a) For renewable inputs, harvest rates should not exceed regeneration rates (nondepletion of the source services of natural capital. (b) For nonrenewable inputs the rate of depletion should be equal to the rate at which renewable substitutes can be developed. If a renewable stock is consciously divested (i.e. exploited nonrenewably), it should be subject to the rule for nonrenewables.

Rule (b) is a 'quasi-sustainability' rule for the exploitation of nonrenewables, based on the fact that they are a capital inventory, and it has been operationalised by El Serafy[1]. The question of what qualifies as a renewable substitute is important, and relevant to strong versus weak sustainability. Weak sustainability would imply acceptance of any asset with the required rate of return. Strong sustainability requires a real rather than a merely financial substitute—e.g., a capital set-aside from petroleum depletion should be invested in new energy supplies, including improvements in energy efficiency, but not in, say, law schools, medical research, or MacDonald's Hamburger franchises.

A point sure to be contested is the assertion that manmade and natural capital are complements. Many economists insist that they are substitutes. Since this really is the key issue, and since Beckerman ignores it, it is necessary to repeat here the case for complementarity.

a. One way to make an argument is to assume the opposite and show that it is absurd. If manmade capital were a near perfect substitute for natural capital then natural capital would be a near perfect substitute for manmade capital. But if so, there would have been no reason to accumulate manmade capital in the first place, since we humans were already endowed by nature with a near perfect substitute. But historically we did accumulate manmade capital—precisely because it is complementary to natural capital.

b. Manmade capital is itself a physical transformation of natural resources which are the flow yield from the stock of natural capital. Therefore, producing more of the alleged substitute (manmade capital)—physically requires more of the very thing being substituted for (natural capital)—the defining condition of complementarity!

c. Manmade capital (along with labour) is an agent of transformation of the resource flow from raw material inputs into product outputs. The natural resource flow (and the natural capital stock that generates it) are the material cause of production; the capital stock that transforms raw material inputs into product outputs is the efficient cause of production. One cannot substitute efficient cause for material cause—as one cannot build the same wooden house with half the timber no matter how many saws and carpenters one tries to substitute. Also, to process more timber into more wooden houses, in the same time period, requires more saws, carpenters, etc. Clearly the basic relation of manmade and natural capital is one of complementarity, not substitutability. Of course one could substitute bricks for timber, but that is the substitution of one resource input for another, not the substitution of capital for resources.[2] In making a brick house one would face the analogous inability of trowels and masons to substitute for bricks.

The complementarity of manmade and natural capital is made obvious at a concrete and commonsense level by asking: what good is a saw-mill without a forest; a fishing boat without populations of fish; a refinery without petroleum deposits; an irrigated farm without an aquifer or river? We have long recognised the complementarity between public infrastructure and private capital—what good is a car or truck without roads to drive on? Following

Lotka and Georgescu-Roegen we can take the concept of natural capital even further and distinguish between endosomatic (within-skin) and exosomatic (outside-skin) natural capital. We can then ask, what good is the private endosomatic capital of our lungs and respiratory system without the public exosomatic capital of green plants that take up our carbon dioxide in the short run, while in the long run replenishing the enormous atmospheric stock of oxygen and keeping the atmosphere at the proper mix of gases—i.e. the mix to which our respiratory system is adapted and therefore complementary.

If natural and manmade capital are obviously complements, how is it that economists have overwhelmingly treated them as substitutes? *First,* not all economists have—Leontier's input-output economics with its assumption of fixed factor proportions treats all factors as complements. *Second,* the formal, mathematical definitions of complementarity and substitutability are such that in the two-factor case the factors must be substitutes.[3] Since most textbooks are written on two-dimensional paper this case receives most attention. *Third,* mathematical convenience continues to dominate reality in the general reliance on Cobb-Douglas and other constant elasticity of substitution production functions in which there is near infinite substitutability of factors, in particular of capital for resources.[4] Thankfully some economists have begun to constrain this substitution by the law of conservation of mass! *Fourth,* exclusive myopic attention to the margin results in very limited and marginal possibilities for substitution obscuring overall relations of complementarity. For example, private expenditure on extra car maintenance may substitute for reduced public expenditure on roads. But this marginal element of substitution (car repairs for road repairs) should not obscure the fact that cars and roads are basically complementary forms of capital.[5] *Fifth,* there may well be substitution of capital for resources in aggregate production functions reflecting a change in product mix from resource-intensive to capital-intensive products. But this is an artefact of changing product aggregation, not factor substitution along a given product isoquant. Also, a new product may be designed that gives the same service with less resource use—e.g., light bulbs that give more lumens per watt. This is technical progress, a qualitative improvement in the state of the art, not the substitution of a quantity of capital for a quantity of resources in the production of a given quantity of a specific product.

No one denies the reality of technical progress, but to call such changes the substitution of capital for resources (or of manmade for natural capital) is a serious confusion. It seems that some economists are counting as 'capital' all improvements in knowledge, technology, managerial skills, etc.—in short, anything that would increase the efficiency with which resources are used. If this is the usage, then 'capital' and resources would by definition be substitutes in the same sense that more efficient use of a resource is a good substitute for having more of the resource. But formally to define capital as efficiency would make a mockery of the neoclassical theory of production, where efficiency is a ratio of output to input, and capital is a quantity of input.

It was necessary, I think, to go deeply into the issue of complementarity because it is the key to strong sustainability, and by omitting it Beckerman failed to deal with the most important issue in the sustainable development debate.

Turning now to other problems, Beckerman thinks that discounting is the proper way to balance present and future claims on the resource base. But a discount rate is part of the price system, and prices allocate subject to a given distribution of ownership. The key question is the given distribution of ownership between different generations, which are different people. If the resource base is thought to belong entirely to the present generation we get one set of prices, including interest (discount) rate. If the resource base is thought to be distributed in ownership over many generations we get an entirely different set of prices, including a different interest rate. Both sets of prices are efficient, given the distribution.[6] Strong sustainability as a constraint is a way of implicitly providing property rights in the resource base to future generations. It says they have ownership claims to as much natural capital as the present—i.e. the rule is to keep natural capital intact. Strong sustainability requires that manmade and natural capital each be maintained intact separately, since they are considered complements: weak sustainability requires that only the sum of the two be maintained intact, since they are presumed to be substitutes. As natural capital more and more becomes the limiting factor the importance of keeping it separately intact increases.

Beckerman recognises that sustainability of consumption is built into the Hicksian definition of income. But he downplays this respectable lineage by saying that Hicks's definition of income is a purely technical concept, containing no moral injunction against capital consumption. While this is true in terms of accounting definitions, it is also rather disingenuous to pretend that the prudential motive of avoiding inadvertent impoverishment by consuming beyond income played no role in Hicks's formulation of the concept. Hicksian income is a concept consciously designed to inform prudential (sustainable) consumption, even though it does not mandate it. Extending the definitional requirement to keep capital intact to natural capital as well as manmade capital is a small step, and one totally within the spirit of Hicks's prudential concerns. And, given that natural capital is now the limiting factor, leaving it out of consideration vitiates the very meaning of income and runs contrary to its prudential motivation.

In sum, I agree with Beckerman that weak sustainability is a muddle, and that definitions in terms of the welfare of future generations are non-operational. However, I have shown that strong sustainability is neither morally reprehensible nor operationally impractical, and that Beckerman's view to the contrary is based on his mistaken definition of strong sustainability. With proper definition strong sustainability retains Beckerman's

blessing as a logical constraint, since it really does limit present welfare maximisation and is not defined implicitly in terms of the same welfare
maximisation that it is supposed to limit. Strong sustainability also provides
a better way of respecting the rights of future generations than does
discounting. Furthermore, it represents a logical extension of the Hicksian
income concept.

For all of the above reasons I believe that sustainable development, properly clarified (as Beckerman rightly demands), is an indispensable concept.
All important concepts are dialectically vague at the margins. I claim that sustainable development is at least as clear a concept as 'money'. Is money really
M1 or M2, or is it M1a? Do we count Eurodollar-based loans in the US money
supply? How liquid does an asset have to be before it counts as 'quasimoney',
etc.? Yet the human mind is clever. We not only can handle the concept of
money, but would have a hard time without it. The same, I suggest, is true for
the concept of sustainable development.

NOTES

1. El Serafy 1988.
2. Regarding the house example I am frequently told that insulation (capital) is a substitute for resources (energy for space heating). If the house is considered the final product, then capital (agent of production, efficient cause) cannot end up as a part (material cause) of the house,
whether as wood, brick, or insulating material. The insulating material is a resource like wood
or brick, not capital. If the final product is not taken as the house but the service of the house in
providing warmth, then the entire house, not only insulating material, is capital. In this case more
or better capital (a well-insulated house) does reduce the waste of energy. Increasing the efficiency with which a resource is used is certainly a good substitute for more of the resource. But
these kinds of waste-reducing efficiency measures (recycling prompt scrap, sweeping up sawdust
and using it for fuel or particle board, reducing heat loss from a house, etc.) are all rather marginal substitutions that soon reach their limit.
3. The usual definition of complementarity requires that for a given constant output a rise
in the price of one factor would reduce the quantity of both factors. In the two factor case both
factors means all factors, and it is impossible to keep output constant while reducing the input
of all factors. But complementarity might be defined back into existence in the two factor case by
avoiding the constant output condition. For example, two factors could be considered complements if an increase in one alone will not increase output, but an increase in the other will—and
perfect complements if an increase in neither factor alone will increase output, but an increase in
both will. It is not sufficient to treat complementarity as if it were nothing more than 'limited
substitutability'. That means that we could get along with only one factor well enough, with only
the other less well, but that we do not need both. Complementarity means we need both, and
that the one in shortest supply is limiting.
4. N. Georgescu-Roegen deserves to be quoted at length on this point because so few people have understood it. He writes the 'Solow-Stiglitz variant' of the Cobb-Douglas function as:

$$Q = K^{a_1} R^{a_2} L^{a_3} \qquad (1)$$

'where Q is output, K is the stock of capital, R is the flow of natural resources used in production,
L is the labour supply, and $a_1 + a_2 + a_3 = 1$ and of course, $a_1 > 0$.
From this formula it follows that with a constant labour power, L_0, one could obtain any Q_0, if the
flow of natural resources satisfies the condition

$$R^{a_2} = \frac{Q_0}{K^{a_1} L_0^{a_3}} \qquad (2)$$

This shows that R may be as small as we wish, provided K is sufficiently large. Ergo, we can obtain a constant annual product indefinitely even from a very small stock of resources R > O, if we decompose R into an infinite series R = ΣR_i with $R_i \rightarrow O$, use R_i in year i, and increase the stock of capital each year as required by (2). But this *ergo* is not valid in actuality. In actuality, the increase of capital implies an additional depletion of resources. And if $K \rightarrow \infty$, then R will rapidly be exhausted by the production of capital. Solow and Stiglitz could not have come out with their conjuring trick had they borne in mind, first, that any material process consists in the transformation of some materials into others (the flow elements) by some agents (the fund elements), and second, that natural resources are the very sap of the economic process. They are not just like any other production factor. A change in capital or labour can only diminish the amount of waste in the production of a commodity: no agent can create the material on which it works. Nor can capital create the stuff out of which it is made. In some cases it may also be that the same service can be provided by a design that requires less matter or energy. But even in this direction there exists a limit, unless we believe that the ultimate fate of the economic process is an earthly Garden of Eden. The question that confronts us today is whether we are going to discover new sources of energy that can be safely used. No elasticities of some Cobb-Douglas function can help us to answer it.' (Georgescu-Roegen 1979)

5. At the margin a right glove can substitute for a left glove by turning it inside out. Socks can substitute for shoes by wearing an extra pair to compensate for thinning soles. But in spite of this marginal substitution, shoes and socks, right and left gloves, etc. are still complements. Basically the same is true for manmade and natural capital. Picture their isoquants as L-shaped, having a 90° angle. Erase the angle and draw in a tiny 90° arc connecting the two legs of the L. This seems close to reality. However, this very marginal range of substitution has been overextrapolated to the degree that even a Nobel Laureate economist has gravely opined that, thanks to substitution, '. . . . the world can, in effect, get along without natural resources.' (Solow 1974)

6. See Norgaard and Howarth 1991.

References

El Serafy, Salah 1988. 'The Proper Calculation of Income from Depletable Natural Resources', in Y. Ahmad, S. El Serafy, and E. Lutz (eds), *Environmental Accounting for Sustainable Development*. Washington, D.C.: The World Bank.

Georgescu-Roegen, N. 1979. 'Comments . . .' in V. Kerry Smith (ed.) *Scarcity and Growth Reconsidered*, p. 98. Baltimore: Resources for the Future and Johns Hopkins Press.

Norgaard, R. and Howarth, R. 1991. 'Sustainability and Discounting the Future', in R. Costanza (ed.) *Ecological Economics*. New York: Columbia University Press.

Solow, Robert 1974. 'The Economics of Resources or the Resources of Economics', *AER*, May, p. 11.

In Defence of Sustainable Development

Henryk Skolimowski

Mr Wilfred Beckerman, of Balliol College, Oxford has written a crisp essay attempting to undermine the meaning of the concept of 'Sustainable Development'. As I read his first arguments, I couldn't agree with him more that the concept is excessively stretched, that there is a lot of sloppy usage, and indeed that a spurious intellectual industry has been created in manufacturing various by-products of Sustainable Development.

Now, my first reaction, after the Brundtland Report (*Our Common Future*) was published, was that there was nothing new in it, and that all it conveyed was already known and discussed in a greater depth in the literature pertaining to Ecophilosophy[1] and environmental ethics. Yet something was new: the very idea of *Sustainable Development*. It struck a middle ground between more radical approaches which denounced all development, and the idea of development conceived as business as usual. The idea of Sustainable Development, although broad, loose and tinged with lots of ambiguity around its edges, turned out to be *palatable* to everybody. This may have been its greatest virtue: it is radical and yet not offensive. The language is very important. Language is tested in time. And the test of the idea of Sustainable Development proved to be positive. The idea has become widely accepted. It allows thinking people to rally around the platform on which a multitude of things can be discussed. It has permitted ordinary people to understand the new economic thinking and the new directions of our civilisation.

Yet the concept is loose and our sense of intellectual respectability is often offended by its ambiguities, as Wilfred Beckerman pointedly argues. We should not worry too much about intellectual respectability. We should worry more about the survival of the species, and the intellectual tools which have inadvertently led us to grave intellectual, moral, existential and ecological crises. Now Mr Beckerman left me behind when he proposed, in his analysis, that the idea of Sustainable Development should be used as a purely technical concept; and he even mentions something about defining it operationally. Who on earth would want to operationalise the idea of Sustainable Development? And to what purposes?

The real debate is not about Sustainable Development. The debate is about the legacy of material progress, about *the sustainability of life itself.* It is clear that the new economic thinking of the 90s is different from the old economic thinking. As Cristovam Buarque spells out in his book *The End of Economics: Ethics and the Disorder of Progress* (Zed Books, 1993); and as Simon Zadek (reviewing this book in the same issue of *Environmental Values* in which Beckerman's piece is published) eloquently summarises, the new economics is impatient with the old one which aspires and pretends to be value neutral, with its inadequacies in accounting environmental costs, with its blindness to qualitative aspects of life, with its crass allegiance to the materialist world view.

Yes, the new economics holds that ethical and environmental components must be built into our theory and explicitly recognised. In this way economics could become a useful tool in understanding our present environmental and economic problems, and could even be a tool for ameliorating our condition. The old economics is a tool of rape and destruction of the environment at large. It is also an instrument justifying (if indirectly) social injustices and inequities, and thereby deepening the chasm between the South and the North, between the poor and the rich.

It is in this context that we must view the debate on the meaning of Sustainable Development. Is the idea ambiguous? Yes. Is the idea useful? Yes, it is very useful. It tries to combine what needs to be combined: the economic and the moral, the idea of justice with the appropriate economic tools which should serve the idea of justice—particularly with regard to the poor and the underprivileged.

The period of cognitive purity is over. We can no longer separate the cognitive and the ethical, especially in economics—but also in exact sciences, for the very idea of objectivity is morally loaded. Even if some neutrality can be claimed for theories of natural science, it is not so in social science, and especially in classical economics: its basic theory implicitly contains utilitarian ethics, and also contains the whole legacy of material progress—which itself is impregnated with moral values and moral prescriptions.

Our intellectual honesty requires that we recognise economic theories as normative, at least as containing the normative substratum. If there is a clash between our intellectual honesty and our intellectual respectability, we must choose the former, for intellectual respectability so often is a euphemism standing for institutional commitment and servitude to the old, while our intellectual honesty is a new moral stance through which we attempt to help the threatened life on the whole Planet.

Mr Beckerman admonishes us that we use vague concepts as a vehicle leading to the amelioration of the environment and of human life. Yes, we do. It is better to muddle through to salvation than go crisply to damnation.

NOTE

1. See for instance: Henryk Skolimowski, *Eco-philosophy, Designing New Tactics for Living.* Marion Boyars, London 1981.

In Defence of Weak Sustainability: A Response to Beckerman

Salah El Serafy[1]

I thought Herman Daly and Michael Jacobs were too hasty to concur with Beckerman that 'weak sustainability' should be dismissed, and especially Daly in offering his congratulations 'for his [Beckerman's] effective demolition of "weak sustainability"'.[2] Now that Beckerman got 'weak sustainability' out of the way, or so he thought, he proceeded to demolish 'strong sustainability' also (*Environmental Values* 4 (1995) pp. 169–79. . . .

I have always thought that 'strong sustainability' was a useful concept, provided that we temper it with the undeniable possibilities of substitution among inputs, both in the process of production, and also (and this is often forgotten) among the final goods and services that constitute ultimate demand. The scope for substitution, though appreciable in certain areas, may in fact pale in comparison with the rising tide of economic scale that is reinforcing the relationship of 'gross complementarity', and inflicting irreparable harm on the environment. Besides, in order for substitution to work, the market should show more sensitivity than it seems able to do towards the ever-changing patterns of scarcity. And we should also be able to distinguish between price signals that are genuinely produced by the interaction of free and 'socially beneficial' market forces, and those that are the product of monopoly, 'exploitation', political pressure, military intervention, and indeed skewed income distributions. It should be clear to Beckerman, for instance, that primary commodities tend to be undervalued on the international markets since the market fails to internalise the full environmental cost of their production. Many of the problems of underdevelopment, I fancy, would be alleviated if the poorer countries received adequate compensation for their primary product exports. In this respect,

Beckerman exhibits a disarmingly simple faith in the ability of the market to indicate 'optimal' prices.

'Weak sustainability' can in fact be viewed as a first step that must be taken by economists without any normative reference to the environment, and once achieved, perhaps it can lead to stronger forms of sustainability. Daly's and Jacobs's strictures against 'weak sustainability' (which incidentally are shared by others[3]) reveal to me not so much a denial on their part of the utility of this concept, but more of an impatience with a weak and diluted objective in the belief, I think, that its pursuit would impede the attainment of their ultimate and stronger goal. Beckerman's reaction to their partial surrender in the face of his initial onslaught should be a lesson to them not to abandon what is in effect their first line of defence!

WEAK SUSTAINABILITY AND SUSTAINABLE DEVELOPMENT

As an economist I have felt much more comfortable to argue for 'weak sustainability' using economic logic alone, and without resort to any value judgment about the environment. But first we should be clear what 'weak sustainability' actually means. Beckerman's definition of 'weak sustainability' is not one that I recognise, although his excuse is that he is following a recent definition proposed by David Pearce. Careful examination, however, shows that Pearce's definition is not that of 'weak sustainability', but of 'sustainable development—a concept, though related, that is quite different. The notion that 'weak sustainability' (as Beckerman asserts) implies that per capita well-being does not diminish over time is certainly not what is generally understood by 'weak sustainability'. Provided that it can be operationally measured, a non-declining per capita level of welfare may well be an excellent benchmark against which development should be assessed, but this has little to do with 'weak sustainability'.

It is therefore wrong of Beckerman to say that 'As it soon became obvious that the 'strong' concept of sustainable development was morally repugnant, as well as totally impracticable, many environmentalists shifted their ground. A new version of the concept was adopted, known in the literature as "weak sustainability".'[4] Daly's readiness to bury weak sustainability should at least have alerted Beckerman to the possibility that he might in fact be misreading the debate.

'Weak sustainability' did not rise from the ashes of 'strong sustainability', but in fact may be said to have preceded it. For 'weak sustainability' has long been recognised as revolving around the correct measurement of income: not income per capita, and certainly not 'development', whether sustainable or otherwise. 'Development' has traditionally been assessed in terms of economic growth, i.e. the rise over time of what passes as the national income and product of a developing country. Leaving aside the elementary fact that development is a much wider concept than the mere expansion of economic activity, growth (alias, development) will itself be questionable if income has not been properly measured. By drawing attention to the fact that proper income measurement is a *sine qua non* for the accurate gauging of growth, I, as well as others, have insisted that capital, *including natural capital,* must be kept intact.[5] This fundamental requirement which has for centuries been recognised by accountants (namely that capital must be kept intact for the proper estimation of income) and which was later to be adopted by successive generations of economists, found expression half a century ago in Hicks's standard definition of income in *Value and Capital*—a definition which is probably acceptable to most economists: in order to ascertain income in the current period, enough from current receipts must be put aside to compensate for capital deterioration so that future income might be sustained. 'Weak sustainability' insists that this rule be obeyed, but also attempts to insert natural capital under the umbrella of 'keeping capital intact'.

CORRECTING INCOME MEASUREMENTS

As is well known, accounting for income is fraught with uncertainties. Approximations and short-cuts have to be resorted to in order to enable a rough, but eminently useful, picture of income to be drawn. These uncertainties, however, have troubled some economists. But this is not the main point here. The main point is that, in order to satisfy 'weak sustainability' the capital that must be kept intact for sustaining future income is not any specific piece of equipment, or a sub-category of overall capital, but capital *in general*. This, Hicks (1974) has dubbed 'fundist capital'.[6] If proper measurement of income is to be ensured, capital in general must be kept intact. This would mean that the stock of natural capital that contributes to production may be reduced, provided that other forms of capital are increased so that capital in general is kept intact. Two things should be borne in mind, however. One is that accounting for income is typically carried out once a year, so that the sustainability of future income implied by keeping capital intact applies to a fairly near horizon which is defined largely by the life expectancy of existing assets. A corollary of this is that in the process of accounting no view is taken of future technological change, though if and when this change should occur, the necessary adjustment to income (via the adjustment of the capital stock) would be made in the light of the *actual* change. As stated earlier, while traditionally 'keeping capital intact' has been confined to produced assets, advocates of 'weak sustainability' would extend this concept to cover also natural resources, especially those which are already implicitly incorporated in conventional national income estimates, albeit at a zero value. However, since in the very long run, the structure of final demand, as well as production techniques, are liable to change, it is obviously not sufficient to rely on accounting principles to ensure longer term sustainability. In other words, 'weak sustainability' will not satisfy the environmentalists.

The other point to remember is that the concern of the national income statistician is primarily focused on income, and only indirectly is this focus shifted to the stock of capital. To the accountant, maintaining capital intact does not spring from any desire to preserve the capital stock as an end in itself, but simply to get a grip on the estimation of income which has to be sustainable if it is to be identified as income at all. Maintaining capital intact, as Beckerman clearly recognises, is merely a technical artifact. But technical as it may be, however, its lack of observance in practice is rife, especially where natural resources are concerned, and this requires correction. It is 'weak sustainability' that is being invoked for this correction.

For most of the developing countries national income accounting methods in use have tended to confuse natural asset liquidation with growth, and the 'development' suggested (by national income measurements) as taking place is not all genuine, and may be characterised as being unsustainable. The growth indicated by those erroneous income measurements was often illusory since the cardinal rule of keeping capital intact was being ignored. The longer a country avoided incurring the cost of cleaning up its environment, and the faster it cut down its forests, eroded its soil, depleted its aquifers, and exhausted its mineral deposits, the faster it appeared to grow. Economists seldom stopped to question the numbers turned out by faulty national income accounting methods, and have continued to use such numbers in all kinds of otherwise sophisticated analysis, leading them frequently to misjudge an economy's progress, and to prescribe inappropriate, and even harmful, economic policies. To economists, 'weak sustainability' in the sense of getting the accounts right, is by no means a redundant luxury.

From Weak to Strong Sustainability

It was understandable, therefore, that many environmentalists should seize on Hicks's definition of income to point out that measurements of income that ignored environmental deterioration may indeed be faulty, and to demand that economists be faithful to their own discipline, insisting that capital be kept intact for the purpose of properly measuring 'sustainable income'. [I put sustainable income between inverted commas because income, to be income at all, must be sustainable.] This totally objective (and 'positive', i.e. value neutral) requirement, that capital, in its fundist sense, be kept intact for the purpose of properly measuring income and its growth, came in time to be called 'weak sustainability'. But this was subsequently 'strengthened' as sustainability got converted to a normative injunction to keep *natural* capital (a sub-category of fundist capital) intact. Thus the emphasis moved from income estimation to preserving the stock of natural capital intact as an end, not as a means to the estimation of income. This took the concept in the direction of 'strong sustainability'.

Later still, attention to proper national income measurement was extended in another direction to individual *projects*, as some writers attempted to promote the concept of a 'sustainable project', claiming that part of the project-yield which can be attributed to resource use (such as the 'user cost') should indeed be re-invested for the purpose of sustaining future income, but it should be re-invested specifically in projects geared to the generation of substitutes to replace the declining natural resource that is being depleted. This move was also in the direction of 'strong sustainability' although it shifted concern from the macro-aggregates to projects. Not only did this extension move the definition of capital away from its fundist concept towards *materialist* capital, but it also introduced (or endorsed) the notion of a 'sustainable project' to which Beckerman seems uncritically to subscribe. To me, projects are good projects if they can produce a surplus—a genuine surplus that is—in the course of their limited life, after which the capital sunk in them, if it had been properly depreciated, may be shifted to new projects capable of yielding acceptable future returns for a while, until they too will expire. Beckerman's naive example of a poor country having to choose between leaving its mineral wealth in the ground and using the proceeds for survival or education,[7] is unworthy of serious consideration. For nobody has ever suggested other than making use of such a resource constructively in order to better the life of its owners. The real issue is not whether or not to exploit such an asset, but how much of the proceeds from this finite resource can properly be regarded as genuine income, available for consumption, and how much needs to be reinvested in order to sustain the same level of consumption into the future.[8]

CONCLUSION

Defining genuine income is of fundamental importance to economists, and it is the proper measurement of that income that will satisfy the 'weak sustainability' criterion. This is a technical or value-free requirement that has little to do with the environment. As such, 'weak sustainability' is indispensable for accurately assessing economic performance. 'Strong sustainability', by contrast, is a normative concept, and relates to the immensely complex stock of environmental assets and properties. Many of these are not easy (in the famous Pigouvian phrase[9]) 'to bring into a relationship with the measuring rod of money'. The fact that parts of the environment seem now to lie beyond what economists regard as their concern, does not necessarily mean that such parts do not exist or that they might not assert themselves as scarce elements in the future. Like Bishop Berkeley's tree, the environment is beheld by society as whole, and it would be imprudent if economists confined their vision to what is regarded as economic now, and did not keep an open mind about what might become economic later. For one thing, resources that had once been considered abundant, such for instance as clean water, have now become quite scarce. I, for one, would not dismiss 'strong sustainability' as cavalierly as Beckerman does.

NOTES

1. Economic Consultant; formerly Senior Advisor, The World Bank, Washington D.C.
2. Daly and Jacobs, *Environmental Values* **4** (1995): respectively, pp. 49–55, and pp. 57–68, each commenting on Beckerman, 'Sustainable Development: Is It a useful Concept?' *Environmental Values* **3** (1994): pp. 191–209.
3. For instance by Victor, 1994.
4. Beckerman, *Environmental Values* **3** (1995), p. 195.
5. See (inter alia) El Serafy, 1981 and 1989.
6. Hicks, 1974, drew a distinction between 'fundist' and 'materialist' capital in the view of successive generations of economists. Fundist capital represented a value or a fund covering all forms of capital in the possession of an individual, a corporation or an economy, whereas materialist capital related to specific pieces of machinery, inventories and the like. I made use of this distinction (El Serafy 1991) to argue for the inclusion of natural resources in (fundist) capital, relying also on the argument that the environment may be regarded as a factor of production. The latter notion I borrowed from Hicks, 1983, where he wrote (pp. 121–122):
   'So it is not necessary, in order that a thing should be a factor, that it should have a price. In order that a thing should have a price, it must be appropriable, but it is not necessary for a thing to be appropriable for it to be a factor of production, in the sense that if it were to be removed, production (or output) would be diminished. Or, more usefully, if a part of it were to be removed, production would be diminished. Which comes to the same thing as saying that the factor must have a marginal product.'
7. Beckerman, 1994. *Environmental Values* 3, p. 193.
8. See El Serafy, 1989.
9. Pigou, 1924, p. 11.

References

El Serafy, Salah. 1981. Absorptive Capacity, the Demand for Revenue and the Supply of Petroleum. *Journal of Energy and Development,* Volume 7, No. 1 (Autumn).
El Serafy, Salah. 1989. The Proper Calculation of Income from Depletable Natural Resources. In Ahmad, Yusuf J., S. El Serafy, and E. Lutz, editors. *Environmental Accounting for Sustainable Development* A UNEP-World Bank Symposium. The World Bank. Washington D.C.
El Serafy, Salah. 1991. The Environment as Capital. In Costanza, Robert, editor. *Ecological Economics: the Science and Management of Sustainability.* Columbia University Press, New York.
Hicks, John R. 1946. *Value and Capital,* Second Edition. Clarendon Press. Oxford.
Hicks, John R. 1974. Capital Controversies: Ancient and Modern. *American Economic Review,* May.
Hicks, John R. 1983. Is Interest the Price of a Factor of Production? In *Classics and Moderns.* Collected Essays on Economic Theory, Volume III. Harvard University Press, Cambridge, Massachusetts.
Pigou, A.C. 1924. *The Economics of Welfare.* Second Edition. Macmillan and Co., London.
Victor, Peter A. 1994. How Strong is Weak Sustainability? In *Modèles de développement soutenable, Des approches exclusives ou complémentaires de la soutebnabilité?* Université Panthéon-Sorbonne, Paris.

EVALUATING A CASE STUDY: STRUCTURING THE ESSAY

In previous sections, you have moved from adopting an ethical theory to weighing and assessing the merits of deeply embedded cost issues and ethical issues conflicts. The process involves (a) choosing an ethical theory (whose point of view you will adopt), (b) determining your professional practice issues and ethical issues lists, (c) annotating the issues lists by examining how embedded each issue is to the essential nature of the case at hand, (d) creating a brainstorming list that includes both key thoughts on the subject and arguments for and against the possible courses of action, (e) comparing pivotal premises in those arguments using ethical considerations as part of the decision-making matrix, (f) making a judgment on which course to take (given the conflicts expressed in d and e, and (g) presenting your ideas in an essay. The essay is your recommendation to a professional review board about what to do in a specific situation.

This section represents stage (g) in this process. If we continue with the IUD case, your essay might be something like the following.

Sample Essay

Executive Summary. Although my profession would advocate my continuing to distribute IUDs to women in less-developed countries and cost issues dictate that I accept ABC Corporation's offer, it is my opinion that to do so would be immoral. Human life is too precious to put anyone at risk for population control. If IUDs are too dangerous to be sold in the United States, then they are too dangerous for women in poor countries as well. People do not give up their right to adequate health protection just because they are poor. For this reason, I am ordering a halt to the distribution of IUDs until such a time that they can be considered safe again. Furthermore, I will step up efforts to distribute alternate forms of birth control (such as the birth control pill) with better packaging that might encourage regular use.

The Introduction. In this case study, I have chosen the point of view of the regional director. This means that I must decide whether to continue distributing IUDs in less-developed countries despite a health hazard to 5 percent of the women who use this form of birth control. I will argue against continuing the distribution based on an argument that examines: (a) the imperatives of my profession, public health; (b) cost implications (c) the imperatives of ethics; and (d) the rights of the women involved. I will contend that after examining these issues, the conclusion must be to cease IUD distribution in less-developed countries until IUDs no longer pose a significant problem to women's health.

The Body of the Essay.   Develop paragraphs along the lines indicated in the introduction and executive summary.

The Conclusion.   Although the dictates of the normal practice of public health and cost considerations would seem to suggest that IUD distribution continue, the ethical imperatives that human life is individually precious and that each woman has a right to safe medical attention overrule the normal practice of the profession. For these reasons, my office will suspend distribution of IUDs until they no longer pose a health risk to the general population.

Comments on the Sample

The sample provides an essay structure that contains a brief epitome and the essay itself. I often encourage my students to come in with their epitome, key issues, arguments for and against, and brainstorming sheets before writing the essay itself. This way I can get an "in-progress" view of the process of composition.

Obviously, the preceding sample represents the briefest skeleton of an essay proposing a recommendation. The length can vary as can any supporting data (charts, etc.) for your position. Your instructor may ask you to present your outcomes recommendation to the entire class. When this is the assignment, remember that the same principles of any group presentation also apply here including any visual aid that will engage your audience. It is essential to include your audience in your argument as it develops.

Whether it is a written report or a group presentation, the methodology presented here should give you a chance to logically assess and respond to problems that contain moral dimensions.

The following are some general questions that some of my students have raised about writing the essay, that is, the ethical outcomes recommendation.

What if I cannot see the other side? This is a common question from students. They see everything as black or white, true or false, but truth is never advanced by prejudice. It is important as rational humans to take every argument at its face value and to determine what it says, determine the objections to the key premises, determine the strongest form of the thesis, and assess the best arguments *for* and *against* the thesis.

What is the best way to reach my assessment of the best alternative? The basic strategy of the essay is to take the best two arguments that you have selected to support the conflicting alternatives and then to focus on that single premise that seems to be at odds with the other argument. At this point, you must ask yourself, Why would someone believe in either argument 1 or argument 2? If you do not know, you cannot offer an opinion—yet.

The rational person seeks to inform herself by getting into the skin of each party. You must understand why a thinking person might think in a particular way. If you deprecate either side, you lessen yourself because you decrease your chances to make your best judgment.

The rational individual seeks the truth. You have no need to burden your psyche with illogical beliefs. Therefore, you will go to great lengths to find the truth of the key premises that you wish to examine.

In the your final essay, you will focus on one of the argument's premises and find the following:

A. The demonstrated truth of the conclusion depends on the premises that support it.

B. If those supporting premises are false, then the conclusion is not proven.

C. Since we have assumed that the premises are all necessary to get us to the conclusion, if we refute one premise, we have refuted the conclusion.

What if I place professional practice issues or cost issues or ethical issues too highly in my assessment of the outcome? The purpose of preparing an embedded issues analysis is to force you to see that not all ethical issues are central to the problem. Some issues can be solved rather easily. If this is the case, then you should do so. When it is possible to let professional practice issues determine the outcome without sacrificing ethical standards, it is your responsibility to do so. Clearly, some ethical principles cannot be sacrificed no matter what the cost. It is *your* responsibility to determine just what these cases are and just which moral principles are "show stoppers."

Are ethical values the only values an individual should consider? Each person holds a number of personally important values that are a part of his or her worldview. These must be taken into account in real situations. Often they mean that although you cannot perform such and such an act, it is not requisite that the organization forgo doing whatever the professional practice issues dictate in that situation. For example, you may be asked to perform a task on an important religious holy day. Since your religion is important to you, you cannot work on that day, but that does not mean that you will recommend the company abandon the task that another person who does not share your value could perform.

What happens when you confuse professional practice issues and ethical issues? This happens often among managers at all levels. The problem is that one set of issues is neglected or is too quickly considered to be surface embeddedness. Stop. Go through the method again step-by-step. It may restore your perspective.

Macro and Micro Cases.*

Macro Cases.

Macro Case 1. You are the head of curriculum development for science at Bellevue Public Schools in Bellevue, Washington. One of the issues that has come before the committee is dissecting fetal pigs in Biology 1. This skill has

---

*For more on macro and micro cases, see the overview on p. 30.

been taught in the course for many years, but now with simulated computer programs, students can get three-dimensional effects without having to use actual fetal pigs.

One member on the committee said that it was strange that we hold so much regard for human children and the human embryo, yet we blithely butcher hundreds of thousands of fetal pigs each year without any compunction. Another member said that pigs are different from humans because they cannot reason; reason makes all the difference. A third member said that pigs are quite intelligent, so that if that were the standard, pigs would fare well. Also, he said that the cutting-edge technology for surgeons is to use computer-assisted graphics that represent anatomy as they perform tricky, experimental operations. If it is good enough for the best surgeons of the world, certainly it is good enough for first-year high school biology students.

A fourth member of the committee said that those surgeons could use computer-assisted models only *because* they have been taught on real dissections. There is no substitute for actual hands-on experience.

The committee is deadlocked and as its head, you must cast the deciding vote. Write a report to the committee explaining why you cast your vote in favor of traditional fetal pig dissection or the new proposal for computer-simulated dissection. Be sure to cite practical issues and ethical issues (including an ethical theory and linking principle).

Macro Case 2.   You are the head of the Meat Inspection Agency within the Department of Agriculture. Your job traditionally has been to ensure that meat is processed in a clean, hygienic environment. However, the head of the House Agriculture Committee has ordered you to review all meat-processing procedures for legislative reform as the result of current attitudes. One such attitude is represented by an orthodox Jewish rabbi from a powerful congressional district in Brooklyn. This rabbi has suggested to you that the procedure of bleeding pork before slaughter is barbaric. This practice dates back thousands of years when no one wanted to eat pork that was slaughtered in the same way as other animals (such as cattle). Pork is clearly seen to be disgusting because of its bloody color. Thus, the practice of bleeding pigs before slaughter was adopted. This practice, the rabbi contends, is cruel because it inflicts pain on the animal in the last minutes of its life. You have thought about this. Pork does not represent the largest portion of the meat market, but it is still significant. If you think as a politician (because of your political appointment), you will decide according to what is politically expedient. When you do so, the status quo wins. However, you want to do the right thing—but what is the right thing? You must submit a draft review in three days. You must include the rabbi's concerns in your report, but you must also come up with your own recommendations. Write a report on this issue basing your reasons on practical and ethical issues (including an ethical theory and linking principle).

Macro Case 3. You are an official for the Environmental Protection Agency (EPA) and have been assigned to review a lumbering proposal for Oregon (near Mount Hood). ABC Company wants to do two things. First, it wants to cut forest lands on this tract of virgin forest (i.e., not cut by humans since recorded time—around 1840) and to replant so that by the time the last section has been harvested, the first will be covered by adult trees at least 80 percent the height of those trees that were cut first. Second, ABC wants to build a road that will accommodate its logging trucks. This will require filling in four wetland sites. However, in accordance with current federal regulations, ABC will establish four new wetland sites and therefore be in complete compliance with the law.

During public hearings, however, many people came forward to note that the lumber proposal will severely disrupt the habitat of a tree frog is unique to this area. This tree frog is the linchpin of an ecosystem, it is the prey of at least twenty species and is the predator of forty-six species. To disrupt this ecosystem, the detractors contend, would be to kill this species of frog and severely disrupt the ecosystem.

Those in favor of the project say that species are becoming extinct all the time; that is the way of nature. Ecosystems are not in some sort of static state that must be preserved but will adapt as conditions demand—this is the way of evolution. This project will employ 1,800 individuals and support more than 8,000 people when all social factors are considered. Will you say to a family on welfare that it must continue to live in poverty because we are concerned about losing a species of tree frog or damaging an ecosystem?

Write a report to your superiors that is due next Tuesday. In it, note the various positions and the arguments for each. Then recommend what to do based on the appropriate facts and ethical theories.

Macro Case 4. You are the head of the South East Asian Commission for Development at the World Bank. Bangladesh has submitted a proposal for the creation of a giant overflow reservoir that will be significant in solving the recurrent problem of flooding in the delta region. In years past (more than 100), people did not live in this region because of the devastation that periodically occurred. However, things are different now; because of overpopulation and the fertile soil, people now live in this region and there is substantial death and human anguish when the flooding occurs regularly.

At first, there seems to be no problem if the agency funds a project that saves lives, increases jobs, and creates hydroelectric power for the country. However, there are problems. First, there is a lack of family planning in the region. One concern involves overpopulation. With no floods to cause deaths, more people will live to reproduce, so the combination of fewer deaths and more births will lead to overpopulation and its related problems. Second, eighty known unique species of flora and fauna will be lost as the result of the ecological disruption. Third, the increase in cheap power generated may cause a boom in industrial development by foreign companies eager to cash in on it and cheap labor. (Bangladesh is one of the poorest nations of the world.)

Write a report to your superior at the World Bank recommending a course of action. Base your recommendation on a survey of the human, ecological, and the ethical factors (mentioning specifically an ethical theory and a linking principle).

Micro Cases.

Micro Case 1. You and your best friend are at odds over the issue of eating meat. Each day, the two of you eat dinner together in the dining hall. Your friend is a vegetarian and claims that you should be, too.

"Why?" you ask.

"Because you have no right to eat another animal. It's immoral. You wouldn't eat your Uncle Harold, would you?" You always hate it when your friend brings up Uncle Harold.

"I'm not eating my uncle; besides, that has nothing to do with it. Harold is a human. This hamburger I'm eating was once a cow. Have you ever seen how small the frontal lobe of a cow is? These animals are not only not rational but are also *stupid!*"

"They may be stupid but they still feel pain. They still value their lives—"

"Just a minute there; *how* can they value their lives when they do not have an abiding sense of self from which they can base their valuing?"

"You're splitting hairs. Every animal values its life. Every animal feels pain. In virtue of these two facts, you must become a vegetarian. Besides, it's good for you."

"That's another issue, but if you are so inclined to ascribe rights to animals, what about their moral responsibilities?"

"Their responsibilities?"

"Yes. Won't you tell the lion that it is immoral to kill the cheetah or zebra?"

"That's no kind of argument. That assumes a model of reason again. You notice that I didn't defend my position in terms of reason but in terms of feeling pain and not wanting to die."

You decide to stop the conversation for the time being. In the interim, you develop a dialogue between yourself and your friend on this issue at length. You want to slant the issue to one of the two sides. (In other words, there must be a winner.) Write this dialogue, grounding it on an ethical theory and in a linking principle.

Micro Case 2. You are a federal government employee at the Transportation Department and live in Gaithersburg, Maryland, a suburb of Washington, D.C. Your commute to work along the I-270 corridor takes you fifty-five minutes each way. You could also take public transit for just a little more door-to-door time. The cost to drive and park is about $0.50 less each day than the cost of public transit. If your child had an emergency during the day at school, you could get to the school in about 40 minutes by car or in around 68 minutes during nonrush hours via public transit.

There has been a big push at work to promote public transportation. One of the flyers handed out recently included the following statement: "The air quality in this region is not improving. You can become a part of the solution by riding public transit"—a catchy phrase. You appreciate the environment; you have a flower garden in your Gaithersburg townhouse. However, you wonder what good your riding the subway and hopping a bus would do. One person isn't that important. All the personal factors point to driving your single-occupancy vehicle. Still, something inside you says that the only way to continue as a people is to lower pollution so that our development does not permanently disfigure the world. You have heard the term "sustainable development," which means that some sacrifices must be made to balance the costs of development.

Write a personal journal entry citing your conflicting positions and then recommending a particular course of action. Feel free to use short- and long-term time frames. Be sure to refer to an ethical theory and any applicable linking principles.

Micro Case 3. You are a family farmer with 80 acres in southwestern Michigan. You do not make enough from farming to sustain your family, so you work as a carpenter during the winter months. You have been approached by XYZ Company (the largest seed company in the world) about buying its genetically altered seeds that are resistant to insects, are hearty in most environmental conditions, and command a premium price at market. The only thing that bothers you is that these big seed companies create a single style of seed and want to pass it off as the only one that is any good. What about the old days in which you carefully selected the seed you would use because you knew how the product would taste? There were many choices then.

In addition, your college-age daughter tells you that these big seed companies will decrease biodiversity by cornering the market on seeds and standardizing products. Even if they cannot create a monopoly, she says, they will greatly decrease biodiversity, which is a bad thing.

You are unsure what to do. You decide to go to the agent of the local grange association for her advice. Create a dialogue between yourself and the agent that highlights issues about biodiversity and your personal worldview. Create views for yourself and the agent, and then give reasons for choosing or not choosing to take XYZ's seeds.

Micro Case 1. You and your spouse have two children. Both of you love children. You lead several youth groups at your church/synagogue/ mosque. Both of your children seem to be well adjusted and a positive bene- fit to the world. You believe that your particular gift in life is being a parent. This is your problem: You want to have a third child, but your mother-in-law, an ardent environmentalist, says that having more than two children is con- trary to the principle of the world's sustainability. Two children will replace two parents who will die. To have more, your mother-in-law contends, will be to overly burden the earth's population problem. You are concerned about the earth, and you recognize the population problem, but you believe that, on the basis of your interests and track record, you will actually be contributing to the world by having another child.

Write a report stating your position and support it with both practical and ethical considerations.

Internet Resources

The following information provides a starting point for finding interesting material on environmental ethics on the Internet. Since much of the Internet experience is following associated links to other sites, these brief, annotated offerings will be the first and not the last point in your exploration.

1. General

http://www.clearinghouse.net/ The Argus Clearinghouse contains a large number of categories. "Environment" and "Science" are good places to start.

http://www.lib.kth.se/~lg/envsite.htm A large collection of general environmental links.

http://www.earthsystems.org/Environment.html This site puts you in touch with a virtual library with many links to eclectic sites in the United States and Canada.

http://envirolink.org Envirolink is a comprehensive site focusing on environmental activism. It offers news and an extensive directory of environmental sites concerned with economic justice.

2. More Focused Sites

http://www.tnc.org This is the site for the Nature Conservancy.

http://www.edf.org This is the site for the Environmental Defense Fund.

http://www.greenpeace.org This is the site for Greenpeace.

http://environlink.org/arrs/peta/index.html This is the site for People for the Ethical Treatment of Animals.

http://www.erraticimpact.com/~ecologic/ This site is more philosophically oriented. It is centered on ecological problems. There are also links to books, film, music, and so on via Amazon.com.

http://www.cep.unt.edu/1SEE.html This is the site for the University of North Texas, a center for environmental research. There are connections to all that is going on at the university as well as in its university press and the journal *Environmental Ethics.*

http://www.bdt.org.br/bioline/ev This is the site for the journal *Environmental Values.*

http://www.ethics.ubc.ca/resources/ This is the site for the Centre for Applied Ethics at the University of British Columbia. It also includes sections on Business Ethics and Medical Ethics.

http://ecoethics.net/ This is a subsite at Harvard's Divinity School. It specializes in environmental ethics and public policy. There is also a link to an extensive bibliography in environmental ethics. The site also includes job opportunities and conferences.

http://www.igc.org/igc/gateway/enindex.html This is the site for the Institute for Global Communications. It is the online home of several liberal organizations offering links to sites on conflict resolution, the environment, peace studies, labor, and women's issues.

Further Readings

General Note. Many works do not fit neatly into a category, so some of these may fit into several. To avoid repetition, I have listed each work only once.

General Works

Attfield, Robin. *The Ethics of Environmental Concern.* New York: Columbia University Press, 1983.

Blackstone, William T., ed. *Philosophy and the Environmental Crisis.* Athens, GA: University of Georgia Press, 1972.

Booth, Douglas. *Valuing Nature: The Decline and Preservation of Old Growth Forests.* Lanham, MD: Rowman and Littlefield, 1993.

Des Jardins, Joseph R. *Environmental Ethics.* Belmont, CA: Wadsworth, 1993.

Goodpaster, K. E., and K. M. Sayre, eds. *Ethics and Problems of the 21st Century.* Notre Dame, IN: Notre Dame University Press, 1979.

Hargrove, Eugene C. *Foundations of Environmental Ethics.* Upper Saddle River, NJ: Prentice Hall, 1989.

Katz, Eric. *Nature as Subject.* Lanham, MD: Rowman and Littlefield, 1997.

Norton, Bryan G. *Toward Unity among Environmentalists.* New York: Oxford University Press, 1991.

Oelschlaeger, Max. *The Idea of Wilderness from Prehistory to the Present.* New Haven, CT: Yale University Press, 1991.

Rapport, David, "Ecosystem Health: More Than a Metaphor?" *Environmental Values* 4.4 (1995), pp. 287–310.

Sterba, James P., ed. *Earth Ethics*. Upper Saddle River, NJ: Prentice Hall, 1995.

Torrance, John, ed. *The Concept of Nature*. New York: Oxford University Press, 1993.

VanDe Veer, Donald, and Christine Pierce, eds. *The Environmental Ethics and Policy Book*. Belmont, CA: Wadsworth, 1993.

The Land Ethic, Deep Ecology, and Social Ecology

Bookchin, Murray. "Recovering Evolution: A Reply to Eckersley and Fox." *Environmental Ethics* 12 (Fall 1990), pp. 253–73.

———. *The Philosophy of Social Ecology: Essays on Dialectical Naturalism*. Toronto: Black Rose Books, 1990.

———. *Remaking Society: Pathways to a Green Future*. Boston: South End Press, 1990.

Callicott, J. Baird. *In Defense of the Land Ethic*. Albany, NY: SUNY Press, 1989.

Callicott, J. Baird, ed. *Companion to the Sand Country Almanac*. Madison, WI: University of Wisconsin Press, 1987.

Cheney, Jim. "Naturalizing the Problem of Evil." *Environmental Ethics* 19.3 (1997), pp. 299–314.

Clark, John. *The Anarchist Moment: Reflections on Culture, Nature and Power*. Toronto: Black Rose Books, 1984.

Collins, Denis, and John Barkdull. "Capitalism, Environmentalism, and Mediating Structures." *Environmental Ethics* 17.3 (1995), pp. 227–44.

Devall, Bill. "Deep Ecology and Radical Environmentalism." *Society and Natural Resources* 4 (1991), pp. 247–58.

———, and George Sessions. *Deep Ecology: Living as if Nature Mattered*. Salt Lake City, UT: Peregrine Smith Books, 1985.

Leopold, Aldo. *A Sand County Almanac: With Essays on Conservation from Round River*. New York: Ballantine Books, 1970.

Meine, Curt. *Aldo Leopold: His Life and Work*. Madison, WI: University of Wisconsin Press, 1989.

Naess, Arne. *Ecology, Community and Lifestyle: Outline of an Ecosophy*. New York: Cambridge University Press, 1989.

Reitan, Eric H. "Deep Ecology and the Irrelevance of Morality." *Environmental Ethics* 18.4 (1996), pp. 411–24.

Shaw, William, "A Virtue Ethics Approach to Aldo Leopold's Land Ethic." *Environmental Ethics* 19.1 (Spring 1997), pp. 53–68.

Tobias, Michael, ed. *Deep Ecology*. San Diego, CA: Avant Books, 1985.

Ecofeminism

Biehl, Janet. *Rethinking Ecofeminist Politics*. Boston: South End Press, 1991.

Caldecott, Leonie, and Stephanie Leland, eds. *Reclaim the Earth: Women Speak Out for Life on Earth*. London: The Women's Press, 1983.

Cook, Julie, "The Philosophical Colonization of Ecofeminism." *Environmental Ethics* 20.3 (1998), pp. 227–46.

Diamond, Irene, and Gloria Feman Orenstein, eds. *Reweaving the World: The Emergence of Ecofeminism.* San Francisco: The Sierra Club, 1990.

Gaard, Greta, ed. *Ecofeminism: Women, Animals, Nature.* Philadelphia: Temple University Press, 1993.

Hypatia (Special Issue on Ecological Feminism) 6 (Spring 1991).

Jaggar, Alison. *Feminist Politics and Human Nature.* Totowa, NJ: Rowman and Littlefield, 1988.

McIntosh, Alastair. "The Emperor Has No Cloths . . . Let Us Paint Our Loincloths Rainbow: A Classical and Feminist Critique of Contemporary Science Policy." *Environmental Values* 5.1 (1996), pp. 3–30.

Merchant, Carolyn. *Radical Ecology: The Search for a Livable World.* New York and London: Routledge, 1993.

Warren, Karen J., and Jim Cheney. "Ecological Feminism and Ecosystems Ecology." *Hypatia* 6 (Spring 1991), pp. 179–97.

Westra, Laura. *An Environmental Proposal for Ethics: The Principle of Integrity.* Lanham, MD: Rowman and Littlefield, 1993.

Worldview Arguments: Religion and Aesthetics

Booth, Annie L. "Learning from Others: Ecophilosophy and Traditional Native American Women's Lives." *Environmental Ethics* 20.1 (1998), pp. 81–100.

Bratton, Susan Power. *Six Billion and More: Human Population Regulation and Christian Ethics.* Louisville, KY: Westminster/John Knox Press, 1992.

Davis, Donald Edward. *Ecophilosophy: A Field Guide to the Literature.* San Pedro, CA: R. and E. Miles, 1989.

Hargrove, Eugene C., ed. *Religion and Environmental Crisis.* Athens, GA: University of Georgia Press, 1986.

Lynch, Tony. "Deep Ecology as an Aesthetic Movement." *Environmental Values* 5.2 (1996), pp. 147–60.

McFague, Sallie. *Theology for an Ecological, Nuclear Age.* Philadelphia: Fortress Press, 1987.

O'Riordan, Tim. "Valuation as Revelation and Reconciliation." *Environmental Values* 6.2 (1997), pp. 169–84.

Raglon, Rebecca Marian Scholtmeijer. "Shifting Ground: Metanarratives, Epistemology, and the Stories of Nature." *Environmental Ethics* 18.1 (1996), pp. 19–38.

Waks, Leonard J. "Environmental Claims and Citizen Rights." *Environmental Ethics* 18.2 (1996), pp. 133–48.

Anthropocentric Justification

Baier, Annette. "For the Sake of Future Generations." In *And Justice for All.* Ed. Tom Regan and Donald VanDe Veer. Totowa, NJ: Rowman and Littlefield, 1982.

DeGeorge, Richard. "The Environment, Rights, and Future Generations." In *Responsibilities to Future Generations.* Ed. Ernest Partridge. Buffalo, NY: Prometheus Books, 1980.

Ehrlich, Anne, and Paul Ehrlich. *The Population Explosion.* New York: Doubleday, 1990.

Ehrlich, Paul. *The Population Bomb.* New York: Ballantine, 1968.

Golding, Martin. "Obligations to Future Generations." *Monist* 56 (1972).

Hayward, Tim. "Anthropocentrism: A Misunderstood Problem." *Environmental Values* 6.1 (1997), pp. 49–64.

Kavka, Gregory. "The Futurity Problem." In *Obligations to Future Generations*. Ed. Brian Barry and R. I. Sikora. Philadelphia: Temple University Press, 1978.

Narveson, Jan. "Future People and Us." In *Obligations to Future Generations*. Ed. Brian Barry and R. I. Sikora. Philadelphia: Temple University Press, 1978.

Parfit, Derek. "On Doing the Best for Our Children." In *Ethics and Population*. Ed. Michael Bayles. Cambridge, MA: Schenkman, 1976.

Warren, Mary Anne, "Future Generations." In *And Justice for All*. Ed. Tom Regan and Donald VanDe Veer. Totowa, NJ: Rowman and Littlefield, 1982.

Biocentric Justification

Brennan, Andres. *Thining about Nature*. Athens, GA: University of Georgia Press, 1988.

Elliot, Robert, and Arran Gare, eds. *Environmental Philosophy*. University Park, PA: University of Pennsylvania Press, 1983.

Regan, Tom. *All That Dwell Therein*. Berkeley, CA: University of California Press, 1982.

Rolston, Holmes III. *Environmental Ethics*. Philadelphia: Temple University Press, 1988.

Scoville, Judith N. "Value Theory and Ecology in Environmental Ethics: A Comparison of Rolston and Neibuhr." *Environmental Ethics* 17.2 (1995), pp. 115–34.

Stone, Christopher. *Earth and Other Ethics*. New York: Harper & Row, 1987.

Applied Environmental Ethics

Afshar, Haleh, ed. *Women, Development and Survival in the Third World*. London: Longman, 1991.

Attfield, Robin, and Barry Wilkins, eds. *International Justice and the Third World*. London: Routledge, 1992.

van Buren, John. "Rights against Polluters." *Environmental Ethics* 17.3 (1995), pp. 259–76.

DeGrazia, David. *Taking Animals Seriously*. New York: Cambridge University Press, 1996.

Hardin, Garrett. *Living within Limits: Ecology, Economics and Population Taboos*. New York: Oxford University Press, 1993.

Hargrove, Eugene C., ed. *The Animals Rights/Environmental Ethics Debate: The Environmental Perspective*. Albany, NY: SUNY Press, 1993.

Jackson, Wes. *New Roots for Agriculture*. Omaha, NE: University of Nebraska Press, 1980.

Regan, Tom. *The Case for Animal Rights*. Berkeley, CA: University of California Press, 1983.

———, and Peter Singer, eds. *Animal Rights and Human Obligations*. Upper Saddle River, NJ: Prentice Hall, 1989.

Ryan, John C. "Conserving Biological Diversity." *State of the World 1992*. New York: Worldwatch, 1992.

Sen, Gita, and Caren Growen. *Development Crises and Alternative Visions*. New York: Monthly Review Press, 1987.

Shrader-Frechette, Kristin S. *Burying Uncertainty: Risk and the Case against Geological Disposal of Nuclear Waste.* Berkeley, CA: University of California Press, 1993.

Singer, Peter. *Animal Liberation: A New Ethics for Our Treatment of Animals.* New York: Avon Books, 1992.

Soule, Judith, and Jon Piper. *Farming in Nature's Image: An Ecological Approach in Agriculture.* Washington, DC: Island Press, 1992.

Stone, Christopher. *Should Trees Have Standing? Toward Legal Rights for Natural Objects.* Los Altos, CA: William Kaufmann, 1974.

Wilson, E. O. "Threats to Biodiversity." In *Biodiversity.* Ed. E. O. Wilson and Frances Peter. Washington, DC: National Academy Press, 1988.

Acknowledgments

Chapter One

Interview with Tamar Datan. Used with permission of Tamar Datan.

Chapter Three

The Land Ethic, Deep Ecology, and Social Ecology

From Aldo Leopold, *A Sand County Almanac: and Sketches Here and There,* Copyright 1949, 1977 by Oxford University Press, Inc. Used by permission of Oxford University Press, Inc.

Reprinted from "The Shallow and the Deep, Long-Range Ecology Movement: A Summary," *Inquiry* 16 (1983), pp. 95–100, by permission of Taylor & Francis, Oslo, Norway.

From Bill Devall and George Sessions, *Deep Ecology: Living as if Nature Mattered* (pp. 65–73). Salt Lake City: Gibbs Smith, publisher [Peregrine Smith Books], 1985. Used with permission.

Reprinted from Murray Bookchin, "The Modern Crisis," with the kind permission of Black Rose Books [http://www.web.net/blackrosebooks].

Ecofeminism

Carolyn Merchant, "Ecofeminism and Feminist Theory," in *Reweaving the World: The Emergence of Ecofeminism,* edited by Irene Diamond and Gloria Orenstein. Copyright © 1990 by Diamond and Orenstein. Reprinted with permission of Sierra Club Books.

Karen J. Warren, "The Power and the Promise of Ecological Feminism," *Environmental Ethics* 12 (Summer 1990): 125–26, 138–45. Reprinted with permission.

Val Plumwood, "Nature, Self and Gender: A Critique of Rationalism," from "Nature, Self and Gender: Feminism, Environmental Philosophy and the Critique of Rationalism," *Hypatia* 6:1 (Spring 1991): 3– 7, 10–22. Reprinted with permission.

Religion and Aesthetics

Eilon Schwartz, "*Bal Tashit:* A Jewish Environmental Precept," *Environmental Ethics* 19:4 (1997): 355–74. Reprinted with permission.

Annie L. Booth and Harvey M. Jacobs, "Ties That Bind: Native American Beliefs as a Foundation for Environmental Consciousness," *Environmental Ethics* 12:1 (1990): 27–35. Reprinted with permission.

J. Baird Callicott, *Earth's Insights: A Multicultural Survey from the Mediterranean Basin to the Australian Outback.* Copyright © 1994 The Regents of the University of California. Reprinted with permission.

Janna Thompson, "Aesthetics and the Value of Nature," *Environmental Ethics* 17:3 (1995): 291–306. Reprinted with permission.

Chapter Five

Anthropocentric Justification

Alan Gewirth, "Human Rights and Future Generations." Original essay written by Alan Gewirth for this volume.

Onora O Neill, "Environmental Values, Anthropocentrism and Speciesism," *Environmental Values* 6 (1997): 127–42. Reprinted by permission of The White Horse Press, Cambridge, England.

Biocentric Justifications

Homes Ralston III, "Environmental Ethics: Values in and Duties to the Natural World," from F. Herbert Bormann and Stephen R. Kellert, eds., *The Broken Circle: Ecology, Economics, and Ethics.* Copyright © 1991 Yale University Press. Reprinted with permission.

Paul Taylor, *Respect for Nature.* Copyright © 1986 by Princeton University Press. Reprinted by permission of Princeton University Press.

Searching the Middle

James P. Sterba, "Reconciling Anthropocentric and Nonanthropocentric Environmental Ethics," *Environmental Values* 3 (1994): 229–44. Reprinted by permission of The White Horse Press, Cambridge, England.

Brian K. Steverson, "On the Reconciliation of Anthropocentric and Nonanthropocentric Environmental Ethics," *Environmental Values* 5 (1996): 349–61. Reprinted by permission of The White Horse Press, Cambridge, England.

James P. Sterba, "Reconciliation Reaffirmed: A Reply to Steverson," *Environmental Ethics* 5 (1996): 363–68. Reprinted by permission of The White Horse Press, Cambridge, England.

Chapter Six

Animal Rights

Peter Singer, *Animal Liberation, 2/e*. New York: Random House, 1990. Reprinted by permission of the author.

Tom Regan, "The Radical Egalitarian Case for Animal Rights," from *In Defence of Animals*, ed. Peter Singer. Copyright © 1985 Basil Blackwell Publishers. Reprinted with permission.

Mary Ann Warren, "A Critique of Regan's Animal Rights Theory," *Between Species* 2:4 (1987). Reprinted with permission.

Biodiversity

Paul M. Wood, "Biodiversity as the Source of Biological Resources: A New Look at Biodiversity Values," *Environmental Values* 6 (1997): 251–68. Reprinted by permission of The White Horse Press, Cambridge, England.

Elliot Sober, "Philosophical Problems for Environmentalism," from B. G. Norton, ed., *The Preservation of Species*. Copyright © 1986 by Princeton University Press. Reprinted by permission of Princeton University Press.

Sustainable Development

Wilfred Beckerman, " 'Sustainable Development': Is It a Useful Concept?" *Environmental Values* 3 (1994): 191–209. Reprinted by permission of The White Horse Press, Cambridge, England.

Herman E. Daly, "On Wilfred Beckerman's Critique of Sustainable Development," *Environmental Values* 4 (1995): 49–55. Reprinted by permission of The White Horse Press, Cambridge, England.

Henryk Skolimowski, "In Defense of Sustainable Development," *Environmental Values* 4 (1995): 69–70. Reprinted by permission of The White Horse Press, Cambridge, England.

Salah El Serafy, "In Defense of Weak Sustainability: A Response to Beckerman," *Environmental Values* 5 (1996): 75–81. Reprinted by permission of The White Horse Press, Cambridge, England.